THE PRESIDENTS OF THE UNITED STATES ON THE PRESIDENTS OF THE UNITED STATES

THE PRESIDENTS OF THE UNITED STATES ON THE PRESIDENTS OF THE UNITED STATES

The Early Republic, George Washington to John Quincy Adams

DAVID ANTHONY CLARK

ISBN: 1981550208
ISBN 13: 9781981550203
Library of Congress Control Number: 2017919178
CreateSpace Independent Publishing Platform
North Charleston, South Carolina

CONTENTS

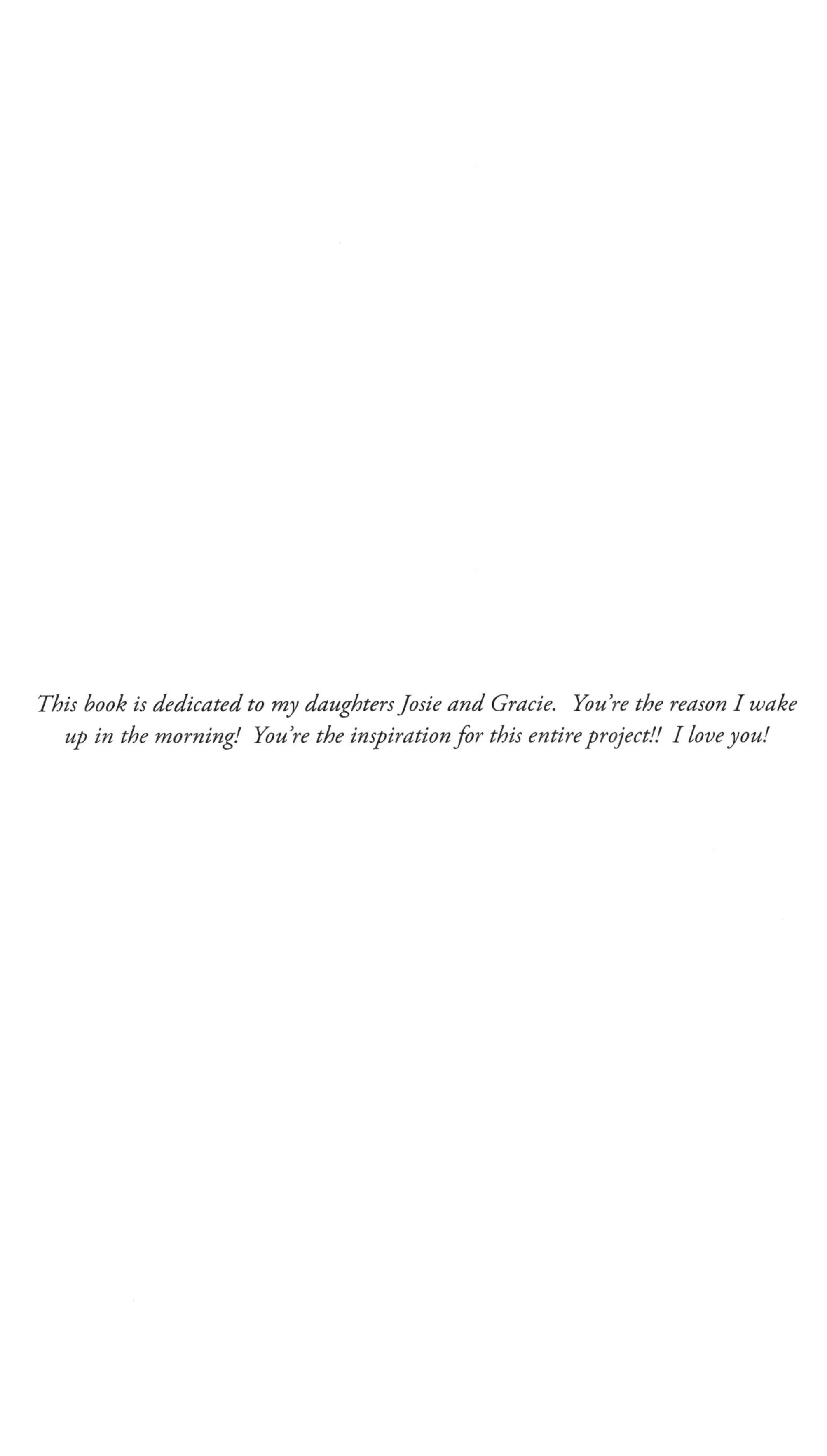

This book is dedicated to my daughters Josie and Gracie. You're the reason I wake up in the morning! You're the inspiration for this entire project!! I love you!

INTRODUCTION

The first six presidents of the United States were, perhaps, the most talented and accomplished succession of leaders the nation has ever known. Their collective tenures as president covered ten terms lasting forty years. All were extremely brilliant in their own right and all were true "Renaissance men" who were as talented at politics and leadership as they were in horticulture, farming, architecture, philosophy, and the knowledge of literature. Four of the six were slave holders, while two vehemently opposed this brutal and dehumanizing practice. Cumulatively, they administered the nation through wars and quasi-wars, rebellions, land acquisitions, trade embargoes, threats of secession, times of economic prosperity and times of economic panic, Indian wars, numerous treaties, and scores of precedents, many of which last to this day. During their collective tenures in office, thirteen new states were added to the Union and the size of the nation grew from 864,746 square miles in 1790 to 1,749,462 square miles at the close of John Quincy Adams's presidency. America's population nearly tripled during the same years growing from roughly 4 million to 13 million citizens. Tragically, the population of slaves in the nation expanded as well, from a population of approximately 700,000 during Washington's first term in office, to over 1.5 million by the end of the Quincy Adams administration.

The first five of the six presidents examined in this work were prominent actors in America's Revolutionary Era and all but one, John Adams, were Virginians. George Washington served as the Commander-in-Chief of the Continental Army which defeated the British forces after 7 years of bloody revolution. John Adams and Thomas Jefferson, while never serving in the military, certainly did a lion's share to create the new nation. Both were prominent members of the Continental Congress and were chosen by their peers to serve on the committee that drafted the Declaration of Independence. Jefferson single-handedly penned that astonishing document to which he and Adams affixed their signatures pledging "to each other," and the other 54 signers from all 13 colonies, "their lives, their fortunes, and their sacred honor." Both George Washington and James Madison signed the United States Constitution. Washington, "the Father of his Country," served as the presiding officer of the Constitutional Convention held in Philadelphia, Pennsylvania in the spring and summer of 1787 and James Madison, "the Father of the Constitution," played a critical role in the document's creation as well as its subsequent ratification. He also maintained a comprehensive record of the Convention's proceedings, providing for posterity a meticulously written account of the creation of the United States Constitution. James Monroe served as an officer in the Continental Army and survived the brutal winter of 1777-1778 with General Washington at Valley Forge. He later rose to the rank of lieutenant colonel in 1780 when he was appointed military commissioner of Virginian by Governor Thomas Jefferson. Thirty-Seven years later, President James Monroe would be nostalgically labeled "the last cocked hat" as he was the final member of the Revolutionary generation to serve as President of the United States. With his knee britches, buckled shoes, powdered wig and brimless triangular hat pointed at the front, back, and top, Monroe served as a visible end to a remarkable era. Even his Secretary of State, John Quincy Adams, poignantly recognized this when writing in his diary that Monroe's life "was long, eventful, and connected with the principal events of our history, from the Declaration of Independence, for a full half-century."

At first glance, John Quincy Adams does not seem to fit with the other five presidents as he was of another generation entirely. It was, however, impossible to ignore him when editing and compiling this work. Perhaps none of the six presidents examined in this book were as well prepared as Quincy Adams to serve as the nation's chief executive. The son of President John Adams, he gained a vast amount of knowledge from his father and served him in several administrative roles. Still, he was apprehensive about making politics his profession. "You recommend to me to attend the town meetings and make speeches; to meet with caucuses and join political clubs," the twenty-six year old wrote to his father. "But I am afraid of all these things." Despite the apprehensions of his eldest son, John Adams constantly encouraged him to strive to meet his potential and the two maintained a long and rich correspondence which provides great insight into both men and the nation they helped shape. Quincy Adams was personally acquainted with George Washington and it was the latter who quickly recognized the brilliance and potential of his vice president's eldest son. "I shall be much mistaken," Washington wrote to John Adams in August of 1795, "if in as short a time as can well be expected, he is not found at the head of the Diplomatic Corps." John Quincy Adams's first appointment as Minister to the Netherlands was commissioned by President Washington in 1793 when the former was just twenty-six. Quincy Adams knew Thomas Jefferson as well and sat as a United

States senator from Massachusetts through much of the latter's presidency. He served as Minister to Great Britain during James Madison's administration and as secretary of state for eight years under President James Monroe. After spending one exacting term as the nation's chief executive (1824-1828), he went on to hold a seat in the United States House of Representatives until his death on February 23, 1848 — nearly half a century after the passing of George Washington. Indeed, the brilliant Quincy Adams shared great insight into his five predecessors in office.

George Washington, John Adams, Thomas Jefferson, James Madison, and James Monroe all sat as delegates to the Continental Congress. John Adams and Thomas Jefferson both served as vice president. Adams, Jefferson, Monroe, and Quincy Adams all acted as foreign ministers representing the United States overseas. Jefferson, Madison, Monroe, and Quincy Adams all served as secretary of state, and these accomplishments only touch on the proverbial "tip of the iceberg" of their many professional and personal achievements. Indeed, they were a remarkable succession of leaders.

This work has sought to capture what each man wrote, thought, and spoke about the office of the President of the United States. Their thoughts are deep, wide-ranging and quite diverse. Their political philosophies, personal habits and individual temperaments greatly colored their unique styles of governance, but upon assuming office, all were extremely conscious of the great trust and enormous responsibility that was placed in their hands. After an examination of their thoughts on the presidency, the work goes on to explore each man in a much deeper and more personal fashion. A great deal of the study captures what they wrote, thought, and spoke about each other. The words and emotions they express range from the kindness and warmth that one would expect to find amidst Revolutionary compatriots unified in their desire to forge a new nation, to the cold and calculated scheming found among political nemeses seeking to fulfill their own personal desires and ambitions. What they wrote to each other is often very different in tone than what they expressed in words to others. If the reader is careful they will notice throughout the work the unfolding of many fascinating and important stories exclusive to each man and the nation they led.

Very few individuals have had the privilege to serve in this magnificent and uniquely American office. The first six men to do so are arguably the most remarkable of all. It took over a decade to research, compile, and organize the many quotes found between these pages and never have they been collected into a single volume. While the work does not include absolutely everything these men ever wrote or spoke about the presidency or one another, it is quite comprehensive and offers a vast amount of extremely interesting and insightful information. The quotes range from the seemingly mundane—such as simple dinner invitations and thoughts about the weather—to the introspective and often anxiety-ridden decisions that helped shape 18th and 19th century America. The methodology used for this study was quite simplistic, though at times somewhat difficult. The deliberate absence of commentary by the editor ensures that the words of the first six presidents remain pure and free from subjective opinion. While some selective editing did take place, it was not done to add to or detract from these men's unique abilities and achievements. Nor was it done to highlight or magnify their personal failures and weaknesses. In short, there was no bias used when compiling this work. Instead, it was created to add a unique and objective window through which to view the office of the American presidency and the first six men to occupy it.

ACKNOWLEDGEMENTS

My interest in American history began in 1982 when I was in the 8th grade. For three nights in November my dad let me stay up late to watch the Civil War mini-series, *the Blue and the Gray,* starring John Hammond and Stacy Keach. This fascinating television series changed my life forever and sent me on a trajectory toward making American history my profession. My appreciation for American history grew at Bishop Manogue Catholic High School in Reno, Nevada in the classroom of the late Brother Ignatius Foster. Brother Ignatius's American history class was the stuff of legend and was—by far—one of the most interesting and academically rigorous courses I have ever taken. I remember pouring over the course textbook each evening after football practice in preparation for Brother's exams. As challenging as the class was, I left it with a much deeper appreciation of American history and a hunger to learn more (although being made to memorize and recite the preambles to both the United States Constitution and Declaration of Independence may have been a bit much).

After graduating high school, I moved to California and attended the University of San Francisco where I completed my undergraduate degree in American history. During my years at U.S.F. I was lucky enough to have had some very talented history professors who took me under their wings and began to mold me into an historian. I would like to thank Tony Fels who was, perhaps, the best professor I have ever had. In addition to taking many of his courses, Dr. Fels directed my Senior Honors Thesis and gently guided me away from law school and toward a career in teaching and for this I will be forever grateful. I would also like to thank Frank Beach, who would consistently amaze me at the amount of knowledge he could impart to his students in one 50-minute history class —and every second of it fascinating.

Upon graduating U.S.F. in 1991 I returned to Reno ready to take on the world. Although, with the economy in recession all I really took on was a little bit of debt and a whole lot of stress. After aimlessly kicking around Reno for a year I decided to join the military and enlisted in the Nevada Air National Guard. Upon being commissioned a second lieutenant at the Academy of Military Science in Knoxville, Tennessee, I was stationed at Sheppard Air Force Base in Wichita Falls, Texas, where I completed the Aircraft Maintenance and Munitions Officer Course. While at Sheppard, I decided to apply to graduate school to pursue a Master of Arts degree in American history. I was accepted to Villanova University located on the Main Line just west of Philadelphia and was extremely excited to attend. What I was not as certain about was how my commander, Colonel Larry Matlock, would feel about my attending a school nearly 3,000 miles from my military responsibilities, and this, just weeks after completing my Air Force technical training. When I broached the subject with him, however, he was extremely warm and supportive. He told me that when I was home from Villanova for winter and summer breaks I could make up the Unit Training Assemblies I would miss while away. I will be forever grateful to Colonel Matlock for allowing me the freedom to pursue my degree at Villanova while remaining an officer in the National Guard. Both experiences have been highlights in my life.

I hold very warm memories of my years at Villanova University. I am particularly grateful to the late James Bergquist who immersed his students in the fascinating world of historiography. It is difficult to put into words how important Dr. Bergquist was to me during those years at Villanova—so to him I will simply say thank you! I also want to thank David Contosta who taught us how to refine our craft as researchers and writers and for guiding fascinating walking tours through the historic neighborhoods of Philadelphia. I would also like to thank Adele Lindenmeyr for all her support and guidance during those incredible years. Most importantly, I would like to thank my good friend and fellow Villanova alum, Ed McNamara. Villanova would not have been the same without his constant friendship and support. Whether the topic is history, Villanova basketball, reminiscing on trips to Sagamore Hill, or serious life issues, Ed has always been there. I would also like to extend a special thanks to Brooks Simpson at Arizona State University for deepening my interest in the American presidency (and yes Dr. Simpson, John Adams did in fact describe James Madison as "withered"). Also, I owe a large debt of gratitude to Dr. John Kaminski at the University of Wisconsin-Madison. Dr. Kaminski provided the inspiration for this project in 2005 during a talk he gave at Arizona State about compiling and editing related historical documents and has offered his help and advice all along the way. I would also like to thank long-time friends Pat Rogers, John York, Charlie Susano, Kevin Williams, and Jeff Eslinger. Due to the wonders of modern technology we can still make each other laugh every day despite the distance! Special thanks also to Regina Mann, Christine Hull, and Lieutenant Colonel Tom Funk for all their support over the years. Also, much thanks to my sisters Kathy, Patricia, and Laura and to my brother Jim, for their love and encouragement and for pretending to listen as I droned on incessantly over the years about my "president's book." It's finally done! Most importantly, I would like to thank my parents, Barbara and Tony, for all their support in everything I have ever done or tried to do.

Lastly, I would like to thank the staffs at the University of Nevada's (old) Getchell Library and (new) Matthewson-IGT Knowledge Center and all of the help they provided in finding the resources needed to compile this study. I would also like to thank *the American Libraries Collection* at Archives.org, the Massachusetts Historical Society at www.masshist.org, and the National Archives' *Founders Online*, for providing incredible material that would have otherwise been out of my reach.

Chapter 1

GEORGE WASHINGTON

I. GEORGE WASHINGTON ON THE PRESIDENCY

1. GEORGE WASHINGTON TO THE MARCHIONESS DE LAFAYETTE APRIL 4, 1784

"From the clangor of arms and the bustle of a camp, freed from the cares of public employment, and the responsibility of office, I am now enjoying domestic ease under the shadow of my own Vine, and my own Fig tree; and in a small Villa, with the implements of Husbandry, and Lambkins around me, I expect to glide gently down the stream of life, 'till I am entombed in the dreary mansions of my Fathers."

2. GEORGE WASHINGTON TO THE MARQUIS DE LAFAYETTE APRIL 28, 1788

"In answer to the observations you make on the probability of my election to the Presidency (knowing me as you do) I need only say, that it has no enticing charms, and no fascinating allurements for me. However, it might not be decent for me to say I would refuse to accept or even to speak much about an appointment, which may never take place: for in so doing, one might possibly incur the application of the moral resulting from that Fable, in which the Fox is represented as inveighing against the sourness of the grapes, because he could not reach them. All that it will be necessary to add, my dear Marquis, in order to show my decided predilection, is, that, (at my time of life and under my circumstances) the encreasing infirmities of nature and the growing love of retirement do not permit me to entertain a wish beyond that of living and dying an honest man on my own farm. Let those follow the pursuits of ambition and fame, who have a keener relish for them, or who may have more years, in store, for the enjoyment."

3. GEORGE WASHINGTON TO ALEXANDER HAMILTON OCTOBER 3, 1788

"Although I could not help observing, from several publications and letters that my name had been sometimes spoken of, and that it was possible the *Contingency* which is the subject of your letter might happen; yet I thought it best to maintain a guarded silence and to seek the counsel of my best friends (which I certainly hold in the highest estimation) rather than to hazard an imputation unfriendly to the delicacy of my feelings. For, situated as I am, I could hardly bring the question into the slightest discussion, or ask an opinion even in the most confidential manner, without betraying, in my judgment, some impropriety of conduct, or without feeling an apprehension, that a premature display of anxiety might be construed into a vain-glorious desire of pushing myself into notice as a candidate. Now, if I am not grossly deceived in myself, I should unfeignedly rejoice, in case the Electors, by giving their votes in favor of some other person, would save me from the dreaded Dilemma of being forced to accept or refuse.

If that may not be, I am, in the next place, earnestly desirous of searching out the truth, and of knowing whether there does not exist a probability that the government would be just as happily and effectually carried into execution without my aid, as with it. I am *truly* solicitous to obtain all the previous information which the circumstances will afford, and to determine (when the determination can with propriety be no longer postponed) according to the principles of right reason, and the dictates of a clear conscience; without too great a reference to the unforeseen consequences, which may affect my person or reputation. Untill that period, I may fairly hold myself open to conviction; though I allow your sentiments to have weight in them; and I shall not pass by your arguments without giving them as dispassionate a consideration, as I can possibly bestow upon them.

In taking a survey of the subject, in whatever point of light I have been able to place it, I will not suppress the acknowledgment, my Dr. Sir that I have always felt a kind of gloom upon my mind, as often as I have been taught to expect, I might, and perhaps must ere long, be called to make a decision. You will, I am well assured, believe the assertion (though I have little expectation it would gain credit from those who are less acquainted with me) that if I should accept it; the acceptance would be attended with more diffidence and reluctance than ever I experienced before in my life. It would be, however, with a fixed and sole determination of lending whatever assistance might be in my power to promote the public, weal, in hopes that at a convenient and an early period, my services might be dispensed with, and that I might be permitted once more to retire—to pass an unclouded evening, after the stormy day of life, in the bosom of domestic tranquility."

4. GEORGE WASHINGTON TO BENJAMIN LINCOLN OCTOBER 26, 1788

"I would willingly pass over in silence that part of your letter, in which you mention the persons who are Candidates for the two first Offices in the Executive, if I did not fear the omission might seem to betray a want of confidence. Motives of delicacy have prevented me hitherto from conversing or writing on this subject, whenever I could avoid it with decency. I may, however, with great sincerity & I believe without offending against modesty or propriety, *say* to *you* that I most heartily wish the choice to which you allude might not fall upon me: and that, if it should, I must reserve to myself the right of making up my final decision, at the last moment when it can be brought into one view, and when the expediency inexpediency of a *refusal* can be more judiciously determined than at present. But be assured, my dear Sir, if from any inducement I shall be persuaded ultimately to accept, it will not be (so far as I know my own heart) from any of a private or personal nature. Every personal consideration conspires to rivet me (if I may use the expression) to retirement. At my time of life and under my circumstances, nothing in this world can ever draw me from it, unless it be a *conviction* that the partiality of my Countrymen had made my services absolutely necessary, joined to a *fear* that my refusal might induce a belief that I preferred the conservation of my own reputation & private ease to the good of my Country. After all, if I should conceive myself in a manner constrained to accept, I call Heaven to witness, that this very act would be the greatest sacrifice of my personal feelings and wishes that ever I have been called upon to make. It would be to forego repose and domestic enjoyment, for trouble, perhaps for public obloquy: for I should consider myself as entering upon an unexplored field, enveloped on every side with clouds and darkness.

From this embarrassing situation I had naturally supposed that my declarations at the close of the war would have saved me; and that my sincere intentions, then publicly made known, would have effectually precluded me for ever afterwards from being looked upon as a Candidate for any office. This hope, as a last anchor of worldly happiness in old age, I had still carefully preserved; until the public papers and private letters from my Correspondents in almost every quarter, taught me to apprehend that I might soon be obliged to answer the question, whether I would go again into public life or not."

5. GEORGE WASHINGTON TO GOUVERNEUR MORRIS NOVEMBER 28, 1788

"As to what you hint respecting myself, towards the close of your letter; I have really but little leisure or inclination to enter on the discussion of a subject so unpleasant to me. You may be persuaded in the first place; that I hope the choice will not fall upon me—and, in the second; that if it should, & if I can with any degree of propriety decline, I shall certainly contrive to get rid of the acceptance."

6. GEORGE WASHINGTON TO JONATHAN TRUMBULL, JR. DECEMBER 4, 1788

"I believe you know me sufficiently well, my dear Trumbull, to conceive that I am very much perplexed and distressed in my own mind, respecting the subject to which you allude. If I should (unluckily for me) be reduced to the necessity of giving an answer to the question, which you suppose will certainly be put to me, I would fain do what is in all respects best. But how can I know what is best, or on what shall I determine? May Heaven assist me in forming a judgment: for at present, I can see nothing but clouds and darkness before me."

7. GEORGE WASHINGTON TO BENJAMIN FISHBOURN DECEMBER 23, 1788

"The future is all a scene of darkness and uncertainty to me, on many accounts. It is known; that when I left the army, it was with a fixed determination, never to be engaged again in any public affairs. Events, which were not then foreseen, have since turned up: but, perhaps, neither those or any which can happen, will be of sufficient urgency to justify me in foregoing my fixed determination and sacrificing my domestic happiness. So much, at present, I can say with the strictest truth; that nothing but a conviction of the indispensable necessity of the measure, can ever induce me to make the sacrifice. That conviction not having been made; it would be improper for me to say any thing whatsoever on the immediate point to which you allude; and because as a farther reason if it should be my fate to administer the government, I will go into it free from engagements of every kind and nature whatsoever making, when the pretentions of every candidate are brought to view as far as my judgment shall direct me, justice, and the public good file sole objects of my pursuits."

8. GEORGE WASHINGTON TO WILLIAM GORDON DECEMBER 23, 1788

"I flatter myself my countrymen are so fully persuaded of my desire to remain in private life; that I am not without hopes and expectations of being left quietly to enjoy the repose, in which I am at present. Or, in all events, should it be their wish (as you suppose it will be) for me to come again on the Stage of public affairs—I certainly will decline it, if the refusal can be made consistently—with what I conceive to be the dictates of property and duty. For the great Searcher of human hearts knows there is no wish in mine, beyond that of living and dying an honest man, on my own farm."

9. GEORGE WASHINGTON TO THE MARQUIS DE LAFAYETTE JANUARY 29, 1789

"I can say little or nothing new, in consequence of the repetition of your opinion, on the expediency there will be, for my accepting the office to which you refer. Your sentiments, indeed, coincide much more nearly with those of my other friends, than with my own feelings. In truth my difficulties encrease and magnify as I draw towards the period, when, according to the common belief, it will be necessary for me to give a definitive answer, in one way or another. Should the circumstances render it, in a manner inevitably necessary, to be in the affirmative: be assured, my dear Sir, I shall assume the task with the most unfeigned reluctance, and with a real diffidence for which I shall probably receive no credit from the world. If I know my own heart, nothing short of a conviction of duty will induce me again to take an active part in public affairs and, in that case, if I can form a plan for my own conduct, my endeavours shall be unremittingly exerted (even at the hazard of former fame or present popularity) to extricate my country from the embarrassments in which it is entangled, through want of credit; and to establish a general system of policy, which if pursued will ensure permanent felicity to the Commonwealth. I think I see a *path*, as clear and as direct as a ray of light, which leads to the attainment of that object. Nothing but harmony, honesty, industry and frugality are necessary to make us a great and happy people. Happily the present posture of affairs and the prevailing disposition of my countrymen promise to co-operate in establishing those four great and essential pillars of public felicity."

10. GEORGE WASHINGTON TO BENJAMIN HARRISON MARCH 9, 1789

"I will therefore declare to you, that, if it should be my inevitable fate to administer the government (for Heaven knows that no event can be less desired by me; and that no earthly consideration short of so general a call, together with a desire to reconcile contending parties as far in me layes, could again bring me into public life) I will go to the chair under no preengagement of any kind or nature whatsoever. But when in it, I will, to the best of my Judg<m>ent, discharge the duties of the office with that impartiality and zeal for the public good, which ought never to suffer connections of blood or friendship to intermingle, so as to have the least sway on decision of a public nature. I may err, notwithstanding my most strenuous efforts to execute the difficult trust with fidelity and unexceptionably, but my errors shall be of the head—not of the heart."

11. GEORGE WASHINGTON TO JAMES MADISON MARCH 30, 1789

"On the subject of lodgings I will frankly declare, I mean to go into none but hired ones. If these cannot be had tolerably convenient (I am not very nice) I would take rooms in the most decent Tavern, till a house can be provided for the more permanent reception of the President. I have already declined a very polite and pressing offer from the Governor, to lodge at his house till a place could be prepared for me; after which should any other of a similar nature be made, there would be no propriety in the acceptance. But as you are fully acquainted with sentiments on this subject, I shall only add, that as I mean to avoid private families on the one hand, so on another, I am not desirous of being placed *early* in a situation for entertaining. Therefore, hired (private) lodgings would not only be more agreeable to my own wishes, but, possibly, more consistent with the dictates of sound policy. For, as it is my wish and intention to conform to the public desire and expectation, with respect to the style proper for the Chief Magistrate to live in, it might be well to know (as far as the nature of the case will admit) what these are before he enters upon it.

After all, something may perhaps have been decided upon with respect to the accommodations of the President, before this letter wd. have reached you that may render this application nugatory. If otherwise, I will sum up all my wishes in one word, and that is to be placed in an independent situation, with the prospect I have alluded to, before me."

12. EXCERPT FROM A SPEECH BY GEORGE WASHINGTON TO THE MAYOR, CORPORATION, AND CITIZENS OF ALEXANDRIA, VIRGINIA APRIL 16, 1789

"Those, who have known me best (and you, my fellow citizens, are from your situation, in that number) know better than any others that my love of retirement is so great, that no earthly consideration, short of a conviction of duty, could have prevailed upon me to depart from my resolution, *'never more to take any share in transactions of a public nature.'* For, at my age, and in my circumstances, what possible advantages could I propose to myself, from embarking again on the tempestuous and uncertain ocean of public - life?"

13. GEORGE WASHINGTON TO JOHN ADAMS MAY 10, 1789

"The President of the United States wishes to avail himself of your sentiments on the following points:

1st. Whether a line of conduct, equally distant from an association with all kinds of company on the one hand and from a total seclusion from Society on the other, ought to be adopted by him? and, in that case, how is it to be done?

2d. What will be the least exceptionable method of bringing any system, which may be adopted on this subject, before the public and into use?

3d. Whether, after a little time, one day in every week will not be sufficient for receiving visits of Compliment?

4th. Whether it would tend to prompt impertinent applications and involve disagreeable consequences to have it known, that the President will, every Morning at eight Oclock, be at leisure to give Audience to persons who may have business with him?

5th. Whether, when it shall have been understood that the President is not to give *general entertainments* in the manner the Presidents of Congress have formerly done, it will be practicable to draw such a line of discrimination in regard to persons, as that Six, eight or ten official characters (including in the rotation the members of both Houses of Congress) may be invited informally or otherwise to dine with him on the days fixed for receiving Company, without exciting clamours in the rest of the Community?

6th. Whether it would be satisfactory to the Public for the President to make about four great entertainments. in a year on such great occasions as...the Anniversary of the Declaration of Independence...the Alliance with France...the Peace with Great Britain...the Organization of the general Government: and whether arrangements of these two last kinds could be in danger of diverting too much of the Presidents time from business, or of producing the evils which it was intended to avoid by his living more recluse than the Presidts. Of Congress have heretofore lived.

7th. Whether there would be any impropriety in the Presidents making informal visits; that is to say, in his calling upon his Acquaintances or public Characters for the purposes of sociability of civility: and what (as to the form of doing it) might evince these visits to have been made in his private character, so as that they may not be construed into visits from the President of the United States? and in what light would his appearance *rarely at Tea* parties be considered?

8th. Whether, during the recess of Congress, it would not be advantageous to the interests of the Union for the President to make the tour of the United States, in order to become better acquainted with their principal Characters and internal Circumstances, as well as to be more accessible to numbers of well- informed persons, who might give him useful information and advices on political subjects?

9th. If there is a probability, that either of the arrangements may take place, which will eventually cause additional expenses, whether it would not be proper that those ideas should come into contemplation, at the time when Congress shall make a permanent provision for the support of the Executive?

REMARKS

On the one side no augmentation can be effected in the pecuniary establishment which shall be made in the first instance, for the support of the Executive. On the other, all monies destined to that purpose beyond the actual expenditures, will be left in the Treasury of the United States or sacredly applied to the promotion of some national objects.

Many things which appear of little importance in themselves and at the beginning, may have great and durable consequences from their having been established at the commencement of a new general government. It will be much easier to commence the administration, upon a well adjusted system, built on tenable grounds, than to correct errors or alter inconveniences after they shall have been confirmed by habit. The President in all matters of business and etiquette, can have no object but to demean himself in his public character, in such a manner as to maintain the dignity of Office, without subjecting himself to the imputation of superciliousness or unnecessary reserve. Under these impressions, he asks for your candid and undisguised Opinions."

14. GEORGE WASHINGTON TO JAMES MADISON MAY 12, 1789

"My dear Sir: To draw such a line for the conduct of the President as will please *every* body, I know is impossible, but to mark out and follow one (which by being consonant with reason) will meet general approbation, may be as practicable as it is desirable. The true medium I conceive must lye in pursuing such a course, as will allow him time for all the official duties of his station. This should be the primary object. The next, to avoid as much as may be, the charge of superciliousness, and seclusion from information by too much reserve and too great a withdraw of himself from company on the one hand, and the inconveniences, as well as reduction of respectability by too free intercourse, and too much familiarity on the other.

Under these impressions I have submitted the enclosed queries for your consideration, and would thank you for your sentiments thereon, with the return of the paper. For the remarks which it contains, it is necessary that some plan should be adopted by the President for his mode of living; that the pecuniary estimates for the department may have an eye therto; and though *secondary*, it is a motive for my brining the matter before you at this time."

15. GEORGE WASHINGTON TO ELÉONOR FRAN, THE COUNT DE MOUSTIERS MAY 25, 1789

"Every one who has any knowledge of my manner of acting in public life, will be persuaded that I am not accustomed to impede the despatch or frustrate the success of business, by a ceremonious attention to idle forms. Any person, of that description, will also be satisfied that I should not readily consent to lose one of the most important functions of my office, for the sake of preserving an imaginary dignity. But, perhaps, if there are rules of proceeding, which have originated from the wisdom of statesmen and are sanctioned by the common consent of Nations, it would not be prudent for a young state to dispense with them altogether, at least, without some substantial cause for so doing. I have myself been induced to think, possibly from the habits of experience, that in general the best mode of conducting negotiations, the detail and progress of which might be liable to accidental mistakes or unintentional misrepresentations, is by writing. This mode, if I was obliged myself to negotiate with any one, I should still pursue. I have, however, been taught to believe, that there is, in most polished nations, a system established, with regard to the foreign as well as the other great Departments, which, from the utility, the necessity, and the reason of the thing, provides that business should be digested and prepared by the Heads of those departments.

The impossibility that one man should be able to perform all the great business of the State, I take to have been the reason for instituting the great Departments, & appointing officers therein, to assist the Supreme Magistrate in discharging the duties of his trust. And, perhaps, I may be allowed to say of myself, that the supreme Magistrate of no State can have a greater variety of important business to perform in person, than I have at this moment. Very many things will doubtless occur to you, Sir, as being incident to the office of President in the commencement of the Government, which cannot be done by the intervention of a third person. You will give me leave to say likewise, that no third person (were there a disposition for it) shall ever have it in his power to erect a wall between me and the Diplomatic Corps; that is to say, to prevent necessary communications. Nor has anybody insinuated that it would be beneath the dignity of a President of the United States occasionally to transact business with a foreign Minister. But in what light the public might view the establishment of a precedent for negotiating the business of a Department, without any agency of the Head of the Department who was appointed for that very purpose, I do not at present pretend to determine: Nor whether a similar practice, in that case, must not of right be extended hereafter to all Diplomatic characters of the same rank."

16. GEORGE WASHINGTON TO DAVID STUART JULY 26, 1789

"While the eyes of America, perhaps of the world, are turned to this government, and many are watching the movements of all those, who are concerned in its administration, I should like to be informed, through so good a medium of the public opinion of both men and measures, and of none more than myself; not so much of what may be thought commendable parts, if any, of my conduct, as of those which are conceived to be of a different complexion. The Man who means to commit no wrong, will never be guilty of enormities; consequently can never be unwilling to learn what is ascribed to him as foibles. If they are really such the knowledge of them in a well disposed mind will go half way towards a reform. If they are not errors he can explain and justify the motives of his actions.

At a distance from the theatre of action truth is not always related without embellishment, and sometimes is entirely perverted from a misconception of the causes which produce the effects that are the subjects of censure. 1. This leads me to think that a system which I found it indispensably necessary to adopt upon my first coming to this city, might have undergone severe strictures and have had motives very foreign from those that govern me assigned as causes therefor; I mean, returning *no* visits; 2. Appointing certain days to receive them generally (not to the exclusion however of visits on any other days under particular circumstances) and 3. at first entertaining no company, and afterwards until I was unable to entertain any at all confining it to official characters. A few days evinced the necessity of the two first in so clear a point of view that, had I not adopted it, I should have been unable to have attended to *any* sort of business unless I had applied the hours allotted to rest and refreshment to this purpose for by the time I had done breakfast, and thence till dinner, and afterwards till bed time I could not get relieved from the ceremony of one visit before I had to attend to another; in a word, I had no leisure to read or to answer the dispatches that were pouring in upon me from all quarters; and with respect to the third matter I early received information through very respectable channels that the adoption thereof was not less essential [than] that of the other two if the President was to preserve the dignity and respect that was due to the first Magistrate, for that a contrary conduct had involved the late Presidents of Congress in insuperable difficulties, and the office (in this respect) in perfect contempt. for the table was considered as a public one, and every person, who could get introduced, conceived that he had a *right* to be invited to it. This, although the Table was always crowded (and with mixed company, and the President considered in no better light than as a Maitre d'Hôtel) was in its nature impracticable and as many offences given as if no table had been kept.

The citizens of this place were well knowing to this fact, and the principal Members of Congress in both Houses were so well convinced of the impropriety and degrading situation of their President, that it was the general opinion that the President of the United States should neither give or receive invitations. Some from a belief, (independent of the circumstances I have mentioned) that this was fundamentally right in order to acquire respect. But to this I had two objections, both powerful in my mind; first, the novelty of it I knew would be considered as an ostentatious shew of mimicry of sovereignty; and secondly that so great a seclusion would have stopped the avenues to useful information from the many, and make me more dependent on that of the few; but to hit on a discriminating medium was found more difficult than it appeared to be at first view. for if the Citizens at large were begun upon no line could be drawn, all of decent appearance would expect to be invited, and I should have been plunged at once into the evil I was endeavoring to avoid. Upon the whole, it was thought best to confine *my* invitations to official characters and strangers of distinction. This line I have hitherto pursued; whether it may be found best to adhere to or depart from it in some measure must be the result of experience and information.

So strongly had the citizens of this place imbibed an idea of the impropriety of my accepting invitations to dinner that I have not received one from any family (though they are remarkable for hospitality, and though I have received every civility and attention possible from them) since I came to the city except dining with the Governor on the day of my arrival, so that, if this should be adduced as an article of impeachment there can be at least *one* good reason adduced for my not dining out; to wit never having been asked to do so."

17. GEORGE WASHINGTON TO CATHERINE MACAULAY GRAHAM JANUARY 9, 1790

"In the first place I thank you for your congratulatory sentiments on the event which has placed me at the head of the American Government; as well as for the indulgent partiality, which it is to be feared, however, may have warped your judgment too much in my favor. But you do me no more than justice in supposing that, if I had been permitted to indulge my first and fondest wish, I should have remained in a private Station. Although neither the present age or Posterity may possibly give me full credit for the feelings which I have experienced on the subject; yet I have a consciousness, that nothing short of an absolute conviction of duty could ever have brought me upon the scenes of public life again."

18. GEORGE WASHINGTON TO CATHERINE MACAULAY GRAHAM JANUARY 9, 1790

"All see, and most admire, the glare which hovers round the external trappings of elevated office. To me there is nothing in it, beyond the luster which may be reflected from its connection with a power of promoting human felicity."

19. GEORGE WASHINGTON TO CATHERINE MACAULAY GRAHAM JANUARY 9, 1790

"If after all my humble but faithful endeavors to advance the felicity of my Country and mankind, I may indulge a hope that my labours have not been altogether without success, it will be the only real compensation I can receive in the closing of life."

20. GEORGE WASHINGTON TO CATHERINE MACAULAY GRAHAM JANUARY 9, 1790

"In our progress towards political happiness my station is new; and if I may use the expression, I walk on untrodden ground. There is scarcely any part of my conduct wch. may not hereafter be drawn into precedent. Under such a view of the duties inherent to my arduous office, I could not but feel a diffidence in myself on the one hand; and an anxiety for the Community that every new arrangement should be made in the best possible manner on the other."

21. GEORGE WASHINGTON TO THE VIRGINIA LEGISLATURE APRIL 27, 1790

"Gentlemen,

With a due sense of the affectionate terms in which your affection is conceived, I offer my best thanks for your congratulations on my election to the Chief Magistracy of a free and enlightened Nation.

If I have been enabled to make use of whatever abilities Heaven has been pleased to confer upon me, with any advantage to our common Country, I consider it not less owing to the fostering encouragement I received in early life from the Citizens of the Commonwealth in which I was born, than to the persevering support I have since experienced from my fellow-Citizens collectively, in the course of their exertions, which, under Divine Providence, saved their Liberties and established their Independence.

However I may have confirmed my professions by my conduct, I can claim no merit for having been involved in the duties of a military command through necessity, or for having retired to the state of a private citizen through inclination. But I may be permitted to avow, that the construction you are pleased to put upon my motives for returning to public life is peculiarly satisfactory to me. Because I receive, from the voice of my Countrymen, the only reward I wished for the sacrifice—a just interpretation of the principles by which, I am conscious, I have been actuated.

Accustomed to have my actions viewed through a favorable medium by my fellow-Citizens in general, and more especially by those of my native State; I can but poorly compensate for such indulgence, by the purest emotions of gratitude, demonstrated in an active devotion to that Republican Government, which is so deservedly the first object of their political attachment.

In looking forward to that awful moment, when I must bid adieu to Sublunary Scenes, I anticipate the consolation of leaving our Country in a prosperous condition. And, while the curtain of separation shall be drawing, my last breath will, I trust, expire in a prayer for the temporal and eternal felicity of those, who have not only endeavoured to gild the evening of my days with unclouded serenity, but extended their desires to my happiness hereafter in a brighter world."

22. GEORGE WASHINGTON TO DAVID STUART JUNE 15, 1790

"In a letter of last year to the (b)est of my recollection, I informed you of the motives, which *compelled* me to allot a day for the reception of idle and ceremonies visits (for it never has prevented those of sociability and friendship in the afternoon, or at any other time) but if I am mistaken in this, the history of this business is simply and shortly as follows. Before the custom was established, which now accommodates foreign characters, Strangers, and others who from motives of curiosity, respect to the Chief Magistrate, or any other cause, are induced to call upon me, I was unable to attend to any business *whatsoever* ; for Gentlemen, consulting their own convenience rather than mine, were calling from the time I rose from breakfast, often before, until I sat down to dinner. This, as I resolved not to neglect my public duties, reduced me to the choice of one of these alternatives, either to refuse them *altogether*, or to appropriate a time for the reception of them. The first would, I well knew, be disgusting to many. The latter, I *expected*, would undergo an imadversion, and blazoning from those who would find fault, *with*, or *without* cause. To please everybody was impossible; I therefore adopted that line of conduct which combined public advantage with private convenience, and which in my judgment was unexceptionable in itself...

These visits are optional. They are made without invitation. Between the hours of three and four every Tuesday I am prepared to receive them. Gentlemen, often in great numbers, come and go, chat with each other, and act as they please. A Porter shows them into the room, and they retire from it when they please, and without ceremony. At their *first* entrance they salute me, and I them, and as many as I can talk to I do. What pomp there is in all this, I am unable to discover. Perhaps it consists in not sitting. To this two reasons are opposed, first it is unusual; secondly, (which is a more substantial one) because I have no room large enough to contain a third of the chairs, which would be sufficient to admit it. If it is supposed that ostentation, or the fashions of courts (which by the by I believe originates oftener in convenience, not to say necessity than is generally imagined) gave rise to this custom, I will boldly affirm that *no* supposition was ever more erroneous; for, if I was to give indulgence to my inclinations, every moment that I could withdraw from the fatigues of my station should be spent in retirement. That they are not proceeds from the sense I entertain of the propriety of giving to every one as free access, as consists with that respect which is due to the Chair of government; and that respect I conceive is neither to be acquired or preserved but by observing a just medium between much state and too great familiarity.

Similar to the above, but of a more sociable kind are the visits every Friday afternoon to Mrs. Washington where I always am. These public meetings and a dinner once a week to as many as my table will hold, with the references *to* and *from* the different Departments of State, and *other* Communications with *all* parts of the Union is as much, if not more, than I am able to undergo; for I have already had within less than a year, two *severe* attacks; the last worse than the first; a third more than probable, will put me to sleep with my fathers; at what distance this may be I know not. Within the last twelve months I have undergone more, and severer sickness than thirty preceding years afflicted me with, put it all together. I have abundant reason however to be thankful that I am so well recovered; though I still feel the remains of the violent affection of my lungs. The cough, pain in my breast, and shortness in breathing not having entirely left me. I propose in the recess of Congress to visit Mount Vernon; but when this recess will happen is beyond my ken, or the ken I believe of any of its members. I am &c."

23. GEORGE WASHINGTON TO DAVID STUART JUNE 15, 1790

"I can truly say I had rather be at Mount Vernon with a friend or two about me, than to be attended at the Seat of Government by the Officers of State and the Representatives of every Power in Europe."

24. GEORGE WASHINGTON TO TOBIAS LEAR SEPTEMBER 5, 1790

"The House Mr. R. Morris had, previous to my arrival, been taken by the Corporation for my residence. It is the best they could get. It is, I believe, the best *single House* in the City; yet, without additions it is inadequate to the *commodious* accomodation of my family. These, I believe, will be made.

The first floor contains only two public rooms (except one for the *upper* Servants). The second floor will have two public (drawing) rooms, & with the aid of one room with the partition in it in the back building will be sufficient for the accomodation of Mrs. Washington & the Children, & their Maids—besides affording me a small place for a private study & dressing room. The third story will furnish you & Mrs. Lear with a good lodging room—a public office (for there is no place below you for one) and two rooms for the gentlemen of the family. The Garret has four good rooms which must serve Mr. & Mrs. Hyde (unless they should prefer the room over the wash house)—William—and such servants as it may not be better to place in the addition (as proposed) to the back building. There is a room over the stable (without a fire place, but by means of a stove) may serve the Coachman & Postilions; and there is a smoke house, which, possibly, may be more useful to me for the accomodation of servants than for smoking of meat. The intention of the addition to the back building is to provide a servants hall, and one or two (as it will afford) lodging rooms for the servants; especially those who are coupled. There is a very good wash house adjoining to the kitchen (under one of the rooms already mentioned). There are good stables, but for 12 horses only, and a coach house which will hold all my carriages."

25. GEORGE WASHINGTON TO JAMES MADISON MAY 20, 1792

"My dear Sir: As there is a possibility if not a probability, that I shall not see you on your return home; or, if I should see you, that it may be on the road and under circumstances which will prevent my speaking to you on the subject we last conversed upon; I take the liberty of committing to paper the following thoughts, and requests.

I have not been unmindful of the sentiments expressed by you in the conversations just alluded to: on the contrary I have again, and again revolved them, with thoughtful anxiety; but without being able to dispose my mind to a longer continuation in the Office I have now the honor to hold. I therefore still look forward to the fulfilment of my fondest and most ardent wishes to spend the remainder of my days (which I can not expect will be many) in ease and tranquility.

Nothing short of conviction that my deriliction of the Chair of Government (if it should be the desire of the people to continue me in it) would involve the Country in serious disputes respecting the chief Magestrate, and the disagreeable consequences which might result therefrom in the floating, and divided opinions which seem to prevail at present, could, in any wise, induce me to relinquish the determination I have formed: and of this I do not see how any evidence can be obtained previous to the Election. My vanity, I am sure, is not of that cast as to allow me to view the subject in this light.

Under these impressions then, permit me to reiterate the request I made to you at our last meeting, namely, to think of the proper time, and the best mode of announcing the intention; and that you would prepare the latter. In revolving this subject myself, my judgment has always been embarrassed. On the one hand, a previous declaration to retire, not only carries with it the appearance of vanity and self importance, but it may be construed into a manoeuvre to be invited to remain. And on the other hand, to say nothing, implies consent; or, at any rate, would leave the matter in doubt, and to decline afterwards might be deemed as bad, and uncandid.

I would fain carry my request to you farther than is asked above, although I am sensible that your compliance with it must add to your trouble; but as the recess may afford you leisure, and I flatter myself you have dispositions to oblige me, I will, without apology desire (if the measure in itself should strike you as proper, and likely to produce public good, or private honor) that you would turn your thoughts to a Valadictory address from me to the public; expressing in plain and modest terms: that having been honored with the Presidential Chair, and to the best of my abilities contributed to the Organization and Administration of the government. that having arrived at a period of life when the private Walks of it, in the shade of retirement, becomes necessary, and will be most pleasing to me; and the spirit of the government may render a rotation in the Elective Officers of it more congenial with their ideas of liberty and safety, that I take my leave of them as a public man; and in bidding them adieu (retaining no other concern than such as will arise from fervent wishes for the prosperity of my Country) I take the liberty at my departure from civil, as I formerly did at my military exit, to invoke a continuation of the blessings of Providence upon it; and upon all those who are the supporters of its interests, and the promoters of harmony, order and good government.

That to impress these things it might, among other things be observed, that we are *all* the Children of the same country; a Country great and rich in itself; capable, and promising to be, as prosperous and as happy as any the Annals of history have ever brought to our view. That our interest, however, deversified in local and smaller matters, is the same in all the great and essential concerns of the Nation. That the extent of our Country, the diversity of our climate and soil, and the various productions of the States consequent to both, are such as to make one part not only convenient, but perhaps indispensably necessary to the other part; and may render the whole (at no distant period) one of the most independant in the world. That the established government being the work of our own hands, with the seeds of amendment engrafted in the Constitution, may by wisdom, good dispositions, and mutual allowances; aided by experience, bring it as near to perfection as any human institution ever aproximated; and therefore, the only strife among us ought to be, who should be foremost in facilitating and finally accomplishing such great and desirable objects; by giving every possible support, and cement to the Union. That however necessary it may be to keep a watchful eye over public servants, and public measures, yet there ought to be limits to it; for suspicions unfounded, and jealousies too lively, are irritating to honest feelings; and oftentimes are productive of more evil than good.

To enumerate the various subjects which might be introduced into such an Address would require thought; and to mention them to you would be unnecessary, as your own judgment will comprehend *all* that will be proper; whether to touch, specifically, any of the exceptionable parts of the Constitu[t]ion may be doubted. All I shall add therefore at present, is, to beg the favor of you to consider: 1st. the propriety of such an Address. 2d. if approved, the several matters which ought to be contained in it; and 3d. the time it should appear: that is, whether at the declaration of my intention to withdraw from the service of the public; or to let it be the closing Act of my Administration; which, will end with the next Session of Congress (the probability being that that body will continue sitting until March,) when the House of Representatives will also dissolve.

'Though I do not wish to hurry you (the cases not pressing) in the execution of either of the publications beforementioned, yet I should be glad to hear from you generally on both; and to receive them in time, if you should not come to Philadelphia until the Session commences, in the form they are finally to take. I beg leave to draw your attention also to such things as you shall conceive fit subjects for Communication on that occasion; and, noting them as they occur, that you would be so good as to furnish me with them in time to be prepared, and engrafted with others for the opening of the Session. With very sincere and Affectionate regard etc."

26. EXCERPT FROM GEORGE WASHINGTON'S SECOND INAUGURAL ADDRESS MARCH 4, 1793

"I am again called upon, by the voice of my country, to execute the functions of its Chief Magistrate. When the occasion proper for it shall arrive, I shall endeavor to honor, and of the confidence which has been reposed in me by the people of the United America.

Previous to the execution of any official act of the PRESIDENT, the Constitution requires an oath of office. This oath I am now about to take, and in your presence; that if it shall be found, during my administration of the Government, I have in any instance, violated, willingly or knowingly, the injunction thereof, I may (besides incurring Constitutional punishment) be subject to the upbraidings of all who are now witnesses of the present solemn ceremony."

27. GEORGE WASHINGTON TO JONATHAN TRUMBULL MARCH 3, 1797

"Although I shall resign the chair of government without a single regret, or any desire to intermeddle in politics again, yet there are many of my compatriots (among whom be assured I place you) from whom I shall part sorrowing; because, unless I meet with them at Mount Vernon it is not likely that I shall ever see them more, as I do not expect that I shall ever be twenty miles from it after I am tranquilly settled there."

28. GEORGE WASHINGTON TO JOHN SINCLAIR MARCH 6, 1797

"On the 11th of December I wrote you a long letter; and intended before the close of the last session of Congress (which ended on the third instant, conformably to the Constitution) to have addressed you again; but oppressed as I was with the various occurences incident thereto, especially in the latter part of it, it has not been in my power to do so during its continuance; and now, the arrangements necessary to my departure from this City—for a more tranquil theatre, and for the indulgence of rural pursuits, will oblige me to suspend my purpose until I am fixed at Mount Vernon, where I expect soon to be; having resigned the chair of government to Mr. John Adams on Friday last; the day on which I completed my second four years administration."

29. GEORGE WASHINGTON TO JOHN QUINCY ADAMS JANUARY 20, 1799

"When I offered my Valedictory Address to the People of the United States, I little thought that any event would arise in my day, that could withdraw me from the retreat in which I expected to pass the remnant of a life (worn down with cares) in ruminating on past scenes, & contemplating the future granduer of this rising Empire—But we know little of ourselves, & much less the designs of Providence."

30. GEORGE WASHINGTON TO JONATHAN TRUMBULL AUGUST 30, 1799

"With respect to the other subject of your letter,[1] I must again express a strong, and ardent wish and desire that, no eye, no tongue, no thought, my be turned towards me for the purpose alluded to therein."

1 Running for a third term as president.

II. JOHN ADAMS ON GEORGE WASHINGTON

1. JOHN ADAMS LETTER TO ABIGAIL ADAMS MAY 29, 1775

"Coll. Washington appears at Congress in his Uniform and, by his great Experience and Abilities in military Matters, is of much service to Us. Oh that I was a Soldier! - - I will be. - - I am reading military Books. - - Every Body must and will, and shall be a soldier."

2. EXCERPT FROM THE AUTOBIOGRAPHY OF JOHN ADAMS JUNE 1775

"I am determined this Morning to make a direct Motion that Congress should adopt the Army before Boston and appoint Colonel Washington Commander of it... I concluded with a Motion in form that Congress would Adopt the Army at Cambridge and appoint a General, that though this was not the proper time to nominate a General, yet as I had reason to believe this was a point of the greatest difficulty, I had no hesitation to declare that I had but one Gentleman in my Mind for that important command, and that was a Gentleman from Virginia who was among Us and very well known to all of Us, a Gentleman whose Skill and Experience as an Officer, whose independent fortune, great Talents and excellent universal Character, would command the Approbation of all America, and unite the cordial Exertions of all the Colonies better than any other Person in the Union. Mr. Washington, who happened to sit near the Door, as soon as he heard me allude to him, from his Usual Modesty darted into the Library Room."

3. JOHN ADAMS TO ABIGAIL ADAMS JUNE 17, 1775

"I can now inform you that the Congress have made choice of the modest and virtuous, the amiable, generous, and brave George Washington, Esquire, to be General of the American army, and that he is to repair, as soon as possible, to the camp before Boston. This appointment will have a great effect in cementing and securing the union of these colonies. The continent is really in earnest, in defending the country... I hope the people of our province will treat the General with all that confidence and affection, that politeness and respect, which is due to one of the most important characters of the world. The liberties of America depend on him, in a great degree."

4. JOHN ADAMS TO ELBRIDGE GERRY JUNE 18, 1775

"There is something charming to me in the conduct of Washington. A gentleman of one of the first fortunes upon the continent, leaving his delicious retirement, his family and friends, sacrificing his ease, and hazarding all in the cause of his country! His views are noble and disinterested. He declared, when he accepted the mighty trust, that he would lay before us an exact account of his expenses, and not accept a shilling for pay. The express waits."

5. EXCERPT FROM THE AUTOBIOGRAPHY OF JOHN ADAMS DECEMBER 1777

"The News of my Appointment [as Minister to France] was whispered about, and General Knox came up to dine with me, at Braintree. The design of his Visit was As I soon perceived to sound me in relation to General Washington. He asked me what my Opinion of him was. I answered with the Utmost Frankness, that I thought him a perfectly honest Man, with an amiable and excellent heart, and the most important Character at that time among Us, for he was the Center of our Union. He asked the question, he said, because, as I was going to Europe it was of importance that the Generals Character should be supported in other Countries. I replied that he might be perfectly at ease on the Subject for he might depend upon it, that both from principle and Affection, public and private I should do my Utmost to support his Character at all times and in all places, unless something should happen very greatly to alter my Opinion of him, and this I have done from that time to this."

6. JOHN ADAMS TO ABIGAIL ADAMS APRIL 6, 1777

"Another report, which has been industriously circulated, is that the General has been made by Congress dictator. But this is as false as the other stories. Congress, it is true, upon removing to Baltimore, gave the General power to raise fifteen battalions, in addition to those which were ordered to be raised before, and to appoint the officers, and also to raise three thousand horse, and to appoint their officers, and also to take necessaries for his army, at an appraised value. But no more. Congress never thought of making him dictator or of giving him a sovereignty. I wish I could find a correspondent who was idle enough to attend to every report, and write it to me. Such false news, uncontradicted, does more or less harm. Such a collection of lies would be a curiosity for posterity."

---

7. JOHN ADAMS TO ABIGAIL ADAMS SEPTEMBER 1, 1777

"General Washington sets a fine example. He has banished wine from his table, and entertains his friends with rum and water. This is much to the honor of his wisdom, his policy, and his patriotism. And the example must be followed by banishing sugar and all imported articles from our families. If necessity should reduce us to a simplicity of dress and diet becoming republicans, it would be a happy and glorious necessity."

---

8. JOHN ADAMS TO ABIGAIL ADAMS SEPTEMBER 2, 1777

"Washington has a great body of militia assembled and assembling, in addition to a grand Continental army. Whether he will strike or not, I can't say. He is very prudent, you know, and will not unnecessarily hazard his army. By my own inward feelings, I judge, I should put more to risk if I were in his shoes, but perhaps he is right."

---

9. EXCERPT FROM JOHN ADAMS'S *TWENTY-SIX LETTERS UPON INTERESTING SUBJECTS RESPECTING THE REVOLUTION OF AMERICA* OCTOBER 10, 1780

"Is it necessary to put the supposition, that General Washington should be corrupted? Is it possible, that so fair a fame as Washington's should be exchanged for gold or for crowns? A character so false, so cruel, so blood-thirsty, so detestable as that of a Monk might betray a trust; but a character so just, so humane, so fair, so open, honorable, and amiable as Washington's, never can be strained with so foul a reproach.

Yet I am fully of opinion, that even if Mr. Washington should go over to the English, which I know to be impossible, he would find none or very few officers or soldiers to go with him. He would become the contempt and execration of his own army as well as of all the rest of mankind."

---

10. JOHN ADAMS'S TO RICHARD CRANCH APRIL 3, 1784

"But my political Career is run. I will wind off as decently as I can, and notwithstanding my family is coming to Europe, I hope in another Year to imitate the General in the only Thing perhaps in which I am capable of imitating him, in Retreat."[2]

11. JOHN ADAMS LETTER TO JOHN LEBB SEPTEMBER 10, 1785

"... Instead of adoring a Washington, mankind should applaud the nation which educated him... The human mind naturally exerts itself to form its character, according to the ideas of those about it. When children and youth hear their parents and neighbors, and all about them, applauding the love of country, of labor, of liberty; and all the virtues, habits, and faculties, which constitute a good citizen, that is, a patriot and a hero, those children endeavor to acquire those qualities, and a sensible and virtuous people will never fail to form multitudes of patriots and heros. I glory in the character of a Washington, because I know him to be only an exemplification of the American character. I know that the general character of the natives of the United States is the same with his, and that the prevalence of such sentiments and principles produced his character and preserved it, and I know there are thousands of others who have in them all the essential qualities, moral and intellectual, which compose it. If his character stood alone, I should value it very little,—I should wish it had never existed; because, although it might have wrought a great event, yet that event would be no blessing. In the days of Pompey, Washington would have been a Ceasar; his officers and partisans would have stimulated him to it; he could not have had their confidence without it; in the time of Charles, a Cromwell; in the days of Phillip the second, a prince of Orange, and would have wished to be Count of Holland. But in America he could have no other ambition than that of retiring."

12. JOHN ADAMS TO THOMAS JEFFERSON OCTOBER 9, 1787

"If General Washington had a Daughter, I firmly believe, she would be demanded in Marriage by one of the Royal Families of France or England, perhaps by both, or if he had a Son he would be invited to come a courting to Europe."

2 On 23 December 1783, George Washington resigned as Commander-in Chief of the Continental Army and returned to private life at his home at Mount Vernon, Virginia.

13. JOHN ADAMS TO THOMAS JEFFERSON MARCH 1, 1789

"In four days, the new Government is to be erected. Washington appears to have an unanimous vote: and there is probably a Plurality if not a Majority in favour of your Friend.—It may be found easier to give Authority, than to yield Obedience."

14. JOHN ADAMS ON GEORGE WASHINGTON APRIL 6, 1789

"That Washington was not a schollar is certain. That he was too illiterate, unlearned, unread for his station and reputation is equally beyond dispute. He had derived little Knowledge from Reading, none from Travel."

15. JOHN ADAMS ADDRESS TO THE UNITED STATES SENATE APRIL 21, 1789

"Were I blessed with powers to do justice to his character, it would be impossible to increase the confidence or affection of his country, or make the smallest addition to his glory. This can only be effected by a discharge of the present exalted trust, on the same principles, with the same abilities and virtues, which have uniformly appeared in all his former conduct, public or private. May I, nevertheless, be indulged to inquire, if we look over the catalogue of the first magistrates of nations, whether they have been denominated presidents or consuls, kings or princes, where shall we find one, whose commanding talents and virtues, whose overruling good fortune, have so completely united all hearts and voices in his favor, who enjoyed the esteem and admiration of foreign nations and fellow citizens with an equal unanimity? Qualities, so uncommon, are no common blessings to the country that possesses them. By those great qualities, and their benign effects, has Providence marked out the head of this nation with a hand, so distinctly visible, as to have been seen by all men, and mistaken by none."

16. JOHN ADAMS TO THOMAS BRAND-HOLLIS JUNE 1, 1790

"Franklin is no more, and we have lately trembled for Washington. Thank God, he has recovered from a dangerous sickness and is likely now to continue many years. His life is of vast importance for us."

17. JOHN ADAMS TO ABIGAIL ADAMS MARCH 25, 1796

"Yesterday I dined at the Presidents with Ministers of State and their Ladies foreign and Domestic. After dinner the Gentlemen drew off after the Ladies and left me alone with the President in close Conversation. He detained me there till Nine o Clock and was never more frank and open upon Politicks. I find his Opinions and sentiments are more like mine than I ever knew before, respecting England and France and our American Parties. He gave me Intimations enough that his Reign would be very short. He repeated it three times at least, that this and that was of no Consequence to him personally, as he had but a very little while to stay in his present situation. This must be a confidential secret."

18. JOHN ADAMS TO ABIGAIL ADAMS DECEMBER 16, 1796

"I shall not suffer so much in retiring as the P[resident] whose tender feelings are excited both by Kindness and Unkindness. I shall retire without much of either to harrow up my soul. It is rather a dull Prospect to see nothing but ones Plougshare between one and the Grave but I am confident I can bear it as well as the P. My Misery will all be over by the Ninth of Feb. if I am released. But that is too long."

19. JOHN ADAMS TO ABIGAIL ADAMS MARCH 3, 1797

"We shall be put to great difficulty to live and that in not one third the Style of Washington."

20. EXCERPT FROM JOHN ADAMS'S FIRST INAUGURAL ADDRESS MARCH 4, 1797

"Such is the amiable and interesting system of government (and such are some of the abuses to which it may be exposed) which the people of America have exhibited to the admiration and anxiety of the wise and virtuous of all nations for eight years under the administration of a citizen who, by a long course of great actions, regulated by prudence, justice, temperance, and fortitude, conducting a people inspired with the same virtues and animated with the same ardent patriotism and love of liberty to independence and peace, to increasing wealth and unexampled prosperity, has merited the gratitude of his fellow-citizens, commanded the highest praises of foreign nations, and secured immortal glory with posterity.

In that retirement which is his voluntary choice may he long live to enjoy the delicious recollection of his services, the gratitude of mankind, the happy fruits of them to himself and the world, which are daily increasing, and that splendid prospect of the future fortunes of this country which is opening from year to year. His name may be still a rampart, and the knowledge that he lives a bulkwark, against all open or secret enemies of his country's peace. This example has been recommended to the imitation of his successors by both Houses of Congress and by the voice of legislatures and the people throughout the nation."

21. JOHN ADAMS TO ABIGAIL ADAMS MARCH 5, 1797

"My dearest Friend, your dearest Friend never had a more trying day than Yesterday. A Solemn Scene it was indeed and it was made more affecting to me by the presence of the General, whose Countenance was as serene and unclouded as the day. He Seemed to me to enjoy a triumph over me. Methought I heard him think Ay! I am fairly out and you fairly in! See which of Us will be happiest. When the Ceremony was over he came and made me a visit and cordially congratulated me and wished my Administration might be happy, Successful and honourable."

22. JOHN ADAMS TO ABIGAIL ADAMS APRIL 14, 1797

"Oh what an enchanting Summer I should have had, if W[ashington] had been P[resident] and I V. P.! But never mind that. We will do our Duty as We are and he could do no more."

23. EXCERPT FROM JOHN ADAMS'S ADDRESS TO THE UNITED STATES SENATE DECEMBER 23, 1799

"The life of our Washington cannot suffer by a comparison with those of other countries who have been most celebrated and exalted by fame. The attributes and decorations of royalty could have only served to eclipse the majesty of those virtues which made him, from being a modest citizen, a more resplendent luminary. Misfortune, had he lived, could hereafter have sullied his glory only with those superficial minds, who, believing that characters and actions are marked by success alone, rarely deserve to enjoy it. Malice could never blast his honor, and envy made him a singular exception to her universal rule. For himself, he had lived enough to life and to glory. For his fellow-citizens, if their prayers could have been answered, he would have been immortal. For me, his departure is at a most unfortunate moment. Trusting, however, in the wise and righteous dominion of Providence, over the passions of men, and the results of their counsels and actions, as well as over their lives, nothing remains for me but humble resignation.

His example is now complete, and it will teach wisdom and virtue to magistrates, citizens, and men, not only in the present age, but in future generations, as long as our history shall be read. If a Trajan found a Pliny, a Marcus Aurelius can never want biographers, eulogists, or historians."

24. JOHN ADAMS TO JOHN TRUMBULL NOVEMBER 18, 1805

"I agree with you that Washington had high talents and great qualities: and that he far surpassed any one who ever acted in the American Theatre. Lee, Gates, Steuben, Green or even Warren or Montgomery, though some of them were much superior to him in science and learning, would not have answered our end so well. Nor would any general in Europe. This opinion I constantly avowed and supported both in Europe and America. Tom Paine has repeatedly asserted in print that I was one of that faction who were for removing him from his command. This is one among many of Paine's lies. I left Congress at York town on the 11th. of November 1777 and never knew of any plan to remove the General. It was in the winter of 1778, if ever that such a scheme was laid or proposed; when I was tumbling among the mountains of waves in the Gulph Stream, the English Channel and the Bay of Biscay.

I agree too, in your opinion that if we could have had our choice of all the military commanders in Europe we should not have found his equal for our purpose. There is reason to suspect that General Conway and some other foreigners, were instigated from France, to supplant the General, to make way for a foreign commander. Before I left Congress in 1777 letters were read in it, from Mr. Deane, one of them enquired whether in any supposable case Congress would consent to supersede General Washington and give the command in Chief to a foreign officer."

25. EXCERPT FROM JOHN ADAMS'S *PROPOSITIONS FOR AMENDING THE CONSTITUTION OF THE UNITED STATES, SUBMITTED BY MR. HILLHOUSE TO THE SENATE, ON THE TWELFTH DAY OF APRIL, 1808, WITH HIS EXPLANATORY REMARKS* 1808

"Notwithstanding all the ardor of popular affection for Washington, and the great, I will not say unlimited confidence in him, congress and the nation were more divided, during the eight years of his administration, than they have been ever since."

26. JOHN ADAMS TO BENJAMIN RUSH JUNE 20, 1808

"Since the death of Washington, you say there has been no Center of Union. But what Center was Washington? He had unanimous Votes as President, but the two houses of Congress and the great Party of the People, were more equally divided under him than they ever have been since. Jonathan Dickenson Serjeant and Dr Hutchinson would have turned him out of his House, if the Yellow fever had not been Sent to save him, and a Majority of the People of the Union would then have applauded Genet, untill John Quincy Adams turned the Tide of popular fury and Delusion. Never was Man under greater obligation to another, than Washington was to that youth, and no Man was more Sensible of it, than Washington himself, as I can prove by indisputable Evidence."

27. JOHN ADAMS TO BENJAMIN RUSH OCTOBER 10, 1808

"Si velis pacem para bellum, is by the Federalists Said to be Washington's Doctrine."[3]

28. JOHN ADAMS TO *THE BOSTON PATRIOT* JUNE 8, 1809

"The Senate was now decidedly federal. During President Washington's whole administration of eight years, his authority in the Senate was extremely weak. The Senate was equally divided in all great constitutional questions, and in all great questions of foreign relations, and such as were the most sharply contested were brought to my decision as Vice President."

3 "If you want peace, prepare for war."

29. JOHN ADAMS TO *THE BOSTON PATRIOT* JUNE 27, 1811

"The base and wicked insinuations that Jefferson or Madison have been bribed or intimidated by Bonaparte—*have my utmost detestation—I should believe it of* Washington *as soon as of either*. There is more reason to suspect that both of them, and Washington too, were too much overawed by the terrors of the British navy, than by any fears of Napoleon."

30. JOHN ADAMS TO JOHN HOLMES AUGUST 10, 1815

"2nd I protest against the application in your 9th page of the magnificent title of Father of his Country to Washington. I could name twenty men, who have merited that appellation more than Washington. I will only mention two & they shall be Virginians. Richard Henry Lee and Patrick Henry. I have sometimes wondered, that popular delirium, called public opinion, has not given this title to Tom Paine!"

31. JOHN ADAMS TO JOHN RANDOLPH, JR. 1816

"When was this goverment, "in the hands of bad Men"? Was Washington a "bad Man"? Was Jefferson a "bad Man"? Is Madison a "bad Man"? Have any of their Ministers been "bad Men"? Have both Houses of Congress for five and twenty years been bad Men? Where then Shall We look to find good Men? The People under Washington from Georgia to New Hampshire, were more discontented than they ever have been Since. His Administration was Supported by Smaller Majorities in both Houses than any Administration since. It was about half and half through his whole Eight years."

32. JOHN ADAMS COMMENTS ON GEORGE WASHINGTON WHILE BEING PAINTED BY GILBERT STUART 1825

"Washington got the reputation of being a great man because he kept his mouth shut."

III. THOMAS JEFFERSON ON GEORGE WASHINGTON

1. THOMAS JEFFERSON ON THE FAME OF GEORGE WASHINGTON DATE?

"Washington's fame will go on increasing until the brightest constellation in yonder heaven shall be called by his name."

2. EXCERPT FROM THOMAS JEFFERSON'S *NOTES ON VIRGINIA* 1782

"'America has not yet produced one good poet.' When we shall have existed as a people as long as the Greeks did before they produced a Homer, the Romans a Virgil, the French a Racine and Voltaire, the English a Shakespeare and Milton, should this reproach be still true, we will inquire from what unfriendly causes it has proceeded, that the other countries of Europe and quarters of the earth shall not have inscribed any name in the roll of poets. But neither has America produced one able mathematician, one man of genius in a single art or a single science. In war we have produced a Washington, whose memory will be adored while liberty shall have votaries, whose name will triumph over time, and will in future ages assume its just station among the most celebrated worthies of the world, when that wretched philosophy shall be forgotten which would have arranged him among the degeneracies of nature."

3. THOMAS JEFFERSON TO PATRICK HENRY JANUARY 12, 1785

"Doctor Franklin and myself became satisfied that no statue could be executed so as to obtain the approbation of those to whom the figure of the original is known, but on an actual view by the artist. Of course no statue of General Washington, which might be a true evidence of his figure to posterity, could be made from his picture. Statues are made every day from portraits; but if the person be living, they are always condemned by those who know him for a want of resemblance, and this furnishes a conclusive presumption that similar representations of the dead are equally unfaithful. Monsr. Houdon, whose reputations is such as to make it his principal object, was so anxious to be the person who should hand down the figure of the General to future ages, that without hesitating a moment, he offered to abandon his business [in Paris], to leave the statues of Kings unfinished, and to go to America to take the true figure by actual inspection and mensuration… We are agreed in one circumstance, that the size shall be precisely that of life. Were we to have executed a statue in any other case, we should have preferred making it somewhat larger than life; because as they are generally a little elevated they appear smaller, but we think it important that some one monument should be preserved of the true size as well as figure, form which all other countries (and our own at any future day when they shall desire it), may take copies, varying them in their dimensions as may suit the particular situation in which they wish to place them. The duty as well as the glory of this presentation we think belongs peculiarly to Virginia. We are sensible that the eye alone considered will not be quite as well satisfied; but connecting the consideration that the whole, and every part of it presents the true size of the life, we suppose the beholders will receive a greater pleasure on the whole."

4. THOMAS JEFFERSON TO WILLIAM CARMICHAEL AUGUST 12, 1788

"Another defect (of the Constitution), the perpetual re-eligibility of the same President, will probably not be cured during the life of General Washington. His merit has blinded our countrymen to the danger of making so important an officer re-eligible. I presume there will not be a vote against him in the United States."

5. THOMAS JEFFERSON TO WILLIAM SHORT FEBRUARY 9, 1789

"Genl. Washington will be president and probably Mr. Adams vice president. So that the constitution will be put under way by those who will give it a fair trial."

6. THOMAS JEFFERSON TO GEORGE WASHINGTON MAY 10, 1789

"Tho' we have not heard of the actual opening of the New Congress, & consequently have not official information of your election as President of the U. S. yet as there never could be a doubt entertained of it, permit me to express here my felicitations, not to yourself, but to my country. Nobody who has tried both public & private life can doubt but that you were much happier on the banks of the Potowmac than you will be at New York.[4] But there was nobody so well qualified as yourself to put our new machine into a regular

4 New York City served as the nation's capital from 1785 to 1788 and 1789 to 1790.

course of action, nobody the authority of whose name could have so effectually crushed the opposition at home, and produced respect abroad. I am sensible of the immensity of the sacrifice on your part. Your measure of fame was full to the brim: and therefore you have nothing to gain. But there are cases wherein it is a duty to risk all against nothing, and I believe this was exactly the case. We may presume too, according to every rule of probability, that after doing a great deal of good you will have found to have lost nothing but private repose."

7. THOMAS JEFFERSON TO NICHOLAS LEWIS FEBRUARY 9, 1791

"Congress will rise on the 3d of March. They have passed an excise bill, which, considering the present circumstances of the Union, is not without objection, and a bill for establishing a bank to which it is objected that they have transcended their powers. There are certainly persons in all the departments who are for driving too fast. Government being founded on opinion, the opinion of the public, even when it is wrong, ought to be respected to a certain degree. The prudence of the President is an anchor of safety to us."

8. THOMAS JEFFERSON TO HARRY INNES MARCH 13, 1791

"It is fortunate that our first executive magistrate is purely and zealously republican. We cannot expect all his successors to be so, and therefore should avail ourselves the present day to establish principles and examples which may fence us against future heresies preached now, to be practiced hereafter."

9. THOMAS JEFFERSON TO GEORGE WASHINGTON MAY 23, 1792

"I consider your continuance at the head of affairs as of the last importance. The confidence of the whole Union is centered on you. Your being at the helm will be more than an answer to every argument which can be used to alarm and lead the people in any quarter, into violence and secession. North and South will hang together if they have you to hang on; and if the first correction of a numerous representation should fail in its effect, your presence will give time for trying others, not inconsistent with the Union and peace of the States. I am perfectly aware of the oppression under which your present office lays on your mind, and of the ardor with which you pant for domestic life. But there is sometimes an eminence of character on which society have such peculiar claims as to control the predilections of the individual for a particular walk of happiness, and restrain him to that alone arising from the present and future benedictions of mankind. This seems to be your condition, and the law imposed on you by Providence in forming your character, and fashioning the events on which it was to operate; and it is to motives like these and not to personal anxieties of mine or others who have no right to call on you for sacrifices, that I appeal, and urge a revisal of it, on the ground of change in the aspect of things. Should an honest majority result from the new and enlarged representation; should those acquiesce whose principles or interests they may control, your wishes for retirement would be gratified with less danger, as soon as that shall be manifest, without awaiting the completion of the second period of four years. One or two sessions will determine the crisis; and I cannot but hope that you can resolve to add more to the many years you have already sacrificed to the good of mankind. The fear of suspicion that any selfish motive of continuance in office may enter into this solicitation on my part, obliges me to declare that no such motive exists. It is a thing of mere indifference to the public whether I retain or relinquish my purpose of closing my tour with the first political renovation of the government. I know my own measure too well to suppose that my services contribute anything to the public confidence or the public utility. Multitudes can fill the office in which you have been pleased to place me, as much to their advantage and satisfaction. I have, therefore, no motive to consult but my own inclination, which is bent irresistibly on the tranquil enjoyment of my family, my farm and my books. I should repose among them, it is true, in far greater security, if I were to know that you remained at the watch; and I hope it will be so."

10. THOMAS JEFFERSON TO GEORGE WASHINGTON MAY 23, 1792

"When you first mentioned to me your purpose of retiring from the government, though I felt all the magnitude of the event, I was in a considerable degree silent. I knew that, to such a mind as yours, persuasion was idle and impertinent; that before forming your decision you had weighed all the reasons for and against the measure, had made up your mind full view of them, and that there could be little hope of changing the result. Pursuing my reflections, too, I knew we were some day to try to walk alone, and if the essay should be made while you should be alive and looking on, we should derive confidence from that circumstance, and resource, if it failed. The public mind, too, was calm and confident, and therefore in a favorable state for making the experiment."

11. EXCERPT FROM THOMAS JEFFERSON'S *THE ANAS* JULY 10, 1792

"My letter to the President, directed to him at Mount Vernon, came to him [in Philadelphia]. He told me of this, and that he would take occasion of speaking with me on the subject. He did so this day. He began by observing that he had put it off from day to day, because the subject was painful, to wit, his remaining in office, which that letter solicited. He said that the declarations he had made when he quitted his military command, of never again acting in public life, was sincere. That, however, when he was called to come forward to set the present government in motion, it appeared to him that circumstances were so changed as to justify a change in his resolution; he was made to believe that in two years all would be well in motion, and he might retire. At the end of two years he found some things still to be done. At the end of the third year, he thought it was not worth while to disturb the course of things, as in one year more his office would expire, and he was decided then to retire. Now he was told there would still be danger in it. Certainly, if he thought so, he would conquer his longing for retirement. But he feared it would be said his former professions of retirement had been mere affectation, and that he was like other men, when once in office he could not quit it. He was sensible, too, of a decay of his hearing; perhaps his other faculties might fall off, and he not be sensible of it. That with respect to the existing causes of uneasiness, he thought there were suspicions against a particular party, which had been carried a great deal too far; there might be *desires*, but he did not believe there were *designs* to change the form of government into a monarchy; that there might be a few who wished it in the higher walks of life, particularly in the great cities, but that the main body of the people in the eastern States were as steadily for republicanism as in the southern. That the pieces lately published, and particularly in Freneau's paper, seemed to have in view the exciting opposition to the government. That this had taken place in Pennsylvania as to the Excise law, according to information he had received from General Hand. That they tended to produce a separation of the Union, the most dreadful of all calamities, and that whatever tended to produce anarchy, tended, of course, to produce a resort to monarchical government. He considered those papers as attacking him directly, for he must be a fool indeed to swallow the little sugar plums here and there thrown out to him. That in condemning the administration of the government, they condemned him, for if they thought there were measures pursued contrary to his sentiment, they must conceive him too careless to attend to them, or too stupid to understand them. That though, indeed, he had signed many acts which he did not approve in all their parts, yet he had never put his name to one which, he did not think, on the whole, was eligible. That as to the Bank, which had been an act of so much complaint, until there was some infallible criterion of reason, a difference of opinion must be tolerated. He did not believe the discontents extended far from the seat of government. He had seen and spoken with many people in Maryland

and Virginia in his late journey. He found the people contented and happy. He wished, however, to be better informed on this head. If the discontent were more extensive than he supposed, it might be that the desire that he should remain in the government was not general."

-⊰⊱-

12. EXCERPT FROM THOMAS JEFFERSON'S *THE ANAS* OCTOBER 1792

"President Washington said that as yet he was quite undecided whether to retire in March or not. His inclinations led him strongly to do it. Nobody disliked more the ceremonies of his office, and he had not the least taste or gratification in the execution of its functions. That he was happy at home alone, and that his presence there was now particularly called for by the situation of Major Washington, whom he thought irrecoverable, and should he get well, he would remove into another part of the country, which might better agree with him. That he did not believe his presence necessary; that there were other characters who would do the business as well or better. Still, however, if his aid was thought necessary to save the cause to which he had devoted his life principally, he would make the sacrifice of a longer continuance. That he, therefore, reserved himself for future decision, and his declaration would be in time if made a month before the day of election. He had desired Mr. [Tobias] Lear to find out from conversation, without appearing to make the inquiry, whether any other person would be desired by anybody. He had informed him, he judged from conversations that it was the universal desire he should continue, and he believed that those who expressed a doubt of his continuance, did it in a language of apprehension, and not of desire. But this, says he, is only from the north; it may be very different in the south. I thought this meant as an opening to me to say what was the sentiment of the south, from which quarter I come. I told him, that as far as I knew, there was but one voice there, which was for his continuance."

-⊰⊱-

13. THOMAS JEFFERSON TO JAMES MADISON JUNE 9, 1793

"The President is not well. Little lingering fevers have been hanging about him for a week or ten days, and have affected his looks most remarkably. He is also extremely affected by the attacks made & kept up on him in the public papers. I think he feels those things more than any person I ever yet met with. I am sincerely sorry to see them. I remember an observation of yours, made when I first went to New York, that the satellites & sycophants which surrounded him had wound up the ceremonials of the government to a pitch of stateliness which nothing but his personal character could have supported, & which no character after him could ever maintain. It appears now that even his will be insufficient to justify them in the appeal of the times to common sense as the arbiter of everything. Naked he would have been sanctimoniously reverenced, but inveloped in the rags of royalty, they can hardly be torn off without laceration."

14. EXCERPT FROM THOMAS JEFFERSON'S, *THE ANAS* AUGUST 1793

"[Secretary of War Henry] Knox in a foolish incoherent sort of speech introduced the Pasquinade lately printed, called the funeral of George W[ashingto]n and James W[ilso]n; King & judge &c. where the President was placed on a guillotine. The Presidt was much inflamed, got into one of those passions when he cannot command himself, ran on much on the personal abuse which had been bestowed on him, defied any man on earth to produce one single act of his since he had been in the govmt which was not done on the purest motives, that he had never repented but once the having slipped the moment of resigning his office, & that was every moment since, that *by god* he had rather be in his grave than in his present situation. That he had rather be on his farm than to be made *emperor of the world* and yet that they were charging him with wanting to be a king. That that *rascal Freneau*[5] sent him 3 of his papers every day, as if he thought he would become the distributor of his papers, that he could see in this nothing but an impudent design to insult him. He ended in this high tone."

15. THOMAS JEFFERSON TO WILLIAM BRANCH GILES DECEMBER 31, 1795

"[George Washington] errs as other men do, but errs with integrity."

16. THOMAS JEFFERSON TO ARCHIBALD STUART JANUARY 4, 1797

"Such is the popularity of the President that the people will support him in whatever he will do or will not do, without appealing to their own reason or to anything but their feelings toward him. His mind has been so long used to unlimited applause that

5 Philip Freneau, 1752-1832, publisher of the *National Gazette,* a newspaper often critical of President Washington.

it could not brook contradiction, or even advice offered unasked. To advice, when asked, he is very open. I have long thought therefore it was best for the republican interest to soothe him by flattering where they could approve his measures, & to be silent where they disapprove, that they not render him desperate as to their affections, & entirely indifferent to their wishes, in short to lie on their oars while he remains at the helm, and let the bark drift as his will and a superintending providence shall direct."

17. THOMAS JEFFERSON TO JAMES MADISON JANUARY 8, 1797

"The President is fortunate to get off just as the bubble is bursting, leaving others to hold the bag. Yet, as his departure will mark the moment when the difficulties begin to work, you will see, that they will be ascribed to the new administration, and that he will have his usual good fortune of reaping credit from the good acts of others, and leaving to them that of his errors."

18. EXCERPT FROM THOMAS JEFFERSON'S, *THE ANAS* FEBRUARY 1, 1800

"Dr. Rush tells me that he had it from Asa Green that when the clergy addressed Genl. Washington on his departure from the govmt, it was observed in their consultation that he had never on any occasion said a word to the public which showed a belief in the Christian religion and they thot they should so pen their address as to force him at length to declare publicly where he was a Christian or not. They did so. However he observed the old fox was too cunning for them. He answered every article of their address particularly except that, which he passed over without notice. Rush observes he never did say a word on the subject in any of his public papers except in his valedictory letter to the Governors of the states when he resigned his commission in the army, wherein he speaks of the benign influence of the Christian religion."

19. EXCERPT FROM THOMAS JEFFERSON'S FIRST INAUGURAL ADDRESS MARCH 4, 1801

"Without pretensions to that high confidence you reposed in our first & greatest revolutionary character whose preeminent services had entitled him to the first place in his country's love, and had destined for him the fairest page in the volume of faithful history, I ask so much confidence only as may give firmness & effect to the legal administration of your affairs."

20. EXCERPT FROM A CIRCULAR WRITTEN BY THOMAS JEFFERSON NOVEMBER 6, 1801

"Having been a member of the first administration under Genl. Washington, I can state with exactness what our course then was. Letters of business came addressed sometimes to the President, but most frequently to the heads of departments. If addressed to himself, he referred them to the proper department to be acted on: if to one of the Secretaries, the letter, if it required no answer, was communicated to the President simply for his information. If an answer was requisite, the Secretary of the department communicated the letter & his proposed answer to the President. Generally they were simply sent back, after perusal, which signified his approbation. Sometimes he returned them with an informal note, suggesting an alteration or a query. If a doubt of any importance arose, he reserved it for conference. By this means he was always in accurate possession of all facts & proceedings in every part of the Union, & to whatsoever department they related; he formed a central point for the different branches, preserved an unity of object and action among them, exercised that participation in the gestion of affairs which his office made incumbent on him, and met himself the due responsibility for whatever was done. During mr. Adams's administration, his long & habitual absences from the seat of government rendered this kind of communication impracticable, removed him from any share in the transaction of affairs, & parcelled out the government in fact among four independent heads, drawing sometimes in opposite directions. That the former is preferable to the latter course cannot be doubted. It gave indeed to the heads of departments the trouble of making up, once a day, a packet of all their communications for the perusal of the President; it commonly also retarded one day their dispatches by mail: but, in pressing cases, this injury was prevented by presenting that case singly for immediate attention; and it produced us in return the benefit of his sanction for every act we did."

21. THOMAS JEFFERSON TO THE EARL OF BUCHAN JULY 10, 1803

"I feel a pride in the justice which your Lordship's sentiments render to the character of my illustrious countryman, Washington. The moderation of his desires, and the strength of his judgment, enabled him to calculate correctly, that the road to that glory which never dies is to use power for the support of the laws and liberties of our country, not for their destruction; and his will accordingly survives the wreck of everything now living."

-꧁꧂-

22. THOMAS JEFFERSON TO DANIEL ECCLESTON NOVEMBER 21, 1807

"That our own nation should entertain sentiments of gratitude and reverence for the great character [Washington]who is the subject of your medallion, is a matter of duty. His disinterested and valuable services to them have rendered it so; but such a monument to his memory by the member of another community, proves a zeal for virtue in the abstract, honorable to him who inscribes it, as to him whom it commemorates. In returning you my individual thanks for the one destined for myself, I should perform but a part of my duty were I not to add an assurance that this testimonial in favor of the first worthy of our country will be grateful to the feeling of our citizens generally."

-꧁꧂-

23. THOMAS JEFFERSON TO DOCTOR WALTER JONES JANUARY 2, 1814

"I am satisfied the great body of republicans think of [Washington] as I do. We were, indeed, dissatisfied with him on his ratification of the British treaty. But this was short lived. We knew his honesty, the wiles with which he was encompassed, and that age had already begun to relax the firmness of his purposes; and I am convinced he is more deeply seated in the love and gratitude of the republicans, than in the Pharisaical homage of the federalist monarchists. For he was no monarchist from preference of his judgment. The soundness of that gave him correct views of the rights of man, and his severe justice devoted him to them. He has often declared to me that he considered our new constitution as an experiment on the practicability of republican government, and with what dose of liberty man could be trusted for his own good; that he was determined the experiment should have a fair trial, and would lose the last drop of his blood in support of it."

-꧁꧂-

24. THOMAS JEFFERSON TO DOCTOR WALTER JONES JANUARY 2, 1814

"I think I knew General Washington intimately and thoroughly; and were I called on to delineate his character, it should be in terms like these.

His mind was great and powerful, without being of the very first order; his penetration strong, though not so acute as that of a Newton, Bacon, or Locke; and as far as he saw, no judgment was ever sounder. It was slow in operation, being little aided by invention or imagination, but sure in conclusion. Hence the common remark of his officers, of the advantage he derived from councils of war, where hearing all suggestions, he selected whatever was best; and certainly no General ever planned his battles more judiciously. But if deranged during the course of the action, if any member of his plan was dislocated by sudden circumstances, he was slow in re-adjustment. The consequence was, that he often failed in the field, and rarely against an enemy in station, as at Boston and York. He was incapable of fear, meeting personal dangers with the calmest unconcern. Perhaps the strongest feature in his character was prudence, never acting until every circumstance, every consideration, was maturely weighed; refraining if he saw a doubt, but, when once decided, going through with his purpose, whatever obstacles opposed. His integrity was most pure, his justice the most inflexible I have ever known, no motives of interest or consanguinity, of friendship or hatred, being able to bias his decision. He was, indeed, in every sense of the words, a wise, a good, and a great man. His temper was naturally high toned; but reflection and resolution had obtained a firm and habitual ascendancy over it. If ever, however, it broke its bonds, he was most tremendous in his wrath. In his expenses he was honorable, but exact; liberal in contributions to whatever promised utility; but frowning and unyielding on all visionary projects and all unworthy calls on his charity. His heart was not warm in its affections; but he exactly calculated every man's value, and gave him a solid esteem proportioned to it. His person, you know, was fine, his stature exactly what one would wish, his deportment easy, erect and noble; the best horseman of his age, and the most graceful figure that could be seen on horseback. Although in the circle of his friends, where he might be unreserved with safety, he took a free share in conversation, his colloquial talents were not above mediocrity, possessing neither copiousness of ideas, nor fluency of words. In public, when called on for a sudden opinion, he was unready, short and embarrassed. Yet he wrote readily, rather diffusely, in an easy and correct style. This he had acquired by conversation with the world, for his education was merely reading, writing and common arithmetic, to which he added surveying at a later day. His time was employed in action chiefly, reading little, and that only in agriculture and English history. His correspondence became necessarily extensive, and, with journalizing his agricultural proceedings, occupied most of his leisure hours within doors. On the whole, his character was, in its mass, perfect, in nothing bad, in few points indifferent; and it may truly be said, that never did nature and fortune combine more perfectly to make a man great, and to place him in the same constellation with whatever worthies have merited from man an everlasting remembrance. For his was the singular destiny and merit, of leading the armies of his country successfully through an arduous war, for the establishment of its independence; of conducting its councils through the birth of a government, new in its forms and principles, until it had settled down into a quiet and orderly train; and of scrupulously obeying the laws through the whole of his career, civil and military, or which the history of the world furnishes no other example."

25. THOMAS JEFFERSON TO DOCTOR WALTER JONES JANUARY 2, 1814

"I do believe that General Washington had not a firm confidence in the durability of our government. He was naturally distrustful of men, and inclined to gloomy apprehensions; and I was ever persuaded that a belief that we must at length end in something like a British constitution, had some weight in his adoption of the ceremonies of levees, birth-days, pompous meetings with Congress, and other forms of the same character, calculated to prepare us gradually for a change which he believed possible, and to let it come on with as little shock as might be to the public mind."

26. THOMAS JEFFERSON TO DOCTOR WALTER JONES JANUARY 2, 1814

"I served with him in the Virginia legislature from 1769 to the Revolutionary war, and again, a short time in Congress, until he left us to take command of the army. During the war and after it we corresponded occasionally, and in the four years of my continuance in the office of Secretary of State, our intercourse was daily, confidential and cordial. After I retired from that office, great and malignant pains were taken by our federal monarchists, and not entirely without effect, to make him view me as a theorist, holding French principles of government, which would lead infallibly to licentiousness and anarchy. And to this he listened the more easily, from my known disapprobation of the British treaty. I never saw him afterwards, or these malignant insinuations should have been dissipated before his just judgment, as mists before the sun. I felt on his death, with my countrymen, that 'verily a great man hath fallen this day in Israel.'"

27. EXCERPT FROM THOMAS JEFFERSON'S *THE ANAS* FEBRUARY 1818

"Could these documents, all, be laid open to the public eye, they might be compared, contrasted, weighed, & the truth fairly sifted out of them, for we are not to suppose that every thing found among Genl. Washington's papers is to be taken as gospel truth. Facts indeed of his own writing & indicting, must be believed by all who knew him; and opinions, which were his own, merit veneration and respect; for few men have lived whose opinions were more unbiased and correct. Not that it is pretended he never felt bias. His passions were naturally strong; but his reason, generally stronger. But the materials from his own pen make probably an almost insensible part of the mass of papers which fill his presses. He possessed the love, the veneration, and confidence of all. With him were deposited suspicions & certainties, rumors & realities, facts & falsehoods, by all those who were, or who wished to be thought, in correspondence with him, and by the many Anonymi who were ashamed to put their names to their slanders. From such Congeries history may be made to wear any hue, with the passions of the compiler, royalist or republican, may chuse to tinge it. Had Genl. Washington himself written from these materials a history of the period they embrace, it would have been a conspicuous monument to the integrity of his mind, the soundness of his judgment, and its powers of discernment between truth & falsehood; principles & pretensions."

28. EXCERPT FROM THOMAS JEFFERSON'S *THE ANAS* FEBRUARY 1818

"Let no man believe that Genl. Washington ever intended that his papers should be used for the suicide of the cause, for which he had lived, and for which there never was a moment in which he would not have died."

29. EXCERPT FROM THOMAS JEFFERSON'S *THE ANAS* FEBRUARY 1818

"[Washington] was true to the republican charge confided to him; & has solemnly and repeatedly protested to me, in our private conversations, that he would lose the last drop of his blood in support of it, and he did this the oftener, and with more earnestness, because he knew my suspicions of Hamilton's designs against it; & wished to quiet them. For he was not aware of the drift, or of the effect of Hamilton's schemes. Unversed in financial projects & calculations, & budgets, his approbation of them was bottomed on his confidence in the man."

30. EXCERPT FROM THOMAS JEFFERSON'S *THE ANAS* FEBRUARY 1818

"Much of this relation is notorious to the world, & many intimate proofs of it will be found in these notes. From the moment, where they end, of my retiring from the administration, the federalists got unchecked hold of Genl. Washington. His memory was already sensibly impaired by age, the firm tone of mind for which he had been remarkable, was beginning to relax, it's energy was abated; a listlessness of labor, a desire for tranquility had crept on him, and a willingness to let others act and even think for him. Like the rest of mankind, he was disgusted with atrocities of the French revolution, and was not sufficiently aware of the difference between the rabble who were used as instruments of their perpetration, and the steady & rational character of the American people, in which he had not sufficient confidence. The opposition too of the republicans to the British treaty, and zealous support of the federalists in that unpopular, but favorite measure of theirs, had made him all their own. Understanding moreover that I disapproved of that treaty, & copiously nourished with falsehoods by a malignant neighbor of mine, who ambitioned to be his correspondent, he had become alienated from myself personally, as from the republican body generally of his fellow citizens; & he wrote the letters to Mr. Adams, and Mr. Carroll, over which, in devotion to his imperishable fame, we must forever weep as monuments of mortal decay."

31. THOMAS JEFFERSON TO WILLIAM JOHNSON JUNE 12, 1823

"What a treasure will be found in General Washington's cabinet, when it shall pass into the hands of as candid a friend to truth as he was himself! When no longer, like Caesar's notes and memorandums in the hands of Anthony, it shall be open to the high-priests of federalism only, and garbled to say so much, and no more, as suits their views!"

32. THOMAS JEFFERSON TO WILLIAM JOHNSON JUNE 12, 1823

"With respect to his farewell address, to the authorship of which, it seems, there are conflicting claims, I can state to you some facts. He had determined to decline re-election at the end of his first term, and so far determined, that he had requested Mr. Madison to prepare for him something valedictory, to be addressed to his constituents on his retirement. This was done, but he was finally persuaded to acquiesce in a second election, to which no one more strenuously pressed him than myself, from a conviction of the importance of strengthening, by longer habit, the respect necessary for that office, which the weight of his character only could effect."

33. THOMAS JEFFERSON TO MARTIN VAN BUREN JUNE 29, 1824

"When, on my return from Europe, I joined the government in March, 1790, at New York, I was much astonished, indeed, at the mimicry I found established of royal forms and ceremonies, and more alarmed at the unexpected phenomenon, by the monarchical sentiments I heard expressed and openly maintained in every company, and among others by the high members of the government, executive and judiciary, (General Washington alone excepted,) and by a great part of the legislature, save only some members who had been of the old Congress, and very few of recent introduction. I took occasion, at various times, of expressing to General Washington my disappointment at these symptoms of a change of principle, and that I thought them encouraged by the forms and ceremonies which I found prevailing, not at all in character with the simplicity of republican government, and looking as if wishfully to those of European courts. His general explanations to me were, that when he arrived at New York to enter on the executive administration of the new government, he observed to those who were to assist him, that placed as he was in an office entirely new to him, unacquainted with the forms and ceremonies of other governments, still less apprized of those which might be properly established here, and himself perfectly indifferent to all forms, he wished them to consider and prescribe what they should be; and the task was assigned particularly to General Knox, a man of parade, and to Colonel Humphreys, who had resided some time at a foreign court. They, he said, were the authors of the present regulations, and that others were proposed so highly strained that he absolutely rejected them. Attentive to the difference of opinion prevailing on this subject, when the term of his second election arrived, he called the Heads of departments together, observed to them the situation in which he had been at the commencement of the government, the advice he had taken and the course he had observed in compliance with it; that a proper occasion had now arrived of revising that course, of correcting it in any particulars not approved in experience; and he desired us to consult together, agree on any changes we should think for the better, and that he should willingly conform to what we should advise."

34. THOMAS JEFFERSON TO MARTIN VAN BUREN JUNE 29, 1824

"The truth is, that the federalists, pretending to be the exclusive friends of George Washington, have ever done what they could to sink his character, by hanging theirs on it, and by representing as the enemy of republicans him, who, of all men, is best entitled to the appellation of the father of that republic which they were endeavoring to subvert, and the republicans to maintain. They cannot deny, because the elections proclaimed the truth, that the great body of the nation approved the republican measures. General

Washington was himself sincerely a friend to the republican principles of our constitution. His faith, perhaps, in its duration, might not have been as confident as mine; but he repeatedly declared to me, that he was determined it should have a fair chance for success, and that he would lose the last drop of his blood in its support, against any attempt which might be made to change it from its republican form. He made these declarations the oftener, because he knew my suspicions that Hamilton had other views, and he wished to quiet my jealousies on this subject."

35. THOMAS JEFFERSON TO MARTIN VAN BUREN JUNE 29, 1824

"General Washington, after the retirement of his first cabinet, and the composition of his second, entirely federal, and at the head of which was Mr. Pickering himself, had no opportunity of hearing both sides of any question. His measures, consequently, took more the hue of the party in whose hands he was. These measures were certainly not approved by the republicans; yet were they not imputed to him, but to the counsellors around him; and his prudence so far restrained their impassioned course and bias, that no act of strong mark, during the remainder of his administration, excited much dissatisfaction. He lived too short a time after, and too much withdrawn from information, to correct the views into which he had been deluded; and the continued assiduities of the party drew him into the vortex of their intemperate career; separated him still farther from his real friends, and excited him to actions and expressions of dissatisfaction, which grieved them, but could not loosen their affections from him. They would not suffer the temporary aberration to weigh against the immeasurable merits of his life; and although they tumbled his seducers from their places, they preserved his memory embalmed in their hearts, with undiminished love and devotion; and there it forever will remain embalmed, in entire oblivion of every temporary thing which might cloud the glories of his splendid life. It is vain, then, for Mr. Pickering and his friends to endeavor to falsify his character, by representing him as an enemy to republicans and republican principles, and as exclusively the friend of those who were so; and had he lived longer, he would have returned to his ancient and unbiased opinions, would have replaced his confidence in those whom the people approved and supported, and would have seen that they were only restoring and acting on the principles of his own first administration."

36. THOMAS JEFFERSON TO MARTIN VAN BUREN JUNE 29, 1824

"My last parting with General Washington was at the inauguration of Mr. Adams, in March, 1797, and was warmly affectionate; and I never had any reason to believe any change on his part, as there certainly was none on mine. But one session of Congress intervened between that and his death, the year following, in my passage to and from which, as it happened to be not convenient to call on him, I never had another opportunity; and as to the cessation of correspondence observed during that short interval, no particular circumstance occurred for epistolary communication, and both of us were too much oppressed with letter-writing, to trouble, either the other, with a letter about nothing."

IV. JAMES MADISON ON GEORGE WASHINGTON

1. JAMES MADISON TO THOMAS JEFFERSON, JUNE 2, 1780

"General Washington has found it of the utmost difficulty to repress the mutinous spirit engendered by hunger and want of pay: and all his endeavours could not prevent an actual eruption of it in two Connecticut regiments, who assembled on the parade with their arms, and resolved to return home or satisfy their hunger by the power of the bayonet."

2. JAMES MADISON TO EDMUND PENDLETON NOVEMBER 27, 1781

"On the same evening arrived our illustrious general, returning on his position to the North river. We shall probably, however, have his company [in Philadelphia] for some days at least, where he will be able to give Congress very seasonable aid in settling the military establishment for the next year, about which there is some diversity of opinion."

3. JAMES MADISON TO JAMES MONROE NOVEMBER 1784

"General Washington arrived here on sunday last, and the Marquis on thursday. The latter came from Boston in a French frigate. They have both been addressed and entertained in the best manner that circumstances would admit."

4. JAMES MADISON TO THOMAS JEFFERSON JANUARY 9, 1785

"The Treasurer is by this act[6] directed to subscribe 50 shares in the Potowmac and 100 shares in the James River Companies, which shall vest in General Washington and his heirs. This mode of adding some substantial to the many honorary rewards bestowed on him was deemed least injurious to his delicacy, as well as least dangerous as a precedent. It was substituted in place of a direct pension, urged on the House by the indiscreet zeal of some of his friends. Though it will not be an equivalent sućcour in all respects, it will save the General from subscriptions which would have oppressed his finances; and if the schemes be executed within the period fixed, may yield a revenue for some years before

6 An act vesting in George Washington shares in the companies created for opening the James and Potomac Rivers for suitable navigation by water going vessels.

the term of his. At all events, it will demonstrate the grateful wishes of his Country, and will promote the object which he has so much at heart. The earnestness with which he espouses the undertaking is hardly to be described, and shews that a mind like his, capable of great views, and which has long been occupied with them, cannot bear a vacancy; and surely he could not have chosen an occupation more worthy of succeeding to that of establishing the political rights of his Country than the patronage of works for the extensive and lasting improvement of its natural advantages; works which will double the value of half the lands within the Commonwealth, will extend its commerce, link with its interests those of the Western States, and lessen the emigration of its citizens by enhancing the profitableness of situations which they now desert in search of better."

5. JAMES MADISON TO THE MARQUIS DE LAFAYETTE MARCH 20, 1785

"Our Legislature made a decent provision for remittances due for 1785 from Virginia to the Treasury of the United States, and very extensive provision for opening our inland navigation. They have passed an act vesting in General Washington a considerable interest in each of the works on James River and Potowmac, but with an honorary rather lucrative aspect. Whether he will accept it or not I cannot say."

6. JAMES MADISON TO THOMAS JEFFERSON APRIL 27, 1785

"I have not learnt with certainty whether General Washington will accept or decline the shares voted him by the Assembly in the companies for opening our rivers. If he does not chuse to take to himself any benefit from the donation, he has, I think, a fine opportunity at once of testifying his disinterested purposes, of shewing his respect for the Assembly, and of rendering a service to his Country. He may accept the gift so far as to apply it to the scheme of opening the rivers, and may then appropriate the revenue which it is hereafter to produce to some patriotic establishment. I lately dropped a hint of this sort to one of his friends, and was told that such an idea had been suggested to him."

7. JAMES MADISON TO THOMAS JEFFERSON OCTOBER 3, 1785

"On my journey I call at Mount Vernon, and had the pleasure of finding the General in perfect health. He had just returned from a trip up the Potomac. He grows more and more sanguine as he examines further into the practicability of opening its navigation. The subscriptions are completed within a few shares, and the work is already begun at some of the lesser obstructions…The General declines the shared voted to him by the Assembly, but does not mean to withdraw the money from the object which it is to aid, and will even appropriate the future tolls, I believe, to some useful public establishment, if any such can be devised that will both please himself and be likely to please the State."

8. JAMES MADISON TO THOMAS JEFFERSON JANUARY 22, 1786

"The donation presented to Genl Washington embarrassed him much. On one side, he disliked the appearance of slighting the bounty of his Country, and of an ostentatious disinterestedness. On the other, an acceptance of reward in any shape was irreconcileable with the law he had imposed on himself. His answer to the Assembly declined in the most affectionate terms the emolument allotted to himself, but intimated his willingness to accept it so far as to dedicate it to some public and patriotic use. This act recites the original act and his answer, and appropriates the future revenue from the shares to such public objects as he shall appoint. He has been pleased to ask my ideas with regard to the most proper objects. I suggest, in general only, a partition of the fund between some institution which would please the philosophical world, and some other which may be of a popular cast. If your knowledge of the several institutions in France or elsewhere should suggest models or hints, I could wish for your ideas on the case, which no less concern the good of the Commonwealth than the character of its most illustrious citizen."

9. JAMES MADISON TO GEORGE WASHINGTON DECEMBER 7, 1786

"DEAR SIR,—Notwithstanding the communications in your favor of the 18th ult°, which has remained until now unacknowledged, it was the opinion of every judicious friend whom I consulted that your name could not be spared from the Deputation to the meeting in May, at Philadelphia. It was supposed, in the first place, that the peculiarity of the Mission, and its acknowledged pre-eminence over every other public object, may possibly reconcile your undertaking it with the respect which is justly due, and which you wish to pay, to the late officers of the Army; and, in the second place, that although you should find that or any other consideration an obstacle to your attendance on the service, the advantage of having your name in the front of the appointment, as a mark of the earnestness of Virginia, and an invitation to the most select characters from every part of the Confederacy, ought at all events to be made use of. In these sentiments I own I fully concurred, and flatter myself that they will at least apologize for my departure from those held out in your letter. I even flatter myself that they will merit a serious consideration with yourself whether the difficulties which you enumerate ought not to give way to them."

10. JAMES MADISON TO GEORGE WASHINGTON DECEMBER 24, 1786

"DEAR SIR,—Your favor of the 16th instant came to hand too late on thursday evening to be answered by the last mail. I have considered well the circumstances which it confidentially discloses, as well as those contained in your preceding favor. The difficulties which they oppose to an acceptance of the appointment, in which you are included, can as little be denied as they can fail to be regretted. But I still am inclined to think that the posture of our affairs, if it should continue, would prevent every criticism on the situation which the contemporary meetings would place you in; and that at least a door could be kept open for your acceptance hereafter, in case the gathering clouds become so dark and menacing as to supersede every consideration but that of our national existence and safety. A suspension of your ultimate determination would be nowise inconvenient in a public view, as the Executive are authorized to fill vacancies, and can fill them at any time; and in any event, three out of seven deputies are authorized to represent the State. How far it may be admissible in another view will depend, perhaps, in some measure, on the chance of your finally undertaking the service, but principally on the correspondence which is now passing on the subject between yourself and the Governor."

11. JAMES MADISON TO THOMAS JEFFERSON MARCH 19, 1787

"General Washington has prudently authorised no expectations of his attendance, but has not either precluded himself absolutely from stepping into the field if the crisis should demand it."

12. JAMES MADISON TO THOMAS JEFFERSON MAY 15, 1787

"DEAR SIR,—Monday last was the day for the meeting of the Convention. The number as yet assembled is but small. Among the few is General Washington, who arrived on

Sunday evening, amidst the acclamations of the people, as well as more sober marks of the affection and veneration which continues to be felt for his character."

-⊰⊱-

13. EXCERPT FROM JAMES MADISON'S *JOURNAL OF THE CONSTITUTIONAL CONVENTION OF 1787* MAY 25, 1787

"M^{r}. Robert Morris informed the members assembled that by the instruction & in behalf, of the deputation of Pen^{a}. he proposed George Washington, Esqr. late Commander in chief for *president* of the Convention. M^{r}. Jno. Rutlidge seconded the motion; expressing his confidence that the choice would be unanimous, and observing that the presence of Genl. Washington forbade any observations on the occasion which might otherwise be proper."

-⊰⊱-

14. EXCERPT FROM JAMES MADISON'S *JOURNAL OF THE CONSTITUTIONAL CONVENTION OF 1787* MAY 25, 1787

"General Washington was accordingly unanimously elected by ballot, and conducted to the Chair by Mr. R. Morris and Mr. Rutlidge; from which in a very emphatic manner he thanked the Convention for the honor they had conferred on him, reminded them of the novelty of the scene of business in which he was to act, lamented his want of better qualifications, and claimed the indulgence of the House towards the involuntary errors which his inexperience might occasion."

-⊰⊱-

15. JAMES MADISON TO EDMUND PENDLETON MAY 27, 1787

"General Washington was called to the chair by a unanimous voice, and has accepted it."

-⊰⊱-

16. JAMES MADISON TO THOMAS JEFFERSON JUNE 6, 1787

"The names of the members will satisfy you that the States have been serious in this business. The attendance of General Washington is a proof of the light in which he regards it. The whole community is big with expectation, and there can be no doubt but that the result will in some way or other have a powerful effect on our destiny."

-⊰⊱-

17. JAMES MADISON TO THOMAS JEFFERSON JUNE 6, 1787

"The day fixed for the meeting of the Convention was the 14th ultimo. On the 25th, and not before seven States were assembled, General Washington was placed, una voce, in the chair."

18. JAMES MADISON TO THOMAS JEFFERSON OCTOBER 8, 1788

"There is no doubt that General Washington will be called to the Presidency. For the vice Presidency are talked of principally Mr. [John] Hancock and Mr. [John] Adams."

19. JAMES MADISON TO THOMAS JEFFERSON OCTOBER 17, 1788

"The Presidency alone unites the conjectures of the public. The Vice President is not at all marked out by the general voice. As the President will be from a Southern State, it falls almost of course for the other part of the Continent to supply the next in rank."

20. JAMES MADISON TO THOMAS JEFFERSON DECEMBER 8, 1788

"Notwithstanding the formidable opposition made to the new federal Government, first, in order to prevent its adoption, and since, in order to place its administration in the hands of disaffected men, there is now both a certainty of its peaceable commencement in March next, and a flattering prospect that it will be administered by men who will give it a fair trial. General Washington will certainly be called to the Executive department. Mr. Adams, who is pledged to support him, will probably be the vice President."

21. JAMES MADISON TO THOMAS JEFFERSON MARCH 29, 1789

"The votes were unanimous with respect to General Washington, as appears to have been the case in each of the States. The secondary votes were given, among the federal members, chiefly to Mr. J. Adams, one or two being thrown away in order to prevent a possible competition for the Presidency."

22. JAMES MADISON TO EDMUND PENDLETON APRIL 8, 1789

"DEAR SIR—, You will not learn without some surprise that the sixth of this month arrived before a quorum was made up in both branches of the new Legislature, and the first of the month before a Quorum was attained in either. The first and only step taken by the Congress was the examination of the ballots for President and vice president. The votes were found, as was expected, to be unanimously given to General Washington; and a sufficient number, though smaller than was expected, to give the secondary dignity to Mr. Adams. The entire number of votes was 69. Mr. Adams had 34 only."

23. JAMES MADISON TO EDMUND RANDOLPH MAY 10, 1789

"No question has been made in this quarter or elsewhere, as far as I have learned, whether the General ought to have accepted the trust.[7] On the contrary, opinions have been unanimous and decided that it was essential to the commencement of the Government, and a duty from which no private considerations could absolve him. The promptitude of his setting out from Mount Vernon was the effect of information of the delay of business here, the impatience of the public mind, and the necessity of his presence to make the Government competent to its first and most urgent objects. His election was known to him with certainty a long time before the ballots were opened, and informally communicated. I believe, before it was regularly notified. It was taken for granted here, that, under the circumstances of the occasion, he would lose no time in repairing to his station, if he meant not to decline it altogether."

24. JAMES MADISON TO THOMAS JEFFERSON MAY 23, 1789

"My last inclosed copies of the President's inaugural Speech, and the answer of the House of Representatives. I now add the answer of the Senate. It will not have escaped you that the former was addressed with a truly republican simplicity to George Washington, President of the United States. The latter follows the example, with the omission of the personal name, but without any other than the Constitutional title. The proceeding on this point was, in the House of Representatives, spontaneous. The imitation by the Senate was extorted. The question became a serious one between the two Houses. J. Adams espoused the cause of titles with great earnestness. His friend, R[ichard] H[enry] Lee, although elected as a Republican enemy to an aristocratic Constitution, was a most zealous second. The projected title was, his Highness

7 Madison is referring to the presidency.

the President of the United States and protector of their liberties. Had the project succeeded, it would have subjected the President to a severe dilemma, and given a deep wound to our infant Government."

25. JAMES MADISON TO SAMUEL JOHNSTON JUNE 21, 1789

"I lost no time in handing to the President the address inclosed in your favor of the 22 of May, and have postponed an acknowledgement of the latter in expectation of being able at the same time to cover the President's answer. This has been and continues to be delayed by a very serious indisposition. We hope that he is not in much danger, but are by no means without our fears also. His disorder commenced in a fever which has greatly reduced him, and is terminating in a very large tumor which, unless it degenerates itself into a dangerous malady, will probably be remedial."

26. JAMES MADISON TO EDMUND RANDOLPH JUNE 24, 1789

"The President has been ill, but is now in a safe way. His fever terminated in an abscess, which was itself alarming, but has been opened with success, and the alarm is now over. His death, at the present moment, would have brought on another crisis in our affairs."

27. JAMES MADISON TO EDMUND RANDOLPH MAY 19, 1790

"The President has been *critically* ill for some days past, but is now, we hope, out of danger; his complaint is a peripneumony, united probably with the Influenza."

28. EXCERPT FROM JAMES MADISON'S *SUBSTANCE OF A CONVERSATION WITH THE PRESIDENT* MAY 5, 1792

"In consequence of a note this morning from the President, requesting me to call on him, I did so; when he opened the conversation by observing, that having some time ago communicated to me his intention of retiring from public life on the expiration of his four years, he wished to advise with me on the *mode* and *time* most proper for making known that intention. He had, he said, spoken with no one yet on those *particular points,* and took this opportunity of mentioning them to me, that I might consider the matter, and give him my opinion before the adjournment of Congress, or my departure from Philadelphia. He had, he said, forborne to communicate his intentions to any other persons whatever but Mr. Jefferson, Col. Hamilton, General Knox, and myself, and of late to Mr. Randolph. Col. Hamilton and Genl Knox, he observed, were extremely importunate that he should relinquish his purpose, and had made pressing representations to induce him to it. Mr. Jefferson had expressed his wishes to the like effect. He had not, however, persuaded himself that his continuance in public life could be of so much necessity or importance as was conceived, and his disinclination to it was becoming every day more and more fixed; so that he wished to make up his mind as soon as possible on the points he had mentioned. What he desired was, to prefer that mode which would be most remote from the appearance of arrogantly presuming on his re-election in case he should not withdraw himself, and such a time as would be most convenient to the public in making the choice of his successor. It had, he said, at first occurred to him, that the commencement of the ensuing session of Congress would furnish him with an apt occasion for introducing the intimation; but besides the lateness of the day, he was apprehensive that it might possibly produce some notice in the reply of Congress that might entangle him in farther explanations.

I replied, that I would revolve the subject as he desired, and communicate the result before my leaving Philadelphia, but that I could not but yet hope there would be no necessity at this time for his decision on the two points he had stated. I told him that when he did me the honor to mention the resolution he had taken, I had forborne to do more than briefly express my apprehensions that it would give a surprise and shock to the public mind, being restrained from enlarging on the subject by an unwillingness to express sentiments sufficiently known to him, or to urge objections to a determination which, if absolute, it might look like affectation to oppose; that the aspect which things had been latterly assuming seemed, however, to impose the task on all who had the opportunity of urging a continuance of his public services; and that, under such an impression, I held it a duty, not indeed to express my wishes, which would be superfluous, but to offer my opinion that his retiring at the present juncture might have effects that ought not to be hazarded; that I was not unaware of the urgency of his inclination, or of the peculiar motives he might feel to withdraw himself from a situation into which it was so well known to myself he had entered with a scrupulous reluctance; that I well recollected the embarrassments under which his mind labored in deciding the question on which he had consulted me, whether it could be his duty to accept his present station after having taken a final leave of public life; and that it was particularly in my recollection that I then entertained and intimated a wish that his acceptance, which appeared to be indispensable, might be known hereafter to have been in no degree the effect of any motive, which strangers to his character might suppose, but of the severe sacrifice which his friends knew he made of his inclinations as a man to his obligations as a citizen; that I owned I had at that time contemplated, and, I believed, suggested, as the most unequivocal though not the only proof of his real motive, a voluntary return to private life as soon as the state of the government would permit; trusting that if any premature casualty should unhappily cut off the possibility of this proof, the evidence known to his friends would in some way or other be saved from oblivion, and do justice to his character; that I was not less anxious on the same point now that I was then; and if I did not conceive that reasons of a like kind to those which required him to undertake still required him to retain, for some time longer, his present station, or did not presume that the purity of his motives would be sufficiently vindicated, I should be the last of his friends to press, or even to wish, such a determination.

He then entered on a more explicit disclosure of the state of his mind; observing that he could not believe or conceive himself any wise necessary to the successful administration of the Government; that, on the contrary, he had from the beginning found himself deficient in many of the essential qualifications, owing to his inexperience in the forms of public business, his unfitness to judge legal questions, and questions arising out of the Constitution; that others more conversant in such matters would be better able to execute the trust; that he found himself, also, in the decline of life, his health becoming sensibly more infirm, and perhaps his faculties also; that the fatigues and disagreeableness of his situation were in fact scarcely tolerable to him; that he only uttered his real sentiments when he declared that his inclination would lead him rather to go to his farm, take his spade in his hand, and work for his bread, than remain in his present situation; that it was evident, moreover, that a spirit of party in the Government was becoming a fresh source of difficulty, and he was afraid was dividing some (alluding to the Secretary of State and Secretary of the Treasury[8]) more particularly connected with him in the administration; that there were discontents among the people which were also shewing themselves more and more, and that although the various attacks against public men and measures had not in general been pointed at him, yet, in some instances, it had been visible that he was the indirect object, and it was probable the evidence would grow stronger and stronger that his return to private life was consistent with every public consideration, and, consequently, that he was justified in giving way to his inclination for it.

I was led by this explanation to remark to him, that however novel or difficult the business might have been to him, it could not be doubted that, with the aid of the

8 Thomas Jefferson and Alexander Hamilton

official opinions and informations within his command, his judgment must have been as competent in all cases as that of any one who could have been put in his place, and, in many cases, certainly more so; that in the great point of conciliating and uniting all parties under a Government which had excited such violent controversies and divisions, it was well known that his services had been in a manner essential; that with respect to the spirit of party that was taking place under the operations of the Government, I was sensible of its existence, but considered that as an argument for his remaining, rather than retiring, until the public opinion, the character of the Government, and the course of its administration, should be better decided, which could not fail to happen in a short time, especially under his auspices; that the existing parties did not appear to be so formidable to the Government as some had represented; that in one party there might be a few who, retaining their original disaffection to the Government, might still wish to destroy it, but that they would lose their weight with their associates by betraying any such hostile purposes; that although it was pretty certain that the other were, in general, unfriendly to republican Government, and probably aimed at a gradual approximation of ours to a mixed monarchy, yet the public sentiment was so strongly opposed to their views, and so rapidly manifesting itself, that the party could not long be expected to retain a dangerous influence; that it might reasonably be hoped, therefore, that the conciliating influence of a temperate and wise administration would, before another term of four years should run out, give such a tone and firmness to the Government as would secure it against danger from either of these descriptions of enemies; that although I would not allow myself to believe but that the Government would be safely administered by any successor elected by the people, yet it was not to be denied, that in the present unsettled condition of our young Government, it was to be feared that no successor would answer all the purposes to be expected from the continuance of the present chief magistrate...In this state of our prospects, which was rendered more striking by a variety of temporary circumstances, I could not forbear thinking that although his retirement might not be fatal to the public good, yet a postponement of it was another sacrifice exacted by his patriotism.

Without appearing to be any wise satisfied with what I had urged, he turned the conversation to other subjects; and when I was withdrawing repeated his request that I would think of the points he had mentioned to me, and let him have my ideas on them before the adjournment. I told him I would do so, but still hoped his decision on the main question would supersede for the present all such incidental questions."

29. EXCERPT FROM JAMES MADISON'S *SUBSTANCE OF A CONVERSATION WITH THE PRESIDENT* MAY 9, 1792

"Understanding that the President was to set out the ensuing morning for Mount Vernon, I called on him to let him know that, as far as I had formed an opinion on the subject he had mentioned to me, it was in favor of a direct address of notification to the public, in time for its proper effect on the election, which I thought might be put into such a form as would avoid every appearance of presumption or indelicacy, and seemed to be absolutely required by his situation. I observed that no other mode deserving consideration had occurred, except the one he had thought of and rejected, which seemed to me liable to the objections that had weighed with him. I added, that if on farther reflection I should view the subject in any new lights, I would make it the subject of a letter, though I retained my hopes that it would not yet be necessary for him to come to any opinion on it. He begged that I would do so, and also suggest any matters that might occur as proper to be included in what he might say to Congress at the opening of their next session; passing over the idea of his relinquishing his purpose of retiring in a manner that did not indicate the slightest assent to it."

30. JAMES MADISON TO GEORGE WASHINGTON JUNE 21, 1792

"DEAR SIR,—Having been left to myself for some days past, I have made use of the opportunity for bestowing on your letter of the 20th ult°, handed to me on the road, the attention which its important contents claimed. The question which it presents for consideration are—1st. At what time a notification of your purpose to retire will be most convenient? 2. What mode will be most eligible? 3. Whether a valedictory address will be requisite or advisable? 4. If either, whether it would be more properly annexed to the notification, or postponed to your actual retirement?

The answer to the first question involves two points: first, the expediency of delaying the notification; secondly, the propriety of making it before the choice of electors takes place, that the people may make the choice with an eye to the circumstances under which the trust is to be executed. On the first point, the reasons for as much delay as possible are too obvious to need recital. The second, depending on the times fixed in the several States, which must be within 34 days preceding the first Wednesday in December, requires that the notification should be in time to pervade every part of the Union by the beginning of November. Allowing six weeks for this purpose, the middle of September, or perhaps a little earlier, would seem a convenient date for the act.

2. With regard to the mode, none better occurs than a simple publication in the newspapers. If it were proper to address it through the medium of the general Legislature, there will be no opportunity. Nor does the change of situation seem to admit a recurrence to the State governments, which were the channels used for the former valedictory address. A direct address to the people, who are your only constituents, can be made, I think, with most propriety, through the independent channel of the press, through which they are, as a constituent Body, usually addressed.

3. On the third question, I think there can be no doubt that such an address is rendered *proper* in itself by the peculiarity and importance of the circumstances which mark your situation, and *advisable* by the salutary and operative lesson of which it may be made the vehicle. The precedent at your military exit might also subject an omission now to conjectures and interpretations which it would not be well to leave room for.

4. The remaining question is less easily decided. Advantages and objections lie on both sides of the alternative. The occasion on which you are *necessarily* addressing the people evidently introduces, most easily and most delicately, any *voluntary* observations that are meditated. In another view, a farewell address before the final moment of departure is liable to the appearance of being premature and awkward. On the opposite side of the alternative, however, a postponement will beget a dryness and an abridgment in the first address little corresponding with the feelings which the occasion would naturally produce both in the author and the objects of it; and though not liable to the above objection, would require a resumption of the subject apparently more forced, and on which the impressions having been anticipated and familiarized, and the public mind diverted, perhaps, to other scenes, a second address would be received with less sensibility and effect than if incorporated with the impressions to the original one. It is possible, too, that, previous to the close of the term, circumstances might intervene in relation to public affairs, or the succession to the Presidency, which would be more embarrassing, if existing at the time of a valedictory appeal to the public, than if unknown at the time of that delicate measure.

On the whole, my judgment leans to the propriety of blending the acts together; and the more so, as the crisis which will terminate your public career will still afford and opportunity, if any immediate contingency should call for a supplement to your farewell observations. But as more correct views of the subject may produce a different result in your mind, I have endeavored to fit the draught enclosed to either determination. You will readily observe that in executing it I have arrived at that plainness and modesty of language which you had I view, and which, indeed, are so peculiarly becoming the character and the occasion; and that I have had little more to do as to the matter than to follow the very just and comprehensive outline which you had sketched. I flatter myself, however, that in everything which has depended on me, much improvement will be made before so interesting a paper shall have taken its last form.

Having thus, sir, complied with your wishes, by proceeding on a supposition that the idea of retiring from public life is to be carried into execution, I must now gratify my own by hoping that a reconsideration of the measure, in all its circumstances and consequences, will have produced an acquiescence in one more sacrifice, severe as it may be, to the desires and interests of your country. I forbear to enter into the arguments which plead for it in my mind, because it would be only repeating what I have already taken the liberty of fully explaining. But I could not conclude such a letter as the present without a repetition of my ardent wishes and hopes that our country may not, at this important conjuncture, be deprived of the inestimable advantage of having you at the head of its counsels.

[*Draught enclosed in the above*]

The period which will close the appointment with which my fellow-citizens have honored me being not very distant, and the time actually arrived at which their thoughts must be designating the citizen who is to administer the Executive Government of the U. S. during the ensuing term, it may be requisite to a more distinct expression of the public voice that I should apprize such of my fellow-citizens as may retain their partiality towards me, that I am not to be numbered among those out of whom a choice is to be made.

I beg them to be assured that the resolution which dictates this intimation has not been taken without the strictest regard to the relation which, as a dutiful citizen, I bear to my country; and that in withdrawing that tender of my services which silence in my situation might imply, I am not influenced by the smallest deficiency of zeal for its future interests, or of grateful respect for its past kindness, but by the fullest persuasion that such a step is compatible with both.

The impressions under which I entered on the present arduous trust were explained on the proper occasion. In discharge of this trust, I can only say that I have contributed towards the organization and administration of the Government the best exertions of which a very fallible judgment was capable. For any errors which may have flowed from this source,

I feel all the regret which an anxiety for the public good can excite; not without the double consolation, however, arising from a consciousness of their being involuntary, and an experience of the candor which will interpret them. If there were any circumstances which could give value to my inferior qualifications for the trust, these circumstances must have been temporary. In this light was the undertaking viewed when I ventured upon it. Being, moreover, still farther advanced into the decline of life, I am every day more sensible that the increasing weight of years renders the private walks of it in the shade of retirement as necessary as they will be acceptable to me. May I be allowed to add that it will be among the highest, as well as the purest enjoyments that can sweeten the remnant of my days, to partake in a private station, in the midst of my fellow-citizens, of that benign influence of good laws under a free Government which has been the ultimate object of all our wishes, and in which I confide as the happy reward of our cares and labors? May I be allowed further to add, as a consideration far more important, that an early example of rotation in an office of so high and delicate a nature may equally accord with the republican spirit of our Constitution, and the ideas of liberty and safety entertained by the people?

(If a farewell address is to be added at the expiration of the term, the following paragraph may conclude the present:)

Under these circumstances, a return to my private station, according to the purposes with which I quitted it, is the part which duty as well as inclination assigns me. In executing it, I shall carry with me every tender recollection which gratitude to my fellow-citizens can awaken, and a sensibility to the permanent happiness of my country that will render it the object of my unceasing vows and most fervent supplications.

(Should no further address be intended, the preceding clause may be omitted, and the present address proceed as follows:)

In contemplating the moment at which the curtain is to drop forever on the public scenes of my life, my sensations anticipate, and do not permit me to suspend, the deep acknowledgments required by that debt of gratitude which I owe to my beloved country for the many honors it has conferred on me, for the distinguished confidence it has reposed in me, and for the opportunities I have thus enjoyed of testifying my inviolable attachment by the most stedfast services which my faculties could render. All the returns I have now to make will be in those vows which I shall carry with me to my retirement and to my grave, that Heaven may continue to favor the people of the United States with the choicest tokens of its beneficence; that their union and brotherly affection may be perpetual; that the free Constitution, which is the work of their own hands, may be sacredly maintained; that its administration in every Department may be stamped with wisdom and with virtue, and that this character may be ensured to it by that watchfulness over public servants and public measures which, on one hand, will be necessary to prevent or correct a degeneracy, and that forbearance, on the other, from unfounded or indiscriminate jealousies, which would deprive the public of the best services by depriving a conscious integrity of one of the noblest incitements to perform them; that, in fine, the happiness of the people of America under the auspices of liberty may be made complete, by so careful a preservation and so prudent a use of this blessing as will acquire them the glorious satisfaction of recommending it to the affection, the praise, and the adoption, of every nation which is yet a stranger to it.

And may we not dwell with well-grounded hopes on this flattering prospect, when we reflect on the many ties by which the people of America are bound together, and the many proofs they have given of an enlightened judgment and a magnanimous patriotism?

We may all be considered as the children of one common country. We have all been embarked in one common cause. We have all had our share in common sufferings and common successes. The portion of the earth allotted for the theatre of our fortunes fulfils our most sanguine desires. All its essential interests are the same; whilst the diversities arising from climate, from soil, and from other local and lesser peculiarities, will naturally form a mutual relation of the parts that must give to the whole a more entire independence than has, perhaps, fallen to the lot of any other nation.

To confirm these motives to an affectionate and permanent union, and to secure the great objects of it, we have established a common Government, which, being free in its principles, being founded in our own choice, being intended as the guardian of our common rights and the patron of our common interests, and wisely containing within itself a provision for its own amendment as experience may point out its errors, seems to promise everything that can be expected from such an institution; and if supported by wise counsels, by virtuous conduct, and by mutual and friendly allowances, must approach as near to perfection as any human work can aspire, and nearer than any which the annals of mankind have recorded.

With these wishes and hopes I shall make my exit from civil life, and I have taken the same liberty of expressing them which I formerly used in offering the sentiments which were suggested by my exit from military life. If, in either instance, I have presumed more than I ought on the indulgence of my fellow-citizens, they will be too generous to ascribe it to any other cause than the extreme solicitude which I am bound to feel, and which I can never cease to feel, for their liberty, their prosperity, and their happiness."

31. JAMES MADISON TO THOMAS JEFFERSON JUNE 10, 1793

"Every Gazette I see (except that of the U. S.) exhibits a spirit of criticism on the anglified complexion charged on the Executive politics. I regret extremely the position into which the P[resident] has been thrown. The unpopular cause of Anglomany is openly laying claim to him. His enemies masking themselves under the popular cause of France are playing off the most tremendous batteries on him. The proclamation was in truth a most unfortunate error.[9] It wounds the national honor, by seeming to disregard the stipulated duties to France. It wounds the popular feelings by a seeming indifference to the cause of liberty. And it seems to violate the forms & spirit of the Constitution, by making the executive Magistrate the organ of the disposition the duty & the interest of the Nation in relation to War & peace, subjects appropriated to other departments of the Government. It is mortifying to the real friends of the P[resident] that his fame & his influence should have been unnecessarily made to depend in any degree on political events in a foreign quarter of the Globe; and particularly so that he should have anything to apprehend from the success of liberty in another country, since he owes his pre-eminence to the success of it in his own. If France triumphs, the ill-fated proclamation will be a millstone, which would sink any other character, and will force a struggle even on his."

32. JAMES MADISON TO THOMAS JEFFERSON JUNE 13, 1793

"I observe that the newspapers continue to criticize the President's proclamation, and I find that some of the criticisms excite the attention of dispassionate and judicious individuals here. I have heard it remarked by such, with some surprise, that the President should have declared the United States to be neutral in the unqualified terms used, when we were so notoriously and unequivocally under *eventual engagements* to defend the American possessions of France. I have heard it remarked, also, that the impartiality on the people was as little reconciliable with their moral obligations as the unconditional neutrality proclaimed by the Government is with the express articles of the Treaty. It has been asked, also, whether the authority of the Executive extended by any part of the Constitution to a declaration of the *Disposition* of the United States on the subject of war and peace? I have been mortified that on these points I could offer no bona fide explanations that ought to be satisfactory. On the last point, I must own my surprise that such a prerogative should have been exercised. Perhaps I may have not attended to some parts of the Constitution with sufficient care, or may have misapprehended its meaning. But, as I have always supposed and still conceive,

9 Washington's Proclamation of Neutrality

a proclamation on the subject could not properly go beyond a declaration of the fact that the United States were at war or peace, and an injunction of a suitable conduct on the citizens. The right to decide the question whether the duty and interests of the United States require war or peace under any given circumstances, and whether their disposition be towards the one or the other, seems to be essentially and exclusively involved in the right vested in the Legislature of declaring war in time of peace, and in the President and Senate of making peace in time of war. Did no such view of the subject present itself in the discussions of the Cabinet? I am extremely afraid that the President may not be sufficiently aware of the snares that may be laid for his good intentions by men whose politics at bottom are very different from his own. An assumption of prerogatives not clearly found in the Constitution, and having the appearance of being copied from a monarchical model, will beget animadversion equally mortifying to him and disadvantageous to the Government. Whilst animadversions of this sort can be plausibly ascribed to the spirit of party, the force of them may not be felt. But all his real friends will be anxious that his public conduct may bear the strictest scrutiny of future times, as well as of the present day; and all such friends of the Constitution would be doubly pained at infractions of it under the auspices that may consecrate the evil till it be incurable."

33. EXCERPT FROM JAMES MADISON'S *HELVIDIUS NUMBER I* AUGUST 24, 1793

"In these disguises they have appeared to claim the attention I propose to bestow on them; with a view to shew, from the publication itself, that under colour of vindicating an important public act, of a chief magistrate, who enjoys the confidence and love of his country, principles are advanced which strike at the vitals of its constitution, as well as at its honor and true interest.

As it is not improbable that attempts may be made to apply insinuations which are seldom spared when particular purposes are to be answered, to the author of the ensuing observations, it may not be improper to premise, that he is a friend to the constitution, that he wishes for the preservation of peace, and that the present chief magistrate has not a fellow-citizen, who is penetrated with deeper respect for his merits, or feels a purer solicitude for his glory."

34. EXCERPT FROM JAMES MADISON'S *SKETCH* SEPTEMBER 2, 1793

"That the eminent virtues and services of our illustrious fellow-citizen, George Washington, President of the United States, entitle him to the highest respect and lasting gratitude of his Country, whose peace, liberty, and safety, must ever remind it of his distinguished agency in promoting the same..."

35. JAMES MADISON TO THOMAS JEFFERSON MARCH 2, 1794

"Genet has been superseded by Fauchét, the Secretary to the Executive Council. The latter has not been here long enough to develop his temper and character. He has the aspect of moderation. His account of things in France is very favorable on the whole. He takes particular pains to assure all who talk with him of the perseverance of France in her attachment to us, and her anxiety that nothing which may have taken place may lessen it on our side. In his interview with the President he held the same language; and I am told by E. Randolph, that the President not only declared explicitly his affectionate solicitude for the success of the Republic,[10] but after he had done so, with great emphasis, desired, in order to be as pointed as possible, that his expressions might be repeated by E[dmund] Randolph, who acted as Interpreter."

36. JAMES MADISON TO THOMAS JEFFERSON MAY 25, 1794

"The influence of the Executive on events, the use made of them, and the public confidence in the President, are an overmatch for all the efforts Republicanism can make. The party of that sentiment in the Senate is compleatly wrecked, and, in the House of Representatives, in a much worse condition than at an earlier period of the Session."

37. JAMES MADISON TO THOMAS JEFFERSON JUNE 1, 1794

"The attempt of this Branch[11] to give the President power to raise an army of 10,000, if he should please, was strangled more easily in the House of Representatives than I had expected. This is the 3d or 4th effort made in the course of the Session to get a powerful

10 French Republic

11 United States Senate

military establishment, under the pretext of public danger, and under the auspices of the President's popularity."

38. JAMES MADISON TO JAMES MONROE DECEMBER 4, 1794

"You will readily understand the business detailed in the newspapers relating to the denunciation of the 'self-created Societies.' The introduction of it by the President was, perhaps, the greatest error of his political life. For his sake, as well as for a variety of obvious reasons, I wished it might be passed over in silence by the House of Representatives. The answer was penned with that view, and so reported. This moderate course would not satisfy those who hope to draw a party advantage out of the President's popularity. The game was to connect the Democratic Societies with the odium of this insurrection;[12] to connect the Republicans in Congress with those Societies; to put the President ostensibly at the head of the other party, in opposition to both, and by these means prolong the illusions in the North, and try a new experiment in the South. To favor the project, the answer of the Senate was accelerated, and so framed as to draw the President into the most pointed reply on the subject of the Societies. At the same time, the answer of the House of Representatives was procrastinated, till the example of the Senate and the commitment of the President could have their full operation. You will see how nicely the House was diverted, and how the matter went off. As yet, the discussion has not been revived by the newspaper combatants. If it should, and equal talents be opposed, the result cannot fail to wound the President's popularity more than anything that has yet happened. It must be seen that no two principles can be either more indefensible in reason, or more dangerous in practice, than that—1. Arbitrary denunciations may punish what the law permits, and what the Legislature has no right by law to prohibit; and that, 2. The Government may stifle all censure whatever on its misdoings; for if it be itself the Judge, it will never allow any censures to be just; and if it can suppress censures flowing from one lawful source, it may those flowing from any other—from the press and from individuals, as well as from Societies, &c."

39. EXCERPT FROM JAMES MADISON'S *POLITICAL OBSERVATIONS* APRIL 20, 1795

"The people of the United States would not merit the praise universally allowed to their intelligence if they did not distinguish between the respect due to the man and the functions

12 The Whiskey Rebellion

belonging to the office. In expressing the former, there is no limit or guide, but the feelings of their grateful hearts. In deciding the latter, they will consult the Constitution; they will consider human nature, and, looking beyond the character of the existing Magistrate, fix their eyes on the precedent which must descend to his successors.

Will it be more than truth to say, that this great and venerable name is too often assumed for what cannot recommend itself, and for what there is neither proof nor probability that its sanction can be claimed? Do arguments fail? Is the public mind to be encountered? There are not a few every ready to invoke the name of WASHINGTON; to garnish their heretical doctrines with his virtues, and season their unpalatable measures with his popularity. Those who take this liberty will not, however, be mistaken; his truest friends will be the last to sport with his influence—above all, for electioneering purpose. And it is but a fair suspicion, that they who draw most largely on that fund are hastening fastest to bankruptcy in their own."

40. JAMES MADISON TO JAMES MONROE FEBRUARY 26, 1796

"It is now pretty certain that the President will not serve beyond his present term. The British party had Jay first in view, as is believed. It is now said Adams is the object."

41. JAMES MADISON TO THOMAS JEFFERSON FEBRUARY 29, 1796

"The President's birthday has been celebrated with unexampled splendor. The crisis explains the policy of this. It is remarkable, however, that the annual motion to adjourn for half an hour to pay the compliment of the day was rejected this year by 50 vs. 38, altho' last year, on the yeas and nays, 13 only voted in the negative."

42. JAMES MADISON TO JAMES MONROE APRIL 18, 1796

"Every eye within and without doors was then turned to the President. The prevailing belief was, that he would send a part, if not the whole, of papers applied for. If he thought any part improper to be disclosed, or if he wished to assert his prerogative without coming to a rupture with the House, it was seen to be easy for him to avoid that extremity by that expedient. You will find by his Message, in answer, that he not only ran into the extreme of an absolute refusal, but assigned reasons worse than the refusal itself. I have no doubt that the advice, and even the Message itself, were contrived in New York, where it was seen that if the rising force of the republicans was not crushed, it must speedily crush the British party, and that the only hope of success lay in favoring an open rupture with the President.[13] It is to be lamented that he so easily lent himself to the stratagem. It was expected that the Message would have produced long and animated discussion. In that expectation I entered into a full comment on it, and in support, at the same time, of the two Resolutions asserting the rights of the House, which you will find in the Newspapers."

43. JAMES MADISON TO JAMES MONROE APRIL 23, 1796

"It is now generally understood that the President will retire. Jefferson is the object on one side; Adams, apparently, on the other. The secondary object still unsettled."

44. JAMES MADISON TO JAMES MONROE MAY 14, 1796

"It is now generally understood that the President will retire. Jefferson is the object on one side; Adams, apparently, on the other."

45. JAMES MADISON TO THOMAS JEFFERSON DECEMBER 19, 1796

"You will see in the answer to the President's speech much room for criticism. You must, for the present, be content to know that it resulted from a choice of evils. His reply to the foreign paragraph indicates a good effect on his mind. Indeed, he cannot but wish to avoid entailing a war on his successor. The danger lies in the fetters he has put on himself, and in the irritation and distrust of the French Government."

46. JAMES MADISON TO THOMAS JEFFERSON JANUARY 29, 1797

"A war with France, and an alliance with Great Britain, enter both into print and conversation; and no doubt can be entertained that a push will be made to screw up the President to that point before he quits the office."

13 Madison is referring to Alexander Hamilton who advised President Washington "to resist in totality" the House's request.

47. JAMES MADISON TO THOMAS JEFFERSON FEBRUARY 1798

"There never was, perhaps, a greater contrast between two characters than between those of the present President and his predecessor; although it is the boast and prop of the present that he treads in the steps of his predecessor. The one, cool, considerate, and cautious; the other, headlong, and kindled into flame by every spark that lights on his passions; the one, ever scrutinizing into the public opinion, and ready to follow, where he could not lead it; the other, insulting it by the most adverse sentiments and pursuits. Washington a hero in the field, yet overweighing every danger in the Cabinet; Adams without a single pretension to the character of a soldier, a perfect Quixotte as a statesman. The former chief magistrate pursuing peace every where with sincerity, though mistaking the means; the latter taking as much pains to get into war as the former took to keep out of it. The contrast might be pursued into a variety of other particulars—the policy of the one in shunning connections with the arrangements of Europe, of the other in holding out the United States as a make-weight in the Balances of power; the avowed exultation of Washington in the progress of liberty every where, and his eulogy on the Revolution and people of France, posterior even to the bloody reign and fate of Robespierre; the open denunciations by Adams of the smallest disturbance of the ancient discipline, order, and tranquility of despotism, &c., &c., &c."

48. JAMES MADISON TO THOMAS JEFFERSON MARCH 12, 1798

"I think the Whigs[14] acted very properly in attending the Birthnight, on the principle of appropriating it to the person, and not to the office of the late President. It is a pity that the nonattendance of the Adamsites is not presented to the public in such a manner, with their names, as to satisfy the real friends of Washington, as well as the people generally, of the true principles and views of those who have been loudest in their hypocritical professions of attachment to him."

49. JAMES MADISON TO PLANTAGENET ECCLESTON 1810

"SIR,—I have duly received the Medallion of General Washington accompanying your favor of Jany 1, and return my thanks for it. The high veneration in which his memory is held in his own Country renders such tokens of respect to it in others at once grateful in themselves, and just titles to esteem in those who, looking beyond a national horizon, can do justice to the worthies and benefactors of mankind, wherever seen or however distant."

14 Federalists

50. JAMES MADISON TO THOMAS JEFFERSON JUNE 27, 1823

"Your statement relating to the farewell address of General Washington is substantially correct. If there be any circumstantial inaccuracy, it is in imputing to him more agency in composing the document than he probably had. Taking for granted that it was drawn up by Hamilton, the best conjecture is, that the General put into his hands his own letter to me suggesting his general ideas, with the paper prepared by me in conformity with them; and if he varied the draught of Hamilton at all, it was by a few verbal or qualifying amendments only. It is very inconsiderate in the friends of General Washington to make the merit of the Address a question between him and Col. Hamilton, and somewhat extraordinary, if countenanced by those who possess the files of the General, where it is presumed the truth might be traced. They ought to claim for him the merit only of cherishing the principles and views addressed to his Country, and, for the Address itself, the weight given to it by his sanction; leaving the literary merit, whatever it be, to the friendly pen employed on the occasion; the rather, as it was never understood that Washington valued himself on his writing talent, and no secret to some that he occasionally availed himself of the friendship of others whom he supposed more practised than himself in studied composition. In a general view, it is to be regretted that the Address is likely to be presented to the public, not as the pure legacy of the Father of his Country, as has been all along believed, but as the performance of another, held in different estimation. It will not only lose the charm of the name subscribed to it, but it will not be surprising if particular passages be understood in new senses, and with applications derived from the political doctrines and party feelings of the discovered author.

At some future day it may be an object with the curious to compare the two draughts, made at different epochs, with each other, and the letter of General Washington with both. The comparison will shew a greater conformity in the first with the tenor and tone of the letter than in the other; and the difference will be more remarkable, perhaps, in what is omitted, than in what is added in the Address as it stands.

If the solicitude of General Washington's connexions be such as is represented, I foresee that I shall share their displeasure, if public use be made of what passed between him and me at the approaching expiration of his first term. Although it be impossible to question the facts, I may be charged with indelicacy, if not breach of confidence, in making them known; and the irritation will be the greater if the authorship of the Address continue to be claimed for the signer of it, since the call on me on one occasion will favor the allegation of a call on another on another occasion."

51. JAMES MADISON TO THOMAS JEFFERSON FEBRUARY 8, 1825

"And on the distinctive principles of the Government of our own State, and of that of the United States, the best guides are to be found in—1. The Declaration of Independence, as the fundamental act of Union of these States. 2. The book known by the title of the "Federalist," being an authority to which appeal is habitually made by all, and rarely declined or denied by any, as evidence of the general opinion of those who framed and those who accepted the Constitution of the United States on questions as to its genuine meaning. 3. The Resolutions of the General Assembly of Virginia in 1799, on the subject of the Alien and Sedition laws, which appeared to accord with the predominant sense of the people of the United States. 4. The Inaugural Speech and Farewell Address of President Washington, as conveying political lessons of peculiar value; and that in the branch of the school of law, which is to treat on the subject of Government, these shall be used as the text and documents of the school."

52. JAMES MADISON TO HENRY COLEMAN AUGUST 25, 1825

"Is it a fact that they had the liberties of their country within their grasp? that the troops then in command, even if led on by their illustrious chief, and backed by the apostates from the revolutionary cause, could have brought under the yoke the great body of their fellow citizens, most of them with arms in their hand, no inconsiderable part fresh from the use of them, all inspired with rage at the fratricidal attempt, and not only guided by the federal head, but organized and animated by their local Governments, possessing the means of appealing to their interests as well as other motives, should such an appeal be required?

I have always believed that if General Washington had yielded to a usurping ambition, he would have found an insuperable obstacle in the incorruptibility of a sufficient portion of those under his command, and that the exalted praise due to him and them was derived, not from a forbearance to effect a revolution within their power, but from a love of liberty and of country, which there was abundant reason to believe no facility of success could have seduced. I am not less sure that General Washington would have spurned a scepter, if within his grasp, than I am that it was out of his reach if he had secretly sighed for it. It must be recollected, also, that the practicability of a successful usurpation by the army cannot well be admitted, without implying a folly or pusillanimity reproachful to the American character, and without casting some shade on the vital principle of popular Government itself."

53. JAMES MADISON TO JOSEPH C. CABELL MARCH 22, 1827

"Every President, from General Washington to Mr. J. Q. Adams, inclusive, has recognised the power of a tariff in favor of manufactures, without indicating a doubt, or that a doubt existed anywhere."

54. JAMES MADISON TO JARED SPARKS MAY 30, 1827

"I thank you, sir, for the dates of the recorded letters from General Washington to me. Of these I do not find on my files those noted in the annexed list; some of which I should be particularly glad to see, unless the answers to them should be among the letters you are forwarding, and should prove sufficient for my purpose. My files contain, besides a number of short notes asking interviews, &c., twenty odd letters from the General, which it appears, from your communication, are not in his letter book. Some of these are of an importance and delicacy which have hitherto kept them from every eye but my own; no occasion before the present having ever raised the question how far the seal might be properly removed from them. It is not easy, considering the exactness of General Washington in preserving copies of his letters, to account for such a deficiency in his Register. Was it his intention that the letters should not be preserved, or were they separately preserved without being entered in the book? and in this case, may they not yet be found? Perhaps a clue may be furnished by a circumstance noted in a letter received from Judge Washington some years ago. Wishing to supply the chasm in the retained copies of my letters to his uncle, I requested the favor of having copies from the source in his possession. In his answer, he was led to remark that 'the papers sent to the Chief Justice, and which are still in Richmond, have been very extensively mutilated by rats, and otherwise much injured by damps, as he not long since informed me.' It seems in every view not amiss that the condition of these papers should be adverted to, before the prolix trouble of copies from my files be incurred.

My letters from the files of General Washington, when received and compared with those of which I have preserved copies, may shew whether the former are short of the number written to him; and thence, perhaps, throw some light on his views with respect to some parts of our correspondence, with the uncertainty nevertheless arising from the casualties at Richmond."

55. JAMES MADISON TO EDWARD EVERETT JUNE 3, 1827

"DEAR SIR,—I offer for your brother and yourself the thanks I owe for the copy of his work on "America." It well sustains the reputation for talents and learning acquired by his former work on "Europe." I have found in the volume many proofs of original as well as enlarged views, and not a few passages of glowing eloquence. With this just tribute I must be allowed to combine the remark, that my trains of thought do not accord with some of his speculations, and that the work is susceptible of improved accuracy from recesses of information which time is gradually laying open. One error into which the author has been led will, I am sure, be gladly corrected. In page 109 it is said of Washington that he 'appears to have wavered for a moment in making up his mind upon the Constitution.' I can testify, from my personal knowledge, that no member of the Convention appeared to sign the Instrument with more cordiality than he did, nor to be more anxious for its ratification. I have, indeed, the most thorough conviction, from the best evidence, that he never wavered in the part he took in giving it his sanction and support.

The error may, perhaps, have arisen from his backwardness in accepting his appointment to the Convention..."

56. JAMES MADISON TO JARED SPARKS APRIL 8, 1830

"I have been looking over such of the letters of General Washington to me, as do not appear on his files. They amount to 28, besides some small confidential notes. Most of the letters are of some importance; some of them are peculiarly delicate, and some equally important and delicate. To make extracts from them is a task I should not wish to undertake. To forward to you the whole for that purpose through the hazard of the mail is liable to the objection, that, as no copies exist, a loss of the originals would be fatal. Under these circumstances it occurs that you may be able to spare a few days for a trip from Washington to Montpelier, where you can review the whole, in affording an opportunity for which I shall think myself justified by the confidence reposed in you by those to whom the memory of Washington was most dear, and by the entire confidence felt by myself."

57. JAMES MADISON TO J. K. PAULDING APRIL 1831

"Everything relating to Washington is already known to the world, or will soon be made known through Mr. Sparks, with the exception of some of those inside views of character and scenes of domestic life which are apart from ordinary opportunities of observation. And it may be presumed that interesting lights will be let in even on those exceptions through the private correspondences in the hands of Mr. Sparks."

58. JAMES MADISON TO GEORGE W. BASSETT APRIL 30, 1833

"DEAR SIR,—I have received your letter of the 25th instant, which requests my company at the laying of the corner-stone of the proposed Monument to the memory of the Mother of Washington.

I feel much regret that my very advanced age, to which is added a continued indisposition, will not permit me to be present on an occasion commemorative of the mother of him who was the Father of his own Country, and has left in his example and his counsels a rich legacy to every country."

59. JAMES MADISON TO JOHN TRUMBULL MARCH 1, 1835

"But as the resolution of Congress limited the number of paintings to four, and the Declaration of Independence, with the events at Saratoga and York, stood forth with irresistible claims, that at Bunker's Hill was yielded to Washington's resignation of his commission as a spectacle too peculiarly interesting, whether as a contrast to the military usurpations so conspicuous in history, or as a lesson and example to leaders of victorious armies who aspire to true glory; and it was a circumstance agreeable to us all that the subjects finally adopted had been the choice of the artist himself, whose pencil had been chosen for the execution of them."

V. JAMES MONROE ON GEORGE WASHINGTON

1. JAMES MONROE TO GENERAL CHARLES LEE JUNE 15, 1780

"When I left you in Phil'a, my wish and expectation was immediately to go to Europe; on my coming to Virginia, being under age, I found it difficult to make such disposition of my property as wo'd admit of it. I meant however to go this fall, & as I wish'd to go in the character of an officer, for that purpose I went up to H'd Q'rs by Phil'a (where I wish'd much to have seen you) to require from [General Washington] & L'd Stirling a certificate of my good conduct. This I meant to present to the Virg'a Assembly & from them procure an appointment. His Excellency gave the letter I co'd have wished & Ld Stirling also treated me with gentlemanly politeness."

2. JAMES MONROE TO GEORGE WASHINGTON AUGUST 15, 1782

"DEAR SIR,—You will pardon the liberty I take in writing you upon a subject w'ch has no relation to the publick interest when I inform you I am induc'd thereto merely from a principle of gratitude to make acknowledgment for the personal service I have rec'd from your Excellency. The introduction you gave me some time since to this State, for the purpose of attaining some military appointment to place me in the service of my country in a line with those worthy citizens, with whom common hardship & danger had nearly connected me, altho' it failed me in that instance has avail'd me in another line. Upon relinquishing my military pursuits, w'ch I did with reluctance, & returning to those studies in w'ch I had been engag'd previous to my joining y'r army, till of late I have been literally a recluse. Having gone thro' that course w'ch in the opinion of Mr. Jefferson to whom I submitted the direction of my studies was sufficient to qualify me in some degree for publick business, in my application to my county in the first instance & in the subsequent appointment of the Assembly to the Executive Council of the State I have had the pleasure to experience y'r friendly letter in my fav'r of essential service to me. If, therefore, I was so fortunate in the manag'ment of my conduct more immediately under y'r eye as to gain y'r good opinion & esteem I flatter myself that in the discharge of the duties of my present office & a faithful observance & attention to the confidence repos'd in me by my country I shall take no step w'ch will entitle me to forfeit theirs or give you cause to repent y'r prepossession in my fav'r. A conscience that I had in some degree merited y'r approbation & that of the Gentlemen of the army with whom I had the honor t associate, gave me a consolation & a pleasure in my subsequent retir'ment, tho' wound'd & chagrin'd at my disappointment from the State, w'ch I co'd not have derived from any other source. If in the line of my present appointment fortune sho'd put it in my power to pay attention to or obey in any instance y'r Excellency's commands believe me she co'd not confer a fav'r on me, I sho'd receive with greater pleasure from her hands. With every sentiment of respect & esteem w'ch y'r great & unwearied service to y'r country & your kind & friendly attention to me can fill my breast I have the honor to be y'r Excellency's most obedient & most humble servant. . ."

3. JAMES MONROE TO THOMAS JEFFERSON JULY 15, 1785

"By M'r and M'rs Macauly Graham I have the pleasure to transmit this. They intend immediately for the south of France and as from yours in March I had reason to suspect you intended thither I have suggested to them the probability of their meeting you in that quarter. This lady is the author of the history under her name. She hath been to Mount Vernon, hath been well receiv'd by Gen'l Washington & returns to Europe under the most favorable impressions of him."

4. JAMES MONROE TO THOMAS JEFFERSON JULY 27, 1787

"With the political world I have had little to do since I left Congress.[15] My anxiety however for the gen'l welfare hath not been diminish'd. The affairs of the federal government are, I believe, in the utmost confusion. The convention is an expedient that will produce a decisive effect. It will either recover us from our present embarrassments or complete our ruin; for I do suspect that if what they recommend sho'd be rejected this wo'd be the case. But I trust that the presence of Gen'l Washington will have great weight in the body itself so as to overawe & keep under the demon of party, & that the signature of his name to whatever act shall be the result of their deliberations will secure its passage thro' the union."

5. JAMES MONROE TO THOMAS JEFFERSON JULY 12, 1788

"The conduct of Genl. Washington upon this occasion has no doubt been right and meritorious. All parties had acknowledged defects in the federal system, and been sensible of the propriety of some material change. To forsake the honorable retreat to which he had retired & risque the reputation he had so deservedly acquir'd, manifested a zeal for the publick interest, that could after so many and illustrious services, & at this stage of his life, scarcely have been expected of him. Having however commenc'd

15 Monroe served as a member of the Continental Congress from 1783 to 1786.

again on the publick theatre, the course which he takes becomes not only highly interesting to him but likewise so to us: the human character is not perfect; if he partakes of those qualities which we have too much reason to believe are almost inseparable from the frail nature of our being, the people of America will perhaps be lost. Be assured his influence carried this Government; for my own part I have a boundless confidence in him nor have I any reason to believe he will ever furnish occasion for withdrawing it. More is to be apprehended if he takes a part in the public councils again, as he advances in age, from the designs of those around him than from any disposition of his own.

In the discussion of the subject an allusion was made I believe in the first instance, by Mr. Henry to an opinion you had given on this subject, in a letter to Mr. Donald. This afterwards became the subject of much inquiry & debate in the house..."

6. JAMES MONROE TO ________ MARCH 31, 1791

"The President has fix'd the location for the federal town. Tis to be on the eastern branch runing thence up the Potow'k some few miles above Georgeton. He proposes to extend it down so as to include alex'a. Whether this will be agreed to or not is incertain. He extends it in any event on boths sides of the river."

7. JAMES MONROE TO JOHN BRECKINRIDGE APRIL 6, 1792

"The representation bill, under discussion when you were here, was lost. A 2'd founded as the other was in the H. of R. upon the ratio of 1 for 30.000 was amended, by adding 8 members one to each State having the highest fraction, in the Senate. The principle of this amendment was that the ratio sho'd be applied to the whole numbers of all the States and not to those of each individual state. This was ultimately acceded to by the other house. Yesterday being the last of the 10 days allotted the President to reject or affix his seal to it, it was returned with his negative, declaring in concise & plain terms that he thought it unconstitutional. This act of decision, firmness, and independence has presented a ray of hope to the desponding mind of the republican party. It inspires them with a confidence that the government contains within itself a resource capable of resisting every encroachment on the publick rights. The decision of that house will be taken today upon the objections of the President; but there is no doubt the bill be lost."

8. JAMES MONROE TO THOMAS JEFFERSON JUNE 27, 1793

"In my last I made some observations evincing the propriety of our neutrality in the present European war, but as that sentiment appears to be general, I refer it now only as a proof that it is likewise mine. It leaves me more at liberty to comment on the conduct of the Executive since, which I do the more freely as I do not know what part you have borne in it. The measure I particularly refer to is the proclamation declaring this neutrality, with the reply to the address of some merchants of Phil'a and the order for the prosecution of two marines who had embarked in a privateer licensed by the French minister. I must confess I had considered the proclamat'n at first only an admonition to the people to mind their own business, and not interfere in the controversy; and in this view altho' I could not perceive the necessity of the measure, yet I was inclined to deem it harmless. As the executive magistrate, the competent authority having not otherwise declared, the President might, if he was distrustful of his constituents, endeavor to restrain them within the limits such authority had prescribed, or rather allowed; if indeed there exists in the government, a right to inhibit the citizens of the States from taking commissions from either of the powers at war & fighting in their service. I did not suppose it was intended as a matter of right to declare what sho'd be the conduct of these States in relation to that controversy. But the reply to the merchants and the prosecution above mentioned seem to denote the contrary, and to shew that the President meant it as such. Upon this construction I deem it both unconstitutional & impolitick.

I cannot conceive upon what principle the right is claimed. I think the position incontrovertible that if he possesses the right to say we shall be neutral, he might say we sho'd not be. The power in both instances must be in the same hands. For if the Executive could say we sho'd be neutral, how could the legislature, that we sho'd war. In truth a right to declare our neutrality, as a distinct authority, cannot exist, for that is only the natural state of things, when the positive power of declaring war is not exerted, and this belongs to the legislature only. Any interference therefore with it, by the Executive, must be unconstitutional & improper."

9. JAMES MONROE TO GEORGE NICHOLAS AUGUST 23, 1793

"The monarchy party among us, which is likewise the British one, are availing themselves of some indiscretions of the French Minister to turn the popularity of the President against the French Revolution. This is the fact."

10. AN EXCERPT FROM JAMES MONROE'S SERIES OF LETTERS TITLED, *AGRICOLA* SEPTEMBER 4, 1793

"The French minister it appears in pressing in some instances, the cause of his country and of liberty, upon the President of the United States, has experienced some disappointments, and which in the fever of his zeal, led him into a declaration, intimating a belief, that the general sentiment of the people of America was, more favourable to his country and to her cause, than our executive councils were: and that he would appeal to this sentiment. But what were the points in controversy, or to whom this declaration was made; whether by memorial to the President, or a convivial party, or intended to be carried into effect, has not been shewn. The only fact which appears is that he at sometime, and at some place, made this declaration; and this has been certified with great pomp and solemnity by Mr. Jay, the present chief justice of the United States, and Mr. King, a senator for the state of New York.

With respect to the supposed disagreement, uninformed on that head as we are, it can only be said with propriety at present, that the public have been too long acquainted with the patriotism of their chief magistrate, and his virtuous exertions in the cause of liberty at home, to suspect that he can be indifferent to that interest abroad, and especially in France to whom we owe so much; and on the other hand, that they are too much attached to the great principles of the French revolution, and to the merits of that magnanimous nation, struggling in the best of causes, to bestow their censure upon any of its upright advocates, and especially her representative, however zealous they may be—that the public judgment should be suspended upon those great points, until facts should be correctly stated, upon which alone it should be formed; and that a different line of conduct would not only prove the parent of error and injustice, but lessen them in the estimation of the candid and impartial throughout the world."

11. AN EXCERPT FROM JAMES MONROE'S SERIES OF LETTERS TITLED, *AGRICOLA* DECEMBER 4, 1793

"It was stated in a former paper, that this unfriendly dis[posit]ion had been shown through the whole of our inter[course] with that nation, for the term specified, but more particularly by the regulation of our commerce, and those [other] acts which had taken place between the two countries, since the commencement of its troubles. And the appointment of a public minister of known monarchic principles, to represent us with that Republic, and the proclamation of the President which parted us from and put us on [the] same footing with it as with the invading powers, notwithstanding the alliance and guarantee by which we were [un]ited were given as proofs of this disposition more latterly."

-⊰⊱-

12. JAMES MONROE TO THOMAS JEFFERSON MAY 26, 1794

"In the Senate it will pass immediately, for the republican party is entirely broken in that branch. Thus it results that thro' the influence of the Executive aided by the personal weight of the President, the republican party notwithstanding its systematic & laborious efforts has been able to accomplish nothing which might vindicate the honor or advance the prosperity of the country."

-⊰⊱-

13. JAMES MONROE TO JAMES MADISON OCTOBER 24, 1795

"I most sincerely hope the President has not & will not ratify this treaty; for if he does, I greatly fear the consequences here [in Paris]. From what I can learn we shall be deemed rather than otherwise in the scale of the coalis'd powers—and under such an impression it will require moderation in any gov't to withhold its resentment. How cautious, therefore, sho'd the President be in hazarding a step of this kind at the present moment, when the slightest circumstance is sufficient to excite indignation, & even to part the two countries for ever."

-⊰⊱-

14. JAMES MONROE TO JAMES MADISON JULY 5, 1796

"DEAR SIR,—Yesterday the Forth of July was celebrated here [in Paris] by the Americans. I intended to have done it, but having given them an entertainment last year they returned the compliment this. You will observe by the copy sent in, that [in the toast] to the American government the term 'executive' is used and not 'president.' The course of the business was as follows: The project [of the celebration] began first with the friends of the British treaty, and fell through, and was then [taken] up by its enemies, and after which the others came in. But the first party had appointed a committee (or rather the second in order) and who conducted the business, the majority of whom were for giving 'the Congress' only, or drinking no toasts. I told them if they would give the 'executive,' I supposed all would be satisfied and I would attend and which I could not otherwise do. The first party however in order were not consulted or disliked what was done and when the toasts [were] gone through, one of them ro[se] and proposed a volunteer in favor of G[enl] Washington

&c. and which was [opposed] by some of the others. This made a loud noise here and perhaps will with you as some slander may in consequence be leveled at me, I therefore give you the facts."

15. JAMES MONROE TO JAMES MADISON JULY 5, 1796

"Paine having resolved to continue in Europe some time longer and knowing it was inconvenient for me to keep him longer in my family and wishing also to treat on our politics which he could not well do in my house, left me some time since. He thinks the President winked at his imprisonment and wished he might die in goal, and bears him resentment for it; also he is preparing an attack upon him of the most virulent kind. Through a third person I have endeavoured to divert him from it without effect.[16] It may be said I have instigated him but the above is the truth."

16. JAMES MONROE TO JAMES MADISON JULY 5, 1796

"...Washington is an honest man."

17. JAMES MONROE TO JAMES MADISON SEPTEMBER 1, 1796

"This letter [from Pickering] corresponds so much with the publication in the New York paper that it tends to create a suspicion they were written by the same hand, but these little Connecticut Jockey tricks are too easily seen through now a days to produce any effect. Poor Washington. Into what hands he has fallen!"

18. JAMES MONROE TO JAMES MADISON DECEMBER 7, 1799

"I annex also an extract of a letter from Gen'l Washington, bearing date three days after my letter of recall, w'h by its stile precludes the idea of his intending any dishonorable imputation

16 Upset and believing that Washington had abandoned him in a French prison, Paine wrote a blistering letter to Washington dated July 30, 1796 in which he accused the President of betraying their friendship. He also charged Washington with public hypocrisy as both a general and president, and concluded the letter by writing "the world will be puzzled to decide whether you are an apostate or an imposter; whether you have abandoned good principles or whether you ever had any,"

against me: unless indeed a strange motive sho'd be assigned for his using *that* stile at *that* time." [17]

19. JAMES MONROE TO JAMES MADISON DECEMBER 7, 1799

"The publication of the extract from Gen'l W's letter without any hostile reference to him, taking the idea in the papers, improved as it may be, but yet without concession in his favor, wo'd turn him against those who have acted under him and have used him to oppress justice & truth. Or he must come out daring the inferences drawn from his letter showing the whole affair referred to take a direct & positively hostile ground against me, & lay himself open to my reply w'h wo'd not be wanting. I think he w'd be silent & leave what I guess as a text to be commented on by the world."

20. JAMES MONROE TO JAMES MADISON AUGUST 10, 1804

"The name of Genl. Washington has been used for party purposes. His death removed him from the scene & gave his memory a claim even from his opponents to that notice which his virtues & services entitled him to, especially in the course of our revolution. That sentiment was wisely respected by the republicans on his demise. Much folly was afterwards displayed by others, in attempts to raise monuments in his favor which neither the circumstances of our country, the modesty or wisdom of our people would justify or sanction. May not however the true course be now struck & executed by the republicans? How would it answer after the next election is decided for them to bring forward a motion to erect the equestrian statue voted at the end of the war? I think that the more liberal acts we do which are founded in justice, the less air of party we give to the course of the government, and the more we tranquilize the publick mind the better the effect will be on all our interests at home and abroad."

21. JAMES MONROE'S RESPONSE TO THE WELCOME ADDRESS GIVEN ON BEHALF OF THE MAYOR, CITY COUNCIL, AND CITIZENS OF TRENTON, NEW JERSEY UPON THE HIS ARRIVAL TO THAT CITY DURING HIS PRESIDENTIAL TOUR OF 1817 JUNE 7, 1817

"I feel very sensibly this kind of attention on the part of the authorities of the city of Trenton—the place where the hopes of the country were revived in the war of the

17 Monroe was recalled as U.S. minister to France on August 22, 1796.

revolution by a signal victory obtained by the troops under the command of General George Washington, after a severe and disastrous campaign."

22. EXCERPT FROM PRESIDENT JAMES MONROE'S RESPONSE TO THE WELCOME ADDRESS GIVEN ON BEHALF OF THE CITIZENS OF BOSTON, MASSACHUSETTS UPON HIS ARRIVAL TO THAT CITY DURING HIS PRESIDENTIAL TOUR OF 1817 JULY 3, 1817

"As no person is more willing than I am, in the discharge of my duty, according to the fair exercise of my judgment, to take example from the conduct of the distinguished men who have preceded me in this high trust, it is particularly gratifying to me to have recalled, by this incident, to the memory of many who are now present, a like visit from the illustrious commander of our revolutionary army: who, by many other important services, had so just a claim to the revered title of father of his country. It was natural that the presence of a citizen, so respected and beloved, who had so eminently contributed to the establishment of this government, and to whom its administration in the commencement had been committed, should inspire and enlighten a virtuous and free people with unlimited confidence in its success, and it is a cause of general felicitation and joy to us all, to find that thirty years successful experiment have justified that confidence and realized our most sanguine hopes in its favor."

23. EXCERPT FROM PRESIDENT JAMES MONROE'S RESPONSE TO THE WELCOME ADDRESS PROVIDED BY THE CIVIC OFFICIALS OF ANNAPOLIS, MARYLAND DURING HIS PRESIDENTIAL TOUR OF 1818 MAY 28, 1818

"In recurring to the period of 1783, when Congress held their session here, you bring to view incidents in the highest degree important. It was then, and here, after a long & arduous struggle, which secured our independence, that the treaty of peace was ratified. It was then, & here, that the illustrious commander of our revolutionary armies, after performing services, which a grateful country can never forget, nor time obliterate, restored his commission to the authority from whom he had received it. To me these events so profoundly interesting to all, were peculiarly imposing and impressive."

24. EXCERPT FROM PRESIDENT JAMES MONROE'S RESPONSE TO THE WELCOME ADDRESS PROVIDED BY THE CIVIC OFFICIALS AND CITIZENS OF GEORGETOWN, VIRGINIA, DURING HIS PRESIDENTIAL TOUR OF 1819 APRIL 22, 1819

"In recurring to the great events which characterize our revolutionary struggle, we see every thing in the conduct of those who guided our councils, and fought our battles, to command our admiration and gratitude. By that great struggle we asserted and achieved our independence; by it was laid the foundation on which our present happy constitution was erected, and our equal rights and liberties completely secured. I concur in the sentiment which you have expressed, that the example of those whose virtues and talents we are so much indebted should be the object of our constant attention, and that the very extraordinary services of him, who has been emphatically call the father of his country, give him a just claim to that venerated title...

To the virtuous councils, which advised, and declared the late war; to the energy, with which it was prosecuted, and to the heroic gallantry of our army, navy, and militia, too much praise cannot be given. That I performed the part allotted to me, to the satisfaction of my fellow citizens, under my patriotic and enlightened predecessor, affords a gratification which I shall not attempt to describe."

25. JAMES MONROE TO JOHN QUINCY ADAMS AUGUST 3, 1820

"I have been assured that the principle relied on above, that the gov't was not responsible for more than I have stated, was decided in the commencement of our gov't, under the administration of Gen'l Washington, in the cases litigated at that time between France and other powers."

26. JAMES MONROE TO THOMAS JEFFERSON SEPTEMBER 6, 1821

"But the great demand which has been and is still made on them, in various ways, in support of institutions & measures on which their highest interest depend, has been so sensibly felt that a like attempt in honor of the memory of General Washington has recently failed in this State, nor has a statue yet been erected to his memory by this nation."

27. EXCERPT FROM JAMES MONROE'S *THE MEMOIR* NOVEMBER 1826

"The favorable opinion of that individual [Washington] was always an object of the highest interest to me. I had served under him as a subaltern, in our revolutionary army, and had witnessed his very exemplary conduct at the most difficult and perilous epochs of that great struggle. I had received his approbation of my conduct in that struggle, and been promoted by him. I was a member of the Revolutionary Congress of 1783, and present when he resigned his commission as Commander in Chief of our Armies, and retired to private life. I knew him at his residence in retirement, as I afterwards did while a member of the Senate; when at the head of the government to which he was called by the unanimous suffrage of his fellow citizens, and I have always cherished the highest respect for his memory, and admired his great virtues and talents."

28. JAMES MONROE TO JOHN MCLEAN DECEMBER 5, 1827

"I was charged with a failure to perform my duty in my first mission, & recalled from it, & censured. The book which I published on my return home, with the official documents which it contains, vindicated me against the charge, and on that ground I then left it.[18] The parties are since dead, and I am now retired to private life. I never doubted the perfect integrity of Genl. Washington, nor the strength, or energy of his mind, and was personally attached to him. I admired his patriotism, and had full confidence in his attachment to liberty, and solicitude for the success of the French revolution. It being necessary to advert to that occurrence, in my communication to the committee which was first appointed by him on my claims, I availed myself of the occasion to express a sentiment corresponding with the above, in his favor, as I likewise did in the memoir since published. The documents published with it prove, in minute detail, not only that I faithfully performed my duty to my country, but exerted my best faculties, on all occasions, in support of his character and fame."

29. EXCERPT FROM THE *AUTOBIOGRAPHY OF JAMES MONROE* 1827-1830

"'On the 15th of June 1775 (says he), a commander-in-chief of all the forces, raised and to be raised for the defense of American liberty, was appointed by unanimous vote of Congress, and his conduct in the discharge of the duties of that high trust, which he held

18 The book Monroe is referring to is his *A View of the Conduct of the Executive in the Foreign Affairs of the United States* (1797).

through the whole of the war, has given an example to the world for talents as a military commander, for integrity, fortitude, and firmness under the severest of trials, for respect to the civil authority and devotion to the rights and liberties of his country, of which neither Rome nor Greece have exhibited the equal.'"

30. EXCERPT FROM THE *AUTOBIOGRAPHY OF JAMES MONROE* 1827-1830

"'I saw him in my earliest youth, in the retreat through Jersey, at the head of a small band, or rather, in its rear, for he was always near the enemy, and his countenance and manner made an impression on me which time can never efface. A lieutenant then in the Third Virginia Regiment, I happened to be on the rear guard at Newark, and I counted the force under his immediate command by platoons as it passed me, which amounted to less than 3,000 men. A deportment so firm, so dignified, so exalted, but yet so modest and composed, I have never seen in any other person.'"

31. EXCERPT FROM THE *AUTOBIOGRAPHY OF JAMES MONROE* 1827-1830

"The success of the enemy in the battles of Long Island and the White Plains, with the capture of Forts Washington and Lee, and the retreat of our army through Jersey, put fairly at issue with the nation the great question whether they were competent and resolved to support their independence, or would sink under the pressure. The councils of the union exhibited a firmness which showed that they were equal to the crisis. The Congress of the United States and the legislatures of all the states were in session, and not the slightest symptom of hesitation was seen in either of those public bodies. The most active efforts were made by all, and with the most faithful cooperation between them, each performing its appropriate duties, to raise and support a force which would meet and defy the enemy in the field the next campaign. General Washington was equally attentive to his duties. He perceived that the British Commander, by the disposition which he had made of his troops, had estimated his success beyond their merit: that he considered the country as essentially conquered. The opportunity for profiting of that error, of depressing the British power, and elevating the hopes and spirits of his country, was favorable, and he resolved to take advantage of it. The force at Trenton was small, but believed by the British commander to be superior to any that he could bring to bear on it."

32. EXCERPT FROM THE *AUTOBIOGRAPHY OF JAMES MONROE* 1827-1830

"General Washington was attentive to the conduct of the enemy. He perceived that the British force extended over a large surface and that the body which was at Germantown was not well supported by that at the city and below it. He resolved to attack it, and with that view made secretly the necessary preparations. Having formed his army into columns, with a suitable commander at the head of each, he advanced on them and commenced the attack on the troops that were encamped near Germantown, who were taken by surprise and driven before him."

33. EXCERPT FROM THE *AUTOBIOGRAPHY OF JAMES MONROE* 1827-1830

"The first session, under his first appointment to Congress, was held at Annapolis and commenced in December, 1783. The Virginia delegation consisted of Mr. Jefferson, Mr. Hardy, Mr. Arthur Lee, John Francis Mercer and himself. The contest for our liberties had succeeded by the complete establishment of our independence. A definitive treaty to that effect had been concluded, and its ratification was among the first acts of that session. The resignation of the Commander-in-chief of all our forces of the commission under which he had acted through the whole war, was a necessary consequence of its termination, and which occurred in an early stage of that session. The scene was highly interesting. The manner in which he took his leave and the sentiment expressed in the audience given him by Congress of the conduct through that arduous struggle was such as evinced the high sense entertained of his merit and became the dignity of the body under whom he had so served. It could not fail to excite the sensibility of Mr. Monroe to reflect that he had served as a lieutenant under him only a few years before."

34. EXCERPT FROM THE *AUTOBIOGRAPHY OF JAMES MONROE* 1827-1830

"From the time that the Constitution was reported from Philadelphia by the Convention who had formed it, the citizens throughout the country became much divided respecting its merits, those opposed to it contending that it would lead to consolidation and monarchy; those who supported it, that its adoption was indispensible to the preservation of the union and of free government. By degrees the parties became violent, each imputing to the other selfish and improper motives. Those in favor of it were called Federalists; those against it; Anti-Federalists. This division was felt in the state assemblies and conventions to whom it was submitted, and in Congress after its adoption, though the confidence reposed in General Washington, who had been unanimously elected to the office of the President, abated considerably its violence."

35. EXCERPT FROM THE *AUTOBIOGRAPHY OF JAMES MONROE* 1827-1830

"The Constitution was ratified by all the state conventions and carried into effect in 1789, and the distinguished citizen who had commanded our Revolutionary armies and presided in the late national Convention was elected to the Chief Executive status by the unanimous suffrage of the whole people. He served in that trust the two first terms, making eight years, and although regarding the novelty of the station, the divisions among ourselves, and the convulsed state of the world at that important epoch, with its bearing on us, his situation was eminently difficult, and some of his measures were not approved by the Republican party, yet he had the peculiar felicity to enjoy to the end of his services and of his life the undiminished confidence of his country. In the arrangement of parties he belonged, by the forces of circumstances, to the Federal, and was in consequence at its head, but he was nevertheless at the head of the nation, not by his office alone, but by the place which he held in the confidence and affections of his fellow citizens. No one suspected him of a desire to promote the establishment of monarchy. His devotion to the rights and liberties of his country and incorruptible integrity had been too fully proved by his long, very eminent and very faithful services to admit any doubt on that point."

36. EXCERPT FROM THE *AUTOBIOGRAPHY OF JAMES MONROE* 1827-1830

"It is believed that no person was ever called to a trust of greater delicacy and difficulty than was our first Chief Magistrate. His greater dread was that of disunion, but it proceeded solely from a disinterested regard for the public welfare. His difficulties arose from the nature of the trust itself: the commencement of a new government with a divided sovereignty respecting which, in some of its powers, a great diversity of sentiment had prevailed and strong parties been formed in the discussions which led to its adoption, which still existed and might be felt in its subsequent movement. No such government had ever existed before because the sovereignty, independent of other peculiarities, had never been divided before, nor can it be divided except where the sovereignty is in the people and the government, a trust created by compact, in which those who discharge its duties have no rights or interests of their own, but are mere agents employed for the purpose.

37. EXCERPT FROM THE *AUTOBIOGRAPHY OF JAMES MONROE* 1827-1830

"For the decision on this question, much allowance ought to be made, and especially to the Chief Magistrate. It cannot be doubted that the leading Federalists were for the exclusion of their opponents. It was, therefore, difficult for him to disregard their council and to separate himself, as it were from them. He was also one of the last of men to take a course which should subject him to the suspicion of pursuing a temporizing policy for any purpose whatever."

38. EXCERPT FROM THE *AUTOBIOGRAPHY OF JAMES MONROE* 1827-1830

"In regard to the President, we are happy to state that the opinion which Mr. Monroe had formed in early life and entertained at the time of his appointment of his transcendent services, exalted merit, and great purity of principle, had undergone no change, even at the period when the burden of his censure lay heaviest on him."

39. EXCERPT FROM THE *AUTOBIOGRAPHY OF JAMES MONROE* 1827-1830

"He well knew that his situation had become peculiarly delicate, by the treaty itself, in its bearing on all the parties and interests connected with it, especially after the decision of the Senate. Had he rejected it, he would have taken on himself the responsibility of all the consequences which would have followed, of a war with England, for example, had that ensued. He was aware also that the popular movements in the United States against the treaty might have formed an additional obstacle to its rejection, as it might have been inferred that it had been produced by those movements, and by intimidation, to which he was the last of men to yield.

Such had been the division of parties, and so great were the excitement and animosity between them at this moment, and so far had the measure advanced, that to have rejected the treaty would have thrown him essentially on that party which was in direct opposition to the whole proceeding. He was instilled to the confidence of the nation, and actually enjoyed it, but in the state in which the affair then stood, he could expect support in the course which he might adopt from one party only. By ratifying the treaty and relying on the party which had supported the policy pursued, he was sure of its uniform and continued support, and might calculate on the acquiescence of the other after the excitement of the moment had passed away. By rejecting it, especially if war with Great Britain should ensue, there was danger that the Federal party would have been offended and the other have afforded only a moderate support. His situation was therefore peculiarly delicate and difficult, not in regard to himself only but the nation, as to the consequences attending his decision. It was known that he hesitated after the British had commenced the seizure of our vessels laden with provisions destined for the ports of France, and it cannot be doubted, had he foreseen the state in which we then were, at a period while the proceeding was under his control, that he would have prevented it. In the decision which he did form, which was to ratify the treaty, he was compelled to view the actual state, and in which we are satisfied that he was governed by the present principles. The recall of Mr. Monroe seemed to be incidental to that decision. Those near him, whose council he had respected and with whom Mr. Monroe had had collision—we allude particularly to Mr. Jay and Mr. Hamilton—would press his recall, and the President might suppose after the ratification of the treaty that his recall and the appointment of another Minister would indicate more tone and have a better effect with the French government."

40. EXCERPT FROM THE *AUTOBIOGRAPHY OF JAMES MONROE* 1827-1830

"He (Monroe) departed immediately for Richmond, accompanied by the venerable Mr. Jefferson to Milton, and by Colonel Randolph and the troop to the boundary line of the county. Many friends saluted him on the road, and as he approached Richmond, he was met by Dr. Foushee and other friends, with whom he entered the city. As they advanced, he was informed by Dr. Foushee that an authentic account had been received of the death of General Washington, an event which shocked and deeply affected him, for it was his intention, now that he was placed on independent ground by the generous confidence of his fellow citizens, to make advances and indicate a desire to restore their former friendly relation. The report made to him by his friend Dr. Edwards of the favorable sentiment expressed of him by the General after his recall, he thought would justify such advance from the station he then held, and it accorded highly with his feelings and principles to make it."

VI. JOHN QUINCY ADAMS ON GEORGE WASHINGTON

1. EXCERPT FROM JOHN QUINCY ADAMS' *ADDRESS TO PRESIDENT WASHINGTON BY THE CITIZENS OF NEWBURYPORT* NOVEMBER 1789

"When by the unanimous suffrages of your countrymen you were called to preside at her councils, the citizens of the town of Newbury Port participated in the general joy arising from a pleasing anticipation of an administration conducted by one to whose exertions they felt themselves so much indebted for their inestimable freedom.

At the present moment they indulge themselves in sentiments in joy resulting from principles perhaps less elevated, but equally dear to their hearts; from the gratification of their affection in beholding personally among them, the friend, the benefactor, the father of his country.

They cannot hope, Sir, to exhibit any peculiar marks of attachment to your person, since in expressing the feelings of the warmest and sincerest gratitude, they could only re-echo the sentiments which are impressed upon the hearts of all their fellow citizens as deeply as upon their own. But in justice to themselves, they think they are authorized to assure you, that in no part of the United States are those sentiments of gratitude and affection more cordial and sincere, than in the town which at this time is honored by your presence."

2. JOHN QUINCY ADAMS TO ABIGAIL ADAMS DECEMBER 5, 1789

"I was not one of the choir who *welcomed* the President to *New England's shore*, upon his arrival here by land. I was, however, in the procession which was formed here to receive him in humble imitation of the Capital. And when he left us, I was one of the *respectable citizens* (as our newspapers term them) who escorted him on horse-back to the lines of New Hampshire… I had the honor of paying my respects to the President upon his arrival in this town, and he did me the honor to recollect that he had seen me a short time before, at New York. I had the honor of spending part of the evening in his presence at Mr. [Jonathan] Jackson's. I had the honor of breakfasting in the same room with him the next morning at Mr. [Tristram] Dalton's. I had the honor of writing the billet which the major general of the county sent him to inform him of the military arrangements he had made for his reception. And I had the honor of draughting an address, which with many alterations and additions (commonly called amendments) was presented to him by the town of Newburyport."

3. JOHN QUINCY ADAMS TO JOHN ADAMS DECEMBER 8, 1792

"Our electors met in this town on Wednesday last, and their votes for President and Vice President were unanimous. This was generally expected here, and the event is supposed to have been nearly if not wholly the same in all the New England states. New York it is imagined was unanimous for Mr. [George] Clinton as V[ice] P[resident]. Their electors are chosen by their legislature, where their Governor has a bare majority, determined to support upon all occasions his party and his politics. From the other states you will probably hear before us. And upon the whole I presume the election will be favorable."[19]

4. EXCERPT FROM AN ARTICLE WRITTEN BY JOHN QUINCY ADAMS UNDER THE SIGNATURE OF "COLUMBUS" DECEMBER 4, 1793

"When the Minister of the French Republic [Edmond Charles Genet] declared his determination to appeal from the decision of the regular and constituted authority, upon the construction of certain treaties, to the people of America, the first sentiments which the declaration excited in the breasts of that people, was the spontaneous emotion of the heart. They considered it as an insolent outrage offered to the man, who was deservedly the object of their grateful affection; as an insult upon the character of their common friend and benefactor, and they spurned the attempt to degrade their Hero, with scorn and disdain. 'The people,' says Junius, 'are seldom mistaken in their *opinions*, in their *sentiments* they are never wrong.' When the Americans were rudely called upon to pronounce upon the conduct of the patriot, whose disinterested virtues and superior talents had been employed in their service through all the vicissitudes of fortune; whose generous magnanimity had supported them in the most distressing moments of national depression; whose expanded patriotism had participated with rapture in the most blissful scenes of national exultation; the glory of their war, and the ornament of their peace; when a beardless foreigner, whose name was scarcely

19 President George Washington was re-elected as president receiving 132 electoral votes. The vote for vice president was split between John Adams (77), George Clinton (50), Thomas Jefferson (4), and Aaron Burr (1).

enrolled upon the catalogue of Liberty; a petulant stripling, whose commission from a friendly power was his only title to their respect, and whose only merit was his country, presumed to place himself in opposition to the *father of their country*, and to call for their approbation to support his claims, they viewed the application as an indignity offered to themselves, and even before their judgment had deliberated upon the merits of the case, they rejected the arrogant pretensions of the foreigner, with pointed indignation."

5. EXCERPT OF AN ARTICLE WRITTEN BY JOHN QUINCY ADAMS UNDER THE SIGNATURE "COLUMBUS" DECEMBER 4, 1793

"Did they[20] strain every nerve to create a distinction in his behalf, and explain his intention of appeal, to be merely an insult upon the person of the Chief Magistrate, and not upon the government of *America?* He was sure to disclaim so frail a discrimination, and to declare that he was incapable of disrespect to the 'Hero of Liberty,' but that his threat was pointed at the government of the Union."

6. AN EXCERPT FROM THE DIARY OF JOHN QUINCY ADAMS JUNE 3, 1794

"When I returned to my lodgings at the close of the evening, upon opening a letter from my father, which I had just before taken from the postoffice I found that it contained information that Edmund Randolph, Secretary of State of the United States, had, on the morning of the day when the letter was dated, called on the writer, and told him that the President of the United States had determined to nominate me to go to the Hague as Resident Minister from the United States. This intelligence was very unexpected, and indeed surprising. I had laid down as a principle, that I never would solicit for any public office whatever, and from this determination no necessity has hitherto compelled me to swerve."

7. AN EXCERPT FROM THE DIARY OF JOHN QUINCY ADAMS JULY 11, 1794

"By the invitation of the President, I attended the reception he gave to *Piomingo* and a number of other Chickasaw Indians. Five Chiefs, seven Warriors, four boys and

20 American supporters of "Citizen" Genet.

an interpreter constituted the company. As soon as the whole were seated, the ceremony of smoking began. A large East Indian pipe was placed in the middle of the Hall. The tube, which appeared to be of leather, was twelve or fifteen feet in length. The President began, and after two or three whiffs, passed the tube to Piomingo; he to the next Chief, and so all round. Whether this ceremony be really of Indian origin, as is generally supposed, I confess I have some doubt. At least these Indians appeared to be quite unused to it, and from their manner of going through it, looked as if they were submitting to a process in compliance with *our* custom. Some of them, I thought, smiled with such an expression of countenance as denoted a sense of *novelty*, and of *frivolity* too; as if the ceremony struck them, not only as new, but also as ridiculous. When it was finished, the President addressed them in a speech which he read, stopping at the close of every sentence for the interpreter to translate it. . . .The President told them that the Chickasaws had always been distinguished as sincere and faithful friends, and that the United States always valued such friends most highly. They said nothing of their own sincerity, and made no answer to the President's compliment."

8. AN EXCERPT FROM THE DIARY OF JOHN QUINCY ADAMS JANUARY 22, 1795

"They spoke of the President, whom, like all Europeans, they called General Washington. Enquired his age;[21] and on being told, said he might still long enjoy his glory; that he was a great man, and they had great veneration for his character."

9. AN EXCERPT FROM THE DIARY OF JOHN QUINCY ADAMS MARCH 18, 1795

"[The Commissioner to Holland] spoke of the President in the most respectful terms, and said he was a great man, and deserving of veneration from all mankind. I told him that such was our opinion in America. 'And it is the general opinion in France, too,' said he. 'There may be some exceptions, because great pains have been taken to prejudice minds against him but in general we know from what a perfidious quarter those pains came, and therefore they have been in general unsuccessful.'"

21 At the time of this entry Washington was just one month shy of his 63rd birthday.

10. AN EXCERPT FROM THE DIARY OF JOHN QUINCY ADAMS APRIL 4, 1795

"Count Löwenhielm spoke in terms of great respect and admiration of the President of the United States, and of the neutral system of policy pursued by the American Government in the present war. Upon the observation that the Regent of Sweden had pursued the same wise policy, he said that it was the example of America which had encouraged it, and the Swedes were obliged to the President of the United States for being the first to stand forward with that example, which encourages them to imitation, and secured to them such great advantages and such exemptions from the common distress in which all the nations are now involved."

11. JOHN QUINCY ADAMS TO JOHN ADAMS MAY 22, 1795

"The President of the United States has so decidedly adopted and maintained the policy of neutrality, and it has proved so advantageous to the country, that it is perhaps an idle apprehension that can imagine it will again be endangered."

12. JOHN QUINCY ADAMS TO JOHN ADAMS SEPTEMBER 12, 1795

"I received two days ago your letter from New York of June 29. It gratified my highest ambition, as it testifies the approbation of the President and the Secretaries upon my conduct and correspondence. . ."

13. JOHN QUINCY ADAM TO TIMOTHY PICKERING NOVEMBER 15, 1795

"The system of policy pursued by the President since the commencement of the present European war has been encountered by so many difficulties and embarrassments, which the wisdom of his government has removed and overcome, that I feel encouraged in the hope that it will be successfully pursued to the end."

14. AN EXCERPT FROM THE DIARY OF JOHN QUINCY ADAMS DECEMBER 1, 1795

"Asked if I had heard any thing of the President's intending to resign. Told him no. He said he had heard such was his determination at the expiration of his present term, in case there should be no troubles in the country. What sort of a soul does this man suppose I have?"

15. JOHN QUINCY ADAMS TO SYLVANUS BOURNE DECEMBER 16, 1795

"The President has not resigned, but there appears to be a most violent attack carried on against him, the object of which is probably to induce his resignation, or his removal at the next election. In this country the same people who derive so much pleasure from the Western Insurrection[22] of the last year, take an equal satisfaction in this circumstance. They seem to anticipate with delight the fall of a man, who has hitherto been the boast of Republicans. Time will show, whether in this instance, as in the former, these exulters have not purchased the skin before the chase was killed.

But Mr. Randolph *has* resigned, and as to the origin of his resignation there are, as usual, two stories. His friends say that it was *only* certain indiscreet communications between him and the French Minister [Jean-Antoine Joseph] Fauchet, and they very much blame the President for having made an *éclat* of a thing, which they think ought to have been overlooked or arranged without noise."

16. JOHN QUINCY ADAMS TO SYLVANUS BOURNE DECEMBER 24, 1795

"The most recent accounts from America contain the usual mixture of sweet and bitter, but with more than an ordinary quality of both ingredients. The attack upon the President is still carried on with that virulence and brutality which have uniformly been characteristic of an American party mingling with a foreign influence."

17. JOHN QUINCY ADAMS TO SYLVANUS BOURNE DECEMBER 24, 1795

"At the present moment if our neutrality be still preserved, it will be due to the President alone. Nothing but his weight of character and reputation, combined with his firmness and political intrepidity, could have stood against the torrent that is still

22 Whiskey Rebellion.

tumbling with a fury that resounds even across the Atlantic. He is now pledged, and he is unmoved. If his system of administration now prevails, ten years more will place the United States among the most powerful and opulent nations on earth. If he fails, though the Demon of Discord may raise a cloud of prejudice and obloquy around the splendor of his fame for the present moment, it will only serve to add a brighter radiance to his future glory. Yet I deprecate this event because the value of his administration will in that case be proved by the deprivation of the blessings it has secured to his country.

This, my good friend, is not the language of a courtier. You and I have known the time when *not to applaud* the man who united all hearts was almost held to a crime. Should that time return again while he lives, *my* tribute of veneration and gratitude shall again remain silent in my heart. But now, when he does not unite all hearts, when on the contrary a powerful party at home, and a mighty influence from abroad, are joining all their forces to assail his reputation and his character, I think it my duty as an American to avow my sentiments as they concern that man."

18. JOHN QUINCY ADAMS TO JOHN ADAMS DECEMBER 29, 1795

"The direct and formal attack upon the President, which has been carried on in the usual style, and which is noticed in your letter, was not unexpected to me, and I think you must have received very soon after the date of yours a letter from me written at the Hague in July or August, containing the opinions I had then formed on that head. That the systematic course of abuse pointed against him, and which was arranged in Europe before it was put in execution in America, is connected with the scheme for dividing the American executive, is perhaps nothing more than a conjecture on my part; but I have little doubt, that it was merely preparatory for the purpose of bringing forward in due time a change of men or of government in our country."

19. JOHN QUINCY ADAMS TO JOHN ADAMS FEBRUARY 10, 1796

"Mr. [Edmund] Randolph's pamphlet had arrived before Mr. Hall, but I had seen only some extracts from it, which were and yet are dealt out in some of the daily papers here.[23] I think he rolls the stone of Sisyphus with a more impetuous recoil than I ever witnessed

23 London, England.

before. I confess I should never have thought that even the delirium of guilt could publish *such* a production, and imagine it would injure the reputation of the President, or defend that of the writer. In my last numbered letter to you I mentioned an opinion that the party in France would perhaps return to the courting system, and I am almost tempted to believe that they advised this publication by way of atonement. For it seems to me impossible that the production should have been given to the world, but by the agency of a person inveterate even to rancor against Mr. Randolph, and disposed to raise the character of the President higher if possible than its former elevation.

But the publication to the world of confidential opinions and sentiments entertained by the President with respect to the European parties and governments, will produce in a degree the effect for which it was calculated. They will produce some mischief. The sensation here upon seeing a proclamation to all the world that the President has been inimical to England, and the friend of the French cause, is very perceptible and very strong. It will not only corroborate and confirm that deep rooted malignity towards us which governs the cabinet, but it alienates and irritates the part of the nation who are well disposed towards us."

20. JOHN QUINCY ADAMS TO JOHN ADAMS FEBRUARY 10, 1796

"The cabinet [in London] have of late affected a great regard for the *Government* of the United States. In this particular too they have coincided with our most virulent anarchists, and have taken all possible pains to countenance and give credit to *their* assertions that the American administrations were upon terms of great harmony with that of Britain. The truth is that the American *Government*, and those who are at the head of its administration, have not upon the earth more rancorous enemies, than the springs which move the executive machine of this country."

21. JOHN QUINCY ADAMS TO JOHN ADAMS APRIL 4, 1796

"There may be another object connected with that of stimulating a rupture with Britain, the success of which may be considered as important towards that purpose. The Presidential elections are to take place in the course of the present year. The experiment of an attack upon the popularity of the President was made the last autumn and winter. It was indeed altogether unsuccessful, but it prepared the way for the repetition of an assault, whenever the circumstances should be favorable to the purpose. The party are inveterate against the President, because they now think him pledged in opposition to their views, and their object has therefore been to impress the French rulers with an opinion that he is inimical to their cause."

-⊰⊱-

22. JOHN QUINCY ADAMS TO JOHN ADAMS APRIL 4, 1796

"All these things are bottomed upon the principle of [Jean-Antoine de Mesmes, Comte] d'Avaux, and perhaps others, which may be supposed to contain powers of personal operation upon the feelings of our first magistrate, will continue to be employed, however discouraging the ill success of the former attempts may have been.

On one hand therefore he will be courted by the prospect of every support from the party, and on the other that of an opposition at least against the unanimity which marked the two preceding elections, will be suffered to be seen, under an expectation that it will have its influence in conciliating the sentiments of the person to the measures of the party. If this should not succeed, the attack of the last season will be renewed with redoubled impetuosity, and if they cannot hope to turn the balance of the election they flatter themselves that at least they can induce retirement or resignation from the disgust of ill treatment. Such it seems according to Fauchet's letter was the policy upon which the persecution against Mr. [Alexander] Hamilton was conducted, and they will have double reasons for pursuing it in this instance.

The removal of the President, however effected in the tactics of the combined French and party powers, is to be followed by a plan for introducing into the American Constitution a Directory instead of a President, and for taking from the supreme Executive the command of the armed force."

-⊰⊱-

23. JOHN QUINCY ADAMS TO CHRISTOPHER GORE JULY 26, 1796

"The intention of the president to retire at the expiration of his present term of service, I fear is unquestionable from what is mentioned in your letter. I have many reasons to regret the circumstance. I do not assent entirely to the opinion very prevalent in Europe, that the destinies of the United States depend solely upon that man, but I really deem his continuance in office, *at present*, of great importance to their welfare. As long as our neutrality shall not be placed beyond all possible danger, I shall always believe the weight of his character and influence very necessary to secure it."

24. JOHN QUINCY ADAMS TO JOHN ADAMS AUGUST 13, 1796

"Mr. Paine is said to be yet writing his pamphlet against the President of the United States and his administration, but he does not now live in the house of Mr. [James] Monroe. . . . The Pamphlet war against the character of the President was begun under the auspices of the French government the last summer. If it is now to be renewed it will be still under their auspices, but they *may* perhaps discover that his personal feelings and fortunes are as inaccessible to their attacks as his fame. But as panegyric and calumny are equally among their means, and they are perfectly indifferent which of them it is they employ, the choice is decided by circumstances only, and they will at an hour's warning be prepared to erect a statue to him who they find they cannot ruin.

But *measures and not men* is their maxim, and their only means of destroying a system is by attacking the person upon whom they suppose its support to depend. It may therefore be expected that the French government and their pamphleteers will from the same batteries only change the direction of their artillery. The object will remain the same, to *force us* out of our neutrality, to deprive us at least of all connections with Britain, and to alter our Constitution to such a form as shall give them a more certain and effectual influence over our national Executive."

25. JOHN QUINCY ADAMS TO JOSEPH PITCAIRN NOVEMBER 13, 1796

"There is a great ignorance of the character and sentiments of the American people in France among those who imagine that any manœuvre of *theirs* could turn an election against the President of the United States. Their invectives and their calumnies may add a few more to the number of his detractors, or take away some who admired him from fashion or from personal motives; but among the great mass of the people he stands fixed as the foundations of the world, and France will find it more easy to go through five and twenty revolutions at home, than to root out that man's merits and services from the memory of Americans, or a proper sense of them from their hearts.

It is probable, however, that if the President persists in his intention to retire, the French will soon forget their political resentments against him. As to his system of policy they will do well to acquiesce in that, for they will not overturn it."

26. JOHN QUINCY ADAMS TO JOHN ADAMS NOVEMBER 25, 1796

"The President's address to the people of the United States of September 17, arrived here some time since. I imagine it will be translated and published in the papers of the country. There are perhaps some characters here who do not perfectly relish it; the observations upon the absurdity of having any *favorite* foreign nation are applicable to other countries, as well as to the United States. Their justice is pointedly felt here, and several persons have mentioned to me the address in terms of the highest satisfaction. But the foreign nation here is something more than a favorite, and it requires a degree of courage by no means universal even to *profess* any sentiments of independence."

27. JOHN QUINCY ADAMS TO JOHAN LUZAC NOVEMBER 25, 1796

"MY DEAR SIR:

"I have just read in the supplement to the *Leyden Gazette* of this morning, under the extract of the news from London, an article which says that General Washington had been induced, from disgust at the ingratitude with which his services have been recently paid, to retire from his eminent station, and to request in a discourse pronounced on the 17th of September, that his fellow citizens would not continue him in high office at the next election.

I shall not examine the inducement which *Englishmen* may have to impute motives to General Washington unworthy of his character, or to attribute ingratitude for public services to the Americans. But my regard for my country and for its brightest ornament makes me anxiously desirous that no aspersion cast upon them should remain in the minds of our *friends*.

I hope in the course of a few days to send you the address of the President to the people of the United States, dated and published (not pronounced) on the 17th of September. You will judge from the paper itself whether the disgust or the ingratitude, which some Englishmen are always ready to discover, because they would be glad to find them in the United States of America, were the motives for the retirement from the Chief Magistracy of the American Union. I flatter myself on the contrary, that you will find his inducements more consistent with the dignity of his character, and with the honor and justice of the American people. At the same time I am sure you will concur in the opinion that it is one of the most interesting papers as a public document, and in every respect worthy of one whose life has been one continued benefaction to his country. I know not whether it can conveniently be inserted in a translation at full length in the *Leyden Gazette*; but I am persuaded that your brother will have the goodness to correct the impression which an imputation, injurious both to the President and the people of the United States, would leave on the public mind in Europe. The reasons assigned by the President himself for declining to be viewed as a candidate for the approaching election are his time of life, his strong inclinations towards a retired life, and the peaceable, calm and prosperous state of affairs in that country, which permit him to retire without apprehending any essential detriment to the public service. At the same time he bears a testimony equally just and honorable to his fellow citizens, for the steady, constant and invariable confidence with which they have always supported him and rewarded his exertions in their service. I mention these circumstances with the more readiness, because I am sure you will be gratified to know that the imputation of disgust to General Washington, and of ingratitude to the Americans, is merely the calumny of English spirits beholding the felicity of the Americans, as Satan is represented beholding that of our first parents in the garden of Eden."

28. JOHN QUINCY ADAMS TO JOHN ADAMS DECEMBER 24, 1796

"I have mentioned that one of the motives of the French Directory in their late proceeding[24] is to influence the American election, or to embarrass the new administration. There is an opinion propagated with great zeal and industry in every part of Europe, that the union and prosperity of the United States are dependent altogether upon the personal character, merits, and popularity of the present President, and that the moment he shall retire from the government we shall fall into irreconcilable dissentions, which will soon be followed by a separation of the northern from the southern states. In England and France, perhaps among some people in this country, these ideas are not simple opinions; they have ripened into *hopes*."

24 The French government rejected Charles Cotesworth Pinckney's credentials as United States Minister to France upon his arrival to that country.

29. JOHN QUINCY ADAMS TO ABIGAIL ADAMS FEBRUARY 8, 1797

"The address of the President declaring his intention to retire from the public service has been republished, translated, and admired all over Europe. But in France the usual arts of French intrigue in all their impudence and all their falsehood have been used against it. The most barefaced forgeries have been palmed upon the public in France under the name of translations and extracts of this address, and I know not whether one faithful French translation of it has appeared in that country. The *Leyden Gazette* has given one here, together with such encomiums upon the piece itself and its author, as both deserve and obtain from every virtuous mind, and has noticed the infidelity of the pretended translations published in the Paris papers. The French Directory, or their guide, have taken a dislike to the principles and fame of Washington, and have, among other of their little projects, undertaken to *run him down.* They have been at work two years upon it, and are now in a perfect frenzy at the thought that he has placed himself beyond the reach of their weapons. Yet they have been unable to succeed generally, even in France, where at the moment the generality of the nation revere his character, and where his name will be remembered with veneration, when they will escape detestation only inasmuch as they shall sink into oblivion. . . ."

30. JOHN QUINCY ADAMS TO GEORGE WASHINGTON FEBRUARY 11, 1797

"As this letter will not come to your hands until after the period which you have fixed upon for retiring from the Chief Magistracy of the Union, I cannot omit the opportunity of expressing the deep concern which, in common with every virtuous American citizen, I have felt upon being informed of your resolution, and the veneration and gratitude with which, as one of the people of the United States, I received your address to them, dated on the 17th of September last. I fervently pray that they may not only impress all its admonitions upon their hearts, but that it may serve as the foundation upon which the whole system of their future policy may rise, the admiration and example of future time; that your warning voice may upon every great emergency recur to their remembrance with an influence equal to the occasion; that it may control the fury of domestic factions and check the encroachments of foreign influence; that it may cement with indissoluble force over our national Union, and secure at once our dignity and our peace.

I beg leave at the same time to offer you, Sir, the tribute of my grateful acknowledgment for the distinguished notice which, in the course of your public administration, you were pleased to bestow on me, by the repeated nomination to places of honor and trust under the government of the United States, to places so far beyond any pretensions or expectations of mine, that they had never been even the subject of a wish, until your favorable opinion called me to them. I cannot deem it improper at this moment to express the gratitude which I must ever feel, and as I know that the only acceptable return for the favors of this nature will in your mind consist in the zealous and faithful discharge of the public service which you were pleased to assign, I shall always consider my personal obligations to you among the strongest motives to animate my industry and invigorate my exertions in the service of my country.

With the most ardent wishes and prayers that the remainder of your life may be as replete with personal and domestic happiness to yourself, as it has hitherto been with benefits to your native land, with usefulness to the world, and dignity to the human character, I have the honor to be most respectfully, &c."

31. JOHN QUINCY ADAMS TO JOSEPH PITCAIRN MARCH 3, 1797

"Paine's letter to the President I have not yet seen.[25] His sort of intermediate station, between the French government and Mr. Monroe, has long since been a subject of animadversion. It has, in the course of Heaven's ways to man, been God's pleasure sometimes to create human beings with mischievous powers more extensive than those of Paine, but none more malignant. Even Madam Roland thought him fit for nothing but destruction. In former publications he has acknowledged that Washington had been his personal friend and patron. This is doubtless the reason why he now reviles him. It was fit that he who, by all his servile adulation of Robespierre could only mitigate his measure of punishment from the guillotine to imprisonment, should now abuse his own benefactor, who uses neither Luxemburgs nor guillotines. There has been a school of philosophers who pretended that private vices were public benefits, but the school of Paine teaches something more. It makes the highest *public virtue* to consist in the most detestable private vices."

32. JOHN QUINCY ADAMS TO WILLIAM VANS MURRAY SEPTEMBER 4, 1798

"You will undoubtedly have seen before this the letter of General Washington accepting the command of the army, and been charmed, though not surprised, at the firmness with which the hero comes forward again in the cause of his country."

25 *A Letter to George Washington, President of the United States of America. On Affairs Public and Private,* 1796.

33. JOHN QUINCY ADAMS TO GEORGE WASHINGTON OCTOBER 29, 1798

"I am happy in having this opportunity to express my warm and cordial participation in the joy, which all true Americans have felt, upon finding again secured to our country the benefit of your important services, by your acceptance of the command of her armies. However much to be regretted is the occasion which has again summoned you from your beloved retirement, there is every reason to hope, that the spirit of firmness and dignity which your example has so powerfully contributed to inspire and maintain, will either obviate the necessity of another struggle for our independence, or once more carry us victoriously and gloriously through it."

34. JOHN QUINCY ADAMS TO WILLIAM VANS MURRAY JANUARY 25, 1800

"There is no more comparison between the power of a President of the United States and a premier consul, than between the character of Washington and Buonaparte. It is satisfactory to see them [the French] returning to their veneration for our venerable patriot hero, whose fame stands upon too durable foundations for them to shake."

35. JOHN QUINCY ADAMS TO WILLIAM VANS MURRAY FEBRUARY 4, 1800

"General Washington we learn from the latest accounts by way of England died after a very short illness on the 15th of December. He is gone to a better world, very few of whose inhabitants were while sojourners in this so deserving of it. If there be in that state room for the exercise of virtue, its powers must be more extensive and less clogged than on this wretched globe. But where all are glorious he will shine with more than a common luster. The world needs some consolation for the loss of such a man."

36. JOHN QUINCY ADAMS TO JOSEPH PITCAIRN FEBRUARY 4, 1800

"I was very much affected with the account of General Washington's death. He is now beyond the reach of all bad passions which have attempted to shed some of their venom even upon him, and his character will remain to all ages a model of human virtue, untarnished with a single vice. The loss of such a man is a misfortune to all mankind. To our country it is a heavy calamity."

37. JOHN QUINCY ADAMS TO WILLIAM VANS MURRAY FEBRUARY 1, 1800

"The report of General Washington's death was but too true. Nothing of him now remains but his immortal spirit, and [one] of the greatest names that ever appeared upon earth for the pride and consolation of the human race. I feel it as an inestimable happiness to have been the contemporary of that man. 'Praise enough for a common mind' says [English poet William] Cowper,

> That Chatham's language was his mother tongue,
> And Wolfe's great name compatriot with his own.

The sentiment is good; but how much more forcibly can we apply it to the name of Washington than it appears in the names chosen by the poet himself to express his idea. . ."

38. JOHN QUINCY ADAMS TO TIMOTHY PICKERING MARCH 8, 1800

"The formal and public tribute of respect, which the first consul [Napoleon] Buonaparte has paid to the memory of our great and ever lamented fellow citizen, Washington, is honorable to himself and I presume will give much pleasure to our country. He has ordered black crapes to be suspended to the flags and colors of the French armies throughout the whole Republic for ten days and that the bust of Washington shall be placed in the Tuileries, with those of many other illustrious military characters of ancient and modern times. And a funeral eulogium, at his desire, was delivered at the Hotel des Invalides, in honor of our great patriot and statesman. Upon this occasion the French minister at this court, General [Pierre de Ruel, marquis de] Beurnonville, with his whole legation, paid me a visit a few days since to testify their sorrow at the loss which the United States have experienced by the death of their most illustrious citizen."

39. JOHN QUINCY ADAMS TO ABIGAIL ADAMS JUNE 12, 1800

"The orations in honor of that honorable man, who only lived in memory as a model for later statesmen and heroes, gave me likewise great pleasure, though not all worthy of the illustrious character they commemorate. Poor as our country unfortunately is in the most elegant departments of literature, I cannot but hope that some native unsophisticated American will be found to give the world a specimen of biography, which may be in its way as useful and as honorable as the life it will record. A subject in every respect so admirable ought to be treated by the wisest head and the most excellent heart in the union."

40. JOHN QUINCY ADAMS TO SKELTON JONES APRIL 17, 1809

"In the winter of 1793 and 1794 I published another series of papers in support of President Washington's administration, in the controversies excited by the French minister Genèt. It was my zeal for the independence of the nation that again impelled me to write, and on this occasion my sentiments happened to accord so well with the prevailing public opinion that these papers were received with much favor, and contributed to give me reputation."

41. JOHN QUINCY ADAMS TO SKELTON JONES APRIL 17, 1809

"In May 1794, I was appointed Minister Resident to the United Netherlands. The circumstances that led to this appointment were never known to me. The nomination was, of course, made by President Washington. I have heard that my name had been mentioned by him to Mr. Jefferson, before his retirement from the Department of State, who had some personal acquaintance with me while I was in France; I have also been told that the papers I have just mentioned[26] had attracted the President's attention, and led him to make inquiries concerning their author. My father was then Vice President, but my appointment was as unexpected to him as to myself.

From 1794 to 1801 I was in Europe, successively employed as a public minister in Holland, England, and Prussia. One of the last acts of President Washington's administration was the nomination of me as Minister Plenipotentiary to the Court of Portugal."[27]

26 Letters of *Columbus*

27 John Quincy Adams never made it to Portugal. His father, President John Adams, changed his commission to that of Minister of Prussia while John Quincy was en route to Lisbon.

42. JOHN QUINCY ADAMS TO WILLIAM PLUMER AUGUST 16, 1809

"I should have been glad to see a little more of this *tendency* in Marshall's *Life of Washington*,[28] than I did find. For Washington was emphatically the man of the whole Union, and I see a little too much of the Virginian in Marshall."

43. AN EXCERPT FROM THE DIARY OF JOHN QUINCY ADAMS NOVEMBER 17, 1821

"But as to this power of the President to take care that the laws of nations be faithfully executed without waiting for an Act of Congress, it had been exercised by President Washington, by seizing and restoring vessels illegally captured at the commencement of the wars of the French Revolution, before any Act of Congress upon the subject, and it was now exercised continually by the admission duty-free of baggage and articles imported by foreign Ministers."

44. AN EXCERPT FROM JOHN QUINCY ADAMS'S *PARTIES IN THE UNITED STATES* JANUARY 1822

"The retirement of President Washington had been prompted by a real weariness and disgust with public life. . . ."

45. EXCERPT FROM THE DIARY OF JOHN QUINCY ADAMS NOVEMBER 1, 1824

"Mr. Crawford told twice over the story of President Washington's having at an early period of his Administration gone to the Senate with a project of a treaty to be negotiated, and been present at their deliberations upon it. They debated it and proposed alterations, so that when Washington left the Senate-chamber he said he would be damned if he ever went there again. And ever since that time treaties have been negotiated by the Executive *before* submitting them to the consideration of the Senate.

The President said he had come into the Senate about eighteen months after the first organization of the present Government, and then heard that something like this had occurred.

28 *The Life of George Washington*, 5 volumes, 1804-1807.

Crawford then repeated the story, varying the words, so as to say that Washington *swore* he would never go to the Senate again."

46. AN EXCERPT FROM JOHN QUINCY ADAMS'S MESSAGE TO THE HOUSE OF REPRESENTATIVES OF THE UNITED STATES MARCH 15, 1826

"Mindful of the advice given by the father of our country in his Farewell Address, that the great rule of conduct for us in regard to foreign nations is, in extending our commercial relations, to have with them as little political connection as possible, and faithfully adhering to the spirit of that admonition, I can not overlook the reflection that the counsel of Washington in that instance, like all the counsels of wisdom, was founded upon the circumstances in which our country and the world around us were situated at the time when it was given; that the reasons assigned by him for his advice were that Europe had a set of primary interests which to us had none or a very remote relation; that hence she must be engaged in frequent controversies, the causes of which were essentially foreign to our concerns; that our *detached* and *distant* situation invited and enabled us to pursue a different course; that by our union and rapid growth, with an efficient Government, the period was not far distant when we might defy material injury from external annoyance, when we might take such an attitude as would cause our neutrality to be respected, and, with reference to belligerent nations, might choose peace or war, as our interests, guided by justice, should counsel.

Compare our situation and the circumstances of that time with those of the present day, and what, from the very words of Washington then, would be his counsels to his countrymen now? Europe has still her set of primary interests, with which we have little or a remote relation. Our distant and detached situation with reference to Europe remains the same. But we were then the only independent nation of this hemisphere, and we were surrounded by European colonies, with the greater part of which we had no more intercourse than with the inhabitants of another planet. Those colonies have now been transformed into eight independent nations, extending to our very borders, seven of them Republics like ourselves, with whom we have an immensely growing commercial, and *must* have and have already important political, connections; with reference to whom our situation is neither distant nor detached; whose political principles and systems of government, congenial with our own, must and will have an action and counteraction upon us and ours to which we can not be indifferent if we would.

The rapidity of our growth, and the consequent increase of our strength, has more than realized the anticipations of this admirable political legacy. Thirty years have nearly elapsed since it was written, and in the interval our population, our wealth, our territorial extension, our power—physical and moral—have nearly trebled. Reasoning upon this state of things from the sound and judicious principles of Washington, must we not say that the period which he predicted as then not far off has arrived; that *America* has a set of primary interests which have none or a remote relation to Europe; that the interference of Europe, therefore, in those concerns should be spontaneously withheld by her upon the same principles that we have never interfered with hers, and that if she should interfere, as she may, by measures which may have a great and dangerous recoil upon ourselves, we might be called in defense of our own altars and firesides to take an attitude which would cause our neutrality to be respected, and choose peace or war, as our interests, guided by justice, should counsel.

The acceptance of this invitation, therefore, far from conflicting with the counsels or the policy of Washington, is directly deducible from and conformable to it..."

47. EXCERPT FROM THE DIARY OF JOHN QUINCY ADAMS DECEMBER 22, 1826

"In the evening I could not write; but read a great part of the letters from General Washington to Henry Lee, which I found deeply interesting. Lee was one of the most distinguished partisan officers of our Revolutionary War, though he rose no higher than to the rank of colonel. But he was in great favor with Washington. From 1791 to 1793 he was Governor of Virginia, and commanded in chief the troops (militia) sent against the Pennsylvania insurgents in 1794. Afterwards Lee was a member of the U. S. House of Representatives, and in that character delivered, by appointment of the House, the funeral eulogy upon Washington."

48. EXCERPTS FROM THE DIARY OF JOHN QUINCY ADAMS APRIL 11 & 15, 1830

"11 April—In my walk this morning I met Chief Justice [John] Marshall near the head of the Avenue, and he walked down with me to its termination, opposite the yard of the Treasury Building. I asked him who, since the decease of the late Judge Washington, was the owner of President Washington's papers. He said he did not know, but that they were now in the possession of Mr. [Jared] Sparks, who was to publish his letters, and some of the letters to him."

"15 April—As I was walking out, I met Mr. Sparks, who was coming to see me, and walked with him round the Capitol Hill. . . I asked him when he expected to publish his correspondence of Washington. He thought there would be a volume out before the end of this year. I asked him how many volumes he supposed would complete the work. He said, ten or twelve. I observe that the English Quarterly Review advised him to retrench the publication and give but little—advice quite natural for Englishmen, who the less they heard about Washington and the American Revolution the better pleased they were.

He said that he had difficulties with the proprietors of the papers; that he could never obtain them from the late Judge Washington till he held out to him the prospect of money to be made by the publication, and his wish was to make the most money from it that he could. The present proprietor, Colonel Washington,[29] now a member of Congress, had the same disposition. It was probable that a collection of four volumes would raise more money than ten or twelve, but he thought that the publication of all those which would be useful as historical documents would be better for the public."

49. EXCERPT TAKEN FROM JOHN QUINCY ADAMS'S *AN EULOGY ON THE LIFE AND CHARACTER OF JAMES MONROE, FIFTH PRESIDENT OF THE UNITED STATES* AUGUST 1831

"Successive bands of warriors had maintained a conflict of seven years' duration, but Washington had been commander of them all. His commission, issued twelve months before the Declaration of Independence, had been commensurate with the war. He was the great military leader of the cause; and so emphatically did he exemplify the position I have assumed, that Providence prepares the characters of men, adapted to the emergencies in which they are to be placed, that, were it possible for the creative power of imagination to concentrate in one human individual person, the cause of American Independence, in all its moral grandeur and sublimity, that person would be no other than Washington."

50. EXCERPT TAKEN FROM JOHN QUINCY ADAMS'S *AN EULOGY ON THE LIFE AND CHARACTER OF JAMES MONROE, FIFTH PRESIDENT OF THE UNITED STATES* AUGUST 1831

"The habit of command takes root so deep in the human heart, that Washington is perhaps the only example in human annals of one in which it was wholly extirpated. In all other records of humanity, the heroes of patriotism have sunk into hereditary Princes. Glorious achievements have always claimed magnificent awards. Washington, receiving from his country the mandate to fight the battles of her freedom, assumes the task at

29 Representative George C. Washington, Maryland.

once with deep humility, and undaunted confidence, disclaiming in advance all reward of profit, which it might be in her power to bestow. After eight years of unexampled perils, labors, and achievements, the warfare is accomplished; the cause in which he had drawn his sword, is triumphant; the independence of his country is established; her union cemented by a bond of confederation, the imperfection of which had not yet been disclosed; he comes to the source whence he first derived his authority, and, in the face of mankind, surrenders the truncheon of command, restores the commission, the object of which had been so gloriously accomplished, and returns to mingle with the mass of his fellow-citizens, in the retirement of private life, and the bosom of domestic felicity."

51. EXCERPTS FROM THE DIARY OF JOHN QUINCY ADAMS FEBRUARY 9, 10, 13, 14, & 22, 1832

9 February—"Attended the joint committee of the two Houses on the proposed centennial celebration of Washington's birthday. They met in the committee-room of the military committee of the Senate. There were twenty-two members of the committee of the House present. Burges, of Rhode Island, and Duncan, of Illinois, were absent. The committee of the Senate consisted of Messrs. Clay, Webster, Chambers, Poindexter, and Bibb. It was agreed that the committees should act and vote separately. Mr. Clay was Chairman of the committee of the Senate, and Mr. Thomas, of Louisiana, who offered the resolution, Chairman of the committee of the House. There was much diversity of opinion, and much trifling debate. McCoy, of Virginia, and Thompson, of Georgia, were for reporting that it would not be expedient to hold any celebration of the day. Thompson made that motion, and, as it was opposed, rather stiffly urged it, till I observed it was a difference of opinion upon an important principle, on which I hoped the question would be fairly taken; upon which Thompson withdrew his motion.

Mr. Clay said there were two modes of celebrating the day which might be proposed: one, by the delivery of a sermon; the other, far less probable, by that of an oration. A motion was then made that Chief-Justice Marshall should be requested to deliver an oration upon that occasion, and, after some discussion, it was adopted. The Chairmen of the two committees were appointed a sub-committee to make the application, and to report his answer to an adjourned meeting of the joint committee to-morrow morning. There was some idle debate on the question whether, in the event of the Chief Justice declining, the sub-committee should be authorized to make application to any other person. Mr. Bell, of Tennessee, said there was but one other person to whom with any sort of propriety application could be made if the Chief

Justice should decline, and he was a member of the House itself. Without direct notice of this allusion, which was to me, I said it would perhaps be best not to anticipate that the Chief Justice would decline. I hoped he would not. If he should, I inclined to the belief that it would be best to make of it a religious ceremony and to have a sermon. The meeting adjourned till to-morrow."

10 February—"Attended the centennial celebration committee. Chief-Justice Marshall declines delivering an oration, alleging his occupation and his infirmities. The letter from the sub-committee to him, and his answer, were read by Mr. Clay. The question what was next to be done ensued. Colonel Drayton offered a resolution that it would be inexpedient to have an oration. Mr. Bell, of Tennessee, Mr. Howard, of Maryland, and Dr. Condict, of New Jersey, intimated the wish that another application should be made. They did not name me, but were understood as referring to me. Dr. Condict had asked me privately whether I would undertake it, and I had noticed to him the objections in the way. Those objections, or others, were felt by a large majority of the committee, and Colonel Drayton's motion was adopted, with my vote and approbation. I was glad to be relieved from the necessity of undertaking this task, for the performance of which the time was too short.

It was then determined that the report should recommend that the two Houses of Congress should adjourn over from the 21st to the 23d of February, and that the Chaplains should be requested to perform divine service on that day; also that the members of Congress should unite with their fellow-citizens in other festivities (a ball).

Then a resolution was proposed to take this opportunity to carry into effect a resolution of Congress for the transporting the remains of Washington to be deposited under the Capitol on that day. This was much debated, and opposed by McCoy, of Virginia, Thompson, of Georgia, and Hall, of North Carolina. But it passed by a large majority. It was proposed by Wickliffe, of Kentucky. The two Chairmen were charged to make the report to the respective Houses, and the committees adjourned."

"13 February—Mr. Thomas, of Louisiana, Chairman of the committee for the House of the joint committee on the centennial celebration, made the joint report of arrangements, and presented two resolutions for carrying into effect the resolution of Congress of 19th December, 1799, to transfer the remains of George Washington to be entombed under the Capitol. These resolutions were debated till half-past five o'clock, and then adopted by yeas and nays—one hundred and nine to seventy-six. They were also debated and passed by yeas and nays in the Senate—twenty-one to fifteen."

"14 February—In the House, General Adair moved a resolution that the President of the United States and the members of the Administration should be invited to attend the ceremony of removing the remains of George Washington for interment under the Capitol. The Judges of the Supreme Court, Charles Carroll of Carrollton, the last surviving signer of the Declaration of Independence, James Madison, a former President of the United States, and the relatives of the Washington family, were added to the invitation. Mr. Cambreleng moved to add to the list the name of the late President of the United States, but at my request withdrew the motion. James Bates, of Maine, moved a resolution that the relative of Martha Washington, G. W. P. Custis, should be requested to permit that the remains of Martha Washington should be removed and deposited under the Capitol with those of her husband. This resolution was adopted, and concurred in by the Senate. They postponed Adair's resolution."

"22 February—Centennial birthday of Washington. The solemnities intended for this day at this place lost all their interest for me by the refusal of John A. Washington[30] to permit the remains of George Washington to be transferred to be entombed under the Capitol – a refusal to which I believe he was not competent, and into the real operative motives to which I wish not to inquire. I did wish that this resolution might have been carried into execution, but this wish was connected with an imagination that this federative Union was to last for ages. I now disbelieve its duration for twenty years, and doubt its continuance for five. It is falling into the sere and yellow leaf. For this, among other reasons, I determined that my celebration of this day should only be by sharing in its devotions. I attended the performance of divine service at the Capitol, where a very ordinary prayer was made by Mr. Post, the Chaplain to the House of Representatives, and a singular, though not ineloquent, sermon was delivered by Mr. Durbin, Chaplain to the Senate. His text was from Revelation, iv. II: 'Thou art worthy, O Lord, to receive glory and honor and power: for Thou hast created all things, and for Thy pleasure they are and were created.' The discourse was not written, nor was it composed to be preserved. It was extemporaneous, and yet well suited to the occasion. It exalted the character of Washington perhaps too much. There were close approaches to the expression of a belief that there was something supernatural in his existence. There seemed little wanting to bring out a theory that he was a second Savior of mankind. That he had a charmed life, and was protected by a special Providence, was explicitly avowed as a belief. The religious character of Washington was dwelt on with great emphasis. The House was well filled, but not crowded. The 148th and 100th Psalms were sung without instrumental music, and a hymn at the close. The Vice-President and Speaker of the House of Representatives

30 George Washington's nephew, John Augustine Washington.

were there, and the Judges of the Supreme Court, but neither the President of the United States nor any member of his Cabinet."

52. AN EXCERPT FROM THE DIARY OF JOHN QUINCY ADAMS NOVEMBER 28, 1837

"I answered a letter yesterday received from Mr. Robert Gilmor, of Baltimore, and it consumed the leisure of the day. It was on the important question whether the inscription upon the Washington monument at Baltimore, commemorating his appointment as Commander-in-Chief of the American armies of the Revolution, should be the 15th of June, 1775, the day of his appointment, or the 19th, the date of his commission."

53. AN EXCERPT FROM THE DIARY OF JOHN QUINCY ADAMS MARCH 23, 1839

"I have determined to accept the invitation of the New York Historical Society to deliver, if I possibly can, an address before them on the 30th of next month, the fiftieth anniversary of the inauguration of George Washington as the first President of the United States. I have brought myself to this conclusion with extreme repugnance, and under a sense of obligation to that Society which I cannot suppress. The subject is rugged with insurmountable difficulties. My reputation, my age, my decaying faculties, have all warned me to decline the task. Yet I cannot resist the pressing and repeated invitations of the Society."

54. AN EXCERPT FROM THE DIARY OF JOHN QUINCY ADAMS APRIL 25, 1839

"Among the felicities of Washington's life is the unity of the two great objects which he had to pursue: first, the war of independence; and, secondly, the establishment of the Constitution of the United States. There is the unity of a Grecian drama in both of them—a tragedy and a comedy. No reputation of a great man can be acquired but by the accomplishment of some great object. But perhaps fortune is the great furnisher of occasions. The Revolutionary age and the Constituent age were the times for great men; the Administrative age is an age of small men and small things."

55. AN EXCERPT FROM THE DIARY OF JOHN QUINCY ADAMS APRIL 30, 1839

"Jubilee of the inauguration of George Washington as first President of the United States. . . At eleven a.m., meeting of the Historical Society at the City Hotel. At noon, short procession to Middle Dutch Church, corner of Nassau Street. Prayer by the pastor; ode by the choir. I delivered an address of two hours; well received."

56. AN EXCERPT FROM THE DIARY OF JOHN QUINCY ADAMS APRIL 18, 1844

"I was all the time laboring with preparation for the ceremony of presenting to the House, and thereby to Congress, in the name of the late William Sidney Winder, the camp-chest of General George Washington, used by him during the Revolutionary War. There are circumstances of deep feeling in this transaction, susceptible of being most invidiously turned against me and giving awkward and perhaps ridiculous aspect of the whole proceeding. There was a letter from General Washington referring to the furniture of this chest, which, after long and anxious search, I found at the National Intelligencer office, in Niles's Register of 13th May, 1843. By agreement with the Speaker, immediately after the reading of the (journal) of the House, I stated that I had this chest to present, and proposed that three o'clock P.M. this day should be fixed for the operation; to which the House assented."

Chapter 2

JOHN ADAMS

I. JOHN ADAMS ON THE PRESIDENCY

1. JOHN ADAMS TO THOMAS JEFFERSON DECEMBER 6, 1787

". . . You are afraid of the one, I of the few. We agree perfectly that the many should have a full, fair, and perfect representation. You are apprehensive of monarchy, I, of aristocracy. I would, therefore, have given more power to the president, and less to the senate. The nomination and appointment to all offices, I would have given to the president, assisted only by a privy council of his own creation; but not a vote or voice would I have given to the senate or any senator unless he were of the privy council. Faction and distraction are the sure and certain consequences of giving to a senate a vote in the distribution of offices. You are apprehensive that the president, when once chosen, will be chosen again and again as long as he lives. So much the better, as it appears to me. You are apprehensive of foreign interference, intrigue, and influence. So am I. But as often as elections happen, the dangers of foreign influence renews. The less frequently they happen, the less danger; and if the same man may be chosen again, it is possible he will be, and the danger of foreign influence will be less. Foreigners, seeing little prospect, will have less courage for enterprise. Elections, my dear sir, to offices which are a great object of ambition, I look at with terror. Experiments of this kind have been so often tried, and so universally found productive of horrors, that there is great reason to dread them. . ."

2. JOHN ADAMS TO GEORGE WASHINGTON MAY 17, 1789

"The office, by its legal authority, defined in the constitution, has no equal in the world, excepting those only which are held by crowned heads; nor is the royal authority in all cases to be compared to it. The royal office in Poland is a mere shadow in comparison with it. The Dogeship in Venice, and the Stadtholdership in Holland, are not so much. Neither dignity nor authority can be supported in human minds, collected into nations or any great numbers, without a splendor and majesty in some degree proportioned to them. The sending and receiving ambassadors, is one of the most splendid and important perogatives of sovereigns, absolute or limited; and this, in our constitution, is wholly in the President. If the state and pomp essential to this great department are not, in a good degree, preserved, it will be in vain for America to hope for consideration with foreign powers."

3. JOHN ADAMS TO ROGER SHERMAN JULY 18, 1789

"The duration of our president is neither perpetual nor for life; it is only for four years; but his power during those four years is much greater than that of an avoyer, a consul, a podestà, a doge, a stadtholder; nay, than a king of Sparta. I know of no first magistrate in any republican government, excepting England and Neuchâtel, who possesses a constitutional dignity, authority, and power comparable to his. The power of sending and receiving ambassadors, of raising and commanding armies and navies, of nominating and appointing and commissioning all officers, of managing the treasurers, the internal and external affairs of the nation; nay, the whole executive power, coextensive with the legislative power, is vested in him, and he has the right, and his is the duty, to take care that the laws be faithfully executed. These rights and duties, these prerogatives and dignities, are so transcendent that they must naturally and necessarily excite in the nation all the jealousy, envy, fears, apprehensions, and opposition, that are so constantly observed in England against the crown."

4. JOHN ADAMS TO ROGER SHERMAN JULY 18, 1789

"A simple sovereignty in one, a few, or many, has no balance, and therefore no laws. A divided sovereignty without a balance, or, in other words, where the division is unequal, is always at war, and consequently has no laws. In our constitution the sovereignty – that is, the legislative power – is divided into three branches. The house and senate are equal, but the third branch, though essential, is not equal. The president must pass judgment upon every law; but in some cases his judgment may be overruled. These cases will be such as attack his constitutional power; it is, therefore certain he has not equal power to defend himself, or the constitution, or the judicial power, as the senate and house have.

Power naturally grows. Why? Because human passions are insatiable. But that power alone can grow which already is too great; that which is unchecked; that which has no equal power to control it. The legislative power, in our constitution, is greater than the executive; it will, therefore, encroach, because both aristocratical and democratical passions are insatiable. The legislative power will increase, the executive will diminish. In the legislature, the monarchical power is not equal either to the aristocratical or democratical; it will, therefore, decrease, while the other will increase. Indeed, I think the aristocratical power is greater than either the monarchical or democratical. That will, therefore, swallow up the other two. . . ."

5. JOHN ADAMS TO JAMES LOVELL SEPTEMBER 1, 1789

"You insinuate that I am accused 'of deciding in favor of the power of the prime, because I look up to that goal.' That I look up to that goal sometimes, is very probable, because it is not far above me, only one step, and it is directly before my eyes, so that I must be blind not to see it. I am forced to look up to it, and bound by duty to do so, because there is only the breath of one mortal between me and it. There was lately cause enough to look up to it, as I did with horror, when that breath was in some danger of expiring. But deciding for the supreme was not certainly the way to render that goal more desirable or less terrible, nor was it the way to obtain votes for continuing in it, or an advancement to it. The way to have insured votes would have been to have given up that power. There is not, however, to be serious, the smallest prospect that I shall ever reach that goal. Our beloved chief is very little older than his second, has recovered his health, and is a much stronger man than I am. A new Vice-President must be chosen before a new President. This reflection gives me no pain, but on the contrary, great pleasure; for I know very well that I am not possessed of the confidence and affection of my fellow-citizens to the degree that he is. I am not of Ceasar's mind. 'The second place in Rome' is high enough for me, although I have a spirit that will not give up its right or relinquish its place. Whatever the world, or even my friends, or even you, who know me so well, may think of me, I am not an ambitious man. Submission to insult and disgrace is one thing, but aspiring to higher situations is another. I am quite contented in my present condition, and should not be discontented to leave it."

6. JOHN ADAMS TO "A RECLUSE MAN" JANUARY 19, 1792

"...I arose in my place, and asked the advice of the senate, in what form should I address him; whether I should say, 'Mr. Washington,' 'Mr. President,' 'Sir,' 'May it please your Excellency,' or what else? I observed that it had been common while he commanded the army to call him 'His Excellency,' but I was free to own it would appear to me better to give him no title but 'Sir,' or 'Mr. President,' than to put him on a level with a governor of Bermuda, or one of his own ambassadors, or a governor of any one of our States. After I had made my observations, a senator arose and said it was an important point, and this was the precise moment to settle it. He therefore moved for a committee of both Houses to consider and report upon it. This is the substance of the charge against me for a passion for titles. For my own part, I freely own that I think decent and moderate titles, as distinctions of offices, are not only harmless, but useful in society, and that in this country, where I know them to be prized by the people as well as their magistrates as highly as by any people or any magistrates in the world, I should think some distinction between the magistrates of the national government and those of the State governments proper. There is not, however, in the United States, personally, a citizen more indifferent upon the subject or more willing to conform to the public will or wish concerning it."

7. JOHN ADAMS TO ABIGAIL ADAMS FEBRUARY 2, 1796

"I will not resist Jupiter. I will resign to his Will. If his Will is that any other should be president I know his Will also is that I should be a Farmer, for he has given me an understanding and a heart, which ought not and cannot and will not bow under Jefferson nor Jay nor Hamilton. It would be wicked in me. It would be countenancing Tyranny, Corruption and Villany in the People."

8. JOHN ADAMS TO ABIGAIL ADAMS FEBRUARY 15, 1796

"In my Opinion there is no more danger in the Change[31] than there would be in changing a Member of the Senate and whoever lives to see it will own me to be a Prophet. If Jay or even Jefferson and one or the other it certainly will be, if the Succession should be passed over, should be the Man, the Government will go on as well as ever. Jefferson could not stir a step in any other system than that which is Jay would not wish it. The Votes will run for three Persons – two I have mentioned. The third being the Heir apparent will not probably be wholly overlook'd. If Jefferson and Jay are President and Vice President,

31 Adams is referring to the election of a new president.

as is not improbable, the other retires without Noise, or Cries or Tears to his farm. If either of those two are President and the other Vice President, he retires without Murmur or Complaint to his farm, forever. If this other should be P[resident] and Jefferson or Jay V[ice] President, four Years more if Life lasts, of Residence in Philadelphia will be his and your Portion, after which Tie shall probably be desirous of imitating the Example of the present Pair: or if by reasons of thought and Fortitude Eight Years should be accomplished, that is the Utmost Limit of time that I will ever continue in public Life at my rate. Be of good Courage therefore and tremble not. I see nothing to appall me and I feel no ill forebodings or faint Misgivings. I have not the Smallest dread of private Life, nor of public – if private Life is to be my Portion my farm and my Mare shall employ the rest of my days."

9. JOHN ADAMS TO ABIGAIL ADAMS MARCH 13, 1796

"I Sometimes think, that if I was in the H[ouse] of R[epresentatives] and could make Speeches there I could throw some Light upon these Things. If Mr. Jefferson should be president, I believe I must put up, as a Candidate for the House. But this is my Vanity. I feel sometimes as if I could Speechify among them, but alas, as, I am too old. It would soon destroy my Health. I declare, however, if I were in that House I would drive out of it some Daemons that haunt it. There are false Doctrines and false Jealousies predominant there at times that it would be easy to exorcise. You see I mind no order in what I write to you."

10. JOHN ADAMS TO ABIGAIL ADAMS APRIL 9, 1796

"I am so fatigued and disgusted with the Insipidity of this dull Life that I am half a Mind to vow that if W[ashington] dont Resign I will. The Old Hero looks very grave of late."

11. JOHN ADAMS TO ABIGAIL ADAMS DECEMBER 7, 1796

"It really Seems to me as if I wished to be left out. Let me See! do I know my own heart? I am not Sure. However all that I seem to dread, is a foolish, mortifying, humiliating, uncomfortable Residence here, for two tedious months after I shall be known to be Skinned, as my Wallmen Speak.

I can pronounce Thomas Jefferson to be chosen P[resident] of the U[nited] S[tates] with firmness and good grace that I dont fear. But here alone abed, by my fireside nobody to Speak to, poring upon my Disgrace and future Prospects – this is Ugly. The 16 of Feb. will soon come and then I take my Leave, for ever. Then for Frugality and Independence. Poverty and Patriotism. Love and a Carrot bed."

---

12. JOHN ADAMS TO ABIGAIL ADAMS JANUARY 1, 1797

"Last Night I had a Visit from Dr. Rush, whose Tongue ran for an hour. So many Compliments, so many old Anecdotes. To be Sure, My Election he said, he had vast pleasure in assuring me since it had been made certain had given vast Satisfaction in [Philadelphia, Pennsylvania]. Even those who had voted for another had a great affection for me."

---

13. JOHN ADAMS TO ABIGAIL ADAMS JANUARY 31, 1797

"The Prices of Things are so extravagantly high [in Philadelphia] that We shall be driven to Extremities to live in any decent style. I must hire and maintain secretaries as well as servants and the purchase of Horses, Carriages. Furniture and the Rent of a House 2666 Dollars & 2/3 a year will Streighten Us and put Us to all manner of shifts. I have a great Mind to dismiss all Levees, Drawing Rooms and Dinners at once. Dinners upon Washingtons Scale I will dismiss and only entertain a few select Friends. They shall have a Republican President in earnest."

---

14. JOHN ADAMS TO ABIGAIL ADAMS MARCH 5, 1797

"My Chariot is finished and I made my first Appearance in it Yesterday. It is Simple but elegant enough. My horses are young but clever. In the Chamber of the House of Representatives, was a Multitude as great as the Space could contain, and I believe Scarcely a dry Eye but Washingtons. The Sight of the Sun Setting full orbit and another rising no less Splendid, was a novelty."

---

15. JOHN ADAMS TO ABIGAIL ADAMS MARCH 9, 1797

"Mrs. Cushing will call upon you and give you an account of what they call The Inauguration. It is the general Report that there was more Weeping than there has ever been at the Representation of any Tragedy. But whether it was from Grief or Joy, whether from the loss of their beloved President, or from the Accession of an unbeloved one, or from the Pleasure of exchanging Presidents without Tumult or from the Novelty of the Thing, or from the sublimity of it, arising from the Multitude present, or whatever other cause I know not. One thing I know I am Being of too much Sensibility to Act any Part well in such an Exhibition. Perhaps there is little danger of my having Such another Scene to feel or behold.

The Stillness and Silence astonishes me. Every body talks of the Tears, the full Eyes, the streaming Eyes, the trickling Eyes &c. but all is Enigma beyond. No one descends to particulars to say Why or wherefore. I am therefore left to Suppose that it is all Grief for the Loss of their beloved."

16. JOHN ADAMS TO ABIGAIL ADAMS MARCH 17, 1797

". . . It would have given me great pleasure to have had some of my family present at my inauguration, which was the most affecting and overpowering scene I ever acted in. I was very unwell, had no sleep the night before, and really did not know but I should have fainted in presence of all the world. I was in great doubt whether to say anything or not besides repeating the oath. And now the world is as silent as the grave. All the Federalists seem to be afraid to approve anybody but Washington. The Jacobin papers damn with faint praise, and undermine with misrepresentation and insinuation. If the Federalists go to playing pranks, I will resign the office, and let Jefferson lead them to peace, wealth, and power if he will."

17. EXCERPT FROM JOHN ADAMS'S ADDRESS TO THE AMERICAN ACADEMY OF ARTS AND SCIENCES AUGUST 23, 1797

"To succeed in the administration of the government of the United States, after a citizen, whose great talents, indefatigable exertions and disinterested patriotism had carried the gratitude of his country and the applause of the world to the highest pitch, was indeed an arduous enterprise. It was not without much diffidence, and many anxious apprehensions that I engaged in the service. But it has been with inexpressible gratitude and pleasure that I have everywhere found, in my fellow-citizens, an almost universal disposition to alleviate the burden as much as possible, by the cheerful and generous support of their affectionate countenance and cordial approbation. Nothing of the kind has more tenderly touched me, than the explicit sanction you have been pleased to express of the measures I have hitherto adopted.

Permit me, gentlemen, to join in your fervent prayers, that the incomprehensible Source of light and of power may direct us all, and crown with success all our efforts to promote the welfare of our country and the happiness of mankind."

18. JOHN ADAMS TO MERCY OTIS WARREN AUGUST 8, 1807

"Your thirty first Chapter, Madam is like Mustard after Dinner as our Friends the French Say; or like the volunteer Toast after a Feast, when the original List is exhausted. After the Termination of the Revolutionary War your Subject was completed. I have no Objection however to follow you. The Same good Will to me appears in the Suppliment as in the Body of the Work. Not the least Notice is taken of my repeated Elections as Vice President, nor of a laborious discharge of the very arduous Duties of that office for Eight Years. Three Successive Elections, two as Vice President and one as President might have convinced you that the People did not believe, the falsehoods that were fabricated concerning my Monarchical or Aristocratical biases which you have so unjustly countenanced. Nay I presume to Say that the People do not believe them at this hour."

19. JOHN ADAMS TO BENJAMIN RUSH JULY 25, 1808

"In one of your letters you say that one half of the people think the Government too strong and the other half too weak. The truth is it is too strong, already, without being just.—Wisdom and justice can never be promoted till the President's office instead of being a Doll and a Whistle, shall be made more independent and more respectable; capable of mediating between two infuriated Parties. Till this is done, the Government will be ride and tye a game at leap frog, one Party once in eight or twelve years leaping over the head and shoulders of the other, kicking and spurring when it rides. If the President must be the head of a Party, and not the President of the Nation, we have no hope of long escaping a civil contest."

20. EXCERPT FROM JOHN ADAMS'S *REVIEW OF THE PROPOSITIONS FOR AMENDING THE CONSTITUTION SUBMITTED BY MR. HILLHOUSE TO THE SENATE OF THE UNITED STATES IN 1808* 1808

"In short, presidents must break asunder their leading strings, and the people must support them in it. They must unite the two parties, instead of inflaming their divisions.

They must look out for merit, wherever they can find it; and talent and integrity must be a recommendation to office, wherever they can find it; and talent and integrity must be a recommendation to office, wherever they are seen, though differing in sentiments from the president, and in an opposite party to that whose little predominance brought him into power.

People of the United States!—you know not half the solicitude of your presidents for your happiness and welfare, nor a hundredth part of the obstructions and embarrassments they endure from intrigues of individuals of both parties. You must support them in their independence, and turn a deaf ear to all the false charges against them. But, if you suffer them to be overawed and shackled in the exercise of their constitutional powers, either by aristocratical or democratical manoevres, you will soon repent of it in bitter anguish. Anarchy and civil war cannot be far off. Whereas, by a steady support of the independence of the president's office, your liberties and happiness will be safe, in defiance of all foreign influence, French or English, and of all popular commotion and aristocratical intrigue."

21. JOHN ADAMS ON HIS DEFEAT FOR RE-ELECTION IN 1800 AND SUBSEQUENT RETIREMENT 1809

"Though I give [Alexander Hamilton] no thanks for this, I most heartily rejoice in it, because it has given me eight years, incomparably the happiest of my life, whereas, had I been chosen President again, I am certain I could not have lived another year. It was utterly impossible that I could have lived through one year more of such labors and cares as were studiously and maliciously accumulated upon me by the French faction and the British faction, the former aided by the republicans, and the latter by Alexander Hamilton and his satellites."

22. JOHN ADAMS TO JOHN ADAMS SMITH DECEMBER 22, 1811

"When I was President I hazarded and sacrificed my popularity to a Navy. In all my Public writings and private conversations, a Navy has been my constant theme. The wooden walls—the floating castles, the swimming batteries the floating citadels of the United States have been my constant toast: how then can it be necessary or proper for me to produce myself before the public."

23. JOHN ADAMS TO BENJAMIN RUSH JUNE 24, 1812

"It is the first duty of a statesman especially of the first Magistrate of a nation to watch and provide for the preservation and safety of his country in all her interests; her agriculture, her commerce, her navigation her fisheries; all her rights on the ocean and on the land; nay I will add her morals her religion, in some degree or other; her liberties; and as indispensable to the preservation of all and every one of these, to preserve a national consciousness of her own right, a national feeling of her own power, a national resentment of national wrongs and injuries."

24. JOHN ADAMS TO JAMES LLOYD MARCH 31, 1815

"As I am not now writing a history of my administration, I will sum up all I have to say in a few words. I left my country in peace and harmony with all the world, and after all my 'extravagant expenses' and 'wanton waste of public money,' I left navy yards, fortifications, frigates, timber, naval stores, manufactories of cannon and arms, and a treasury full of five millions of dollars. This was all done step by step, against perpetual opposition, clamors and reproaches, such as no other President ever had to encounter, and with a more feeble, divided, and incapable support than has ever fallen to the lot of any administration before or since. For this I was turned out of office, degraded and disgraced by my country; and I was glad of it. I felt no disgrace, because I felt no remorse. It has given me fourteen of the happiest years of my life; and I am certain I could not have lasted one year more in that station, shackled in the chains of that arbitrary faction."

25. JOHN ADAMS TO JAMES MADISON JUNE 17, 1817

"There is nothing more irrational, absurd or ridiculous, in the Sight of Philosophy, than the Idea of hereditary Kings and Nobles: Yet all the Nations of the Earth civilized Savage and brutal have adopted them. Whence this universal and irresi[s]table Propensity? How Shall it be controuled, restrained corrected, modified or managed?"

II. GEORGE WASHINGTON ON JOHN ADAMS

1. GEORGE WASHINGTON TO JOHN ADAMS JANUARY 15, 1776

"I am exceedingly sorry I did not know that you were in this place today. Our want of Men and arms is such, as to render it necessary for me to get the best advice possible of the most eligeble mode of obtaining of them. I adjourned the Council of Officers today, untill I could be favourd with your opinion (together with that of others of the General Court) on these heads. They meet again tomorrow at 11 O'clock (head Quarters) when I should take it exceedingly kind of you to be present."

2. GEORGE WASHINGTON TO MAJOR GENERAL PHILIP SCHUYLER JANUARY 18, 1776

"In Order that proper Measures might be adopted I called a Council of General Officers, and upon Mr. John Adams and other members of influence of the General Courts, and laid before them your letter & proposition—After due consideration of their importance they determined that the provinces of Massachusetts and Colonies of Connecticut and New Hampshire should each immediately raise a regiment to continue in service for one year, and to march forthwith to Canada agreeable to the rout proposed in your letter to Congress."

3. GEORGE WASHINGTON TO BENJAMIN LINCOLN NOVEMBER 14, 1788

"There is good sense in the answers given by Mr. Adams to the questions of Doctor Calkoen, combined with an extensive knowledge of the interests and resources of this Country. If there be in some instances an exageration of our force, it is not a matter of wonder—but the tenor of the whole performance rather affords a subject for admiration that so much accurasy should have been discovered in representations, mostly drawn from recollection. Indeed I was very much pleased with the perusal & doubt not but the work must have been well calculated to answer the good purposes for which it was intended."

4. GEORGE WASHINGTON TO BENJAMIN LINCOLN JANUARY 31, 1789

". . . in Maryland and this State, it is probable Mr. John Adams will have a considerable number of the votes of Electors. Some of those gentlemen will have been advised that this measure would be entirely agreeable to me, and that I considered it to be the only way to prevent the election of an Antifederalist."

5. GEORGE WASHINGTON TO HENRY KNOX MARCH 2, 1789

"The results of the late Elections will not only soon be known; but the effect of them must soon be discovered. Of the nine Representatives (annon'd) for [Virginia], 6 are decided friends of the Government and the 10th. (yet unknown) from Kentuckey it is expected from the Account which has been received from thence will carry with him a similar disposition. To hear that the Votes have run in favor of Mr. Adams gives me pleasure."

6. GEORGE WASHINGTON TO HENRY KNOX JANUARY 1, 1790

"From different channels of information, it seemed probable to me (even before the receipt of your letter) that Mr. John Adams would be chosen Vice President. He will doubtless make a very good one: and let whoever may occupy the first seat, I shall be entirely satisfied with that arrangement for filling the second office."

7. EXCERPT FROM THE DIARY OF GEORGE WASHINGTON'S DIARY APRIL 6, 1790

"Tuesday 6th. Sat for Mr. Savage, at the request of the Vice-President, to have my Portrait drawn for him."

8. GEORGE WASHINGTON TO JOHN ADAMS JUNE 14, 1790

"The President of the United States and Mrs. Washington request the pleasure of the Vice-Presidents and Mrs. Adams's company to dinner on Thursday next *at four* o'clock, an answer is desired."

9. JOHN ADAMS TO ABIGAIL ADAMS QUOTING GEORGE WASHINGTON DECEMBER 7, 1796

"The P[resident] was pleased to say that 'Mr. Adams's Intelligence was very good, and his Penetration and foresight very great.'"

10. GEORGE WASHINGTON TO HENRY KNOX MARCH 2, 1797

"As early in next week as I can make arrangements for it, I shall commence my journey for Mount Vernon. To morrow, at dinner, I shall, as a servant of the public, take my leave of the President Elect, of the foreign characters, heads of Departments, &ca. And the day following, with pleasure, I shall witness the inauguration of my Successor to the Chair of government."

11. GEORGE WASHINGTON TO BARTHOLOMEW DANDRIDGE APRIL 3, 1797

"Dear Sir: Mr. Lear informs me that the president has declined, finally to take any part of the furniture in the Green drawing room and that you were requested to have the lustre in the middle of it packed up and sent round to this place."

12. GEORGE WASHINGTON TO OLIVER WOLCOTT, JR. MAY 29, 1797

"The President has, in my opinion, placed matters upon their true ground in his speech to Congress. The crisis calls for an unequivocal expression of the public mind, and the speech will, mediately, or immediately, bring this about. Things ought not, indeed can not remain longer in their present state; and it is time the People should be thoroughly acquainted with the political situation of this country, and the causes which have produced it, that they may either give active & effectual support to those to whom they have entrusted the Administration of the government (if they approve the principles on which they have acted); or sanction the conduct of their opposers, who have endeavoured to bring about a change, by embarrassing all its measures—not even short of foreign means."

13. GEORGE WASHINGTON TO JOHN ADAMS JUNE 17, 1798

"Dear Sir: I have heard with much pleasure, that you contemplate a visit to the City designated for the permanent Seat of Government of the U. States, in the course of the Summer, or in early in Autumn.

It is unnecessary, I hope, for me in that event, to express the satisfaction it would give Mrs. Washington and me to see Mrs. Adams, yourself and Company in the shade of our Vine and Fig tree; but I shall request that while you remain in these parts, that you would make Mount Vernon your Head Quarters. It is but about 17 Miles by land, and less by water from the Federal City; and only half that distance from Alexandria, which is on the direct route between them."

14. GEORGE WASHINGTON TO JOHN ADAMS JUNE 17, 1798

"I pray you to believe that, no one has read the various approbatory Addresses, which have been presented to you, with more heart-felt satisfaction than I have done; nor are there any who more sincerely wish that your Administration of the Government may be easy, happy and honorable to yourself, & prosperous for the Country."

15. GEORGE WASHINGTON TO JOHN ADAMS JULY 4, 1798

"I have delayed no time, unnecessarily, since I had the honor of receiving your very obliging favour of the 22d. Ulto. to thank you for the polite and flattering sentiments you have been pleased to express relatively to me;—and to assure you, that as far as it is in my power to support your Administration, and to render it easy, happy & honorable, you may command me without reserve.—"

16. GEORGE WASHINGTON TO JOHN ADAMS JULY 13, 1798

"Dear Sir: I had the honour on the evening of the 11th. instant to receive from the hands of the Secretary of War, your favour of the 7th. announcing, that you had, with the advice and consent of the Senate appointed me 'Lieutenant General and Commander in Chief of all the Armies raised, or to be raised for the Service of the U.S.'

I cannot express how greatly affected I am at this New proof of public confidence, and the highly flattering manner in which you have been pleased to make the communication; at the sametime I must not conceal from you my earnest wish, that the choice had fallen on a man less declined in years, and better qualified to encounter the usual vicissitudes of War."

17. GEORGE WASHINGTON TO JOHN ADAMS JULY 13, 1798

"It was not possible for me to remain ignorant of, or indifferent to, recent transactions. The conduct of the Directory of France towards our Country; their insidious hostility to its Government; their various practices to withdraw the affections of the People from it; the evident tendency of their Arts and those of their Agents to countenance and invigorate opposition; their disregard of solemn treaties and the laws of Nations; their war upon our defenceless Commerce; their treatment of our Minister of Peace, and their demands amounting to tribute, could not fail to excite in me corresponding sentiments with those my countrymen have so generally expressed in their affectionate Addresses to you. Believe me, Sir, no one can more cordially approve of the wise and prudent measures of your Administration. They ought to inspire universal confidence and will no doubt, combined with the state of things call from Congress such laws & means as will enable you to meet the full force and extent of the Crisis."

18. GEORGE WASHINGTON TO JOHN ADAMS JULY 13, 1798

"Satisfied therefore, that you have sincerely wished and endeavoured to avert war, and exhausted to the last drop, the cup of reconciliation, we can with pure hearts appeal to Heaven for the justice of our cause, and may confidently trust that kind Providence who has heretofore, and so often, signally favoured the People of these United States."

19. GEORGE WASHINGTON TO JOHN ADAMS SEPTEMBER 25, 1798

"With all the respect which is due to your public station, and with the regard I entertain for your private character, the following representation is presented to your consideration.—If in the course of it, any expression should escape me which may appear to be incompatible with either,—let the purity of my intentions;—and a due respect for my own character, be received as an apology.—

The subject on which I am about to address you, is not less delicate in its nature, than it is interesting to my feelings.—It is the change which you have directed to be made in the relative rank of the Major Generals, which I had the honor of presenting to you, by the Secretary of War;—the appointment of an Adjutant General *after* the first nomination was rejected;—and the *prepared* state you are in to appoint a third, if the second should decline, without the least intimation of the matter to me."

20. GEORGE WASHINGTON TO JOHN ADAMS SEPTEMBER 25, 1798

"We are now, near the end of September, and not a man recruited, nor a Battalion Officer appointed, that has come to my knowledge. The consequence is, that the spirit and enthusiasm which prevailed a month or two ago and would have produced the *best* men in a short time, is evaporating *fast*, and a month or two hence may induce but few, and those perhaps of the *worst* sort to Inlist. Instead therefore of having the augmented force in a state of preparation, and under a course of discipline, it is now to be *raised* and possibly may not be in existence when the Enemy is in the field; we shall have to meet veteran Troops inured to conquest with Militia or raw recruits; the consequences of which is not difficult to conceive or foretell."

21. GEORGE WASHINGTON TO JOHN ADAMS MARCH 3, 1799

"I sincerely pray, that in the discharge of these arduous and important duties committed to you, your health may be unimpaired, and that you may long live to enjoy those blessings which must flow to our Country, if we should be so happy as to pass this critical period in an honorable and dignified manner, without being involved in the horrors and calamities of War."

22. GEORGE WASHINGTON TO JONATHAN TRUMBULL JULY 21, 1799

"Lengthy as this letter is, I cannot conclude it without expressing an *earnest* wish that some intimate & confidential friend of the Presidents would give him to understand that, his long absence from the Seat of Government in the present critical conjuncture, affords matter for severe animadversion by the friends of government; who speak of it with much disappobation; while the other Party chuckle at and set it down as a favorable omen for themselves. It has been suggested to me to make this Communication, but I have declined it, conceiving that it would be better received from a private character—m<ore> in the habits of social intercourse and friendship."

23. GEORGE WASHINGTON TO JAMES MCHENRY AUGUST 11, 1799

"Is the President returned to the Seat of Government? When will he return? His absence (I mention it from the best motives) gives much discontent to the friends of the government, while its enemies chuckle at it, & think it a favorable omen for them."

24. GEORGE WASHINGTON TO JAMES MCHENRY AUGUST 11, 1799

"The President has a choice of difficulties before him, in this business; If he pursues the line he marked out, *all* the consequences cannot be foreseen: If he relinquishes it, it will be said to be a piece with all the other Acts of the Administration—unmeaning if not wicked, deceptious—&ca—&ca—&ca; and will arm the opposition with fresh weapons, to commence new attacks upon the Government, be the turn given to it, and reasons assigned what they may."

III. THOMAS JEFFERSON ON JOHN ADAMS

1. THOMAS JEFFERSON TO JAMES MADISON FEBRUARY 14, 1783

"His vanity is a lineament in his character which had entirely escaped me. His want of taste I had observed. Notwithstanding all this he has a sound head on substantial points, and I think he has integrity. I am glad therefore that he is of the commission & expect he will be useful in it.[32] His dislike of all parties, and all men, by balancing his prejudices, may give them some fair play to his reason as would a general benevolence of temper. At any rate honesty may be extracted even from poisonous weeds."

2. THOMAS JEFFERSON TO WILLIAM STEPHENS SMITH OCTOBER 22, 1786

"Will you undertake to prevail on Mr. Adams to set for his picture & on Mr. [Mather] Brown to draw it for me? I wish to add to those of other principal American characters which I have or shall have: & I had rather it should be original than a copy."

3. THOMAS JEFFERSON TO JOHN ADAMS FEBRUARY 20, 1787

"I learn with real pain the resolution you have taken of quitting Europe. Your presence on this side the Atlantic gave me a confidence that, if any difficulties should arise within my department, I should always have one to advise with, on whose counsels I could rely. I shall now feel bewidowed."

4. THOMAS JEFFERSON TO JAMES MADISON 1787

"He is vain, irritable, and a bad calculator of the force and probable effect of the motives which govern men. This is all the ill which can possibly be said of him. His is as disinterested as the Being who made him. He is profound in his views, and accurate in his judgment, except where knowledge of the world is necessary to form a judgment. He is so

32 Jefferson is referring to Adams's appointment as a commissioner to France

amiable that I pronounce you will love him, if ever you become acquainted with him. He would be, as he was, a great man in Congress."

5. THOMAS JEFFERSON TO JAMES MADISON JULY 29, 1789

"The President's title as proposed by the senate was the most superlatively ridiculous thing I ever heard of.[33] It is a proof the more of the justice of the character given by Doctor Franklin to my friend [Adams]. Always an honest one [?] often a great one but sometimes absolutely mad."

6. THOMAS JEFFERSON TO GEORGE WASHINGTON MAY 8, 1791

"I am afraid the indiscretion of a printer has committed me with my friend Mr. Adams, for whom, as one of the most honest & disinterested men alive, I have cordial esteem, increased by long habits of concurrence in opinion in the days of his republicanism; and even since his apostacy to hereditary monarchy & nobility, tho' we differ, we differ as friends should do."

7. THOMAS JEFFERSON TO JAMES MADISON MAY 9, 1791

"I though no more of this and heard no more till the pamphlet appeared to my astonishment with my note at the head of it. I never saw J. B. Smith or the printer either before or since. I had in view certainly the doctrines of Davila. I tell the writer [John Adams] freely that he is a heretic, but certainly never meant to step into a public newspaper with that in my mouth."

8. THOMAS JEFFERSON TO JAMES MADISON JULY 10, 1791

"A Boston paper has declared that Mr. Adams 'has no more concern in the publication of the writings of *Publicola*, than the author of the "Rights of Man" himself.' If the equivoque here were not intended, the disavowal is not entirely credited, because not from Mr. Adams himself, and because the style and sentiments raise so strong a presumption.

33 Adams put forth the title "*His Highness, the President of the United States of America, and Protector of their Liberties*," which was voted down in favor of simply "*The President of the United States*."

Besides, to produce any effect he must disavow Davila and the Defence of the American Constitutions. A host of writers have risen in favor of Paine, and prove that in this quarter, at least, the spirit of republicanism is sound. The contrary spirit of the high officers of government is more understood than I expected. Colonel Hamilton avowing that he never made a secret of his principles, yet taxes the imprudence of Mr. Adams in having stirred the question, and agrees that 'his business is done.'"

9. THOMAS JEFFERSON TO JOHN ADAMS JULY 17, 1791

"That you and I differ in our ideas of the best form of government is well known to us both: but we have differed as friends should do, respecting the purity of each other's motives, and confining our differences of opinion to private conversation. And I can declare with truth in the presence of the almighty that nothing was further from my intention or expectation than to have had either my own or your name brought before the public on this occasion. The friendship and confidence which has so long existed between us required this explanation from me, and I know you too well to fear any misconstruction of the motives of it. Some people here who would wish me to be, or to be thought, guilty of improprieties, have suggested that I was Agricola, that I was Brutus etc. etc. I never did in my life, either by myself or by any other, have a sentence of mine inserted in a newspaper without putting my name to it; and I believe I never shall."

10. THOMAS JEFFERSON TO JOHN ADAMS AUGUST 30, 1791

"I received some time ago your favor of July 29, and was happy to find that you saw in it's true point of view the way in which I had been drawn into the scene which must have been so disagreeable to you. The importance which you still seem to allow to my note, and the effect you suppose it to have had tho unintentional in me, induce me to shew you that it really had no effect. Paine's pamphlet, with my note, was published here about the 2d. week in May. Not a word ever appeared in the public papers on the subject for more than a month; and I am certain not a word on the subject would ever have been said had not the writer, under the name of Publicola[34], at length undertaken to attack Mr. Paine's principles, which were the principles of the citizens of the U. S. Instantly a host of writers attacked Publicola in support of those principles. He had thought proper to misconstrue a figurative expression in my note; and these writers so far noticed me as to place the expres-

34 *Publicola* was in fact written by Adams's son, John Quincy. Jefferson knew this at the time this letter was written.

sion in it's true light. But this was only an incidental skirmish preliminary to the general engagement, and they would not have thought me worth naming, had not he thought proper to bring me on the scene. His antagonists, very criminally in my opinion presumed you to be Publicola, and on that presumption hazarded a personal attack on you. No person saw with more uneasiness than I did, this unjustifiable assault, and the more so, when I saw it continued after the printer had declared you were not the author. But you will perceive from all this, my dear Sir, that my note contributed nothing to the production of these disagreeable pieces. As long as Paine's pamphlet stood on it's own feet, and on my note, it was unnoticed. As soon as Publicola attacked Paine, swarms appeared in is defence. To Publicola then and not in the least degree to my note, this whole contest is to be ascribed and all it's consequences.

You speak of the execrable paragraph in the Connecticut paper. This it is true appeared before Publicola. But it had no more relation to Paine's pamphlet and my note, than to the Alcoran. I am satisfied the writer of it had never seen either; for when I past through Connecticut about the middle of June, not a copy had ever been seen by anybody either in Harford or New Haven, nor probably in that whole state: and that paragraph was so notoriously the reverse of the disinterestedness of character which you are known to possess by every body who knows your name, that I never heard a person speak of the paragraph but with an indignation in your behalf, which did you entire justice. This paragraph then certainly did not flow from my note, any more than the publications which Publicola produced. Indeed it was impossible that my note should occasion your name to be brought into question; for so far from naming you, I had not even in view of any writing which I might suppose to be yours, and the opinions I alluded to were principally those I had heard in common conversation from a sect aiming at the subversion of the present government to bring in their favorite form of a King, lords, and commons.

Thus I hope, my dear Sir, that you will see me to have been as innocent *in effect* as I was in intention. I was brought before the public without my own consent, and from the first moment of seeing the effort of the real aggressor in this business to keep me before the public, I determined that nothing should induce me to put pen to paper in the controversy. The business is now over, and I hope it's effects are over, and that our friendship will never be suffered to be committed, whatever use others may think proper to make of our names."

11. THOMAS JEFFERSON TO THOMAS PINCKNEY DECEMBER 3, 1792

"The occasion of electing a Vice-President has been seized as a proper one for expressing the public sense on the doctrines of the monocrats. There will be a strong vote against Mr. Adams, but the strength of his personal worth and his service will, I think, prevail over the demerit of his political creed."

12. THOMAS JEFFERSON TO JAMES MADISON DECEMBER 17, 1796

"I have no expectation that the Eastern states will suffer themselves to be so much outwitted, as to be made the tools for bringing in P[inckney] instead of A[dams] I presume they will throw away their second vote. In this case, it begins to appear possible, that there may be an equal division where I had supposed the republican vote would have been considerably minor. It seems also possible, that the Representatives may be divided. This is a difficulty from which the constitution has provided no issue. It is both my duty & inclination, therefore, to relieve the embarrassment, should it happen; and in that case, I pray you and authorize you fully, to solicit on my behalf that mr. Adams may be preferred. He has always been my senior, from the commencement of my public life, and the expression of the public will being equal, this circumstance ought to give him the preference. And when so many motives will be operating to induce some of the members to change their vote, the addition of my wish may have some effect to preponderate the scale."

13. THOMAS JEFFERSON TO JOHN ADAMS DECEMBER 28, 1796

"DEAR SIR,—The public & the papers have been much occupied lately in placing us in a point of opposition to each other. I trust with confidence that less of it has been felt by ourselves personally. I the retired canton where I am, I learn little of what is passing: pamphlets I see never: papers but a few; and the fewer the happier. Our latest intelligence from Philadelphia at present is of the 16th inst. But tho' at that date your election to the first magistracy seems not to have been known as a fact, yet with me it has never been doubted. I knew it impossible you should lose a vote north of the Delaware, and even if that of Pennsylvania should be against you in the mass, yet that you would get enough South of that to place your succession out of danger. I have never one single moment expected a different issue; & tho' I know I shall not be believed, yet it is not the less true that I have never wished it. My neighbors as my compurgators could aver that fact, because they see my occupations & my attachment to them. Indeed it is impossible that you may be cheated of your succession by a trick worthy of the subtlety of your arch-friend of New York who has been able to make of your real friends tools to defeat their and your just wishes. Most probably he will be disappointed as to you; and my inclinations place me out of his reach. I leave to others the sublime delights of riding in the storm, better pleased with sound sleep and a warm birth below, with the society of neighbors, friends & fellow-laborers of the earth, than of spies & sycophants. No one then will congratulate you with purer disinterestedness than myself. The share indeed which I may have had in the late vote, I shall still value highly, as an evidence of the share I have in the esteem of my fellow citizens. But while in this point of view, a few votes less would be little sensible, the difference in the effect of a few more would be very sensible and oppressive to me.[35] I have no ambition to govern men. It is a painful and thankless office. Since the day too on which you signed the treaty of Paris our horizon was never overcast. I devoutly wish you may be able to shun for us this war by which our agriculture, commerce & credit will be destroyed. If you are, the glory will be all your own; and that your administration may be filled with glory, and happiness to yourself and advantage to us is the sincere wish of on who tho' in the course of our own voyage thro' life, various little incidents have happened or been contrived to separate us, retains still for you the solid esteem of the moments when we were working for our independence, and sentiments of respect & affectionate attachment."

14. THOMAS JEFFERSON TO JAMES MADISON JANUARY 22, 1797

"My letters inform me that mr. A speaks of me with great friendship, and with satisfaction in the prospect of administering the government in concurrence with me. I am glad of the first information, because tho I saw that our ancient friendship was affected by a little leaven, produced partly by his constitution, partly by the contrivance of others, yet I never felt a diminution of confidence in his integrity, and retained a solid affection for him. His principles of government I knew to be changed, but conscientiously changed."

15. THOMAS JEFFERSON TO JAMES MADISON JANUARY 30, 1797

"Mr. A[dams] & myself were cordial friends from the beginning of the revolution. Since our return from Europe, some little incidents have happened, which were capable of affecting a jealous mind like his. The deviation from that line of politics on which we had been united, has not made me less sensible of the rectitude of his heart; and I wished him to know this, & also another truth, that I am sincerely pleased at having escaped the late draught for the helm, and have not a wish which he stands in the way

35 Jefferson lost to Adams in the 1796 presidential election by 3 electoral votes.

of. That he should be convinced of these truths, is important to our mutual satisfaction, & perhaps to the harmony & good of the public service. But there was a difficulty in conveying them to him, & a possibility that the attempt might do mischief there or somewhere else; & I would not have hazarded the attempt, if you had not been in place to decide upon it's expediency. It is now become unnecessary to repeat it by a letter. I have had occasion to write to Langdon, in answer to one from him, in which I have said exactly the things which will be grateful to mr. A[dams] & no more. This I imagine will be shewn to him."

16. EXCERPT FROM THOMAS JEFFERSON'S, *THE ANAS* MARCH 2, 1797

"…Mr. Adams, in the first moments of enthusiasm of the occasion, (his inauguration,) forgot party sentiments, and as he never acted on any system, but was always governed by the feeling of the moment, he thought, for a moment, to steer impartially between the parties; that Monday, the 6th of March [1797], being the first time he had met his cabinet, on expressing ideas of this kind, he had been at once diverted from them, and returned to his former party views."

17. EXCERPT FROM THOMAS JEFFERSON'S, *THE ANAS* DECEMBER 26, 1797

"[John] Langdon tells me that at the 2d election of Pr[esident] & V[ice] P[resident] of U S. when there was a considerable vote given to [George] Clinton in opposition to Mr. Adams, he took occasion to remark it in conversation in the Senate chamber with Mr. A[dams] who gritting his teeth said 'Damn 'em Damn 'em Damn 'em you see that an elective government will not do.' He also tells me that Mr. A[dams] in a late conversation said 'Republicanism must be disgraced, Sir.'"

18. THOMAS JEFFERSON TO EDMUND PENDLETON JANUARY 29, 1799

"If the understanding of the people could be rallied to the truth on this subject,[36] by exposing the dupery practised on them, there are so many other things about to bear on them fa-

36 The current negotiations with France and the XYZ Affair, both mentioned earlier in the letter.

vorably for the resurrection of their republican spirit, that a reduction of the administration to constitutional principles cannot fail to be the effect. These are the Alien & Sedition laws, the vexations of the stamp act, the disgusting particularities of the direct tax, the additional army without an enemy, & recruiting officers lounging at every court house, a navy of 50. ships, 5. million to be raised to build it, on the usurious interest of 8. per cent., the perseverance in war on our part, when the French government shows such an anxious desire to keep at peace with us, taxes of 10. millions now paid by 4. millions of people, and yet a necessity, in a year or two, of raising 5. millions more for annual expences. These things will immediately be bearing on the public mind, and if it remain not still blinded by a supposed necessity, for the purpose of maintaining our independence & defending our country, they will set things to rights, I hope you will undertake this statement."

19. THOMAS JEFFERSON TO DOCTOR BENJAMIN RUSH OCTOBER 4, 1803

"Mr. Adams was then Vice President, & I thought Genl. W[ashington] had his eye on him, whom he certainly did not love."

20. THOMAS JEFFERSON TO ABIGAIL ADAMS JUNE 13, 1804

"Mr. Adams's friendship & mine began at an earlier date. It accompanied us thro' long & important scenes. The different conclusions we had drawn from our political reading & reflections, were not permitted to lessen mutual esteem; each party being conscious they were the result of an honest conviction in the other. Like differences of opinion existing among our fellow citizens, attached them to one or the other of us, and produced a rivalship in their minds which did not exist in ours. We never stood in one another's way; for if either had been withdrawn at any time, his favorers would not have gone over to the other, but would have sought for some one of homogeneous opinions. This consideration was sufficient to keep down all jealously between us, & to guard our friendship form any disturbance by sentiments of rivalship."

21. THOMAS JEFFERSON TO ABIGAIL ADAMS JUNE 13, 1804

"I can say with truth, that one act of Mr. Adams's life, and one only, ever gave me a moment's personal displeasure. I did consider his last appointments to office as personally unkind. They were from among my most ardent political enemies, from whom no faithful co-operation could ever be expected; and laid me under the embarrassment of acting thro' men whose views were to defeat mine, or to encounter the odium of putting others in their places. It seems but common justice to leave a successor free to act by instruments of his own choice. If my respect for him did not permit me to ascribe the whole blame to the influence of others, it left something for friendship to forgive, and after brooding over it for some little time, and not always resisting the expression of it, I forgave it cordially, and returned to the same state of esteem & respect for him which had so long subsisted."

22. THOMAS JEFFERSON TO ABIGAIL ADAMS JULY 22, 1804

"With respect to the calumnies and falsehoods which writers and printers at large published against Mr. Adams, I was as far from stooping to any concern or approbation of them, as Mr. Adams was respecting those of Porcupine, Fenno, or Russell, who published volumes against me for every sentence vended by their opponents against Mr. Adams. But I never supposed Mr. Adams had any participation in the atrocities of these editors, or their writers. I knew myself incapable of that base warfare, & believed him to be so. On the contrary, whatever I may have thought of the acts of the administration of that day, I have ever borne testimony to Mr. Adams' personal worth; nor was it ever impeached in my presence without a just vindication of it on my part. I never supposed that any person who knew either of us, could believe that either of us meddled in that dirty work."

23. THOMAS JEFFERSON TO DOCTOR BENJAMIN RUSH JANUARY 16, 1811

"I receive with sensibility your observations on the discontinuance of friendly correspondence between Mr. Adams and myself, and the concern you take in its restoration. This discontinuance had not proceeded from me, nor from the want of sincere desire and of effort on my part, to renew our intercourse. You know the perfect coincidence of principle and of action, in the early part of the Revolution, which produced a high degree of mutual respect and esteem between Mr. Adams and myself. Certainly no man was ever truer than he was, in that day, to those principles of rational republicanism which, after the necessity of throwing off our monarchy, dictated all our efforts in the establishment of a new government. And although he swerved, afterwards, towards the principles of the English constitution, our friendship did not abate on that account."

24. THOMAS JEFFERSON TO DOCTOR BENJAMIN RUSH JANUARY 16, 1811

"The nation at length passed condemnation on the political principles of the federalists, by refusing to continue Mr. Adams in the Presidency. On the day on which we learned in Philadelphia the vote of the city of New York, which it was well known would decide the vote of the State, and that, again, the vote of the Union, I called on Mr. Adams on some official business. He was very sensibly affected, and accosted me with these words: 'Well, I understand that you are to beat me in this contest, and I will only say that I will be as faithful a subject as any you will have.' 'Mr. Adams,' said I, 'this is no personal contest between you and me. Two systems of principles on the subject of government divide our fellow citizens into two parties. With one of these you concur, and I with the other. As we have been longer on the public stage than most of those now living, our names happen to be more generally known. One of these parties, therefore, has put your name at its head, the other mine. Were we both to die to-day, to-morrow two other names would be in the place of ours, without any change in the motion of the machinery. Its motion is from principle, not from you or myself.' 'I believe you are right,' he said, 'that we are but passive instruments, and should not suffer this matter to affect our personal dispositions.'"

25. THOMAS JEFFERSON TO DOCTOR BENJAMIN RUSH JANUARY 16, 1811

"A little time and reflection effaced in my mind this temporary dissatisfaction with Mr. Adams, and restored me to that just estimate of his virtues and passions, which a long acquaintance had enabled me to fix. And my first wish became that of making his retirement easy by any means in my power; for it was understood that he was not rich. I suggested to some republican members of the delegation from his State, the giving him, either directly or indirectly, an office, the most lucrative in that State, and then offered to be resigned, if they thought he would not deem it affrontive. They were of the opinion he would take great offence at the offer; and moreover, that the body of republicans would consider such a step in the outset as arguing very ill of the course I meant to pursue. I dropped the idea therefore, but did not cease to wish for some opportunity of renewing our friendly understanding."

-⁂-

26. THOMAS JEFFERSON TO DOCTOR BENJAMIN RUSH JANUARY 16, 1811

"I have the same good opinion of Mr. Adams which I ever had. I know him to be an honest man, an able one with his pen, and he was a powerful advocate on the floor of Congress. He has been alienated from me, by belief in the lying suggestions contrived for electioneering purposes, that I perhaps mixed in the activity and intrigues of the occasion. My most intimate friends can testify that I was perfectly passive. They would sometimes, indeed, tell me what was going on; but no man ever heard me take part in such conversations; and none ever misrepresented Mr. Adams in my presence without my asserting his just character. With very confidential persons I have doubtless disapproved of the principles and practices of his administration. This was unavoidable. But never with those with whom it could do him any injury. Decency would have required this conduct from me, if disposition had not; and I am satisfied Mr. Adams' conduct was equally honorable towards me. But I think it part of his character to suspect foul play in those of whom he is jealous, and not easily to relinquish his suspicions."

-⁂-

27. THOMAS JEFFERSON TO DOCTOR BENJAMIN RUSH JANUARY 16, 1811

"And then followed those scenes of midnight appointment, which have been condemned by all men. The last day of his political power, the last hours, and even beyond midnight, were employed in filling all offices, and especially permanent ones, with the bitterest federalists, and providing for me the alternative, either to execute the government by my enemies, whose study it would be to thwart and defeat all my measures, or to incur the odium of such numerous removals from office, as might bear me down. A little time and reflection effaced in my mind this temporary dissatisfaction with Mr. Adams, and restored me to that just estimate of his virtues and passions, which a long acquaintance had enabled me to fix."

-⁂-

28. THOMAS JEFFERSON TO BENJAMIN RUSH DECEMBER 5, 1811

"In Boston they[37] fell into company with Mr. Adams, and by his invitation passed a day with him at Braintree. He spoke out to them everything which came uppermost, and as it occurred to his mind, without any reserve; and seemed most disposed to dwell on those things which happened during his own administration. He spoke of his *masters*, as he called his Heads of departments, as acting above his control, and often against his opinions. Among many other topics, he adverted to the unprincipled licentiousness of the press against myself, adding, 'I always loved Jefferson, and I still love him.'

This is enough for me. I only needed this knowledge to revive towards him all the affections of the most cordial moments of our lives. Changing a single word only in Dr. Franklin's character of him, I knew him to be always an honest man, often a great one,, but sometimes incorrect and precipitate in his judgments; and it is known to those who have ever hear me speak of Mr. Adams, that I have ever done him justice myself, and defended him when assailed by others, with the single exception as to political opinions. But with a man possessing so many other estimable qualities, why should we be dissocialized by mere differences of opinions in politics, in religion, in philosophy, or anything else. His opinions are as honestly formed as my own. Our different views of the same subject are the result of a difference in our organization and experience.

I never withdrew from the society of any man on this account, although many have done it from me; much less should I do it from one with whom I had gone through, with hand and heart, so many trying scenes. I wish, therefore, but for an opposite occasion to express to Mr. Adams my unchanged affections for him. There is an awkwardness which hangs over the resuming a correspondence so long discontinued, unless something could arise which should call for a letter. Time and chance may perhaps generate such an occasion, of which I shall not be wanting in promptitude to avail myself. From this fusion of mutual affections, Mrs. Adams is of course separated. It will only be necessary that I never name her. In your letters to Mr. Adams, you can, perhaps, suggest my continued cordiality towards him, and knowing this, should an occasion of writing first present itself to him, he will perhaps avail himself of it, as I certainly will, should it first occur to me. No ground for jealousy now existing, he will certainly give fair play to the natural warmth of his heart. Perhaps I may open the way in some letter to my old friend [Elbridge] Gerry, who I know is in habits of the greatest intimacy with him.

37 Two of Thomas Jefferson's "neighbors and friends."

I have thus, my friend, laid open my heart to you, because you were so kind as to take an interest in healing again revolutionary affections, which have ceased in expression only, but not in their existence."

29. THOMAS JEFFERSON TO JOHN ADAMS JANUARY 21, 1812

"A letter from you calls up recollections very dear to my mind. It carries me back to the times when, beset with difficulties and dangers, we were fellow laborers in the same cause, struggling for what is most valuable to man, his right of self-government. Laboring always at the same oar, with some wave ever ahead threatening to overwhelm us and yet passing harmless under our bark, we knew not how, we rode through the storm with heart and hand, and made a happy port. Still we did not expect to be without rubs and difficulties; and we had them. First the detention of the Western posts: then the coalition of Pilnitz, outlawing our commerce with France, and the British enforcement of the outlawry. In your day French depredations: in mine English, and the Berlin and Milan decrees: now the English orders of council, and the piracies they authorize: when these shall be over, it will be the impressment of our seamen, or something else: and so we have gone on, and so we shall go on, puzzled and prospering beyond example in the history of man. And I do believe we shall continue to growl, [i.e., grow] to multiply and prosper until we exhibit and association, powerful, wise and happy, beyond what has yet been seen by men."

30. THOMAS JEFFERSON TO JOHN ADAMS JANUARY 21, 1812

"Sometimes indeed I look back to former occurrences, in remembrance of our old friends and fellow laborers, who have fallen before us. Of the signers of the Declaration of Independance I see now living not more than half a dozen on your side of the Potomak, and, on this side, myself alone.[38] You and I have been wonderfully spared, and myself with remarkable health, and a considerable activity of body and mind. I am on horseback 3. or 4. hours of every day; visit 3. or 4. times a year a possession I have 90 miles distant,[39] performing the winter journey

38 Ten signers of the Declaration of Independence were alive in 1812 to include both Jefferson and Adams, Elbridge Gerry (d. 1814) and Robert Treat Paine (d. 1814) of Massachusetts, William Ellery (d.1820) of Rhode Island, William Floyd (d. 1821) of New York, Benjamin Rush (d. 1813) and George Clymer (d. 1813) of Pennsylvania, Thomas McKean (d. 1817) of Delaware, and Charles Carroll (d. 1832) of Maryland. Cappon, *The Adams-Jefferson Letters*, vol. II, (Chapel Hill, 1959), p. 292.

39 Jefferson is referring to his retreat, Poplar Forest in Bedford County, Virginia. Cappon, *The Adams-Jefferson Letters*, vol. II, (Chapel Hill, 1959), p. 292.

on horseback. I walk little however; a single mile being too much for me; and I live in the midst of my grandchildren, one of whom has lately promoted me to be a great grandfather.[40] I have heard with pleasure that you also retain good health, and a greater power of exercise in walking than I do. But I would rather have heard this from yourself, and that, writing a letter, like mine, full of egotisms, and of details of your health, your habits, occupations and enjoyments, I should have the pleasure of knowing that, in the race of life, you do not keep, in it's physical decline, the same distance ahead of me which you have done in political honors and achievements. No circumstances have lessened the interest I feel in these particulars respecting yourself; none have suspended for one moment my sincere esteem for you; and I now salute you with unchanged affections and respect."

31. THOMAS JEFFERSON TO WILLIAM P. GARDNER FEBRUARY 19, 1813

"[Adams] was the pillar of it's[41] support on the floor of Congress, it's ablest advocate and defender against the multifarious assaults it encountered. For many excellent persons opposed it on doubts whether we were provided sufficiently with the means of supporting it, whether the minds of our constituents were yet prepared to receive it &c. who, after it was decided, united zealously in the measures it called for."

32. THOMAS JEFFERSON TO JOHN ADAMS JUNE 15, 1813

"In truth, my dear Sir, we were far from considering you as the author of all the measures we blamed. They were placed under the protection of your name, but we were satisfied they wanted much of your approbation. We ascribed them to their real authors, the Pickerings, the Wolcotts, the Tracys, the Sedwicks, *et id genus omne,* with whom we supposed you in a state of duresse. I well remember a conversation with you in the morning of the day on which you nominated to the Senate a substitute for Pickering, in which you expressed a just impatience under 'the legacy of secretaries which General Washington had left you,' and whom you seemed, therefore, to consider as under public protection. Many other incidents showed how differently you would have acted with less impassioned advisers; and subsequent events have proved that your minds were not together. You would do me great injustice, therefore, by taking to yourself what was intended for

40 Jefferson's first great grandchild was John Warner Bankhead (b. 1810). Cappon, *The Adams-Jefferson Letters,* vol. II, (Chapel Hill, 1959), p. 292.

41 Declaration of Independence

men who were then your secret, as they are now your open enemies. Should you write on the subject, as you propose, I am sure we shall see you place yourself farther from them than from us."

33. THOMAS JEFFERSON TO JOHN ADAMS MAY 5, 1817

"You certainly acted wisely in taking no notice of what the malice of [Timothy] Pickering could say of you. Were such things to be answered, our lives would be wasted in the filth of fendings and provings, instead of being employed in promoting the happiness and prosperity of our fellow citizens. The tenor of your life is the proper and sufficient answer. It is fortunate for those in public trust, that prosperity will judge them by their works and not by the malignant vituperations and invectives of the Pickerings and Gardiners of their age. [42] After all, men of energy of character must have enemies; because there are two sides to every question, and taking one with decision, and acting on it with effect, those who take the other will of course be hostile in proportion as they feel that effect. Thus, in the revolution, Hancock and the Adamses were the raw-head and bloody bones of tories and traitors who yet knew nothing of you personally but what was good."

34. EXCERPT FROM THOMAS JEFFERSON'S, *THE ANAS* FEBRUARY 4, 1818

"Mr. Adams had originally been a republican. The glare of royalty and nobility, during his mission to England, had made him believe their fascination a necessary ingredient in government, and Shay's rebellion, nor sufficiently understood where he then was, seemed to prove that the absence of want and oppression was not a sufficient guarantee of order. His book on the American constitutions having made known his political bias, he was taken up by the monarchical federalists, in his absence, and on his return to the U. S. he was by them made to believe that the general disposition of our citizens was favorable to monarchy."

42 Timothy Pickering was dismissed as Secretary of State on May 12, 1800 by President John Adams due to the former's criticism of Adams's handling of the XYZ Affair. Pickering was also consistently critical of Adams.

35. EXCERPT FROM THOMAS JEFFERSON'S, *THE ANAS* FEBRUARY 4, 1818

"Mr. Adams, I am sure, has been long since convinced of the treacheries with which he was surrounded during his administration. He has since thoroughly seen that his constituents were devoted to republican government, and whether his judgment is re-settled on it's ancient basis, or not, he is conformed as a good citizen to the will of the majority, and would now, I am persuaded, maintain it's republican structure with zeal and fidelity belonging to his character. For even an enemy has said 'he is always an honest man, & often a great one.' But in the fervor of the furry and follies of those who made him their stalking horse, no man who did not witness it, can form and idea of their unbridled madness, and the terrorism with which they surround themselves."

36. THOMAS JEFFERSON TO JAMES MADISON AUGUST 30, 1823

"Had Mr. Adams been so restrained, Congress would have lost the benefit of his bold and impressive advocations of the rights of Revolution. For no man's confident and fervid addresses, more than Mr. Adams', encouraged and supported us through the difficulties surrounding us, which, like the ceaseless action of gravity weighed on us by night and by day."

37. THOMAS JEFFERSON TO JAMES MADISON AUGUST 30, 1823

"Mr. Adams supported the Declaration with zeal and ability, fighting fearlessly for every word of it."

38. THOMAS JEFFERSON TO JAMES MONROE MARCH 27, 1824

"Fortune had disjointed our first affections, and placed us in opposition in every point. This separated us for a while. But on the first intimation thro' a friend, we re-embraced with cordiality, recalled our ancient feelings and dispositions, and every thing was forgotten but our first sympathies. I bear ill-will to no human being."

39. EXCERPT FROM DANIEL WEBSTER'S INTERVIEW WITH THOMAS JEFFERSON DECEMBER 1824.

"John Adams was our Colossus on the floor. He was not graceful, nor elegant, nor remarkably fluent; but he came out, occasionally, with a power of thought and expression that moved us from our seats."

40. LETTER FROM THOMAS JEFFERSON TO ________ JANUARY 21, 1826

"Add to this, that the statement I have given to [William Branch Giles] on the subject of Mr. Adams, is entirely honorable to him in every sentiment and fact it contains. There is not a word in it which I would wish to recall. It is one which Mr. Adams himself might willingly quote, did he need to quote anything. It was simply that during continuance of the embargo, Mr. Adams informed me of a combination (without naming anyone concerned in it,) which had for its object a severance of the Union, for a time at least. That Mr. Adams and myself not being then in the habit of mutual consultation and confidence, I considered it as the stronger proof of the purity of his patriotism, which was able to lift him above all party passions when the safety of his country was endangered. Nor have I kept this honorable fact to myself. During the late canvas, particularly, I had more than one occasion to quote it to persons who were expressing opinions respecting him, of which this was a direct corrective. I have never entertained for Mr. Adams any but sentiments of esteem and respect; and if we have not thought alike on political subjects, I yet never doubted the honesty of his opinions, of which the letter in question, if published, will be an additional proof."

IV. JAMES MADISON ON JOHN ADAMS

1. JAMES MADISON TO THOMAS JEFFERSON FEBRUARY 11, 1783

"Congress yesterday received from Mr. Adams several letters dated September, not remarkable for anything unless it be a fresh display of his vanity, and prejudice against the French court, and his venom against Doctor Franklin."

2. JAMES MADISON TO JAMES MONROE APRIL 12, 1785

"The appointment of Mr. A[dams] to the Court of G[reat] B[ritain] is a circumstance which does not contradict my expectations; nor can I say that it displeases me. Upon Geographical considerations N. E. will always have one of the principle appointments, and I know of no individual from that quarter, who possesses more of their confidence, or would possess more of that of the other States; nor do I think him so well fitted for any Court of equal rank, as that of London, I hope it has removed all obstacles to the establishment of Mr. Jefferson at the Court of France."

3. JAMES MADISON TO JAMES MONROE DECEMBER 30, 1785

"In the course of the debates no pains were spared to disparage the Treaty by insinuations against Congress, the Eastern States, and the negociators of the Treaty, particularly J. Adams."

4. JAMES MADISON TO THOMAS JEFFERSON JUNE 6, 1787

"Mr. Adams' Book[43] which has been in your hands of course, has excited a good deal of attention. An edition has come out here and another is on the press at N. York. It will probably be much read, particularly in the Eastern States, and contribute with other circumstances to revive the predilections of this Country for the British Constitution. Men of learning find nothing new in it, Men of taste many things to criticize. And men without either, not a few things, which they will not understand. It will nevertheless be read, and praised, and become a powerful engine in forming the public opinion. The name

43 *A Defense of the Constitutions of Government of the United States of America*, 3 vols., 1787-1788.

and character of the Author, with the critical situation of our affairs, naturally account for such an effect. The book also has merit, and I wish many of the remarks in it, which are unfriendly to republicanism, may not receive fresh weight from the operations of our Government."

---

5. JAMES MADISON TO THOMAS JEFFERSON OCTOBER 24, 1787

"Mr. Adams has received permission to return, with thanks for his services. No provision is made for supplying his place, or keeping up any representation there. Your reappointment for three years will be notified from the office of F[oreign] Affrs."

---

6. JAMES MADISON TO GEORGE WASHINGTON FEBRUARY 11, 1788

"'I inclose a newspaper containing the propositions communicated by Mr. Hancock to the Convention on thursday last. Mr. Adams who contrary to his own sentiments has been hitherto silent in Convention, has given his Public and explicit approbation of Mr. Hancock's propositions. We flatter ourselves that the weight of these two characters will ensure our success; but the event is not absolutelcy certain."

---

7. JAMES MADISON TO THOMAS JEFFERSON OCTOBER 17, 1788

"The Presidency alone unites the conjectures of the public. The vice president is not at all marked out by the general voice. As the president will be from a Southern State, it falls almost of course for the other part of the Continent to supply the next in rank. South Carolina may however think of Mr. Rutledge unless it should be previously discovered that votes will be wasted on him. The only candidates in the Northern States brought forward with their known consent are Hancock and Adams, and between these it seems probable the question will lie. Both of them are objectionable & would I think be postponed by the general suffrage to several others if they would accept the place. Hancock is weak ambitious a courtier of popularity, given to low intrigue, and lately reunited by a factious friendship with S. Adams. J. Adams has made himself obnoxious to many, particularly in the Southern States by the political principles avowed in his book. Others recollecting his cabal during the war against general Washington, knowing his extravagant self-importance, and considering his preference of an unprofitable dignity to some place of emolument better adapted to private fortune as a proof of his having an eye to the presidency, conclude that he would not be a very cordial second to the General, and that an impatient ambition might even intrigue for a premature advancement. The danger would be the greater if particular factious characters, as may be the case, should get into the public councils. Adams it appears, is not unaware of some of the obstacles to his wish, and thro a letter to Smith has thrown out popular sentiments as to the proposed president."

8. JAMES MADISON TO GEORGE WASHINGTON NOVEMBER 5, 1788

"The public conversation seems to be not yet settled on the Vice President. Mr. Hancock & Mr. Adams have been most talked of. The former *it is said* rejects the idea of any secondary station; and the latter does not unite the suffrages of his own State, and is unpopular in many other places. As other candidates however are not likely to present themselves, and New England will be considered as having strong pretensions, it seems not improbable that the question will lie between the Gentlemen above named."

9. JAMES MADISON TO THOMAS JEFFERSON DECEMBER 8, 1788

"Notwithstanding the formidable opposition made to the new federal Government, first in order to prevent its adoption, and since in order to place its administration in the hands of disaffected men, there is now both a certainty of its peaceable commencement in March next, and a flattering prospect that it will be administered by men who will give it a fair trial. General Washington will certainly be called to the Executive department. Mr. Adams who is *pledged to support him* will probably be the vice president."

10. JAMES MADISON TO THOMAS JEFFERSON MARCH 29, 1789

"A few days will, therefore, fit the Body for the first step, to wit, opening the Ballots for the President and Vice President. I have already said that General Washington will be the first by a unanimous suffrage. It is held to be certain that Mr. Adams, though refused a great many votes from different motives, will have the second appointment."

11. JAMES MADISON TO THOMAS JEFFERSON MAY 23, 1789

"My last inclosed copies of the President's inaugural Speech and the answer of the House of the Representatives. I now add the answer of the Senate. It will not have escaped you that the former was addressed with a truly republican simplicity to G. W. President of the U. S. The latter follows the example, with the omission of the personal name, but with out any other than the constitutional title. The proceeding on this point was in the House of Reps. spontaneous. The imitation by the Senate was extorted. The question became a serious one between the two houses. J. Adams espoused the cause of titles with great earnestness. His friend R. H. Lee tho elected as a republican enemy to an aristocratic constitution was a most zealous second. The projected title was—His Highness the President of the United States and Protector of Their Liberties. Had the project succeeded it would have subjected the president to a severe dilemma and given a deep wound to our infant government."

12. JAMES MADISON TO THOMAS JEFFERSON MAY 12, 1791

"I had seen Payne's pamphlet[44] with the preface of the Philadelphia Editor. It immediately occurred that you were brought into the Frontispiece in the manner you explain. But I had not foreseen the particular use made of it by the British partisans. Mr. Adams can least of all complain. Under a mock defense of the Republican Constitutions of his Country, he attacked them with all the force he possessed, and this in a book with his name to it whilst he was the Representative of his Country at a foreign Court.[45] Since he had been the 2d. Magistrate in the new Republic, his pen has constantly been at work in the same cause; and tho' his name has not been prefixed to his anti republican discourses, the author has been as well known as if that formality had been observed.[46] Surely if it be innocent & decent in one servant of the public thus to write attacks against its Government, it cannot be very criminal or indecent in another to patronize a written defence of the principles on which that Government is founded."

13. JAMES MADISON TO THOMAS JEFFERSON JUNE 27, 1791

"Mr. Adams seems to be getting faster & faster into difficulties. His attack on Payne, which I have not seen, will draw the public attention to his obnoxious principles, more than everything he has published."

---

44 Thomas Paine's The *Rights of Man*, 1791.

45 *A Defense of the Constitutions of Governments of the United States of America*, 3 vols., 1787-1788.

46 Madison is referring to Adams's *Discourses on Davila*, 1790.

14. JAMES MADISON TO THOMAS JEFFERSON JULY 13, 1791

"Beckley has just got back from his eastern trip. He says that the partizans of Mr. Adams's heresies in that quarter are perfectly insignificant in point of number; that particularly in Boston he is become distinguished for his unpopularity; that Publicola is probably the manufacture of his son, out of materials furnished by himself, and that the publication is generally as obnoxious in New England as it appears to be in Pennsylvania. If young Adams be capable of giving the dress in which Publicola presents himself, it is very probable he may have been made the Editor of his father's doctrines.

I hardly think the printer would so directly disavow the fact if Mr. Adams was himself the writer. There is more of method, also, in the arguments, and much less of clumsiness and heaviness in the style, than characterize his writings."

15. EXCERPT FROM JAMES MADISON'S *SUBSTANCE OF A CONVERSATION WITH THE PRESIDENT* MAY 5, 1792

"With respect to Mr. Adams, his monarchical principles, which he had not concealed, with his late conduct on the representation bill, had produced such a settled dislike among republicans every where, & particularly in the Southern States, that he seemed to be out of the question. It would not be in the power of those who might be friendly to his private character & willing to trust him in a public one, notwithstanding his political principles to make head against the torrent."

16. JAMES MADISON TO EDMUND PENDLETON DECEMBER 6, 1792

"The election of a vice P[resident] has excited in this quarter considerable animation and called forth comparative portraits of the political characters of Mr. Adams & Governor [George] Clinton the only candidates brought into the field. The former has been exhibited in all its monarchical features; and the latter in the anti federal colors it worse in 1788. There are not sufficient data here to calculate with certainty the event of the contest. The probability is rather favorable to Mr. A[dams]; but not in such a degree as to prevent pretty keen apprehensions among his friends. As the opposition to him is leveled entirely against his political principles, and is made under very great disadvantages, the extent of it, whether successful or not, will satisfy him that the people at large are not yet ripe to his system."

17. AN EXCERPT FROM JAMES MADISON'S *POLITICAL OBSERVATIONS* APRIL 20, 1795

"Soon after the peace, Mr. Adams, the present Vice President of the United States, was appointed Minister Plenipotentiary to the British Court. The measure was the more respectful as no mutual arrangement had been premised between the two countries, nor any intimation received from Great Britain that the civility should be returned; nor was the civility returned during the whole period of his residence. The manner in which he was treated, and the United States though him, his protracted exertions and the mortifying inefficacy of them are too much in the public remembrance to need a rehearsal."

18. JAMES MADISON TO JAMES MONROE FEBRUARY 26, 1796

"It is now pretty certain that the President will not serve beyond his present term. The British party had Jay first in view, as is believed. It is now said Adams is the object."

19. JAMES MADISON TO THOMAS JEFFERSON DECEMBER 5, 1796

"It is not improbable that Pinckney will step in between the two who have been treated as the principals in the question. It is even suspected that this turn has been secretly meditated from the beginning, in a quarter where the *leading* zeal for Adams has been affected. This Jockeyship is accounted for by the enmity of Adams to Banks and funding systems, which is now become public, and by an apprehension that he is too headstrong to be a fit puppet for the intriguers behind the screen."

20. JAMES MADISON TO THOMAS JEFFERSON DECEMBER 19, 1796

"The returns from N. Hampshire Vermont, S. C. & Georgia are still to come in, & leave the event of the Election in some remaining uncertainty. It is but barely possible that Adams my fail of the highest number."

21. JAMES MADISON TO THOMAS JEFFERSON DECEMBER 19, 1796

"On the whole, it seems *essential* that you should not refuse the station which is likely to be your lot.[47] There is reason to believe, also, that your neighbourhood to Adams may have a valuable effect on his councils particularly in relation to our external system. You know that his feelings will not enslave him to the example of his predecessor. It is certain that his censures of our paper system & the intrigues at new York for setting [Thomas] P[inckney] above him, have fixed an enmity with the British faction. Nor should it pass for nothing, that the true interest of new england particularly requires reconciliation with France as the road to her commerce, add to the whole that he is said to speak of you now in friendly terms and will no doubt be soothed by your acceptance of a place subordinate to him. It must be confessed however that all these calculations are qualified by his political principles and prejudices. But they add weight to the obligation, from which you must not withdraw yourself."

22. JAMES MADISON TO THOMAS JEFFERSON DECEMBER 25, 1796

"Dear Sir,—I cannot yet entirely remove the uncertainty in which my last left the election. Unless the Vermont election, of which little has, of late, been said, should contain some fatal vice in it, Mr. Adams may be considered as the President elect. Nothing can deprive him of it but a general run of the votes in Georgia, Tennessee, and Kentucky, in favour of Mr. Pinckney, which is altogether contrary to the best information."

23. JAMES MADISON TO THOMAS JEFFERSON JANUARY 8, 1797

"The election is not likely to terminate in the equilibrium of votes, for which the Constitution has not provided. If the Vermont votes should be valid, as is now generally supposed, Mr. Adams will have 71 and you 68, Pinckney being in the rear of both. It is to be hoped that the nicety, and, in truth, the unpropitious casualty of the choice of Mr. A., will lessen the evil of such an ostensible protest by this Country against Republicanism. Your acceptance of a share in the administration will not fail to aid this tendency."

24. JAMES MADISON TO THOMAS JEFFERSON JANUARY 15, 1797

"The last mail brought me your favor of January 1, inclosing an unsealed one for Mr. A[dams] & submitting to my discretion the eligibility of delivering it. In exercising this

47 Madison is writing about Jefferson's probable election to the vice presidency.

delicate trust I have felt no small anxiety, arising by no means however from an apprehension that a free exercise of it could be in collision with your real purpose, but from a want of confidence in myself, & the importance of a wrong judgment in this case. After the best consideration I have been able to bestow, I have been led to suspend the delivery of the letter, till you should have an opportunity of deciding on the sufficiency or insufficiency of the following reasons. 1. It is certain that Mr. Adams, on his coming to this place, expressed to different persons a respectful cordiality towards you, & manifested a sensibility to the candid manner in which your friends had in general conducted the opposition to him. And it is equally known that your sentiments towards him personally have found their way to him in the most conciliating form. This being the state of things between you, it deserves to be considered whether the idea of bettering it is not outweighed by the possibility of changing it for the worse. 2. This is perhaps a general air on the letter which betrays the difficulty of your situation in writing it, and it is uncertain what the impression might be resulting from this appearance. 3. It is certain that Mr. A. is fully apprized of the trick aimed at by his Pseudo friends of N. Y. and there may be danger of his suspecting in mementos on that subject, a wish to make his resentment an instrument for revenging that [of] others. A hint of this kind was some time ago dropped by a judicious & sound man who lives under the same roof, with a wish that even the Newspapers might be silent on that point. 4. May not what is said, of 'the sublime delights of riding in the storm, &c,' be misconstrued into a reflection on those who have no distaste to the helm at the present crisis? You know the temper of Mr. A. better than I do: but I have always conceived it to be rather a ticklish one. 5. The tenderness due to the zealous & active promoters of your election, makes it doubtful whether their anxieties & exertions ought to be depreciated by anything implying the unreasonableness of them. I know that some individuals who have deeply committed themselves, & probably incurred the political enmity at least of the P. elect, are already sore on this head. 6. Considering the probability that Mr. A.'s course of administration may force an opposition to it from the Republican quarter, & the general uncertainty of the posture which our affairs may take, there may be real embarrassments from giving written possession to him, of the degree of compliment & confidence which your personal delicacy & friendship have suggested.

I have ventured to make these observations because I am sure you will equally appreciate the motive & the matter of them; and because I do not view them as inconsistent with the duty & policy of cultivating Mr. Adam's favorable dispositions, and giving a fair start to his Executive career. As you have, no doubt retained a copy of the letter I do not send it back as you request. It occurs however that if the subject should not be changed in your view of it, by the reasons which influence mine, & the delivery of the letter be accordingly judged expedient, it may not be amiss to alter the date of it; either by writing the whole over again, or authorizing me to correct that part of it."

25. JAMES MADISON TO THOMAS JEFFERSON JANUARY 20, 1797

"A war with France, and an alliance with Great Britain, enter both into print and conversation; and no doubt can be entertained that a push will be made to screw up the President to that point before he quits the office. The strides latterly made with so much inconsistency, as well as weakness, in that direction, prepare us for receiving every further step without surprise. No further discovery has been made of the mind of the President elect. I cannot prevail on myself to augur much that is consoling from him."

26. JAMES MADISON TO THOMAS JEFFERSON FEBRUARY 5, 1797

"I reserve for a verbal communication the indications by which we judge the prospect from the accession of Mr. A. to the helm. They are not, I conceive, very flattering."

27. JAMES MADISON TO THOMAS JEFFERSON FEBRUARY 11, 1797

"Dear Sir—After several little turns in the mode of conveying you notice of your election, recurrence was had to the precedence of leaving the matter to the Senate, where, on the casting vote of Mr. Adams, the notification was referred to the President of the U. States, in preference to the Pres. of the Senate. You will see in the papers the state of the votes, and the manner of counting and proclaiming them. You will see, also, the intimation given by Mr. A. of the arrangement he had made for taking the oath of office. I understand he has given another intimation which excites some curiosity, and gives rise to several reflections, which will occur to you; it is, that he means to take the advice of the Senate, on coming into office, whether the offices held during pleasure are, or are not, vacated by the political demise of his predecessor. This is the substance. I do not aim at or know the terms of the question, of which previous notice is there given, that the members of the Senate may the better make up their opinions. What room is there for such a question at all? Must it not have been settled by precedent? On what principle is the Senate to be consulted? If this step be the result of deliberation and system, it seems to shew—1. That the maxims of the British Government are still uppermost in his mind. 2. That the practice of his predecessor are not laws to him, or that he considers a second election of the same person as a continuation of the same reign. 3. That the Senate is to be brought more into Executive agency than heretofore."

28. JAMES MADISON TO JAMES MONROE DECEMBER 17, 1797

"I have not recd. a line from Philada. on the subject of the Speech, or indeed on any other. To me no explanation of the phenomenon is necessary, having been on the ground for observing the progressive apostasy from the principles of our Revolution & Governments, which marked the period of your absence. If events should not be unpropitious to the Monarchical party, you may prepare yourself for still more wonderful indications of its spirit & views. Those who tolerate at present the fashionable sentiments, will soon be ready to embrace & avow them. The active characters who promoted Mr. A. to his station, knowing him to be what he is, can not at bottom have been much averse to his political tenets, and will find in the spirit of party & in personal attachments & animosities, sufficient motives to go all lengths with him. Let us hope however that the tide of evil is nearly at its flood, and that it will ebb back to the true mark of which it has overpassed."

29. JAMES MADISON TO THOMAS JEFFERSON FEBRUARY 1798

"I am glad to find the public opinion to be taking the turn you describe on the subject of arming. For the public opinion alone can now save us from the rash measures of our hotheaded Executive: it being evident from some late votes of the House of Representatives, particularly in the choice of Managers for the Impeachment, that a majority there as well as in the Senate are ready to go as far as the control of their constituents will permit."

30. JAMES MADISON TO THOMAS JEFFERSON FEBRUARY 1798

"There never was perhaps a greater contrast between two characters than between those of the present President & his predecessor, altho' it is the boast & prop of the present that he treads in the steps of his predecessor. The one cool considerate & cautious, the other headlong & kindled into flame by every spark that lights on his passions: the one ever scrutinizing into the public opinion, and ready to follow where he could not lead it; the other insulting it by the most adverse sentiments & pursuits. W.

a hero in the field, yet overweighing every danger in the Cabinet—A. without a single pretension to the character of a soldier, a perfect Quixotte as a statesman: the former chief magistrate pursuing peace every where with sincerity, tho' mistaking the means; the latter taking as much pains to get into a war, as the former took to keep out of it. The contrast might be pursued into a variety of other particulars—the policy of the one in shunning connections with the arrangements of Europe, of the other in holding out the U. S. as a makeweight in the Balances of power; the avowed exultation of W. in the progress of liberty every where, & his eulogy on the Revolution & people of France posterior even to the bloody reign & fate of Robespierre—the open denunciations by Adams of the smallest disturbance of the ancient discipline order & tranquility of despotism, &c &c &c."

31. JAMES MADISON TO THOMAS JEFFERSON MARCH 12, 1798

"I think the Whigs acted very properly in attending the Birth-night, on the principle of appropriating it to the person, and not to the office of the late President. It is a pity that the nonattendance of the Adamsites is not presented to the public in such a manner, with their names, as to satisfy the real friends of Washington, as well as the people generally, of the true principles and views of those who have been loudest in their hypocritical professions of attachment to him."[48]

32. JAMES MADISON TO THOMAS JEFFERSON APRIL 2, 1798

"The President's message is only a further development to the public, of the violent passions, & heretical politics, which have been long privately known to govern him. It is to be hoped however that the H. of Reps will not hastily eccho them. At least it may be expected that before war measures are instituted, they will recollect the principle asserted by 62 vs. 37, in the case of the Treaty, and insist on a full communication of the intelligence on which such measures are recommended. The present is a plainer, if it be not a stronger case, and

48 First Lady Abigail Adams wrote to her sister on February 5, 1798 explaining why the first couple did not attend the birthday celebration. "These Philadelphians," she wrote, "have the least feeling of real genuine politeness of any people with whom I am acquainted. As an instance of it, they are about to celebrate, not the Birthday of the first Magistrate of the union as such, but of General Washington's Birthday, and have had the politeness to send invitations to the President, Lady and family to attend it. . . I do not know when my feelings of contempt have been more called forth. That the Virginians should celebrate that day is natural and proper if they please, and so may any others who choose. But the propriety of doing it in the Capitol. . .and inviting the head of the Nation to come and do it too, in my view is ludicrous beyond compare. I however, bite my lip and say nothing, but I wanted to vent my indignation upon paper." (*Abigail Adams Papers*, Library of Congress).

if there has been sufficient defection to destroy the majority which was then so great & so decided, it is the worst symptom that has yet appeared in our Councils. The constitution supposes, what the History of all Govts demonstrates, that the Ex. is the branch of power most interested in war, & most prone to it. It has accordingly with studied care, vested the question of war in the Legisl. But the Doctrines lately advanced strike at the root of all these provisions, and will deposit the peace of the Country in that Department which the Constitution distrusts as most ready without cause to renounce it. For if the opinion of the P. not the facts & proofs themselves are to sway the judgment of Congress, in declaring war, and if the President in the recess of Congress create a foreign mission, appt. the minister, negociate a War Treaty, without the possibility of a check even from the Senate, untill the measures present alternatives, overruling the freedom of its judgment; if again a Treaty when made obliges the Legis. to declare war contrary to its judgment, and in pursuance of the same doctrine, a law declaring war, imposes a like moral obligation, to grant the requisite supplies until it be formally repealed with the consent of the P. & Senate, it is evident that the people are cheated out of the best ingredients in their Govt., the safeguards of peace which is the greatest of their blessings. I like both your suggestions in the present crisis. Congress ought clearly to prohibit arming, & the P. ought to be brought to declare on what ground he undertook to grant an indirect licence to arm. The first instructions were no otherwise legal than as they were in pursuance of the law of Nations, & consequently in execution of the law of the land. The revocation of the instructions is a virtual change of the law, & consequently a usurpation by the Ex. of a legislative power. It will not avail to say that the law of Nations leaves this point undecided, & that every nation is free to decide it for itself. If this be the case, the regulation being a Legislative not an Executive one, belongs to the former, not the latter Authority; and comes expressly within the power, 'to define the law of Nations,' given to Congress by the Constitution. I do not expect however that the Constitutional party in the H. of R. is strong enough to do what ought to be done in the present instance. Your 2 ⊠ idea that an adjournment for the purpose of consulting the constituents on the subject of war, is more practicable because it can be effected by that branch alone if it pleases, & because an opposition to such a measure will be more striking to the public eye. The expedient is the more desirable as it will be utterly impossible to call forth the sense of the people generally before the season will be over, especially as the Towns, &c., where there can be most despatch in such operation are on the wrong side and it is to be feared that a partial expression of the public voice, may be misconstrued or miscalled, an evidence in favor of the war party. On what do you ground the idea that a decln of war requires 2/3ds of the Legislature? The force of your remark however is not diminished by this mistake, for it remains true, that measures are taking or may be taken by the Ex. that will end in war, contrary to the wish of the Body which alone can declare it."

33. JAMES MADISON TO THOMAS JEFFERSON APRIL 15, 1798

"The effect of the President's speech in France is less to be wondered at, than the speech itself, with other follies of a like tendency is to be deplored. Still the mode & degree of resisting them is rather meeting folly with folly, than consulting the true dignity & interest which ought to prescribe such cases. . . .This interesting fact must nevertheless finally take possession of thinking minds; and strengthen the suspicion, that whilst the Ex. were pursuing ostensible plans of reconciliation, and giving instructions which might wear that tendency, the success of them was indirectly counterworked by every irritation & disgust for which opportunities could be found in official speeches & messages, answers to private addresses harangues in Congress and the vilest insults & calumnies of Newspapers under the patronage of the Government."

34. JAMES MADISON TO THOMAS JEFFERSON APRIL 15, 1798

"The discovery of Mr. A.'s dislike to the City of Washington will cause strong emotions. What sort of conscience is that which feels an obligation on the Govt to remove thither, and a liberty to quit it the next day? The objection to the magnificence of the President's House belongs to a man of very different principles from those of Mr. A. The increase of expense therefore without a probable increase of salary in proportion, must be the real ground of objection."

35. JAMES MADISON TO THOMAS JEFFERSON MAY 13, 1798

"The successful use of the Despatches in kindling a flame among the people, and of the flame in extending taxes armies & prerogatives, are solemn lessons which I hope will have their proper effect when the infatuation of the moment is over. The management of foreign relations appears to be the most susceptible of abuse, of all the trusts committed to a Government, because they can be concealed or disclosed, or disclosed in such parts & at such times as will best suit particular views; and because the body of the people are less capable of judging & are more under the influence of prejudices, on that branch of their affairs, than of any other. Perhaps it is a universal truth that the loss of liberty at home is to be charged to provisions agst. danger real or pretended from abroad....If he [Adams] finds it thus easy to play on the prepossessions of the people for their own Govt. agst. a foreign, we ought not to be disappointed if the same game should have equal success in the hands of the Directory."

36. JAMES MADISON TO THOMAS JEFFERSON MAY 20, 1798

"The President, also, seems to be co-operating for the same purpose. Every answer he gives to his addressers unmasks more and more his principles & views. His language to the young men at Pha. Is the most abominable & degrading that could fall from the lips of the first magistrate of an independent people, & particularly from a Revolutionary patriot. It throws some light on his meaning when he remarked to me, 'that there was not a single principle the same in the American & French Revolutions;' & on my alluding to the contrary sentiment of his predecessor expressed to Adêt on the presentment of the Colours, added, 'that it was false let who would express it.' The abolition of Royalty was it seems not one of his Revolutionary principles. Whether he always made this profession is best known to those, who knew him in the year 1776.—The turn of the elections in N. Y. is proof that the late occurrences have increased the noise only & not the number of the Tory party."

37. JAMES MADISON TO THOMAS JEFFERSON JUNE 3, 1798

"But the palpable urgency of the Ex. & its partisans to press war in proportion to the apparent chance of avoiding it, ought to open every eye to the hypocrisy which has hitherto deceived so many good people. Should no such consequence take place it will be a proof of infatuation which does not admit of human remedy. It is said, and there are circumstances which make me believe it, that the hotheaded proceedings of Mr. A. are not well relished in the cool climate of Mount Vernon. This I think may fairly be inferred from the contrast of characters and conduct, but if it has been expressed it must have been within a very confidential circle."

38. JAMES MADISON TO THOMAS JEFFERSON JUNE 10, 1798

"The answers of Mr. Adams to his addressers form the most grotesque scene in the tragicomedy acting by the Govermt. They present not only the grossest contradictions to the maxims measures & language of his predecessor and the real principles & interests of his Constituents, but to himself. He is verifying completely the last feature in the character drawn of him by Dr. F[ranklin], however his title may stand to the two first, 'Always an honest man, often a wise one, but sometimes wholly out of his senses.'"[49]

49 Madison in quoting Benjamin Franklin who in 1783 stated about Adams: "He means well for his country, is always an honest man, often a wise one, but sometimes, and in some things absolutely out of his senses." (L.H. Butterfield, ed., *Diary and Autobiography of John Adams*. vol. I (Cambridge: Belknap Press, 1961), p. lxiii.

39. JAMES MADISON TO THOMAS JEFFERSON DECEMBER 29, 1798

"The President's speech corresponds pretty much with the idea of it which was preconceived. It is the old song, with no other variation of the tune than the spirit of the moment was thought to exact. It is evident, also, that he rises in his pitch as the echoes of the Senate and House of Representatives embolden him, and particularly that he seizes with avidity that of the latter flattering his vigilance and firmness against illusory attempts on him, without noticing, as he was equally invited, the allusion to his pacific professions."

40. JAMES MADISON TO THOMAS JEFFERSON FEBRUARY 8, 1799

"I have had a glance at (Elbridge) Gerry's communications & the P.s Report on it. It is impossible for any man of candor not to see in the former an anxious desire on the part of France for accommodation, mixed with the feelings which Gerry satisfactorily explains. The latter a narrow understanding and a most malignant heart."

41. JAMES MADISON TO THOMAS JEFFERSON JANUARY 10, 1801

"I would not wish to discourage any attentions which friendship, prudence, or benevolence may suggest in his behalf, but I think it not improper to remark, that I find him infinitely sunk in the estimation of all parties. The follies of his administration, the oblique stroke at his Predecessor in the letter to [Tench] Coxe, and the crooked character of that to T. Pinkney, are working powerfully agst. him, added to these causes is the pamphlet of H[amilton], an open *Letter Concerning the Public Conduct and Character of John Adams*] which, tho' its recoil has perhaps more deeply wounded the author, than the object it was discharged at, has contributed not a little to overthrow the latter staggering as he before was in the public esteem."

42. JAMES MADISON TO THOMAS JEFFERSON JANUARY 10, 1801

"I find that the vote of Kentucky establishes the tie between the Republican characters,[50] and consequently throws the result into the hands of the House of Representatives. Desperate as some of the adverse party there may be, I can scarcely allow myself to be-

50 Democratic-Republicans Thomas Jefferson and Aaron Burr each received 73 Electoral votes to Federalist John Adams's 65. Because Jefferson and Burr received the same number of Electoral votes, the election would be decided by the House of Representatives.

lieve that enough will not be found to frustrate the attempt to strangle the election of the people, and smuggle into the Chief Magistracy the choice of a faction. It would seem that every individual member who has any standing or stake in society, or any portion of virtue or sober understanding, must revolt at the tendency of such a maneuver. Mr. Adams should give his sanction to it, if that should be made a necessary ingredient? or that he would not hold it his duty or his policy, in case the present House should obstinately refuse to give effect to the Constitution, to appoint, which he certainly may do before his office expires, as early a day as possible after that event for the succeeding House to meet and supply the omission? Should he disappoint a just expectation in either instance, it will be an omen, I think, forbidding the steps towards him which you seem to be meditating."

43. JAMES MADISON TO THOMAS JEFFERSON FEBRUARY 28, 1801

"The conduct of Mr. A. is not such as was to have been wished or perhaps, expected. Instead of smoothing the path for his successor, he plays into the hands of those who are endeavoring to strew it with as many difficulties as possible; and with this view does not manifest a very squeamish regard to the Constn. Will not his appts. to offices, not vacant actually at the time, even if afterwards vacated by acceptances of the translations, be null?"

44. JAMES MADISON TO JOHN ADAMS OCTOBER 12, 1816

"The favorable judgment you are so good as to express on the course of my administration, cannot but be very gratifying to me; not merely for the immediate value I set on it, but as an encouraging presage of the light in which my endeavours in the service of my country will be hereafter viewed by those most capable of deciding on them."

45. JAMES MADISON TO JOSEPH DELAPLAINE MARCH 20, 1817

"P.S. I thank you for the offer, just recd. to procure me a copy of the Portrait of Mr. Adams; but as I would prefer a likeness of him at the date of his Chief Magistracy, I suspend an acceptance of your proposal, untill I shall ascertain that my wish can not be attained."

46. JAMES MADISON TO JOHN ADAMS MAY 22, 1817

"Dear Sir,—I have received your favor of April 22d, with the two volumes bearing the name of Condorcet. If the length of time they remained in your hands had been in the least inconvenient to me, which was not the case, the debt would have been overpaid by the interesting observations into which you were led by your return of them.

The idea of a Government "in one centre," as expressed and espoused by this Philosopher and his theoretic associates, seems now to be every where exploded. And the views which you have given of its fallacy will be a powerful obstacle to its revival any where."

47. JAMES MADISON TO JOHN ADAMS MAY 22, 1817

"I have always been much gratified by the favorable opinion you have been pleased occasionally to express of the public course pursued while the Executive trust was in my hands, and I am very thankful for the kind wishes you have added to a repetition of it. I pray you to be assured of the sincerity with which I offer mine, that a life may be prolonged which continues to afford proofs of your capacity to enjoy and make it valuable."

48. JAMES MADISON TO JOHN ADAMS AUGUST 7, 1818

"Your remark is very just on the subject of Independence. It was not the offspring of a particular man or a particular moment...Our forefathers brought with them the germ of Independence in the principle of self-taxation. Circumstances unfolded and perfected it."

49. JAMES MADISON TO THOMAS JEFFERSON SEPTEMBER 6, 1823

"I am glad you have put on paper a correction of the apocryphal tradition, furnished by Pickering, of the Draught of the Declaration of Independence. If he derived it from the misrecollections of Mr. Adams, it is well that the alterations of the original paper proposed by the latter, in his own handwriting, attest the fallibility of his aged memory. Nothing can be more absurd than the cavil that the Declaration contains known and not new truths. The object was to assert, not to discover truths, and to make them the basis of the Revolutionary act. The merit of the Draught, therefore, could only consist in a lucid communication of human rights, in a condenses enumeration of the reasons for such an exercise of them, and in a style and tone appropriate to the great occasion, and to the spirit of the American people."

50. JAMES MADISON TO R. PETERS SEPTEMBER 8, 1826

"The lights and lessons afforded by our Revolution, on all subjects most interesting to that condition, are already diffusing themselves in every direction, and form a source of peculiar gratification to those who had any part in the great event. Fortunately, we are not excluded from the number. If we cannot associate our names with the two luminaries who have just sunk below the horizon,[51] leaving inextinguishable traces behind, we have at least a place in the galaxy of faithful citizens who did their best for their country when it most needed their services."

51. JAMES MADISON TO JAMES K. PAULDING APRIL 1831

"In relation to Mr. John Adams, I had no personal knowledge of him till he became Vice President of the United States, and then saw no side of his private character which was not visible to all; whilst my chief knowledge of his public character and career was acquired by means now accessible, or becoming so, to all. His private papers are said to be voluminous; and when open to public view, will doubtless be of much avail to a biographer. His official correspondence during the Revolutionary period, just published, will be found interesting both in a historical and biographical view. That he had a mind rich in ideas of its own, as well as in its learned store; with an ardent love of Country, and the merit of being a colossal champion of its Independence, must be allowed by those most offended by the alloy in his Republicanism, and the fervors and flights originating in his moral temperament."

51 John Adams and Thomas Jefferson both died on July 4, 1826. Jefferson passed at 12:50 P.M. and Adams followed approximately six hours later.

V. JAMES MONROE ON JOHN ADAMS

1. JAMES MONROE TO BENJAMIN HARRISON FEBRUARY 14, 1784

"Sir,

Since our last dispatches from Mr. Adams we have not recd. nothing from our Missions in Europe. By these we were informed of his and Mr. Jay's arrival in London, but as Congress hath appointed neither of these Gent'n to that court, nor directed the scene of Negotiation even with that power to be chang'd from Paris, we presume their attendance there is merely on a private visit."

2. JAMES MONROE TO BENJAMIN HARRISON MAY 14, 1784

"Sir

At length our foreign affairs are put upon as excellent an establishment as we could desire as respectable talents as these States possess are the characters eminent for integrity & attachment to the publick interest collected also in such manner from the different parts of the Union as to possess a knowledge of the local interests of the whole are concentrated into three gentlemen Mr. Adams, Mr. Franklin & Mr. Jefferson who are employed in the negotiation of our commercial treaties abroad."

3. JAMES MONROE TO JAMES MADISON JULY 6, 1785

"By the packet we are informed that Mr. Adams had arrived in London, been presented to the King & well received. The ceremonial had only taken place when his dispatches were forwarded, so that he had not proceeded to business."

4. JAMES MONROE TO THOMAS JEFFERSON AUGUST 15, 1785

"Mr. Adams seems to suppose the principle object in his mission to the court of London was the formation of a treaty; but the contrary was certainly the case: it was merely to conciliate & prevent a variance which seemed to threaten at that time. He might however readily make this mistake under the present instructions. A treaty is not expected & I am satisfied the majority here wish all propositions on that head to cease, at least for the present, and untill our restrictions on their commerce have effected a different disposition."

5. JAMES MONROE TO THOMAS JEFFERSON JULY 25, 1791

"The contest of Burke & Paine, as revived in America with the different publications on either side is much the subject of discussion in all parts of [Virginia] Adams is universally believed to be the author of Publicola & the principles he avows, as well as those of Mr. B. as universally reprobated."

6. JAMES MONROE TO THOMAS JEFFERSON JULY 25, 1791

"At present it appears unsettled, especially as Adams is not the avowed author of Publicola, and so many writers have taken up the subject in your favor."

7. JAMES MONROE TO JAMES MADISON SEPTEMBER 18, 1792

"At Richmond it is conceived that the fate of election of V. P. will in great measure affect the question & that his opponents are in some parts embarked before the publick against him. This I suppose they have gathered from the north."

8. JAMES MONROE TO JAMES MADISON OCTOBER 9, 1792

"Afloat as the business is with the certainty of reproach from that party let the event be what it may, I should not hesitate to aid Burr in opposition to Adams. If he could succeed, it might have its good effects and could not possibly do any mischief—so that in truth 'tis very difficult to act, informed as we now are, with propriety."

9. EXCERPT FROM JAMES MONROE AND JAMES MADISON'S *THE VINDICATION OF MR. JEFFERSON* OCTOBER 20, 1792

"Catullus, whom I consider as the American, says, in effect, that the publication by Mr. John Adams, upon the subject of government, has been written so obscurely that no person could tell whether he was an advocate for hereditary orders or not; of course, that it would bear either construction. I had concluded, from the perusal I once gave that voluminous and ponderous work that the equivocation, intended, had been covered so thin a veil that no person would mistake his sentiments on that point. Indeed I have always understood, it was acknowledged by his more intimate friends, that its principal merit consisted in the Candor with which he supported, at the risk of his popularity, that kind of government. It is with reluctance mention this gentleman; I should not have done it had his friends not brought him forward."

10. AN EXCERPT FROM JAMES MONROE'S *A VIEW OF THE CONDUCT OF THE EXECUTIVE, IN THE FOREIGN AFFAIRS OF THE UNITED STATES, CONNECTED WITH THE MISSION TO THE FRENCH REPUBLIC, DURING THE YEARS 1794, 5, & 6*

"In the beginning of November 1796, I received a letter from the Secretary of State of the 22d of August, announcing my recall by the President of the United States. In this letter the Secretary refers me for the motives of that measure, to his former letter of the 12th of June. He adds, however, in *this* that the President was further confirmed in the propriety of that measure by other concurring circumstances, but of which he gave no detail."

11. AN EXCERPT FROM JAMES MONROE'S *A VIEW OF THE CONDUCT OF THE EXECUTIVE, IN THE FOREIGN AFFAIRS OF THE UNITED STATES, CONNECTED WITH THE MISSION TO THE FRENCH REPUBLIC, DURING THE YEARS 1794, 5, & 6*

"It is well known, that the executive administration has heretofore guided all our measures; pursuing, in many instances, a course of policy equally contrary to the public feeling, and the public judgment: And it was natural to expect that the administration would now be held highly responsible for the embarrassments it has thus brought upon our country."

12. AN EXCERPT FROM JAMES MONROE'S *A VIEW OF THE CONDUCT OF THE EXECUTIVE, IN THE FOREIGN AFFAIRS OF THE UNITED STATES, CONNECTED WITH THE MISSION TO THE FRENCH REPUBLIC, DURING THE YEARS 1794, 5, & 6*

"But the administration has attempted by this attack on me, to shield itself from the censure it justly apprehended, in the hope of throwing the blame on others; a finesse which ought not to succeed."

13. JAMES MONROE TO TIMOTHY PICKERING JULY 6, 1797

"I request this statement as a matter of right and upon the principle that altho the Executive possesses the power to censure & remove a public minister, yet it is a power which ought to be exercised according to the rules of Justice: which only are too well defined, by the Principles of our government, to require illustration here."

14. JAMES MONROE TO TIMOTHY PICKERING JULY 19, 1797

"If you supposed that I would submit in silence to the injurious imputations that were raised against me by the administration you were mistaken. I put too high a value upon the blessing of an honest fame, & have too long enjoyed that blessing, in the estimation of my countrymen, to suffer myself to be robbed of it by any description of persons, under any pretence whatever.

Nor can I express my astonishment which the present conduct of the administration excites in my mind; for I could not believe till it was verified by the event, after having denounced me to my countrymen as a person who had committed some great act of misconduct, & censured me for such supposed act by deprivation from office, that when I called upon you for a statement of the charge against me, with the facts by which you support it, I should find you disposed to evade my demand & shrink from the inquiry. Upon what principle does the administration take this ground, and what are its motives for it?

Do you suppose or contend that the power committed to the Executive by the Constitution, to remove and censure a public minister, or any other public servant, has authorized it so to do, without a sufficient cause? Or that the Executive is not accountable to the publick & the party injured for such an act, in like manner as it is accountable for any and every other act, it may perform by virtue of the Constitution? Upon what principle is a discrimination founded, which presumes restraints in certain cases, against the abuse of Executive power, and leaves that power without restraint in all other cases? And how do you designate, or where draw the line between these two species of power, so opposite in their nature & character? This doctrine is against the spirit of our Constitution which provides a remedy for every injury. It is against the spirit of elective government, which considers every public functionary as a public servant. It becomes the meridian of those countries only, where the monarch inherits the territory as his patrimony, and the people who inhabit it as his slaves."

15. JAMES MONROE TO TIMOTHY PICKERING JULY 19, 1797

"I have been injured by the Administration and I have a right to redress. Imputations of misconduct have been by it raised against me, and I have a right to vindicate myself against them."

16. JAMES MONROE TO TIMOTHY PICKERING JULY 31, 1797

"I think proper now to observe that when I called upon you for an explanation of the motives of the Administration in making this attack upon me it was not with a view to derive any information, for myself. I have been too long and too well acquainted with the political conduct, principles and views of the Administration, not to know what its motives were in that respect without any aid from you."

17. JAMES MONROE TO TIMOTHY PICKERING JULY 31, 1797

"I forbear to discuss again the solidity of that principle which supposes every public officer of the United States (the judges excepted) a menial servant to the President: a principle which if established, banishes from the bosom of every such officer all regard for country; every noble and patriotic sentiment, and makes him dependent, not upon the integrity and propriety of his own conduct, but upon the personal favor of his supervisor. If such were the case what confidence could the people of America repose in any public functionary, since after he gets into office he sinks into a machine and ceases to be a watchful centinel over the public rights and interests. If such were the case the principles and practiced of our free government are departed from, and the most slavish doctrines of the most slavish governments are introduced in their stead. And that such must be the case is obvious if the Executive can exercise the *discretion* you speak of, in the *pleasurable* manner you contend for, and without accounting for any of its acts, or the motives of them in any case to the party injured, the public, or any person whatever."

18. JAMES MONROE TO TIMOTHY PICKERING JULY 31, 1797

"Much has been said and done by the Administration, not simply to exculpate itself, from all blame in that respect, but to criminate others, and when called upon to state and substantiate its charges what has been the result? Let your letters shew."

19. JAMES MONROE TO TIMOTHY PICKERING JULY 31, 1797

"Tis now time to close this subject and bring into view an important question which must be decided on. Has the Administration performed its duty to its country in these great concerns and aquitted itself to the public as it ought to have done? In my judgment it has not."

20. JAMES MONROE TO THOMAS JEFFERSON NOVEMBER 1797

"...I want to have nothing to do with the government or rather the administration."

21. JAMES MONROE TO THOMAS JEFFERSON FEBRUARY 19, 1798

"DEAR SIR,—Your favor in answer to mine by Mr. Giles gives me much comfort. I had almost concluded that the administration would carry the product for arming our merchant vessels & thus involve us in war with France & Spain. That view of our affairs was a disquieting one, but yet I was satisfied, as the war, in its consequences, would rouse the publick attention, that the result would be favorable to republican government & disgraceful to the administration. I was satisfied the people would shrink from it as from a pestilence, whereby the administration would soon stand alone & become an object of publick scorn. But if we can get right without the aid of such a scourge, happy indeed will it be for us. And nothing is wanting to get us right but a knowledge of our affairs among the people which nothing will so essentially contribute to diffuse as able, free, & comprehensive discussion on the part of the friends of republican government in the House of Representatives. I believe no administration was ever before in such a dilemma, for if it carries its measures, it must be disgraced, & if it does not carry them, it must be so likewise. Mr. Adams may thank himself for this. You did every thing in your power to unite the people under this administration, & to give him in negotiation the aid of the republican character & interest to support the pretentions of our country & not without hazard to yourself. But this he spurred with a degree of wantonness of which there is no example. He would have none in his ranks but tried men, whose political creed corresponded with his own. My opinion is if this measure is carried we have war, & if rejected, the tone of the French government will change, since the regard they bear for America, especially when thus pronounced through a constitutional organ against war, will immediately operate. The House of Representatives may, therefore, prevent war if it carries its measures & stands firm. But what is then the situation of the country? An unhappy one, it is true, but still better than in war. Its unhappiness, however, proceeds from the past misconduct of the administration, which seeking war and favoring the cause of the kings against France, has so compromitted itself that it cannot become a useful organ of the publick sentiment, to extricate us from the dilemma into which it has brought us."

22. JAMES MONROE TO THOMAS JEFFERSON FEBRUARY 25, 1798

"If we had had no ministers abroad through this war, I am sure we should have had no dispute with France. And Mr. [52]Adams's appointment of his son to the mission, was a most reprehensible act. If you had appointed (being in his place) a near relation to such an office, the noise which the royalists would have made, would never have ceased."

23. JAMES MONROE TO THOMAS JEFFERSON APRIL 8, 1798

"Mr. A: will never surprise me by any acts of the wild & extravagant kind. If he was in a sober and discreet manner to repair the breach between this country & France heal the wounds his predecessor has given to the reputation & interest of his country I should be surprised. His passion is to outdo his predecessor & thus I expect to find no difference between the knight of the present day and the former one, than what superior violence of his passion may lead to...Let the issue be what it may, I mean as to the passage or rejection

52 John Quincy Adams was appointed Minister to Prussia in 1798 by his father, President John Adams.

of Mr. A's propositions, I date from the present epoch, the decline & perhaps the ruin of the party."

24. JAMES MONROE TO THOMAS JEFFERSON MAY 4, 1798

"The course of the admn. does not surprise me. It is a consistent one. I think, however, the admn. will overwhelm itself by its folly and madness."

25. JAMES MONROE TO THOMAS JEFFERSON MAY 14, 1798

"There is a meeting in town to-day of the merchants to address the President as other places have done Eastward of this approving his measures. There is a party in opposition of great respectability, so that the issue is uncertain."

26. JAMES MONROE TO THOMAS JEFFERSON JUNE 16, 1798

"Dear Sir,—The last communication of our Envoys was the last from you. By it nothing is more obvious than that France intends not to make war on us, so that our administration has the merit exclusively of precipitating us into that state: if it exists, or takes place hereafter, of which there can be little doubt, if there is any of its existence, at the present time. France has been roused against us by the administration, who have never lost a moment to keep her resentment at the height, by multiplying the causes of initiation daily, for otherwise the contempt she naturally has for the administration & respect she naturally has for the nation, would wear it away & leave us in peace. But since the late acts of Congress the appeal is to another tribunal. The triumph of the administration in the representative branch, cuts asunder the only remaining link between the two nations, & gives the American people *war* which with the administration they now invite."

27. JAMES MONROE TO THOMAS JEFFERSON JUNE 16, 1798

"Still if we would skulk off with the same ignominy we have bourne thro' the whole of the war, 'tis possible we might escape a terrible scourging. For that state, I think the former administration would be disposed to do, declaring at the same time, it meant nothing by the late acts beyond the limits of the strictest neutrality. But our present Viceroy would I think even in that state be for fighting, to make the last effort in favor of his book[53] that the state of the world would admit of, in the hope also of displaying himself to the same advantage in the field as a soldier, as he thinks he has done as a man of science in the rebublick of letters. It is really an astonishing spectacle to behold such a nation as this is, containing so many enlightened men, such a virtuous & entelligent yeomanry, such an active and grasping body of merchants, dandled about against the obvious interests & principles of every class, as it were by an old woman!"

28. JAMES MONROE TO THOMAS JEFFERSON JUNE 16, 1798

"With respect to myself I am inclined to think I should take no step in consequence of the late attack of Adams, but remain as I am quiet. A further attack on me of the violent kind if not supported by proof cannot otherwise than injure them. Should, however, the subject come before the House of Representatives I am of opinion my friends should unite in a call for the charge against me &c. and promote otherwise so far as depends on them—in *any form most eligible* to the other party an inquiry. The late outrage if they do not go further, must appear intemperate & dishonorable. And if they go further, I think it will appear worse, for it will make the subject better understood by the people. For me to come forward will place me in some degree in the attitude of an assailant, I mean by calling on Adams in any form, and circumstanced as the countries are make me appear as fighting the cause of France against my own country. It will be proper I think, that such a coloring to the adverse party, however unjustly in fact, should be avoided."

29. JAMES MONROE TO JAMES MADISON JUNE 1798

"I was attacked by the late President and censured. I replied to the denunciation, criminating the adverse party, to which they have not replied. Mr. Adams has volunteered it against me and taken in that respect the ground of his predecessor. But this, in truth, is no new ground for him, for altho' his speech to Congress at the extry. Session was not so harsh & illiberal as his late reply to the people of Lancaster, yet it was in principle the same. His conduct towards me was equally hostile: he took all his measures before my arrival, tho' it was known I had sailed & would soon arrive, and altho' (if peace were his object or reconcilement of any kind) it was to be presumed, from the manner of my

53 John Adams's *A Defense of the Constitutions of Governments of the United States of America, 3 vols., 1787-1788.*

farewell from the French govt., that I could give useful counsel to promote that end. His language too was as harsh towards me as he could well make it, by indirect allusion, if such it could be called. Now, indeed, he has been more explicit, owing I presume to the dominant fortunes of his party, having a decided preponderance in the H. of Reps. as well as in the Senate, and according to appearances, if not in truth, the publick opinion on his side. It is possible this attack may be made as the forerunner to other measures against me, such as an impeachment & trial by the Senate. Be the object what it may it becomes me to act with mature counsel in the course I take. A conflict with him & his party at the present time must be on terms disadvantageous to me: yet I am not afraid of it. I may have erred and can myself name acts which as now advised, from prudential motives, I would have avoided but I was true to my country. I do not think a pursuit of me can benefit them with an impartial or even an honest publick; certainly it cannot with posterity. It may even injure them and the *more* according to the violence of it. There are two ways of acting, one by taking no notice of this outrage: the other by cabling on the author for an explanation of his motive. For the first it may be urged that as he has only echoed the calumny of his predecessor in a manner as loose and vague as his predecessor urged it, that it does not become me to notice it, or any other attack not accompanied with a specific charge. For the second it may be urged that by not calling on him, I rather decline a revival of the controversy & leave the adversary in some sort in possession of the ground. The question should be examined not by the impression of the moment but mathematically, if I may so say, and the course taken which will bear the test here after when our heads are deposited below the surface. I am ready to take any course which you advise & suggest these points for consideration. As things stand am I a defendant or otherwise, and if so what is the charge? Does not Adams's situation and age preclude the idea of making the affair personal, and if it does can I approach him otherwise than to vindicate myself against a charge? If their object is to push the affair will they not be gratified that I again furnish them with a pretext? Will they not in that case push forward whether I do or not. & whether will it be better to meet than wait to attack? You will readily see that these questions turn on the effect which any measure may have on the publick mind, without much regard to the merits of the controversy."

30. JAMES MONROE TO JAMES MADISON JUNE 1798.

"Standing however on upright ground, and knowing that my conduct was useful to my country, I am ready if deemed advisable to repair immediately to Phila., and rush Mr. Adams to an explanation. Perhaps the discussion might be of real & essential publick utility, as the incident might be taken advantage of to tell some truths as well as develop some principles of importance at the present time."

31. JAMES MONROE TO JAMES MADISON JUNE 24, 1798

"If Mr. Lee or any one else gives a note or written reply to my queries, he had better not let it be known he has given such, or been applied to as the more these gentry (the administration) are kept in the dark of my views or intentions, the better."

32. JAMES MONROE TO JAMES MADISON JUNE 24, 1798

"I rather think, everything considered, that contempt is the best notice that can be shown in the calumnies of Mr. Addison, —at least for the present, as also the dishonorable & unmanly attack of our insane President. I should gain nothing by encountering with a subaltern, & a principal must lose by an attack on me if he does not furnish proof. Mr. Adams has placed himself in a dilemma by this measure. If he proceeds in his denunciation, my moderation as to what is past, will at least secure me a candid hearing in my defense, for such it then will be. And if he does not proceed, what he has done, will be considered as at least an intemperate and in respect to himself, to go no further, unmerited outrage."

33. JAMES MONROE TO JAMES MADISON JUNE 24, 1798

"Let the President denounce; the House of Representatives impeach & the Senate try me. I will not shrink from the trial, but readily obey the summons...".

34. JAMES MONROE TO THOMAS JEFFERSON NOVEMBER 16, 1798

"I see the late Declarations of the French government have greatly changed the state of affairs, and improved the situation of the republican party. The improvement will be seen either in a direct change of policy in the President, adopting conciliatory measures, lessening expenses at home, promoting the dismission of the military for a repeal of unconstitutional & obnoxious laws; in which case we get what we want or by his taking an opposite course, in which case his reputation is gone, for the people will then understand him. If he takes the latter course he must furnish a motive for it."

35. JAMES MONROE TO THOMAS JEFFERSON NOVEMBER 16, 1798

"Adams might be wounded much thro' this channel—his book (if necessary to go back so far) and replies to addresses expose him greatly."

36. JAMES MONROE TO JAMES MADISON NOVEMBER 22, 1799

"When Mr. Adams made his attack on me, I was at a stand for awhile, whether to notice it or not; I then wrote the enclosed letter to Mr. Dawson, who returned it with other papers as he passed last summer, which contains some of the considerations which induced me to be silent. I sent it to show the state of my mind at that time. Perhaps the present more favorable state of affairs would authorise a publication of those documents at present, since from a farther proof of the injury done me in the first case, as outset of the present system of policy towards France, or rather towards America, some illustrations might be given to later occurrences."

37. JAMES MONROE TO JUDGE JOSEPH PRENTIS DECEMBER 23, 1799

"The act of my recall brought before the public the evidence necessary to enable it to judge of my conduct & that of the administration and it cannot otherwise than be delightful to me to find, under its gradual progress of truth, the public mind pronouncing itself with such decision on the right side."

38. JAMES MONROE TO THOMAS JEFFERSON JANUARY 4, 1800

"I have thought it beneath me to make a more direct attack on Mr. Adams, and perhaps at present impolitick. Yet the publick mind ought not to be suffered to lose any portion of its republican tone by taking a position short of what it will bear."

39. JAMES MONROE TO THOMAS JEFFERSON JANUARY 4, 1800

"...I am strongly impressed with a belief if A. puts himself in the hands of the British faction, an attempt will be made to carry the Sedition Law here, as an electioneering trick, in the course of the summer. They must be deprived of a plausible pretext, in which case, an *attempt* will dishonor them, & their systems of standing armies &c. become a burden to themselves."

40. JAMES MONROE TO JAMES MADISON JUNE 4, 1800

"Every anticipation of the views of the admn. in this State seems to have been verified, or so many facts established as to put beyond a doubt the original design. A Grand Jury well chosen for the purpose, presented to old Callendar, a petit Jury found him guilty, and the court pronounc'd judgmt. angst. him for sedition, fining him 200. dolrs. & imprisoning him 9. months from yesterday, being precisely, the residue of Mr. Adam(s's) administration."

41. JAMES MONROE TO JAMES MADISON NOVEMBER 7, 1800

"From the north we have nothing new except the publication of a pamphlet by Hamilton, the object of which is to decry Adams, and throw the British or anti republican vote on Pinckney. I have not read it but am inclined to believe from what I have heard of the work, it will do their whole party more harm than good. I am told it unmasks the views of that party too much not to injure it."

42. JAMES MONROE TO JOHN ADAMS DECEMBER 30, 1800

"Sir,—It would give me great pleasure to have it in my power, on your arrival at the seat of government of this commonwealth, to pay you the attention to which your office entitles you. But you have in that office made an attack on me, by which you attempted to injure my character in the estimation of my countrymen. This attack too was the more extraordinary because it was unprovoked by me, unconnected with the subject before you, & repeating transactions which preceded your appointment to your present office; of course, when I was not responsible to you, nor you to the public for my conduct. Under such circumstance, I consider any attention from me to you, without some provisions & suitable explanation on your part, subscribing to the unjust denunciation you made against me, as being highly improper on mine. It is nevertheless much my wish to pay you that attention provided it can be done on terms that will justify me to my own feelings, as well as to the judgment of an enlightened community in so doing, to myself, to you, and the public. The object of this therefore is to invite you to make such an explanation on the above subject as will obviate this difficulty, and enable me to perform an office, which in that case would be an agreeable one, because it would exempt me from any improper imputation.

Your own conscience of the injury done me on that occasion, will to a generous mind suggest the proper redress, and I can assure you that I shall meet a spirit of conciliation on your part with a like temper on mine."

43. EXCERPT FROM JAMES MONROE'S LOOSE MANUSCRIPTS NOTES NOVEMBER-DECEMBER 1800

"A note founded on the denunciation by Mr. Adams in his reply to address from the people of Lancaster." Draft #1

"J. M. was recalled under imputations of misconduct by Mr. W[ashington] who retired, leaving in office the ministers who were parties to his recall. Mr. A[dams], who succeeded Mr. W[ashington] continued in office the same ministers and adopted his system of policy in all other respects. Of J. M. it is true he made no mention by name, but yet referred to him in his speech to Congress in the extraordinary session, in a manner to recognize the censure that was leveled at him by his predecessor.

When J. M. arrived in the U. S. he called on the administration for an explanation of the motives of his recall, & was answered by the Secretary of State that a succeeding president was not bound to answer for or explain the motives of the acts of his predecessor, intending to create a belief there was just cause of complaint against J. M. tho' none was communicated or avowed."

44. EXCERPT FROM JAMES MONROE'S LOOSE MANUSCRIPTS NOTES NOVEMBER-DECEMBER 1800

"A note founded on the denunciation by Mr. Adams in his reply to address from the people of Lancaster." Draft #1

"Of late Mr. Adams has denounced J. M. in a reply to an address to the people of Lancaster as a person 'disgraced for misconduct &c.' But no example of misconduct was given or specific charge alleged."

45. EXCERPT FROM JAMES MONROE'S LOOSE MANUSCRIPTS NOTES NOVEMBER-DECEMBER 1800

"A note founded on the denunciation by Mr. Adams in his reply to address from the people of Lancaster." Draft #1

"The merits of J. Monroes conduct, as likewise that of the administration, seem to be fully before the public, in J. M's view of the administration, and on ground favorable to J. M., much turpitude being shown in the conduct of the administration & none in that of J. M."

46. EXCERPT FROM JAMES MONROE'S LOOSE MANUSCRIPTS NOTES NOVEMBER-DECEMBER 1800

"A note founded on the denunciation by Mr. Adams in his reply to address from the people of Lancaster." Draft #1

"J. M. has already replied to this denunciation, and Mr. A[dams] has injured & is still injuring the country by the course of policy, he has pursued. The truth is, J. M. and the administration are equally in judgment before the people & equally true it is, that the present opinion will be influenced, by extraneous causes or such as have no connection with the past conduct of either party, by which alone it ought strictly to be decided. The public will judge of the *past acts* of both parties in a great measure by their *present acts*, altho' the state of things had already changed, & the *present* were the inevitable result of the *past*, which is never adopted on principle in a different situation of affairs. As things now are, France stands arraigned as the enemy of our Country. She is so by law, passed by the regular authority of the Government, and in the public opinion to all appearances in many parts of the Union, if not the greater part, disposed to consider any pressure, on the administration, connected with its measures towards France, as a pressure in favor of France, against our country. Thus the administration has gained for the present, against those who have honestly & wisely opposed its measures, by the preacceptancy, violence & extremity of those measures."

47. EXCERPT FROM JAMES MONROE'S LOOSE MANUSCRIPTS NOTES NOVEMBER-DECEMBER 1800

"A note founded on the denunciation by Mr. Adams in his reply to address from the people of Lancaster." Draft #2

"'I have seen in a gazette from Richmond republished from one of Phila, in a reply from Mr. Adams P. of the U. S. the following passage—

I have seen an address from the people of Lancaster to Mr. Adams P. of the U. S. & his reply about which papers were published in the gazettes of Phila, & afterwards throughout the Union. In Mr. A's reply is the following passage:'

Every one who reads this reply to the &c will perceive that I am the person Mr A designates by the terms 'disgraced minister, dismissed in displeasure for misconduct.' Since I was the minister who was dismissed by our administration & who took leave of the Directory of France upon the occasion to which he refers. I therefore am the person whom he denounces to his country in terms thus harsh & opprobrious since every one knows that I was the minister who &c."

48. EXCERPT FROM JAMES MONROE'S LOOSE MANUSCRIPT NOTES CIRCA 1800

"It is to be observed that the merits of J. M.'s conduct & of the conduct of the administration also are fully before the public, and resting on ground favorable to J. M. Much turpitude is shown in the conduct of the administration & none in that of J. M. The whole of Mr. A's administration too has tended to prove the charges alleged against that of his predecessor, to which Mr. A's administration is only a postscript. It merits consideration whether general denunciations without specific charges & proof are not best answered by silent contempt. Whether such a conduct on the part of Mr. A's being in union with his general conduct, which is intemperate and unpolitick as every days experience shews, will not contribute to lessen him in public estimation & whether that tendency will not be more promoted by J. M.'s reserve than by any step he might take, especially as in the present state of affairs any act he might take might exhibit him as contending for France against his own country. But if any step is taken, he may adopt either of the following—Calumniated by Mr. W[ashington] who retired from the administration leaving the ministries in office, who were parties to my removal.

Mr A[dams] successor of Mr. W[ashington] continued in office the same ministers & otherwise adopted his system of policy in all respects. Of me it is true he made no mention, but yet he referred to me in a manner to recognize the reproach that was levelled at me by his predecessor.

When I (M) arrived he called on the administration for an explanation of the motives of my recall & was answered by the Secty of State that a succeeding President was not responsible for the acts of his predecessor, or might not choose to give an explanation of the motives of such acts. In other respects the answer was equivocal, intended to create a belief there existed a just cause of complaint against me, whilst more was communicated or even avowed by the government.

J. M. then published his views of the conduct of the administration &c. Lately he was denounced by Mr A in a reply to an address, as a person who was disgraced for misconduct &c But no example of misconduct was stated or specific charge adduced."

49. JAMES MONROE TO THOMAS JEFFERSON MARCH 3, 1801

"You see that Adams has done everything in his power to embarrass your administration. In some of his appointments, too, he has nominated his enemies to strengthen his party. This shews that personal hatreds are sacrificed to the good of the cause."

50. JAMES MONROE TO GEORGE WILLIAM ERVING MARCH 5, 1801

"We will look forward to a better state of things under a better & wiser administration."

51. JAMES MONROE TO THOMAS JEFFERSON MAY 4, 1801

"The cession of the marine hospital at Norfolk was the subject, which was concluded, Mr. Adams having replied to my letter. I afterwards wrote him in compliance with a resolution of the General Assembly, respecting the conduct of the British Consul at Norfolk who was charged with receiving of P. Read and sending to one of the British Islands, a person who was said to be a mutineer on board the Hermione Frigate, and I sent him at the same time all the documents relative to that transaction. To the last letter I recd. no answer. Perhaps he discovered that I was making a question of the kind above suggested, & was resolved to oppose my doctrine; perhaps the communication offended him as it brought to his memory his conduct in the case of Robins; perhaps his other duties at that late period of his service rendered it impossible for him to act on it. But be the motive of his silence what it might, the fact of his omission to answer prevents my considering the point as being absolutely settled by him."

52. JAMES MONROE TO COLONEL JOHN TAYLOR SEPTEMBER 10, 1810

"Some doubted my integrity; many thought I had been too long from home, and had lost in Britain some part of those sound principles for which they had once given me credit, as Mr. Adams was said to have done before me."

53. JAMES MONROE TO COLONEL JOHN TAYLOR SEPTEMBER 10, 1810

"I knew also that I had in my hands ample means wherewith to put my own conduct in an unquestionable light, and thereby to annoy them, but still I could not use those means for those purposes. I had pursued that course on a former occasion, as you well know, and it was one which was most consistent with my natural disposition and general views of policy, but then I had to contend in favor of free government against a system of oppression, and the contest was maintained, not with my old friends, but with such men as Adams…for I could not consider Washington a party to it."

54. JAMES MONROE TO JOHN ADAMS JUNE 3, 1811

"Sir,—I have had the honor to receive your letter of the 25 ulto in which you are so good as to express a wish for my success in the discharge of the duties of the important & difficult office to which I have been lately appointed by the President. For the obliging communication, I beg you to accept my sincere acknowledgement.

Permit me to reciprocate this friendly sentiment & to assure you that I most earnestly hope, that you may enjoy the residue of your days, all the satisfaction and happiness of which our nature is susceptible."

55. JAMES MONROE TO JOHN ADAMS FEBRUARY 15, 1813

"I had the pleasure to receive from you some time since a letter which excited much my feelings. Having highly respected in my life the great abilities and virtuous firmness which you displayed in our revolutionary struggle; having always entertained the utmost confidence in your independence of foreign influence, in your integrity, patriotism, and attachment to our happy Union, I could never be indifferent either to what concerned your welfare, or to your sentiments and disposition towards me. In acknowledging that communication permit me to assure you that your opinion on the subject to which it related had much weight with me. My sincere wish is that no innocent person should fail to obtain redress, and I am persuaded, whatever may have been the character of the original transaction, that many innocent persons have suffered. I am aware that this calamity affecting one portion of the Union only produces an injurious effect, and think that consideration in itself ought to have much weight. My hope is that this cause of inquietude and complaint may be settled on just principles, & to the satisfaction of all parties. Your favorable opinion of their claim tends much to promote that result."

56. JAMES MONROE TO ABIGAIL ADAMS APRIL 10, 1813

"Dear Madam,—I fear that the pressure of much business, and an anxiety to write fully to Mr. Adams in reply to his kind letter, made me delay it longer than I ought to have done. I now return you the letter which he had the goodness to submit to my perusal, & with many thanks to him. The sentiments which it conveys do honor to the head & heart of the author."

57. JAMES MONROE TO JOHN QUINCY ADAMS AUGUST 17, 1818

"On arriving at Quincy I have to request that you will be so good as to present my respectful regards to your father and mother, with the assurance of my best wishes for the tranquility and happiness of their future lives. To your father I owe a letter which I will write him sometime hereafter."

58. JAMES MONROE TO JOHN ADAMS JULY 4, 1817

"Dear Sir—

I regret that I could not have the pleasure of seeing you again before you left town, which I found that you had done, when I called yesterday at our lodgings. I wanted to communicate more full with you, respecting the part I ought to take, in the ceremonies of this day. It is possible you may be in town today in which case I may still enjoy that advantage."

59. JAMES MONROE TO JOHN ADAMS FEBRUARY 20, 1820

"Dear Sir,—I have the pleasure to forward to you by the mail of this day a copy of the Journal of the Convention which formed the constitution of the U States.

This instrument having secured to us, & to our latest posterity, as I trust and believe, the great blessings of the revolution, I always look with profound respect & regard to those who contributed as much as you three have done to the accomplishment of that great event.

Congress having appropriated a copy for you, & one for Mr. Jefferson, & likewise for Mr. Madison, I have charged myself with the exn. of so much of the resolution as relates to each of you.

I avail myself of this opportunity to acknowledge your kind attentions on former occasions, & to assure you of the great interest which I take in the preservation of your health & happiness, being with the greatest respect & regard very sincerely yours."

VI. JOHN QUINCY ADAMS ON JOHN ADAMS

1. JOHN QUINCY ADAMS TO JOHN ADAMS AUGUST 30, 1786

"The class did me the honor to choose me among the theses collectors, and for the mathematical part. Little did I think, when you gave me those lessons at Auteuil, which you called our suppers, that they would be productive of this effect."

2. JOHN QUINCY ADAMS TO JOHN ADAMS JUNE 30, 1787

"At an exhibition which took place at the beginning of April, I delivered the inclosed piece upon the profession of the law. Two of my classmates performed at the same time, one of which spoke upon physic and the other upon divinity. The comparative utility of these professions was the topic, and the performance was honored with the approbation of the audience. It may savour perhaps of vanity in me to mention this circumstance, and I should have said nothing of it was it not from the hope that it would afford satisfaction to the best of parents."

3. JOHN QUINCY ADAMS TO JOHN ADAMS MARCH 19, 1790

"I hope I shall ever feel suitably grateful for the tender solicitude which you express with respect to my future prospects, and I trust I shall always be sufficiently sensible of the weight and importance of your advice and directions to regulate my conduct."

4. JOHN QUINCY ADAMS TO JOHN ADAMS APRIL 5, 1790

"I know not but that I shall incur your censure for departing even in this instance from the line which I have prescribed to myself, and losing the lawyer in the politician; and still more for the freedom with which I have expressed myself upon public men and measures. If I should on this occasion meet with your disapprobation, I shall without difficulty observe a more prudent silence upon these subjects in the future. The opinions which I have heard expressed are no evidence of the general opinion even throughout the Commonwealth, but in some instances they have been the opinions of men whose influence is great and extensive. But if the information contained in this letter should compensate your mind for its tediousness, I shall from time to time continue to give you a similar supply. In the meantime I remain your affectionate son."

5. JOHN QUINCY ADAMS TO JOHN ADAMS SEPTEMBER 21, 1790

"To avoid an early matrimonial connection, was one of the principles which I think I have heard you say was recommended to you by Mr. [Jeremiah] Gridley. Happiness in life I am fully persuaded must be derived principally from domestic attachments; but a foundation must be laid before the superstructure can be erected. I hope I am in no danger from this quarter."

6. EXCERPT FROM JOHN QUINCY ADAMS' *LETTERS OF PUBLICOLA* NO. XI JULY 27, 1791

"The papers under the signature of PUBLICOLA have called forth a torrent of abuse, not upon their real author nor upon the sentiments they express, but upon a supposed author, and supposed sentiments.

With respect to the author, not one of the conjectures that have appeared in the public prints has been well grounded. The Vice President neither wrote nor corrected them; he did not give his sanction to an individual sentiment contained in them, nor did they 'go to the press under the assumed patronage of his son.'"

7. JOHN QUINCY ADAMS TO THOMAS BOYLSTON ADAMS FEBRUARY 1, 1792

"I happened however quite accidentally to be present at the meeting and was nominated by Dr. [Charles] Jarvis, to be a member of the Committee, and was accordingly chosen. He was indeed the last man in this town from whom I should have expected such a nomination, and I cannot very readily account for his motives. Dr. Welsh asked him what his object was; and he answered, 'that this country was under great obligations to my father, and he thought it very proper that some notice should be taken of his son…".

8. JOHN QUINCY ADAMS TO JOHN ADAMS DECEMBER 8, 1792

"Our electors met in this town [Boston] on Wednesday last, and their votes for President and Vice President were unanimous. This was generally expected here, and the event is supposed to have been nearly if not wholly the same in all the New England states. New York it is imagined was unanimous for Mr. [George] Clinton as V[ice] P[resident]. Their electors are chosen by their legislature, where their Governor has a bare majority, determined to support upon all occasions his party and politics. From the other states you will probably hear before us. And upon the whole I presume the election will be favorable."[54]

9. JOHN QUINCY ADAMS TO JOHN ADAMS DECEMBER 16, 1792

"There has been upon my mind a strong sentiment of delicacy which has kept me silent in the midst of all the scurrility of which you have been the object. The charges which private malice and public faction have employed as instruments against you, have been so despicable in themselves, that common sense and common honesty must have felt some degradation in descending to the refutation of them. I have thought that where they could have any possible effect, sober reason and plain truth could not counteract it, because the minds affected must be too blind or too wicked to feel the operation of just sentiments."

10. JOHN QUINCY ADAM TO JOHN ADAMS DECEMBER 22, 1792

"If we are truly informed the election of President and Vice President is decided by the votes of which we have already heard, and which extend no further than Maryland. From the indication of the disposition of the people I feel much personal gratification, as it shows that the aspersions of private malice and of public faction have had no success in shaking the reverence and affection which your countrymen entertained for you, and which you have so richly deserved of them...".

54 George Washington was re-elected president with 132 Electoral votes. John Adams was re-elected vice president receiving 77 followed by George Clinton 50, Thomas Jefferson 4, and Aaron Burr 1.

11. AN EXCERPT FROM THE DIARY OF JOHN QUINCY ADAMS JUNE 3, 1794

"On Sunday the 8th, my father arrived at Quincy from Philadelphia, and on Tuesday the 10th I went from Boston to Quincy to see him. I found that my nomination[55] had been as unexpected to him as to myself, and that he had never uttered a word upon which a wish on his part could be presumed that a public office should be conferred upon me. His opinion on the subject agreed with my own; but his satisfaction at the appointment is much greater than mine."

12. JOHN QUINCY ADAMS TO JOHN ADAMS JULY 27, 1794

"I have written very freely to you, Sir, upon this subject, because I wish to have the sanction of your opinion and your advice. The principle which I have adopted has been so consonant to your own practice, and has been in my mind so clearly the result of your instructions, that I think it cannot but meet with your approbation. Perhaps the time upon which I have fixed may not preserve so accurately the medium as I should wish, and if you are of that opinion, I must solicit you for the result of your reflections in writing, if it be not too inconvenient. Your kindness will excuse the unceasing egotism of this letter, which could admit of no apology, were it not directed to the indulgence of a parent, for the purpose of obtaining the guidance of paternal wisdom…".

13. JOHN QUINCY ADAMS TO JOHN ADAMS JUNE 27, 1795

"I received two or three days since your favors of March 26, April 21 and 26, all together, and I know not how to express the pleasure they gave me. The first and dearest of all my wishes is personally to give satisfaction, and obtain the approbation of my parents, and in a public capacity to justify the confidence in me by the appointment I now hold. This wish is in both parts so abundantly gratified by the warm and cordial expressions used in your letters, that I have nothing left to desire but a continuance of that kindness and indulgence which I have always experienced from you, and which the government has been pleased to bestow upon my first performances in their service."

55 John Quincy Adams is referring to his nomination to the Hague as Resident Minister from the United States.

14. JOHN QUINCY ADAMS TO JOHN ADAMS JUNE 27, 1795

"Every suggestion or intimation of advice from you will always be received with gratitude by me, because I know from long experience, that it will operate to my own advantage in its use."

15. JOHN QUINCY ADAMS TO CHARLES ADAMS SEPTEMBER 15, 1795

"You may observe that there are many people who wish to raise a jealousy between Mr. Jay and another public character nearly connected with us.[56] It appears to me very probable that such attempts will be made, and I hope with you that they will prove abortive; but if I have one wish in my heart more forcible than any other, it is that the occasion for which you suppose the plan is laid may never happen. Whoever may be the successor of the present first magistrate will hold a situation so uncomfortable and so dangerous, that there is nothing in its possession to make it desirable. I am so far from looking on that place as an object worthy of ambition, that if my unequivocal wishes could decide the point on the supposition of the contingency, which we all deprecate, the election would be declined in the most decisive and explicit manner."

16. JOHN QUINCY ADAMS TO JOHN ADAMS OCTOBER 31, 1795

". . . all advice from you will always have, great weight in my mind."

17. JOHN QUINCY ADAMS TO JOHN ADAMS JULY 21, 1796

"In writing to you I never know when to finish."

18. JOHN QUINCY ADAMS TO JOHN ADAMS AUGUST 13, 1796

"Your indifference concerning the event of a possible future competition; the determination to be altogether passive, and the intrepidity with which the prospects of either decision are contemplated, I readily believe; and rejoice in believing them, because I have no doubt but that the transaction will call for the exercise of all those qualities in an eminent

56 John Adams.

degree. Besides the innumerable sources of opposition all native Americans, and the principles of which are so fully unfolded in your great political work,[57] you will expect all the art and intrigue of France, and all its weight and influence concerted with the American adverse party in formal array displayed against you. Their talents at political manœver are well known and appreciated by you. The range of their means, comprehending every thing that can be achieved and limited by no scruple of general morality, is understood. The popularity of their pretexts, the terror of their brilliant success in war, and the natural disposition among men of cringing before the insolence of victory, are duly estimated. You will also be prepared, I presume, for an opposition equally malignant though more concealed and perhaps, during the first period altogether inactive, from the rival influence of Great Britain; nor are you unaware of the dangers to which the station at the helm will be exposed at the most tempestuous political season that the world perhaps ever witnessed, when the elements of civil society are rapidly and inevitably returning to chaos in Europe, and at a moment when the fame of the predecessor has heaped to such accumulation the burden of the successor's task. All I am well convinced has been maturely weighed. It remains for me as a man, as an American, and as your son only to say *quod felix faustumque sit!* . . .".

19. JOHN QUINCY ADAMS TO JOHN ADAMS NOVEMBER 25, 1796

"Before this letter reaches you the elections for President and Vice President will be completed, and it will doubtless decide as to your continuance in the public service."

20. JOHN QUINCY ADAMS TO JOHN ADAMS JANUARY 14, 1797

"I *hope* that to the future President of the United States, whoever he may be, the peace of his country, its honor, and its justice will be as dear as they are to the present, and while every honest voice is uttering admiration, and every human heart ejaculating blessings to the name of Washington, that his successor, by exhibiting a continuance of the same wisdom, firmness and moderation, will prove to the sceptics in political speculation, that the American soil is fruitful to those virtues, and the American people determined to support them."

57 John Adams's *A Defense of the Constitutions of Governments of the United States of America,* 3 vols., 1787-1788.

21. JOHN QUINCY ADAMS TO JOHN ADAMS FEBRUARY 3, 1797

"From the returns of the most recent date, the accuracy of which must however be considered as very questionable, it would seem that a bare majority of the suffrages has called you to the post of the highest eminence and danger, while that which you now hold will in the terms of the Constitution be assigned to Mr. Jefferson; and the difference of numbers amounts to not more than two or three votes. Whether Mr. Jefferson will choose to serve the public in the second station, or if he should refuse, what measures will be taken in a case for which no special provision seems to have hitherto made either by the Constitution of the laws, it is useless for me to anticipate. What other questions or difficulties may arise or be started, it were equally needles to conjecture. As I presume you will not reject this call of your country, the time for observations upon the evils of the situation is past, and my duty henceforth will only be to transmit the most accurate information that I can collect of the state of our affairs in this country [the Netherlands] particularly and in Europe generally, as well as of the general complexion of European affairs from time to time."

22. JOHN QUINCY ADAMS TO JOHN ADAMS FEBRUARY 7, 1797

"It would be very needless for me to tell you, that in this country [the Netherlands] your name is remembered with respect and attachment by the people of all parties. The proofs of it which I have observed ever since I have been in the country, are innumerable, and most particularly since the recent American elections have become an object of immediate notice and attention."

23. AN EXCERPT FROM THE DIARY OF JOHN QUINCY ADAMS MARCH 4, 1797

"The day upon which the new Administration of the United States commences, and I am still uncertain what the elections have decided. Everything has contributed to accumulate anxiety upon this event in my mind. Futurity laughs at our foresight. I can only pray for the happiness and prosperity of my country. Wrote a letter to my father."

24. JOHN QUINCY ADAMS TO JOHN ADAMS MARCH 18, 1797

"We have not yet any authentic account concerning the issue of the American elections. That which is current and which I gather from the public newspapers states the choice of President as being ascertained, and that Mr. Jefferson is Vice President. A report prevails that he will serve in that office, which I cordially hope to be true, because I still confidently trust that the purposes which may exist in such a case, to divide and set in opposition against each other the two first officers of the Union will be disappointed. The welfare, the dearest interests of a common country are at stake. I am sure that their benefit and security will be your only object. I firmly hope and believe they will also be that of your old friend and fellow patriot."

25. JOHN QUINCY ADAMS TO JOHN ADAMS APRIL 30, 1797

"One of my friends at Paris has sent me an extract from a Philadelphia newspaper of March 6, containing an account of the commencement of the new administration, and the speeches of the President and Vice President upon their installation in their respective offices. It was impossible that anything should give me a more soothing hope, a more pleasing consolation, than the prospect of union and harmony between the two first officers of the government. Of your sentiments, indeed, I could need no formal declaration. I know them very well; but the solemn assurance given by Mr. Jefferson of his attachment to the Constitution, of his conviction concerning the importance of the Union, and of his esteem for you, gave me a satisfaction the more pointed, because I had seen all the attempts which have been so long and so variously pursued to set at variance and opposition two characters who have so often been united in rendering the most important services to the common country; and because I am profoundly convinced that there never was a time, or occasion, which more imperiously called for a concert of talents, and virtues, and influence, of the most respected citizens throughout the Union, to meet the trials that are preparing for us, or rather that are at this moment bearing upon us."

26. JOHN QUINCY ADAMS TO JOHN ADAMS MAY 20, 1797

"Among the papers enclosed there is one (that of the 10th) containing a pretended extract of a letter from Philadelphia, giving an account of the manner in which the anniversary of the treaty with France was celebrated, and also of the opening and counting the votes for President and Vice President at the late election. You will see with what effrontery it lies in speaking of you, and with how much malignity it states first an equality of force between two factions in America, and next your attachment to one that is for an union with England."

27. JOHN QUINCY ADAMS TO JOHN ADAMS JUNE 7, 1797

". . . I shall reconcile myself to continue my residence in Europe as long as circumstances will permit, or as will be in any manner proper; remembering that even were it possible for me to recede from a rigorous principle of exclusion for me (which I never can believe), it is at least my duty never to accept any public office whatever under your nomination. From that duty I shall not swerve. But I should not have renewed a subject upon which I have heretofore expressed my sentiments, but for an intimation that the late President has expressed a wish that you would not withhold promotion from me if I should deserve it. His approbation and good opinion are indeed more precious to me than any promotion whatever. The distinction by which he thinks my promotion by you reconcileable with his own practice while he held the office, may as it respects any other person be just. I cannot admit it to myself."

28. JOHN QUINCY ADAMS TO JOHN ADAMS JULY 2, 1797

"Infinite pains have been taken there [France] to spread universally the idea that there are in America only two parties, the one entirely devoted to France and the other to England. You have been in the Paris newspapers expressly represented as at the head of the latter, and Mr. Jefferson of the former. The English too have been much disposed to countenance the same idea."

29. JOHN QUINCY ADAMS TO ABIGAIL ADAMS FEBRUARY 5, 1798

"I am very glad that I was not sent to France, for there is so much *personal* malignity among the men in power in that country against my father, that they would have felt a special satisfaction in treating me with more than common indignity, and in defeating every attempt by me for a reconciliation between the two governments. . .

. . .Of the *personal* malignity which I have above noticed, there has been for years past incessant proofs many of which I have heretofore noticed; it continues still indefatigable. You will have the plainest evidence of the arts used by the Directory and their creatures, to give the color of a personal quarrel to the differences between the governments. They do not only make personal complaints against the President, but they have made their creatures in Holland (creatures which since then they have without ceremony kicked out of doors themselves,) complain against me simply because they bear a personal malice against him, and of course against anyone connected with him."

30. JOHN QUINCY ADAMS TO WILLIAM VANS MURRAY JUNE 7, 1798

". . . the most indefatigable pains are taken to throw the blame of a rupture [with France] upon our government, or rather upon the President personally, and there are men enough among us of consequence and influence most heartily disposed to second this purpose."

31. JOHN QUINCY ADAMS TO WILLIAM VANS MURRAY OCTOBER 30, 1800

"To return to a subject of greater importance, I repeat my felicitations upon the happy issue of your embassy to Paris. As this mission was the origin of that very strange division of the federal party, which will probably transfer the office of President at the impending election into the hands of their opponents, I confess I have felt more than ordinary solicitude that it might terminate successfully. It is so essential to the nature of mankind to judge of things merely from events, that I could not have seen without some degree of mortification the defection of so many persons of abilities and influence from their party and their chief, apparently justified by the results of events. As things have terminated it seems to me that no man of common sense will henceforth dispute the wisdom of a measure which proved so injurious to the personal influence of the man at the head of our government. Under this conviction I feel myself now perfectly at ease with regard to the issue of the election. The President may now go out of office with at least as much honor and dignity as he could desire from being continued in office, and if the same measure which has given an honorable peace to his country should deprive him of his reelection, it will but prove the more victoriously that he acted in his station, not as the man of a party, but as the man of the whole nation."

32. JOHN QUINCY ADAMS TO JOHN ADAMS NOVEMBER 25, 1800

"All these [newspaper reports] concur in representing the state of parties and the temper of the public mind in such a state, as to leave scarce a doubt but that a change will take place at the ensuing election, which will leave you at your own disposal, and furnish one more example to the world, how the most important services to the public and a long laborious life, anxiously and *successfully* devoted to their welfare, are rewarded in popular governments.

As I know that from the earliest period of your political life you have always made up your account to meet sooner or later such treatment in return for every sacrifice and every toil, I hope and confidently believe that you will be prepared to bear this event with calmness and composure, if not with indifference; that you will not suffer it to prey upon your mind, or affect your health; nor even to think more hardly of your country than she deserves. Her truest friends I am persuaded will more keenly feel your removal from the head of her administration than yourself. Your long settled and favorite pursuits of literature and of farming will give you full employment, and prevent that craving void of the mind which is so apt to afflict statesmen out of place; which conjures up a spectre to haunt them, or embitters them against their own species in a degree that renders their own lives miserable.

In your retirement you will have not only the consolation of a consciousness that you have discharged all the duties of a virtuous citizen, but the genuine pleasure of reflecting, that by the wisdom and firmness of your administration you left that very country in safe and honorable peace, which at the period of your entrance into office was involved in dangerous and complicated disputes with more than one formidable foreign power. That without the smallest sacrifice of national honor and dignity you have succeeded in settling a quarrel with France which, under any other system of conduct than that which you pursued, would at this moment have burst into a most ruinous and fatal war, or could only be pacified by disgraceful and burthensome humiliations. The merit of this system, too, is so entirely and exclusively your own, that we are told it was disapproved by almost all the principal leaders of the party friendly to the constitution and the union, the great supporters of your last election. Nay, the general opinion is, that to this defection of your friends, originating solely in your adherence to the system you had adopted against their opinions, must be ascribed your removal from the chair at this time. Indeed, my dear sir, if this be the case, it is not your fame of honor that will suffer by the result. The common and vulgar herd of statesmen and warriors are so wont to promote on every occasion their private and personal interest at the expense of their country, that it will be a great and glorious preëminence for you to have exhibited an example of the contrary, of a statesman who made the sacrifice of his own interest and influence to the real and unquestionable benefit of his country."

33. JOHN QUINCY ADAMS TO JOHN ADAMS NOVEMBER 25, 1800

"Let then a thinking and impartial man compare the situation of the United States on the 4th of March, 1797, when you assumed the functions of their first Executive magistrate, with their situation on the same day 1801, when I here suppose they will cease. Let him observe them at the first period, at the point of war to every appearance inevitable with France and Spain, yet at the same time having the highest reason to complain against the treatment of Great Britain. At the last period in full and, as far as human foresight can judge, is safe and permanent peace with all these powers. And let him ask himself how much of this favorable change ought justly to be ascribed to you; had you been the man of one great party which divides the people of the United States, you might have purchased peace by tribute under the name of loans and bribes, under that of presents, by sacrificing with pleasure, as one of the leaders of that party formally avowed his disposition to do, the rights of the Union to the pleasure of France by answering her injuries with submission and her insults with crouching. Had you been the man of the other party, you would have lost the only favorable moment for negotiating peace to the best advantage, and at this moment would have seen the United States at open war with an enemy in the highest exultation of victory, without an ally and, in the general opinion of the world if not in real truth, little better than once more a colony of Great Britain. In resisting, therefore, with all the energy which your constitutional power enabled you to exercise and all your personal influence could excite among your countrymen, the violence of France, you saved the honor of the American name from disgrace and prepared the way for obtaining fair terms of reconciliation. By sending the late mission you restored an honorable peace to the nation, without tribute, without bribes, without violating any previous engagement, without the abandonment of any claim of right, and without even exciting the resentment of the great enemy of France. You have, therefore, given the most decisive proof that in your administration you were the man not of any party, but of the whole nation, and if the eyes of faction will shut themselves against the value of such a character, if even the legal and constitutional judgment of your country as expressed by their suffrages at an election will be insensible to it, you can safely and confidently appeal from the voice of heated and unjust passions, to that of cool and equitable reason, from the prejudices of the present to the sober decision of posterity."

34. JOHN QUINCY ADAMS TO THOMAS BOYLSTON ADAMS DECEMBER 3, 1800

"You speak of it as a problematic point, whether the federalists will divide at the new election; by all the accounts from America it appears unquestionable that they will, and I consider already the result as perfectly ascertained. You are so extremely discreet about the original cause of the difference which has ended in a scission of the friends to government and order, that I know not even to this day what it is imputable to. But if the last mission to France was the point, every real friend of the President and of our country will rejoice that he adopted and persisted in that measure, though it should be at the expense of his election. There has been no one period since the commencement of our present national government, when the aspect of our affairs with relation to foreign states has been so favorable as at the present moment."

35. JOHN ADAMS TO THOMAS BOYLSTON ADAMS DECEMBER 20, 1800

"To ascribe the dissolution of the army to the President is ridiculous; but to whomsoever it is due, the measure was a good one, as such a number of troops could now be of no service, and would only have served to burthen the union with additional debt. If a President of the United States to secure his reëlection must sacrifice his country's interests to his party's passions and prejudices, Heaven be thanked that the present chief magistrate disdained to set the example."

36. JOHN QUINCY ADAMS TO THOMAS BOYLSTON ADAMS DECEMBER 27, 1800

"I am sensible that by being removed from the turbulent and disgusting scene of perpetual electioneering I am spared many a detail of vexation, which I should otherwise be obliged to suffer, and probably none will ever again take place, in which I shall feel so near and strong an interest, as in that which at this moment is decided. Its result is not equivocal, and in my opinion (which on this occasion cannot well be impartial) is far from doing honor to the discernment, or to the gratitude of the people, upon whose voice the issue depended. The administration of the present President, however hurtful to his personal interest and influence, has been in the highest degree useful and honorable to his country. Whether that of his successor will be equally distinguished for its wisdom and firmness, as little influenced by party men and party measures, and as much devoted to the welfare of the whole nation, it is for time to determinate. Never since the period of our revolution has there been a moment of more imminent danger, and more complicated embarrassment for the United States than that when the President entered upon his office. Never have they enjoyed a moment of tranquility and safety, so strongly grounded and so probably permanent. The danger and embarrassment had been only the consequence of unfortunate circumstances. More fortunate circumstances have contributed a share to produce the safety and tranquility. But these themselves would not have sufficed. His merit in effecting them, however, it may be disputed or disregarded now, I am confident will one day be acknowledged and duly appreciated."

37. JOHN QUINCY ADAMS TO THOMAS BOYLSTON ADAMS DECEMBER 27, 1800

"Perhaps the severest of all the trials of virtue is that of finding benefits returned with injuries, and her devotion with ingratitude. Were I therefore not acquainted with the genuine energy of your father's character, and the pure magnanimity of his soul, my keenest feelings at this time would arise from concern at what the effect of this event would be upon his mind. I fondly hope he will meet it as far as human nature will admit with real indifference, that he will sincerely pardon the infatuation of his countrymen, and consider it with compassion rather than with resentment. This temper of mind, of extremest difficulty in such a case to attain, is however so essentially necessary for his own happiness and that of his family and friends, that the bare possibility of his feeling uncontrolled that irritation so natural to a generous spirit under such treatment, gives me more anxiety than every other consideration.

I am not without some apprehensions on this occasion arising from another source. Although his principles of economy are as rigorous as can consist with a mind which appreciates money at its true value, and his practice has always been sufficiently conformable to his theory, to keep his estate free from serious and permanent embarrassment, yet he has been so far from growing rich in the service of the public, that it is not improbable he may in his retirement have occasion for money. I therefore authorize and direct you to consider all and every part of my property in your hands, whether of principal or interest, as subject at all times to his disposal for his own use. If you are certain (as you have means of information which I cannot at this distance possess) that he will have no occasion for this, you will not mention to him that I have given you this instruction, for I wish not to make a show of offering service where it is not wanted; but unless you are thus sure, let him know I have given you this order, and that it is my most urgent request he would use it whenever it may suit his convenience."

38. JOHN QUINCY ADAMS TO THOMAS BOYLSTON ADAMS DECEMBER 30, 1800

"[Your letter] mentions that Tench Coxe had published a private letter which your father wrote to him eight years ago, and containing something (I am yet ignorant what) to the disadvantage of General Pinckney. Likewise that Mr. Hamilton had published a pamphlet against your father and highly recommending General Pinckney as President. Now if these are the instances which you thought would surprise me, your conjecture was natural but not accurate. Coxe and Hamilton I knew had both become political enemies of the President. That their enmity was bitter I had no doubt, because it was unjust, and I had no reason to suppose that either of the men would scruple at such a mode of manifesting his enmity. It is an old maxim of prudence always to treat an enemy as if he might one day become your friend; and a knowledge of mankind will too often prescribe an alteration of the rule, and direct us always to treat a friend as if he might one day become your enemy."

39. JOHN QUINCY ADAMS TO THOMAS BOYLSTON ADAMS DECEMBER 30, 1800

"With the scanty information I can collect I distrust my own opinions upon American affairs. But from what I do see, it is impossible for me to avoid the supposition that the ultimate necessary consequence, if not the ultimate object of both the extreme parties which divide us, will be a dissolution of the Union and civil war. Your father's policy was certainly to steer between the shoals on one side, and the rocks on the other. But as both factions have turned their arms against him, and the people themselves have abandoned him, there is too much reason to expect that the purpose common to the two opposite factions will be effected."

40. JOHN QUINCY ADAMS TO WILLIAM VANS MURRAY JANUARY 27, 1801

"So far am I then from having any concern in the future about the French negotiation, that I confidently believe it will be considered as one of the President's most distinguished services, and the greater the opposition against it by those who, under the name of his friends, would have been his leaders, the more honorable I am persuaded the result will prove to him."

41. JOHN QUINCY ADAMS TO ABIGAIL ADAMS MARCH 10, 1801

"My mind has deeply shared in all the anxieties, and disappointments, and afflictions, both of a public and private nature which have befallen you, crowded into so short a space of time. The loss of my brother Charles,[58] the illness of my father, and the manner in which his country rewarded a life of labors devoted to their service, were all events which I know must call forth the fortitude and energy of his soul and yours."

42. JOHN QUINCY ADAMS TO ABIGAIL ADAMS MARCH 10, 1801

"The illness of my father and the result of the election I was informed of at the same time by the English and German newspapers. Five weeks have since elapsed, during which I have not had a single line from America. Mr. Murray, my constant and valuable correspondent, has informed me very lately that he had seen in a New York paper a paragraph stating my father's having recovered from his fever, which it was a great consolation for me to hear from any quarter, and which I hope will soon be made certain to me by more direct intelligence. The issue of the election I could not suppose would be an object of indifference to him; but I knew he had always been impressed fully with the sentiment that every man who serves the public must look upon the injustice of men, so far as it concerns himself, in the same light as upon the ills of nature; the shocks that flesh is heir to—a fever or a clap of thunder—which are neither to be denied for real evils, nor to be complained of as avoidable. Political disappointment is perhaps one of the occasions in human life which requires the greatest portion of philosophy, and although philosophy has very little power to assuage the keenness of our feelings, she has at least the power to silence the voice of complaint. To be relieved from the labors and responsibility of such a station as that of an American President, is a great consolation for all the pain of being removed from it, and will I hope have its full weight as such.

What the influence of the change in our administration upon the reputation and fortunes of our country may be, I do not think it necessary to inquire, and am altogether unable to foresee. For the *past* alone my father has anything on this score to answer. For the future the whole responsibility rests upon the people themselves. If they find themselves after the experience of their new system more prosperous than they have been under the old, the pure and generous spirit of patriotism will rejoice in their prosperity, and forget their injustice. But if the principles to which they have thought proper to transfer their trust should prove delusive, and bring upon them the miseries of broken public faith, of disunion, or of war, deeply will their sufferings be lamented by the pure and virtuous

58 Charles Adams, May 29, 1770 – November 30, 1800, was President John Adams's third child.

friend of his country; but he will find comfort in the reflection that he had done all in his power to ward off these calamities, and that the people would not have composed themselves to their effects but by first abandoning him.

I have hitherto for the last four years written seldom to my father, because I knew that all my public correspondence will be laid before him. For the future, however, (while I remain in Europe) I shall write oftener to inform him of the principal political events which may occur. I say while I remain in Europe, because I am in expectation of my recall immediately upon the new President's coming into office. He will doubtless have nothing personal against me, but my mission here has been one of the most powerful objections made against the policy of his predecessor, and I presume, therefore, will be one of the first objects that he will think it expedient to reform."

43. JOHN QUINCY ADAMS TO JOHN ADAMS MARCH 24, 1801

"With respect to you as these events affect you personally, it is not for me to tell you that the leaders (as they are called) of the federal party, or at least many of them, are the persons who *at heart* will feel the sincerest pleasure at the loss of your election. After the first moment of secret exultation at the issue, your successor will feel that the contested place is not a bed of roses, and his enjoyments in it, if any such he finds, will often be dashed by the consciousness that in justice it was not his proper place. His friends and partisans who put him in it, will many of them feel the same unacknowledged rankling in the breast at his elevation, as those of the other party did at yours; and amid the general pleasure of a party triumph, every single heart will yearn with some individual mortification. But the federal great men, the men of profound genius and all comprehensive talents, who are alone qualified for the government of empires; the lynx-eyed statesmen and the lionhearted warriors, who look down with eyes of pity upon your services, while for party purposes they extol them, and think you might do for President, since there was no hope of getting the place for themselves—these are the people who in the general run of federalism will find the soothing consolation, that in the misfortunes of our best friends there is always something *not displeasing*. How many of these characters there are, I am not near enough to observe. It is a breed common to all ages of the world, and to every civilized nation. I trust you will not feel distressed at their comforts any more than at the loud mouthed triumphs of your avowed enemies."

44. JOHN QUINCY ADAMS TO ABIGAIL ADAMS APRIL 14, 1801

"I learn with extreme satisfaction that under all these circumstances my father has retained his health and spirits. I have ever been fully convinced of his vigor and energy of mind, and was persuaded it would ever bear him up on these occasions, as it had done in many former instances of difficulty, danger, and disappointment. I knew that he was aware that in contributing to found a great republic, he was not preparing a school for public gratitude; that bad passions and bad practices would produce the same effects there, that they had in all other ages and climates with similar governments; and that he himself would in all probability be one of the most signal instances of patriotism sacrificed to intrigue and envy."

45. JOHN QUINCY ADAMS TO THOMAS BOYLSTON ADAMS AUGUST 27, 1802

"You have seen two letters from your father [John Adams] to S. Adams, written in 1790, lately published in the newspapers. They have been attacked with characteristic violence and bitterness, by the fifty-dollar men at Washington, Worcester and Boston. They are defended in the *Boston Gazette*. The first publication was to defeat the basest misrepresentations, which were circulating here by the paid slanderers, who had seen them, by the treachery of the old prophet, and who were affirming that the letters in so many words urged the establishment of an hereditary monarchy and nobility in this country, and named the families of which this nobility was to be composed. Judge how much the publication has exasperated those fellows, by taking the lie out of their mouths and holding it up to the public view."

46. JOHN QUINCY ADAMS TO JOHN ADAMS DECEMBER 11, 1804

"I received together last evening your two favors of 30th ultimo and 2nd instant, for which I most sincerely return you my thanks. In the dreary path which I am now compelled to tread, it is cheering to the spirits and gives the most pleasing consolation to have occasionally the benefit of your correspondence."

47. JOHN QUINCY ADAMS TO JOHN ADAMS DECEMBER 11, 1804

"In making and reiterating the request that you would commit to writing memoirs of your own life, I did not expect that it would consist of recollections altogether pleasing.

I am well aware that the pictures both of men and events, which your unalterable regard to truth would often render necessary, must be marked with very dark shades. But such must be the fate of every man who distinguishes himself in any eminent manner among his fellow men; and I was and remain decided in the opinion, that a work of this kind from you would be extremely useful both to your family and your country. I am persuaded from the vigor and accuracy of your judgment, neither vanity nor disappointment would suffer you to misrepresent or mistake any material part of the narrative, and that you would always have a due control over all the natural instigations of self-complacency and importance, which must continually occur to a man writing of himself."

48. JOHN QUINCY ADAMS TO JOHN ADAMS JANUARY 24, 1805

"I have never in my gloomiest moments considered my situation as of so trying or severe a nature as was yours during the whole period of our revolutionary controversy; but you had the advantage of a great and powerful consolation which totally fails to me, and that was, the honor and profit which you never failed to derive from your profession. I have had experience and acquired self-knowledge enough to be convinced that from my profession [attorney] neither profit nor honor will ever derive to me."

49. JOHN QUINCY ADAMS TO JOHN ADAMS MARCH 14, 1805

". . . I have been induced by two motives to give you the detail contained in this and my last letter. The one, because the transactions which I have related may be the precursors of events more highly momentous, and as such deserve peculiarly to be noted down; and the other, because I was desirous to make you some return for the excellent letters I have received from you in the course of the winter, and which my engagements at the time compelled me to leave unanswered. I thought the narrative might afford you some amusement, and knew it would furnish you a fund for useful reflections, of which I indulge the hope of sharing the benefit. . . ".

50. JOHN QUINCY ADAMS TO SKELTON JONES APRIL 17, 1809

"My father took his degree of Bachelor of Arts in 1755, and that of master, 1758. There has been lately published in the *Monthly Anthology* a letter written by him in the year 1755, and in the twentieth year of his age. Written to one of his youthful companions, and in which the probability of the severance of the colonies from the mother-country, the causes from which that event would naturally proceed, and the policy by which Britain might prevent it, are all indicated with the precision of prophecy. The date of this letter, the age at which it was written, and the standing in society of the writer at the time, are circumstances which render it remarkable."

51. JOHN QUINCY ADAMS TO SKELTON JONES APRIL 17, 1809

"In the eleventh year of my age my father took me with him to France, where he was sent as a joint Commissioner with Benjamin Franklin, and Arthur Lee, at the Court of Versailles. We sailed from Boston in February, 1778, and arrived at Bordeaux in the beginning of April of the same year. Before that time my education had been that of the common schools, interrupted by the convulsions of the times, but supplied by the substituted care and attention of both my parents. My obligations to them in this respect are *such* as gratitude can never repay *to them*. The impression resulting from it upon my own mind has been, that of a special duty incumbent upon me to pay the debt of the former age to that which is to succeed, and to reward my parents by transferring the same obligations to my children."

52. JOHN QUINCY ADAMS TO SKELTON JONES APRIL 17, 1809

"We arrived at Boston 1 August, 1779. The Massachusetts Convention for forming ac constitution was then just about to assemble. My father was elected a member of that body, and drew the original plan of the constitution which, with some modifications made by the Convention, was afterwards adopted, and is still the constitution of this Commonwealth."

53. JOHN QUINCY ADAMS TO SKELTON JONES APRIL 17, 1809

"From 1794 to 1801 I was in Europe, successively employed as a public minister in Holland, England, and Prussia. One of the last acts of President Washington's administration was the nomination of me as Minister Plenipotentiary to the Court of Portugal. But on my way from The Hague to Lisbon, I received a new commission which changed my destination to Berlin. The nomination of me to this mission was made by my father, and has been represented as an office bestowed upon me by him. It was even asserted in the public newspapers that I had received the separate outfit of these different appointments."

54. JOHN QUINCY ADAMS TO WILLIAM EUSTIS JUNE 22, 1809

"What I did stake was enough to make me feel no slight gratification in the daily accumulating public evidence, that I was not mistaken. And whether I live long enough to survive the passions, and prejudices, and personal enmities which my conduct and the course of events have brought upon me or not, I have no fear that either my father or myself will leave to the after ages a name, at which my children will ever have occasion to blush."

55. JOHN QUINCY ADAMS TO JOHN ADAMS APRIL 30, 1810

"I believe nobody will now deny, that the time has come to which you foretold, when nobody would believe you, that that the very name of republicanism is more detested in France than that of monarchy ever was at the moment of its destruction."

56. JOHN QUINCY ADAMS TO JOHN SINGLETON COPLEY APRIL 29, 1811

"It is I believe the only full length picture of my father as large as life that ever has been painted, and perhaps the only one that will remain after him. Mr. Stuart was engaged by the legislature of Massachusetts to paint one to be placed in the hall of the House of Representatives, and in pursuance of this engagement he actually took a likeness of his face. But Mr. Stuart thinks it the prerogative of genius to disdain the performance of his engagements, and he did disdain the performance of that. There is in America no other painter capable of executing a work, which I should wish to see preserved, and considering my father's age, it is more than probable that hereafter your portrait of him will be an *unique*. You will easily judge therefore how anxious I am for its preservation."

57. JOHN QUINCY ADAMS TO JOHN ADAMS JUNE 7, 1811

". . . I know of no human law more unerring than your example."

58. JOHN QUINCY ADAMS TO JOHN ADAMS JUNE 7, 1811

"There is neither office, dignity, honor nor emolument, in the gift of man, single or collective, upon this spot of earth, which could for a moment counterbalance the anguish that I should feel in giving by any voluntary act of mine a serious pang to you."

59. JOHN QUINCY ADAMS TO JOHN ADAMS JUNE 25, 1811

"Your disposition to draw from everything that you read, whether poetry, romance of history, speculations upon government, with your own description of this state of mind, delighted me exceedingly; not only as I could see in it the likeness of the picture, but as it struck me with the accuracy of self observation in the painter. I rejoiced that meditation upon government, as resulting from and combined with the nature of man, has been throughout your life the most strongly marked feature in your character, because I am convinced that your country has already derived great benefit from this cause and its effects, and because I am equally confident that posterity will derive still more advantage from them. Though you will expect no thanks from your country, perhaps none from posterity, for any good they may enjoy in consequence of your labors, it is my deliberate opinion that this very propensity of your mind is the principal cause, if not the exclusive one, of the *balance* established as the great and fundamental principle of the American Constitution. Other men may claim details, many of them very ill suited to the system. Some are useful, some injurious and some absurd, but the balance is yours and yours alone. How long it will last I shall not undertake to say; but there it is in the general Constitution, and in most of the particular ones. Let the powers of earth and the other place be conjured as they have been against it, they can devise nothing to take the place of this balance without falling into anarchy or despotism. In your own country mankind have, therefore, to a certain extent and to a very great extent, listened to you and to nature. So far as they have listened to you, their systems of government have hitherto proved highly prosperous. But whatever our future history is destined to be, the principle of the balance is now so deeply rooted in our institutions, that it can nor more be eradicated from them than your agency in introducing it can be contested."

60. JOHN QUINCY ADAMS TO JOHN ADAMS JUNE 25, 1811

"There is so much of this thing called praise which springs from friendship, from prejudice, from party spirit, from flattery, from interest, and even from the bad passions, that I consider very little of it as genuine, and set but a low value upon it. I value your applause, because I consider it as evidence of a duty, one of the greatest duties discharged."

61. JOHN QUINCY ADAMS TO BENJAMIN WATERHOUSE AUGUST 28, 1811

"I have also seen some of the numbers addressed to the People of the United States, and published in the newspapers by Mr. Pickering. As I had long known this man's honesty, and in particular his regard to truth, was subordinate to the violence of his passions and to his vanity, I was not at all surprised either at the coarseness or at the falsehood of his attacks upon the reputation of my father. His primary object in writing at that time was so obviously to secure his own reëlection, that it was natural for him to *suspect* others of passions as selfish and contracted as his own, and with him, *suspicion* confirmed by a proper dose of hatred is systematically equivalent to proof. I certainly felt indignant at the effusions of his malice against my father, but as there was no immediate effect injurious to him that they could produce, I should have thought them in America, as I think them here, deserving only of silent contempt. My father's reputation with posterity has a foundation which it is not in such men as Pickering to shake."

62. JOHN QUINCY ADAMS TO JOHN ADAMS MARCH 22, 1813

"She [Madame Anne Louise Germaine de Staël] soon asked me if I was related to the celebrated Mr. A. the author of the book upon government. I said I had the happiness of being his son. She replied that she had read it and admired it very much."

63. JOHN QUINCY ADAMS TO JOHN ADAMS SEPTEMBER 3, 1813

"This day thirty years ago you signed a definitive treaty of peace between the United States of America and Great Britain, and here am I authorized together with two others of our fellow citizens to perform the same service, but with little prospect of a like successful issue."

64. JOHN QUINCY ADAMS TO ABIGAIL ADAMS MARCH 30, 1814

"I feel an inclination almost irresistible to give my father the whole budget of my feelings and opinions upon this new effort to reconcile two countries which seem incapable of living either at peace or at war with each other. But mindful of an admonition in one of his last letters, I must reserve my thoughts until they can be imparted without restraint, in the freedom of direct conversation. I may simply add that I expect to have this pleasure before the close of the year."

65. JOHN QUINCY ADAMS TO ABIGAIL ADAMS OCTOBER 25, 1814

"This is the day of jubilee! the fiftieth year since your marriage is completed! By the blessing of Heaven my dear father can look back to all the successions of years since that time with the conscious recollection that it was a happy day. The same pleasing remembrance I flatter myself is yours; and may that gracious being who has hitherto conducted you together through all the vicissitudes of an eventful life still watch over you! Still reserve for you many years of health and comfort and of mutual happiness!"

66. JOHN QUINCY ADAMS TO JOHN ADAMS APRIL 8, 1816

"Your indifference as to the result of the elections to the Presidency of the United States and to the office of governor of your own Commonwealth of Massachusetts, which I find avowed in your favor of 7th of February, is the best of all possible political symptoms. It proves first, that you consider all the candidates as more likely to fill the respective stations, if suited to them, with credit to themselves and usefulness to the country. Secondly, that you consider no important principle of administration, external and internal, to be involved in the issue. Thirdly, that the violence of party spirit continues to subside among us, and that there are no conflicting interests to immediate operation threatening our national union, or the unutterable horrors of civil war."

67. AN EXCERPT FROM THE DIARY OF JOHN QUINCY ADAMS JUNE 2, 1816

"I told [Sir James Mackintosh] I did not believe Dr. Franklin wished for the Revolution – nor Washington. He asked me if any the leading men had. I said, perhaps my father, Samuel Adams, and James Otis."

68. JOHN QUINCY ADAMS TO ABIGAIL ADAMS OCTOBER 15, 1816

". . . oh, that I could make a visit to my father."

69. JOHN QUINCY ADAMS TO JOHN ADAMS OCTOBER 29, 1816

"As for you, my dear and ever honored father, though you never like Frederick stole anything from anybody, and although you have been all your life doing as you would be done by, yet your theory and your practice do not always coincide. Your great example does not strengthen all your laws. You inquire into the why and wherefore as curiously as any man, whether pious Christians like Sir Isaac Newton, or reprobate atheists like Diderot and the Baron d'Holbach. Now my theory is more like your practice, and my practice more like your theory. I never took much delight in reasoning high upon

Fix'd fate, free will, foreknowledge absolute;

but I have always thought that they are favorite contemplations of the brightest human intellects, and independent of revelation, it is only by such researches that the mind of man can arrive at the idea of God. All reasoning upon such subjects leads to that, and that is the foundation of all morality."

70. JOHN QUINCY ADAMS TO JOHN ADAMS NOVEMBER 2, 1818

"My Ever Dear and Revered Father:

By a letter from my son John, I have this day been apprised of that afflictive dispensation of Providence which has bereft you of the partner of your life; me of the tenderest and most affectionate of Mothers, and our species of one whose existence was virtue, and whose life was a perpetual demonstration of the moral excellence of which human nature is susceptible. How shall I offer your consolation for your loss when I feel that my own is irreparable? Where shall I entreat you to look for comfort in that distress which earth has nothing to assuage? Ten days have elapsed since we received in a letter from Harriet Welsh, the first intimation of my mother's illness; and in every anxious hour, from mail to mail, I have felt that I ought to write to you, and endeavor to soothe by the communion of sorrows, of hopes and fears, that anguish which I knew was preying upon your heart. Do not impute, my dear and only Parent, the silence that I have kept to neglect of that sacred duty which I owe to you. If I have refrained even from good words, it was because in the agitation of my own heart I knew not how to order my speech, nor whether on receiving my letter, it would come to you seasonably to sympathize with your tears of gratitude or of resignation.

The pangs of dissolution are past, and my Mother, I humbly hope, is a spirit, purified even from that little less than heavenly purity which in her existence here was united with the lot of mortality. I am advised that you have endured the agony of her illness with the fortitude that belongs to your character; that after the fatal event that fortitude rose, as from you I should have expected, with renewed elasticity from the pressure under which it had been bowed down. Will the deep affliction of your son now meet in congenial feeling with your own, without probing the wound which it is the dearest of his wishes to alleviate? Let me hear from you, my dearest father, let me hear from you soon. And may the blessings of that God, whose tender mercies are over all his works, still shed rays of heavenly hope and comfort over the remainder of your days.

Your distressed but ever affectionate and dutiful son."

---

71. AN EXCERPT FROM THE DIARY OF JOHN QUINCY ADAMS MARCH 14, 1820

"An account, preceding the mail from New York, announced the arrival there of a vessel from Liverpool bringing the intelligence of the death of the British King, George the Third, and of the Duke of Kent. It had first been known here yesterday. The papers this day received confirmed it. The Duke of Kent died on the 24th of January, and the King the 29th of the same month. George the Third had reigned sixteen years the sovereign of this country. I suppose there are about half a million souls in this Union who were once his subjects: four-fifths of that number born his subjects – of whom I was one. The forty-fourth year is revolving since the people of North America cast off their allegiance to him and declared their independence. Of the fifty-six signers of that instrument, only four are at this day numbered among the living – John Adams, of Massachusetts, my father, Thomas Jefferson, of Virginia, William Floyd, of New York, and Charles Carroll, of Carrollton, Maryland."

---

72. EXCERPT FROM JOHN QUINCY ADAMS'S *PARTIES IN THE UNITED STATES* JANUARY 1822

". . . The Administration of Mr. Adams was a continuation of that of Washington. All the heads of the executive departments appointed by Washington continued in office. There was a large and decided majority of the Federal Party in the Senate, but a very small one in the House of Representatives. The parties throughout the country were in nearly equal numbers, and in a temper of great and increasing bitterness against each other.

During the second term of President Washington's administration the foundation of the navy had been laid. It had then, and long before, even during the Revolutionary War, been a favorite object to his successor."

73. EXCERPT FROM THE DIARY OF JOHN QUINCY ADAMS AUGUST 25, 1823

"Just at one we arrived at my father's house, and I was deeply affected at meeting him. Within the two last years since I had seen him, his eyesight has grown dim, and his limbs stiff and feeble. He is bowed with age, and scarcely can walk across a room without assistance."

74. EXCERPT FROM THE DIARY OF JOHN QUINCY ADAMS SEPTEMBER 6, 1824

"At about eleven we took a hack, and came out to my father's house at Quincy. The infirmities of age have much increased upon my father since I was here last year. His sight is so dim that he can neither write nor read. He cannot walk without aid, and his hearing is partially affected. His memory yet remains strong, his judgment sound, and his interest in conversation considerable."

75. EXCERPT FROM THE DIARY OF JOHN QUINCY ADAMS SEPTEMBER 8, 1824

"The remainder of this day I passed in conversation with my father. He bears his condition with fortitude, but is sensible to all its helplessness. His mind is still vigorous, but cannot dwell long upon any one subject. Articles of news and of political speculation in the newspapers are read to him, on which he remarks with sound discernment. He receives some letters, and dictates answers to them. In general the most remarkable circumstance of his present state is the total prostration of his physical powers, leaving his mental faculties scarcely impaired at all."

76. EXCERPT TAKEN FROM THE DIARY OF JOHN QUINCY ADAMS SEPTEMBER 15, 1824

"Quincy spoke to me confidentially respecting the state and prospects of my father's health. He wrote under my father's dictation his will, and is appointed joint executor of it with myself. I have not seen it. I have hope that my personal attentions may yet contribute to the comfort of his declining days, and with gratitude to Providence observe the still vigorous energies of his mind."

77. EXCERPT FROM THE DIARY OF JOHN QUINCY ADAMS SEPTEMBER 24, 1824

"This day we took our departure to return to Washington. I took leave of my father with a heavy and foreboding heart. Told him I should see him again next year."

78. EXCERPTS FROM THE DIARY OF JOHN QUINCY ADAMS JULY 8-21, 1826

"*July 8.* — The mail this morning brought me three letters. One, dated the 3d, from my brother Charles's daughter, Mrs. Susan B. Clark, informing me that my father's end was approaching; that she wrote me because my brother was absent in Boston; that Dr. Holbrook, who was attending as his physician, thought he would probably not survive two days, and certainly not more than a fortnight. The second was from my brother, written on the morning of the 4th, announcing that, in the opinion of those who surrounded my father's couch, he was rapidly sinking; that they were sending an express for my son in Boston, who might perhaps arrive in time to receive his last breath. The third was from my brother's wife to her daughter Elizabeth to the same purport, and written in much distress."

"*July 9.* – We stopped half an hour, between seven and eight, at Ross's Tavern, and reached Merrill's, at Waterloo, where we breakfasted, before eleven. Mr. Merrill told me that he had come this morning out from Baltimore, and was informed there that my father had died on the 4th of this month about 5 o'clock in the afternoon. From the letters which I had yesterday received, this event was so much expected by me that it had no sudden and violent effect on my feelings.

My father had nearly closed the ninety-first year of his life – a life illustrious in the annals of his country and of the world. He had served to great and useful purpose his nation, his age, and his God. He is gone, and may the blessing of Almighty Grace have attended him to his account! I say not, 'May my last end be like his!' – it were presumptuous. The time, the manner, the coincidence with the decease of Jefferson, are visible and palpable marks of divine favor, for which I would humble myself in grateful and silent adoration before the Ruler of the universe. For myself, all that I dare to ask is that I may live the remnant of my days in a manner worthy of him from whom I came, and, at the appointed hour of my Maker, die as my father has died, in peace with God and man, sped to the regions of futurity with the blessings of my fellow-men."

"*July 12.* – My son George came in shortly after, and was with me till near one in the morning. He informed me of the circumstances of my father's last moments, and of those attending the funeral. George himself was on the 4th in Boston, expecting to attend with his company at the celebration of the day. An express was sent for him, and he came out about noon. My father recognized him, looked upon him, and made an effort to speak, but without success. George was with him at the moment when he expired, a few minutes before six in the evening. Mr. Quincy, who, on the 4th, delivered an oration at Boston, came out the next morning. The arrangements for the funeral were made with his concurrence. It took place on Friday, the 7th. There was a great concourse of people from this and the neighboring towns. Mr. Whitney delivered a sermon from I Chronicles xxix. 28: 'He died in a good old age, full of days and honor.' About two thousand persons took a last look at his lifeless face, and all that was mortal of John Adams was deposited in the tomb."

"*July 13.* – After breakfast I came out with my two sons, George and John, to Quincy. I found at my father's house my brother with his family. Everything about the house is the same. I was not fully sensible of the change till I entered his bedchamber, the place where I had last taken leave of him, and where I had most sat with him at my two last yearly visits to him at this place. That moment was inexpressibly painful, and struck me as if it had been an arrow to the heart. My father and my mother have departed. The charm which has always made this house to me an abode of enchantment is dissolved; and yet my attachment to it, and to the whole region round, is stronger than I ever felt it before. I feel it is time for me to begin to set my house in order, and to prepare for the church-yard myself."

"*July 14.* – Company occupied most of the day. My reflections upon my own situation and duties engrossed the remainder, so that I found barely time for writing to my wife. My father, by his will, has given me the option of taking this house and about ninety-three acres of land round it, upon securing the payment of ten thousand dollars, with interest, in three years from the time of his decease. After making this request, he made a donation to the town of parts of the lands, detaching eight acres on the road, of the grounds opposite to the house, but leaving the condition unaltered. It is repugnant to my feelings to abandon this place, where for near forty years he has resided, and where I have passed many of the happiest days of my life. I shall within two or three years, if indulged with life and health, need a place of retirement. Where else should I go? This will be a safe and pleasant retreat where I may pursue literary occupations as long and as much as I can take pleasure in them. I cannot sufficiently anticipate my own dispositions to know whether the country will for the whole remnant of my days fill up my time and attention so much as to sustain the interest of existence. From an active and much agitated life to pass suddenly and forever to a condition of total retirement, and almost of solitude, is a trial to which I cannot look without . . . concern."

"*July 16.* – Heard Mr. Whitney from I Corinthians xv. 19: 'If in this life only we have hope in Christ, we are of all men most miserable.' A discourse somewhat occasional upon the decease of my father. But he preached a sermon at the funeral. I have at no time felt more deeply affected by that event than on entering the meeting-house and taking in his pew the seat which he used to occupy, having directly before me the pew at the left of the pulpit, which was his father's, and where the earliest devotions of my childhood were performed. The memory of my father and mother, of their tender and affectionate care, of the times of peril in which we then lived, and of the hopes and fears which left their impressions upon my mind, came over me, till involuntary tears started from my eyes."

"*July 21.* – Dr. Holbrook, who as a physician attended my father, gave me some particulars of his last days. He retained his faculties till life itself failed. . . On Tuesday morning an express was sent for my son George, who was at Boston attending the celebration of the day. He came out immediately; was here between noon and one. He was recognized by my father, who made an effort to speak to him, but without success. George received his expiring breath between five and six in the afternoon. He had in the morning been removed from one bed to another, and then back. Mrs. Clark said to him that it was the 4th of July, the fiftieth anniversary of independence. He answered, 'It is a great day. It is a good day.' About one in the afternoon he said, 'Thomas Jefferson survives,' but the last word was indistinctly and imperfectly uttered. He spoke no more. He had sent as a toast to the celebration at Quincy, 'Independence forever.' Dr. Holbrook said his death was the mere cessation of the functions of nature, by old age, without disease."

"*Aug. 2.* – At eleven I went to the Senate-chamber in the State House, where the Governor and Lieutenant-Governor, Thomas L. Winthrop, with the Mayor and authorities of the city, were assembled, and when we went in procession to Faneuil Hall, and heard a eulogy upon John Adams and Thomas Jefferson by Mr. Daniel Webster. The prayers were performed by Mr. Charles Lowell. There was a funeral symphony, anthem, and dirge. The streets from the State House to the hall were thronged with a greater concourse of people than I ever witnessed in Boston. The hall itself was crowded to the utmost of its capacity. Mr. Webster was about two hours and a half in delivering his discourse, during which attention held the whole assembly mute."

79. EXCERPT FROM THE DIARY OF JOHN QUINCY ADAMS SEPTEMBER 28, 1836

"There are many considerations which make this exceedingly hazardous at my time of life, but after long deliberation I have concluded that there is a duty for me to perform — a duty to the memory of my father; a duty to the character of the people of New England; a duty to truth and justice. If controversy is made, I shall have an arduous and probably a very unthankful task to perform, and may sink under it; but I will defend my father's fame."

80. EXCERPT FROM THE DIARY OF JOHN QUINCY ADAMS OCTOBER 18, 1842

". . . I went to Cambridge this morning, and attended the meeting of the Committee of Overseers, to examine the state of the University, and the autumnal exhibition. We went with Mr. Quincy first to the new dining-hall, around which all the portraits are ranged, new varnished and freshened; but the best of them all, the full length portrait of my father, painted by Copley in 1783, has been damaged by a hole punched through the canvas on the shoulder."

Chapter 3

THOMAS JEFFERSON

I. THOMAS JEFFERSON ON THE PRESIDENCY

1. THOMAS JEFFERSON TO A. DONALD FEBRUARY 7, 1788

"There is another strong feature in the new constitution, which I as strongly dislike. That is, the perpetual re-eligibility of the President. Of this I expect no amendment at present, because I do not see that anybody has objected to it on your side of the water.[59] But it will be productive of cruel distress to our country, even in your day and mine. The importance to France and England, to have our government in the hands of a friend or a foe, will occasion their interference by money, and even by arms. Our President will be of much more consequence to them than a King of Poland. We must take care, however, that neither this, nor any other objection to the new form, produces a schism in our Union."

2. THOMAS JEFFERSON TO GEORGE WASHINGTON MAY 2, 1788

"I had intended to have written a word to your Excellency on the subject of the new constitution, but I have already spun out my letter to an immoderate length. I will just observe, therefore, that according to my ideas, there is a great deal of good in it. There are two things, however, which I dislike strongly. 1. The want of a declaration of rights... 2. The perpetual re-eligibility of the President. This, I fear, will make that an office for life, first, and then hereditary. I was much an enemy to monarchies before I came to Europe. I am ten thousand times more so, since I have seen what they are. There is scarcely an

59 Jefferson is writing from Paris, France.

evil known in these countries, which may not be traced to their king, as its source, nor a good, which is not derived from the small fibers of republicanism existing among them. I can further say, with safety, there is not a crowned head in Europe, whose talents or merits would entitle him to be elected a vestryman, by the people of any parish in America. However, I shall hope, that before there is danger of this taking place in the office of President, the good sense and free spirit of our countrymen, will make the changes necessary to prevent it."

3. THOMAS JEFFERSON TO EDWARD CARRINGTON MAY 27, 1788

"Re-eligibility makes him [the President of the United States] an officer for life, and the disasters inseperable from an elective monarchy, render it preferable, if we cannot tread back that step, that we should go forward & take refuge in an hereditary one. Of the correction of this Article however I entertain no present hope, because I find it has scarcely excited an objection in America. And if it does not take place ere long, it assuredly never will. The natural progress of things is for liberty to yield, & government to gain ground. As yet our spirits are free. Our jealousy is only put to sleep by the unlimited confidence we all repose in the person to whom we all look to as our president. After him inferior characters may perhaps succeed and awaken us to the danger which his merit has led us into."

4. THOMAS JEFFERSON TO JAMES MADISON APRIL 27, 1795

"For as to myself, the subject had been thoroughly weighed & decided on, & my retirement from office had been meant from all office high or low, without exception. I can say, too, with truth, that the subject had not been presented to my mind by any vanity of my own. I know myself & my fellow citizens too well to have ever thought of it. But the idea was forced upon me by continual insinuations in the public papers, while I was in office. As all these came from a hostile quarter, I knew that their object was to poison the public mind as to my motive, when they were not able to charge me with facts. But the idea being once presented to me, my own quiet required that I should face it & examine it. I did so thoroughly, & had no difficulty to see that every reason which had determined me to retire from the office I then held, operated more strongly against that which was insinuated to be my object. I decided then on those general grounds which could alone be present to my mind at the time, that is to say, reputation, tranquility, labor; for as to public duty, it could not be a topic of consideration in my case. If these general considerations were sufficient to ground a firm resolution never to permit myself to think of the office, or to be thought for it, the special ones which have supervened on my retirement, still more insuperably bar the door to it. My health is entirely broken down within the last eight months; my age requires that I should place my affairs in a clear state; these are sound if taken care of, but capable of considerable dangers if longer neglected; and above all things, and delights I feel in the society of my family, and the agricultural pursuits in which I am so eagerly engaged. The little spice of ambition which I had in my younger days has long since evaporated, and I set still less store by a posthumous than present name. In stating to you the heads of reasons which have produced my determination, I do not mean an opening for future discussion, or that I may be reasoned out of it. The question is forever closed with me; my sole object is to avail myself of the first opening ever given me from a friendly quarter (and I could not with decency do it before), of preventing any division of loss of votes, which might be fatal to the Republican interest. If that has any chance of prevailing, it must be by avoiding the loss of a single vote, and by concentrating all its strength on one object. Who this should be, is a question I can more freely discuss with anybody than yourself."

5. THOMAS JEFFERSON TO EDWARD RUTLEDGE DECEMBER 27, 1796

"These are hard wages for the services of all the active and healthy years of one's life. I had retired after five and twenty years of constant occupation in public affairs, and total abandonment of my own. I retired much poorer than when I entered the public service, and desired nothing but rest and oblivion. My name, however, was again brought forward, without concert or expectation on my part; (on my salvation I declare it.) I do not as yet know the result, as a matter of fact; for in my retired canton we have nothing later from Philadelphia than of the second week of this month. Yet I have never one moment doubted the result. I knew it was impossible Mr. Adams should lose a vote north of the Delaware, and that the free and moral agency of the South would furnish him an abundant supplement. On principles of public respect I should not have refused; but I protest before my God, that I shall, from the bottom of my heart, rejoice at escaping. I know well that no man will ever bring out of that office the reputation which carries him into it. The honey moon would be as short in that case as in any other, and its moments of extasy would be ransomed by years of torment and hatred. I shall highly value, indeed, the share which I may have had in the late vote, as an evidence of the share I hold in the esteem of my countrymen."[60]

60 In the election of 1796, John Adams received 71 electoral votes to Thomas Jefferson's 68.

6. THOMAS JEFFERSON TO JAMES MADISON DECEMBER 17, 1797

"The first whish of my heart was, that you should have been proposed for the administration of the government. On your declining it, I wish any body rather than myself; and there is nothing I so anxiously hope, as that my name may come out either second or third. These would be indifferent to me; as the last would leave me at home the whole year, & the other two-thirds of it."

7. THOMAS JEFFERSON TO JAMES SULLIVAN FEBRUARY 9, 1797

"DEAR SIR—I have many acknolegments to make for the friendly anxiety you are pleased to express in your letter of Jan 12, for my undertaking the office to which I have been elected. The idea that I would accept the office of President, but not that of Vice President of the U S, had not its origin with me. I never thought of questioning the free exercise of the right of my fellow citizens, to marshal those whom they call into their service according to their fitness, nor ever presumed that they were not the best judges of these. Had I indulged a wish in what manner they should dispose of me, it would precisely have coincided with what they have done. Neither the splendor, nor the power, nor the difficulties, nor the fame or defamation, as may happen, attached to the first magistracy, have any attractions for me. The helm of a free government is always arduous, & never was ours more so, than at a moment when two friendly people are like to be committed in war by the ill temper of their administrations. I am so much attached to my domestic situation, that I would not have wished to leave it at all. However, if I am to be called from it, the shortest absences & most tranquil station suit me best."

8. THOMAS JEFFERSON TO ELBRIDGE GERRY MAY 13, 1797

"When I retired from [the nation's capital] & the office of Secy of state, it was in the firmest contemplation of never more returning here. There had indeed been suggestions in the public papers, that I was looking towards a succession to the President's chair, but feeling a consciousness of their falsehood, and observing that the suggestions came from hostile quarters, I considered them as intended merely to excite public odium against me. I never in my life exchanged a word with any person, on the subject, till I found my name brought forward, generally, in competition with that of mr. Adams. Those with whom I the communicated, could say, if it were necessary, whether I met the call with desire, or even with a ready acquiescence, and whether from the moment of my first acquiescence, I did not devoutly pray that the very thing might happen which has happened. The second office of this government is honorable & easy, the first but a splendid misery."

9. EXCERPT FROM THOMAS JEFFERSON'S FIRST INAUGURAL ADDRESS MARCH 4, 1801

"With experience enough in subordinate stations to know the difficulties of this the greatest of all, I have learnt to expect that it will rarely fall to the lot of imperfect man to retire from this station with the reputation & the favor which bring him into it."

10. THOMAS JEFFERSON TO THOMAS M'KEAN MARCH 9, 1801

"DEAR SIR—I have to acknolege the receipt of your favor of Feb. 20, and to thank you for your congratulations on the event of the election. Had it terminated in the elevation of Mr. Burr, every republican would, I am sure, have acquiesced in a moment; because, however it might have been variant from the intentions of the voters, yet it would have been agreeable to the Constitution. No man would more cheerfully have submitted than myself, because I am sure the administration would have been republican, and the chair of the Senate permitting me to be at home 8. months in the year, would, on that account, have been much more consonant to my real satisfaction."

11. THOMAS JEFFERSON TO MOSES ROBINSON MARCH 23, 1801

"I sincerely wish with you, we could see our government so secured as to depend less on the character of the person in whose hands its trusted. Bad men will sometimes get in, and with such an immense patronage, may make great progress in corrupting the public mind and principles. This is a subject with which wisdom and patriotism should be occupied."

12. THOMAS JEFFERSON TO ELBRIDGE GERRY MARCH 3, 1804

"I sincerely regret that the unbounded calumnies of the federal party have obliged me to throw myself on the verdict of my country for trial, my great desire having been to retire, at the end of the present term, to a life of tranquility; and it was my decided purpose when

I entered into office. They force my continuance. If we can keep the vessel of State as steadily in her course for another four years, my earthly purpose will be accomplished, and I shall be free to enjoy, as you are doing, my family, my farm, and my books."

13. THOMAS JEFFERSON TO JOHN DICKINSON JANUARY 13, 1807

"I have tired you, my friend, with a long letter. But your tedium will end in a few lines more. Mine has yet two years to endure. I am tired of an office where I can do no more good than many others, who would be glad to be employed in it. To myself, personally, it brings nothing but unceasing drudgery & daily loss of friends. Every office becoming vacant, every appointment made, *me donne un ingrate, et cent ennemies.*[61] My only consolation is in the belief that my fellow citizens at large give me credit for good intentions. I will certainly endeavor to merit the continuance of that good-will which follows well-intended actions, and their approbations will be the dearest reward I can carry into retirement."

14. THOMAS JEFFERSON TO M. DUPONT DE NEMOURS MARCH 2, 1809

"After using every effort which could prevent or delay our being entangled in the war with Europe, that seems now our only resource. The edicts of the two belligerents, forbidding us to be seen on the ocean, we met by an embargo. This gave us time to call home our seamen, ships and property, to levy men and put our seaports into a certain state of defense. We have now taken off the embargo, except as to France and England and their territories, because fifty millions of exports, annually sacrificed, are the treble of what war would cost us; besides, that by war we should take something, and lose less than at present. But to give you a true description of the state of things here, I must refer you to Mr. [Edward] Coles, the bearer of this, my secretary, a most worthy, intelligent and well-informed young man, whom I recommend to your notice, and conservation of our affairs. His description and fidelity may be relied on. I expect he will find you with Spain at your feet, but England still afloat, and a barrier to the Spanish colonies. But all these concerns I am now leaving to be settled by my friend Mr. Madison. Within a few days I retire to my family, my books and farms; and having gained the harbor myself, I shall look on my friends still buffeting the storm with anxiety indeed, but not with envy. Never did a prisoner, released from his chains, feel such relief as I shall on shaking off the shackles of power. Nature intended me for the tranquil pursuits of science, by rendering them my supreme delight.

61 "give me one hundred ungrateful enemies."

But the enormities of the times in which I have lived, have forced me to take a part in resisting them, and to commit myself on the boisterous ocean of political passions. I thank God for the opportunity of retiring from them without censure, and carrying with me the most consoling proofs of public approbation."

15. EXCERPT FROM THOMAS JEFFERSON'S ADDRESS "TO THE CITIZENS OF WASHINGTON" MARCH 4, 1809

"It is very gratifying to me that the general course of my administration is approved by my fellow citizens, and particularly that the motives of my retirement are satisfactory. I part with the powers entrusted by my country, as with a burthen of heavy bearing; but it is with sincere regret that I part with the society in which I have lived here. It has been the source of much happiness to me during my residence at the seat of government, and I owe it much for its kind dispositions. I shall ever feel a high interest in the prosperity of the city, and an affectionate attachment to its inhabitants."

16. THOMAS JEFFERSON TO MESSRS. BLOODGOOD AND HAMMOND SEPTEMBER 30, 1809

"The very friendly sentiments which my republican fellow citizens of the city and county of New York have been pleased to express through yourselves as their organ, are highly gratifying to me, and command my sincere thanks; and their approbation of the measures pursued, while I was entrusted with the administration of their affairs, strengthens my hope that they were favorable to the public prosperity. For any errors which may have been committed, the indulgent will find some apology in the difficulties resulting from the extraordinary state of human affairs, and the astounding spectacles these have presented. A world in arms and trampling on all those moral principles which have heretofore been deemed sacred in the intercourse between nations, could not suffer us to remain insensible of all agitation."

17. THOMAS JEFFERSON TO WILLIAM DUANE AUGUST 12, 1810

"While I cherish with feeling the recollections of my friends, I banish from my mind all political animosities which might disturb its tranquility, or the happiness I derive from my present pursuits. I have thought it among the most fortunate circumstances of my late administration that, during its eight years continuance, it was conducted with a cordiality and harmony among all the members, which never were ruffled on any, the greatest or smallest occasion. I left my brethren with sentiments of sincere affection and friendship, so rooted in the uniform tenor of a long and intimate intercourse, that the evidence of my own senses alone ought to be permitted to shake them."

18. THOMAS JEFFERSON TO SAMUEL H. SMITH AUGUST 2, 1823

"DEAR SIR—I agree with you in all the definitions of your favor of July 22. of the qualificns necessary for the chair of the US. and I add another. He ought to be disposed rigorously to maintain the line of power marked by the constitution between the two co-ordinate governments, each sovereign & uffeting in it's department, the states as to everything relating to themselves and their state, the General government as to everything relating to things or persons out of a particular state. The one may be strictly called the Domestic branch of government which is sectional but sovereign, the other the foreign branch of government co-ordinate with the other domestic & equally sovereign on it's own side of the line. The federalists baffled in their schemes to monarchise us, have given up their name, which the Hartford Convention had made odious, and have taken shelter among us and under our name. But they have not only changed the point of attack. On every question of the usurpation of State powers by the Foreign or Genl govmt, the same men rally together, force the line of demarcation and consolidate the government. The judges are at their head as heretofore, and are their entering wedge. The true old republicans stand to the line, and will I hope die on it if necessary. Let our next president be aware of this new party principle and firm in maintaining the constitutional line of demarcation."

II. GEORGE WASHINGTON ON THOMAS JEFFERSON

1. GEORGE WASHINGTON TO THOMAS JEFFERSON FEBRUARY 10, 1783

"I feel myself much flattered by your kind rememberance of me in the hour of your departure from this Continent and for the favourable Sentiments you are pleased to entertain of my Services for our common Country. To merit the approbation of good and virtuous Men is the height of my ambition; and will be a full compensation for all my toils and sufferings in the long and painful contest we have been engaged."

2. GEORGE WASHINGTON TO THE MARQUIS DE LAFAYETTE MAY 10, 1786

"The favourable terms in which you speak of Mr Jefferson gives me great pleasure: he is a man of whom I early imbibed the highest opinion."

3. GEORGE WASHINGTON TO RICHARD HENDERSON JUNE 19, 1788

"As to the European Publications respecting the United States, they are commonly very defective...of books at present existing, Mr. Jefferson's 'Notes on Virginia' will give the best idea of this part of the Continent to a Foreigner."

4. GEORGE WASHINGTON TO THOMAS JEFFERSON JANUARY 21, 1790

"I consider the successful Administration of the general Government as an object of almost infinite consequence to the present and future hapiness of the Citizens of the United States. I consider the Office of Secretary for the Department of State as *very* important on many accts: and I know of no person, who, in my judgment, could better execute the Duties of it than yourself."

5. GEORGE WASHINGTON TO JAMES MADISON FEBRUARY 20, 1790

"My dear Sir: I return Mr. Jefferson's letter with thanks for the perusal of it. I am glad he has resolved to accept the appointment of Secretary of State, but sorry it is so repugnant to his own inclinations, that it is done."

6. GEORGE WASHINGTON TO THOMAS JEFFERSON OCTOBER 18, 1792

"Why then, when some of the best Citizens in the United States—Men of discernment—Uniform and tired Patriots, who have no sinister views to promote, but are chaste in their ways of thinking and acting are to be found, some on one side, and some on the other of the questions which have caused these agitations, should either of you be so tenacious of your opinions as to make no allowances for those of the other?"

7. GEORGE WASHINGTON TO THOMAS JEFFERSON OCTOBER 18, 1792

"My dear Sir

I did not require the evidence of the extracts which you enclosed me, to convince me of your attachments to the Constitution of the United States, or of your disposition to promote the general welfare of this Country. But I regret—deeply regret—the difference in opinions which have arisen, and divided you and another principal Officer of the Government; and wish, devoutly, there could be an accommodation of them by mutual yieldings."

8. GEORGE WASHINGTON TO EDMUND RANDOLPH DECEMBER 24, 1793

"My dear Sir: It was my wish, for many reasons (needless to enumerate) to have retained Mr. Jefferson in administration, to the end of the present Session of Congress, but he is so decidedly opposed to it, that I can no longer hint this to him...Mr. Jefferson will quit it the last day of this month and proposes to set out for Virginia a few days afterwards."

9. GEORGE WASHINGTON TO THOMAS JEFFERSON JANUARY 1, 1794

"Dear Sir: I yesterday received, with sincere regret your resignation of the office of Secretary of State. Since it has been impossible to prevail upon you, to forego any longer the indulgence of your desire for private life; the event, however anxious I am to avert it, must be submitted to.

But I cannot suffer you to leave your Station, without assuring you, that the opinion, which I had formed, of your integrity and talents, and which dictated your original nomination, has been confirmed by the fullest experience; and that both have been eminently displayed in the discharge of your duties.

Let a conviction of my most earnest prayers for your happiness accompany you in your retirement; and while I accept with the warmest thanks your solicitude for my welfare, I beg you to believe that I always am &c."

10. GEORGE WASHINGTON TO HENRY LEE AUGUST 26, 1794

"With respect to the words said to have been uttered by Mr. Jefferson, they would be enigmatical to those who are acquainted with the characters about me, unless supposed to be spoken ironically; and in that case they are too injurious to me, and have too little foundation in truth, to be ascribed to him."

11. GEORGE WASHINGTON TO THOMAS JEFFERSON JULY 6, 1796

"As you have mentioned the subject yourself, it would not be frank, candid, or friendly to conceal, that your conduct has been represented as derogatory from that opinion *I* had conceived you entertained of me. That to your particular friends and connextions you have described, and they have denounced me, as a person under a dangerous influence; and that, if I would listen *more* to some *other* opinions, all would be well. My answer invariably has been, that I had never discovered anything in the conduct of Mr. Jefferson to raise suspicions, in my mind, of his insincerity; that if he would retrace my public conduct while he was in the Administration, abundant proofs would occur to him, that truth and right decisions, were the *sole* objects of my pursuit; that there were as many instances within his *own* knowledge of my having decided *against*, as in *favor of* the opinions of the person evidently alluded to; and moreover, that I was no believer in the infallability of the politics, or measures of *any man living*. In short, that I was no party man myself, and the first wish of my heart was, if parties did exist, to reconcile them."

III. JOHN ADAMS ON THOMAS JEFFERSON

1. EXCERPT FROM THE AUTOBIOGRAPHY OF JOHN ADAM'S AUGUST 19, 1776

"Jefferson in those days never failed to agree with me, in every Thing of a political nature."

2. EXCERPT FROM THE DIARY OF JOHN ADAMS 1782-1804

"The Committee had several meetings, in which were proposed the Articles of which the Declaration was to consist, and minutes made of them. The Committee then appointed Mr. Jefferson and me, to draw them up in form, and cloath them in a proper Dress. The Sub Committee met, and considered the Minutes, making such Observations on them as then occurred: when Mr. Jefferson desired me to take them to my Lodgings and make the Draught. This I declined and gave several reasons for declining. 1. That he was a Virginian and I a Massachusettensian. 2. that he was a southern Man and I a northern one. 3. That I had been so obnoxious for my early and constant Zeal in promoting the Measure, that any draught of mine, would undergo a more severe Scrutiny and Criticism in Congress, than one of his composition. 4thly and lastly and that would be reason enough if there were no other, I had a great Opinion of the Elegance of his pen and none at all of my own. I therefore insisted that no hesitation should be made on his part. He accordingly took the Minutes and in a day or two produced to me his Draught. Whether I made of suggested any corrections I remember not. The Report was made to the Committee of five, by them examined, but whether altered or corrected in any thing I cannot recollect. But in substance at least it was reported to Congress where, after a severe Criticism, and striking out several of the most oratorical Paragraphs it was adopted on the fourth of July 1776, and published to the World."

3. EXCERPT FROM THE DIARY OF JOHN ADAMS 1782-1804

"The Committee of Independence, were Thomas Jefferson, John Adams, Benjamin Franklin, Roger Sherman and Robert R. Livingston. Mr. Jefferson had been now about a Year a Member of Congress, but had attended his Duty in the House but a very small part of the time and when there had never spoken in public: and during the whole Time I satt with him in Congress, I never heard him utter three Sentences together. The most of a Speech he ever made in my hearing was a gross insult on Religion, in one or two Sentences, for which I gave him immediately the Reprehension, which he richly merited. It will naturally be enquired, how it happened that he was appointed on a Committee of such importance. There were more reasons than one. Mr. Jefferson had the Reputation of a masterly Pen. He had been chosen Delegate in Virginia, in consequence of a very handsome public Paper[62] which he had written for the House of Burgesses, which had given him the Character of a fine Writer. Another reason was that Mr. Richard Henry Lee was not beloved by the most of his Colleagues from Virginia and Mr. Jefferson was sett up to rival and supplant him. This could be done only by the Pen, for Mr. Jefferson could stand no competition with him or any one else in Elocution and public debate."

4. JOHN ADAMS TO JAMES WARREN AUGUST 27, 1784

"I received yours of the 29 of June by Mr. Jefferson whose appointment [as Minister to France] gives me great pleasure. He is an old Friend with whom I have often had occasion to labour at many a knotty Problem, and in whose Abilities and Steadiness I always found great Cause to confide. The appointment of this Gentleman and that of Mr. Jay and Mr. Dana, are excellent Symtoms."

5. JOHN ADAMS TO ELBRIDGE GERRY DECEMBER 12, 1784

"Jefferson is an excellent hand. You could not have sent a better. He appears to me to be infected with no Party Passions or national prejudices, or any Partialities, but for his own Country... Since our Meeting upon our new Commissions, our affairs have gone on with the utmost Harmony and nothing has happened to disturb our Peace. I wish this Calm may continue, and believe it will."

6. JOHN ADAMS TO RICHARD CRANCH APRIL 27, 1785

"I shall part with Mr. Jefferson, with great Regret, but as he will no doubt be placed at Versailles, I shall be happy in a Correspondence of Friendship, Confidence, and Affection with the Minister at this Court, which is a very fortunate Circumstance, both for me, and the public."

62 *Summary View of the Rights of British America*

7. JOHN ADAMS TO HENRY KNOX DECEMBER 15, 1785

"You can Scarcely have heard a Character too high of my Friend and Colleague Mr. Jefferson, either in point of Power or Virtues. My Fellow Labourer in Congress, eight or nine years ago, upon many arduous Tryals, particularly in the draught of our Declaration of Independence and in the formation of our Code of Articles of War, and Laws for the Army. I have found him uniformly the same wise and prudent Man and Steady Patriot. I only fear that his unquenchable Thirst for knowledge may injure his Health."

8. JOHN ADAMS TO THOMAS JEFFERSON JULY 29, 1791

"I thank you, Sir, very sincerely for writing to me upon this occasion. It was high time that you and I should come to an explanation with each other. The friendship that has subsisted for fifteen years without the smallest interruption, and, until this occasion without the slightest suspicion, ever has been and still is very dear to my heart. There is no office which I would not resign, rather than give a just occasion to one friend to forsake me. Your motives for writing to me I have not a doubt were the most pure and the most friendly; and I have no suspicion that you will not receive this explanation from me in the same friendly light."

9. JOHN ADAMS TO THOMAS JEFFERSON JULY 29, 1791

"You observe, 'that you and I differ in our ideas of the best form of government, is well known to us both.' But, my dear Sir, you will give me leave to say that I do not know this. I know not what your idea is of the best form of government. You and I have never had a serious conversation together, that I can recollect, concerning the nature of government. The very transient hints that have ever passed between us have been jocular and superficial, without ever coming to an explanation. If you suppose that I have, or ever had, a design or desire of attempting to introduce a government of Kings, Lords, and Commons, or in other words, an hereditary executive, or an hereditary senate, either into the government of the United States or that of any individual State, you are wholly mistaken. There is not such a thought expressed or intimated in any public writing or private letter, and I may safely challenge all mankind to produce such a passage, and quote the chapter and verse. If you have ever put such a construction on any thing of mine, I beg you would mention it to me, and I will undertake to convince you that it has no such meaning."

10. JOHN ADAMS TO ABIGAIL ADAMS DECEMBER 28, 1792

"I am really astonished at the blind Spirit of Party which has Lived on the whole soul of this Jefferson. There is not a Jacobin in France more devoted to faction. He is however Selling off his Furniture and his Horses: He has been I believe a greater fool than I have, and run farther in Debt by his French Dinners and Splendid Living. Farewell for me all that Folly forever. Jefferson may for what I know pursueing my example and finding the Blanket too short taking up his feet. I am sure all the offices of Government must hall in their horns as I have done."

11. JOHN ADAMS TO JOHN QUINCY ADAMS JANUARY 3, 1793

"The public papers will inform you that Mr. Jefferson has resigned and that Mr. Randolph is appointed Secretary of State. . . The motives to Mr. Jefferson's resignation are not assigned, and are left open to the conjectures of a speculating world. I also am a speculator in the principles and motives of men's actions and may guess as well as others 1. Mr. Jefferson has a habit as well as a disposition to expensive living, and as his salary was not adequate to his luxury, he could not subdue his pride and vanity as I have done, and proportion his style of life to his revenue. 2. Mr. Jefferson is in debt as I have heard to an amount of seven thousand pounds before the war, so that I suppose he cannot afford to spend his private income in the public service. 3. Mr. Jefferson has been obliged to lower his note in politicks. Paine's principles when adopted by Genet, were not found so convenient for a Secretary of State. 4. He could not rule the roast in the ministry. He was often in a minority. 5. Ambition is the subtlest beast of the intellectual and moral field. It is wonderfully adroit in concealing itself from its owner, I had almost said from itself. Jefferson thinks he shall by this step get a reputation of a humble modest, meek man, wholly without ambition or vanity. He may even have deceived himself into this belief. But if the prospect opens, the world will see and he will feel, that he is as ambitious as Oliver Cromwell though no soldier. 6. At other moments he may mediate the gratification of his ambition; Numa was called from the forrests to be King of Rome. And if Jefferson, after the death or resignation of the President should be summoned from the familiar Society of Egeria, to govern the country forty years in peace and piety, so be it. 7. The tide of popular sentiment in Virginia runs not so rapidly in favour of Jacobinical feelings as it did—though the Party were a minority and carried every member at the last election, there are symptoms of increasing federalism in Virginia. A wise man like Jefferson foreseeth the evil and hideth himself—But after all I am not very anxious what were his motives.—Though his desertion may be a loss to us, of some talents, I am not sorry for it on the whole, because his soul is poisoned with ambition and his temper imbittered against the Constitution and Administration I think."

-⁂-

12. JOHN ADAMS TO ABIGAIL ADAMS FEBRUARY 3, 1793

"Mr. Jefferson was polite enough to accompany me so you see We are still upon Terms. I wish somebody would pay his Debt of Seven Thousand Pounds to Britain and the Debts of all his Countrymen and then I believe his Passions would subside his reason return; and the whole Man and his whole State become good Friends of the Union and its Govt. Silence however on this head, or at least great Caution."

-⁂-

13. JOHN ADAMS TO ABIGAIL ADAMS DECEMBER 26, 1793

"I am told Mr. Jefferson is to resign tomorrow. I have so long been in the habit of thinking well of his Abilities and general good dispositions, that I cannot but feel some regret at this Event: but his want of Candour, his obstinate Prejudices both of Aversion and Attachment his real Partiality in Spite of all his Pretensions and his low notions about many things have so nearly reconciled me to it, that I will not weep. Whether he will be chosen Governor of Virginia, or whether he is to go to France, in Place of Mr. Morris I know not. But this I know that is he is neglected at Monticello he will soon see a Spectre like the disgraced Statesman in Gill Blass, and not long afterwards will die, for instead of being the ardent pursuer of Science that some think him, I know he is indolent, and his soul is prisoned with Ambition. Perhaps the Plan is to retire, till his Reputation magnifies enough to force him into the Chair in Case. So be it, if it is thus ordained."

-⁂-

14. JOHN ADAMS TO ABIGAIL ADAMS JANUARY 6, 1794

"Jefferson went off Yesterday, and a good riddance of bad ware. I hope his Temper will be more cool and his Principles more reasonable in Retirement than they have been in office. I am almost tempted to wish he may be chosen Vice President at the next Election for there if he could do no good, he could do no harm. He has Talents I know, and Integrity I believe: but his mind is now poisoned with Passion Prejudice and Faction."

-⁂-

15. JOHN ADAMS LETTER TO THOMAS JEFFERSON MAY 11, 1794

"If I had Your Plantation and your Labourers I should be tempted to follow your Example and get out of the Fumum et Opes Strepitumque Romae ['the smoke, the wealth, the din of Rome'] which I abominate."

16. JOHN ADAMS TO ABIGAIL ADAMS DECEMBER 20, 1796

"It is supposed to be certain that Mr. Jefferson cannot be P[resident] and a narrow Squeak it is as the Boys say, whether he or [Thomas] P[inckney] shall be Daddy Vice: a Character that I shall soon relinquish whether I am or not the Person whom they now toast under the Title of 'The President elect. I have been Dady Vice long enough."

17. JOHN ADAMS TO ABIGAIL ADAMS DECEMBER 27, 1796

"According to present Appearances, Jefferson will be Daddy Vice, and between you and me I expect you will soon see a more ample Provision made for him, that he may live in Style and not be obliged to lodge at Taverns and ride in Stage Coaches. I See plainly enough that when your Washingtons and Adams's are stowed away our dear Country will have a gay Government. I cannot help these injudicious Extreams into which People will run, nor these invidious Partialities."

18. JOHN ADAMS TO ABIGAIL ADAMS JANUARY 1, 1797

"[Dr. Benjamin Rush] met Mr. Madison in the Street and ask'd him if he thought Mr. Jefferson would accept the Vice Presidency. Mr. Madison answered there was no doubt of that. Dr. Rush replied that he had heard Some of his Friends doubt it. Mr. Madison took from his Pocket a Letter from Mr. Jefferson himself and gave it to the Dr. to read. In it he tells Mr. Madison that he had been told there was a Possibility of a Tye between Mr. Adams and himself. If this should happen says he, I beg of you, to Use all your Influence to procure for me the Second Place, for Mr. Adams's Services have been longer, more constant and more important than mine, and Something more in the complimentary strain about qualifications &c."

19. JOHN ADAMS TO ABIGAIL ADAMS JANUARY 3, 1797

"Mr. Jeffersons Letter to Mr. Madison was Yesterday in the mouth of every one. It is considered as Evidence of his Determination to accept—of his Friendship for me–And of his Modesty and Moderation."

20. JOHN ADAMS TO ABIGAIL ADAMS JANUARY 5, 1797

"I dined yesterday with Dr. Rush who desired me to send the inclosed oration upon a weak Democrat whom he is pleased to call a great Philosopher, Astronomer, and Republican. We must put up with the Vagaries of our flighty friend."

21. JOHN ADAMS TO HENRY KNOX MARCH 30, 1797

"It is a delicate thing for me to speak of the late election. To myself, personally, 'my election' might be a matter of indifference or rather of aversion. Had Mr. Jay, or some others, been in question, it might have less mortified my vanity, and infinitely less alarmed my apprehensions for the public. But to see such a character as Jefferson, and much more such an unknown as Pinckney, brought over my head, and trampling on the bellies of hundreds of other men infinitely his superiors in talents, services, and reputation, filled me with apprehensions for the safety of us all. It demonstrated to me that, if the project succeeded, our Constitution could not have lasted four years.[63] We should have been set afloat, and landed, the Lord knows where."

22. JOHN ADAMS TO JAMES MCHENRY JUNE 1800

"Hamilton is an intriguant—the greatest intriguant in the World—a man devoid of every moral principle—a Bastard, and as much a foreigner as [Albert] Gallatin. Mr. Jefferson is an infinitely better man; a wiser one, I am sure, and, if President, will act wisely. I know it, and would rather be Vice President under him, or even Minister Resident at the Hague, than indebted to such a being as Hamilton for the Presidency."

63 Alexander Hamilton's plan to have Thomas Pinckney elected president

23. JOHN ADAMS TO ELBRIDGE GERRY DECEMBER 30, 1800

". . . Your anxiety for the issue of the election is, by this time, allayed. How mighty a power is the spirit of party! How decisive and unanimous it is! Seventy-three for Mr. Jefferson and seventy-three for Mr. Burr. May the peace and welfare of the country be promoted by this result! But I see not the way as yet. In the case of Mr. Jefferson, there is nothing wonderful; but Mr. Burr's good fortune surpasses all ordinary rules, and exceeds that of Bonaparte."

24. JOHN ADAMS TO *THE BOSTON PATRIOT* JUNE 8, 1809

"I have great reason to believe, that Mr. Jefferson came into office with the same spirit that I did—that is, with a sincere desire of conciliating parties, as far as he possibly could, consistently with his principles."

25. EXCERPT FROM JOHN ADAMS'S *CORRESPONDENCE ORIGINALLY PUBLISHED IN THE BOSTON PATRIOT* 1809

"I will not take leave of Mr. Jefferson in this place, without declaring my opinion that the accusations against him of blind devotion to France, of hostility to England, of hatred to commerce, of partiality and duplicity in his late negotiations with the belligerent powers, are without foundation."

26. JOHN ADAMS TO JOSEPH WARD JANUARY 8, 1810

"The Repeal of the taxes as well as the neglect of the Navy were great errors in my judgment as well as yours: but they were both national errors. The general voice of the Nation declared loudly for both. Jefferson was chosen for this very purpose: and his Administration was infinitely more popular than Washington's or mine. He had through his eight years a majority of six to one in the Senate and of two three or four to one in the House. The Nation stood by him to his last moment, absolutely petitioned him to serve again, and would have chosen him by a greater majority than Mr. Madison had. I know that Mr. Jefferson has studied Natural History more than politicks and has laboured more to acquire a sweetness of style than to capture the profound and muddy bottoms of the policy of modern or ancient nations: but I believe he sincerly acted for what he thought the public good, and I am not much disposed harshly to condemn him and still less to blacken him and slander him for being carried away by the public opinion which was at the same time so flattering and delightful to himself. Of all the measures of his Administration I the most cordially condemn the repeal of the Judiciary Law. I give him up to censure for this: but even here I must give up the Legislature and the nation with him. In this point the Nation ought, above all others, loudly and decidedly to have pronounced against him: because their Constitution and their own security demanded it."

27. JOHN ADAMS TO DR. BENJAMIN RUSH DECEMBER 25, 1811

"I perceive plainly enough, Rush, that you have been teasing Jefferson to write to me, as you did me some time ago to write to him. You gravely advise me 'to receive the olive branch,' as if there had been a war; but there has never been any hostility on my part, nor that I know, on his. When there has been no war, there can be no room for negotiations of peace.

Mr. Jefferson speaks of my political opinions; but I know of no difference between him and myself relative to the Constitution, or to forms of government in general. In measures of administration, we have differed in opinion. I have never approved the repeal of the judicial law, the repeal of taxes, the neglect of the navy; and I have always believed that his system of gunboats for a national defence was defective. To make it complete, he ought to have taken a hint from Moliére's *"Femmes précieuses,"* of his learned ladies, and appointed three of four brigades of horse, with a Major-General, and three of four brigadiers, to serve on board his galleys of Malta. I have never approved his non-embargo, or any non-intercourse, or non-importation laws.

But I have raised no clamors nor made any opposition to any of these measures. The nation approved them; and what is my judgment against that of the nation? On the contrary, he disapproved of the alien law and sedition law, which I believed to have been constitutional and salutary, if not necessary.

He disapproved of the eight per cent loan, and with good reason. For I hated it as much as any man, and the army, too, which occasioned it. He disapproved, perhaps, of the partial war with France, which I believed, as far as it proceeded, to be a holy war. He disapproved of taxes, and perhaps the whole scheme of my administration, &c., and so perhaps did the nation. But his administration and mine are passed away into the dark backwards, and are now of no more importance than the administration of the old Congress in 1774 and 1775.

We differed in opinion about the French Revolution. He thought it wise and good, and that it would end in the establishment of a free republic. I saw through it, to the end of it, before it broke out, and was sure it could end only in a restoration of the Bourbons, or a military despotism, after deluging France and Europe in blood. In this opinion I differed from you as much as from Jefferson; but all this made me no more of an enemy to you than to him, nor to him than to you. I believe you both to mean well to mankind and your country. I might suspect you both to sacrifice a little to the infernal Gods, and perhaps unconsciously to suffer your judgments to be a little swayed by a love of popularity, and possibly by a little spice of ambition.

In the point of republicanism, all the difference I ever knew or could discover between you and me, or between Jefferson and me, consisted,

1. In the difference between speeches and messages. I was a monarchist because I thought a speech more manly, more respectful to Congress and the nation. Jefferson and Rush preferred messages.
2. I held levees once a week, that all my time might not be wasted by idle visits. Jefferson's whole eight years was a levee.
3. I dined a large company once or twice a week. Jefferson dined a dozen every day.
4. Jefferson and Rush were for liberty and straight hair. I thought curled hair was as republican as straight.

In these, and a few other points of equal importance, all miserable frivolities, that Jefferson and Rush ought to blush that they ever laid any stress upon them, I might differ; but I never knew any points of more consequence on which there was any variation between us."

28. JOHN ADAMS TO DR. BENJAMIN RUSH DECEMBER 25, 1811

"You exhort me to 'forgiveness and love of enemies,' as if I considered, or had ever considered, Jefferson as my enemy. This is not so; I have always loved him as a friend. If I ever received or suspected any injury from him, I have forgotten it long and long ago, and have no more resentment against him than against you."

29. JOHN ADAMS TO DR. BENJAMIN RUSH DECEMBER 25, 1811

"But why do you make so much ado about nothing? Of what use can it be for Jefferson and me to exchange letters? I have nothing to say to him, but to wish him an easy journey to heaven, when he goes, which I wish may be delayed as long as life shall be agreeable to him. And he can have nothing to say to me, but to bid me make haste and be ready. Time and chance, however, or possibly design, may produce ere long a letter between us."

30. JOHN ADAMS TO THOMAS JEFFERSON FEBRUARY 3, 1812

"Sitting at My Fireside with my Daughter [Abigail Adams] Smith, on the first of February My Servant brought me a Bundle of Letters that struck my Eye had the Post Mark of Milton 23. Jany. 1812. Milton is the next Town to Quincy and the Post Office in it is but three Miles from my House. How could the Letter be so long in coming three miles? Reading the Superscription, I instantly handed the Letter to Mrs. Smith. Is that not Mr. Jeffersons hand? Looking attentively at it, she answered it is very likely it. How is it possible a Letter from Mr. Jefferson, could get into the Milton Post office? Opening the Letter I found it, indeed from Monticello in the hand and with the Signature of Mr. Jefferson: but this did not much diminish my Surprize. How is it possible a Letter can come from Mr. Jefferson to me in seven or Eight days? I had no Expectation of an Answer, thinking the Distance so great and the Roads so embarrassed under two or three Months. This History would not be worth recording but for the Discovery it made of a Fact, very pleasing to me, vizt. that the Communication between Us is much easier, surer and may be more frequent than I had ever believed or suspected to be possible."

31. JOHN ADAMS TO THOMAS JEFFERSON MAY 1, 1812

"I have uniformly treated the charges of corruption which I have read in newspapers and pamphlets and heard from the pulpit against you and Mr. Madison with contempt and indignation. I believe in the integrity of both, at least as undoubtingly as in that of Washington. In the measures of administration I have neither agreed with you or Mr. Madison. Whether you or I were right posterity must judge; I have never approved of non importations, non intercourses, or embargoes for more than six weeks. I never have approved and never can approve of the repeal of the taxes the repeal of the judiciary system, or the neglect of the Navy. You and Mr. Madison had as good a right to your opinions as I had to mine, and I must acknowledge the nation was with you, but neither your authority nor that of the nation has convinced me: nor, I am bold to pronounce will convince posterity."

32. JOHN ADAMS TO DR. BENJAMIN RUSH DECEMBER 27, 1812

"On the 16th. Jan. 1804 I wrote to a correspondent 'I wish Jefferson no ill: I envy him not. I Shudder at the calamities which I fear his conduct is preparing for his Country, from a mean thirst of popularity, an inordinate ambition, and a want of Sincerity.'"

33. JOHN ADAMS TO RICHARD RUSH NOVEMBER 24, 1814

"Mr. Jefferson lives at Monticello the lofty Mountain. I live at *Montezillo* a little Hill."

34. JOHN ADAMS TO JAMES LLOYD APRIL 5, 1815

"The halcyon days of New England prosperity were the first six years of Mr. Jefferson's administration. Was this felicity owing to the wisdom, the virtue, or the energy of Mr. Jefferson? Or was it the natural, necessary, and unavoidable effect of the universal peace and tranquility abroad and at home, and with universal nature, civilized and savage, entailed upon him by his predecessor, in spite of friends and enemies?"

35. JOHN ADAMS TO THOMAS JEFFERSON FEBRUARY 2, 1817

"I find that all our Young Gentlemen who have any *Nous,* and can afford to travel, have an ardent Curiosity to visit, what shall I say? the Man of the Mountain? The Sage of Monticello? Or the celebrated Philosopher and Statesman of Virginia? They all apply to me for Introduction. In hopes of softening asperities and promoting Union, I have refused none whom I thought Men of Sense."

36. JOHN ADAMS TO THOMAS JEFFERSON MAY 26, 1817

"I congratulate you and Madison and Monroe, on your noble employment in founding a University. From Such a noble Tryumvirate, the world will expect something very great and very new. But if it contains any thing quite original, and very excellent, I fear the prejudices are too deeply rooted to suffer it to last long, though it may be accepted at first. It will not always have three such colossal reputations to support it."

37. JOHN ADAMS TO THOMAS JEFFERSON NOVEMBER 10, 1823

"Your last letter was brought to me from the Post office when at breakfast with my family. I bade one of the misses open the budget; she reported a letter from Mr. Jefferson and two or three newspapers. A letter from Mr. Jefferson, says I, I know what the substance is before I open it. There is no secrets between Mr. Jefferson and me, and I cannot read it; therefore you may open and read it. When it was done, it was followed by a universal exclamation, The best letter that ever was written, and round it went through the whole table—How generous! how noble! How magnanimous! I said that it was just such a letter as I expected, only it was infinitely better expressed. A universal cry that the letter ought to be printed. No, hold, certainly not without Mr. Jefferson's express leave."

IV. JAMES MADISON ON THOMAS JEFFERSON

1. JAMES MADISON TO EDMUND RANDOLPH MAY 1, 1781

"A letter which I received a few days ago from Mr. Jefferson gives me a hope that he will lend his succor in defending the title of Virginia. He professes ignorance of the ground on which the report of the committee places the controversy. I have exhorted him not to drop his purpose, and referred him to you as a source of copious information on the subject. I wish much you and he could unite your ideas on it."

2. JAMES MADISON TO PHILIP MAZZEI JULY 7, 1781

"Governor Jefferson had a very narrow escape. The members of the Government rendezvoused at Stanton, where they soon made a House. Mr. Jefferson's year having expired, he declined a re-election, and General Nelson has taken his place."

3. JAMES MADISON TO EDMUND PENDLETON DECEMBER 25, 1781

"It gives me great pleasure to hear of the honorable acquittal of Mr. Jefferson. I know his abilities, & I think I know his fidelity & zeal for his Country so well, that I am persuaded it was a just one. We are impatient to know whether he will undertake the new service to which he is called."

4. JAMES MADISON TO THOMAS JEFFERSON JANUARY 15, 1782

"The result of the attack on your administration was so fully anticipated that it made little impression on me. If it had been consistent with your sentiments and views to engage in the service to which you were called, it would have afforded me both unexpected and singular satisfaction, not only from the personal interest I felt in it, but from the important aid which the interest of the State would probably have derived from it."

5. JAMES MADISON TO JAMES MADISON, SR. MAY 20, 1782

"If Mr. Jefferson will be so obliging as to superintend the legal studies of William I think he cannot do better than prosecute the plan he has adopted.[64] The interruption occasioned by the Election of Mr. Jefferson although inconvenient in that respect, is by no means a decisive objection against it."

6. JAMES MADISON TO EDMUND RANDOLPH JUNE 11, 1782

"Great as my partiality is to Mr. Jefferson, the mode in which he seems determined to revenge the wrong received from his country does not appear to me to be dictated either by philosophy or patriotism. It argues, indeed, a keen sensibility and strong consciousness of rectitude.[65] But this sensibility ought to be as great towards the relentings as the misdoings of the Legislature, not to mention the injustice of visiting the faults of this body on their innocent constituents."

7. JAMES MADISON TO EDMUND RANDOLPH AUGUST 13, 1782

"In compiling the evidence of our title, I suppose you will, of course, be furnished with all Mr. Jefferson's lights. I have lately seen a fact stated by him, which shows clearly the ideas entertained by Virginia with respect to her territorial limits subsequent to the resumption of the charter."

8. EXCERPT FROM JAMES MADISON'S *DEBATES IN THE CONGRESS OF THE CONFEDERATION, FROM NOVEMBER 4TH, 1782, TO FEBRUARY 13TH, 1783* NOVEMBER 12, 1782

"The reappointment of Mr. Jefferson as Minister Plenipo: for negotiating peace was agreed to unanimously and without a single adverse remark. The act took place in consequence of its being suggested that the death of Mrs. [Martha Wayles Skelton] Jefferson had probably changed the sentiments of Mr. J. with regard to public life, & that all the reasons which led to his original appointment still existed and indeed, had acquired additional force from the improbability that Mr. Laurens would actually assist in the negotiation."

64 Madison is referring to his younger brother William Taylor Madison, 1762-1843.

65 Jefferson had decided to take a sabbatical from public life.

9. JAMES MADISON TO THOMAS JEFFERSON AUGUST 11, 1783

"At the date of my letter in April I expected to have had the pleasure by this time of being with you in Virginia. My disappointment has proceeded from several dilatory circumstances on which I had not calculated. My journey to Virginia tho' still somewhat contingent in point of time cannot now be very long postponed. I need not I trust renew my assurance that it will not finally stop on this side of Monticello."

10. JAMES MADISON TO JAMES MADISON, SR. MAY 13, 1784

"Mr. Jefferson has been appointed an associate with Dr. Franklin and Mr. Adams in forming commercial treaties and will proceed immediately to Europe. He takes the place of Mr. Jay who is returning to America and who is to be the Secretary of F(oreign) affairs if he will accept the office."

11. JAMES MADISON TO THOMAS JEFFERSON MAY 15, 1784

"The arrangement which is to carry you to Europe has been made known to me by Mr. Short who tells me he means to accompany or follow you. With the many reasons which make this event agreeable, I cannot but mix some regret that your aid towards a revisal of our State Constitution will be removed. I hope however for your license to make use of the ideas you were so good as to confide to me, so far as they may be necessary to forward the object."

12. EXCERPT FROM JAMES MADISON'S "SPEECHES IN THE VIRGINIA CONVENTION" JUNE 12, 1788

"But the honorable member, in order to influence our decision, has mentioned the opinion of a citizen [Jefferson] who is an ornament to this state. When the name of this distinguished character was introduced, I was much surprised. Is it come to this, then, that we are not to follow our own reason? Is it proper to introduce the opinions of respectable men, not within these walls? If the opinion of an important character were to weigh on this occasion, could we not adduce a character equally great on our side? Are we, who (in the honorable gentleman's opinion) are not to be governed by an erring world, now to submit to the opinion of a citizen beyond the Atlantic? I believe, that were that gentleman now on this floor, he would be for the adoption of this constitution. I wish his name had never been mentioned. I wish every thing spoken here, relative to his opinion, may be suppressed if our debates should be published. I know that the delicacy of his feelings will be wounded, when he will see in print what has and may be said, concerning him on this occasion. I am, in some measure, acquainted with his sentiments on this subject. It is not right for me to unfold what he has informed me. But I will venture to assert, that the clause now discussed, is not objected to by Mr. Jefferson. He approves of it, because it enables the government to carry on its operations. –He admires several parts of it, which have been reprobated with vehemence in this house. He is captivated with the equality of suffrage in the senate, which the honorable gentleman [Mr. Henry] calls the rotten part of this constitution. But, whatever be the opinion of that illustrious citizen, considerations of personal delicacy should dissuade us from introducing it here."

13. JAMES MADISON TO EDMUND RANDOLPH JULY 2, 1788

"There are public letters just arrived from Jefferson. The contents are not yet known. His private letters to me & others refer to his public political views. I find that he is becoming more and more a friend to the new Constitution, his objections being gradually dispelled by his own further reflections on the subject. He particularly renounces his opinion concerning the expediency of a ratification by 9 & a refusal by 4 States, considering the mode pursued by Massachusetts as the only rational one, but disapproving some of the alterations recommended by that State. He will see still more room for disapprobation in the reconsideration of other States. The defects of the Constitution which he continues to criticize are the omission of a bill of right, and the principle of rotation at least in the Executive Department."

14. JAMES MADISON TO THOMAS JEFFERSON JANUARY 24, 1790

"I take for granted that you will before the receipt of this, have known the ultimate determination of the President on your appointment.[66] All that I am able to say on the subject is that a universal anxiety is expressed for your acceptance, and to repeat my declarations that such an event will be more conducive to the general good, and perhaps to the very objects you have in view in Europe, than your return to your former station."

66 On October 10, 1789 President George Washington informed Thomas Jefferson of the latter's appointment to serve as the nation's first Secretary of State.

15. JAMES MADISON TO EDMUND RANDOLPH, MARCH 21, 1790

"Mr. Jefferson is not yet [in New York City]. The bad roads have retarded him. We expect him today or tomorrow. I am this instant told he is come."

16. JAMES MADISON TO JAMES MONROE JUNE 1, 1790

"Mr. Jefferson has had a tedious spell of the head-ache. It has not latterly been very severe, but is still not absolutely removed."

17. EXCERPT FROM JAMES MADISON'S *SUBSTANCE OF A CONVERSATION WITH THE PRESIDENT* MAY 5, 1792

". . . with respect to Mr. Jefferson his extreme repugnance to public life & anxiety to exchange it for his farm & his philosophy made it doubtful with his friends whether it would be possible to obtain his own consent; and if obtained, whether local prejudices in the Northern States, with the views of Pennsylvania in relation to the seat of Government, would not be a bar to his appointment."

18. JAMES MADISON TO EDMUND PENDLETON DECEMBER 6, 1792

"It is probable that Mr. Jefferson will not remain very long in his public station; but it is certain that his retirement is not to be ascribed to the Newspaper calumnies which may have had that in view."

19. JAMES MADISON TO THOMAS JEFFERSON MAY 27, 1793

"I feel for your situation but you must bear it. Every consideration private as well as public requires a further sacrifice of your longings for the repose of Monticello, you must not make your final exit from public life till it will be marked with justifying circumstances which all good citizens will respect, & to which your friends can appeal. At the present crisis, what would the former think, what could the latter say? The real motives, whatever they might be would either not be admitted or could not be explained; and if they should be viewed as satisfactory at a future day, the intermediate effects would not be lessened & could not be compensated."

20. JAMES MADISON TO THOMAS JEFFERSON AUGUST 20, 1793

". . . This hurries me; And has forced me to hurry what will be inclosed herewith, particularly the last No. V, which required particular care in the execution. I shall be obliged to leave that & the greater part of the other Nos to be transcribed, sealed up & forwarded in my absence. It is certain therefore that many little errors will take place. As I cannot let them be detained till I return, I must pray you to make such corrections as will not betray your hand. In pointing & *erasures* not breaking the sense, there will be no difficulty. I have already requested you to make free with the latter. You will find more quotations from the Fed t. Dash them out if you think the most squeamish critic could object to them. In N°. 5. I suggest to your attention a long preliminary remark into which I suffered myself to be led before I was aware of the prolixity. As the piece is full long without it, it had probably better be lopped off. The propriety of the two last paragraphs claims your particular criticism. I would not have hazarded them without the prospect of your revisal, & if proper your erasure. That which regards Spain &c may contain unsound reasoning, or be too delicate to be touched in a Newspaper. The propriety of the last, as to the President's answers to addressers depends on the truth of the fact, of which you can judge. I am not sure that I have seen all the answers. My last was of the 12th, & covered the 2 first Nos. of H[elvidiu]s. I am assured that it was put into the post office on tuesday evening. It ought therefore to have reached you on saturday last."

21. JAMES MADISON TO THOMAS JEFFERSON DECEMBER 19, 1796

"The returns from N. Hampshire, Vermont, S. C., & Georgia are still to come in, & leave the event of the Election in some remaining uncertainty. It is but barely possible that Adams may fail of the highest number. It is highly probable, tho' not absolutely certain, that Pinkney will be third only on the list. You must prepare yourself therefore to be summoned to the place Mr. Adams now fills. I am aware of the objections arising from the inadequateness of the of the place to the sacrifices you would be willing to make to a greater prospect of fulfilling the patriotic wishes of your friends; and from the irksomeness of being at the head of a body whose sentiments are at present so little in unison with your own. But it is expected that as you had made up your mind to obey the call of your country, you will let it decide on the particular place where your services are to be rendered. It may even be said, that as you submitted to the election knowing the contingency involved in it, you are bound to abide by the event whatever it may be. On the whole, it seems *essential* that you should not refuse the station which is likely to be your lot. There is reason to believe, also, that your neighborhood to Adams may have a valuable effect on his councils particularly in relation to our external system. You know that his feelings will not enslave him to the example of his predecessor. It is certain that his censures of our paper system & the intrigues at new York for setting Pinkney above him, have fixed an enmity with the British faction. Nor should it pass for nothing, that the true interest of new england particularly requires reconciliation with France as the road to her commerce, add to the whole that he is said to speak of you now in friendly terms and will no doubt be soothed by your acceptance of a place subordinate to him. It must be confessed however that all these calculations are qualified by his political principles and prejudices. But they add weight to the obligation, from which you must not withdraw yourself."

22. JAMES MADISON TO JAMES MADISON, SR. MARCH 12, 1797

"I wrote you by the last mail, and add this by Mr. Jefferson. Lest my last letter should by any possibility have miscarried, I repeat my request that my name may not be suffered to get on the Pole for the County election. If Mr. Jefferson should call & say anything to counteract my determination I hope it will be regarded as merely expressive of his own wishes on the subject, & that it will not be allowed to have the least effect."

23. JAMES MADISON TO JAMES MONROE NOVEMBER 10, 1800

"In this region of, Country, the elections have exceeded our hopes. In this County, our of more than 350 votes, 7 only were on the wrong ticket. I hear that in Frederick, the Jefferson ticket prevailed in the proportion of 3 to 1."

24. JAMES MADISON TO JAMES MONROE NOVEMBER 10, 1800

"I cannot apprehend any danger of a *surprize* that would throw Mr. Jefferson out of the primary station. I cannot believe that any such is intended, or that a single *republican* vote would abandon him. The worst, therefore, that could possibly happen, would be a tie, that would appeal to the House of Representatives, where the candidates would certainly, I think, be arranged properly, even on the recommendation of the secondary one."

25. JAMES MADISON TO JAMES MONROE JANUARY 19, 1804

"The Spanish Minister at length broke the subject to me, in Stile of complaint, and with an appeal to the universal practice in Europe, as well as the preceding practice here, in support of the precedence of foreign Ministers & their families over those of the Country; and wished that the President's decision might be obtained & made known. You can judge of his distaste for such a subject. He thought it best nevertheless in order to put an end if possible to these little disquietudes which sometimes & with some tempers swell into serious embarrassments, that some decision as far as depended on him should be formed & communicated to the diplomatic gentlemen. The pêle mêle readily occurred as the most convenient in itself, and the most consonant to the principles of the Country. The Spanish & British Ministers were accordingly informed; that in all hospitable scenes such would be the practice, that on the arrival of a foreign Minister, as there must be a first visit, it would be expected from him, his family however receiving the first visit; and that on public occasions, such as an inaugural Speech, a place would be provided for the foreign & domestic Ministers with any others who might be invited on the part of the Govt; all of whom would in such place be in pêle mêle. On mentioning this to Mr. Merry, he went into a candid disclosure of his feelings, which I found had been deeply wounded, and a recital of causes, some of which had never been dreampt of. His first complaint was that altho' he had according to instructions waited on the President at his audience, in the fullest dress, he had been recd, not even in such a dress as the P. generally has on in the afternoon, but in plainer dress of the morning. He was told that the P. did not observe these distinctions of dress, more than others in this country, and that he had recd. a Danish Minister, the only one who had come hither during his administration, in the same plain manner. This circumstance therefore could not have deserved attention."

26. JAMES MADISON TO JAMES MONROE FEBRUARY 16, 1804

"I collect that the cavil at the pele mele here established turns much on the alledged degradation of ministers and envoies to a level with chargés d'affaires. The truth is, and I have so told Mr. Merry that this is not the idea; that the President did not mean to decide anything as to their comparative grades or importance; that these would be estimated as heretofore; that among themselves they might fix their own ceremonies, and that even at the President's table they might seat themselves in any subordination they pleased. All he meant was that no seats were to be designated for them, nor the order in which they might happen to sit to be any criterion of the respect them. It may not be amiss to recollect that under the old Congress, as I understand, and even in the ceremonies attending the introduction of the new Govt the foreign ministers were placed according to the order in which their Govt. acknowledged by Treaties the Independence of the U. States. In this point of view the pêle mêle is favorable both to G. B. and to Spain.

I have, I believe already told you that the President has discountenanced the handing first to the table the wife of a head of department applying the general rule of pele mele to that as to other cases.

The Marquis d'Yrujo joined with Merry in refusing an invitation from the President & has throughout made a common cause with him not however approving all the grounds taken by the latter. His case is indeed different and not a little awkward; having acquiesced for nearly three years in the practice against which he now revolts. Pichon being a chargé only, was not invited into the pretensions of the two Plent. He blames their contumacy but I find he has reported the affair to his government which is not likely to patronize the cause of Merry & Yrujo.

Thornton has also declined an invitation from the President. This shews that he unites without necessity with Merry. He has latterly expressed much jealousy of our views founded on little and unmeaning circumstances.

The manners of Mrs. M[erry] disgust both sexes and all parties."

27. JAMES MADISON TO JAMES MONROE NOVEMBER 9, 1804

"The President's message goes to you by this opportunity. The Tableau which it presents cannot fail to strengthen his administration at home, and to increase the weight of the United States abroad. His re-election is certain;"

28. JAMES MADISON TO JAMES MONROE MARCH 10, 1806

"The President is just taken with one of his afflicting periodical headaches. We hope, from some symptoms, that it will be less severe than his former ones."

29. EXCERPT FROM JAMES MADISON'S *FIRST INAUGURAL ADDRESS* MARCH 4, 1809

"It is my good fortune, moreover, to have the path in which I am to tread lighted by examples of illustrious services successfully rendered in the most trying difficulties by those who have marched before me. Of those of my immediate predecessor it might least become me here to speak. I may, however, be pardoned for not suppressing the sympathy with which my heart is full in the rich reward he enjoys in the benedictions of a beloved country, gratefully bestowed for exalted talents zealously devoted through a long career to the advancement of its highest interest and happiness."

30. JAMES MADISON TO THOMAS JEFFERSON FEBRUARY 12, 1819

"I have not been able to learn a tittle of your health since I saw you. It has, I hope, been entirely re-established. I congratulate you on the success of the Report to the Legislature on the subject of the University. It does not yet appear what steps have been taken by the Governor towards giving effect to the law."

31. JAMES MADISON TO JAMES MONROE FEBRUARY 13, 1819

"I have heard nothing from or of Mr. Jefferson since the visit of Dr. Eustis & myself to Monticello. I mentioned to you the state of his health at that time & our hopes that it would be soon entirely restored. It is to be wished that he may witness & guide the launching of the Institution which he put on the stocks, and the materials for which were supplied from his Stores."

32. JAMES MADISON TO RICHARD RUSH MAY 1, 1822

"I have not overlooked what you intimate in regard to Mr. Jefferson, who approaches his *octogenary climacteric* with a *mens sana in corpore sano.*[67] The vigor of both is, indeed, very remarkable at his age. He bears the lamented failure of our Legislature to enable the University to go into immediate action with a philosophic patience, supported by a patriotic hope that a succeeding Representation of the people will better consult their interest and character."

33. JAMES MADISON TO THOMAS RITCHIE AUGUST 13, 1822

"The Enquirer of the 6th very properly animadverts on the attempts to pervert the historical circumstances relating to the draught of the Declaration of Independence. The fact that Mr. Jefferson was the author, and the nature of the alterations made in the original, are too well known, and the proofs are too well preserved, to admit of successful misrepresentation."

34. JAMES MADISON TO TENCH COXE FEBRUARY 21, 1823

"I have forwarded the letters, with the printed papers, to Mr. Jefferson. I know well the respect which he, as well as myself, attaches to your communications. But I have grounds to believe, that with me, also, he has yielded to the considerations and counsels which dissuade us from taking part in measures relating to the Presidential election. And certainly, if we are to judge of the ability with which the comparative pretensions of the candidates will be discussed, by the samples sent us, the public will be sufficiently enabled to decide understandingly on the subject."

35. JAMES MADISON TO TENCH COXE MARCH 1, 1823

"Mr. Jefferson has just returned your two letters and papers. Supposing that I had yet to acknowledge them, he annexes a line requesting me to do it for him also; observing that it would hurt him much to leave unnoticed an old friend, and that the difficulty of using his pen with his crippled hand had compelled him to abandon writing but from the most urgent necessities. I find he thinks it best to abstain strictly

67 "Jefferson approaches 80 years old with a sound mind in a sound body."

from the Presidential election, not even expressing a sentiment on the subject of the Candidates."

-⊰⊱-

36. JAMES MADISON TO TENCH COXE NOVEMBER 3, 1823

"Your solicitude for the memory of Franklin, to whom his Country and the human race owe so much, is highly praiseworthy. I cannot say what particular knowledge Mr. Jefferson's files or recollections may possess that could aid in securing posthumous justice. A future day may unlock the former; but his great age, and his devotion of what remains of time and strength to the establishment of a University, forbid, I believe, any present expectations from him."

-⊰⊱-

37. JAMES MADISON TO A. B. WOODWARD SEPTEMBER 11, 1824

"You have fallen into a mistake in ascribing the Constitution of Virginia to Mr. Jefferson, as will be inferred from the animadversions on it in his "Notes on Virginia." Its origin was with George Mason, who laid before the committee appointed to prepare a plan a very broad outline, which was printed by the committee for consideration, and, after being varied on some points and filled up, was reported to the Convention, where a few further alterations gave it the form in which it now stands. The declaration of rights was subsequently from the same hand. The preamble to the Constitution was probably derived in great measure, if not wholly, from the funds of Mr. Jefferson, the richness of which in such materials is seen in the Declaration of Independence, as well as elsewhere. The plan of Mr. Jefferson, annexed to one of the editions of his "Notes on Virginia," was drawn up after the Revolutionary war, with a view to correct the faults of the existing Constitution, as well as to obtain the authentic sanction of the people."

-⊰⊱-

38. JAMES MADISON TO THE REVEREND FREDERICK BEASLEY DECEMBER 22, 1824

"You seem to have allotted me a greater share in this undertaking than belongs to me.[68] I am but one of seven managers, and one of many pecuniary benefactors. Mr. Jefferson has been the great projector and the mainspring of it."

-⊰⊱-

68 Founding the University of Virginia.

39. JAMES MADISON TO GEORGE THOMSON JUNE 30, 1825

"Your old friend, Mr. Jefferson, still lives, and will close his illustrious career by bequeathing to his Country a magnificent Institute for the advancement and diffusion of knowledge; which is the only Guardian of true liberty, the great cause to which his life has been devoted."

40. JAMES MADISON TO THOMAS JEFFERSON FEBRUARY 24, 1826

"I had noticed the disclosures at Richmond with feelings which I am sure I need not express, any more than the alleviation of them by the sequel. I had not been without fears that the causes you enumerate were undermining your estate. But they did not reach the extent of the evil. Some of these causes were, indeed, forced on my attention by my own experience. Since my return to private life, (and the case was worse during my absence in public,) such have been the unkind seasons, and the ravages of insects, that I have made but one tolerable crop of tobacco, and but one of wheat; the proceeds of both of which were greatly curtailed by mishaps in the sale of them. And having no resources but in the earth I cultivate, I have been living very much throughout on borrowed means. As a necessary consequence, my debts have swelled to an amount which, if called for at the present conjuncture, would give to my situation a degree of analogy to yours. Fortunately, I am not threatened with any rigid pressure, and have the chance of better crops and prices, with the prospect of a more leisurely disposal of the property, which must be a final resort."

41. JAMES MADISON TO THOMAS JEFFERSON FEBRUARY 24, 1826

"You do not overrate the interest I feel in the University, as the temple through which alone lies the road to that of Liberty. But you entirely do my aptitude to be your successor in watching over its prosperity. It would be the pretension of a mere worshiper, 'remplacer,' the Tutelary Genius of the sanctuary. The best hope is in the continuance of your cares, till they can be replaced by the stability and self-growth of the Institution. Little reliance can be put even on the fellowship of my services. The past year has given me sufficient intimation of the infirmities in wait for me. In calculating the probabilities of survivorship, the inferiority of my constitution forms an equation, at least, with the seniority of yours."

42. JAMES MADISON TO THOMAS JEFFERSON MARCH 10, 1826

"You cannot look back to the long period of our private friendship and political harmony with more affecting recollections than I do. If they are a source of pleasure to you, what ought they not [to] be to me? We cannot be deprived of the happy consciousness of the pure devotion to the public good with which we discharge the trusts committed to us. And I indulge a confidence that sufficient evidence will find its way to another generation, to ensure, after we are gone, whatever of justice may be withheld whilst we are here. The political horizon is already yielding, in your case at least, the surest auguries of it. Wishing and hoping that you may yet live to increase the debt which our Country owes you, and to witness the increasing gratitude which alone can pay it, I offer you the fullest return of affectionate assurances."

43. JAMES MADISON TO NICHOLAS P. TRIST JULY 6, 1826

"DEAR SIR,—I have just received your of the 4th. A few lines from Dr. Dunglison had prepared me for such a communication; and I never doubted that the last scene of *our* illustrious friend would be worthy of the life which it closed.[69] Long as this has been spared to his Country and to those who loved him, a few years more were to have been desired for the sake of both. But we are more than consoled for the loss by the gain to him; and by the assurance that he lives and will live in the memory and gratitude of the wise and good as a luminary of science, as a votary of liberty, as a model of patriotism, and as a benefactor of human kind. In these characteristics I have known him, and not less in the virtues and charms of social life, for a period of fifty years, during which there has not been an interruption or diminution of mutual confidence and cordial friendship for a single moment, in a single instance. What I feel, therefore, now, need not, I should say, cannot, be expressed. If there be any possible way in which I can *usefully* give evidence of it, do not fail to afford me an opportunity. I indulge a hope that the unforeseen event will not be permitted to impair *any* of the beneficial measures which were in progress or in project. It cannot be unknown that the anxieties of the deceased were for others, not for himself."

44. JAMES MADISON TO GOVERNOR JOHN TYLER AUGUST 4, 1826

"DEAR SIR,—I have received your favor of the 31 ult., inclosing a copy of your Oration on the death of Mr. Jefferson, in which you so eloquently express what is felt by all, as a

---

69 Thomas Jefferson

just tribute to his exalted name, and a grateful commemoration of his invaluable services to his Country and to his fellow-men."

45. JAMES MADISON TO SAMUEL H. SMITH NOVEMBER 4, 1826

"DEAR SIR,—I have received your letter of October 25th, requesting from me any information which could assist you in preparing a Memoir of Mr. Jefferson for the Columbian Institute. Few things would give me more pleasure than to contribute to such a task, and the pleasure would certainly be increased by that of proving my respects for your wishes. I am afraid, however, I can do little more than refer you to other sources, most of them probably already known to you.

It may be proper to remark that Mr. Thomas Jefferson Randolph, legatee of the manuscripts of Mr. Jefferson, is about to publish forthwith a Memoir left by his grandfather, in his own handwriting, and if not in every part intended by him for the press, is thought to be throughout in a state well fitted for it. The early parts are, I believe, purely, and, in some instances, minutely biographical; and the sequel, embracing a variety of matter, some of it peculiarly valuable, is continued to his acceptance of the Secretaryship of State under the present Constitution of the United States. Should this work appear in time, it would doubtless furnish your pencil with some of the best material for your portrait.

The period between his leaving Congress in 1776, and his mission to France, was filled chiefly by his labours on the Revised Code, by the preparation of his "Notes on Virginia," an *obiter performance*, his Governorship of that State, and his service as a member of Congress, and of the Committee of the States at Annapolis.

The Revised Code, in which he had a masterly share, exacted, perhaps, the most severe of his public labours. It consisted of 126 bills, comprising and recasting the whole Statutory Code, British and Colonial, then admitted to be in force, or proper to be adopted, and some of the most important articles of the unwritten law, with original laws on particular subjects; the whole adapted to the Independent and Republican form of Government. The work, though not enacted in the mass, as was contemplated, has been a mine of Legislative wealth; and a model, also, of statutory composition, containing not a single *superfluous* word, and preferring always words and phrases of a meaning fixed as much as possible by oracular treatises or solemn adjudications. His "Notes on Virginia" speak for themselves.

For his administration of the Government of Virginia, the latter chapters of the 4th Volume of Burk's history, continued by Girardin, may be consulted. They were written with the advantage of Mr. Jefferson's papers opened fully by himself to the author. To this may now be added the letter just published, from Mr. Jefferson to Major H. Lee, which deserves particular notice, as an exposure and correction of historical errors and rumored falsehoods, assailing his reputation.

His services at Annapolis will appear in the Journal of Congress of that date. The answer of Congress to the Resignation of the Commander-in-Chief, and important document, attracts attention by the shining traces of his pen.

His diplomatic agencies in Europe are to be found in the unpublished archives at Washington, or in his private correspondences, as yet under the seal of confidence. The memoir in the hands of his grandson will probably throw acceptable lights on this part of his history.

The University of Virginia, as a temple dedicated to science and liberty, was, after his retirement from the political sphere, the object nearest his heart, and so continues to the close of his life. His devotion to it was intense, and his exertions unceasing. It bears the stamp of his genius, and will be a noble monument of his fame. His general view was to make it a nursery of Republican patriots, as well as genuine scholars. You will be able to form some idea of the progress and scope of the Institution from the two inclosed Reports from the Rector for the Legislature of the State, (the intermediate Report is not at hand,) which, as they belong to official sets, you will be so good as to send back at your entire leisure. I may refer, also, to a very graphic and comprehensive Exposè of the present state of the University, lately published in the National Intelligencer, which will have fallen under your eye.

Your request includes "his general habits of study." With the exception of an intercourse in a session of the Virginia Legislature in 1776, rendered slight by the disparities between us, I did not become acquainted with Mr. Jefferson till 1779, when, being a member of the Executive Council, and he the Governor, an intimacy took place. From that date we were for the most part separated by different walks in public and private life till the present Government of the U. States brought us together; first, when he was Secretary of State and I a member of the House of Representatives, and next, after an interval of some years, when we entered in another relation the service of the U. States in 1801. Of his earlier habits of study, therefore, I cannot particularly speak. It is understood that whilst at College [William and Mary] he distinguished himself in all the branches of knowledge taught there, and it is known that he never ceased to cultivate them. The French language he had learned when very young, and became very familiar with it, as he did with the literary treasures which it contains. He read, and at one time spoke, the Italian, also, with a competent knowledge of the Spanish; adding to both the Anglo-Saxon, as a root of the English and an element in legal philology. The law itself he studies to the bottom, and in its greatest breadth, of which proofs were given at the Bar, which he attended for a number of years, and occasionally throughout his career. For all the fine arts he had a more than common taste; and in that of architecture, which he studies both in its useful and its ornamental characters, he made himself an adept; and [as?] the variety of orders and styles executed according to his plan, founded on the Grecian and Roman models, and under his superintendence, in the buildings of the University, fully exemplify. Over and above these acquirements, his miscellaneous reading was truly remarkable; for which he derived leisure from the methodical and indefatigable application of the time required for indispensable objects, and particularly from his rule of never letting the sun rise before him. His relish for books never forsook him, not even in his infirm years; and in his devoted attention to the rearing of the University, which led him often to express his regret that he was so much deprived of that luxury by the epistolary tasks which fell upon him, and which consumed his health as well as his time. He was certainly one of the most learned men of the age. It may be said of him, as has been said of others, that he was a walking library; and, what can be said but of few of such prodigies, that the genius of philosophy ever walked hand in hand with him.

I wish, sir, I could have made you a communication less imperfect. All that I can say beyond it is, that if, in the progress of your pen, any particular point should occur on which it may be supposed I could add any thing to your information from other sources, I shall cheerfully obey a call as far as may be in my power.

The subject of this letter reminds me of the "History of the Administration of Mr. Jefferson," my copy of which, with other things, disappeared from my collection during my absence from the care of them. It would be agreeable to me now to possess a copy; and if you can *conveniently* favor me with one, I shall be greatly obliged."

46. JAMES MADISON TO GENERAL LA FAYETTE NOVEMBER 1826

"You will never doubt that your happiness is very dear to me; and I feel the sentiment growing stronger as the loss of others dear to us both shortens the list to which we belong.

That which we have lately sustained at Monticello is irreparable, but was attended with every circumstance that could soothe us under it. I wish I was not obliged to add, "with one affecting exception." His family, so long in the lap of all the best enjoyments of life, is threatened with the contrast of pinching poverty. The expenses of his numerous household, his extensive hospitalities, and a series of short crops and low markets, to which are to be added old debts contracted in public service abroad, and new ones for which private friendship had made him responsible; all these causes together had produced a situation of which he seems not to have been fully aware, till it was brought home to his reflections by the calls of creditors, (themselves pressed by the difficulties of the times,) and by the impossibility of satisfying them without a complete sacrifice of his property, perhaps not even by that, at such a crisis. In this posture of things, he acquiesced in an appeal to the Legislature for the privilege of a lottery. This was granted, and arrangements made which promised relief, with a residuary competence for his beloved daughter and her children. The general sensation produced by the resort to a lottery, and by the occasion for it, unfortunately led some of his most enthusiastic admirers to check the progress of the measure by attempting to substitute patriotic subscriptions, which they were so sanguine as to rely on, till the sad event on the 4th of July benumbed, as it ought not to have done, the generous experiment; with a like effect, which ought still less to have happened, on the lottery itself. And it is now found that the subscriptions do not exceed ten or twelve thousand dollars, and the tickets but a very inconsiderable number, whilst the debts are not much short of one hundred thousand dollars; an amount which a forced sale, under existing circumstances, of the whole estate, (*negroes* included,) would not perhaps reach. Faint hope exist that renewed efforts may yet effectuate such a sale of tickets as may save something for the family; and fainter ones, that the Legislature of the State may interpose a saving hand. God grant it! But we are all aware of the difficulties to be encountered there. I well know, my dear sir, the pain which this melancholy picture will give you, by what I feel at the necessity of presenting it. I have duly adverted to the generous hint as to the East Florida location. But for any immediate purpose, it is, in any form whatever, a resource perfectly dormant, and must continue so too long for the purpose in question. Your allusion to it is, nevertheless, a proof of the goodness which dwells in your heart, and whenever known, will be so regarded. The urgency of particular demands has induced the executor, Thomas Jefferson Randolph, who is the legatee of the manuscripts, to undertake an immediate publication of a memoir, partly biographical, partly political and miscellaneous, left in the handwriting of his grandfather, the proceeds of which he hopes will be of critical use; and if prompt and extensive opportunities be given for subscriptions, there may be no disappointment. The work will recommend itself not only by personal details interwoven into it, but by *Debates in Congress* on the *question of* Independence, and other very important subjects coeval with its Declaration, as the debates were taken down and preserved by the illustrious member. The memoir will contain, also, very interesting views of the origin of the French Revolution, and its progress and phenomena. during his diplomatic residence in Paris, with reflections on its tendencies and consequences. A trial will probably be made to secure the copyright of the publication both in England and in France. In the latter case, your friendly counsel will of course be resorted to; and I mention it that you may, in the mean time, be turning the subject in your thoughts. The manuscripts of which the memoir makes a part are great in extent, and doubtless rich in matter; and *discreet* extracts may, perhaps, prove a further pecuniary resource, from time to time; but how soon, and in what degree, I have not the means of judging. Mrs. Randolph, with her two youngest children, left Montpellier some days ago on her way to pass the winter with Mrs. Coolidge. Such a change of scene had become essential to her health, as well as to her feelings. She has made up her mind for the worst results; a merit which quickens the sympathy otherwise so intense. She was accompanied by her son, Thomas J. Randolph, who will endeavour to make arrangements with the Northern printers for the volume to be published. It will be an octavo of about three hundred pages."

47. JAMES MADISON TO SAMUEL H. SMITH FEBRUARY 2, 1827

"DEAR SIR,—I have received, with your favor of January 24, a copy of your biographical memoir of Thomas Jefferson, delivered before the Columbian Institute; and I cannot return my thanks without congratulating the Institute on its choice of the hand to which the preparation of the memoir was assigned. The subject was worthy of the scientific and patriotic body which espoused it, and the manner in which it has been treated worthy of the subject. The only blemishes to be noted on the face of the memoir, are the specks in which the partiality of a friend betrays itself towards one of the names occasionally mentioned."

48. JAMES MADISON TO JOSEPH C. CABELL MARCH 18, 1827

"I am truly sorry for the failure of the Legislature to do what was so much due to the character of the State, and to the merits and memory of Mr. Jefferson. The footing on which the meetings of the Visitors are put is a valuable accommodation to them, as is the loan authorized an acceptable one to the creditors of the University. One of them was with difficulty dissuaded lately from appealing to the law for his debt. I hope they will all be a little patient now."

49. JAMES MADISON TO JOSEPH C. CABELL MARCH 18, 1827

"That a tariff for the encouragement of manufactures may be abused by its excess, by its partiality, or by a noxious selection of its objects, is certain. But so may the exercise of every constitutional power; more especially that of imposing indirect taxes, though limited to the object of revenue. And the abuse cannot be regarded as a breach of fundamental compact till it reaches a degree of oppression so iniquitous and intolerable as to justify civil war, or disunion pregnant with wars, then to be foreign ones. This distinction may be a key to the language of Mr. Jefferson, in the letter you alluded to. It is known that he felt and expressed strongly his disapprobation of the existing Tariff and its threatened increase."

50. JAMES MADISON TO NICHOLAS BIDDLE MAY 17, 1827

"DEAR SIR,—I thank you very sincerely for the copy of your 'Eulogium on Thomas Jefferson.' I have derived from it the peculiar pleasure which so happy a portraiture could not fail to afford one who intimately knew, and feelingly admired, the genius, the learning, the devotion to public liberty, and the many private virtues of the distinguished original. Ably and eloquently as the subject has been handled, all must see that it had not been exhausted; and you are, I am sure, alone in regretting that what remained for some other hand, fell into yours.

Pardon me for remarking that you have been led into an error, in the notice you take of the Revised Code provided for by the first Independent Legislature of Virginia. The Revisors were in number not three, but five, viz: Mr. Jefferson, Mr. Pendleton, Mr. Wythe, Col. Geo. Mason, and Col. Thomas L. Lee. The last died, and Col. Mason resigned; but not before they had joined in a consultative meeting. In the distribution of the work among the others, Mr. Wythe was charged with the British Statutes, Mr. Pendleton with the Colonial laws, and Mr. Jefferson with certain parts of the common law, and the new laws called for by the new state of the country.

The portion executed by Mr. Jefferson was, perhaps, the severest of his many intellectual labours. The entire Report, as a model of technical precision and perspicuous brevity, and particularly as comprising samples of the philosophical spirit which ennobled his Legislative policy, may, in spite of its Beccarian illusions, be worthy of a place among the collections of the society of which he was once the presiding member; and if a copy be not already there, it will be a pleasure to me to furnish one.

In page 9th of the Eulogium, I observe an erratum with respect to the age of Mr. Jefferson, when his summary of American Rights was penned; which the reader, however, may correct, by recurring to the date of his birth, previously mentioned, or adverting to his age afterwards mentioned, when the Declaration of Independence was drawn."

51. JAMES MADISON TO HENRY D. GILPIN OCTOBER 25, 1827

"DEAR SIR,—I was duly favored with yours of the 9th instant. accompanied by your 'Life of Thomas Jefferson,' which I have read with the double pleasure it affords; being valuable for its historic materials as well as for its biographical portrait of the highly distinguished individual."

52. JAMES MADISON TO HENRY D. GILPIN OCTOBER 25, 1827

"143 Hair not *red*, but between *yellow and red.*

144 Nose rather under, certainly not above, common size.

Broweris' bust in plaister, from his mode of taking it, will, probably, shew a perfect likeness.

I know not that I could give any aid to the use made of the public materials before you, or add any particular anecdotes not to be found in some of the obituary eulogies of Mr. Jefferson. I had, myself, but a very slight acquaintance with him, till he became Governor of Virginia, in 1779, at which time I was a member of the Executive Council, and so continued for some months thereafter. Should the proposed republication of your 'Sketch' not take place before the appearance of his papers understood to be in preparation for the press, they will doubtless avail you much when putting the last hand on it."

53. JAMES MADISON TO GENERAL LA FAYETTE FEBRUARY 20, 1828

"I wish I could give you fuller and better accounts of the Monticello affairs. Neither Virginia, nor any other State, has added to the provision made for Mrs. Randolph by South Carolina and Louisiana; and the lottery, owing to several causes, has entirely failed.

The property sold, consisting of *all* the items except the lands and a few pictures and other ornaments, was fortunate in the prices obtained. I know not the exact amount, but a balance of debt remains which, I fear, in the sunken value and present unsalableness of landed property, will require for its discharge a more successful use of the manuscripts proper for the press than is likely to be soon effected. A prospectus has been lately published by Mr. Jefferson Randolph, extending to 3 or 4 octavo volumes, and considerable progress is made, I understand, in selecting (a very delicate task) and transcribing (a tedious one) the materials for the edition. In this country, also, subscriptions in the extent hoped for will require time; and arrangements are yet to be made for cotemporary publications in England and France, in both of which they are, as they ought to be, contemplated. I have apprized Mr. Randolph of your friendly dispositions with respect to a French edition, &c.; for which he is very thankful, and means to profit by. From this view of the matter, we can only flatter ourselves that the result will be earlier than the promise, and prove adequate to the occasion. If the difficulties in the way of the enlarged plan of publication can be overcome, and the work have a sale corresponding with its intrinsic merits, it cannot fail to be very productive. A memoir making a part of it will be particularly attractive in France, portraying as it does the Revolutionary scenes, whilst Mr. Jefferson was in Paris. Is there not some danger that a censorship may shut the press against such a publication? I fear the translator will be obliged to skip over parts, at least; and those perhaps among the most interesting. . . .

. . . I was aware when I saw the printed letter of Mr. Jefferson, in which he animadverts on licentious printers, that if seen in Europe it would receive the misconstruction, or rather perversion, to which you allude. Certain it is that no man more than Mr. Jefferson regarded the freedom of the press as an essential safeguard to free Government, to which no man could be more devoted than he was; and that he never could, therefore, have expressed a syllable or entertained a thought unfriendly to it."

54. JAMES MADISON TO JAMES MAURY APRIL 5, 1828

"I am sorry I cannot give you a satisfactory account of the prospects for the Monticello family. The examples of South Carolina and Louisiana have been followed by no other States, not even by Virginia. The scheme of a lottery fell through entirely. The personal estate, except a few article of ornamental furniture, was sold better than was expected; leaving, however, a balance of debts, which a sale of the landed at this time would probably not meet. It is proposed to publish, at an early day, three or four volumes of Mr. Jefferson's manuscripts, which may prove a considerable resource, if circumstances should do justice to their intrinsic value."

55. JAMES MADISON TO NICHOLAS P. TRIST APRIL 23, 1828

"DEAR SIR,—I have received your favor of the 17th, and thank you for the copy of Mr. Jefferson's letter to Mr. Norvell, on the deceptive and licentious character of the press. My answer to the letter of General La Fayette, to the abuse abroad of that of Mr. Jefferson, in decrying the liberty of the press, appealed for an antidote to the known attachment of Mr. Jefferson to a free press, as a necessary guardian of free Government, to which no man could be more devoted than he was."

56. JAMES MADISON TO JOSEPH C. CABELL DECEMBER 5, 1828

"DEAR SIR,—I have received, though somewhat tardily, your letter of November 20. Since mine of the 10th acknowledged it, I have written you two others requesting further corrections of my remarks on the 'Tariff,' addressed in both instances to Edgewood, with a duplicate of the last forwarded to Richmond.

Has not the passage in Mr. Jefferson's letter to Mr. Giles, to which you allude, denouncing the assumptions of power by the General Government, been in some respects misunderstood? 'They assume,' he says, '*indefinitely*, that also over agriculture and manufactures.' It would seem that, writing confidentially, and probably in haste, he did not discriminate with the care he otherwise might have done, between an assumption of power and an abuse of power; relying on the term 'indefinitely' to indicate an excess of the latter, and to imply an admission of a *definite* or reasonable use of the power to regulate trade for the encouragement of manufacturing and agricultural products. This view of the subject is recommended by its avoiding a variance with Mr. Jefferson's known sanctions, in official acts and private correspondence, to a power in Congress to encourage manufactures by commercial regulations. It is not easy to believe that he could have intended to reject *altogether* such a power. It is evident from the context that his language was influenced by the great injustice, impressed on his mind, of a measure charged with the effect of taking the earnings of one, and that the most suffering class, and putting them into the pockets of another, and that the most flourishing class. Had Congress so regulated an impost for revenue merely, as in the view of Mr. Jefferson, to oppress one section of the Union and favor another, it may be presumed that the language used by him would have been not less indignant, though the tariff, in that case, could not be otherwise complained of than as an abuse, not as a usurpation of power; or, at most, as an abuse violating the spirit of the Constitution, as every unjust measure must that of every Constitution, having justice for a cardinal object. No Constitution could be lasting without an habitual distinction between an abuse of legitimate power and the exercise of a usurped one. It is quite possible that there might be a latent reference in the mind of Mr. Jefferson to the reports of Mr. Hamilton and Executive recommendations to Congress favorable to indefinite power over both agriculture and manufactures."

57. EXCERPT FROM JAMES MADISON'S *OUTLINE* SEPTEMBER 1829

"In No. XI of 'Retrospects,' [by Gov. Giles,] in the Richmond Enquirer of Sept. 8, 1829, Mr. Jefferson is misconstrued, or, rather, *misstated*, as making the State governments and the Government of the United States *foreign* to each other; the evident meaning, or rather, the express language of Mr. Jefferson being, 'the *States* are foreign to each other, in the portions of sovereignty not granted, as they were in the entire sovereignty before the grant,' and not that the State governments and the Government of the United States are foreign to each other. As the State governments participate in appointing the functionaries of the General Government, it can no more be said that they are altogether foreign to each other, than that the people of a State and its governments are foreign."

58. JAMES MADISON TO PROFESSOR GEORGE TUCKER APRIL 30, 1830

"DEAR SIR,—I have received yours of March 29, in which you intimate your purpose of undertaking a biography of Mr. Jefferson. It will be a good subject in good hands; and I wish you may succeed in procuring the means of doing full justice to both. I know not that I shall be able to make any important contributions. I was a stranger to Mr. Jefferson till he took his seat, in 1776, in the first Legislature under the Constitution of Virginia, formed in that year. The acquaintance with him then made was very slight. During a part of the time he was Governor I was a member of the Council. Our acquaintance then became intimate, and a friendship took place which was one for life.

From this sketch you will perceive that I can know nothing of the first half of his career; and during the other half the materials for a biographer are to be found chiefly in the public archives, and among his voluminous manuscripts, partly in print, partly in the hands of his legatee. All these, with the connecting links and appropriate reflections, cannot fail to supply what will make a work highly interesting in itself, and be a rich offering to a future historian.

I hope you will also find a due portion of the anecdotic spices and gems with which you will well know how to sprinkle such a work. Should any occur to me or be recalled by particular enquiries, it will give me great pleasure to comply with your wishes. Mr. Jefferson's letters to me amount to hundreds; but they have not been looked into for a long time, with the exception of a few of latter dates. As he kept copies of all his letters throughout the period, the originals of those to me exist, of course, elsewhere."

59. JAMES MADISON TO JOSEPH C. CABELL MAY 31, 1830

"Having never concealed my opinion of the nullifying doctrine of South Carolina, I did not regard the allusion to it in the Whig, especially as the manner of the allusion showed that I did not obtrude it. I should have regretted a publication of my letters, because they did not combine with the opinion the views of the subject which support it. I have latterly been drawn into a correspondence with an advocate of the doctrine, which led me to a review of it in some extent, and particularly to a vindication of the proceedings of Virginia in 1798-99, against the misuse made of them. You will see in vol. iii, page 429, of Mr. Jefferson's Correspondence, a letter to W. C. Nicholas, proving that he had nothing to do with the Kentucky resolutions of 1799, in which the word 'nullification' is found. The resolutions of that State in 1798, which were drawn by him, and have been republished with the proceedings of Virginia, do not contain that or any equivalent word."

60. JAMES MADISON TO EDWARD EVERETT SEPTEMBER 10, 1830

"DEAR SIR,—Since my last letter, in which I expressed a belief that there was no ground for supposing that the Kentucky Resolutions of 1799, in which the term 'nullification' appears, were drawn by Mr. Jefferson, I infer from a manuscript paper containing the term just noticed, that although he probably had no agency in the draft, nor even any knowledge of it at the time, yet that the term was borrowed from that source. It may not be safe, therefore, to rely on his to Mr. W. C. Nicholas, printed in his Memoir and

Correspondence, as a proof that he had no connexion with, or responsibility for, the use of such a term on such an occasion. Still, I believe that he did not attach to it the idea of a constitutional right in the sense of South Carolina, but that of a natural one in cases justly appealing to it."

61. JAMES MADISON TO MRS. MARGARET H. SMITH SEPTEMBER 1830

"I have received, my dear madam, the very friendly, and, I must add, very flattering letter, in which you wish from my own hand some reminiscence marking the early relations between Mr. Jefferson and myself, and involving some anecdote concerning him that may have a place in a manuscript volume you are preparing as a legacy for your son.

I was a stranger to Mr. Jefferson [till] the year 1776, when he took his seat in the first Legislature under the Constitution of Virginia, then newly formed; being at the time myself a member of that Body, and for the first time a member of any public Body. The acquaintance made with him on that occasion was very slight; the distance between our ages being considerable, and other distances much more so. During part of the time whilst he was Governor of the State, a service to which he was called not long after, I had a seat in the Council, associated with him. Our acquaintance then became intimate, and a friendship was formed which was for life, and which was never interrupted in the slightest degree for a single moment.

Among the occasions which made us immediate companions was the trip in 1791 to the borders of Canada, to which you refer. According to an understanding between us, the observations in our way through the northern parts of New York and the newly settled vicinity of Vermont, to be noted by him, were of a miscellaneous cast, and part at least noted on the birch bark of which you speak. The few observations devolving on me related chiefly to agricultural and economic objects. On recurring to them, I find the only interest they contain is in the comparison they may afford of the infant State with the present growth of the settlements through which we passed; and I am sorry that my memory does not suggest any particular anecdote, to which yours must have alluded.

The scenes and subjects which had occurred during the session of Congress which had just terminated at our departure from New York, entered of course into our itinerary conversations. In one of those scenes, a dinner party, at which both of us were present, I recollect now, though not perhaps adverted to then, an incident, which, as it is characteristic of Mr. Jefferson, I will substitute for a more exact compliance with your request.

The new Constitution of the U. States having been just put into operation, forms of Government were the uppermost topics everywhere, more especially at a convivial board; and the question being started as to the best mode of providing the Executive chief, it was, among other opinions, boldly advanced that a hereditary designation was preferable to any elective process that could be devised. At the close of an eloquent effusions against the agitations and animosities of a popular choice, and in behalf of birth, as, on the whole, affording even a better chance for a suitable head of the Government, Mr. Jefferson, with a smile, remarked that he had heard of a University somewhere in which the Professorship of Mathematics was hereditary. The reply, received with acclamations, was a *coup de grace* to the anti-republican heretic."

62. JAMES MADISON TO ROBERT WALSH JANUARY 25, 1831

"The situation of Mr. Jefferson during the critical period of the Presidential contest in the House of Representatives was equally marked by its peculiarity and its importance. He saw the whole Government in a state of convulsion; he saw the danger of an absolute interregnum in its Executive branch, the consequences of which could not be foreseen; he saw what he regarded the will of the people about to be trampled upon, and the party whose ascendency he believed to be of vital importance to the cause of Republican Government attempted to be broken down; whilst the escape from all these dangers presented to him was through pledges which might be stigmatized as an ambitious intrigue and a purchase of success at the expense of those principles and feelings which he avowed and held inviolable. Happily, the course of circumstances fulfilled his patriotic wishes without the sacrifice which the accomplishment of them had seemed to require.

The situation of Mr. Bayard was also peculiar and trying. He was justly struck with horror at the prospects of an interregnum in the Government, so full of evils and so fatal in its example; and he was scarcely less alarmed at the danger which threatened, what he held to be, a vital policy of his country. But holding, at the same time, in his hands the event on which every thing depended, he availed himself of the opportunity of terminating the crisis in a manner which prevented the calamity he most dreaded, and provided, as he believed, and adequate security against the other.

Before dismissing the subject, a word may be proper with respect to the charge in the publication against Mr. Jefferson, of leaving the memorandum referring to Mr. Bayard's deposition for posthumous use, when the means of refuting it might be lost.

The suit of Gillespie and Smith, which led to the deposition of Mr. Bayard, is said to have been a fictitious one, instituted for the purpose of obtaining and perpetuating testimony against the purity of Mr. Jefferson's conduct during the Presidential election of 1801. The cause, it is understood, never was brought to trial; and it is inferred, from a resort to the source which furnished the copies of the depositions of Mr. Bayard and General Smith, that the depositions were never published. Of their existence, however, (and in a custody supposed by Mr. Jefferson to be unfriendly,) and in the passage in that of Mr. Bayard testifying that he (Mr. Jefferson) had authorized General Smith to accede for him to certain conditions on which his election to the Presidency might be obtained, Mr. Jefferson, it seems, was apprized from some friendly quarter. With this knowledge of a shaft that might posthumously inflict a deep wound on his reputation, could he do less than provide a shield against it by recording with his own hand the falsity of the charge, and the affirmance of its falsity at the moment of his doing so, by the individual named as the authority for the charge? What is now before the public proves that a weapon was in reserve by which a posthumous assault on his reputation might be made; and if there be unfairness in the case let candor pronounce on which side it is chargeable—in that of Mr. Jefferson, not of the deponents, (doubtless involuntary,) but of the parties to the suit which rendered the precaution necessary."

63. JAMES MADISON TO JAMES K. PAULDING APRIL 1831

"With Mr. Jefferson I was not acquainted till we met as members of the first Revolutionary Legislature of Virginia, in 1776; I had, of course, no personal knowledge of his early life. Of his public career, the records of his country give ample information; and of the general features of his character, with much of his private habits, and of his peculiar opinions, his writing before the world, to which additions are not improbable, are equally explanatory. The obituary eulogiums, multiplied by the epoch and other coincidences of his death, are a field where some things not unworthy of notice may perhaps be gleaned. It may, on the whole, be truly said of him, that he was greatly eminent for the comprehensiveness and fertility of his genius, for the vast extent and rich variety of his acquirements, and particularly distinguished by the philosophic impress left on every subject which he touched. Nor was he less distinguished for an early and uniform devotion to the cause of liberty, and systematic preference of a form of

Government squared in the strictest degree to the rights of man. In the social and domestic spheres, he was a model of the virtues and manners which must adorn them."

-⊰⊱-

64. JAMES MADISON TO __________ TOWNSEND OCTOBER 18, 1831

"You ask 'whether Mr. Jefferson was really the author of the Kentucky Resolutions of 1799.' The inference that he was not is as conclusive as it is obvious, from his letter to Col. Wilson Carey Nicholas of September 5, 1799, which expressly declines, for reasons stated, preparing anything for the Legislature of that year.

Again, 'whether the father of the Mr. Nicholas referred to in the letter of December 11, 1821, as having introduced the resolutions of 1798 into the Kentucky Legislature, be not the same individual to whom Mr. Jefferson alludes as the brother of Col. Wilson Carey Nicholas, in a letter addressed to the latter on the 5th September, 1799, vol. iii, p. 420.' He was the elder brother, and his name George. He died prior to the Kentucky resolutions of 1799.

What might or would have been the meaning attached to the term 'nullify' by Mr. Jefferson, is to be gathered from his language in the resolutions of 1798 and elsewhere, as in his letter to Mr. Giles, December 25, 1825, viz, to extreme cases, as alone justifying a resort to any forcible relief. That he ever asserted a right in a single State to arrest the execution of an act of Congress, the arrest to be valid and permanent unless reversed by three-fourths of the States, is countenanced by nothing known to have been said or done by him. In his letter to Major Cartwright, he refers to a Convention as a peaceable remedy for conflicting claims of power in our compound Government; but whether he alluded to a convention as prescribed by the Constitution, or brought about by any other mode, his respect for the will of majorities, as the vital principle of Republican Government, makes it certain that he could not have meant a convention in which a minority of seven States was to prevail over seventeen, either in amending or expounding the Constitution.

Whether the debates in Kentucky on the resolutions of 1798-99 were preserved, and whether anything similar to the explanatory report in Virginia took place, are points upon which I have no information. If there be any contemporary evidence explanatory of the Virginia resolutions beyond the documents referred to in the letter of August, 1830, to Mr. Everett, it is not within my present recollection. It may doubtless exist in pamphlets or newspapers not yet met with, and still more in private letters not yet brought to light.

I have noticed, in a paper headed 'Nullification Theory,' published in the Richmond Enquirer of the 20th of September, views of Mr. Jefferson's opinions, which may perhaps throw light on the object of your letter."

65. JAMES MADISON TO NICHOLAS P. TRIST DECEMBER 1831

"To view the doctrine [nullification] in its true character, it must be recollected that it asserts a right in a single State to stop the execution of a federal law, although in effect stopping the law everywhere, until a Convention of the States could be brought about by a process requiring an uncertain time; and finally, in the Convention, when formed, a vote of seven States, if in favour of the veto, to give it a prevalence over the vast majority of seventeen States. For this preposterous and anarchical pretension there is not a shadow of countenance in the Constitution; and well that there is not, for it is certain that, with such a deadly poison in it, no constitution could be sure of lasting a year; there having scarcely been a year since ours was formed without a discontent in some one or other of the States, which might have availed itself of the nullifying prerogative. Yet this has boldly sought a sanction under the name of Mr. Jefferson, because, in his letter to Major Cartwright, he held out a Convention of the States, as, with us, a peaceable remedy, in cases to be decided in Europe by intestine wars. Who can believe that Mr. Jefferson referred to a Convention summoned at the pleasure of a single State, with an interregnum during its deliberations; and, above all, with a rule of decision subjecting nearly three-fourths to one-forth? No man's creed was more opposed to such an inversion of the republican order of things."

66. JAMES MADISON TO NICHOLAS P. TRIST MAY 1832

"Allowances also ought to be made for a habit in Mr. Jefferson, as in others of great genius, of expressing in strong and round terms impressions of the moment."

67. JAMES MADISON TO NICHOLAS P. TRIST DECEMBER 23, 1832

"It is remarkable how closely the nullifiers, who make the name of Mr. Jefferson the pedestal for their colossal heresy, shut their eyes and lips whenever his authority is ever so clearly and emphatically against them."

68. JAMES MADISON TO JUDGE BUCKNER THRUSTON MARCH 1, 1833

"Your letter of the 13th instant was duly received with a copy of Judge Cranch's Memoir of President Adams, to which is annexed your Latin epitaph, embracing the coincidences in the lives and deaths of him and of President Jefferson."

69. JAMES MADISON TO PROFESSOR GEORGE TUCKER JULY 6, 1833

"It is observable that Mr. Jefferson, in his letter of March 15, '89, says, 'this instrument [the Constitution of U. S.] forms us into *one State,* for certain objects,' &c. In a number of other places, if I mistake not, he speaks of the Constitution as making us one people and one nation for certain purposes. Yet his authority is made to support the doctrine that the States have parted with none of their sovereignty or nationality."

70. JAMES MADISON TO W. C. RIVES OCTOBER 21, 1833

"Mutius, in his anxiety to discredit the opinions of J. M., endeavours to discredit the 'Federalist,' in which he bore a part, by observing, 'that the work was no favourite with Mr. Jefferson.' Mutius is probably ignorant of, and will be best answered by, the fact that Mr. Jefferson proposed, that, with the Declaration of Independence, the Valedictory of General Washington, and the Resolutions and Report of 1798-99, the Federalist should be, as it now is, a text-book in the University. He describes it as 'being an authority to which appeal is habitually made by all, and rarely declined or denied by any, as evidence of the general opinion of those who framed and of *those who accepted* the Constitution of the United States, on questions as to its general meaning.' [He speaks of the Federalist 'as being, in his opinion, the best commentary on the principles of Government that ever was written.'. . .]."

71. JAMES MADISON TO MAJOR HENRY LEE MARCH 3, 1834

"The crisis at which I accepted the Executive appointment under Mr. Jefferson is well known. My connexion with it, and the part I had borne in promoting his election to the Chief Magistracy, will explain my yielding to his pressing desire that I should be a member of his Cabinet."

72. EXCERPT FROM JAMES MADISON'S *ON NULLIFICATION* 1835-36

"The amount of this modified right of nullification is, that a single State may arrest the operation of a law of the United States, and institute a process which is to terminate in the ascendency of a minority over a large majority in a republican system, the characteristic rule of which is, that the major will is the ruling will. And this new-fangled theory is attempted to be fathered on Mr. Jefferson, the apostle of republicanism, and whose own words declare that 'acquiescence in the decision of the majority is the vital principle of it.'"

73. EXCERPT JAMES MADISON'S *ON NULLIFICATION* 1835-36

"Well might Virginia declare, as her Legislature did by a resolution of 1833, that the resolutions of 1798-99 gave no support to the nullifying doctrine of South Carolina. And well may the friends of Mr. Jefferson disclaim any sanction to it or to any *constitutional* right of nullification from his opinions. His meaning is fortunately rescued from such imputations by the very document procured from his files and so triumphantly appealed to by the nullifying partisans of every description. In this document the remedial right of nullification is expressly called a *natural* right, and, consequently, not a right derived from the Constitution, but from abuses or usurpations, releasing the parties to it from their obligation."

74. JAMES MADISON TO GEORGE TUCKER JUNE 27, 1836

"Apart from the value put on such a mark of respect from you in a dedication of your 'Life of Mr. Jefferson' to me, I could only be governed in accepting it by my confidence in your capacity to do justice to a character so interesting to his country and to the world; and, I may be permitted to add, with whose principles of liberty and political career mine have been so extensively congenial."

V. JAMES MONROE ON THOMAS JEFFERSON

1. JAMES MONROE TO THOMAS JEFFERSON SEPTEMBER 9, 1780

"DEAR SIR,—Your kindness & attention to me in this & a variety of other instances has really put me under such obligations to you that I fear I shall hardly ever have it in my power to repay them. But believe me in whatever situation of life ye chance of fortune may place me, no circumstance can happen wch. will give me such pleasure or make me so happy, at present or during my progress thro' life, as to have it in my power to convince you of ye proper impressions they have made on me. A variety of disappointments with respect to ye prospects of my private fortune previous to my acquaintance with your Excellency, upon w'ch I had built as on ground w'ch co'd not deceive me, & w'ch fail'd in a manner w'ch co'd not have been expected, perplex'd my plan of life & expos'd me to inconveniences w'ch had nearly destroy'd me. In this situation had I not form'd a connection with you I sho'd most certainly have retir'd from society with a resolution never to have enter'd on ye stage again. I co'd never have prevail'd on myself to have taken an introduction to ye Country, or to have deriv'd any advantages or even to have remain'd in connection with one by whom I felt myself injur'd, but whose near relationship & situation in life put it in his power to serve me. In this situation you became acquainted with me & undertook ye direction of my studies & believe me I feel that whatever I am at present in ye. opinion of others or whatever I may be in the future has greatly arisen from y'r friendship. My plan of life is now fix'd, has a certain object for its views & does not depend on other chance or circumstance further that ye same events may effect ye. publick at large. In ye late instance when we were threatened by an invasion from ye south, our prospects were so gloomy & ye. danger so imminent that I thought it ye duty of every citizen to turn out & bear a part in repelling ye invasion. The attention of y'r Excellency & Council paid me in calling on me to perform ye. duties of so important a trust as so critical a time if it had gone no further than intimating ye. good opinion you severally entertain'd of me, I knew did me honor & gave me more pleasure than any pecuniary compensation I cod. possibly derive from it. I was happy in undertaking ye charge with a view of performing some service to ye country& also of assuring you, that even in an affair w'ch had so distant a relation to you, how effectually you might command my small services. My plan of taking nothing for any little service I might do ye publick in this cause did not commence with my late employment: during ye. greater part of my service in ye. army I had not my expenses borne, I as in this instance, I have only acted ye part w'ch ye opinion of ye duty I owe to ye publick dictated & w'ch many worthy Republicans are now acting without even a similar compensation, it is my wish not to deviate from it. Under ye present direction my prospects are fix'd & altho' my private fortune is but small still it is sufficient for my maintenance in ye pursuit of them... You will forgive ye liberty I have taken in writing you a letter of this kind. Y'r kindness has really led me into it. & at ye same time it enables me to explain some part of my conduct I am happy that it gives me an opportunity of assuring you how just a sense I have of y'r good offices."

2. JAMES MONROE TO THOMAS JEFFERSON JUNE 18, 1781

"DEAR SIR,—I some time since address'd a letter to you from a small estate of mine in King George wither I had retir'd to avoid ye enemy from ye one I lately dispos'd of on ye Patommack river. I had then ye pleasure to congratulate you on ye safe retreat from Richmond to Charlottesville & anticipated ye joy y'r self & family must have felt on y'r arrival at Monticello from wh. ye misfortune of ye times has long separated you. I lament y'r felicity on that head was of but short duration. I hope howe'er that neither y'rself nor Mrs. Jefferson has sustain'd injury from these obtrusions of ye enemy... Wither you continue in your determination to retire from office I hope to see both y'rself & family in ye course of ye year. If we [*mutilated*] & in ye former instance I sho'd find you at Stanton on my way to ye Springs. Otherwise God knows where we shall be. Be so kind as to make my best respects to Mrs. Jefferson & believe me with ye great esteem & regard yr. friend & servant, Jas. Monroe."

3. JAMES MONROE TO THOMAS JEFFERSON OCTOBER 1, 1781

"DEAR SIR,—I propos'd to myself the pleasure of visiting y'r self & family before this at Monticello but ye prospects below & ye arrival of Gen'l Washington in ye State induc'd me to postpone ye trip of pleasure to ye less agreeable one..."

4. JAMES MONROE TO THOMAS JEFFERSON OCTOBER 1, 1781

"I sho'd be happy to wait on you before I sail & shall be sincerely sorry to leave ye continent without wishing y'r self & family health & happiness in person, but as we sail ye 10th or 12th of next month from some port south of Portsmouth & I have much business to transact in these days I shall be at home, am unfortunately depriv'd of that pleasure. I have to desire of you a letter to each of our Ministers & also y'r advice upon ye plan I had better pursue as also where I had better visit. Since my return from Richm'd I have liv'd a very sedentary life upon a small estate I have in King Georges in course of w'h time have read all ye books you mention on ye subject of law."

5. JAMES MONROE TO THOMAS JEFFERSON MAY 6, 1782

"DEAR SIR,—Mr. Short being just setting out for Monticello I am happy to take ye opportunity to assure you how sincerely I thank you for ye late instance of y'r kindness and attention to me w'h I particularly value as a testimony of y'r. regard for me, & at ye same time to assure you that nothing but a series of disappointments in ye vessels I had appointed to sail in, depriv'd me of ye opportunity of availing myself in that instance of ye advantage it w'd have given me. Mr. Short will inform you of my appointm't in ye House, upon declining ye other plan, & how very anxiously I wish y'r. arrival & how very sincerely I join ye better part of this community in my desire that a few days more will give us y'r. aid in ye House & Society to y'r. friends."

6. JAMES MONROE TO THOMAS JEFFERSON MAY 11, 1782

"It is publickly said here that ye people of y'r country inform'd you in times of less difficulty & danger than ye present to please you, but that now they had call'd you forth into publick office to serve themselves. This is a language w'ch has been often us'd in my presence & you will readily conceive that as it furnishes those who argue on ye fundamental maxims of a republican government with ample field for declamation, the conclusion has always been, you sho'd not decline ye service of yr country. The present is generally conceiv'd to be an important era w'ch of course makes y'r attendance particularly necessary, & as I have taken ye liberty to give you ye publick opinion & desire upon this occasion, & as I am warmly interested in whatever concerns ye publick interest or has relation to you, it will be unnecessary to add it is earnestly ye desire of, Dear Sir, y'r sincere friend and servant..."

7. JAMES MONROE TO THOMAS JEFFERSON MAY 14, 1784

"I very sensibly feel your absence not only in the solitary situation in w'h you have left me but upon many other accounts."

8. JAMES MONROE TO THOMAS JEFFERSON DECEMBER 14, 1784

"It seems to be an opinion generally given into that a minister shall be appointed to the Court of Britain. That one shall also be appointed to take the place of Franklin; whom the former will be, is altogether incertain but I think it beyond a doubt you will be the latter. It is also probable that you may be appointed to negotiate that particular business with Spain but this is only probable. If Franklin hath left France it may be proper you shod not leave the court in case of that appointment. The French gentn here are very desirous of it."

9. JAMES MONROE TO JAMES MADISON MARCH 6, 1785

"I suppose Jefferson will shortly be appointed in the room of Franklin to the court of France."

10. JAMES MONROE TO THOMAS JEFFERSON AUGUST 15, 1785

"How is Miss Patsy? How is Short? How are they pleas'd with France? I must observe that Congress seem to expect the court of France will send a Minister here. To visit you wod. give me infinite pleasure. Whether I shall be able or not depends on circumstances. If I do it will be in the Spring after Congress adjourn or at least the most importt. business is finish'd."

11. JAMES MONROE TO THOMAS JEFFERSON JANUARY 19, 1786

"Accept my acknowledgements for yr. book wh. I have read with great pleasure & improvement & be assur'd I will keep it as private as you might wish, until you shall consent to its publication wh. I hope will be the case. [70] I shod. suppose the observations you have made on the subject [of slavery] you allude to wd. have a very favorable effect, since no consideration wd. induce them but a love for the rights of man & for your country. Whether I shall be able to visit you is still doubtful. My dependence is almost altogether on the bar...the sooner I return to it the better it will be for me."

70 Monroe is referencing Jefferson's *Notes on Virginia* which he had sent to Monroe with an injunction of secrecy.

12. JAMES MONROE TO THOMAS JEFFERSON MAY 11, 1786

"You will be supris'd to hear that I have form'd the most interesting connection in human life, with a young lady in this town, as you know my plan was to visit you before I settled myself. But having form'd an attachment to this young Lady (a Miss Kortright, the daughter of a gentn. of respectable character & connections in this State tho' injured in his fortunes by the late war) I have found that I must relinquish all other objects not connected with her."

13. JAMES MONROE TO THOMAS JEFFERSON JULY 27, 1787

"Mrs. Monroe hath added a daughter to our society who tho' noisy, contributes greatly to its amus'ment. She is very sensibly impress'd with your kind attention to her, & wishes an opportunity of shewing how highly she respects & esteems you."

14. JAMES MONROE TO THOMAS JEFFERSON JULY 27, 1787

"You mentioned in yr last the injury you had sustain'd in yr. wrist. How did it happen? I hope you found yr trip to the south of advantage—yr. Daughters I hope are well—nothing be assur'd will give me more pleasure than to hear from you frequently. If I can be of service in yr private affrs. in any line…I beg you to command me. It will always be convenient for me to attend to anything of that kind, either in person or by a suitable messenger."

15. JAMES MONROE TO THOMAS JEFFERSON APRIL 10, 1788

"DEAR SIR,—I must depend on your kindness to pardon my omission in not writing you oftener, for I will not pretend to justify it. I shod. have wrote you as before, and can give no satisfactory reason even to myself why I have not, for that my communications will not be of much importance I do not urge as an excuse. I will however make amends in the future."

16. JAMES MONROE TO JAMES MADISON OCTOBER 26, 1788

"I have lately clos'd a bargain with Colo. Nicholas for his property in Charlotteville & 300 acres contiguous to it, within one mile…I shall not move to it I believe; but feel a pleasure in having it in my power to take a residence so convenient to Mr. Jefferson when it may suit me."

17. JAMES MONROE TO THOMAS JEFFERSON FEBRUARY 15, 1789

"It has always been my wish to acquire property near Monticello. I have lately accomplish'd it by the purchase of Colo. G. Nicholas improvements in Charlotteville & 800 acres of land within a mile, on the road to the R. fish Gap...Whether to move up immediately or hereafter when I shall be so happy as to have you as a neighbor I have not determin'd. In any event it puts it within my reach to be contiguous to you when the fatigue of publick life, shod. dispose you for retirement, and in the interim will enable me in respects to your affairs, as I shall be frequently at Charlottville as a summer retreat, and in attendance on the district court there to render you some service. You will I doubt not command me with that freedom the pleasure I shall have in executing your desires will authorize."

18. JAMES MONROE TO THOMAS JEFFERSON MARCH 5, 1790

"Mr. Jefferson is in town & will sit out in a day or two for New York—his daughter has been lately married to Mr. Randolf...".

19. JAMES MONROE TO THOMAS JEFFERSON JUNE 17, 1791

"Upon political subjects we perfectly agree, & particularly in the reprobation of all measures that may be calculated to elevate the government above the people, or place it in any respect without its natural boundary."

20. JAMES MONROE TO THOMAS JEFFERSON JULY 25, 1791

"The contest of Burke & Paine, as reviv'd in America with the different publications on either side is much the subject of discussion in all parts of this State. Adams is universally believ'd to be the author of Publicola & the principles he avows, as well as those of Mr. B. as universally reprobated. The character of the public officers is likewise pretty well known. At first it was doubted whether you wod. not be compell'd to give your sentiments fully to the publick,—whether a respect for yourself & the publick opinion wod. not require it of you. Whilst the fever was at the highest opinion preponderated in favor of it. At present it appears unsettled, especially as Adams is not the avow'd author of Publicola, and so many writers have taken up the subject in your favor. Your other engagements wh. employ so much of yr. time necessarily, are certainly to be taken into the calculation & must have great weight. The publick opinion however will before long fully disclose itself on the subject of government, and as an opportunity has & is in some measure offer'd you to give the aid of yr. talents & character to the republican scale, I am aware you must have experienc'd some pain in repressing yr. inclinations on the subject. Your sentiments indeed, if they had been previously question'd, are made known as well by the short note prefix'd to Paines pamphlet, as a vol: cod. do it."

21. JAMES MONROE TO THOMAS JEFFERSON SEPTEMBER 3, 1793

"I have been long sensible that yr. departure,[71] & especially since the publick mind has been so much agitated, wod. be severely felt & vehemently opposed by a particular character. If I mistake not he fears to be left exposed, in the society of those who would be left behind with him after yr. departure. If yr. opinions had more weight upon the questions agitated, I shod. believe the desire for yr. continuance was not dictated by self-love. Permit me to add that I consider yr. situation, the most important & interesting that can be conceived. Its importance is felt by the opposite party in such a degree that altho in one view they wod. be gratified by yr. retreat, yet they fear greater injury to themselves, from that event than yr. continuance, and therefore wish it. They know the solidity of yr. principles founded on reason & reflection, and in case the republican party shod. pass that boundary, count upon yr. restraining them; because they well know that that party repose an unlimited confidence in you."

22. JAMES MONROE TO THOMAS JEFFERSON MARCH 3, 1794

"DEAR SIR,—The avidity with which I knew you sought retirement and peace, undisturbed by political occurrences, with the further consideration that no event of any importance had taken place since you left us, prevented my trespassing on you sooner. I am perfectly satisfied you will find in that retirement a contentment & tranquility not to be hoped for in publick life. And yours will be the greater because you carry to it, notwithstanding the importance and even turbulent scenes you have passed through, not only the approbation of yr. own heart, & of yr. countrymen generally, but the silence & of course the constrained approbation of yr. enemies."

71 Monroe is writing about Thomas Jefferson's desire to resign as President Washington's Secretary of State, which he later did on December 31, 1793.

23. JAMES MONROE TO THOMAS JEFFERSON MARCH 3, 1794

"I look forward with pleasure to the period, and it shall be no distant one, when I shall occupy as your neighbor the adjoining farm. To this end all my plans will hereafter have an undeviating reference. . .".

24. JAMES MONROE TO THOMAS JEFFERSON JUNE 17, 1794

"DEAR SIR,—The urgent pressure of the Executive for my immediate departure has deprived me of the pleasure of seeing you before I sailed.[72] I sincerely regret this for many reasons but we can not control impossibilities—will you forward me a cypher, & letters for yr. friends remaining in Paris to the care of Mr. R[andolph] as soon as possible, they may probably reach Paris as soon as I shall—I beg you to add whatever occurs which may be useful where I am going to the cause in which I am engaged, or to myself in advocating it. Being well acquainted with the theatre on which I am to act, it will be much yr. power to give me hints of that kind which may be serviceable."

25. JAMES MONROE TO THOMAS JEFFERSON SEPTEMBER 7, 1794

"I rely upon yr. self & Mr. [Joseph] Jones in planning the many little tho' very important matters for me abt. my farm. Such as fixing the place for my house orchards & the like. It will not be very long before we join you...".

26. JAMES MONROE TO JAMES MADISON JUNE 13, 1795

"I beg of you in particular to show my communications always to Mr. Jefferson, who I suspect declines intentionally a correspondence from a desire to enjoy free from interruption the comforts of private life."

27. JAMES MONROE TO THOMAS JEFFERSON JUNE 27, 1795

"We wish most sincerely to get back & shall certainly do it, as soon as a decent respect for appearances will permit, especially if the present system of policy continues. I wish much to hear from you having written you several times but recd. not a line since my

72 Monroe was appointed as United States Minister to France.

appointment here. Is there anything in this quarter you wish to command of books or any other; or can I serve you in any respect whatever? you will of course command me if I can be serviceable."

28. JAMES MONROE TO THOMAS JEFFERSON NOVEMBER 18, 1795

"DEAR SIR,—Your favor of the 26 of May did not reach me until lately, owing as I presume to its having been committed to some private hand and by whom it was retained to be delivered personally until that prospect was abandoned. I was extremely gratified by it as it led me into a society which is very dear to me & often uppermost in my mind. I have, indeed, much to reproach myself for not having written you and others of our neighbors more frequently, but I have relied much on you not only to excuse me personally, but to make my excuse to others, by assuring them how little of my time remains from publick & other duties, for those with whom by the strong claims of friendship I have a right to take liberties. Before this, however, you have doubtless recd. mine of June last and wch. gave a short sketch of affrs. here, so that culpable as I am, still I am less so than I might have been.

I accept with great pleasure your proposal to forward my establishment on the tract adjoining you, in the expectation, however, that you will give yourself no further trouble in it than by employing for me a suitable undertaker who will receive from you the plan he is to execute, that you will draw on me for the money to pay him, & make my plantation one of the routes you take when you ride for exercise, at which time you may note how far the execution corresponds with the plan. With this view I shall look out for a model to be forwarded you as soon as possible, subjecting it to yr. correction, & give you full power to place my house orchards &c. where you please, and to draw on me by way of commencement for the sum of 1,000 dols. to be paid where you please 3 months after it is presented."

29. JAMES MONROE TO THOMAS JEFFERSON NOVEMBER 18, 1795

"You have I presume seen the new [French] constitution & will I doubt not concur with me that altho' defective when tested by those principles which the light of our hemisphere has furnished, yet it is infinitely superior to any thing ever seen before on this side of the Atlantic."

30. JAMES MONROE TO JAMES MADISON JANUARY 20, 1796

"Mr. Jefferson proposes to have a house built for me on my plantation near him & to wh. I have agreed under conditions that will make the burden as light as possible upon him. For this purpose I am about to send 2 plans to him submitting both to his judgment & contemplate accepting the offer of a skilful mason here who wishes to emigrate & settle with us, to execute the work. I wish yrself & Mr. Jones to see the plans & council with Mr. Jefferson on the subject."

31. JAMES MONROE TO JAMES MADISON JULY 5, 1796

"I most earnestly hope that Mr. Jefferson will be elected and that he will serve. If he is elected every thing will most probably be right here from that moment and afterwards on the other side of the channel. And in my opinion there never was such an opportunity offered for the acquisition of fame in the restoration of national credit abroad and at home as is now present presented, independent of the gratification an honest mind will always feel in rendering useful service to his country. He will be able at the same time that he secures the preponderating republican councils and gives stability to republican government, to conciliate the well meaning of the other party and thus give peace to his country."

32. JAMES MONROE TO JAMES MADISON JULY 30, 1796

"I rejoice that you pay attention to the improvement of my farm near you, since we look to it as a place of comfort from the unquiet theatre on wch. we now stand; for to me & in more views than one it has been a very unquiet one indeed."

33. JAMES MONROE TO THOMAS JEFFERSON JULY 12, 1797

"I think you should acknowledge your letter to Mazzei stating that it was a private one and brought to public view without your knowledge or design; that the man to whom it was addressed had lived long as your neighbour & was now in Pisa whither it was addressed: that you do think that the principles of our Revolution and of Republican government have been substantially swerved from of late in many respects; have often expressed this sentiment which as a free man you had a right to express in your public places & in the walks of private life &c. according to the letter: That you declined saying anything about it till you got home to examine how correct the letter was. This brings the question before the public & raises the spirits of the honest part of the community."

34. JAMES MONROE TO THOMAS JEFFERSON OCTOBER 15, 1797

"DEAR SIR,—I shall send Mr. Bache to-morrow about two. thirds of my narrative and the residue by the next post…It becomes necessary that I give the publication a title, and therefore I wish yr. opinion upon that point. I subjoin one wch. is subject to your correction.[73] You mentioned some time since the propriety of my discussing the question whether a minister was that of his country or the admn. It is a plain one, but yet I will thank you to put on paper what occurs to you on it, any time within a day or two & send it to me."

35. JAMES MONROE TO THOMAS JEFFERSON FEBRUARY 12, 1798

"Nothing or very little is done to yr. house since you left it—& I suppose will not till you return."

36. JAMES MONROE TO THOMAS JEFFERSON FEBRUARY 19, 1798

"You did every thing in yr. power to unite the people under [Adams's] admin; & to give him in negotiation the aid of the republican character & interest to support the pretentions of our country & not without hazard to yr. self."

37. JAMES MONROE TO THOMAS JEFFERSON APRIL 14, 1798

"I shall attend to it for the future having no confidence in the admn., in any respect. The royalists are at a point wch. perplexes them & of course they will play a desperate game. Yet I hope the people will take alarm at their projects & forsake them, in wch. case, their fall is inevitable, but this requires temper as well as firmness in the republicans to turn the crisis to good acct. in favor of republican govt. These virtues I think

73 Monroe's first proposed title was *A View of the conduct of the admn. in the management of our foreign affairs for the year 1794, 5 and 6 by an appeal to the official instructions & correspondence of James Monroe, late minister p: of the U. States to the French republick; to wch. is prefix'd an introductory narrative by the sd. James Monroe.* His second proposal was, *A view of the conduct of the Executive of the U. States in the management of the affrs. of those States with foreign powers for the years 1794 &c.*

will be displayed by the members of that party. Their attacks on you will not injure you. They impose the necessity of great caution angst. casualties & false friends, but this you will have."

38. JAMES MONROE TO THOMAS JEFFERSON JUNE 1, 1798

"DEAR SIR,—I have yours of 21 ulto. and very sincerely thank you for the interest you take in what concerns my welfare; of which indeed I have heretofore had so many proofs as long since to have ceased to make acknowledgements."

39. JAMES MONROE TO THOMAS JEFFERSON DECEMBER 16, 1800

"DEAR SIR,—We are yet ignorant of the issue of the election; that is, whether you are ahead of the secondary object. It is believed that every other point is settled."[74]

40. JAMES MONROE TO THOMAS JEFFERSON JANUARY 18, 1801

"It is said here that Marshall has given an opinion in conversation with Stoddard, that in case 9 states shod. not unite in favor of one of the persons chosen, the legislature may appoint a Presidt. till another election is made, & that intrigues are carrying on to place us in that situation."

41. JAMES MONROE TO THOMAS JEFFERSON MARCH 3, 1801

"The spirit of the republican party must be supported and preserved, which can only be done by a bold and magnanimous policy. When you came into the admn. of this State the firmness and decision which you shewed in the case of Hamilton at the time when Washington suffered our people to perish in the jails & prison-ships of N. York, by a pusillanimous and temporizing policy, advanc'd yr. fame & served the cause.[75] The publick opinion expects some tone to be given yr. admn. immediately & it will not long balance before it is formed, on the subject of what they are to expect from it. There is

74 In the presidential election of 1800 Jefferson tied Aaron Burr with 73 electoral votes throwing the election into the House of Representatives. John Adams received 65.

75 Jefferson served as Governor of Virginia from 1779-1781.

a conflict of principle & either democracy,—that is the govt. of the people,—or royalty must prevail. The opposing parties can never be united, I mean the leaders of them; because their views are as opposite as light & darkness. You always had the people and now have the govt. on yr. side, so that the prospect is a favorable as cod. be wished. At the same time it must be admitted you have much trouble and difficulty to encounter. Many friends may grow cool from disappointment; the violent who have their passions too much excited, will experience mortification, in not finding them fully gratified; in addition to which it is to be observed, that the discomfited tory party, profiting of past divisions & follies wch. have contributed much to overwhelm them, will recruit their scattered force agnst. us."

42. JAMES MONROE TO THOMAS JEFFERSON MARCH 3, 1801

"Your difficulties will indeed be great, yet I trust and believe you will surmount them, if you will pursue the dictates of yr. excellent judgment rather than the benevolent suggestions of yr. heart."

43. JAMES MONROE TO THOMAS JEFFERSON MARCH 18, 1801

"Your address has been approved by every description of persons here. It is sound and strong in principle, and grateful to the opposite party. With your judgment, views and principles it is hardly possible you shod. go wrong. Indeed I count on the good effects of yr. admn. being felt in favor of republican govt. abroad as well as at home. Still there are dangers in yr. way which it is necessary to shun. These are seen by you and therefore it may be useless for me to notice them."

44. JAMES MONROE TO THOMAS JEFFERSON MARCH 18, 1801

"It was also on this principle that you came into the admn. one whose past conduct entitled him to the confidence of the republicans, and secured him the unrelenting hatred & persecution of their opponents. The object now is to restore the govt. to its principles, amend its defects, reform abuses and introduce order and economy in the admn."

45. JAMES MONROE TO THOMAS JEFFERSON MARCH 18, 1801

"I am persuaded that much of the unhappiness and misery to wch. our society has been subject, is owing to such conduct in the federal officers in every State. It is to be feared too, such men will never contribute much to the restoration of that harmony, in whose destruction, they had so distinguished an agency. By retaining them in office you will give a proof of tolerance, moderation & forbearance, which must command the respect of the benevolent. Your situation is new and has its difficulties which I doubt not all parties will consider & make allowance for."

46. JAMES MONROE TO THOMAS JEFFERSON MAY 23, 1801

"I have many motives personal as well as publick to support yr. admn., not one to embarrass it."

47. JAMES MONROE TO THOMAS JEFFERSON JUNE 15, 1801

"You will perceive that I invite your attention to a subject of great delicacy and importance, one which in a peculiar degree involves the future peace, tranquility and happiness of the good people of this Commonwealth. I do it, however, in a confidence, you will take that interest in it, which we are taught to expect from your conduct through life, which gives you so many high claims to our regard."

48. JAMES MONROE TO THOMAS JEFFERSON JUNE 20, 1801

"At what time will you be at Monticello? I hope to have the pleasure of seeing you in Albemarle while I am there. The season begins to approach when it becomes dangerous for those accustomed to a better climate to stay here."

49. AN EXCERPT FROM JAMES MONROE'S *TO THE SPEAKERS OF THE HOUSE OF DELEGATES, AND OF THE SENATE* DECEMBER 7, 1801

"I have no hesitation to declare, that I consider the late election to the Executive of the United States, as having essentially contributed to secure to us the enjoyment of the blessings for which we contended in our revolution. The manner too by which the publick will was declared on that great occasion, was not less honorable to the government of the people, than the act itself was important to their cause. No strife, no unbecoming violence, no popular tumult, were heard of. Tranquility, order, and a dignified but unimposing solicitude prevailed in every quarter. A great and useful example have we thus exhibited to an interested and beholding world. An example which proves, how competent the people are to self government! How wise and faithful in the exercise of the most important acts of sovereignty! From this declaration of the publick sentiment, and the administration which was formed by it, I calculate on everything that ought to be expected from the conduct of wise and virtuous men; peace and respect from foreign powers; a republican tone in the government and its measures; economy in the disbursement of publick moneys; the restoration of social harmony, and a thousand other blessings which belong to our situation, and which we ought to enjoy."

50. JAMES MONROE TO THOMAS JEFFERSON APRIL 25, 1802

"The mild republican course of your admn. has tended to put at repose the republicans & relieve from further apprehension the federalists. In such a state of things the former have little motive for exertion. Having overthrown their adversaries they think it beneath their character to pursue them further. Many from the habit of activity they have acquired, from independence of spirit, rivalry or other cause, begin to separate from each other & even criticise the measures of reform that are proposed. But shod the federalists rally under the judiciary, and threaten anything serious it is presumable that the republicans will revive from their lethargy and resume their former tone. These ideas having occurr'd to me on this subject I have thought proper to submit them to yr. consideration."

51. JAMES MONROE TO THOMAS JEFFERSON JUNE 11, 1802

"SIR,—I find by your letter of the 3d. that you think Sierra Leone, on the coast of Africa, a suitable place for the establishment of our insurgent slaves, that it may also become so for those who are or may hereafter be emancipated, and that you are disposed to obtain the assent of the company to such a measure through our minister in London, while your attention will be directed in the interim to such other quarters as may enable us to submit a more enlarged field to the option of our Assembly."

52. JAMES MONROE TO THOMAS JEFFERSON MARCH 7, 1803

"The resolutions of Mr. Ross prove that the federal party will stick at nothing to embarrass the administration and recover its lost power."

53. EXCERPT TAKEN FROM JAMES MONROE'S *JOURNAL OR MEMORANDA—LOUISIANA* MAY 1, 1803

"I accompanied my colleague to the Palace of the Louvre, where I was presented by him to the Consul[76]...After dinner when we retired into the saloon, the first Consul came up to me and asked whether the federal city grew much, I told him it did. 'How many inhabitants has it?' It is just commencing, there are two cities near it, on above, the other below, on the great river Potomack, which two cities if counted with the federal city would make a respectable town, in itself it contains only two or three thousand inhabitants. 'Well; Mr. Jefferson, how old is he?' About sixty. 'Is he married or single?' He is not married. 'Then he is a garcon.' No he is a widower. 'Has he children?' Yes two daughters who are married. 'Does he reside always at the federal city?' Generally. 'Are the publick buildings there commodious, those for the Congress and President especially?' They are."

54. JAMES MONROE TO JAMES MADISON MAY 18, 1803

"The purchase of the whole of Louisiana, tho' not contemplated is nevertheless a measure founded on the principles and justified by the policy of our instructions, provided it be thought a good bargain. The only difference between the acquisition we have made, and that which we were instructed to make in that respect, is, that a favorable occasion presenting itself which indeed was not anticipated by the administration, in the measures which led to that event and laid the foundation for it, we have gone further than we were instructed to do. But the extent of that acquisition does not destroy the motive which existed before of acquiring the Floridas, nor essentially diminish it. In our instructions the idea entertained by the President of the value of that country is defined. It is to be presumed that under existing circumstances it may be had at a cheaper rate, since its importance to Spain is much diminished. And altho' the sum to be paid for Louisiana is considerable, yet the period at which that portion which is applicable to the government of France is to be paid, is so remote, and such delays are incident

76 Monroe is referring to France's First Consul, Napoleon Bonaparte.

to that which will be received by our citizens, that it is to be presumed the payment of what it would be proper to stipulate for the Floridas, would subject our treasury to no embarrassment."

55. JAMES MONROE TO THOMAS JEFFERSON MAY 18, 1803

"I most earnestly hope that what is done here, and may be done in pain, will not only prove an ample vindication of the measures of your administration during the last cession of Congress, when contrasted with the rash and extravagant projects that were opposed to them, but lay the solid foundation of great and permanent happiness to our country. To have contributed in any degree to carry into effect those measures, and justify the wisdom and benevolence of the policy which dictated them, if the result is approved, will always be a source of much delight to me."

56. JAMES MONROE TO JAMES MADISON JULY 20, 1803

"I made a communication similar in substance to what I had already done to the Minister, to which I added that it was the wish of the President that I should assure [Napoleon Bonaparte] before my departure of his high respect & esteem for him personally & for the French Nation, and of his earnest desire to preserve peace & friendship with it. The first Consul reciprocated the sentiments toward the President and the U. S. in strong terms. He said that he considered the President as a virtuous and enlightened man, who understood and pursued the interest of his country, as a friend of liberty and equality."

57. JAMES MONROE TO JAMES MADISON JULY 20, 1803

"Had the disposition of the first Consul to make the cession been produced by any but the measures of our government and country taken together, but more especially by the firm & dignified yet conciliatory conduct of the President, he would not have postponed the discussion of the subject till he was apprized of those measures…".

58. JAMES MONROE TO JAMES MADISON JULY 20, 1803

"I affirm however, with perfect confidence in the opinion, that notwithstanding these favorable circumstances, we should not have succeeded had the amiable relations between America & France been broken, or had the President have taken an attitude of menace toward that power, or any other than precisely that which he did take."

59. JAMES MONROE TO JAMES MADISON AUGUST 15, 1803

"I consider the present moment an all important one in our history, and that much, perhaps everything, depends on what is done by our government in its several branches. If the treaty is ratified, so that the President is left free to carry it into effect, the most prompt and decisive measures appear to me to be necessary on his part. My advice is that he order the troops down immediately to take post at New Orleans. In a mild and friendly manner the Spaniards should see that he expects they will surrender the territory promptly. Perhaps they will give it up without delay or equivocation. If they do not & our government does not take an imposing attitude the favorable moment may pass & everything be lost. If the affair is whiled away by negotiation, France may assume the character of meditation between us, and a year hence a bargain be made up by compromise much to our injury. But if the President pushes the affair with decision and promptitude, the First Consul will find himself bound by honor & interest to take a part in it which must be in the present juncture in favor of the United States. He must interpose so as to compel Spain to yield & put us in possession of the territory we have bought and paid France for. Should the Spaniards delay, the incident may probably furnish another occasion for the President to give a new proof of the energy of his character, and the happy effects of his administration."

60. JAMES MONROE TO THOMAS JEFFERSON SEPTEMBER 20, 1803

"The national institute is perhaps the strongest body in France, the Executive excepted. You should stand well with that body, and it appears to me important that you preserve your footing with it...They have the highest respect & attachment for you, and are delighted with your attention."

61. JAMES MONROE TO THOMAS JEFFERSON SEPTEMBER 20, 1803

"If I contribute in any degree to aid your administration in the confirmation of the just principles on which it rests, & promotion of the liberty & happiness of my country, it will prove in more than one view a delightful mission to me."

62. JAMES MONROE TO JAMES MADISON DECEMBER 15, 1803

"It is with highest satisfaction I learn that the treaty and conventions with France are ratified by the President with the advice of the Senate; that the ratifications are exchanged; and that the ceded territory will be taken possession of immediately by our troops. These events are of incalculable advantage to our country, as they secure to us the great object on which its happiness is so dependent. By taking possession of the territory the business may be considered as essentially concluded. It is impossible that we should ever be disturbed in the enjoyment of it. Spain would never be able to molest us, if she should have the inclination; nor can any other power be so disposed if it had the ability. The promptitude and decision with which the object is pursued, will I am persuaded reflect much honor on our councils, while it produces the happiest effect in our concerns with every European power. Had the President hesitated to take possession of the country, other powers might have been prompted thereby to intermeddle in the affr."

63. JAMES MONROE TO JAMES MADISON DECEMBER 17, 1803

"The decisive step taken by the President will I think put an end to the affair in a mode very honorable to his admn."

64. JAMES MONROE TO JAMES MADISON JANUARY 9, 1804

"Every circumstance that has come to my knowledge since my last, tends to confirm the doctrine it contains, that no time was to be lost in taking possession of Louisiana, after the exchange of ratifications.

It gives me great pleasure to find that the President has adopted the most decisive measures for that purpose. I hope to hear in a few weeks that the ceded territory is in our possession, and the jurisdiction of the U. States acknowledged in every part of it."

65. JAMES MONROE TO JAMES MADISON JANUARY 9, 1804

"If the President had relied on France to put us in possession of the territory, much time might have been whiled away in negotiation, and everything lost. But by taking immediate possession everything is secured."

66. JAMES MONROE TO BARBÉ MARBOIS FEBRUARY 14, 1804

"The manner in which the President expresses himself in his message to Congress of the enlarged liberal & friendly policy which governed the first Consul in the transaction shews in strong terms the sense which he entertains of it. May it seal forever the friendship of the two nations."

67. JAMES MONROE TO JAMES MADISON AUGUST 10, 1804

"It seems to me clear that nothing will redound so much to the honor of the present administration, or strengthen it so much at home, as the preservation of peace with [England] thro' the present war, on fair and respectable terms. It will likewise add much to its credit abroad, which is already high by the adjustment of the business with France, and the tranquility of our interior. Every year of peace which we enjoy gives new strength to our government, & country, & contributes to confirm the opinion of Europe, in favor of our being an independent nation guided by an enlightened policy."

68. JAMES MONROE TO JAMES MADISON AUGUST 10, 1804

"Never one sentiment of an opposite kind has escaped me in publick or private intercourse. Merchants of distinction here [London] have admitted that they have been agreeably disappointed in Mr. Jefferson's admn."

69. JAMES MONROE TO M. TALLEYRAND NOVEMBER 8, 1804

"Before the conclusion of the late treaty between the U States & France, your Excellency will recollect that it was an object of the President, to acquire of Spain by amicable arrangement, Florida, it being a portion of her territory which she held Eastward of the Mississippi."

70. JAMES MONROE TO THOMAS JEFFERSON OCTOBER 24, 1805

"By remaining here for the present, this govt. will be deprived of any pretext for declining an arrangement of our affairs, & an opportunity will be offered to profit of the disposition at home, shewn by our govt. & people and occurrences on the Continent. Had I any knowledge of your wishes in this respect I shod. instantly comply with them; that is did I know that you wished me to come home, I would do it by the first good vessel. But having no idea of what you desire I have been altogether at a loss what to do."

⁂

71. JAMES MONROE TO JAMES MADISON JANUARY 10, 1806

"The President's message which I have just received, is what I wished it to be. It opens the question between the U States and this country [Great Britain], and also with Spain, in a manner to shew that our government understands its rights and interests and will vindicate them, while it makes it equally evident that if a misunderstanding takes place between us and either of them, it will be owing to such power and not to us. It combines well moderation and firmness."

⁂

72. AN EXCERPT FROM JAMES MONROE'S *NOTES RESPECTING OUR DIFFERENCES WITH SPAIN* MAY 28, 1803

"To purchase [Florida from Spain] is a legitimate mode of acquisition for nations as well as individuals, and has been always practiced. It is also an honorable one much more so than that which has been usually resorted to. The opponents to this doctrine will find it difficult to prove that it is more honorable to acquire the property of another by robbery & murder than by paying for it a fair equivalent. If the American government makes a bad bargain or in other respects submits to dishonorable conditions, a high responsibility awaits the act. Besides it is more than probable from what we have seen of the divisions of Congress on the subject, that such a treaty would not be ratified. There is however no cause to apprehend such a result. The career of President Jefferson has been so far, too eminently useful to his country & honorable to himself, to justify the anticipation of it."

⁂

73. JAMES MONROE TO THOMAS JEFFERSON JUNE 15, 1806

"DEAR SIR,—If I was not personally your friend and did not wish success to your administration, from the interest I take in your welfare, as in that of the country, I should not write you with the freedom I propose to do in this letter. It is my intention to enter fully into some topicks which are of very high importance to your reputation as to the best interest of the U States, & I do it in confidence that you will see in it a proof of the sincerity of the motive which prompts me to it."

74. JAMES MONROE TO THOMAS JEFFERSON JULY 8, 1806

"You are so good as to offer me either of the governments of Louisiana & to intimate that they shall be kept open some time for my answer. I should be very sorry if any injurious delay proceeded from that cause; I hasten therefore to prevent it. At one time I was inclined to think that it might suit me to accept the appointment at New Orleans, for reasons which I then took the liberty to mention to Mr. Madison & yourself. To these the removal of some friends there to whom we are much attached, had added another very interesting one. But from the period of my answer to yours on that subject in 1804, I relinquish all thoughts of it."

75. JAMES MONROE TO JOHN RANDOLPH NOVEMBER 12, 1806

"Many of the great features which make the character of the admn., are unquestionably sound. It is incorruptible to foreign influence; it is respectful of & watchful over the public rights; it is friendly to free government; it is honest in the administration of the publick money. It is certainly desirous of avoiding foreign wars, & securing to our virtuous people the blessings of peace. Many may think that it has acquitted itself in the present crisis of affairs, with a superior skill & dexterity in the management of those of our country, while others may be satisfied that it has sank under the weight of the crisis, & shown an absolute want of those great qualities which the occasion called for. Be this as it may, as I cannot suppose, that other defects than those of the first class are attributable to it, my decided opinion is, that it is best for the interest of our country, at the present epoch especially, that they shod. not be brought into view to be made the ground of attack upon the administration."

76. JAMES MONROE TO THOMAS JEFFERSON FEBRUARY 27, 1808

"I can assure you that no occurrences of my whole life ever gave me so much concern as some which took place during my absence abroad, proceeding from the present administration. I allude more especially to the mission of Mr. Pinckney with all the circumstances connected with that measure, and the manner in which the treaty which he and I formed, which was in fact little more than a project was received. I do not wish to dwell on those subjects. I resolved that they should not form any motive of my publick or private conduct, and I proceeded to execute my publick duty in the same manner, & to support and advance to the utmost of my power your political & personal fame, as if they had not occurred. The latter object has been felt thro' life by me scarcely as a secondary one, for from the high respect which I have entertained for your publick service, talents & virtues I have seen the national interest, and your advancement and fame so intimately connected, as to constitute essentially the same cause. Besides I have never forgotten the proofs of kindness & friendship which I received from you in early life."

77. JAMES MONROE TO THOMAS JEFFERSON FEBRUARY 27, 1808

"...I shall never cease to take a deep interest in your political fame & personal happiness."

78. JAMES MONROE TO THOMAS JEFFERSON MARCH 22, 1808

"To do you an injury or indeed any one in the administration, never entered into my mind, for while I laboured under a conviction, not only that I had been injured but that the friendly feelings which you had so long entertained for me had ceased to exist, the only sentiment which I indulged in consequence of it was that of sorrow. At present I am happy to say that all doubts of your friendship towards me having experienced any change is completely done away, and that the only anxiety which I feel is to satisfy you, that the impression was not taken on light ground, nor imputable to communications made me by persons out of the administration."

79. JAMES MONROE TO THOMAS JEFFERSON MARCH 22, 1808

"These were the circumstances which produc'd the impression which I have acknowledged in the commencement of this letter, that your friendship had been withdrawn from me. But the assurances which you now make me & the perfect knowledge which I have of your rectitude & sincerity have completely effac'd that impression and restored to my mind that entire I friendly confidence which it had always been accustomed to cherish.

I am perfectly satisfied that you never meant to injure me & that a belief that I had suffered by any act to which you were an innocent party would give you great pain."

80. JAMES MONROE TO THOMAS JEFFERSON APRIL 18, 1808

"I had the pleasure to receive some days past your favor of the 11th & that of the 13 to day. Being perfectly satisfied by the explanations & assurances which you had given me in your preceding letters that I had taken an improper idea of yr. disposition towards me, the details contained in your last one were not necessary in that view. I receive them however with great interest because in giving them you afford me a new proof of your friendship."

81. JAMES MONROE TO __________ JULY 13, 1808

"I would invariably speak handsomely of the President of his disinterestedness in retiring, his unquestionable merit, & certain fame, his attachment to both parties & indifference to the result. I would give him credit where due, & say no more, avoiding any harsh imputation agnst him…".

82. JAMES MONROE TO L. W. TAZEWELL OCTOBER 30, 1808

"The first was not to identify myself with the admn. I had been pushed, as it were, aside, by it. In rejecting the treaty it had by implication censured me: I thought that I had done right in what I had done, and did not think it comported with what I owed to myself, or the publick, to come in, inlist under its banners [illegible] as a [illegible] in favor of the embargo &c. I answered Mr. Madison's objections to the treaty & afterwards remained quiet, giving the administration all the aide which [illegible] where I disapproved could give it, and the unreserved & constant expression of my approbation where I did approve."

83. JAMES MONROE TO L. W. TAZEWELL OCTOBER 30, 1808

"I have known & esteemed him long; his life has been useful; and altho' I suffered much from those measures in more than one respect, yet I feel an interest in his future tranquility & happiness."

84. JAMES MONROE TO THOMAS JEFFERSON FEBRUARY 2, 1809

"...in a situation of great personal delicacy you looked only to the good of your country, & that the last act of your administration was employed, in a distinguished effort to preserve its peace, liberty & union."

85. JAMES MONROE TO THOMAS JEFFERSON FEBRUARY 2, 1809

"We have been long neighbors & friends & it will be my object to cherish through life those interesting relations."

86. JAMES MONROE TO COLONEL JOHN TAYLOR SEPTEMBER 10, 1810

"The early stages of Mr. Jefferson's administration were attended with as great and brilliant success as ever occurred to any government. The latter period was undoubtedly unfortunate in some important points. I concur with an opinion expressed in one of your papers, that the rejection of the British treaty, and adoption of the embargo, were among his principal errors. Those led to others, and produced also various abortive projects, some of them of a nature with those that were resorted to by the preceding administrations. Whether Mr. Jefferson gave his sanction to the latter schemes, or *they* were the projects of others only, I know not, but I have rather supposed the latter was the case."

87. JAMES MONROE TO COLONEL JOHN TAYLOR SEPTEMBER 10, 1810

"I cannot think that Mr. Jefferson would consent to any measure which violated the principles of free government, or weakened its foundations. I think also that Mr. Jefferson is sincerely attached to those principles."

88. JAMES MONROE TO COLONEL JOHN TAYLOR SEPTEMBER 10, 1810

"Had Mr. Jefferson closed on that ground he would have carried home with him more content than has I fear fallen to his lot, and as illustrious a fame as the Chief Magistrate of any country ever retired with. As it is, we must all recollect that in a long and active life, and in conjunctures of great difficulty, and even danger, he has been firm and incorruptible in support of the rights of his country, and the people, and in paying him the tribute of respect justly due for those important services, look with indulgence on his errors, from which none, even the most perfect, are free."

89. JAMES MONROE TO COLONEL JOHN TAYLOR SEPTEMBER 10, 1810

"The correspondence with Mr. Jefferson I published at the close of the scene, to shew that the relation of friendship which had so long subsisted was preserved between us. As that relation imposed on me an obligation of a certain character, I wished that the nature and extent of it should be known to the public."

90. JAMES MONROE TO COLONEL JOHN TAYLOR NOVEMBER 19, 1810

"I did hope when the admn. changed, and Mr. Jefferson came into power, that all distinctions of parties would have been firmly levelled by the wisdom and success of his admn.; that we should all (with a few incurable exceptions only) have become republicans. He too was penetrated with the great idea, as appeared by his inaugural speech, but he soon relinquished the hope of realizing it...".

91. JAMES MONROE TO THOMAS JEFFERSON APRIL 3, 1811

"Dear Sir,—An unexpected change has taken place in my situation since I had last the pleasure to see you. An invitation from the President to enter into the department of state will take me to Washington. Having accepted the office, I set out tomorrow in the stage to commence its duties...I shall always be happy to hear from you and to receive your opinions on publick measures."

92. JAMES MONROE TO THOMAS JEFFERSON MARCH 9, 1812

"I hope that you continue to enjoy good health. It would give me great pleasure to be able to make a visit to my farm for a few days & to have opportunity of seeing you & other friends."

93. JAMES MONROE TO THOMAS JEFFERSON JUNE 16, 1813

"DEAR SIR,—At the commencement of the war I was decidedly of your opinion, that the best disposition which could be made of our little navy, would be to keep it in a body in a safe port, from which I might sally only, on some important occasion, to render essential service."

94. JAMES MONROE TO THOMAS JEFFERSON OCTOBER 4, 1814

"Nothing but the disasters here, and the duties which have devolved on me, in consequence, the most burthensome that I have ever encountered, would have prevented my writing you long since, as well as more recently. I have devoted this morning to a full communication to you, but have been pressed by committees, on military topics, till the period has passed. You shall hear from me again in a few days."

95. JAMES MONROE TO THOMAS JEFFERSON OCTOBER 10, 1814

"I shall be happy to promote the disposition of your library in the manner you propose, tho' I regret that you are to be deprived of such a resource & consolation in your retirement."

96. JAMES MONROE TO THOMAS JEFFERSON APRIL 23, 1817

"Such exist now, relative to which, if I cannot make you the visit in contemplation, I will write you soon; and if I can, I shall have a better opportunity of communicating in person. For the interest which you take in my success, which is always very gratifying & consoling to me, I am truly thankful."

97. JAMES MONROE TO THOMAS JEFFERSON OCTOBER 5, 1819

"I lament the pecuniary embarrassment, which has spread, over our Union, & particularly the instance, which has occurr'd in Richmond, which has so essentially injured you."

99. JAMES MONROE TO THOMAS JEFFERSON FEBRUARY 19, 1820

"DEAR SIR,—I forwarded to you by this days Mail a copy of the Journal of the Convention which formed the Constitution of the U States. By the Acts of Congress providing for the distribution of them, one is allowed to you, & likewise to Mr. Madison & to Mr. Adams."

99. JAMES MONROE TO THOMAS JEFFERSON NOVEMBER 25, 1822

"DEAR SIR,—We have all been very much distress'd, at the accounts recently receiv'd, of the misfortune you have sustain'd, in the fracture of your arm, or at least of one of its bones. We hope that it has not been so serious, as has been represented, & that you are rapidly recovering from it."

100. EXCERPT FROM JAMES MONROE'S *THE GENESIS OF THE MESSAGE OF 1823; CONTEMPORANEOUS CORRESPONDENCE ON ITS RECEPTION AND EFFECTS* 1823

"A study of the birth of that principle in the policy of the United States of non-intervention in the affairs of Europe and of repelling the interference of European nations in the affairs of America, carries us back to Washington's Farewell Address which clearly suggests it; through the adherence to the principle he pointed out, by his successors; to the broader terms in which Jefferson set it forth in considering the interests of North and South America the same and that the object of both should be to 'exclude all European influence from this hemisphere' and that it was important that the nations of America should join in an American system of policy 'totally independent of and unconnected with those of Europe'; to this epoch when—the times and circumstances rendering it necessary—it was proclaimed in the Message of 1823."

101. EXCERPT FROM JAMES MONROE'S *THE GENESIS OF THE MESSAGE OF 1823; CONTEMPORANEOUS CORRESPONDENCE ON ITS RECEPTION AND EFFECTS* 1823

"Mr. Jefferson thinks them more important than anything that has happened since the Revolution. He is for acceding to the proposals, with a view to pledging Great Britain against the Holy Allies; though he thinks the Island of Cuba would be a valuable and important acquisition to our Union."

102. JAMES MONROE TO THOMAS JEFFERSON MARCH 22, 1824

"DEAR SIR,—Such has been the pressure on me of late, that I have not had a moment, to pay attention or even answer the calls of my friends. I have felt that I had fail'd, both to you and to Mr. Madison."

103. JAMES MONROE TO THOMAS JEFFERSON MARCH 22, 1824

"My particular motive is, to state to you a communication which was lately made to me by Mr. [Robert] Livingston. He assur'd me, that it was an object of deep interest to him, to know that you entertain'd no unkind feelings towards him—that he earnestly wished to be restor'd to the footing which he held in your estimation some 25 years since. I told him, that I was satisfied the intimation of that sentiment, on his part, would be gratifying to you. If you are willing that I should say any thing to him on the subject, trace what it shall be and I shall be happy to be the organ."

104. JAMES MONROE TO THOMAS JEFFERSON JULY 12, 1824

"I regret much that it is not now in my power to fix any period, at which time I may with certainty promise myself the pleasure of seeing you. Mrs. Monroe's health is such as not to permit her to undertake the journey, and is also subjected to such occasional unfavorable changes, as to make it difficult for me to leave her for any length of time. It was my intention to have visited Albemarle, more than a month since, but I was prevented by that and other causes. I shall take her to Loudon County in a day or two, which the elevation of the country, & air, resemble, what we have so long profited of, in Albemarle, & should the change prove advantageous to her, I will continue my journey thither. But this is so uncertain, that I must beg of you, not to permit your mov'ment to depend in the slightest degree on mine. Whether I go over at the same time suggested or not, I shall endeavor to see you in the autumn, when many concerns foreign & domestic will probably have reach'd a stage to require the most profound attention, and on which I shall be happy to confer freely with you & Mr. Madison."

105. JAMES MONROE TO THOMAS JEFFERSON OCTOBER 18, 1824

"It is my earnest desire to visit Albemarle, & to pass a day, with you, and one with Mr. Madison, before the commenc'ment of the Session. If I do, it must be soon, as I must be back, early in the next month, to prepare for that event."

106. JAMES MONROE TO THOMAS JEFFERSON FEBRUARY 13, 1826

". . . I have this moment receiv'd a paper from Richmond, which gives an account of your application to the legislature, for the grant of a lottery for the sale of your estate, to relieve you from embarrassment. I cannot express the concern which this view of your affairs has given me, altho' I can readily conceive the causes which have led to it. They are such as the State, and indeed the whole Union, must feel."

107. JAMES MONROE TO THOMAS JEFFERSON FEBRUARY 23, 1826

"DEAR SIR,—I mention'd in a letter which I lately wrote to you, that I had seen in a paper from Richmond, a notice of an application which you had made to the legislature, for permission to sell a large portion of your estate, by lottery, for the payment of your debts, and that I should write you again on the subject. Since then I have been much indisposed, with the influenza, from which, I have not yet intirely recover'd. I have been much concern'd to find, that your devotion to the public service, for so great a length of time & at so difficult an epoch, should have had so distressing an effect, on your large private fortune, and my regret is the greater, from the interest I take, in what relates to your family as well as to yourself. It is a concern, in which I am satisfied, the people will take a deep interest, and that the legislature will grant to you, who have such very high claims on your country, what it seldom refuses to any one, cannot be doubted. As soon as I saw that notice, I communicated it to my friends in New York, and particularly to Mr. Gouverneur, with a request, that they would promote the object, and which they will do. I shall do the same to others in other quarters. My motive in this, is, to assure you that if in any way, I may be useful to you, it will be very gratifying to me, to be apprized of it."

108. AN EXCERPT FROM JAMES MONROE'S *THE MEMOIR OF JAMES MONROE, ESQ.* 1826

"The President preferred a different policy. He resolved to make an experiment of a pacific character, by a special mission, with intention to resort to war, so far as depended on him, should that mission fail. In that emergency, he demanded my service, and nominated and appointed me to France and Spain, without consulting me, but with a perfect knowledge that I should not decline the mission. Independent of any favourable opinion which the President might have entertained of me personally, arising from the very friendly relations which had so long existed between us in public and in private life, there were considerations known to the public, which, had weight with him in making the appointment."

109. AN EXCERPT FROM THE *AUTOBIOGRAPHY OF JAMES MONROE* 1827-1830

"His [Monroe] father and uncle had intended him for the bar, to which his mind had by preference been directed. To raise the regiment to which he had been recently appointed, he was now replaced in Williamsburg, near the college which he had left three and a half years before. Mr. Jefferson, a very enlightened and distinguished revolutionary patriot and one of the most eminent lawyers in the state, was then its governor, and John Francis Mercer, Mr. Monroe's friend who had left the college and entered the Third Regiment with him, had by accepting the office of aide-de-camp to Major General Charles Lee, lost also his rank in the line and in consequence retired from the army, was then engaged with several other distinguished youths in the study of law under Mr. Jefferson, among whom was William Short and Archibald Stuart, who were likewise students at the college. Mr. Monroe immediately re-entered the college, resumed his study of general science in it, and on the introduction by Judge Jones to Mr. Jefferson, to whom he was already well known by the letter above referred to, he engaged in the study of the law under him and persevered in it until he obtained a license to practice in the courts of the state."

110. AN EXCERPT FROM THE *AUTOBIOGRAPHY OF JAMES MONROE* 1827-1830

"His election to Congress having been made in the spring session of 1783, to take effect in December, he was invited by Mr. Jefferson to pass the interval with him at his residence in Albemarle, with which he complied. Mr. Jefferson urged him to establish himself in that county, assuring him that it would connect him with the western counties, from which he could throw into his hands much business, which he should be happy to do. Having formed a strong attachment to Mr. Jefferson by the relation which had before existed between them, and having become acquainted with many respectable families and citizens in the county during his visit he resolved to make the establishment suggested, and with that view, to purchase a tract of land then for sale in the neighborhood, belonging to Mr. Marks, who had intended to move to Georgia, which tract now belongs to Mr. Rogers and Dr. Everett."

111. AN EXCERPT FROM THE *AUTOBIOGRAPHY OF JAMES MONROE* 1827-1830

"Mr. Jefferson, who had been a member of Congress in 1776, who drew the Declaration of Independence, was afterwards Governor of the State of Virginia and then a member of Congress, was appointed a Minister Plenipotentiary, and associated with Doctor Franklin and Mr. Adams, with authority to form a commercial treaty with all the principal powers in Europe with whom such treaties had not already been concluded."

112. AN EXCERPT TAKEN FROM THE *AUTOBIOGRAPHY OF JAMES MONROE* 1827-1830

"On the 3d of June, 1784, Congress adjourned to meet at Trenton on the 30th of October following, having previously appointed a committee of the states to remain in session during the recess.

During this session Mr. Jefferson and Mr. Monroe, having taken a house and lived together, had agreed to visit in the recess our northwestern frontier, passing by Pittsburgh to Detroit, thence by Lakes Erie and Ontario, taking a view of the falls of Niagra between them, to the St. Lawrence and back through Vermont and New York to Trenton to which place Congress would adjourn...Mr. Jefferson's appointment to Europe prevented their proposed excursion together. Mr. Monroe, however, resolved to execute the plan himself, so far as he might be able, and in which he apprehended no difficulty, the Indians having sued for peace, and the whole route, when on land, being within our limits."

113. AN EXCERPT TAKEN FROM THE *AUTOBIOGRAPHY OF JAMES MONROE* 1827-1830

"While engaged on his farm, his attention was drawn, in the commencement of December, 1799, to a citizen of Richmond who was well known to and respected by him, Colonel Alexander Quarrier, who approached him in the field and delivered a dispatch which had been committed to him by the Speaker of the two Houses of the General Assembly, and of which he added that he was happy to be the bearer. On perusing the dispatch, Mr. Monroe found that it announced to him his election to the office of Chief Magistrate of the state, with a request that he would repair to Richmond to take on himself the duties of the office as soon as it might be convenient to him. He resolved to depart without delay. He required one day only to make such arrangement of his private affairs as would admit of his absence. Early on the ensuing morning, Mr. Jefferson, his venerable neighbor and friend, called on him, and immediately afterwards, Colonel Thomas M. Randolph arrived with a troop of horse to manifest their respect for him personally and for the decision of the General Assembly in electing him to the office of Chief Magistrate. He departed immediately for Richmond, accompanied by the venerable Mr. Jefferson to Milton, and by Colonel Randolph and the troop to the boundary line of the county."

114. AN EXCERPT TAKEN FROM THE *AUTOBIOGRAPHY OF JAMES MONROE* 1827-1830

"At this moment an incident occurred which deeply affected the interest of the western states and roused the indignation of the union. By the treaty of San Ildephonso, between France and Spain, which was concluded on October 1st, 1800, the latter had ceded to the former the province of Louisiana and had suppressed, at the instance of the former, as was inferred, our right of deposit at New Orleans, which was secured by our treaty with Spain of 1795. The act justified war. To which ever government it might be imputed, and many were prepared to risk it by removing the obstruction by force. The President preferred a different policy. He resolved to make the experiment of a special mission, and with that view nominated and appointed him in that character to both France and Spain, without consulting him."

115. AN EXCERPT TAKEN FROM THE *AUTOBIOGRAPHY OF JAMES MONROE* 1827-1830

"Other considerations operated with peculiar force. The intimate and cordial friendship and great harmony in political life which he [Monroe] had so long enjoyed with the President [Jefferson] and Secretary of State [Madison], with his high respect for their talents and merit, rendered it impossible for him to decline a cooperation with them in support of this great cause in which they were engaged."

VI. JOHN QUINCY ADAMS ON THOMAS JEFFERSON

1. EXCERPT FROM JOHN QUINCY ADAMS'S *LETTERS OF PUBLICOLA* JUNE 8, 1791

"It is my intention to submit to the public a few observations which have occurred to me upon the perusal of this pamphlet, which has so clear and valid a title to the public attention.[77] But I must here observe that I wish to avoid every appearance of disrespect either to the real parent of this production or to the gentleman who has stood its sponsor in this country.[78] Both these gentlemen are entitled to the gratitude of their countrymen; the latter still renders important services in a very dignified station. He is a friend to free inquiry upon every subject, and he will not be displeased to see the sentiments which he has made his own by a public adoption canvassed with as much freedom as is consistent with the reverence due to his character."

2. JOHN QUINCY ADAMS TO JOSEPH PITCAIRN NOVEMBER 13, 1796

"You think they [France] will endeavor to promote the election of Mr. Jefferson, and you are probably right; but if Jefferson is elected, I speak with confidence in saying that he will inflexibly pursue the same general system of policy which is now established. Perhaps even you may smile and hesitate in believing this prophecy. I *may* be mistaken, but have no doubt myself upon the subject, and am willing to have my conjectures judged by the test of events."

3. JOHN QUINCY ADAMS TO JOSEPH PITCAIRN DECEMBER 2, 1796

"In speaking so confidently as I did in my last letter as to the policy which Mr. Jefferson will pursue, if placed at the head of our Union, I did not speak from any direct information, or indeed from any other source than my general opinion of his character, and my firm conviction that he could not pursue any other. There is but one variation in the material policy of the American government which could be attempted, and that is a variation from a neutral system to a warlike one. Our friends, as you call them, will no doubt urge

77 Thomas Paine's *Rights of Man*

78 Secretary of State Thomas Jefferson

this as they have done hitherto, or perhaps more incautiously still. But they deceive themselves in imagining that there is a great part of the people in America inclined to become a party in the war. The immense majority of the people is determined upon the preservation of peace, and would very soon show the most pointed disapprobation of any measure on the part of the executive tending toward a different direction. If the advisers whom you justly apprehend should prevail to the adoption of any important change of system, the popular voice and opinion would soon correct their influence. There would therefore be a firmness of necessity, which would prevent any essential evil consequences from a facility of character, which I think with you is indubitable. As to any little variations of detail or of parade, I do not take them at all into the account. With respect to France, Mr. Jefferson would undoubtedly do everything to conciliate and harmonize, that the justice and honor of the United States would permit. Has not the same thing been invariably practiced by the present President? If more is expected, or required; if the unquestionable rights and substantial interests of the American people are demanded as a sacrifice to the humors or the ambitious purposes of whomsoever, Mr. Jefferson is not the man who will make himself the instrument of any such designs. This is an opinion so strongly fixed in my mind, that I have no doubt whatever upon the subject. If I should ever find that this judgment is erroneous, I shall be no less surprised than grieved at the proof."

4. JOHN QUINCY ADAMS TO SYLVANUS BOURNE DECEMBER 22, 1796

"Suppose its effects should be to turn the election? This is probably one of its principal objects, but should it succeed, what then? Is the devil to be raised, or are we to be set all by the ears for having a Virginian instead of a New England man for President? One honest and able man instead of another? Indeed these ideas may pass among Europeans, but they are not worthy of an American."

5. JOHN QUINCY ADAMS TO JOSEPH PITCAIRN JANUARY 31, 1797

"I see a proposal in the House of Delegates of *Virginia* unanimously adopted, to address the President with a declaration of their profound regret at his determination to retire from the public service. Can France possibly believe that Mr. Jefferson, or any other man, would dare to start away from that system of administration which Washington has thus sanctioned, not only by his example, but by his retirement?

Nay, in my mind I have no doubt but that if, instead of Jefferson, the ex-Vicomte de Barras himself were President of the United States, he could not stagger the system."

6. JOHN QUINCY ADAMS TO WILLIAM VANS MURRAY FEBRUARY 24, 1801

"Now if B[urr] should be placed at the first post, would J[efferson] remain at the second? And if he did, would there be for four years together a cordial union of sentiments and of measures between them and the friends of both? The design of their party was to place J[efferson] first and B[urr] second. If the order should be inverted, neither of them could change it back; and if acquiescing in it the party should afterwards continue to harmonize, I should really begin to believe that human nature is turning over a new leaf. If they once divided, it seems to me that whatever Mr. B[urr]'s dispositions are, he could not do any essential harm, and the principal evil that would flow from the choice would be to see a man President of the United States whom not one citizen of the whole Union would have wished to see in that station."

7. JOHN QUINCY ADAMS TO RUFUS KING JANUARY 18, 1802

"The measures recommended by the President at the opening of the session are all popular, in all parts of the Union; but they are all undergoing a scrutiny in the public newspapers, more able and more severe, then they will probably meet in either House of Congress. A writer in the *New York Evening Post*, said to be General Hamilton, has undertaken particularly to point out great and comprehensive errors of system in the message, and his doctrines find great approbation among the federalists, and among all those who consider themselves as the profound thinkers of the nation. These papers will without doubt be transmitted to you by your friends at New York and, with the President's message and the report from the Secretary of the Treasury, will give you the fairest view of what our administration and our opposition are at this time."

8. JOHN QUINCY ADAMS TO RUFUS KING OCTOBER 8, 1802

"The newspapers have been chiefly filled with personal attacks upon the President and Vice President, coming from different and perhaps opposite quarters — all arising originally from divisions in their own party. These divisions have occasioned animosities of no small inveteracy between individuals. You have doubtless been better informed of the transactions at New York than it would be in my power to inform you. The warfare there has been between the friends of Mr. Burr and those of the Clinton family. In Virginia the principal batteries have been pointed at Mr. Jefferson by a Scotsman named [James Thomas] Callender, of whom you have probably heard heretofore. He writes under the influence of personal resentment and revenge; but the effect of his publications upon the reputation of the President has been considerable."

9. EXCERPT FROM JOHN QUINCY ADAMS'S, *THE REPERTORY, NO. III* OCTOBER 30, 1804

"The reduction of the army to a peace establishment was, indeed, a thing which on the complete restoration of peace, would have followed, of course, under any administration. The work had been chiefly accomplished before Mr. Jefferson's elevation, and in all probability this subject would have slept in peace, but for the opportunity it afforded of hoisting in that ingenious execration against standing armies in time of peace, a *sentiment*, the justice of which I shall not contest, any more than the propriety of its expression in any commendation of Mr. Jefferson."

10. EXCERPT FROM JOHN QUINCY ADAMS'S, *THE REPERTORY, NO. III* OCTOBER 30, 1804

"Of the purchase of Louisiana I shall not now undertake to discuss the policy. That it is a great and important feature of Mr. Jefferson's administration is unquestionable true. Whether it will prove a blessing of a curse to this Union, it is only future time that can determine. This much we know, that the price of the purchase will be paid almost entirely by the Eastern and Atlantic states. Thus much we know, that when admitted as members of the Union, the whole weight and power of the purchased territories will be thrown into the scale of southern and western influence. In the relative situation of the United States, New England and the Maritime States have been constantly declining in power and consequence; they must continue to decline in proportion as the growth of the southern and western parts shall be more rapid than theirs. This vibration of the centre of power, being founded in nature, cannot be resisted, and as good citizens it is our duty to acquiesce in the event; but to this increasing ascendancy of the south and west, the acquisition of Louisiana adds an immense force, never contemplated in the original compact of these states. We are still to learn whether this excessive southern preponderance will be enjoyed with moderation, or used with generosity. Should it prove otherwise, and the present symptoms are by no means favorable, the people of America will have no cause to thank Mr. Jefferson for his Louisiana bargain."

11. EXCERPT FROM JOHN QUINCY ADAMS'S, *THE REPERTORY, NO. IV* NOVEMBER 2, 1804

"In order to set this observation in its true light and to show its full importance, we must again remark, that if the mode of choosing electors by single districts were established throughout the Union, Mr. Jefferson and his administration would lose so many electors, that his re-election would be doubtful in the highest degree. It is at least certain that they dared not make the experiment."

12. EXCERPT FROM JOHN QUINCY ADAMS'S, *THE REPERTORY, NO. V* NOVEMBER 6, 1804

"In a moral and political view, this representation of slaves is alike objectionable. The number of those miserable beings already existing in some States is such as to occasion the most serious alarm in all humane and thinking minds. Mr. Jefferson has said that the populace of large cities no more add strength to the body politic, than sores to the body natural. If this comparison be just the slaves of our southern neighbors are abscesses of the deepest and most dangerous matter to our national body."

13. EXCERPT FROM JOHN QUINCY ADAMS'S, *THE REPERTORY, NO. V* NOVEMBER 6, 1804

"The President of the United States belongs to that part of the State of Virginia which, by the effect of the iniquitous mode of representation now established, sends at least two representatives to Congress, where upon principles of equal rights, they ought to send but one. His personal and local interests are, of course, in opposition to the proposed amendment, and there is no doubt but all his influence will be exerted against it. If we judge of the party which now governs this Union by their acts, it will appear that their whole political system centres in personal attachment to him and his views, while on the other part his system consists in substituting them instead of the nation. The destruction of the judiciary independence; the persevering system of turning out honest men from office to introduce partisans in their place; and the amendment to the Constitution, carried through with such extreme precipitation, and at such heavy expense to the people of this country, for the sole purpose of securing his re-election, are all explained by this solution, and can be explained by no other."

14. JOHN QUINCY ADAMS TO JOHN ADAMS NOVEMBER 3, 1804

"Mr. Jefferson thinks that on the return of any of these armed vessels, if they should have fought with a French privateer and killed one of her men, *our* judges ought to hang every man on board the American vessel for murder. He draws his inference from the common law principle, that homicide committed in support of an unlawful act is murder. But common law rules should not be applied to the objects which essentially belong to the laws of nations. I questioned the accuracy of his argument, but asked him why the government had not interposed to *prevent* the arming of these vessels at New York. He said the law would not bear them out in such interference, though he admitted it had been done at an early period of the late war. This he first said was by virtue of a temporary law; but afterwards recollecting himself said it had been done without a law and submitted to. But that had it been contested, the authority of the government would not have been supported for the measure. Hence I concluded we shall have a law for such an authority at the approaching session."

15. JOHN QUINCY ADAMS TO JOHN ADAMS NOVEMBER 1804

"A coincidence of your opinion with that of the President of the United States would be more than enough to stagger me in any point upon which I should have formed a different one. It makes me, therefore, peculiarly mistrust that which I entertain on this subject. The President's position was that *our judges* ought to hang American citizens who should have committed homicide in resisting the execution of French revenue laws in the West Indies. And he gave to support his reasoning the *common law* principle, that homicide committed in support of an *unlawful* act is murder. In this opinion you say he was right. I can only reply what I replied to him: That I had always considered it as a settled maxim that *no nation takes notice of the revenue or colonial laws of another nation;* and therefore that our judges could not hang Americans in the case he put, for homicide in support of acts which to *our judges* were not unlawful."

16. JOHN QUINCY ADAMS TO JOHN ADAMS NOVEMBER 1804

"It is indeed very apparent that popularity bears a strong resemblance to the itch by its contagion, and the President, who has himself enough of the itch of popularity, may congratulate himself upon its wide spread in Massachusetts. I consider the revolution there as completed, and that in the spring both our executive and legislature will pass into other hands and other principles."

17. AN ENTRY FROM JOHN QUINCY ADAMS'S DIARY NOVEMBER 23, 1804

". . . Dined with the President. Mrs. Adams did not go. The company were Mr. R. Smith, Secretary of the Navy, and his lady, Mr. and Mrs. Harrison, Miss Jenifer and Miss Mouchette, Mr. Brent, and the President's two sons-in-law, with Mr. Burwell, his private secretary. I had a good deal of conversation with the President. The French Minister just arrived had been this day first presented to him, and appears to have displeased him by the profusion gold lace on his clothes. He says they must get him down to a plain frock coat, or the boys in the streets will run after him as a sight. I asked if he had brought his *Imperial* credentials, and was answered he had. Mr. Jefferson then turned the conversation towards the French Revolution, and remarked how *contrary to all expectations* this great *bouleversement* had turned out. It seemed as if every thing in that country for the last twelve or fifteen years had been a DREAM; and who could have imagined that such an *ébranlement* would have come to this? He thought it very much to be wished that they could now return to the Constitution of 1789, and call back *the Old Family.* For although by that Constitution the Government was much too weak, and although it was defective in having a Legislature in only one branch, yet even thus it was better than the present form, where it was impossible to perceive *any limits.* I have used as near as possible his very words; for this is one of the most unexpected phases in the waxing and waning opinions of this gentleman concerning the French Revolution. He also mentioned to me the extreme difficulty he had in finding fit characters for appointments in Louisiana, and said he would now give *the creation* for a young lawyer of good abilities, and who could speak the French language, to go to New Orleans as one of the Judges of the Superior Court in the Territory. The salary was about two thousand dollars. We had been very lucky in obtaining one such Judge in Mr. Prevost of New York, who had accepted the appointment, and was perfectly well qualified, and he was in extreme want of another. I could easily have named a character fully corresponding to the one he appeared so much to want. But if his observations were meant as a *consultation* or an intent to ask whether I knew any such person I could recommend, he was not sufficiently explicit. Though if they were not, I know not why he made them to me. He further observed that both French and Spanish ought to be made primary objects of acquisition in all the educations of our young men. As to Spanish, it was so easy that he had learned it, with the help of Don Quixote lent him by Mr. Cabot, and a grammar, in the course of a passage to Europe, on which he was but nineteen days at sea. But Mr. Jefferson tells large stories. At table he told us that when he was at Marseilles he saw there a Mr. Bergasse, a famous manufacturer of wines, who told him that he would make him any sort of wine he would name, and in any quantities, at six or eight sols the bottle. And though there should not be a drop of the genuine wine required in his composition, yet it should so perfectly imitate the taste that the most refined connoisseur should not be able to tell which was which. You never can be an hour in this man's company without something of the marvellous like these stories. His genius is of the old French school. It conceives better than it combines."

18. JOHN QUINCY ADAMS TO JOHN ADAMS DECEMBER 11, 1804

"The French Minister, General Turreau, has called upon me. His family has not yet arrived. The President complains that he glitters too much with gold lace, and hopes in time to get him down to a plain frock coat. The Legion of Honor has a bauble at the buttonhole so closely resembling the old *Croix de St. Louis,* that it requires an opera glass to discover the difference between them. The President told me that the best thing which could now happen to the French nation would be to *recall the old family!!!* and take up the Constitution of 1791. For that although that constitution made the government *too weak!!* and was *defective* in having a legislature in one branch! yet even that would be better than the present unlimited domination. I hope he does not talk so to any body who will carry his words to the Emperor Napoleon."

19. AN EXCERPT FROM THE DIARY OF JOHN QUINCY ADAMS JANUARY 11, 1805

". . . Dined at the President's, with my wife. General Smith and his brother of the navy, Mr. William Smith, formerly a member of Congress, from Baltimore, Mr. Williams and his two daughters, Mrs. Hall and Mrs. Hewes, were there. So was the Vice-President. The President appeared to have his mind absorbed by some other object, for he was less attentive to his company than usual. His itch for telling prodigies, however, is unabated. Speaking of the cold, he said he had seen Fahrenheit's thermometer, *in Paris*, at twenty degrees below zero, and that, not for a single day, but that for six weeks together it stood *thereabouts*. 'Never once in the whole time,' said he, 'so high as zero, which is *fifty* degrees below the freezing point.' These were his own words. He knows better than all this; but he loves to excite wonder. Fahrenheit's thermometer never since Mr. Jefferson existed was at twenty degrees below zero in Paris. It was never for six weeks together so low as twenty degrees above zero. Nor is Fahrenheit's zero fifty degrees below freezing point. I asked him upon what foundation he had, in his *Notes on Virginia*, spoken of the river Potomac as common to Virginia and Maryland. He said it was in *the compact* between the States – that the character of Maryland had included the bed of the river, but the compact had made it common. It is singular, however, if this be the case, that among the vouchers expressly given in the book this compact is not at all mentioned, though a compact with Pennsylvania is. He added, however, that as to all the arguments inferred from these facts in the debate of the House of Representatives (alluding to Mr. J. Randolph's arguments), he considered them as mere metaphysical subtleties, and that they ought to have no weight. This conversation was interrupted by the entrance of General Turreau and Captain Marin; immediately after which we took leave."

20. AN EXCERPT FROM THE DIARY OF JOHN QUINCY ADAMS FEBRUARY 13, 1805

". . . At precisely twelve the two Houses met in convention. The Vice-President opened the duplicate returns, and the votes were read and minuted down by the tellers. There was some question on the accuracy of the returns from the State of Ohio: but they were finally received. The whole number of electors and of votes was one hundred and seventy-six, of which one hundred and sixty-two were for Thomas Jefferson as President and George Clinton as Vice-President, and fourteen for Charles Cotesworth Pinckney as President and Rufus King as Vice-President."

21. JOHN QUINCY ADAMS TO JOHN ADAMS MARCH 14, 1805

"President Jefferson is reported to have said to a member of the Senate, that impeachment was but a clumsy engine to get rid of judges. His warmest friends in both houses of Congress are, I believe, by this time tolerably well convinced of the same thing."

22. AN EXCERPT FROM THE DIARY OF JOHN QUINCY ADAMS NOVEMBER 25, 1805

". . . After returning to Mrs. Decharm's, Mr. John Vaughn called on me, as did Dr. Rush. The object of the latter was to inform me of a conversation which he had with Mr. Madison, the Secretary of State, in the course of the last summer, respecting me. Mr. Madison, he said, had expressed himself in very favorable terms of me, and had told him that the President's opinion of me was equally advantageous, and that it was his wish to employ me on some mission abroad, if I was desirous of it. The Doctor therefore intimated that I might govern myself accordingly, and take much measures to manifest my views as I should think expedient. I told him that I had heretofore received suggestions of a similar nature; that I was obliged to Mr. Jefferson and Mr. Madison for their good opinion; that I never had, and I hoped I never should ask for any office of any man, and certainly never should solicit Mr. Jefferson for any place whatsoever; that all I could say to him was, that if Mr. Jefferson should nominate me for any office abroad to which he thought me competent, I would not refuse it merely because the nomination should come from him. He said this assurance was entirely satisfactory, and that he believed the apprehension of a disdainful refusal was the only thing which could deter Mr. Jefferson from offering me an appointment. I assured him there was no office in the President's gift for which I had any wish, and that, without being rich, I possessed the means of maintaining my family without feeling the necessity of any public station."

23. AN EXCERPT FROM THE DIARY OF JOHN QUINCY ADAMS NOVEMBER 30, 1805

". . . The President mentioned a late act of hostility committed by a French privateer near Charleston, South Carolina, and said that we ought to assume as a principle that the neutrality of our territory should extend to the Gulf Stream, which was a natural boundary, and within which we ought not to suffer any hostility to be committed. Mr. Gaillard observed that on a former occasion in Mr. Jefferson's correspondence with Genet, and by an act of Congress at that period, we had seemed only to claim the usual distance of three miles from the coast; but the President replied that he had then assumed that principle because Genet by his intemperance forced us to fix on some point, and we were not then prepared to assert the claim of jurisdiction to the extent we are in reason entitled to; but he had then taken care expressly to reserve the subject for future consideration, with a view to this same doctrine for which he now contends. I observed that it might be well, before we ventured to assume a claim so broad, to wait for a time when we should have a force competent to maintain it. But in the mean time, he said, it was advisable to *squint at it*, and to accustom the nations of Europe to the idea that we should claim it in future."

24. AN EXCERPT FROM THE DIARY OF JOHN QUINCY ADAMS FEBRUARY 25, 1806

". . . I dined at the President's, with a company of fifteen members of both Houses, all federalists, and consisting chiefly of the delegations from Massachusetts and Connecticut. Mr. White, of Delaware, was also there. I came home early in the evening, and spent it in writing. Conversing with the President on public affairs, he told me that he understood Mr. Gregg's proposition was to be abandoned, and that the question would be between *Mr. Nicholson's* resolutions or nothing. I said it seemed probable that *nothing* would eventually have the preference. He said that then we must abandon our carrying trade, for that unless something were done in aid of negotiation of Great Britain would never yield on this point. His own preference is manifestly for Nicholson's resolution, which is indeed a renewal of his own project in 1794, then produced in Congress by Mr. Madison. He appeared not well pleased when I intimated the suspicion that *nothing* would be done. So he probably counts on the success of Nicholson's motion."

25. AN EXCERPT FROM THE DIARY OF JOHN QUINCY ADAMS FEBRUARY 16, 1807

". . . The President was less cheerful in his manners than usual, but told some of his customary staring stories. Among the rest, he said that before he went from Virginia to France he had some ripe pears sewed up in tow bags, and that when he returned six years afterwards he found them in a perfect state of preservation – self-candied."

26. AN EXCERPT FROM THE DIARY OF JOHN QUINCY ADAMS NOVEMBER 3, 1807

". . . Mr. Jefferson said that the Epicurean philosophy came nearest to the truth, in his opinion, of any ancient system of philosophy, but that it had been misunderstood and misrepresented. He wished the work of Gassendi concerning it had been translated. It was the only accurate account of it extant. I mentioned Lucretius. He said that was only a part – only the *natural* philosophy. But the *moral* philosophy was only to be found in Gassendi.

Dr. Mitchell mentioned Mr. Fulton's steamboat as an invention of great importance. To which Mr. Jefferson, assenting, added, 'and I think his torpedoes a valuable invention too.' He then enlarged upon the certainty of their effect, and adverted to some of the obvious objections against them, which he contended were not conclusive. Dr. Mitchell's conversation was very various, of chemistry, of geography, and of natural philosophy; of oils, grasses, beasts, birds, petrifactions, and incrustations; Pike and Humboldt, Lewis and Barlow, and a long train of et cetera – for the Doctor knows a little of everything, and is communicative of what he knows – which makes me delight in his company. Mr. Jefferson said that he had always been extremely fond of agriculture, and knew nothing about it, but the person who united with other sciences the greatest agricultural knowledge of any man he knew was Mr. Madison. He was the bet farmer I the world. On the whole, it was one of the most agreeable dinners I have had at Mr. Jefferson's."

27. JOHN QUINCY ADAMS TO JOHN ADAMS NOVEMBER 30, 1807

"I remain of my first opinion on my arrival [to Washington, D. C.]. The President's policy is *procrastination,* and if Great Britain does not wage *complete* war upon us, we shall end with doing nothing this session. . . ."

28. AN EXCERPT FROM THE MEMOIRS OF JOHN QUINCY ADAMS DECEMBER 31, 1807

". . . On most of the great national questions now under discussion, my sense of duty leads me to support the Administration, and I find myself of course in opposition to the federalists in general. But I have no communication with the President other than that in the regular order of business in the Senate. In this state of things my situation calls in a particular manner for prudence; my political prospects are declining, and as my term of service draws near its close, I am constantly approaching to the certainty of being restored to the situation of a private citizen."

29. JOHN QUINCY ADAMS TO HARRISON GRAY OTIS MARCH 31, 1808

"The embargo, however, is a restriction always under our own control. It was a measure altogether of defence and of experiment. If it was injudiciously or over-hastily laid, it has been every day since its adoption open to a repeal: if it should prove ineffectual for the purposes which it was meant to secure, a single day will suffice to unbar the doors. Still believing it a measure justified by the circumstances of the time, I am ready to admit that those who thought otherwise may have had a wiser foresight of events, and a sounder judgment of the then existing state of things than the majority of the national legislature, and the President."

30. AN EXCERPT FROM THE DIARY OF JOHN QUINCY ADAMS MARCH 11, 1808

". . . I reached the Capitol this morning rather later than usual, and found the Senate in session. The Vice-President had been formally complaining of the President for a mistake which was really his own. The message of the twenty-six of February was read in public because the Vice-President on receiving it had not noticed the word '*confidential*' written on the outside cover. This had been told in the newspapers, and commented on as evidence of Mr. Clinton's *declining years*. He thinks it was designedly done by the President to ensnare him and expose him to derision. This morning he asked Mr. Otis for a certificate that the message was received in Senate without the word 'confidential;' which Otis declining to do, he was much incensed with him, and spoke to the Senate in anger, concluding by saying that he thought the *Executive* would have had more magnanimity than to have treated him thus."

31. JOHN QUINCY ADAMS TO GEORGE BOYD MAY 14, 1808

"It is I believe known to both to Mr. Madison and to Mr. Jefferson, that I have no personal favor whatsoever to ask of either, and an application in behalf of any person connected with me would appear a departure from those principles to which in all consistency I ought to adhere."

32. JOHN QUINCY ADAMS TO ORCHARD COOK AUGUST 22, 1808

"There has been a meeting of the inhabitants of [Boston], in which a petition to the President was voted, requesting him to suspend the embargo in whole or in part, and if he has any doubt of his power, to call Congress together immediately."

33. JOHN QUINCY ADAMS TO LOUISA CATHERINE ADAMS MARCH 5, 1809

"Immediately after the ceremony was performed the President and his lady received company at their own house. I paid my visit with your mama and Mr. and Mrs. Hellen. It was not at the President's house, which Mr. Jefferson has not yet left. He was with the company who visited his successor."

34. JOHN QUINCY ADAMS TO EZEKIEL BACON JUNE 15, 1809

"I have always thought that the complaints of the English government in regard to this partial exclusion were not without foundation. And it was on this principle, that when the *law*, upon which Mr. Jefferson's excluding Proclamation issued, passed in Congress, I opposed it with all my most fruitless zeal. I mean the law of 3 March, 1805. Under that law I considered the President as bound in duty to issue the Proclamation, and after it was issued the nation was bound to support it. But there never was a law enacted while I say in Congress, which I more strenuously opposed, and my negative vote stands recorded with only three others on the Senate's journals. None of those who have since abused Mr. Jefferson for issuing his Proclamation as that law required, would then join me in voting against the *law*."

35. JOHN QUINCY ADAMS TO WILLIAM EUSTIS OCTOBER 26, 1811

"I have read also in the English newspapers some late lucubrations of Mr. Pickering to prove his old fable of a compact between Mr. Jefferson and Napoleon that the United States should go to war with England. If Pickering believes this himself, it is by means of the process with which Shakespeare says a man works himself up 'to credit his own lye;' but Pickering is cunning enough to see that a war with England may be unavoidable, and *then* he thinks to batter down the administration with this foolish tale of its having been concerted with France beforehand."

36. JOHN QUINCY ADAMS TO ABIGAIL ADAMS MAY 28, 1812

"You will ere this have ample reason to be convinced that Mr. J's rule of taking the exact counterpart of England's interest for the anticipation of her practical policy is not likely to fail at this time."

37. JOHN QUINCY ADAMS TO ABIGAIL ADAMS MARCH 25, 1813

"It is said that opposition to the war with England is the connecting principle which has brought together parties hitherto heterogeneous. But were General Pinckney and Mr. King less averse to the British war than Mr. Clinton and Mr. Ingersoll? Or have the federalists voted for those gentlemen upon the same basis as their representatives, and voted for Mr. Burr not for the sake of choosing him but for that of excluding Mr. Jefferson?"

38. JOHN QUINCY ADAMS TO ABIGAIL ADAMS MAY 16, 1817

"I am aware that by the experience of our history under the present constitution, Mr. Jefferson alone of our four Presidents has had the good fortune of a Cabinet harmonizing with each other and with him through the whole period of his administration."

39. JOHN QUINCY ADAMS TO CHRISTOPHER HUGHES JUNE 22, 1818

"It was a maxim of Mr. Jefferson's, which I find is also approved by Mr. Monroe, that Americans, and especially young Americans, should for their own sake, as well as for that of their country, make no long residences in a public capacity at the courts of Europe. He thought the air of those regions so unfriendly to American constitutions that they always required after a few years to be renovated by the wholesome republican atmosphere of their own country. The practice of the present administration will be altogether conformable to these principles."

40. EXCERPT FROM THE DIARY OF JOHN QUINCY ADAMS OCTOBER 20, 1821

"Jefferson and Madison did attain power by organizing and heading a system of attack upon the Washington Administration, chiefly under the banners of State rights and State sovereignty. They argued and scolded against all implied powers, and pretended that the Government of the Union had no powers but such as were expressly delegated by the Constitution. They succeeded. Mr. Jefferson was elected President of the United States, and the first thing he did was to purchase Louisiana—an assumption of implied power greater in itself and more comprehensive in its consequences than all the assumptions of implied powers in the twelve years of the Washington and Adams Administrations put together. Through the sixteen years of the Jefferson and Madison Administrations not the least regard was paid to the doctrines of rejecting implied powers, upon which those gentlemen had vaulted into the seat of government, with the single exception that Mr. Madison negatived a bill for applying public money to the public internal improvement of the country. But the same Mr. Madison signed a bill for incorporating a Bank of the United States, against which he and all the Virginian party had stubbornly contended as unconstitutional, because *express* power was not given to the Congress to incorporate banks."

41. JOHN QUINCY ADAMS TO ROBERT WALSH JUNE 21, 1822

"When I see Mr. Jefferson, with the snows of fourscore winters upon his head and with all the claims of a life devoted to the service of his country and of mankind to the veneration of all, hunted in the face of evidence as a fraudulent peculator of a sum less than 1200 dollars by 'a native of Virginia' with a malignity and pertinacity equal to but not surpassing the address and cunning of the accusation, I am willing to forget the charges equally false and equally base of the same native of Virginia against myself. That his charges against me are all as false as that against Mr. Jefferson I affirm, and have proved to the satisfaction of the Committee of Congress upon the expenditures in the Department of State."

42. JOHN QUINCY ADAMS TO LOUISA CATHERINE ADAMS AUGUST 28, 1822

". . . my reason for going to the theatre now is that as yet I can do nothing else with the evening. This reason will soon cease. We have had Booth. We now have a man by the name of Wilson, and next week we are to have Cooper, all tragedy heroes. But I prefer Jefferson to them all. The broader the farce, the more I enjoy it."

43. AN EXCERPT FROM THE DIARY OF JOHN QUINCY ADAMS SEPTEMBER 27, 1822

". . . Mr. Calhoun has a most ardent desire that the island of Cuba should become a part of the United States, and says that Mr. Jefferson has the same. There are two dangers to be averted by that event; one, that the island should fall into the hands of Great Britain; the other, that it should be revolutionized by the negroes. Calhoun says Mr. Jefferson told him two years ago that we ought, at the first possible opportunity, to take Cuba, though at the cost of a war with England; but as we are not now prepared for this, and as our great object must be to gain time, he thought we should answer this overture by dissuading them from their present purpose, and urging them to adhere at present to their connection with Spain."

44. JOHN QUINCY ADAMS TO THE FREEHOLDERS OF WASHINGTON, WYTHE, GRAYSON, RUSSELL, TAZEWELL, LEE AND SCOTT COUNTIES, VIRGINIA DECEMBER 28, 1822

"In entertaining these sentiments it is certainly with all the regard and veneration due from me to Mr. Jefferson, as to one of the men to whom the nation owes its deepest debt of gratitude. I am charged by General Smyth with an attempt to ridicule Mr. Jefferson. An expression, distorted and misrepresented in the kennel newspapers of the present day, is the support which the General has for this accusation. Of that expression and of the cause from which it proceeded, I will not now speak. If the animosities of political contention are not to be eternal, it is time to consign that subject to silence. But I address you in the face of our common country, and I hope and trust this paper will pass under the eye of Mr. Jefferson himself. I say, without fear of being disavowed by him, that he will not approve of the use of his name by any one for the purpose of casting odium upon me. And I take this opportunity to add that I deprecate with equal earnestness the unauthorized use by any one of his name to obtain favor of any kind for me."

45. AN EXCERPT FROM JOHN QUINCY ADAMS'S *PARTIES IN THE UNITED STATES* JANUARY 1822

"The opposition to a naval establishment had been so great during the administration of Washington that a small, temporary armament and the building of six frigates was all that it had een possible to effect. The opposition had the support of Mr. Jefferson's opinions. His aversion to the navy was both sectional and political. The first and most important uses of a navy are found in the protection of commercial interests; these were not of primary consideration in the mind of Mr. Jefferson. But a navy was also an engine of power; it would contribute greatly to the strength of the general government. Mr. Jefferson thought it had a squinting to monarchy — upon both these grounds he opposed it, and the then styled Republican Party sustained him."

46. AN EXCERPT FROM JOHN QUINCY ADAMS'S *PARTIES IN THE UNITED STATES* JANUARY 1822

"The feeling of indignation at this outrage was almost universal among the people, but it did not extend to the leaders of the Federal Party, who had formed in 1804 the project of a separate Northern confederacy.[79] They had wrought themselves up into such an abhorrence of and terror of Bonaparte and such an admiration of Great Britain, together with such a belief that Mr. Jefferson was secretly and corruptly in league with Napoleon, that they believed or affected to believe that this affair had been intentionally provoked by Mr. Jefferson to produce a war with Great Britain. I have heard that sentiment expressed by more than one of the persons who afterwards became very conspicuous in the opposition, and I was informed by a person in whose veracity I have perfect confidence that one of them made no scruple of saying, and did say in his hearing, that Mr. Jefferson was sold to France for money."

47. AN EXCERPT FROM JOHN QUINCY ADAMS'S *PARTIES IN THE UNITED STATES* JANUARY 1822

"During the eight years of Mr. Jefferson's administration, the political party principle, with the Republican Party, had absorbed all others, and its result was to resolve the whole into his personal influence. One of the consequences of this was to throw all the sectional influence operating upon the people of the Northern states into the hands of the Federalists. Mr. Jefferson found the convenience of this so great that towards the close of his life he intimated in his confidential letters that he considered 'the party division of Whig and Tory the most wholesome which could exist in any government, and well worthy of being nourished, to keep out those of a more dangerous character.' It was this party division of Whig and Tory which had given to Mr. Jefferson a personal influence almost dictatorial, and he had availed himself of it not only to overthrow the administration of his predecessor, but also to establish the principle as an axiom of government that commerce is but the handmaid of agriculture – the very axiom of the Tories in England when those names had any significancy there. But the efficacy of Mr. Jefferson's Whig party machinery arose from the fact that, at the time when he wielded it, all Europe was divided upon it as a standard of parties, and Napoleon was the head of the Whigs in Europe as Mr. Jefferson was their head in America. The party division of Whig and Tory was certainly all-sufficient for them; but if it is to be used to break down the tenure of judicial office under the government of the United States, or to restore the relative condition of commerce

79 Adams was referring to the practice of British impressment of sailors from U. S. ships on the high seas, specifically the *Chesapeake.*

to servitude under another interest by the annihilation of the navy, or to turn back the progress of internal improvements in ghastly horror at the phantom of consolidation, it is devoutly to be hoped that it may not be nourished, even to keep out others which might seem to him more dangerous."

48. JOHN QUINCY ADAMS TO THE FREEHOLDERS OF WASHINGTON, WYTHE, GRAYSON, RUSSELL, TAZEWELL, LEE AND SCOTT COUNTIES, VIRGINIA DECEMBER 28, 1822

"I declare to you that not one of the votes which General Smyth has called from an arduous service of five years in the Senate of the Union, to stigmatize them in the face of the country, was given from any of the passions or motives to which he ascribes them; that I never gave a vote either in hostility to the administration of Mr. Jefferson, or in disregard to republican principles, or in aversion to republican patriots, or in favor of the slave trade, or in denial of due protection to commerce. I will add, that having often differed in judgment with many of the best and wisest men of this Union of all parties, I have never lost sight either of the candor due to them in the estimate of their motives, or of the difficulties with which it was my duty to maintain the result of my own opinions in opposition to theirs."

49. AN EXCERPT FROM JOHN QUINCY ADAMS'S *PARTIES IN THE UNITED STATES* JANUARY 1822

"The retirement of President Washington had been prompted by a real weariness and disgust of with public life, that of Mr. Jefferson by political principle. He had entertained the opinion that there should have been a constitutional interdict upon the re-eligibility of the President, and he was willing in this respect to sanction his doctrine by his example."

50. AN EXCERPT FROM THE DIARY OF JOHN QUINCY ADAMS MAY 23, 1824

". . . Mr. Hay spoke, as he always does, with extreme bitterness of Mr. Jefferson, whom he declares to be one of the most insincere men in the world. He reminded me of a letter written by Mr. Jefferson to Mr. Monroe in 1818-19, upon my controversial papers with Spain, and relating to the Seminole War. They were in a style even of extravagant encomium. Precisely at the same time, Hay says, Ritchie, of Richmond, told him that Mr. Jefferson had spoken of the same papers in terms of severe reprobation to a gentleman from whom he had it. Hay said he told Ritchie that that gentleman lied; but he knew better: the gentleman was Edward Coles, and he had told the truth. Mr. Jefferson! – his enmity to Mr. Monroe was inveterate, though disguised, and he was at the bottom of all the opposition to Mr. Monroe in Virginia."

51. AN EXCERPT FROM THE DIARY OF JOHN QUINCY ADAMS MAY 18, 1824

". . . G. Sullivan came and took leave. Spoke of his visits to Mr. Jefferson and Mr. Madison, the latter of whom, he said, appeared cordially disposed to this Administration; Mr. Jefferson less so, and particularly with regard to Mr. Clay."

52. AN EXCERPT FROM THE DIARY OF JOHN QUINCY ADAMS JULY 1, 1826

". . . Governor Barbour proposed that on the 4th instant, after the usual ceremonies at the Capitol, he should address the audience, and invite an immediate subscription for the benefit of Mr. Jefferson. Says he proposes to give a hundred dollars himself. Mr. Rush came in while we were speaking of it. I doubted the expediency of the measure, and its success; and thought it would be more likely to succeed if a meeting should be called and a subscription raised as elsewhere. Governor Barbour says the late rains have done immense and irreparable damage to his estate – his loss many thousands."

53. AN EXCERPT FROM THE DIARY OF JOHN QUINCY ADAMS JULY 3, 1826

". . . Dr. Watkins called to say that he and Mr. Asbury Dickins, two members of the Committee of Arrangements, would attend me to the Capitol to-morrow. He also showed me the answers from the surviving signers of the Declaration of Independence and ex-Presidents, declining the invitations to attend the celebration here. Mr. Jefferson's is in the freest style; my father's is signed with his own hand;"

54. AN EXCERPT FROM THE DIARY OF JOHN QUINCY ADAMS JULY 6, 1826

". . . Governor Barbour brought information of the decease of Mr. Jefferson at Monticello on the 4th inst., at ten minutes past one in the afternoon — a strange and very striking coincidence. It became a question whether the event should be noticed by some act of the Administration. Several measures suggested themselves, and were taken for further consideration. The precedent in the case of General Washington's decease was adverted to and examined. But the Congress were then in session, and, excepting the orders for military honors, all was done at the recommendation and by resolutions of that body. We now concluded that general orders to the army and navy would be proper and indispensible, and would reflect till to-morrow on the expediency of issuing a proclamation to the people."

55. AN EXCERPT FROM THE DIARY OF JOHN QUINCY ADAMS JULY 7, 1826

". . . Henry Lee called, and told me that he had been last week to Monticello to consult some papers relating to the Revolutionary War in Mr. Jefferson's possession, and of which he had promised Mr. Lee the perusal. He was there last week, on Thursday, when Mr. Jefferson was, though ill, yet able to converse with him on the subject, and hoped to be able to examine the papers with him in a few days. But from that time Mr. Jefferson grew worse, and on Sunday Lee gave up all expectation of seeing the papers, and left Monticello and Charlottesville, and returned."

56. AN EXCERPT FROM THE DIARY OF JOHN QUINCY ADAMS JULY 21, 1826

". . . Mrs. Clark said to him [John Adams] that it was the 4th of July, the fiftieth anniversary of independence. He answered, 'It is a great day. It is a good day.' About one in the afternoon he said, 'Thomas Jefferson survives,' but the last word was indistinctly and imperfectly uttered."

57. AN ENTRY FROM THE DIARY OF JOHN QUINCY ADAMS NOVEMBER 7, 1830

". . . By the Constitution of the United States, the President is re-eligible as long as he lives. Washington, Jefferson, and Madison voluntarily retired after one re-election, and

Jefferson no doubt intended to make the example a practical exposition of constitutional principle."

58. AN EXCERPT FROM THE DIARY OF JOHN QUINCY ADAMS JANUARY 11, 1831

"I . . . read about fifty pages of the first volume of Jefferson's *Memoirs*. He states that he began his autobiography on the 6th of January, 1821, in the seventy-seventh year of his age. . . The account of his childhood and youth is short, and not boastful; but there are no confessions. He tells nothing but what redounds to his own credit. He is like the French lady who told her sister she did not know how it happened, 'mais il n'y a que moi au monde qui a toujours raison.' Jefferson, by his own narrative, is always in the right. This is not uncommon to writers of their own lives. Dr. Franklin was more candid. Mr. Jefferson names the teachers from whom he learnt Greek, Latin, and French, and speaks gratefully of William Small, a Scotchman, professor of mathematics at William and Mary College, who became attached to him, and probably fixed the destinies of his life. It is rather intimated than expressly told that Small initiated him in the mysteries of free-thinking and irreligion, which did fix the destinies of his life. Loose morals necessarily followed. If not an absolute atheist, he had no belief in a future existence. All his ideas of obligation or retribution were bounded by the present life. His duties to his neighbor were under no stronger guarantee than the laws of the land and the opinions of the world. The tendency of this condition upon a mind of great compass and powerful resources is to produce insincerity and duplicity, which were his besetting sins through life."

59. AN EXCERPT FROM THE DIARY OF JOHN QUINCY ADAMS JANUARY 12, 1831

". . . I finished the memoir of Jefferson's life, which terminates on the 21st of March, 1790, when he arrived at New York to take upon him the office of Secretary of State. There it ends; and there, as a work of much interest to the present and future ages, it should have begun. It is much to be regretted that he did not tell his own story from that time until his retirement from the office of President of the United States in 1809. It was then that all the good and all the evil parts of his character were brought into action. His ardent passion for liberty and the rights of man; his patriotism; the depth and compass of his understanding; the extent and variety of his knowledge, and the enviable faculty of applying it to his own purposes; the perpetual watchfulness of public opinion, and the pliability of principle and temper with which he accommodated to it his own designs and opinions; — all these were in ceaseless operation during those twenty years; and with them were combined a rare mixture of infidel philosophy and epicurean morals, of burning ambition and of a stoical self-control, of deep duplicity and of generous sensibility, between which two qualities, and a treacherous and inventive memory, his conduct towards his rivals and opponents appears one tissue of inconsistency. His treatment of Washington, of Knox, of my father, of Hamilton, of Bayard, who made him President of the United States, and, lastly, of me, is marked with features of perfidy worthy of Tiberius Caesar or Louis the Eleventh of France. This double-dealing character was often imputed to him during his life, and was sometimes exposed. His letter to Mazzei, and the agonizing efforts which he afterwards made to explain it away; his most insidious attack upon my father with his never-ceasing professions of respect and affection for his person and character; and his letter to Giles concerning me, in which there is scarcely a single word of truth — indicate a memory so pandering to the will that in deceiving others he seems to have begun by deceiving himself."

60. AN EXCERPT FROM THE DIARY OF JOHN QUINCY ADAMS JANUARY 25, 1831

". . . Read a few stanzas of *Childe Harold*, and further in the correspondence of Jefferson, till the letter of 28th of May, 1781, to General Washington, announcing his long-declared resolution of retiring from the oppression of his office as Governor of Virginia to private life. . . Where was he from June, 1781, to the close of the war? No mortal can tell from the memoir or the correspondence. In that very June, 1781, at the moment when he resigned his office as Governor of Virginia, he was appointed one of the Ministers for negotiating peace with Great Britain, then, he says, expected to be effected through the mediation of the Empress of Russia. He declined this appointment, he says, for the same reasons for which he had declined in 1776. And what were they? Take his words: 'such was the state of my family that I could not leave it, nor could I expose it to the dangers of the sea, and of capture by the British ships, then covering the ocean. I saw, too, that the laboring oar was really at home, where much was to be done of the most permanent interest, in new-modelling our Governments, and much to defend our fanes and firesides from the desolations of an invading enemy, pressing on our country on every point.' The first of these reasons are mere private considerations. He could not leave his family, and would not expose his family to capture by British ships. John Adams three times exposed himself and two boys to capture by British ships during the war. He left his wife, daughter, and one infant son to the protection of his country. John Jay's wife and children went with him. Dr. Franklin went safe in 1776, as Jefferson would have gone if he had been with him. Henry Laurens was taken and sent to the Tower, and harshly treated; but his son was not even imprisoned, and was allowed to visit him; and so might it have been with Mr. Jefferson if he had gone, with or without his family, and been taken. There are dangers which a high-souled man engaged in a sacred cause must encounter and not flinch from. To assign them as reasons for declining the post of honor savors more of the Sybarite than of the Spartan. They remind one of the certain lord, neat, trimly dressed, who but for those vile guns would himself have been a soldier. As to the other reason, of staying at home to defend our fanes and firesides, it certainly did not apply to Mr. Jefferson either in 1776, when there was neither actual nor threatened invasion of Virginia, or in June, 1781, when Mr. Jefferson had slunk from that very defence into the inactive safety of a private citizen. Perhaps Mr. Jefferson was sufficiently punished for his dereliction of the cause by the humiliating necessity under which he has been of drawing a veil over this portion of his life. 'Pends-toi, brave Crillon,' wrote Henry of Navarre to one of his heroic followers, 'nous avons vaincu, et tu n'y etois pas.'"

---

61. AN EXCERPT FROM THE DIARY OF JOHN QUINCY ADAMS JANUARY 27, 1831

". . . In the evening I read a few pages of Jefferson's correspondence . . . Mr. Jefferson's love of liberty was sincere and ardent — not confined to himself, like that of most of his fellow slave-holders. He was above that execrable sophistry of the South Carolinian nullifiers, which would make of slavery the corner-stone to the temple of liberty. He saw the gross inconsistency between the principles of the Declaration of Independence and the fact of negro slavery, and he could not, or would not, prostitute the faculties of his mind to the vindication of that slavery which from his soul he abhorred. Mr. Jefferson had not the spirit of martyrdom. He would have introduced a flaming denunciation of slavery into the Declaration of Independence, but the discretion of his colleagues struck it out. He did insert a most eloquent and impassioned argument against it in his Notes upon Virginia; but on that very account the book was published almost against his will. He projected a plan of general emancipation in his revision of the Virginia laws, but finally presented a plan of leaving slavery precisely where it was. And in his memoirs he leaves a posthumous warning to the planters, that they must at no distant day emancipate their slaves, or that worse will follow; but he withheld the publication of his prophecy till he should himself be in the grave."

---

62. AN EXCERPT FROM THE DIARY OF JOHN QUINCY ADAMS MARCH 8, 1831

". . . It is a doctrine of the medical faculty that bodily exercise to be salutary should be taken with a vacant mind; such is the precept of Mr. Jefferson. . . At certain seasons, however, the propensity becomes too strong for me. I walk and muse and pour forth premeditated verse, which it takes me six or nine months to lay by and resume to find it good for nothing. It never appears so to me when I compose it."

63. AN EXCERPT FROM THE DIARY OF JOHN QUINCY ADAMS JULY 16, 1834

". . . That which absorbed the largest portion of the day was a research respecting the origin of committees of correspondence in the approach of our war for independence. George Tucker, Professor of Moral Philosophy at the University of Virginia, recently wrote me a letter or enquiry upon this subject. He is writing the life of Thomas Jefferson, and enquires whether any committees of correspondence were appointed by the Legislature of the Colony of Massachusetts Bay before 1773. Jefferson claims the invention of committees of correspondence for Virginia, and it has become a controverted point of history."

64. AN EXCERPT FROM JOHN QUINCY ADAMS'S EULOGY, *LIFE OF JAMES MADISON* JUNE 8, 1836

". . . The influence of Mr. Jefferson over the mind of Mr. Madison was composed of all that genius, talent, experience, splendid public services, exalted reputation, added to congenial tempers, undivided friendship and habitual sympathies of interest and of feeling could inspire. Among the numerous blessings which it was the rare good fortune of Mr. Jefferson's life to enjoy was that of uninterrupted, disinterested, and efficient friendship of Madison."

65. AN EXCERPT FROM JOHN QUINCY ADAMS'S EULOGY, *LIFE OF JAMES MADISON* JUNE 8, 1836

"The controversies of conflicting neutral and belligerent rights continued through the whole of Mr. Jefferson's administration, during the latter part of which they were verging rapidly to war. He had carried the policy of peace perhaps to an extreme. His system of defence by commercial restrictions, dry-docks, gun-boats and embargoes was stretched to its last hair's breadth of endurance. Far be it from me, my fellow citizens, to speak of this system or of its motives with disrespect. If there be a duty, binding in chains more adamantine than all the rest the consequences of a Chief Magistrate of this Union, it is that of preserving peace with all mankind – peace with other nations of the earth – peace among the several States of this Union – peace in the hearts and temper of our own people. Yet must a President of the United States never cease to feel that his charge is to maintain the rights, the interests and the honor no less than the peace of his country – nor will he be permitted to forget that peace must be the offspring of two concurring wills. That to seek peace is not always to ensure it. He must remember, too, that a reliance upon the operation of measures, from their effect on the *interests*, however clear and unequivocal, of nations, cannot be safe against a counter current of their passions. That nations, like individuals, sacrifice their peace to their pride, to their hatred, to their envy, to their jealousy, and even to the craft which the cunning of hackneyed politicians not unfrequently mistake for policy. That nations, like individuals, have sometimes the misfortune of losing their senses, and that lunatic communities, which cannot be confined in hospitals, must be resisted in arms, as a single maniac is sometimes restored to reason by the scourge. That national madness is infectious, and that a paroxysm of it in one people, especially when generated by the Furies that presides [*sic*] over war, produces a counter paroxysm in their adverse party. Such is the melancholy condition as yet of associated man. And while in the wise but mysterious dispensations of an overruling Providence man shall so continue, the peace of every nation must depend not alone upon its own will, but upon that concurrently with the will of all others.

And such was the condition of the two mightiest nations of the earth during the administration of Mr. Jefferson. Frantic, in fits of mutual hatred, envy and jealousy against each other; meditating mutual invasion and conquest, and forcing the other nations of the four quarters of the globe to the alternative of joining them as allies or encountering them as foes. Mr. Jefferson met them with moral philosophy and commercial restrictions, with dry-docks and gun-boats – with non-intercourses, and embargoes, till the American nation were told that they could not be kicked into a war, and till they were taunted by a British statesman in the Imperial Parliament of England, with their five frigates and their striped bunting.

Mr. Jefferson pursued his policy of peace till it brought the nation to the borders of internal war. An embargo of fourteen months' duration was at last reluctantly abandoned by him, when it had ceased to be obeyed by the people, and State courts were ready to pronounce it unconstitutional. A non-intercourse was then substituted in its place, and the helm of State passed from the hands of Mr. Jefferson to those of Mr. Madison, precisely at the moment of this perturbation of earth and sea threatened with war from abroad and at home, but with the principle definitely settled that in our intercourse with foreign nations reason, justice and commercial restrictions require live-oak hearts and iron or brazen mouths to speak, that they may be distinctly heard, or attentively listened to, but the distant ear of foreigners, whether French or British, monarchical or republican."

66. AN EXCERPT FROM THE DIARY OF JOHN QUINCY ADAMS AUGUST 29, 1836

"To refresh my memory on these subjects [the Alien and Sedition Acts], and to retrace the history of those controversies more accurately, I read over the portion of Jefferson's correspondence during that period, published by his grandson. It shows his craft and duplicity in very glaring colors. I incline to the opinion that he was not altogether conscious of his own insincerity, and deceived himself as well as others. His success through a long life, and especially from his entrance upon the office of Secretary of State under Washington until he reached the Presidential chair, seems, to my imperfect vision, a slur upon the moral government of the world. His rivalry with Hamilton was unprincipled on both sides. His treatment of my father was double-dealing, treacherous, and false beyond all toleration. His letter to Mazzei, and his subsequent explanations of it, and apologies for it, show that he treated Washington, as far as he dared, no better than he did my father; but it was Washington's popularity that he never dared to encounter. His correspondence now published proves how he dreaded and detested it. His letter to my father, at the first competition between them for the Presidency, the fawning dissimulation of his first address as Vice-President to the Senate, with his secret machinations against him from that day forth, show a character in no wise amiable or fair; but his attachment to those of his friends whom he could make useful to himself was thoroughgoing and exemplary. Madison moderated some of his excesses, and refrained from following others."

67. AN EXCERPT FROM THE DIARY OF JOHN QUINCY ADAMS AUGUST 30, 1836

"I wrote little, and continued reading the letters of Jefferson from 1793 till August, 1803, published by his grandson. His duplicity sinks deeper and deeper into my mind. His hatred of Hamilton was unbounded; of John Marshall, most intense; of my father, tempered with compunctious visitings, always controlled by his ambition. They had been cordial friends and co-operators in the great cause of independence, and as joint Commissioners abroad after the Peace of 1783; there had then been a warm and confidential intimacy between them, which he never entirely shook off, but which he sacrificed always to his ambition, and, at the last stage of his life, to his envy and his poverty; for he died insolvent, and on the very day of his death received eleemosynary donations from the charity of some of those whom he had most deeply injured. This circumstance is not creditable to his country. She ought not to have suffered a man, who had served her as he had, to die with his household wanting the necessities of life. But it was the natural consequence of the niggardly doctrines which his political system had imposed upon him, and which he had passed off upon the country for patriotism. Among his slanders upon the Administration of my father was the charge of extravagance in diplomatic expenditure; and when he sent Mr. Monroe on the Louisiana mission to France, he wrote to him that he could not have an outfit, and that the refusal of outfits was one of his reforms upon extraordinary missions. The end of all which was, that Mr. Monroe obtained not only the outfit, but gratuities and allowances more than any other Minister abroad has ever had, and died leaving still unsatisfied claims. I am compelled to draw many other harsh conclusions against this great man from his now published letters."

68. AN EXCERPT FROM JOHN QUINCY ADAMS'S *ADDRESS TO HIS CONSTITUENTS* SEPTEMBER 17, 1842

". . . . Washington and Jefferson, themselves slaveholders, living and dying, bore testimony against it;"

69. AN EXCERPT FROM JOHN QUINCY ADAMS'S *ADDRESS TO HIS CONSTITUENTS* SEPTEMBER 17, 1842

"The utter and unqualified inconsistency of slavery, in any of its forms, with the principles of the North American Revolution, and the Declaration of our Independence, has so forcibly struck the Southern champions of our rights that the abolition of slavery and the emancipation of slaves was a darling project of Thomas Jefferson from his first entrance into public life to the last years of his existence."

Chapter 4

JAMES MADISON

I: JAMES MADISON ON THE PRESIDENCY

1. EXCERPT FROM JAMES MADISON'S *VIRGINIA PLAN* MAY 29, 1787

"7. Resd. that a National Executive be instituted; to be chosen by the National Legislature for the term of years, to receive punctually at stated times a fixed compensation for the services rendered, in which no increase or diminution shall be made so as to affect the Magistracy, existing at the time of increase or diminution, and to be ineligible a second time; and that besides a general authority to execute the National laws, it ought to enjoy the Executive rights vested in Congress by the Confederation.

8. Resd. that the Executive and a Convenient number of the National Judiciary, ought to compose a Council of revision with authority to examine every act of the National Legislature before it shall operate, & every act of a particular Legislature before a Negative thereon shall be final; and that the dissent of the said Council shall amount to a rejection, unless the Act of the National Legislature be again passed, or that of a particular Legislature be again negatived by ___ of the members of each branch."

2. EXCERPT FROM JAMES MADISON'S NOTES WRITTEN DURING THE CONSTITUTIONAL CONVENTION IN PHILADELPHIA JUNE 1, 1787

"Mad: agrees wth. Wilson in his definition of executive powers—executive powers ex vi termini, do not include the Rights of war & peace &c. but the powers shd. be confined and defined—if large we shall have the Evils of elective Monarchies—probably the best plan will be a single Executive of long duration wth. a Council, with liberty to depart from their Opinion at his peril—."

3. EXCERPT FROM JAMES MADISON'S NOTES WRITTEN DURING THE CONSTITUTIONAL CONVENTION IN PHILADELPHIA JUNE 1, 1787

Mr. Madison thought it would be proper, before a choice shd. be made between a unity and a plurality in the Executive, to fix the extent of the Executive authority; that as certain powers were in their nature Executive, and must be given to that departmt. whether administered by one or more persons, a definition of their extent would assist the judgment in determining how far they might be safely entrusted to a single officer. He accordingly moved that so much of the clause before the Committee as related to the powers of the Executive shd. be struck out & that after the words 'that a national Executive ought to be instituted' there be inserted the words following viz. 'with the power to carry into effect, the national laws, to appoint to offices in cases not otherwise provided for, and to execute such other powers "not Legislative nor Judiciary in their nature," as may from time to time be delegated by the national Legislature.'"

4. EXCERPT FROM JAMES MADISON'S NOTES WRITTEN DURING THE CONSTITUTIONAL CONVENTION IN PHILADELPHIA JUNE 1, 1787

"Mr. Maddison observed that to prevent a Man from holding an Office longer than he ought, he may for malpractice be impeached and removed;—he is not for any ineligibility."

5. EXCERPT FROM JAMES MADISON'S NOTES WRITTEN DURING THE CONSTITUTIONAL CONVENTION IN PHILADELPHIA JUNE 4, 1787

"We must introduce the Checks, which will destroy the measures of an interested majority—in this view a negative in the Ex: is not only necessary for its own safety, but for the safety of a minority in Danger of oppression from an unjust and interested majority—The independent condition of the Ex. who has the Eyes of all Nations on him will render him a just Judge—add the Judiciary and you increase the respectability—"

6. EXCERPT FROM JAMES MADISON'S NOTES WRITTEN DURING THE CONSTITUTIONAL CONVENTION IN PHILADELPHIA JULY 19, 1787

"Mr. Madison. If it be a fundamental principle of free Govt. that the Legislative, Executive & Judiciary powers should be *separately* exercised, it is equally so that they be *independently* exercised. There is the same & perhaps greater reason why the Executive shd. be independent of the Legislature, than why the Judiciary should: A coalition of the two former powers would be more immediately & certainly dangerous to public liberty. It is essential then that the appointment of the Executive should either be drawn from some source, or held by some tenure, that will give him a free agency with regard to the Legislature. This could not be if he was to be appointable from time to time by the Legislature. It was not clear that an appointment in the 1st. instance even with an ineligibility afterwards would not establish an improper connection between the two departments. Certain it was that the appointment would be attended with intrigues and contentions that ought not to be unnecessarily admitted. He was disposed for these reasons to refer the appointment to some other source. The people at large was in his opinion the fittest in itself. It would be as likely as any that could be devised to produce an Executive Magistrate of distinguished Character. The people generally could only know & vote for some Citizen whose merits had rendered him an object of general attention & esteem. There was one difficulty however of a serious nature attending an immediate choice by the people. The right of suffrage was much more diffusive in the Northern than the Southern States; and the latter could have no influence in the election on the score of the Negroes. The substitution of electors obviated this difficulty and seemed on the whole to be liable to fewest objections."

7. EXCERPT FROM JAMES MADISON'S NOTES WRITTEN DURING THE CONSTITUTIONAL CONVENTION IN PHILADELPHIA JULY 20, 1787

"Mr. Madison thought it indispensable that some provision should be made for defending the Community agst the incapacity, negligence or perfidy of the chief Magistrate. The limitation of the period of his service, was not a sufficient security. He might lose his capacity after his appointment. He might pervert his administration into a scheme of peculation or oppression. He might betray his trust to foreign powers. The case of the Executive Magistracy was very distinguishable, from that of the Legislature or of any other public body, holding offices of limited duration. It could not be presumed that all or even a majority of the members of an Assembly would either lose their capacity for discharging, or be bribed to betray, their trust. Besides the restraints of their personal integrity

& honor, the difficulty of acting in concert for purposes of corruption was a security to the public. And if one or a few members only should be seduced, the soundness of the remaining members, would maintain the integrity and fidelity of the body. In the case of the Executive Magistracy which was to be administered by a single man, loss of capacity or corruption was more within the compass of probable events, and either of them might be fatal to the Republic."

8. EXCERPT FROM A SPEECH MADE BY JAMES MADISON DURING THE CONSTITUTIONAL CONVENTION IN PHILADELPHIA JULY 21, 1787

"Instead therefore of contenting ourselves with laying down the Theory in the Constitution that each department ought to be separate & distinct, it was proposed to add a defensive power to each which should maintain the Theory in practice. In so doing we did not blend the departments together. We erected effectual barriers for keeping them separate. The most regular example of this theory was in the British Constitution. Yet it was not only the practice there to admit the Judges to a seat in the legislature, and in the Executive Councils, and to submit to their previous examination all laws of a certain description, but it was part of their Constitution that the Executive might negative any law whatever; a part of *their* Constitution which had been universally regarded as calculated for the preservation of the whole. The objection agst. a union of the Judiciary & Executive branches in the revision of the laws, had either no foundation or was not carried far enough. If such a Union was an improper mixture of powers, or such a Judiciary check on the laws, was inconsistent with the Theory of a free Constitution it was equally so to admit the Executive to any participation in the making of laws; and the revisionary plan ought to be discarded altogether."

9. EXCERPT FROM A SPEECH DELIVERED BY JAMES MADISON DURING THE CONSTITUTIONAL CONVENTION IN PHILADELPHIA JULY 25, 1787

"Mr. Madison. There are objections agst. every mode that has been, or perhaps can be proposed. The election must be made either by some existing authority under the Natil. or State Constitutions—or by some special authority derived from the people—or by the people themselves. The two Existing authorities under the Natl. Constitution wd. be the Legislative & Judiciary. The latter he presumed was out of the question. The former was in his Judgment liable to insuperable objections. Besides the general influence of that mode on the independence of the Executive, 1. the election of the Chief Magistrate would agitate & divide the legislature so much that the public interest would materially suffer by it. Public bodies are always apt to be thrown into contentions, but into more violent ones by such occasions than by any others. 2. the candidate would intrigue with the Legislature, would derive his appointment from the predominant faction, and be apt to render his administration subservient to its views. 3. The Ministers of foreign powers would have and make use of, the opportunity to mix their intrigues & influence with the Election. Limited as the powers of the Executive are, it will be an object of great moment with the great powers of Europe who have American possessions, to have at the head of our Governmt. a man attached to their respective politics & interests. No pains, nor perhaps expense, will be spared, to gain from the Legislature and appointmt. favorable to their wishes. Germany & Poland are witnesses of this danger. In the former, the election of the Head of Empire, till it became in a manner hereditary, interested all Europe, and was much influenced by foreign interference. In the latter, altho' the elective Magistrate has very little real power, his election has at all times produced the most eager interference of for[e]ign princes, and has in fact at length slid entirely into foreign hands. The existing authorities in the States are the Legislative, Executive & Judiciary. The appointment of the Natl. Executive by the first, was objectionable in many points of view, some of which had been already mentioned. He would mention one which of itself would decide his opinion. The Legislatures of the States had betrayed a strong propensity to a variety of pernicious measures. One object of the Natl. Legislre. was to controul this propensity. One object of the Natl. Executive, so far as it would have a negative on the laws, was to controul the Natl. Legislature, so far as it might be infected with a similar propensity. Refer the appointment of the Natl. Executive to the State Legislatures, and this controuling purpose may be defeated. The Legislatures can & will act with some kind of regular plan, and will promote the appointmt. of a man who will not oppose himself to a favorite object. Should a majority of the Legislatures at the time of election have the same object, or different objects of the same kind, The Natl. Executive would be rendered subservient to them. An appointment by the State Executives, was liable among other objections to this insuperable one, that being standing bodies, they could & would be courted, and intrigued with by the Candidates, by their partizans, and by the Ministers of foreign powers. The State Judiciarys had not & he presumed wd. not be proposed as a proper source of appointment. The option before us then lay between an appointment by Electors chosen by the people—and an immediate appointment by the people. He thought the former mode free from many of the objections which had been urged agst. it, and greatly preferable to an appointment by the Natl. Legislature. As the electors would be chosen for the occasion, would meet at once, & proceed immediately to an appointment, there would be very little opportunity for cabal, or corruption. As a further precaution, it might be required that they should meet at some place, distinct from the seat of Govt. and even that no person within a certain distance of the place at the time shd. be eligible. This Mode however had been rejected, so recently & by so great a majority that it probably would not be proposed anew. The remaining mode was an election by the people or rather by the qualified part of them, at large. With all its imperfections he liked this best. He would not repeat either the general argumts. for or the objections agst. this mode. He would only take notice of two difficulties which he admitted to have weight. The first arose from the disposition in the people to prefer a Citizen of their own State, and the disadvantage this wd. throw on the smaller States. Great as this objection might be he did not think it equal to such as lay agst. every other mode which had been proposed. He thought too that some expedient might be hit upon that would obviate it. The second difficulty arose from the disproportion of qualified voters in the N. & S. States, and the disadvantages which this mode would throw on the latter. The answer to this objection was 1. that this disproportion would be continually decreasing under the influence of the Republican laws introduced in the S. States, and the more rapid increase of their population. 2. That local considerations must give way to the general interest. As an individual from the S. States he was willing to make the sacrifice."

10. EXCERPT FROM JAMES MADISON'S NOTES WRITTEN DURING THE CONSTITUTIONAL CONVENTION IN PHILADELPHIA SEPTEMBER 12, 1787

"Mr. Madison. [T]he President was to be elected by the Legislature and for seven years. He is now to be elected by the people and for four years."

11. JAMES MADISON TO THOMAS JEFFERSON OCTOBER 24, 1787

"The first of these objects as it respects the Executive, was peculiarly embarrassing. On the question whether it should consist of a single person, or a plurality of co-ordinate members, on the mode of appointment, on the duration in office, on the degree of power, on the re-eligibility, tedious and reiterated discussions took place. The plurality of co-ordinate members had finally but few advocates. Governour Randolph was at the head of them. The modes of appointment proposed were various, as by the people at large—by electors chosen by the people—by the Executives of the States—by the Congress, some preferring a joint ballot of the two Houses—some a separate concurrent ballot allowing to each a negative on the other house—some a nomination of several canditates [*sic*] by one House, out of whom a choice should be made by the other. Several other modifications were started. The expedient at length adopted seemed to give pretty general satisfaction to the members. As to the duration in office, a few would have preferred a tenure during good behavior—a considerable number would have chosen to do so, in case an easy & effectual removal by impeachment could be settled. It was much agitated whether a long term, seven years for example, with a subsequent & perpetual ineligibility, or a short term with a capacity to be re-elected, should be fixed. In favor of the first opinion were urged the danger of a gradual degeneracy of re-elections from time to time, into first a life and then a hereditary tenure, and the favorable effect of an incapacity to be reappointed, on the independent exercise of the Executive authority. On the other side it was contended that the prospect of necessary degradation, would discourage the most dignified characters from aspiring to the office, would take away the principal motive to the faithful discharge of its duties—the hope of being rewarded with a reappointment, would stimulate ambition to violent efforts for holding over the constitutional term—and instead of producing an independent administration, and a firmer defence of the constitutional rights of the department, would render the officer more indifferent to the importance of a place which he would soon be obliged to quit for ever, and more ready to yield to the incroachmts. of the Legislature of which he might again be a member. The questions concerning the degree of power turned chiefly on the appointment to offices, and the controul on the Legislature. An *absolute* appointment to all offices—to some offices—to no offices, formed the scale of opinions on the first point. On the second, some contended for an absolute negative, as the only possible mean of reducing to practice, the theory of a free Government which forbids a mixture of the Legislative & Executive powers. Others would be content with a revisionary power to be overruled by three fourths of both Houses. It was warmly urged that the judiciary department should be associated in the revision."

12. EXCERPT FROM JAMES MADISON'S *THE FEDERALIST*, NO. XXXIX JANUARY 16, 1788

"The executive power will be derived from a very compound source. The immediate election of the President is to be made by the States in their political characters. The votes allotted to them are in a compound ratio, which considers them partly as distinct and coequal societies, partly as unequal members of the same society. The eventual election, again, is to be made by that branch of the legislature which consists of the national representatives; but in this particular act they are to be thrown into the form of individual delegations, from so many distinct and coequal bodies politics. From this aspect of government it appears to be of a mixed character, presenting at least as many *federal* as *national* features."

13. EXCERPT FROM A SPEECH GIVEN BY JAMES MADISON IN THE VIRGINIA RATIFYING CONVENTION JUNE 18, 1788

"Mr. *Madison.* Mr. Chairman—I will take the liberty of making a few observations which may place this in such a light as may obviate objections. It is observable, that none of the honorable members objecting to this, have pointed out the right mode of election. It was found difficult in the convention, and will be found so by any Gentleman who will take the liberty of delineating a mode of electing the president, that would exclude those inconveniences which they apprehend. I would not contend against some of the principles laid down by some gentlemen if the interests of some states only were to be consulted. But there is a great diversity of interests. The choice of the people ought to be attended to. I have found no better way of selecting the man in whom they place the highest confidence, than that delineated in the plan of the convention—nor has the gentleman told us. Perhaps it will be found impracticable to elect him by the immediate suffrages of the people. Difficulties would arise from the extent and population of the states. Instead of this, the people choose the electors. This can be done with ease and convenience, and will render the choice more judicious. As to the eventual voting by states, it has my approbation. The lesser states, and some large states, will be generally pleased by that mode. The deputies from the small states argued, (and there is some force in their reasoning) that when the people voted, the large states evidently had the advantage over the rest, and without varying the mode, the interests of the little states might be neglected or sacrificed. Here is a compromise. For in the eventual election, the small states will have the advantage. In so extensive a country, it is probable that many persons will be voted for, and the lowest of the five highest on the list may not be so inconsiderable as he supposes. With respect to the possibility, that a small number of votes may decide his election, I do not know how, nor do I think that a bare calculation of possibility ought to govern us. One honorable gentleman has said, that the eastern states may, in the eventual election, choose him. But in the extravagant calculation he has made, he has been obliged to associate North-Carolina and Georgia, with the five smallest northern states. There can be no union of interests or sentiments between states so differently situated.

The honorable member last up has committed a mistake in saying, there must be a majority of the *whole* number of electors appointed. A majority of votes, equal to a majority of the electors appointed will be sufficient. Forty-six is a majority of ninety-one, and will suffice to elect the president. . ."

14. JAMES MADISON TO THOMAS JEFFERSON OCTOBER 17, 1788

"The States which have adopted the New Constitution are all proceeding to the arrangements for putting it into action in March next. Penn[a] alone has as yet actually appointed Deputies, and that only for the Senate. My last mentioned that these were Mr. R[obert] Morris and Mr. [William] McClay. How the other elections there and elsewhere will run is a matter of uncertainty. The Presidency alone unites the conjectures of the public. The Vice President is not at all marked out by the general voice. As the President will be from a Southern State, it falls almost of course for the other part of the Continent to supply the next in rank. South Carolina may, however, think of Mr. [John] Rutledge, unless it should be previously discovered that votes will be wasted on him."

15. JAMES MADISON TO THOMAS JEFFERSON MAY 9, 1789

"Inclosed is the Speech of the President, with the Address of the House of Representatives, and his reply. You will see in the caption of the address that we have pruned the ordinary stile of the degrading appendages of Excellency, Esquire, &c., and restored it to its naked dignity.[80] Titles to both the President and Vice President were formally and unanimously condemned by a vote of the House of Representatives. This, I hope, will shew to the friends of Republicanism that our new Government was not meant to substitute either Monarchy or Aristocracy, and that the genius of the people is as yet adverse to both."

16. EXCERPT FROM A SPEECH DELIVERED BY REPRESENTATIVE JAMES MADISON MAY 11, 1789

"I do not conceive titles to be so pregnant with danger as some gentlemen apprehend. I believe President of the United States, clothed with all the powers given in the Constitution, would not be a dangerous person to the liberties of America, if you were to load him with all the titles in Europe or Asia. We have seen superb and august titles given, without conferring power and influence, or without even obtaining respect. One of the most impotent sovereigns in Europe has assumed a title as high as human invention can devise; for example, what words can imply a greater magnitude of power and strength than that of High Mightiness? This title seems to border almost upon impiety; it is assuming the preeminence and omnipotence of the Deity; yet this title, and many others cast in the

80 In the House's reply to President Washington's Inaugural Speech they simply addressed him as "George Washington, President of the United States."

same mould, have obtained a long time in Europe, but have they conferred power? Does experience sanction such an opinion? Look at the Republic I have alluded to, and say if their present state warrants the idea?

I am not afraid of titles, because I fear the danger of any power they could confer, but I am against them because they are not very reconcilable with the nature of our Government or the genius of the people. Even if they were proper in themselves, they are not so at this juncture of time. But my strongest objection is founded in principle; instead of increasing, they diminish the true dignity and importance of a Republic, and would in particular, on this occasion, diminish the true dignity of the first magistrate himself. If we gave titles, we must either borrow or invent them. If we have recourse to the fertile fields of luxuriant fancy, and deck out an airy being of our own creation, it is a great chance but its fantastic properties would render the empty phantom ridiculous and absurd. If we borrow, the servile imitation will be odious, not to say ridiculous also; we must copy from the pompous sovereigns of the East, or follow the inferior potentates of Europe; in either case, the splendid tinsel or gorgeous robe would disgrace the manly shoulders of our chief. The more truly honourable shall we be, by showing a total neglect and disregard to things of this nature; the more simple, the more Republican we are in our manners, the more rational dignity we shall acquire."

17. EXCERPT FROM A SPEECH BY JAMES MADISON IN THE UNITED STATES HOUSE OF REPRESENTATIVES MAY 19, 1789

"It is said, that it comports with the nature of things, that those who appoint, should have the power of removal, but I cannot conceive that this sentiment is warranted by the constitution; I believe it would be found very inconvenient in practice. It is one of the most prominent features of the constitution, a principle that pervades the whole system, that there should be the highest possible degree of responsibility in all the executive officers thereof; any thing therefore which tends to lessen this responsibility is contrary to its spirit and intention, and unless it is saddled upon us expressly by the letter of that work, I shall oppose the admission of it into any aspect of the legislature. Now, if the heads of the executive department are subjected to removal by the president alone, we have in him security for the good behavior of the officer: If he does not conform to the judgment of the president, in doing the executive duties of his office, he can be displaced; this makes him responsible to the great executive power, and makes the president responsible to the public for the conduct of the person he has nominated and appointed to aid him in the administration of his department; but if the president shall join in a collusion with this officer, and continue a bad man in office, the case of impeachment will reach the culprit, and drag him forth to punishment. But if you take the other construction, and say, he shall not be displaced, but by and with the advice and consent of the senate, the president no is no longer answerable for the conduct of the officer; all will depend upon the senate. You here destroy a real responsibility without obtaining even the shadow; for no gentleman will pretend to say, the responsibility of the senate can be of such a nature as to afford substantial security. But why, it may be asked, was the senate joined with the president in appointing to office, if they have no responsibility? I answer, merely for the sake of advising, being supposed, from their nature, better acquainted with the characters of the candidates than an individual; yet even here the president is held to the responsibility he nominates, and with their consent appoints; no person can be forced upon him as an assistant by any other branch of the government.

There is another objection to this construction, which I consider of some weight, and shall therefore mention to the committee. Perhaps there was no argument urged with more success, or more plausibly grounded, against the constitution, under which we are now deliberating, that that founded on the mingling of the executive and legislative branches of government in one body. It has been objected, that the senate have too much of the executive power even, by having a controul over the president in the appointment to office. Now, shall we extend this connection between the legislative and executive departments, which will strengthen the objection, and diminish the responsibility we have in the head of the executive? I cannot but believe, if gentlemen weigh well these considerations, they will think it safe and expedient to adopt the clause."

18. JAMES MADISON TO THOMAS JEFFERSON MAY 23, 1789

"My last inclosed copies of the President's inaugural Speech, and the answer of the House of Representatives. I now add the answer of the Senate. It will not have escaped you that the former was addressed with a truly republican simplicity to George Washington, President of the United States. The latter follows the example, with the omission of the personal name, but without any other than the Constitutional title. The proceeding point was, in the House of Representatives, spontaneous. The imitation by the Senate was extorted. The question became a serious one between the Two Houses. J. Adams espoused the cause of titles with great earnestness. His friend, R. H. Lee, although elected as a Republican enemy to an aristocratic Constitution, was a most zealous second. The projected title was, his Highness the President of the United States and protector of their liberties. Had the project succeeded, it would have subjected the President to a severe dilemma, and given a deep wound to our infant Government."

19. JAMES MADISON TO EDMUND RANDOLPH MAY 31, 1789

"Among the subjects on the anvil is the arrangement of the subordinate Executive departments. A unity in each has been resolved on, and an amenability to the President alone, as well as to the Senate by way of impeachment. Perhaps it would not be very consistent with the Constitution to require the concurrence of the Senate in removals. The Executive power seems to be vested in the President alone, except so far as it is qualified by an express association of the Senate in appointments; in like manner as the Legislative is vested in Congress, under the exception in favour of the President's qualified negative. Independently of this consideration, I think it best to give the Senate as little agency as possible in Executive matters, and to make the President as responsible in them. Were the heads of departments dependent on the Senate, a faction in this branch might support them against the President, distract the Executive department, and obstruct the public business. The danger of undue power in the President from such a regulation is not to me formidable. I see and *politically feel* that that will be the weak branch of the Government. With a full power of removal, the President will be more likely to spare unworthy officers through fear than to displace the meritorious through caprice or passion. A disgusted man of influence would immediately form a party against the administration, endanger his re-election, and at least go into one of the Houses and torment him with opposition."

20. EXCERPT OF A SPEECH DELIVERED BY JAMES MADISON IN THE UNITED STATES HOUSE OF REPRESENTATIVES JUNE 16, 1789

"I am clearly of the opinion with [Representative William L. Smith] from South-Carolina, that we ought in this and every other case to adhere to the constitution, so far as it will serve as a guide to us, and that we ought not to be swayed in our decisions by the splendor of the character of the present chief magistrate, but to consider it with respect to the merit of men who, in the ordinary course of things, may be supposed to fill the chair. I believe the power here declared is a high one, and in some respects a dangerous one; but in order to come to a right decision on this point, we must consider both sides of the question. The possible abuses which may spring from the single will of the first magistrate, and the abuse which may spring from the combined will of the executive and the senatorial qualification.

When we consider that the first magistrate is to be appointed at present by the suffrages of three millions of people, and in all human probability in a few years time by double that number, it is not to be presumed that a vicious or bad character will be selected. If the government of any country on the face of the earth was ever effectually guarded against the election of ambitious or designing characters to the first office of state, I think it may with truth be said to be the case under the constitution of the United States. With all the infirmities incident to a popular election, corrected by the particular mode of conducting it, as directed under the present system, I think we may fairly calculate, that the instances will be very rare in which an unworthy man will receive that mark of the public confidence which is required to designate the president of the United States. Where the people are disposed to give so great an elevation to one of their fellow citizens, I own that I am not afraid to place my confidence in him; especially when I know he is impeachable for any crime or misdemeanor, before the senate, at all times; and that at all events he is impeachable before the community at large every four years, and liable to be displaced if his conduct shall have given him umbrage during the time he has been in office. Under these circumstances, although the trust is a high one, and in some degree a dangerous one, I am not sure but it will be safer here than placed where some gentlemen suppose it ought to be.

It is evidently the intention of the constitution that the first magistrate should be responsible for the executive department; so far therefore as we do not make the officers who are to aid him in the duties of that department responsible to him, he is not responsible to his country. Again, is there no danger that an officer when he is appointed by the concurrence of the senate, and has friends in that body, may chuse rather to risk his establishment on the favor of that branch, than rest it upon the discharge of his duties to the satisfaction to the executive branch, which is constitutionally authorised to inspect and controul his conduct? And if it should happen that the officers connect themselves with the senate, they may mutually support each other, and for want of efficacy reduce the power of the president to a mere vapor, in which case his responsibility would be annihilated, and the expectation of it unjust. The high executive officers, joined in cabal with the senate, would lay the foundation of discord, and end in an assumption of the executive power, only to be removed by a revolution in the government. I believe no principle is more clearly laid down in the constitution than that of responsibility."

21. EXCERPT FROM A SPEECH DELIVERED BY JAMES MADISON IN THE UNITED STATES HOUSE OF REPRESENTATIVES JUNE 17, 1789

"But there is another part of the constitution no less explicit than the one on which the gentleman's doctrine is founded, it is that part which declares, that the executive power shall be vested in a president of the United States. The association of the senate with the president exercising that particular function, is an exception to this general rule; and exceptions to general rules, I conceive, are ever to be taken strictly. But there is another part of the constitution which inclines in my judgment, to favor the construction I put upon it; the president is required to take care that the laws be faithfully executed. If the duty to see the laws faithfully executed be required at the hands of the executive magistrate, it would seem that it was generally intended he should have that species of power which is necessary to accomplish that end. Now if the officer when once appointed, is not to depend upon the president for his official existence, but upon a distinct body (for where there are two negatives required either can prevent the removal), I confess I do not see how the president can take care that the laws be faithfully executed. It is true by a circuitous operation, he may obtain an impeachment, and even without this it is possible he may obtain the concurrence of the senate for the purpose of displacing an officer; but would this give that species of control to the executive magistrate which seems to be required by the constitution? I own if my opinion was not contrary to that entertained by what I suppose to be the minority on this question, I should be doubtful of being mistaken, when I discovered how inconsistent that construction would make the constitution with itself. I can hardly bring myself to imagine the wisdom of the convention who framed the constitution, contemplated such incongruity.

There is another maxim which ought to direct us in expounding the constitution, and is of great importance. It is laid down in most of the constitutions or bills of rights in the republics of America, it is to be found in the political writings of the most celebrated civilians, and is every where held as essential to the preservation of liberty, That the three great departments of government be kept separate and distinct; and if in any case they are blended, it is in order to admit a partial qualification in order more effectually to guard against an entire consolidation. I think, therefore, when we review the several parts of this constitution, when it says that the legislative powers shall be vested in a Congress of the United States under certain exceptions, and the executive power vested in the president with certain exceptions, we must suppose they were intended to be kept separate in all cases in which they are not blended, and ought consequently to expound the constitution so as to blend them as little as possible.

Every thing relative to the merits of the question as distinguished from a constitutional question, seems to turn on the danger of such a power vested in the president alone.

But when I consider the checks under which he lies in the exercise of this power, I own to you I feel no apprehensions but what arise from the dangers incidental to the power itself; for dangers will be incidental to it, vest it where you please. I will not reiterate what was said before with respect to the mode of election, and the extreme improbability that any citizen will be selected from the mass of citizens who is not highly distinguished by his abilities and worth; in this alone we have no small security for the faithful exercise of this power. But, throwing that out of the question, let us consider the restraints he will feel after he is placed in that elevated station. It is to be remarked that the power in this case will not consist so much in continuing a bad man in office, as in the danger of displacing a good one. Perhaps the great danger, as has been observed, of abuse in the executive power, lies in the improper continuance of bad men in office. But the power we contend for will not enable him to do this; for if an unworthy man be continued in office by an unworthy president, the house of representatives can at any time impeach him, and the senate can remove him, whether the president chuses or not. The danger then consists merely in this: the president can displace from office a man whose merits require that he should be continued in it. What will be the motives which the president can feel for such abuse of his power, and the restraints that operate to prevent it? In the first place, he will be impeachable by this house, before the senate, for such an act of maladministration; for I contend that the wanton removal of meritorious officers would subject him to impeachment and removal from his own high trust. But what can be his motives for displacing a worthy man? It must be that he may fill the place with an unworthy creature of his own. Can he accomplish this end? No; he can place no man in the vacancy whom the senate shall not approve; and if he could fill the vacancy with the man he might chuse, I am sure he would have little inducement to make an improper removal. Let us consider the consequences. The injured man will be supported by the popular opinion; the community will take side with him against the president; it will facilitate those combinations, and give success to those exertions which will be pursued to prevent his re-election. To displace a man of high merit, and who from his station may be supposed a man of extensive influence, are considerations which will excite serious reflections beforehand in the mind of any man who may fill the presidential chair; the friends of those individuals, and the public sympathy will be against him. If this should not produce his impeachment before the senate, it will amount to an impeachment before the community, who will have the power of punishment by refusing to re-elect him. But suppose this persecuted individual, cannot obtain revenge in this mode; there are other modes in which he could make the situation of the president very inconvenient, if you suppose him resolutely bent on executing the dictates of resentment. If he had not influence enough to direct the vengeance of the whole community, he may probably be able to obtain an appointment in one or other branch of the legislature; and being a man of weight, talents and influence in either case, he may prove to the president troublesome indeed. We have seen examples in the history of other nations, which justifies the remark I now have made. Though the prerogatives of the British king are great as his rank, and it is unquestionably known that he has a positive influence over both branches of the legislative body, yet there have been examples in which the appointment and removal of ministers has been found to be dictated by one or other of those branches. Now if this is the case with an hereditary monarch, possessed of those high prerogatives and furnished with so many means of influence; can we suppose a president elected for four years only dependent upon the popular voice impeachable by the legislature? Little if at all distinguished for wealth, personal talents, or influence from the head of the department himself; I say, will he bid defiance to all these considerations, and wantonly dismiss a meritorious and virtuous officer? Such abuse of power exceeds my conception: If any thing takes place in the ordinary course of business of this kind, my imagination cannot extend to it on any rational principle. But let us not consider the question on one side only; there are dangers to be contemplated on the other. Vest this power in the senate jointly with the president, and you abolish at once that great principle of unity and responsibility in the executive department, which was intended for the security of liberty and the public good. If the president should possess alone the power of removal from office, those who are employed in the execution of the law will be in their proper situation, and the chain of dependence be preserved; the lowest officers, the middle grade, and the highest, will depend, as they ought, on the president, and the president on the community. The chain of dependence therefore terminates in the supreme body, namely, in the people; who will possess besides, in aid of their original power, the decisive engine of impeachment. Take the other supposition, that the power should be vested in the senate, on the principle that the power to displace is necessarily connected with the power to appoint. It is declared by the constitution, that we may by law vest the appointment of inferior officers, in the heads of departments, the power of removal being incidental, as stated by some gentlemen. Where does this terminate? If you begin with the subordinate officers, they are dependent on their superior, he on the next superior, and he on whom?—on the senate, a permanent body; a body, by its particular mode of election, in reality existing for ever; a body possessing that proportion of aristocratic power which the constitution no doubt thought wise to be established in the system, but which some have strongly excepted against: And let me ask gentlemen, is there equal security in this case as in the other? Shall we trust the senate, responsible to individual legislatures, rather than the person who is responsible to the whole community? It is true the senate do not hold their offices for life, like aristocracies recorded in the historic page; yet the fact is they will not possess that responsibility for the exercise of executive powers which would render it safe for us to vest such powers in them. But what an aspect will this give to the executive? Instead of keeping the departments of government distinct, you make the executive a two-headed monster, to use the expression of [Samuel Livermore] from New Hampshire; you destroy the great principle of responsibility, and perhaps have the creature divided in its will, defeating the very purposes for which an unity in the executive was instituted. These objections do not lie against such an arrangement as the bill establishes. I conceive that the president is sufficiently accountable to the community; and if this power is vested in him, it will be vested where its nature requires it should be vested; if any thing in its nature is executive it must be that power which is employed in superintending and seeing that the laws are faithfully executed; the laws cannot be executed but by officers appointed for that purpose; therefore those who are over such officers naturally possess the executive power. If any other doctrine be admitted, what is the consequence? You may set the senate at the head of the executive department, or you may require that the officers hold their places during the pleasure of this branch of the legislature, if you cannot go so far as to say we shall appoint them; and by this means you link together two branches of the government which the preservation of liberty requires to be constantly separated.

Another species of argument has been urged against this clause. It is said, that it is improper, or at least unnecessary to come to any decision on this subject. It has been said by one gentleman, that it would be officious in this branch of the legislature to expound the constitution, so far as it relates to the division of power between the president and senate; it is incontrovertibly of as much importance to this branch of the government as to any other, that the constitution should be preserved entire. It is our duty, so far as it depends upon us, to take care that the powers of the constitution be preserved entire to every department of government; the breach of the constitution in one point, will facilitate the breach in another; a breach in this point may destroy that equilibrium by which the house retains its consequence and share of power; therefore we are not chargeable with an officious interference; besides, the bill, before it can have effect, must be submitted to both those branches who are particularly interested in it; the senate may negative, or the president may object if he thinks it unconstitutional.

But the great objection drawn from the source to which the last arguments would lead us is, that the legislature itself has no right to expound the constitution; that wherever its meaning is doubtful, you must leave it to take its course, until the judiciary is called upon to declare its meaning. I acknowledge, in the ordinary course of government, that the exposition of the laws and constitution devolves upon the judicial. But, I beg to know, upon what principle it can be contended, that any one department draws from the constitution greater powers than another, in marking out the limits of the powers of the several departments. The constitution is the charter of the people to the government; it specifies certain great powers as absolutely granted, and marks out the departments to exercise them. If the constitutional boundary of either be brought into question, I do not see that any one of these independent departments has more rights than another to declare their sentiments on that point.

Perhaps this is an omitted case. There is not one government on the face of the earth, so far as I recollect, there is not one in the United States, in which provision is made for a particular authority to determine the limits of the constitutional division of power between the branches of the government. In all systems there are points which must be adjusted by the departments themselves, to which no one of them is competent. If it cannot be determined in this way, there is no resource left but the will of the community, to be collected in some mode to be provided by the constitution, or one dictated by the necessity of the case. It is therefore a fair question, whether this great point may not as well be decided, at least by the whole legislature, as by a part, by us as well as by the executive or judicial? As I think it will be equally constitutional, I cannot imagine it will be less safe, that the exposition should issue from the legislative authority than any other; and the more so, because it involves in the decision the opinions of both those departments whose powers are supposed to be affected by it. Besides, I do not see in what way this question could come before the judges, to obtain a fair and solemn decision; but even if it were the case that it could, I should suppose, at least while the government is not led by passion, disturbed by faction, or deceived by any discoloured medium of light; but while there is a desire in all to see, and be guided by the benignant ray of truth, that the decision may be made with the most advantage by the legislature itself.

My conclusion from these reflections is, that it will be constitutional to retain the clause; that it expresses the meaning of the constitution as must be established by fair construction, and a construction which, upon the whole, not only consists with liberty, but is more favorable to it than any one of the interpretations that have been proposed."

22. EXCERPT FROM A SPEECH DELIVERED BY JAMES MADISON IN THE UNITED STATES HOUSE OF REPRESENTATIVES DECEMBER 11, 1790

"The constitution makes it the duty of the President to recommend to the consideration of Congress, such measures, as he shall judge necessary and expedient, and give information of the state of the union. Hence it may be inferred, that it is our duty to attend to what he shall judge necessary to be done: at least no gentleman would allow that we might become so disrespectful as to lose sight of them altogether. Then the only way remaining to answer his speech, is to concur with him in all those points, which are clearly and fully understood: and when we find them not clear, we may then say, 'it is incumbent on us to take such measures into due consideration'; thereby pledging ourselves, not only to consider a subject, but not binding the house to agree to it."

23. AN EXCERPT FROM JAMES MADISON'S "CONSOLIDATION" WRITTEN IN *THE NATIONAL GAZETTE* DECEMBER 5, 1791

"Much has been said, and not without reason, against a consolidation of the States into one government. Omitting lesser objections, two consequences would probably flow from such a charge in our political system, which justify the cautions used against it. *First*, it would be impossible to avoid the dilemma, of either relinquishing the present energy and responsibility of a *single* executive magistrate, for some plural substitute, which by dividing so great a trust might lessen the danger of it; or suffering so great an accumulation of powers in the hands of that officer, as might by degrees transform him into a monarch. The incompetency of one Legislature to regulate all the various objects belonging to the local governments, would evidently force a transfer of many of them to the executive department; whilst the increasing splendour and number of its prerogatives supplied by this source, might prove excitements to ambition too powerful for a sober execution of the elective plan, and consequently strengthen the pretexts for an hereditary designation of the magistrate. . . ."

24. JAMES MADISON TO EDMUND PENDLETON FEBRUARY 21, 1792

"On another point, the Bill certainly errs. It provides that in case of a double vacancy, the Executive powers shall devolve on the President pro tempore of the Senate, and he failing, on the Speaker of the House of Representatives. The objections to this argument are various: 1. It may be questioned whether these are *officers* in the Constitutional sense. 2. If officers, whether both could be introduced. 3. As they are created by the Constitution, they would probably have been there designated if contemplated for such a service, instead of being left to the Legislative section. 4. Either they will retain their *Legislative* stations, and then incompatible functions will be blended; or the incompatibility will supersede those stations, and then those being the substratum of the adventitious functions, these must fail also. The Constitution says, Congress may declare *what officers, &c.*, which seems to make it not an appointment or a translation, but an annexation of one office or trust to another office. The House of Representatives proposed to substitute the Secretary of State, but the Senate disagreed, and there being much delicacy in the matter it was not pressed by the former."

25. EXCERPT FROM JAMES MADISON'S *HELVIDIUS* NUMBER 2 AUGUST 24, 1793

"Several pieces with the signature of PACIFICUS were lately published, which have been read with singular pleasure and applause, by the foreigners and degenerate citizens among us, who hate our republican government, and the French revolution; whilst the publication seems to have been too little regarded, or too much despised by the steady friends to both.

Had the doctrines inculcated by the writer, with the natural consequences from them, been nakedly presented to the public, this treatment might have been proper. Their true character would then have struck every eye, and been rejected by the feelings of every heart. But they offer themselves to the reader in the dress of an elaborate dissertation; they are mingled with a few truths that may serve them as a passport to credulity; and they are introduced with professions of anxiety for the preservation of peace, for the welfare of the government, and for the respect due to the present head of the executive, that may prove a snare to patriotism.

In these disguises they have appeared to claim the attention I propose to bestow on them; with a view to shew, from the publication itself, that under colour of vindicating an important public act, of a chief magistrate, who enjoys the confidence and love of his country, principles are advanced which strike at the vitals of its constitution, as well as at its honor and true interest.

As it is not improbable that attempts may be made to apply insinuations which are seldom spared when particular purposes are to be answered, to the author of the ensuing observations, it may not be improper to premise, that he is a friend to the constitution, that he wishes for the preservation of peace, and that the present chief magistrate has not a fellow-citizen, who is penetrated with deeper respect for his merits, or feels a purer solicitude for his glory.

This declaration is made with no view of courting a more favorable ear to what may be said than it deserves. The sole purpose of it is to obviate imputations which might weaken the impressions of truth; and which are more likely to be resorted to, in proportion as solid and fair arguments may be wanting.

The substance of the first piece, sifted from its inconsistencies and its vague expressions, may be thrown into the following propositions:

That the powers of declaring war and making treaties are, in their nature, executive powers:

That being particularly vested by the constitution in other departments, they are to be considered as exceptions out of the general grant to the executive department:

That being, as exceptions, to be construed strictly, the powers not strictly within them, remain with the executive:

That the executive consequently, as the organ of intercourse with foreign nations, and the interpreter and executor of treaties, and the law of nations, is authorised, to expound all articles of treaties, those involving questions of war and peace, as well as others; to judge of the obligations of the United States to make war or not, under any casus federis or eventual operation of the contract, relating to war; and, to pronounce the state of things resulting from the obligations of the United States, as understood by the executive:

That in particular the executive had authority to judge whether in the case of the mutual guaranty between the United States and France, the former were bound by it to engage in the war:

That the executive has, in pursuance of that authority, decided that the United States are not bound: And,

That its proclamation of the 22d of April last, is to be taken as the effect and expression of that decision.

The basis of the reasoning is, we perceive, the extraordinary doctrine, that the powers of making war and treaties, are in their nature executive; and therefore comprehended in the general grant of executive power, where not specially and strictly excepted out of the grant.

Let us examine this doctrine; and that we may avoid the possibility of mistating the writer, it shall be laid down in his own words: a precaution the more necessary, as scarce any thing else could outweigh the improbability, that so extravagant a tenet should be hazarded, at so early a day, in the face of the public.

His words are—'Two of these (exceptions and qualifications to the executive powers) have been already noticed—the participation of the Senate in the *appointment of officers*, and the *making of treaties.* A *third* remains to be mentioned—the right of the legislature to *declare war, and grant letters of marque and reprisal.*[81]

---

81 Syrett, Harlod C. and Jacob E. Cooke, eds. *The Papers of Alexander Hamilton,* "Pacificus" no. I, vol. 15, June 1793-January 1794, (New York: Columbia University Press, 1987), p. 39.

Again—'It deserves to be remarked, that as the participation of the Senate in the *making treaties*, and the power of the legislature to *declare war*, are *exceptions* out of the general *executive power*, vested in the President, they are to be construed *strictly*, and ought to be extended no farther than is essential to their execution.'[82]

If there be any countenance to these positions, it must be found either 1st, in the writers, of authority, on public law; or 2d, in the quality and operation of the powers to make war and treaties; or 3d, in the constitution of the United States.

It would be of little use to enter far into the first source of information, not only because our own reason and our own constitution, are the best guides; but because a just analysis and discrimination of the powers of government, according to their executive, legislative and judiciary qualities are not to be expected in the works of the most received jurists, who wrote before a critical attention was paid to those objects, and with their eyes too much on monarchical governments, where all powers are confounded in the sovereignty of the prince. It will be found however, I believe, that all of them, particularly Wolfius, Burlamaqui, and Vattel, speak of the powers to declare war, to conclude peace, and to form alliances, as among the highest acts of the sovereignty; of which the legislative power must at least be an integral and preeminent part.

Writers, such as Locke and Montesquieu, who have discussed more particularly the principles of liberty and the structure of government, lie under the same disadvantage, of having written before these subjects were illuminated by the events and discussions which distinguish a very recent period. Both of them too are evidently warped by a regard to the particular government of England, to which one of them owed allegiance;* and the other professed an admiration bordering on idolatry. Montesquieu, however, has rather distinguished himself by enforcing the reasons and the importance of avoiding a confusion of the several powers of government, than by enumerating and defining the powers which belong to each particular class. And Locke, notwithstanding the early date of his work on civil government, and the example of his own government before his eyes, admits that the particular powers in question, which, after some of the writers on public law he calls *federative*, are really *distinct* from the *executive*, though almost always united with it, and *hardly to be separated into distinct hands*. Had he not lived under a monarchy, in which these powers were united; or had he written by the lamp which truth now presents to lawgivers, the last observation would probably never have dropt

82 Ibid, 42.

**The chapter on prerogative, shews how much the reason of the philosopher was clouded by the royalism of the Englishman.*

from his pen. But let us quit a field of research which is more likely to perplex than to decide, and bring the question to other tests of which it will be more easy to judge.

2. If we consult for a moment, the nature and operation of the two powers to declare war and make treaties, it will be impossible not to see that they can never fall within a proper definition of executive powers. The natural province of the executive magistrate is to execute laws, as that of the legislature is to make laws. All his acts therefore, properly executive, must pre-suppose the existence of the laws to be executed. A treaty is not an execution of laws: it does not pre-suppose the existence of laws. It is, on the contrary, to have itself the force of a *law*, and to be carried into *execution*, like all *other laws*, by the *executive magistrate*. To say then that the power of making treaties which are confessedly laws, belongs naturally to the department which is to execute laws, is to say, that the executive department naturally includes a legislative power. In theory, this is an absurdity—in practice a tyranny.

The power to declare war is subject to similar reasoning. A declaration that there shall be war, is not an execution of laws: it does not suppose pre-existing laws to be executed: it is not in any respect, an act merely executive. It is, on the contrary, one of the most deliberative acts that can be performed; and when performed, has the effect of *repealing* all the *laws* operating in a state of peace, so far as they are inconsistent with a state of war: and of *enacting* as *a rule for the executive*, a *new code* adapted to the relation between the society and its foreign enemy. In like manner a conclusion of peace *annuls* all the *laws* peculiar to a state of war, and *revives* the general *laws* incident to a state of peace.

These remarks will be strengthened by adding that treaties, particularly treaties of peace, have sometimes the effect of changing not only the external laws of the society, but operate also on the internal code, which is purely municipal, and to which the legislative authority of the country is of itself competent and complete.

From this view of the subject it must be evident, that although the executive may be a convenient organ of preliminary communications with foreign governments, on the subjects of treaty or war; and the proper agency for carrying into execution the final determinations of the competent authority; yet it can have no pretensions from the nature of the powers in question compared with the nature of the executive trust, to that essential agency which gives validity to such determinations.

It must be further evident that, if these powers be not in their nature purely legislative, they partake so much more of that, than of any other quality, that under a constitution leaving them to result to their most natural department, the legislature would be without a rival in its claim.

Another important inference to be noted is, that the powers of making war and treaty being substantially of a legislative, not an executive nature, the rule of interpreting exceptions strictly, must narrow instead of enlarging executive pretensions on those subjects.

3. It remains to be enquired whether there be any thing in the constitution itself which shews that the powers of making war and peace are considered as of an executive nature, and as comprehended within a general grant of executive power.

It will not be pretended that this appears from any *direct* position to be found in the instrument.

If it were *deducible* from any particular expressions it may be presumed that the publication would have saved us the trouble of the research.

Does the doctrine then result from the actual distribution of powers among the several branches of the government? Or from any fair analogy between the powers of war and treaty and the enumerated powers vested in the executive alone?

Let us examine.

In the general distribution of powers, we find that of declaring war expressly vested in the Congress, where every other legislative power is declared to be vested, and without any other qualification than what is common to every other legislative act. The constitutional idea of this power would seem then clearly to be, that it is of a legislative and not an executive nature.

This conclusion becomes irresistible, when it is recollected, that the constitution cannot be supposed to have placed either any power legislative in its nature, entirely among executive powers, or any power executive in its nature, entirely among legislative powers, without charging the constitution, with that kind of intermixture and consolidation of different powers, which would violate a fundamental principle in the organization of free governments. If it were not unnecessary to enlarge on this topic here, it could be shewn, that the constitution was originally vindicated, and has been constantly expounded, with a disavowal of any such intermixture.

The power of treaties is vested jointly in the President and in the Senate, which is a branch of the legislature. From this arrangement merely, there can be no inference that would necessarily exclude the power from the executive class: since the senate is joined with the President in another power, that of appointing to offices, which as far as relate to executive offices at least, is considered as of an executive nature. Yet on the other hand, there are sufficient indications that the power of treaties is regarded by the constitution as materially different from mere executive power, and as having more affinity to the legislative than to the executive character.

One circumstance indicating this, is the constitutional regulation under which the senate give their consent in the case of treaties. In all other cases the consent of the body is expressed by a majority of voices. In this particular case, a concurrence of two thirds at least is made necessary, as a substitute for the other branch of the legislature, which on certain occasions, could not be conveniently a party to the transaction.

But the conclusive circumstance is, that treaties when formed according to the constitutional mode, are confessedly to have the force and operation of *laws*, and are to be a rule for the courts in controversies between man and man, as much as any *other laws*. They are even emphatically declared by the constitution to be "the supreme law of the land."

So far the argument from the constitution is precisely in opposition to the doctrine. As little will be gained in its favour from a comparison of the two powers, with those particularly vested in the President alone.

As there are but few it will be most satisfactory to review them one by one.

'The President shall be commander in chief of the army and navy of the United States, and of the militia when called into the actual service of the United States.'

There can be no relation worth examining between this power and the general power of making treaties. And instead of being analogous to the power of declaring war, it affords a striking illustration of the incompatibility of the two powers in the same hands. Those who are to *conduct a war* cannot in the nature of things, be proper or safe judges, whether *a war ought* to be *commenced*, *continued*, or *concluded*. They are barred from the latter functions by a great principle in free government, analogous to that which separates the sword from the purse, or the power of executing from the power of enacting laws.

'He may require the opinion in writing of the principle officers in each of the executive departments upon any subject relating to the duties of their respective offices; and he shall have power to grant reprieves and pardons for offences against the United States, except in case of impeachment.' These powers can have nothing to do with the subject.

'The President shall have power to fill up vacancies that may happen during the recess of the senate, by granting commissions which shall expire at the end of the next session.' The same remark is applicable to this power, as also to that of 'receiving ambassadors, other public ministers and consuls.' The particular use attempted to be made of this last power will be considered in another place.

'He shall take care that the laws shall be faithfully executed and shall commission all officers of the United States.' To see the laws faithfully executed constitutes the essence of the executive authority. But what relation has it to the power of making treaties and war, that is, of determining what the *laws shall be* with regard to other nations? No other certainly that what subsists between the powers of executing and enacting laws; no other consequently, than what forbids a coalition of the powers in the same department.

I pass over the few other specified functions assigned to the President, such as that of convening of the legislature, &c. &c. which cannot be drawn into the present question.

It may be proper however to take notice of the power of removal from office, which appears to have been adjudged to the President by the laws establishing the executive departments; and which the writer has endeavored to press into his service. To justify any favourable inference from this case, it must be shewn, that the powers of war and treaties are of a kindred nature to the power of removal, or at least are equally within a grant of executive power. Nothing of this sort has been attempted, nor probably will be attempted. Nothing can in truth be clearer, that that no analogy, or shade of analogy, can be traced between a power in the supreme officer responsible for the faithful execution of the laws, to displace a subaltern officer employed in the execution of the laws; and a power to make treaties, and to declare war, such as these have been found to be in their nature, their operation, and their consequences.

Thus it appears that by whatever standard we try this doctrine, it must be condemned as no less vicious in theory than it would be dangerous in practice. It is countenanced neither by the writers on law; nor by the nature of the powers themselves; nor by any general arrangements or particular expressions, or plausible analogies, to be found in the constitution.

Whence then can the writer have borrowed it?

There is but one answer to this question.

The power of making treaties and the power of declaring war, are *royal prerogatives* in the *British government*, and are accordingly treated as Executive prerogatives by *British commentators.*

We shall be the more confirmed in the necessity of this solution of the problem, by looking back to the æra of the constitution, and satisfying ourselves that the writer could not have been misled by the doctrines maintained by our own commentators on our own government. That I may not ramble beyond prescribed limits, I shall content myself with an extract from a work which entered into a systematic explanation and defense of the constitution, and to which there has frequently been ascribed some influence in conciliating the public assent to the government in the form proposed. Three circumstances conspire in giving weight to this contemporary exposition. It was made at a time when no application to *persons* or *measures* could bias: The opinion given was not transiently mentioned, but formally and critically elucidated: It related to a point in the constitution which must consequently have been viewed as of importance in the public mind. The passage relates to the power of making treaties; that of declaring war, being arranged with such obvious propriety among the legislative powers, as to be passed over without particular discussion.

'Tho' several writers on the subject of government place that power *(of making treaties)* in the class of *Executive authorities*, yet this is *evidently* an *arbitrary disposition.* For if we attend *carefully,* to its operation, it will be found to partake *more* of the *legislative* than of the *executive* character, though it does not seem strictly to fall within the definition of either of them. The essence of the legislative authority, is to enact laws; or in other words, to prescribe rules for the regulation of the society. While the execution of the laws and the employment of the common strength, either for this purpose, or for the common defense, seem to comprize *all* the functions of the *Executive magistrate.* The power of making treaties is *plainly* neither the one nor the other. It relates neither to the execution of the subsisting laws, nor to the enaction of new ones, and still less to an exertion of the common strength. Its objects are contracts with foreign nations, which have the *force of law*, but derive it from the obligations of good faith. They are not rules prescribed by the sovereign to the subject, but agreements between the sovereign and sovereign. The power in question seems therefore to form a distinct department, and to belong properly neither to the legislative nor to the executive. The qualities elsewhere detailed as indispensable in the management of foreign *negociations*, point out the executive as the most fit agent in those transactions: whilst the vast importance of the trust, and the operation of treaties *as Laws,* plead strongly for the participation of the whole or a part of the *legislative body* in the office of making them.'

It will not fail to be remarked on this commentary, that whatever doubts may be started as to the correctness of its reasoning against the legislative nature of the power to make treaties: it is *clear, consistent,* and *confident,* in deciding that the power is *plainly* and *evidently* not an *executive power.*"

26. EXCERPT FROM JAMES MADISON'S *HELVIDIUS* NUMBER 2 AUGUST 31, 1793

"Whatever difficulties may arise in defining the executive authority in particular cases, there can be none in deciding on an authority clearly placed by the constitution in another department. In this case the constitution has decided what shall not be deemed an executive authority; tho' it may not have clearly decided in every case what shall be so deemed. The declaring of war is expressly made a legislative function. The judging of the obligations to make war, is admitted to be included as a legislative function. Whenever then a question occurs whether war shall be declared, or whether public stipulations require it, the question necessarily belongs to the department to which these functions belong—And no other department can be *in the execution of its proper functions,* if it should undertake to decide such a question."

27. EXCERPT FROM JAMES MADISON'S *HELVIDIUS* NUMBER 2 AUGUST 31, 1793

"A concurrent authority in two independent departments to perform the same function with respect to the same thing, would be as awkward in practice, as it is unnatural in theory.

If the legislature and executive have both a right to judge of the obligations to make war or not, it must sometimes happen, though not at present, that they will judge differently. The executive may proceed to consider the question to-day, may determine that the United States are not bound to take part in a war, and *in the execution of its functions* proclaim that determination to all the world. To-morrow, the legislature may follow in the consideration of the same subject, may determine that the obligations impose war on the United States, and *in the execution of its functions,* enter into a *constitutional declaration*, expressly contradicting the *constitutional proclamation.*

In what light does this present the constitution to the people who established it? In what light would it present to the world, a nation, thus speaking, thro' two different organs, equally constitutional and authentic, two opposite languages, on the same subject and under the same existing circumstances?

But it is not with the legislative rights alone that this doctrine interferes. The rights of the judiciary may be equally invaded. For it is clear that if a right declared by the constitution to be legislative, and actually vested by it in the legislature, leaves, notwithstanding, a similar right in the executive whenever a case for exercising it occurs, *in the course of its functions:* a right declared to be judiciary and vested in that department may, on the same principle, be assumed and exercised by the executive *in the course of its functions:* and it is evident that occasions and pretexts for the latter interference may be as frequent as for the former. So again the judiciary department may find equal occasions in the execution of *its* functions, for usurping the authorities of the executive: and the legislature for stepping into the jurisdiction of both. And thus all the powers of government, of which a partition is so carefully made among the several branches, would be thrown into absolute hotchpot, and exposed to a general scramble."

28. EXCERPT FROM JAMES MADISON'S *HELVIDIUS* NUMBER 4 SEPTEMBER 14, 1793

"Every just view that can be taken of this subject, admonishes the public, of the necessity of a rigid adherence to the simple, the received and the fundamental doctrine of the constitution, that the power to declare war including the power of judging of the causes of war is *fully* and *exclusively* vested in the legislature: that the executive has no right, in any case to decide the question, whether there is or is not cause for declaring war: that the right of convening and informing Congress, whenever such a question seems to call for a decision, is all the right which the constitution has deemed requisite or proper: and that for such more than for any other contingency, this right was specially given to the executive.

In no part of the constitution is more wisdom to be found than in the clause which confides the question of war or peace to the legislature, and not to the executive department. Besides the objection to such a mixture of heterogeneous powers: the trust and the temptation would be too great for any one man: not such as nature may offer as the prodigy of many centuries, but such as may be expected in the ordinary successions of magistracy. War is in fact the true nurse of executive aggrandizement. In war a physical force is to be created, and it is the executive will which is to direct it. In war the public treasures are to be unlocked, and it is the executive hand which is to dispense them. In war the honors and emoluments of office are to be multiplied; and it is the executive patronage under which they are to be enjoyed. It is in war, finally, that laurels are to be gathered, and it is the executive brow they are to encircle. The strongest passions, and most dangerous weaknesses of the human breast; ambition, avarice, vanity, the honorable or venial love of fame, are all in conspiracy against the desire and duty of peace.

Hence it has grown into an axiom that the executive is the department of power most distinguished by its propensity to war: hence it is the practice of all states, in proportion as they are free, to disarm this propensity of its influence.

As the best praise then that can be pronounced on an executive magistrate, is, that he is the friend of peace; a praise that rises in its value, as there may be a known capacity to shine in war: so it must be one of the most sacred duties of a free people, to mark the first omen in the society, of principles that may stimulate the hopes of other magistrates of another propensity, to intrude into questions on which its gratification depends. If a free people be a wise people also, they will not forget that the danger of surprise can never be so great, as when the advocates for the prerogative of war, can sheathe it in a symbol of peace.

The constitution has manifested a similar prudence in refusing to the executive the *sole* power of making peace. The trust in this instance also, would be too great for the wisdom, and the temptations too strong for the virtue, of a single citizen. The principal reasons on which the constitution proceeded in its regulation of the power of treaties, including treaties of peace, are so aptly furnished by the work already quoted more than once, that I shall borrow another comment from that source.

'However proper or safe it may be in a government where the executive magistrate is an hereditary monarch to commit to him the entire power of making treaties, it would be utterly unsafe and improper to entrust that power to an elective magistrate of four years duration. It has been remarked upon another occasion, and the remark is unquestionably just, that an hereditary monarch, though often the oppressor of his people, has personally too much at stake in the government to be in any material danger of being corrupted by foreign powers. But that a man raised from the station of a private citizen to the rank of chief magistrate, possessed of but a moderate or slender fortune, and looking forward to a period not very remote, when he may probably be obliged to return to the station from which he was taken, might sometimes be under temptations to sacrifice his duty to his interest, which it would require superlative virtue to withstand. An avaricious man might be tempted to betray the interests of the state to the acquisition of wealth. An ambitious man might make his own aggrandizement, by the aid of a foreign power, the price of his treachery to his constituents. The history of human conduct does not warrant that exalted opinion of human virtue, which would make it wise in a nation, to commit interests of so delicate and momentous a kind as *those which concern its intercourse* with the rest of the world, to the *sole* disposal of a magistrate, created and circumstanced, as would be a President of the United States.'[83]

I shall conclude this paper and this branch of the subject, with two reflections, which naturally arise from this view of the Constitution.

The first is, that as the personal interest of an hereditary monarch in the government, is the *only* security against the temptation incident to a commitment of the delicate and momentous interests of the nation which concern its intercourse with the rest of the world, to the disposal of a single magistrate, it is a plain consequence, that every addition that maybe made to the *sole* agency and influence of the Executive, in the intercourse of the nation with foreign nations, is an increase of the dangerous temptation to which an *elective and temporary* magistrate is exposed; and an *argument* and *advance* towards the security afforded by the personal interests of an *hereditary* magistrate.

Secondly, As the constitution has not permitted the Executive *singly* to conclude or judge that peace ought to be made, it might be inferred from that circumstance alone, that it never meant to give it authority, *singly*, to judge and conclude that war ought not to be made. The trust would be precisely similar and equivalent in the two cases. The right to say that war ought not to go on, would be no greater than the right to say that war ought to begin. Every danger of error or corruption, incident to such a prerogative in one case, is incident to it in the other. If the Constitution therefore has deemed it unsafe or improper in the one case, it must be deemed equally so in the other case."

---

83 Syrett, Harlod C., and Jacob E. Cooke. *The Papers of Alexander Hamilton, "The Federalist* No. 75," vol. 4, January 1787-May 1788, (New York: Columbia University Press, 1963), pp. 629-630.

29. EXCERPT FROM JAMES MADISON'S *POLITICAL OBSERVATIONS* APRIL 20, 1795

"The constitution expressly and exclusively vests in the legislature the power of declaring a state of war: it was proposed, that the executive might, in the recess of the legislature, declare the United States to be in a state of war.

The constitution expressly and exclusively vests in the legislature the power of raising armies: it was proposed, that in the recess of the legislature, the executive might, as its pleasure, raise or not raise an army of ten, fifteen, or twenty-thousand men.

The constitution expressly and exclusively vests in the legislature the power of creating offices: it was proposed, that the executive, in the recess of the legislature, might create offices, as well as appoint officers for an army of ten, fifteen, or twenty-thousand men.

A delegation of such powers would have struck, not only at the fabric of our constitution, but at the foundation of all well organized and well checked governments.

The separation of the power of declaring war, from that of conducting it, is wisely contrived, to exclude the danger of its being declared for the sake of its being conducted.

The separation of the power of raising armies, from the power of commanding them, is intended to prevent the raising of armies for the sake of commanding them.

The separation of the power of creating offices, from that of filling them, is an essential guard against the temptation to create offices, for the sake of gratifying favorites, or multiplying dependents.

Where would be the difference between the blending of these incompatible powers, by surrendering the legislative part of them into the hands of the executive, and by assuming the executive part of them into the hands of the legislature? In either case the principle would be equally destroyed, and the consequences equally dangerous."

30. JAMES MADISON TO THOMAS JEFFERSON APRIL 2, 1798

"The constitution supposes, what the History of all governments demonstrates, that the Executive is the branch of power most interested in war, and most prone to it. It has, accordingly, with studied care, vested the question of war in the Legislature."

31. JAMES MADISON TO THE GENERAL ASSEMBLY OF VIRGINIA JANUARY 23, 1799

"But this bill contains other features, still more alarming and dangerous.[84] It dispenses with the trial by jury; it violates the judicial system; it confounds legislative, executive, and judicial powers; it punishes without trial; and it bestows upon the President despotic power over a numerous class of men. Are such measures consistent with out constitutional principles? And will an accumulation of power so extensive in the hands of the Executive, over aliens, secure to natives the blessings of republican liberty?"

32. JAMES MADISON TO THOMAS JEFFERSON MARCH 15, 1800

"It is not to be denied that the Constitution might have been properly more full in prescribing the election of President and Vice President; but the remedy is an amendment to the Constitution, and not legislative interference. It is evident that this interference ought to be, and was meant to be, as little permitted as possible; it being a principle of the Constitution that the two Departments should be independent of each other, and dependent on their Constituents only. Should the spirit of the Bill be followed up, it is impossible to say how far the choice of the Executive my be drawn out of the constitutional hands and subjected to the management of the Legislature. The danger is the greater, as the Chief Magistrate for the time being may be bribed into the usurpations by so shaping them as to favor his re-election. If this licentiousness in constructive perversions of the Constitution continue to increase, we shall soon have to look into our code of laws, and not the charter of the people, for the form, as well as the powers of our Government. Indeed, such an unbridled spirit of construction as has gone forth in sundry instances would bid defiance to any possible parchment securities against usurpation."

84 Madison is referring to the Alien and Sedition Acts

33. EXCERPT FROM JAMES MADISON'S FIRST INAUGURAL ADDRESS MARCH 4, 1809

"Unwilling to depart from examples of the most revered authority, I avail myself of the occasion now presented to express the profound impression made on me by the call of my country to the station to the duties of which I am about to pledge myself by the most solemn of sanctions. So distinguished a mark of confidence, proceeding from the deliberate and tranquil suffrage of a free and virtuous nation, would under any circumstances have commanded my gratitude and devotion, as well as filled me with an awful sense of the trust to be assumed. Under the various circumstances which give peculiar solemnity to the existing period, I feel that both the honor and the responsibility allotted to me are inexpressibly enhanced."

34. EXCERPT FROM JAMES MADISON'S FIRST INAUGURAL ADDRESS ON ASSUMING THE RESPONSIBILITIES OF PRESIDENT MARCH 4, 1809

"Assuring myself that under every vicissitude the determined spirit and united councils of the nation will be safeguards to its honor and its essential interests, I repair to the post assigned me with no other discouragement than what springs from my own inadequacy to its high duties. If I do not sink under the weight of this deep conviction it is because I find some support in a consciousness of the purposes and a confidence in the principles which I bring with me into this arduous service."

35. EXCERPT FROM JAMES MADISON'S SECOND INAUGURAL ADDRESS MARCH 4, 1813

"About to add the solemnity of an oath to the obligations imposed by a second call to the station in which my country heretofore placed me, I find in the presence of this respectable assembly an opportunity of publicly repeating my profound sense of so distinguished a confidence and of the responsibility united with it. The impressions on me are strengthened by such an evidence that my faithful endeavors to discharge my arduous duties have been favorably estimated, and by a consideration of the momentous period at which the trust has been renewed. From the weight and magnitude now belonging to it I should be compelled to shrink if I had less reliance on the support of an enlightened and generous people, and felt less deeply a conviction that the war with a powerful nation, which forms so prominent a feature in our situation, is stamped with that justice which invites the smiles of Heaven on the means of conducting it to a successful termination."

36. EXCERPT OF A MESSAGE FROM JAMES MADISON TO THE UNITED STATES SENATE JULY 6, 1813

"I have received from the committee appointed by the resolution of the Senate of the 14th day of June a copy of that resolution, which authorizes the committee to confer with the President on the subject of the nomination made by him of a minister plenipotentiary to Sweden.

Conceiving it to be my duty to decline the proposed conference with the committee, and it being uncertain when it may be convenient to explain to the committee, and through them to the Senate, the grounds of my so doing, I think it proper to address the explanation directly to the Senate. Without entering into a general review of the relations in which the Constitution has placed the several departments of the Government to each other, it will suffice to remark that the Executive and Senate, in the cases of appointments to office and of treaties, are to be considered as independent of and co-ordinate with each other. If they agree, the appointments or treaties are made; if the Senate disagree, they fail. If the Senate wish information previous to their final decision, the practice, keeping in view the constitutional relations of the Senate and the Executive, has been either to request the Executive to furnish it or to refer the subject to a committee of their body to communicate, either formally or informally, with the head of the proper department. The appointment of a committee of the Senate to confer immediately with the Executive himself appears to lose sight of the co-ordinate relation between the Executive and the Senate which the Constitution has established, and which ought therefore to be maintained.

The relation between the Senate and House of Representatives, in whom legislative power is concurrently vested, is sufficiently analogous to illustrate that between the Executive and Senate in making appointments and treaties. The two Houses are in like manner independent of and co-ordinate with each other, and the invariable practice of each in appointing committees of conference and consultation is to commission them to confer not with the co-ordinate body itself, but with a committee of that body; and although both branches of the Legislature may be too numerous to hold conveniently a conference with committees, were they to be appointed by either to confer with the entire body of the other, it may be fairly presumed that if the whole number of either branch were not too large for the purpose the objection to such a conference, being against the principle as derogating from the co-ordinate relations of the two Houses, would retain all its force.

I add only that I am entirely persuaded of the purity of the intentions of the Senate in the course they have pursued on this occasion, and with which my view of the subject makes it my duty not to accord, and that they will cheerfully furnish with all the suitable information in possession of the Executive in any mode deemed consistent with the principles of the Constitution and settled practice under it."

37. JAMES MADISON TO JOHN ARMSTRONG AUGUST 13, 1814

"On viewing the course which the proceedings of the War Department have not unfrequently taken, I find that I owe it to my own responsibility, as well as to other considerations, to make some remarks on the relations in which the Head of the Department stands to the President, and to lay down some rules for conducting the business of the Department which are dictated by the nature of those relations.

In general, the Secretary of War, like the Heads of the other Departments, as well by express statue as by the structure of the Constitution, acts under the authority and subject to the decisions and instructions of the President, with the exception of cases where the law may vest special and independent powers in the Head of the Department.

From the great number and variety of subjects, however, embraced by that Department, and the subordinate and routine character of a great portion of them, it cannot be either necessary or convenient that proceedings relative to every subject should receive a previous and positive sanction of the Executive. In cases of that minor sort, it is requisite only that they be subsequently communicated, as far and as soon as a knowledge of them can be useful or satisfactory.

In cases of higher character and importance, involving necessarily, and in the public understanding, a just responsibility of the President, the acts of the Department ought to be either prescribed by him or preceded by his sanction."

38. JAMES MADISON TO JAMES MONROE SEPTEMBER 24, 1822

"As I understand the case presented in the other paper enclosed, it turns on the simple question, whether the Senate have a right, in their advice and consent, to vary *the date* at which, according to the nomination of the President, an appointment to office is to take effect.

The subject continues to appear to me in the light which I believe I formerly intimated. The power of appointment, when not otherwise provided by the Constitution, is vested in the President and the Senate. Both must concur in the act; but the act must originate with the President. He is to nominate, and their advice and consent are to make the nomination an appointment. They cannot give their advice and consent without his nomination, nor, of course, differently from it. In so doing they would originate or nominate, so far as the difference extended, and it would be *his*, not their, advice and consent which consummated the appointment. If the President should nominate A to be an officer from the 1st day of January preceding, it is evident, that for the period not embraced by the nomination of the President, the nomination would originate with the Senate, and would require his subsequent sanction to make it a joint act. During that period, therefore, it would be an appointment made by the nomination of the Senate with the advice and consent of the President, not the President with the advice and consent of the Senate.

The case is not essentially changed by supposing the President to nominate A to an office from the 1st day of May following. Here, also, the nomination of the President would not be pursued, and the Constitutional order of appointment would be transposed. Its intention would be violated, and he would not be bound by his nomination to give effect to the advice and consent of the Senate. The proceeding would be a nullity. Nor would this result from pure informality. The President might have as [?] just objections to a postponement. The change in the date might have an essential bearing on the public service, and a collateral or consequential one on the rights or pretensions of others in the public service. In fact, if the Senate, in disregard of the nomination of the President, would postpone the commencement of an appointment for a single day, it could do it for any period, however remote; and whatever might be the intermediate change of things, the date may be as material a part of the nomination as the person named in it."

39. JAMES MADISON TO GEORGE HAY AUGUST 23, 1823

"The difficulty of finding an unexceptionable process for appointing the Executive organ of a Government such as that of the United States was deeply felt by the Convention; and as the final arrangement of it took place in the latter stage of the session, it was not exempt from a degree of hurrying influence produced by fatigue and impatience in all such bodies, though the degree was much less than usually prevails in them.

The part of the arrangement which casts the eventual appointment on the House of Representatives voting by States was, as you presume, an accommodation to the anxiety of the smaller States for their sovereign equality, and the jealousy of the larger towards the cumulative functions of the Senate. The agency of the House of Representatives was thought safer, also, than that of the Senate, on account of the greater number of its members. I might, indeed, happen that the event would turn on one or two States having one or two representatives only; but even in that case the representations of most of the States being numerous, the House would present greater obstacles to corruption than the Senate, with its paucity of members. It may be observed, also, that, although for a certain period the evil of State votes given by one or two individuals would be extended by the introduction of new States, it would be rapidly diminished by growing populations within extensive territories. At the present period the evil is at its maximum. Another census will leave none of the States, existing or in embryo, in the numerical rank of Rhode Island and Delaware; nor is it impossible that the progressive assimilation of local institutions, laws, and manners, may overcome the prejudices of those particular States against an incorporation with their neighbours.

But with all possible abatements, the present rule of voting for President by the House of Representatives is so great a departure from the Republican principle of numerical equality, and even from the Federal rule, which qualifies the numerical by a State equality, and is so pregnant, also, with a mischievous tendency in practice, that an amendment of the Constitution on this point is justly called for by all its considerate and best friends.

I agree entirely with you in thinking that the election of presidential electors by districts is an amendment very proper to be brought forward at the same time with that relating to the eventual choice of President by the House of Representatives. The district mode was mostly, if not exclusively, in view when the Constitution was framed and adopted; and was exchanged for the general ticket and the legislative election as the only expedient for baffling the policy of the particular States which had set the example. A constitutional establishment of that mode will doubtless aid in reconciling the smaller States to the other change, which they will regard as a concession on their part. And it may not be without a value in another important respect. The States, when voting for President by general tickets or by their Legislatures, are a string of beads; when they make their elections by districts, some of these differing in sentiment from others, and sympathizing with that of districts in other States, they are so knit together a to break the force of those geographical and other noxious parties which might render the repulsive too strong for the cohesive tendencies within the political system.

It may be worthy of consideration whether, in requiring elections by districts, a discretion might not be conveniently left with the States to allot two members to a single district. It would manifestly be an important proviso that no new arrangement of districts should be made within a certain period previous to an ensuing election of President.

Of the different remedies you propose for the failure of a majority of electoral votes for any one candidate, I like best that which refers the final choice to a joint vote of the two Houses of Congress, restricted to the two highest names on the electoral lists. It might be a question whether the *three* instead of the *two* highest names might not be put within the choice of Congress, inasmuch as it not unfrequently happens that the candidate third on the list of votes would, in a question with either of the two first, out-vote him, and, consequently, be the real preference of the voters. But this advantage of opening a wider door and a better chance to merit may be outweighed by an increased difficulty in obtaining a prompt and quiet decision by Congress with three candidates before them, supported by three parties, no one of them making a majority of the whole.

The mode which you seem to approve, of making a *plurality* of electoral votes a definitive appointment, would have the merit of avoiding the legislative agency in appointing the Executive; but might not, by multiplying hopes and chances, stimulate intrigue and exertion, as well as incur too great a risk of success to a very inferior candidate? Next to the propriety of having a President the real choice of a majority of his constituents, it is desirable that he should inspire respect and acquiescence by qualifications not suffering too much by comparison.

I cannot but think, also, that there is a strong objection to undistinguishing votes for President and Vice President, the highest number appointing the former, the next the latter. To say nothing of the different services (except in a rare contingency) which are to be performed by them, occasional *transpositions* would take place, violating equally the mutual consciousness of the individuals and the public estimate of their comparative fitness.

Having thus made the remarks to which your communication led with a frankness which I am sure you will not disapprove, whatever errors you may find in them, I will sketch for your consideration a substitute which has occurred to myself for the faulty part of the Constitution in question:

'The electors to be chosen in districts, not more than two in any one district, and the arrangement of the districts not to be alterable within the period of ------ previous to the election of President. Each elector to give two votes, one naming his first choice, the other his next choice. If there be a majority of all the votes on the first list for the same person, he of course to be President; if not, and there be a majority (which may well happen) on the other list for the same person, he then to be the final choice; if there be no such majority on either list, then a choice to be made by joint ballot of the two Houses of Congress from the two names having the greatest number of votes on the two lists taken together.' Such a process would avoid the inconvenience of a second resort to the electors, and furnish a double chance of avoiding an eventual resort to Congress. The same process might be observed in electing the Vice President.

Your letter found me under some engagements which have retarded a compliance with its request, and may have also rendered my view of the subject presented in it more superficial than I have been aware. This consideration alone would justify my wish not to be brought into the public discussion. But there is another, in the propensity of the moment to view everything however abstract from the presidential election in prospect, through a medium connecting it with that question; a propensity the less to be excused, as no previous change of the Constitution can be contemplated, and the more to be regretted, as opinions and commitments formed under its influence may become settled obstacles at a practicable season."

40. JAMES MADISON TO THOMAS JEFFERSON JANUARY 14, 1824

"You have, probably, noticed that the manner in which the Constitution, as it stands, may operate in the approaching election of President, is multiplying projects for amending it. If electoral districts, and an eventual decision by joint ballot of both Houses of Congress, could be established, it would, I think, be a real improvement; and as the smaller States would approve the one, the larger the other, a spirit of compromise might adopt both."

41. JAMES MADISON TO JAMES MONROE NOVEMBER 16, 1827

"The case stated by General Jackson is a very strong one, but does not altogether preclude questions as to the degree of immediate urgency, as to the distinction between the authority of a military office and of the National Executive; nor if the invading act be stamped with the *character of war*, between the Executive and Legislative authority. The only case in which the Executive can enter on a war, undeclared by Congress, is when a state of war has 'been actually' produced by the conduct of another power, and then it ought to be made known as soon as possible to the Department charged with the war power. Such a case was the war with Tripoli during the administration of Mr. Jefferson."

42. JAMES MADISON TO ROBERT LEE FEBRUARY 22, 1830

"The question of re-eligibility in the case of a President of the United States admits of rival views, and is the more delicate because it cannot be decided with equal lights from actual experiment. In general, it may be observed, that the evils most complained of are less connected with that particular question than with the process of electing the Chief Magistrate, and the powers vested in him. Among these, the appointing power is the most operative in relation to the purity of Government and the tranquility of republican Government, and it is not easy to find a depository for it more free from the dangers of abuse. The powers and patronage of a Chief Magistrate, whether elected for a shorter term and re-eligible for a second, or for a longer, without that capacity, might not, in their effect, be very materially different, though the difference might not be unimportant.

It should not be forgotten that many inconveniences are inseparable from the peculiarity of a federal system of Government, while such a Government is essential to the complete success of republicanism in any form."

43. JAMES MADISON TO JAMES HILLHOUSE MAY 1830

"DEAR SIR,—I have received your letter of the 10th instant, with the pamphlet containing the proposed amendments of the Constitution of the United States, on which you request my opinion and remarks.

Whatever pleasure might be felt in a fuller compliance with your request, I must avail myself of the pleas of the age I have reached, and of the control of other engagements, for not venturing on more than a few observations suggested by a perusal of what you have submitted to the public.

I readily acknowledge the ingenuity which devised the plan you recommend, and the strength of reasoning with which you support it. I cannot, however, but regard it as liable to the following remarks:

1. The first that occurs is, that the large States would not exchange the proportional agency they now have in the appointment of the Chief Magistrate, for a mode placing the largest and smallest States on a perfect equality in that cardinal transaction. New York has in it, even now, more than thirteen times the weight of several of the States, and other States according to their magnitudes would decide on the change with correspondent calculations and feelings.

The difficulty of reconciling the larger States to the equality in the Senate, is known to have been the most threatening that was encountered in framing the Constitution. It is known, also, that the powers committed to that body, comprehending, as they do, Legislative, Executive, and Judicial functions, was among the most serious objections, with many, to the adoption of the Constitution.

2. As the President elect would generally be without any previous evidence of national confidence, and have been in responsible relations only to a particular State, there might be danger of State partialities, and a certainty of injurious suspicions of them.
3. Considering the ordinary composition of the Senate, and the number (in a little time nearly fifty) out of which a single one was to be taken by pure chance, it must often happen that the winner of the prize would want some of the qualities necessary to command the respect of the nation, and possibly be marked with some of an opposite tendency. On a review of the composition of that body, through the successive periods of its existence (antecedent to the present, which may be an exception,) how often will names present themselves which would be seen with mortified feelings at the head of the nation! It might happen, it is true, that, in the choice of Senators, an eventual elevation to that important trust might produce more circumspection in the State Legislatures. But so remote a contingency could not be expected to have any great influence; besides that, there might be States not furnishing at the time characters which would satisfy the pride and inspire the confidence of the States and the People.

4. A President not appointed by the nation, and without the weight derived from its selection and confidence, could not afford the advantage expected from the qualified negative on the acts of the Legislative branch of the Government. He might either shrink from the delicacy of such an interposition, or it might be overruled with too little hesitation by the body checked in its career.
5. In the vicissitudes of party, adverse views and feelings will exist between the Senate and President. Under the amendments proposed, a spirit of opposition in the former to the latter would probably be more frequent than heretofore. In such a state of things, how apt might the Senate be to embarrass the President, by refusing to concur in the removal of an obnoxious officer! how prone would be a refractory officer, having powerful friends in the Senate, to take shelter under that authority, and bid defiance to the President! and, with such discord and anarchy in the Executive department, how impaired would be the security for a due execution of the laws!
6. On the supposition that the above objection would be overbalanced by the advantage of reducing the power and the patronage now attached to the Presidential office, it has generally been admitted, that the heads of departments at least, who are at once the associates and the organs of the Chief Magistrate, ought to be well disposed towards him, and not independent of him. What would the situation of the President, and what might be the effect on the Executive business, if those immediately around him, and in daily consultation with him, could, however adverse to him in their feelings and their views, be fastened upon him by a Senate disposed to take side with them? The harmony so expedient between the President and heads of departments, and among the latter themselves, has been too liable to interruption under an organization apparently so well providing against it.

I am aware that some of these objections might be mitigated, if not removed; but not, I suspect, in a degree to render the proposed modification of the Executive department an eligible substitute for the one existing: at the same time, I am duly sensible of the evils incident to the existing one, and that a solid improvement of it is a desideratum that ought to be welcomed by all enlightened patriots.

In the mean time, I cannot feel all the alarm you express at the prospect for the future as reflected from the mirror of the past. It will be a rare case that the Presidential contest will not issue in a choice that will not discredit the station, and not be acquiesced in by the unsuccessful party, as it must do, the appeal to be again made at no very distant day to the will of the nation. As long as the country shall be exempt from a military force, powerful in itself and combined with a powerful faction, liberty and peace will find safeguards in the elective resource and the spirit of the people. The dangers which threaten our political system, least remote, are perhaps of other sorts and from other sources.

I will only add to these remarks what is, indeed, sufficiently evident, that they are too hasty and too crude for any other than a private, and than an indulgent eye."

44. JAMES MADISON TO HENRY CLAY JUNE 1833

"It is obvious that the Constitution meant to allow the President an adequate time to consider the bills, &c., presented to him, and to make his objections to them; and, on the other hand, that Congress should have time to consider and overrule the objections. A disregard on either side of what it owes to the other must be an abuse for which it would be responsible under the forms of the Constitution. An abuse on the part of the President, with a view sufficiently manifest, in a case of sufficient magnitude to deprive Congress the opportunity of overruling objections to their bills, might doubtless be a ground for impeachment. But nothing short of the signature of the President, or a lapse of ten days without a return of his objections, or an overruling of the objections by two-thirds of each House of Congress, can give legal validity to a bill."

II: GEORGE WASHINGTON ON JAMES MADISON

1. GEORGE WASHINGTON TO JAMES MADISON MARCH 31, 1787

"My Dear Sir: At the sametime that I acknowledge the receipt of your obliging favor of the 21st. ult. From New York I promise to avail myself of your indulgence of writing only when it is convenient to me. If this should not occasion a relaxation on your part, I shall become very much your debtor, and possibly like others in similar circumstances (when the debt is burthensome) may feel a disposition to apply the spunge, or what is nearly a-kin to it, pay you off in depreciated paper, which being legal tender, or what is tantamount, being *that* or *nothing,* you cannot refuse. You will receive the nominal value, and that you know quiets the conscience, and makes all things easy, with the debtor."

2. GEORGE WASHINGTON TO JAMES MADISON OCTOBER 10, 1787

"I scarcely think any powerful opposition will be made to the Constitutions being submitted to a Convention of this State. if it is given, it will be there at which I hope you will make it convt. to be present. explanations will be wanting, and none can give them with more accuracy and propriety than yourself."

3. GEORGE WASHINGTON TO JAMES MADISON JUNE 23, 1788

"I hear with real concern of your indisposition. At Fredericksburgh (on a visit to my aged and infirm mother) I understand that you intended to proceed immediately from Richmond to New York, when the Convention shall have arisen. Relaxation must have become indispensably necessary for your health, and for that reason I presume to advise you to take a little respite from business and to express a wish that part of the time might be spent under this roof on your journey thither. Moderate exercise, and books occasionally, with the mind unbent, will be your best restoratives. With much truth I can assure you that no one will be happier in your company than your sincere and Affecte. etc."

4. GEORGE WASHINGTON TO HENRY LEE   SEPTEMBER 22, 1788

"Probably, prudence, wisdom, and patriotism were never more essentially necessary than at the present moment; and so far as it can be done in an irreproachably direct manner, no effort ought to be left unessayed to procure the election of the best possible characters to the new Congress. On their harmony, deliberation and decision every thing will depend. I heartily wish Mr. Madison was in our Assembly, as I think, with you, it is of unspeakable importance Virginia should set out in her federal measures under right auspices."

5. GEORGE WASHINGTON TO JAMES MADISON   SEPTEMBER 28, 1789

"I am very troublesome, but you must excuse me. Ascribe it to friendship and confidence, and you will do justice to my motives."

III. JOHN ADAMS ON JAMES MADISON

1. JOHN ADAMS TO ABIGAIL ADAMS APRIL 28, 1796

"Mr. Madison looks worried to death. Pale, withered, haggard."

2. JOHN ADAMS TO ABIGAIL ADAMS JANUARY 14, 1797

"Mr. Madison is to retire. It Seems the Mode of becoming great is to retire. Madison I Suppose after a Retirement of a few Years is to be President or V.P. It is marvellous how political Plants grow in the Shade."

3. AN EXCERPT FROM JOHN ADAMS'S *TO THE PRINTERS OF THE BOSTON PATRIOT* MARCH 1801

"I asked [Thomas Jefferson] what he thought of sending Mr. Madison to France, with or without others. 'Is it determined to send to France at all?' 'Determined! Nothing is determined until it is executed,' smiling. 'So it does.' 'But why not? I thought it deserved consideration.' 'So it does.' 'But suppose it determined, what do you think of sending Mr. Madison?' 'Is it determined to send Mr. Madison?' 'No; but it deserves consideration.' 'Sending Mr. Madison will make dire work among the passions of our parties in Congress, and out of doors, through the States!' 'Are we forever to be overawed and directed by party passions?' All of this conversation on my part was with the most perfect civility, good humor, and indeed familiarity; but I found it excited a profound gloom and solemn countenance in my companion, which after some time broke out in, 'Mr. President, we are willing to resign.' Nothing could have been more unexpected to me than this observation; nothing was farther from my thoughts than to give any pain or uneasiness. I had said nothing that could possibly displease, except pronouncing the name of Madison. I restrained my surprise, however, and only said, I hope nobody will resign; I am satisfied with all the public officers."

4. AN EXCERPT FROM JOHN ADAMS'S *TO THE PRINTERS OF THE BOSTON PATRIOT* MARCH 1801.

"Upon further inquiries of the other heads of departments and of other persons, I found that party passions had so deep and extensive roots, that I seriously doubted whether the Senate would not negative Mr. Madison, if I should name him.[85] Rather than to expose him to a negative, or a doubtful contest in the Senate, I concluded to omit him."

5. JOHN ADAMS TO JOHN TRUMBULL JULY 27, 1805

"Mr. Madison I have been told has the most extensive and influential Family Connections of any Man in Virginia."

6. JOHN ADAMS TO JOHN TRUMBULL NOVEMBER 18, 1805

"Jefferson's Party I have always considered as a Non Entity, a mere Phantom a mere Stalking Horse to Mr. Madison's. Jefferson is not, never was, and never will be their man. Washington himself was not. It is Mr. Madison who has the radical interests of Virginia. As the Tories were compelled to bring forward Washington in order to hoist Hamilton upon his shoulders, so the Virginians were obliged to raise Jefferson in order to lift up Madison."

7. JOHN ADAMS TO BENJAMIN RUSH MARCH 26, 1806

"Mr. Madison, you Say in one of your Letters acquitted me of any intention to change the Constitution of the Union or the individual states, and I Solemnly assure, you, I never had a wish in my heart or a thought in my head of Attempting an Alteration in this respect."

8. JOHN ADAMS TO MERCY OTIS WARREN AUGUST 8, 1807

"After all this the two Houses of Congress resolved that the President Should be received in the Senate Chamber by the Vice President. I arose from the Chair and respectfully asked the direction of the Senate, by what Style I should address him? by the Title of

85 Adams wanted to appoint Madison as Minister Plenipotentiary to France.

Sir, your Honour your Excellency, or any other? A Senator arose and moved that a Committee Should be appointed to consider what Title Should be affixed to the office. Mr Richard Henry Lee I think was Chairman of the Committee and he drew the Report made it to the House and it was accepted by a large Majority among whom were Mr Lee himself and Several others as determined Republicans as any in the United States or in the World. The Report gave the Title of His Highness to the President. It was Sent down to the House. There the Members were more equally divided. Mr Madison was in doubt what was best to be done. The repulsive force began to be felt between Madison and Hamilton. They had acted contended and wrote in concert hitherto in the formation recommendation and Adoption of the national Constitution. The Moment was now Arrived when they must divide. Washington should have appointed Madison Secretary of State when he appointed Hamilton Secretary of the Treasury. This would have continued the Harmony between them. Madison visited Washington to know his Sentiments. I knew his Sentiments before. He had conversed with me before on the Subject And I know that his opinion was in favour of a Title. I know not all that passed between Washington and Madison because I was not present; but this I believe to be the Truth from Information that I ought to credit. Washington was far from expressing any disapprobation of a Title; So far that he thought a decent Tittle to the Office to be useful and proper but he wanted no Title himself and was convinced from what he heard, in Conversation and read in the public Papers, that if the Title of Highness was given it would excite such a popular Clamour, that Congress would either be obliged to rescind it or it would produce Such a prejudice against the National Government as would do more harm than good. Mr Madison! Am I right in this? I appeal to you. If you contradict me, I will give it up.—"

9. JOHN ADAMS TO JOHN QUINCY ADAMS JANUARY 8, 1808

"As to electioneering you and I may as well have nothing to do with it: but if I must vote for Madison or Monroe I should not hesitate to prefer Madison as at present informed."

10. JOHN ADAMS TO JOHN QUINCY ADAMS FEBRUARY 19, 1808

"The dinner given in London to Mr. Munroe, will not give him in my opinion the preference to Mr. Madison. If this latter Gentleman is chosen he will not continue more than four years. He will be turned out as I was. One system cannot last more than twelve years. The present system will not shine in history. Its measures have not been wise, nor its morals pure, nor its religion divine; if it has had any. I apprehend it will not redound to your popularity or mine to support it. But it must be supported, however unpopular it may be hereafter. We have no other way to defend ourselves against the Sharks and Panthers."

11. JOHN ADAMS TO BENJAMIN RUSH JUNE 20, 1808

"You ask 'Shall We rally round the Standard of a popular Chief'? I know not whom you mean. I am determined to rally round the Standard of the President, as far as I can in honor, whether Mr Pinkney Mr Clinton or Mr Madison be the Man. I will engage in no systematical and universal opposition to any Man. We must rally round our Government, or be undone."

12. JOHN ADAMS TO BENJAMIN RUSH OCTOBER 10, 1808

"The Embargo I presume must be relaxed. If not it will either produce a general violation of it, which will cost more than foreign War to Suppress it, or it will turn out of office at least in New England every Man who Supports it. There will not be a Select Man nor a Representative left who will advocate the Administration. The Same Spirit will increase in the middle and even in the Southern and Western States. Mr. Madison's Administration will be a Scene of Distraction and Confusion if not of Insurrections and Civil War, and foreign War at the Same time both with France and England if the Embargo is not lightened."

13. JOHN ADAMS TO JOHN QUINCY ADAMS DECEMBER 23, 1808

"If the shackles continue on our commerce they will produce an animosity and a rancour which will give much uneasiness to Mr. Jefferson's successor and be very prejudicial to the public service, as well as ruinous to the morals interests and habits of obedience of the people. The Federal party will increase daily. That you will say will be a blessing, but it may be obtained at too dear a rate."

14. JOHN ADAMS TO BENJAMIN RUSH MARCH 4, 1809

"Jefferson expired and Madison came to Life last night at twelve O Clock. Will you be So good as to take a Nap, and dream for my Instruction and Edification a Character of Jefferson and his Administration? I pity poor Madison. He comes to the helm in such a storm as I have seen in the Gul[f] Stream, or rather such as I had to encounter in the Government in 1797. Mine was the worst however, because he has a great Majority of the officers and Men attached to him."

15. JOHN ADAMS TO FRANÇOIS ADRIAAN VAN DER KEMP APRIL 4, 1811

"You Speak of Political Sins in the P[resident]—Pray what are those sins? 'In Adam's fall we sinned all,' but I really know of no more sins committed by Madison than by Washington, Adams or Jefferson."

16. JOHN ADAMS TO BENJAMIN WATERHOUSE MARCH 11, 1812

"If I had a vote I should give it to Mr. Madison at the next Election; because I know of no Man who would do better. At present the general Government are approaching nearer and nearer to my System."

17. JOHN ADAMS TO BENJAMIN RUSH MAY 18, 1812

"My confidence in the integrity of Mr. Jefferson and Mr. Madison, in their love of their Country, and the sincerity of their desires to serve its interests and promote its prosperity, is still entire. Of their genius, talents, learning, industry, I am fully convinced, as all the rest of the world is. But either they are shallow statesmen of I am a natural fool. There is no other alternative or dilemma. Mr. Madison has more correct ideas; but as he has been borne up under the wing of Mr. Jefferson he has been always shackled with Mr. Jefferson's visions and prejudices."

18. JOHN ADAMS TO THOMAS JEFFERSON MAY 21, 1812

"The embargo and the vote against any augmentation of the Navy, more than the taxes and the threats or prospect of war, have raised a storm in Massachusetts and New York which has hurled [Elbridge] Gerry out of his chair and electrified and revolutionised all the subsequent elections. How far the hurricane or the earthquake will extend I know not: but if it should not essentially hazard Mr. Madison's election I fear it will embarrass if not parrallyze his Administration."

⁂

19. JOHN ADAMS TO BENJAMIN RUSH JULY 3, 1812

"Mr. Madison nor Mr. Jefferson ever pretended to be advocates for a democratical government. The great body of the people who have supported them have taken the name of Republicans; and all the most sound solid and intelligent part of them would be allarmed at the prospect of a democratical government and offended at being called Democrats."

⁂

20. JOHN ADAMS TO BENJAMIN RUSH JULY 10, 1812

"The object of all this spiritual and temporal bluster, is to get Madison out. But who to get in? Jay,? Clinton,? Pinkney? Highly as I esteem the first and ignorant as I am of any objections to the other two I own I prefer Madison to all three, at the present moment. John Randolph's conscience recollect the insolence of himself and party on their tryumph. But I am the less anxious on this point because I know that, bring in who they will, he cannot essentially or materially depart from Madison's present system. Madison and Madisonians however should consider, that whoever succeeds him will cherrish a Naval Defense. And if he is rejected, it will be because he has not sufficiently advocated, as I was turned out because I too explicitly recommended it."

⁂

21. JOHN ADAMS TO WILLIAM STEPHENS SMITH NOVEMBER 12, 1812

"But to be serious I see no prospect of uniting this Nation in any other Man better than in Madison. To turn him out, at this time would be such a wound to all the southern and western States who are now the great sufferers by the war, and in the most distress and danger, that I know not what would be the consequence."

⁂

22. JOHN ADAMS LETTER TO JAMES MADISON NOVEMBER 17, 1812

"My Election to the Presidents office, was but by a majority of one or at most two votes. Mr. Jeffersons was by no majority of the people and by a majority of one only in the house after thirty or 40 votes had been equally divided between him and Mr Burr. Mr Jeffersons second election was by a great majority and his third would have been by a greater still if he had not declined. Your Election was I believe by as great a majority as his second. I have entertained hopes that no such meager Elections as mine and Mr Jeffersons first, would ever have been seen again, Indeed I wished, hoped, and expected that your second Election would have been more unanimous than any since Washingtons. I still am confident that your re-Election is certain but by all appearances it will be by a smaller majority than your first."

23. JOHN ADAMS TO WILLIAM KETELTAS NOVEMBER 25, 1812

"In the same page eleventh, you speak of a 'portion of our own people who palsy the arm of the nation.' There is too much truth in this. When I was exerting every nerve to vindicate the honor, and demand a redress of the wrongs of the nation against the tyranny of France, the arm of the nation was palsied by one party. Now Mr. Madison is acting the same part, for the same ends, against Great Britain, the arm of the nation is palsied by the opposite party."

24. JOHN ADAMS TO JOHN QUINCY ADAMS NOVEMBER 30, 1812

"It is now ascertained that Mr. Madison and Mr. Gerry will be chosen by considerable majorities; though the whole federal Party turn'd their coats, apostatized from their principles and voted for an implacable republican."

25. JOHN ADAMS LETTER TO JAMES MADISON FEBRUARY 2, 1813

"I am very apprehensive that the liberties I So frequently take of writing to you, will appear importunate, if not impertinent. But I beg it may be fully understood that none of my letters are to be answered; and that I shall perfectly acquiesce, in your decisions well knowing the multiplicity of Candidates, the difficulty of making the Selections and that The President is the only Ultimate and rightful Judge."

26. JOHN ADAMS TO JAMES MADISON MAY 14, 1813

"If I could now mount my horse, with my saddle bags under me, and my Portmanteau behind as I did from 1774 to 1778, I would visit you at Washington, provided I could be invisible to all but you for the sake of conversing without reserve, upon the state of the Nation."

27. JOHN ADAMS TO RICHARD RUSH JULY 15, 1813

"The talents, the scholarship, the genius, the learning of Jefferson and Madison are not disputed; but their total incapacity for practical government or war, is unblushingly asserted, and I must say not much disputed by any party or individual here."

28. JOHN ADAMS TO RICHARD RUSH SEPTEMBER 6, 1813

"I rejoice that Mr. Madison's health continues to improve; especially as it confutes an afflicting report, that he lives by laudanum and could not hold out four months. His Life is of great importance. The malicious report is contradicted and now understood by the public, to be false."

29. JOHN ADAMS TO THOMAS JEFFERSON SEPTEMBER 22, 1813

"Could the quiveration of my nerves and the inflammation of my eyes be cured, and my age diminished by twenty or thirty years, I would attend you in these researches with infinitely more pleasure than I would George the Fourth, Napoleon, Alexander, or Madison. But only a few hours, a few moments remain for your old friend."

30. JOHN ADAMS TO RICHARD RUSH OCTOBER 8, 1813

"I rejoice that Mr. Madison is well: may he long continue to live and be well; and to see the good work of the war prospering in his hands; for a more necessary war, was never undertaken. It is necessary against England; necessary to convince France, that we are something: and above all necessary to convince ourselves, that we are not, nothing. Know thyself, was never a more important precept to man, or nation."

31. JOHN ADAMS TO THOMAS MCKEAN OCTOBER 30, 1814

"In my humble opinion, if there now is, ever was, or ever can be a just war between one nation and another, my quasi war with France and Madison's present war with Great Britain, are two among the most just and honest wars that ever were waged."

32. JOHN ADAMS TO JAMES LLOYD JANUARY 1815

"It would give me great pleasure to dilate on the various parts of your letter, and mark the many points in which I fully agree with you, as well as the few which are not so clear to me; but I shall confine myself at the present to those things which personally relate to myself and my administration. You say, Sir, that 'I built upon the sand.' And so, indeed, I did. I had no material for a foundation, but a rope of it. The union of States was at that time nothing better. In this respect I was in a worse situation than Mr. Madison is at this hour."

33. JOHN ADAMS TO JAMES LLOYD JANUARY 1815

"And how was I elected? By a majority of one, or at most two votes. And was this majority strong enough to support a war, especially against France? Mr. Madison can now scarcely support a war against England, a much more atrocious offender, elected as he was, and supported as he is, by two thirds of the votes."

34. JOHN ADAMS TO JOHN TAYLOR MARCH 5, 1815

"You who are a lawyer know, that the word crown is a technical term to signify the executive power: and Mr. Madison has as good a crown as Louis 18 or George the third, and better too than either."

35. JOHN ADAMS TO THOMAS MCKEAN JULY 6, 1815

"Mr. Madison's administration has proved great points long disputed in Europe and America.

1. He has proved, that an administration under our present Constitution can declare war.
2. That it can make peace.

3. That money or no money, government or no government, Great Britain can never conquer this country or any considerable part of it.
4. That our officers and men by land are equal to any from Spain and Portugal.
5. That our trans-Alleghanian States, in patriotism, bravery, enterprise, and perseverance, are at least equal to any in the Union.
6. That our navy is equal, *cateris paribus,* to any that ever floated."

36. JOHN ADAMS TO THOMAS JEFFERSON AUGUST 24, 1815

"Mr. Madison's Note of the Convention of 1787 or 1788 are consistent with his indefatigable Character. I shall never see them; but I hope Posterity will."

37. JOHN ADAMS TO THOMAS MCKEAN NOVEMBER 26, 1815

"Washington and Jefferson have introduced a custom of retiring after eight years, and Madison, it is said, will follow their example. I am not enamored with this practice. I may be wrong."

38. JOHN ADAMS TO DR. J. MORSE DECEMBER 5, 1815

"If such was the spirit of the English church in America, and equally in Virginia, before the revolution, can you wonder that men so enlightened as Richard Henry Lee and his brothers, Patrick Henry, Chancellor Wythe, Chief Justice Pendleton, Mr. Jefferson, Mr. Madison, &c., though they had been all educated in that church, became afterwards disciples of Locke, Blackburne, Furneaux, and William Penn, and united in destroying all ecclesiastical establishments in that State?"

39. JOHN ADAMS TO JOHN QUINCY ADAMS DECEMBER 19, 1815

"Mr. Madison has opened the 14th Congress with a message, I will not say such as I should have written, because I never could write so well, but such as I would have dictated to him if he had called me to his counsel and asked my advice."

40. JOHN ADAMS TO THOMAS JEFFERSON FEBRUARY 2, 1817

"I forgot one thing that I intended to say. I pitty our good Brother Madison. You and I have had Children and Grand Children and great grand Children. Though they have cost us Grief, Anxiety, often Vexation, and some times humiliation; Yet it has been cheering to have them hovering about Us; and I verily believe they have contributed largely to keep Us alive. Books cannot always expel Ennui. I therefore pity Brother Madison and especially his Lady. I pitty him more, because notwithstand[ing] a thousand Faults and blunders, his Administration has acquired more glory, and established more Union, than all his three Predecessors, Washington Adams and Jefferson, put together."

41. JOHN ADAMS TO JAMES MADISON APRIL 22, 1817

"The accidental discovery of your books in my library, and the name of Condorcet, have drawn my thoughts to a subject, which I had long since endeavored to forget, as wholly desperate. I fear, Sir, you will wish that I had feloniously appropriated your books to my own use, rather than have returned them with so impertinent a letter. I return them with thanks for the loan of them, and with thanks for your long, laborious, able, and successive services to your country."

42. JOHN ADAMS TO JAMES MADISON JUNE 17, 1817

"There is nothing within the narrow Compass of human knowledge more interesting, than the Subject of your letters."

43. JOHN ADAMS TO JAMES MADISON JUNE 17, 1817

"May you live to a greater age than mine, and be able to die with brighter prospects for your species than can fall to the lot, of Your Friend."

44. JOHN ADAMS TO JOHN QUINCY ADAMS JANUARY 13, 1818

"I am well informed that Mr. Madison has complete minutes of the proceedings and debates in the convention taken down by himself on the spot at the time: which, if that gentleman could be persuaded to consent to their publication, would be an excellent commentary on all that remains in paper."

45. JOHN ADAMS TO J. H. TIFFANY MARCH 31, 1819

"The Federalist is a valuable work, and Mr. Madison's part in it as respectable as any other. But his distinction between a republic and a democracy cannot be justified. A democracy is as really a republic as an oak is a tree, or a temple a building. There are, in strictness of speech and in the soundest technical language, democratical and aristocratical republics, as well as an infinite variety of mixtures of both."

IV. THOMAS JEFFERSON ON JAMES MADISON

1. THOMAS JEFFERSON TO JAMES MADISON DECEMBER 8, 1784

"I once hinted to you the project of seating yourself in the neighborhood of Monticello, and my sanguine wished made me look on your answer as not absolutely excluding the hope. Monroe is decided in settling there, and is actually engaged in the endeavor to purchase. [William] Short is the same. Would you but make it a 'partie quarrée,' I should believe that life had still some happiness in store for me. Agreeable society is the first essential in constituting the happiness, and, of course, the value of our existence. And it is a circumstance worthy great attention when we are making first our choice of a residence. Weigh well the value of this against the difference in pecuniary interest, and ask yourself which will add most to the sum of your felicity though life. I think that, weighing them in this balance, your decision will be favorable to all our prayers. Looking back with fondness to the moment when I am again to be fixed in my own country, I view the prospect of this society as inestimable. I find you thought it worth while to pass the last summer in exploring the woods of America, and I think you were right. Do you not think the men and arts of this country would be worth another summer? You can come in April, pass the months of May, June, July, August, and most of September here, and still be back to the commencement of real business in the assembly following, which I would not have you absent from. You shall find with me a room, bed, and plate, if you will do me the favor to become one of the family; as you would be here only for the summer season, I think your outfit of clothes need not cost you more than 50 guineas, and perhaps the attendance on the theatres and public entertainments, with other small expenses, might be half a guinea or three quarters a day. Your passage backward and forward would, I suppose, be 60 or 70 guineas more. Say that the whole would be 200 guineas. You will for that have purchased the knowledge of another world. I expect Monroe will come in the spring, and return to congress in the fall. If either this object, or the one preceding, for settling you near Monticello, can be at all promoted by the use of the money which the assembly have given me for my share in the revisal, make use of it freely, and be assured it can in no other way be applied so much to my gratification. The return of it may wait your perfect convenience."

2. THOMAS JEFFERSON TO WILLIAM SHORT FEBRUARY 9, 1789

"A vast majority of Antifederalists have got into the assembly of Virginia, so that Mr. [Patrick] Henry is omnipotent there. Mr. Madison was left out as a Senator by 8. or

9. votes and Henry has so modelled the districts for representatives as to tack Orange to counties where he himself has great influence that Madison may not be elected into the lower federal house, which was the place Madison had wished to serve in, & not the Senate. Henry pronounced a Philippic against Madison in open assembly, Madison being then at Philadelphia."

3. THOMAS JEFFERSON TO JAMES MADISON DECEMBER 28, 1794

"The changes in your house, I see, are going on for the better, and even the Augean herd over your heads are slowly purging off their impurities. Hold on then, my dear friend, that we may not shipwreck in the meanwhile. I do not see, in the minds of those with whom I converse, a greater affliction than the fear of your retirement; but this must not be, unless to a more splendid & a more efficacious post. There I should rejoice to see you; I hope I may say, I shall rejoice to see you. I have long had much in my mind to say to you on that subject. But double delicacies have kept me silent. I ought perhaps to say, while I would not give up my own retirement for the empire of the universe, how I can justify wishing one whose happiness I have so much at heart as yours, to take the front of the battle which is fighting for my security. This would be easy enough to be done, but not at the heel of a lengthy epistle."

4. THOMAS JEFFERSON TO JAMES MADISON APRIL 27, 1795

"I expressed my hope of the only change of position I ever wished you to make, and I expressed it with entire sincerity, because there is not another person in the U S. who being placed at the helm of our affairs, my mind would be so completely at rest for the fortune of our political bark. The wish too was pure, & unmixed with anything respecting myself personally."

5. THOMAS JEFFERSON TO JAMES MADISON SEPTEMBER 21, 1795

"[Alexander] Hamilton is really a colossus to the anti-republican party. Without numbers, he is an host within himself. They have got themselves into a defile, where they might be finished; but too much security on the republican part will give time to his talents & indefatigableness to extricate them. We have had only middling performances to oppose to him. In truth, when he comes forward, there is nobody but yourself who can meet him. His adversaries having begun the attack, he has the advantage of answering them, & remains unanswered himself. A solid reply might yet completely demolish what was too feebly attacked, and has gathered strength from the weakness of the attack. The merchants were certainly (except those of them who are English) as open mouthed at first against the treaty as any. But the general expression of indignation has alarmed them for the strength of the government. They have feared the shock would be too great, and have chosen to tack about & support both treaty & government, rather than risk the government. Thus it is, that Hamilton, [John] Jay, &c., in the boldest act they ever ventured on to undermine the government, have the address to screen themselves, & direct the hue & cry against those who wish to drag them into light. A bolder party-stroke was never struck. For it certainly is an attempt of a party, which finds they have lost their majority in one branch of the Legislature, to make a law by the aid of the other branch & of the executive, under color of a treaty, which shall bind up the hands of the adverse branch from ever restraining the commerce of their patron-nation. There appears a pause at present in the public sentiment, which may be followed by a revulsion. This is the effect of the desertion of the merchants, of the President's chiding answer to Boston & Richmond, of the writings of Curtius & Camillus, and of the quietism into which people naturally fall after first sensations are over. For god's sake take up your pen, and give a fundamental reply to Curtius & Camillus."

6. THOMAS JEFFERSON TO JAMES MADISON DECEMBER 17, 1796

"The first wish of my heart was, that you should have been proposed for the administration of the government."

7. THOMAS JEFFERSON TO PEREGRINE FITZHUGH APRIL 9, 1797

"I wish it were in my power to satisfy you with respect to the sentiments expressed by my friend Mr. Madison in the general Convention. But the papers in my possession are under a seal which I have not broken yet, and wish not to break, till I have time to give them a thorough perusal and consideration. Two things may be safely said; 1st. When a man whose life has been marked by its candor, has given a latter opinion contrary to a former one, it is probably the result of further inquiry, reflection and conviction. This is a sound answer, if the contrariety of sentiment as to the treaty-making power were really expressed by him on the former and latter occasion, as was alleged by you. But, 2d. As no man weighs more maturely than Mr. Madison before he takes a side on any question, I do not expect he has changed either his opinion on that subject, or the expression of it, and therefore I presume the allegation founded in some misconception or misinformation."

8. THOMAS JEFFERSON TO JAMES MADISON JUNE 1, 1797.

"[Charles Cotesworth] Pinckney (the Genl), John Marshall & [Francis] Dana are nominated envoys extraordinary to France. Charles Lee consulted a member from Virginia to know whether Marshall would be agreeable. He named you, as more likely to give satisfaction. The answer was, 'Nobody of mr. Madison's way of thinking will be appointed.'"

9. THOMAS JEFFERSON TO JAMES MADISON APRIL 5, 1798.

"You will see in [John] Fenno[86] two numbers of a paper signed Marcellus. They promise much mischief, and are ascribed, without any difference of opinion, to Hamilton. You must, my dear Sir, take up your pen against this champion. You know the ingenuity of his talents; & there is not a person but yourself who can foil him. For heaven's sake, then take up your pen, and do not desert the public cause altogether."

10. THOMAS JEFFERSON TO JAMES MADISON JANUARY 16, 1799

"In a society of members, between whom & yourself is great mutual esteem & respect, a most anxious desire is expressed that you would publish your debates of the Constitution. That these measures of the army, navy & direct tax will bring about a revulsion of public sentiment is thought certain, & that the constitution will then receive a different explanation. Could those debates be ready to appear critically, their effect would be decisive. I beg of you to turn this subject in your mind. The arguments against it will be personal; those in favor of it moral; and something is required from you as a set-off against the sin of your retirement."

86 John Fenno's *Gazette of the United States* served as Alexander Hamilton's mouthpiece.

11. THOMAS JEFFERSON TO JAMES MADISON FEBRUARY 5, 1799

"The public sentiment being now on the creen, and many heavy circumstances about to fall into the republican scale, we are sensible that this summer is the season for systematic energies & sacrifices. The engine is the press. Every man must lay his purse & his pen under contribution. As to the former, it is possible I may be obliged to assume something for you. As to the latter, let me pray & beseech you to set apart a certain portion of every post day to write what may be proper for the public. Send it to me while here, & when I go away I will let you know to whom you may send, so that your name shall be sacredly secret. You can render such incalculable services in this way, as to lessen the effect of our loss of your presence here."

12. THOMAS JEFFERSON TO M. DUPONT MARCH 2, 1809

"I leave everything in the hands of men so able to take care of them, that if we are destined to meet misfortunes, it will be because no human wisdom could avert them."

13. THOMAS JEFFERSON TO M. LE BARON HUMBOLDT MARCH 6, 1809

"You will know before this reaches you, that Mr. Madison is my successor. This ensures to us a wise and honest administration."

14. THOMAS JEFFERSON TO JAMES MADISON MARCH 17, 1809

"I feel great anxiety for the occurrences of the ensuing four or five months. If peace can be preserved, I hope and trust you will have a smooth administration. I know no government which would be so embarrassing in war as ours."

15. THOMAS JEFFERSON TO WILSON CARY NICHOLAS MAY 25, 1809

"As to the merits of the result of our measures against England, Mr. Madison is justly entitled to his full share of all the measures of my administration. Our principles were the same, and we never differed sensibly in the application of them. I am glad therefore that my enemies, & hope that my friends will do him justice as to this & all our other measures."

16. THOMAS JEFFERSON TO DOCTOR ELIJAH GRIFFITH MAY 28, 1809

"In the electoral election, Pennsylvania really spoke in a voice of thunder to the monarchists of our country, and while that State constitutes so firm, with the solid mass of republicanism to the South and West, such efforts as we have lately seen in the anti-republican portion of our country cannot ultimately affect our security. Our enemies may try their cajoleries with my successor. They will find him as immovable in his republican principles as him whom they have honored with their peculiar enmity. The late pacification with England gives us a hope of eight years of peaceable and wise administration, within which time our revenue will be liberated from debt, and be free to commence that splendid course of public improvement and wise application of the public contributions, of which it remains for us to set the first example."

17. THOMAS JEFFERSON TO ROBERT SMITH JUNE 10, 1809

"From the characters now associated in the administration, I have no doubt of the continuance of the same cordiality so interesting to themselves and to the public; and great as are the difficulties and dangers environing our camp, I sleep with perfect composure, knowing who are watching for us."

18. THOMAS JEFFERSON TO MESSRS. BLOODGOOD AND HAMMOND SEPTEMBER 30, 1809

"Your approbations of the reasons which induce me to retire from the honorable station in which my fellow citizens had placed me, is a proof of your devotion to the true principles of our constitution. These are wisely opposed to all perpetuations of power, and to every practice which may lead to hereditary establishments; and certain I am that any services which I could have rendered will be more than supplied by the wisdom and virtues of my successor."

19. THOMAS JEFFERSON TO GENERAL THADDEUS KOSCIUSKO FEBRUARY 25, 1810

"My successor, to the purest principles of republican patriotism, adds a wisdom and foresight second to no man on earth."

20. THOMAS JEFFERSON TO WILLIAM DUANE AUGUST 12, 1810

"Anxious, in my retirement, to enjoy undisturbed repose, my knowledge of my successor and late coadjutors, and my entire confidence in their wisdom and integrity, were assurances to me that I might sleep in security with such watchmen at the helm, and that whatever difficulties and dangers should assail our course, they would do what could be done to avoid or surmount them. In this confidence I envelope myself, and hope to slumber on to my last sleep. And should difficulties occur which they cannot avert, if we follow them in phalanx, we shall surmount them without danger."

21. LETTER FROM THOMAS JEFFERSON TO DAVID HOWELL DECEMBER 15, 1810

"I enjoy, in recollection, my ancient friendships, and suffer no new circumstances to mix alloy with them. I do not take the trouble of forming opinions on what is passing among them, because I have such entire confidence in their integrity and wisdom as to be satisfied all is going right, and that every one is doing his best in the station confided to him."

22. THOMAS JEFFERSON TO PRESIDENT JAMES MADISON APRIL 24, 1811

"I am sure you will pursue steadily your own wise plans, that peace, with the great belligerents at least, will be preserved until it becomes more losing than war, & that the total extinction of the national debt, & liberation of our revenues, for defense in war and improvement in peace, will seal your retirement with the blessings of your country. For all this, & for your health & happiness I pray to God fervently."

23. THOMAS JEFFERSON TO THOMAS C. FLOURNEY OCTOBER 1, 1812

"Servile inertness is not what is to save our country; the conduct of a war requires the vigor and enterprise of younger heads. All such undertakings, therefore, are out of the question with me, and I say so with the greater satisfaction, when I contemplate the person to whom the executive powers were handed over. You probably do not know Mr. Madison personally, or at least intimately, as I do. I have known him from 1779, when he first came into the public councils, and from three and thirty years' trial, I can say conscientiously that I do not know in the world a man of purer integrity, more dispassionate, disinterested and devoted to genuine republicanism; nor could I, in the whole scope of America and Europe, point out a more abler head. He may be illy seconded by others, betrayed by the Hulls and Arnolds of our country, for such there are in every country, and with sorrow and suffering we know it. But what man can do will be done by Mr. Madison. I hope, therefore, there will be no difference among republicans as to his re-election, and we shall know his value when we have to give him up, and to look at large for his successor."

24. THOMAS JEFFERSON TO WILLIAM DUANE OCTOBER 1, 1812

"If our operations have suffered or languished from any want of energy in the present head which directs them, I have so much confidence in the wisdom and conscientious integrity of Mr. Madison, as to be satisfied, that however torturing to his feelings, he will fulfil his duty to the public and to his own reputation, by making the necessary change. Perhaps he may be preparing it while we are talking about it; for all these things I am uninformed."

25. THOMAS JEFFERSON TO JAMES MADISON MAY 21, 1813

"Although it is probable there may not be an idea here which has not been maturely weighed by yourself, and with a much broader view of the whole field, yet I have frankly hazarded them, because possibly some of the facts or ideas may have escaped in the multiplicity of the objects engaging your notice, and because in every event they will cost you but the trouble of reading. The importance of keeping open a water which covers wholly or considerably five of the most productive States, containing three-fifths of the population of the Atlantic portion of our Union, and of preserving their resources for the support of the war, as far as the state of war and the means of the confederacy will admit; and especially if it can be done for less than is contributed by the Union for more than one single city, will justify our anxieties to have it effected. And should my views of the subject be even wrong, I am sure they will find their apology with you in the purity of the motives of personal and public regard which induce a suggestion of them. In all cases I am satisfied you are doing what is for the best, as far as the means put into your hands will enable you, and this thought quiets me under every occurrence, and under every occurrence I am sincerely, affectionately and respectfully yours."

26. THOMAS JEFFERSON TO JAMES MONROE MAY 30, 1813

"I thank you for the communication of the President's Message, which has not yet reached us through the public papers. It is an interesting document, always looked for with anxiety, and the late one is equally able as interesting. I hope Congress will act in conformity with it, in all its parts. The unwarrantable ideas often expressed in the newspapers, and by persons who ought to know better, that I intermeddle in the Executive councils, and the indecent expressions, sometimes, of a hope that Mr. Madison will pursue the principles of my administration, expressions so disrespectful to his known abilities and dispositions, have rendered it improper in me to hazard suggestions to him, on occasions even where ideas might occur to me, that might accidentally escape him. This reserve has been strengthened, too, by a consciousness that my views must be very imperfect, from the want of a correct knowledge of the whole ground."

27. THOMAS JEFFERSON TO JOHN WAYLES EPPS SEPTEMBER 9, 1814

"Nobody who knows the President can doubt but that he has honestly done everything he could to the best of his judgment. And there is no sounder judgment than his."

28. THOMAS JEFFERSON TO JAMES MADISON MARCH 23, 1815

"I sincerely congratulate you on the peace, and, more especially on the eclat with which the war has closed. The affairs of New Orleans was fraught with useful lessons to ourselves, our enemies, and our friends, and will powerfully influence our future relations with the nations of Europe. It will show them we mean to take no part in their wars, and count no odds when engaged in our own."

29. THOMAS JEFFERSON TO THOMAS LEIPER JUNE 12, 1815

"My friendship for Mr. Madison, my confidence in his wisdom and virtue and my approbation of all his measures, and especially of his taking up at length the gauntlet against England, is known to all whom I have ever conversed or corresponded on these measures. The word *federal*, or its synonym *lie*, may therefore be written under every word of Mr. Ralph's paragraph. I have ransacked my memory to recollect any incident which might have given countenance to any particle of it, but I find none. For if you will except the bringing into power and importance those who were enemies to himself as well as to the principles of republican government, I do not recollect a single measure of the President which I have not approved. Of those under him, and of some very near him, there have been many acts of which we have all disapproved, and he more than we. We have at times dissented from the measures, and lamented the dilatoriness of Congress. I recollect an instance the first winter of the war, when, from sloth of proceedings, an embargo was permitted to run through the winter, while the enemy could not cruise, nor consequently restrain the exportation of our whole produce, and was taken off in the spring, as soon as they could resume their stations. But this procrastination is unavoidable. How can expedition be expected from a body which we have saddled with an hundred lawyers, whose trade is talking? But lies, to sow division among us, is so stale an artifice of the federal prints, and are so well understood, that they need neither contradiction nor explanation. As to myself, my confidence in the wisdom and integrity of the administration is so entire, that I scarcely notice what is passing, and have almost ceased to read newspapers. Mine remain in our post office a week or ten days, sometimes, unasked for. I find more amusement in studies to which I was always more attached, and from which I was dragged by the events of the times in which I have happened to live."

30. THOMAS JEFFERSON TO JOHN ADAMS AUGUST 10-11, 1815

"Do you know that there exists in MS. The ablest work of this kind yet executed, of the debates of the Constitutional convention of Philadelphia in 1788 [ie., 1787]? The whole of everything said and done there was taken down by Mr. Madison, with a labor and exactness beyond comprehension."

31. THOMAS JEFFERSON TO JOHN ADAMS *MAY 5, 1817*

"I do not entertain your apprehensions for the happiness of our brother Madison in a state of retirement. Such a mind as his, fraught with information and with matter for reflection, can never know *ennui*. Besides, there will always be work enough cut out for him to continue his active usefulness to his country. For example, he and Monroe (the President) are now here on the work of a collegiate institution to be established in our neighborhood, of which they and myself are three of six visitors. This, if it succeeds, will raise up children for Mr. Madison to employ his attention through life."

32. THOMAS JEFFERSON TO THOMAS RITCHIE DECEMBER 25, 1820

"So, also, as to the two Presidents, late and now in office, I know them both to be of principles as truly republican as any men living. If there be anything amiss, therefore, in the present state of our affairs, as the formidable deficit lately unfolded to us indicates, I ascribe it to the inattention of Congress to their duties, to their unwise dissipation and waste of public contributions. They seemed, some little while ago, to be at a loss for objects whereon to throw away the supposed fathomless funds of the treasury."

33. EXCERPT FROM THE *AUTOBIOGRAPHY OF THOMAS JEFFERSON* JANUARY 6, 1821

"Mr. Madison came into the House in 1776. a new member and young; which circumstances, concurring with his extreme modesty, prevented his venturing himself in debate before his removal to the Council of State in Nov. 77. From thence he went to Congress, then consisting of few members. Trained in these successive schools, he acquired a habit of self-possession which placed at ready command the rich resources of his luminous and discriminating mind, & of his extensive information, and rendered him the first of every assembly afterwards of which he became a member. Never wandering from his subject into vain declamation, but pursuing it closely in language pure, classical, and copious, soothing always the feelings of his adversaries by civilities and softness of expression, he rose to the eminent station which he held in the great National convention of 1787. and in that of Virginia which followed, he sustained the new constitution in all its parts, bearing off the palm against the logic of George Mason, and the fervid declamation of Mr. [Patrick] Henry. With these consummate powers were united a pure and spotless virtue which no calumny has ever attempted to sully. Of the powers and polish of his pen, and of the wisdom of his administration in the highest office of the nation, I need say nothing. They have spoken, and will forever speak for themselves."

34. THOMAS JEFFERSON TO JAMES MADISON FEBRUARY 17, 1826

"The friendship which has subsisted between us, now half a century, and the harmony of our political principles and pursuits, have been sources of constant happiness to me through that long period. And if I remove beyond the reach of attentions to the University [of Virginia], or beyond the bourne of life itself, as I soon must, it is a comfort to leave that institution under your care, and an assurance that it will not be wanting. It has also been a great solace to me, to believe that you are engaged in vindicating to posterity the course we have pursued for preserving to them, in all their purity, the blessings of self-government, which we had assisted too in acquiring for them. If ever the earth has beheld a system of administration conducted with a single and steadfast eye to the general interest and happiness of those committed to it, one which, protected by truth, can never know reproach, it is that to which our lives have been devoted. To myself you have been a pillar of support through life. Take care of me when dead, and be assured that I shall leave with you my last affections."

35. EXCERPT FROM THOMAS JEFFERSON'S WILL MARCH 1826

"I give my friend James Madison, of Montpellier, my gold-mounted walking staff of animal horn, as a token of the cordial and affectionate friendship which for nearly now an half century, has united us in the same principles and pursuits of what we have deemed for the greatest good of our country."

V. JAMES MONROE ON JAMES MADISON

1. JAMES MONROE TO JAMES MADISON DECEMBER 18, 1784

"I heartily wish we had a better cypher, as it is dangerous to trust those subjects upon which I wish most confidently to correspond with you thus to chance & the curiosity of vicious or idle people. In [Trenton, New Jersey] I cannot procure a scribe, can you in Richmond?"

2. JAMES MONROE TO JAMES MADISON JULY 12, 1785

"What say you to a trip to the Indian treaty to be held on the Ohio—some time in August or September—I have thoughts of it & should be happy in your company. We might meet somewhere on the way or perhaps you have thoughts of a trip this way. Packets sail every week eastward to Rhode Island & Boston—a stage is also established to lake George & the communication over lake Champlain to Montreal and Quebec easy & expeditious. Agreeable company may be found either way."

3. JAMES MONROE TO JAMES MADISON JULY 15, 1786

"DEAR SIR,—I had the pleasure to receive yours from Philadelphia yesterday but so late that I could not answer it sooner. I hope you have before this recovered from your fatigue, indeed I advise your prosecution of your journey here as soon as possible as the preferable place for that purpose. I should be happy you could give us as much of your time as possible here for reasons more self interested. Of these we shall confer when we meet."

4. JAMES MONROE TO JAMES MADISON SEPTEMBER 12, 1786

"I sincerely wish you to suffer no anxiety, and to put yourself to no inconvenience upon our private affair—I have no occasion for the money untill about the 5. Or 10th. of October to help to remove me to Virginia and even then it will be in my power to do without it, with tolerable convenience, if you should find it inconvenient to command it. Believe me it will put me to no inconvenience."

5. JAMES MONROE TO THOMAS JEFFERSON OCTOBER 12, 1786

"Mr. Madison & myself have been desirous if possible of forming an engagement for land in this State which would hereafter put us at ease. He promised me to advise you of it and to tell you of our little plan. If it were an object with you to sell your property in my estimation a better opportunity cannot present itself."

6. JAMES MONROE TO JAMES MADISON MAY 23, 1787

"DEAR SIR,—My leisure furnishes me with the opportunity but the country around does not with the materials to form a letter worthy your attention. The scale of my observations is a narrow one & confined entirely within my room: & the subjects of my researches in which I am but seeking to make some proficiency, as I should only detail to you the sentiments of others, give me nothing to supply the deficiency."

7. JAMES MONROE TO JAMES MADISON MAY 23, 1787

"I have to acknowledge your kind attention to my affairs in New York & particularly for the dispatch of my furniture & the advance I find you have been under the necessity of making for me. I am sorry to find it probable that my share of Mordicai's effects (when obtained) will not even reimburse this sum. At what time I shall be able to make up the deficiency as well as remit the amount & for the completion of our contract with Taylor I cannot precisely say. I have hopes of effecting it soon, but can give no assurance with certainty."

8. JAMES MONROE TO THOMAS JEFFERSON JULY 27, 1787

". . . Governor [Edmund Randolph], I have reason to believe is unfriendly to me & hath shewn (If I am well informed) a disposition to thwart me; Madison, upon whose friendship I have calculated, whose views I have favored, and with whom I have held the most confidential correspondence since you left the continent, is in strict league with him & hath I have reason to believe concurred in arrangements unfavorable to me; a suspicion supported by some strong circumstances that this is the case, hath given me great uneasiness—however in this I may be disappointed & wish it may be so."

-☙❧-

9. JAMES MONROE TO THOMAS JEFFERSON FEBRUARY 15, 1789

"This Commonwealth was divided into 10 districts from each of which a member was to be placed in the House of Representatives. A competition took place in many, and in this, consisting of Albemarle, Amherst, Fluvanna, Goochland, Louisa, Spotsylvania, Orange and Culpeper, between Mr. Madison and myself. He prevailed by a large majority of about 300. It would have given me concern to have excluded him, but those to whom my conduct in publick life had been acceptable, pressed me to come forward in this Government on its commencement; and that I might not lose an opportunity of contributing my feeble efforts, in forwarding an amendment of its defects, nor shrink from the station those who confided in me would wish to place me, I yielded. As I had no private object to gratify so a failure has given me no private concern."

-☙❧-

10. JAMES MONROE TO JAMES MADISON MARCH 5, 1790

"DEAR SIR,—I flattered myself I should have been able by this, to have remitted you my proportion of the balance due Mr. Taylor for the land we bought of him—but my endeavors have been ineffectual, nor do any prospects that I have, warrant a hope, I shall be able to command it, within any short period of time. Thus circumstanced it would be more agreeable to me to disengage myself from the contract. Perhaps it might suit you to take the whole—if so I doubt not I should accede with pleasure, to whatever might be agreeable to you—otherwise it may be advisable to propose it to Mr. Taylor, as I fear it will not be in my power to raise the money in time for his purpose—nor is it agreeable to me to keep him longer in suspense."

-☙❧-

11. JAMES MONROE TO THOMAS JEFFERSON OCTOBER 16, 1792

"We expect Mr. Madison here to-morrow & to set out on the 20th together. We may possibly stay a day at Mount Vernon, so that avoiding accidents we shall be in Philadelphia certainly by the 28 or 30th."

-☙❧-

12. JAMES MONROE TO THOMAS JEFFERSON OCTOBER 14, 1793

"DEAR SIR,—The fatigue of my late journey & some concerns which require immediate attention will deprive me of the pleasure of being at Monticello till after ye. arrival of Mr. Madison which will be on Wednesday—unless the funeral of his brother should detain him longer, which however is not expected."

13. JAMES MONROE DEEMING POWER OF ATTORNEY TO JAMES MADISON JUNE 17, 1794

"Mr. Madison will be pleased to receive from Gen'l Wilkinson, or draw on him for the sum of three hundred dollars or thereabouts (due me by him) according as the Gen'l shall direct—He will likewise receive whatever is obtained from Gen'l Bradley from the sale of our Vermont property, or otherwise from the sale or upon account of it—He will likewise be pleased, in case he is applied to, to give advice as to the course to be taken for obtaining justice against J. Kortright and others under the will [of] L. Kortright (father of Mrs. M.) of New York—and whatever he does in the above will be satisfactory & binding on me."

14. JAMES MONROE TO JAMES MADISON SEPTEMBER 2, 1794

"DEAR SIR,—Tomorrow will make one month since our arrival here, and such have been my engagements that altho. I resolved that I would begin a letter to you every succeeding day yet when the day arrived it was not in power heretofore. You will readily conceive that the variety of the objects to which I have been forced to attend, many of which requiring the utmost effort of my judgment, all delicate and interesting and you will readily admit my embarrassment when you know that I have not had a single person (Mr. Skipwith excepted and who is new in this line) with whom I could confidentially confer. I wished not to write you a superficial letter, but whether I shall be forced to hurry this is what I cannot at present determine."

15. JAMES MONROE TO JAMES MADISON FEBRUARY 25, 1795

". . . we are happy to hear you have added a particular associate to the circle of our friends & to whom you will make our best respects[87]—Sincerely I am your friend & servant."

87 Monroe is alluding to Madison's marriage to 26 year-old Dolley Payne Todd. The two married on September 15, 1794.

16. JAMES MONROE TO JAMES MADISON FEBRUARY 20, 1796

"Your China will go from hence in the course of a few days when I will send you an invoice of it. It is a plain neat service, sufficient in number & cheap. If you will permit me I will procure for you in the course of the present year furniture for a drawing room, consisting of the following articles. 1. Chairs, suppose 12. or 18.—2d. two tables or three after the taste which we prefer—3d. a sofa, perhaps 2. These all of tapestry & to suit, if to be had, the curtains we sent you, either one or the other sett. 4th. a clock to stand on the chimney piece, & which chimney piece I will send also, of marble, if you wish it. I wish you to send me a list of what other things you want & especially of books, & I will provide & send or bring them with me when I return home. I will procure every thing as cheap as possible, & adjust the amount when I have occasion for it."

17. JAMES MONROE TO THOMAS JEFFERSON JULY 30, 1796

"I have just heard that I am charged with having become a speculator here [in Paris], with other things still more exceptionable, & God knows what. I send, therefore, by this opportunity to Mr. Madison an ample refutation of these charges, advising that they be published if my friends think fit. He will probably see you on the occasion."

18. JAMES MONROE TO THOMAS JEFFERSON JULY 13, 1797

"You are fortunate in having our friend Madison near you."

19. JAMES MONROE TO JAMES MADISON SEPTEMBER 24, 1797

"I wish you to come up in the course of the week when most convenient to you. We beg you also to make our best respects to Mrs. Madison and request her to accompany you. We will be very happy to see her provided she can submit to our accommodation of which you can give an account having an upper room in one of our offices, there being no additional room as you suppose. But we will do all in our power to make it tolerable."

20. JAMES MONROE TO JAMES MADISON JULY 13, 1799

"DEAR SIR,—Have you ever received your wine from Mr. Yard? Presuming you had not, I intimated in a letter by Dr. Bache to Mr. Yard requesting mine to be forwarded to the care of Governor Jefferson, Richmond, that if yours had not already been I doubted not it would be agreeable to you, it should be by the same route. I hope we shall receive it, since to me it will be a most acceptable accommodation having had none of any kind for a long time; and if it is really of the quality we are taught to expect of it, it will also be of importance to you. If you have not written for it (as you probably did by Dr. Bache as I desired him to mention the subject to you) had you not better yet do it?"

21. JAMES MONROE TO JAMES MADISON JULY 13, 1799

"Can you not come up & stay a day or two with us? Your skill in architecture & farming would be of great use to me at present. I am much engaged in both & take more interest, especially in the latter, tho' under discouraging circumstances, than at any former time. We promise to do everything in our power to make a like visit to Mrs. Madison agreeable, to whom we beg our best regards as we also do to the old gentleman & Lady."

22. JAMES MONROE TO JAMES MADISON NOVEMBER 22, 1799

"DEAR SIR,—I was yesterday at Monticello when Mr. Jefferson informed me he proposed setting out on the next (this) morning on a visit to you, to remain a day & return. Considering your present publick engagement, the business before the legislature & the part you will necessarily take in it, with his publick station, I was immediately impressed with an idea the trip had better be declined & so observed. He said he had omitted writing to you lately as he intended to visit you. I told him it would certainly compromise you both; it would immediately appear throughout the Continent. Under this consideration he declined the trip, in the persuasion an interview might be had, by your making me a visit, at my new house, to which I move tomorrow. There would be nothing extraordinary in your coming up to assist me in arrangements there, and bringing Mrs. Madison with you, which I earnestly wish you to do next week. We will repay the debt hereafter with interest. Our house is unfinished in all respects, the yard in confusion, &c, but you shall have a warm chamber & be made as comfortable as we can make you. Perhaps I have done wrong in interfering, and may have avoided one evil by preferring a worse one. This often happens where the intention is known to be good. But yet the present does not appear to me to be an example of that kind."

23. JAMES MONROE TO JAMES MADISON AUGUST 13, 1800

"Most earnestly do we wish we could make it convenient to execute our engagements with you and Mrs. Madison, for we feel, especially myself, that we have as yet illy acquitted ourselves to you, but as my duty calls me at present to Richmond, and a visit to you would subject me to the same fatigue as heretofore, I fear it will not be in my power. If we do not visit you again you will ascribe it to the true cause which you know too well to doubt its solidity. When you come to Richmond in the fall, as you most probably will, we beg you to bring Mrs. M. with you, as it will be perfectly convenient for us to accommodate you and highly agreeable. A fortnight's residence with us there will make the retreat for the winter more desirable in the mountains. We shall have more leisure too for many topics of conversation than we have had of late. Present our best regards to Mrs. M. & sisters as also to the old gentleman & lady & Miss Fanny."

24. JAMES MONROE TO JAMES MADISON AUGUST 14, 1800

"DEAR SIR,—I wrote you two days since & sent the letter to Charlottesville. It is only this moment that I recollect I omitted to enquire whether you had heard of the overseer you promised to endeavor to engage for me. I shall take no step relying on him till I hear from you. Perhaps he would be satisfied with £50. as it is in a healthy country, and the entire command of the plantation in his hands. But you will do the best you can; since my last child has had no relapse of his former complaints, but I have received a notice which shows I ought to be at Richmond. I wish I had more command of my time, that I might be with you some days before I go down."

25. JAMES MONROE TO THOMAS JEFFERSON SEPTEMBER 20, 1803

"I have declined writing you, as I should have done frequently, had I not thought it better to continue the communication uninterrupted, publick and private, thro' Mr. Madison.

It was of the same advantage to you as if I had written to you, without the inconvenience of hasarding a compromitment of you."

26. JAMES MONROE TO JAMES MADISON JUNE 28, 1804

"I have written you a very long letter; if it gives any hint that may be useful I have attained my object in it. If it does not you will I am satisfied give me credit for the motive."

27. JAMES MONROE TO JAMES MADISON OCTOBER 13, 1807

"DEAR SIR,—I arrived [in Norfolk, Virginia] to day, with my family in the American ship the Augustus in 28. days from Portsmouth. It is my intention to set out for Richmond without delay, & leaving my family there, to proceed thence to Washington, for the purpose of giving you all the information in my power respecting our affairs with the British government. We are much exhausted by fatigue & sickness on the voyage, & there will be difficulty in getting the means of conveying us to Richmond with any degree of comfort, so that I do not expect to leave this till tuesday or to be able to move with much rapidity till I leave that place, but you may be assured that I will be with you as soon as I can."

28. JAMES MONROE TO THOMAS JEFFERSON FEBRUARY 27, 1808

"I informed Mr. Madison when I was at Washington that I should write him a letter in reply to his of May 20th, 1807 on the subject of the treaty to answer some of his objections to it, and place in a just light the conduct of the American Commissioners in that transaction. I informed him also that as I wished to couch that letter in the most amicable terms, if he should find any passage in it, which failed in that respect, I should be happy to alter it, having in view only a fair vindication of my conduct. I have almost concluded the letter & shall forward it in the course of the next week, the early part of it if possible, my private concerns have subjected me to much interruption, or I should have finished it sooner."

29. JAMES MONROE TO THOMAS JEFFERSON FEBRUARY 27, 1808

"No one better knows than I do the merit of Mr. Madison, and I can declare that should he be elected he will have my best wishes for the success of his administration, as well on account of the great interest which I take in what concerns his welfare as in that of my country. It will not lessen my friendship for him which is sincere & strong."

30. JAMES MONROE TO JAMES MADISON MARCH 5, 1808

"DEAR SIR,—I have the pleasure to enclose you my letter on the subject of the late treaty, in conformity with what passed between us when I was at Washington. I have had many other objects to attend to or I should have sent it to you much sooner. I have to repeat what I mentioned to you at Washington, that if there should be any remark in it which in the slightest degree departed from the friendship and respect I bear the administration, which it was desired that I should modify I will be happy to do it. To write anything in vindication of my conduct is most distressing to me; but it was impossible to avoid it, after receiving your letter."

31. JAMES MONROE TO L. W. TAZEWELL OCTOBER 30, 1808

"The state of affairs, especially if our negotiations abroad have failed, which there is much reason to fear has been the case, affords unhappily too great a facility to the demonstration. It will also make an awful appeal to the patriotism even of the best friends and firmest supporters of Mr. Madison. Those not bound to him by stronger ties than such as connect them with the liberty & happiness of their country, ought to hesitate & most probably will hesitate before they take that step. But those who are free to act as their judgment dictates, who are capable of reviewing with impartiality the existing crisis & its dangers, who are already well informed or willing to receive information, who possess sufficient integrity & firmness, or even a due sense of responsibility to their constituents, will have less difficulty in deciding the course which they ought to pursue."

32. JAMES MONROE TO RICHARD BRENT FEBRUARY 25, 1810

". . . Mr. Madison had it in his power, when he came into office, to avail himself and the publick of my services, had it been an object, and that in doing so he would have displayed some magnanimity, that there was but one proposition which he could have made me, or I have accepted, which was to have invited me into the Cabinet in the place he had lately held: that in respect to the military line, I was not desirous of obtaining an office in it, intimating that I should be willing to serve in that line, only in case of an emergency."

33. JAMES MONROE TO COLONEL JOHN TAYLOR SEPTEMBER 10, 1810

"Had I been at home, and the Republicans been willing to place the government in the hands of Mr. Madison, I would have been among the first to promote it. In consideration of his more advanced years, longer services, and just claims, and of the friendship which had so long subsisted between us, I should not have consented to be put in opposition to him. But our affairs had taken such a direction in my absence, so little had an appeal been made with me to generous motives, so completely in truth was I put into a state of duress, that there seemed to be left me no alternative than that of an unworthy submission, or some course which shewed an independence of mind, and a consciousness of integrity. Abandoning then for these reasons, of a public and private nature, the idea of such an attack, and with it all pretension to the government, even the most remote, it remained to settle what kind of attitude I should take. Mr. Madison had criticised the treaty with Great Britain in terms which I thought it did not deserve. Had his criticism operated on her government only it would have been a matter of indifference to me what he said of it. But after the sanction which he had given to that act, though nothing more than a project in respect to our government, it was impossible to excite a public prejudice against it without imparting some portion of its effect to the character of the Ministers who formed it. Here then was a fair ground on which to rest: one which I thought it my duty to occupy. It was one which appeared to me to be free from all the objections that were applicable to the other, and of a nature sufficiently distinct from the administration to shew any independence of it. It has not I presume escaped your attention that my letter from Richmond in reply to that of Mr. Madison alluded to, was written with a view to all these objects."

34. JAMES MONROE TO COLONEL JOHN TAYLOR SEPTEMBER 10, 1810

"Since my return to the United States I have had little communication with the government on public affairs. I was called to Washington last Spring, reluctantly, as you know, to settle my account with the government. The reception given me by the President and officers under him was kind and friendly, and I experienced from them a just and fair conduct to the object which carried me there. But no confidential communication took place between us. Having no resentment for the past, I shewed none. And finding that much interest was taken in what concerned me, I was not insensible to it."

35. LETTER FROM JAMES MONROE TO COLONEL JOHN TAYLOR SEPTEMBER 10, 1810

"I have no desire of a closer connection with the administration than now exists. It is not probable that any ever will take place between us. I do not see the ground on which it can, for should the invitation be given, which is highly improbable, I most certainly would not accept it otherwise than on conditions the most honorable to myself, among which the approbation of those friends who lately supported me in my claims, not to office but to character, would be held an indispensable one."

36. JAMES MONROE TO JAMES MADISON MARCH 23, 1811

"DEAR SIR,—Your letter of the 20th. instant reached me yesterday morning. The subject which it presents to my view is highly interesting, and has received all the consideration which so short a time has enabled me to bestow on it. My wish to give you an early answer, in compliance with your request, has induced me to use all the despatch which the delicacy and importance of the subject would permit.

The proof of your confidence which the proposition communicated by your letter affords is very gratifying to me, and will always be remembered with great satisfaction.

I have no hesitation in saying that I have every disposition to accept your invitation to enter into the Department of State. But in deciding this question, on your part as well as on mine, some considerations occur which claim attention from us both, and which candour requires to be brought into view, and weighed at this time.

My views of policy towards the European powers are not unknown. They were adopted on great consideration, and are founded in the utmost devotion to the publick welfare. I was sincerely of opinion, after the failure of the negotiation with Spain, or rather France, that I was for the interest of our country, to make an accommodation with England, the great maritime power, even on moderate terms, rather than hazard war, or any other alternative. On that opinion I acted afterwards, while I remained in office, and I own that I have since seen no cause to doubt its soundness. Circumstances have in some respects changed, but still my general views of policy are the same."

⁂

37. JAMES MONROE TO JAMES MADISON MARCH 23, 1811

"If I come into the government my object will be to render to my country, and to you, all the service in my power, according to the light, such as it is, of my knowledge and experience, faithfully, and without reserve. It would not become me to accept a station, and to act a part in it, which my judgment and conscience did not approve, and which I did not believe would promote the publick welfare & happiness. I could not do this, nor would you wish me to do it.

If you are disposed to accept my services under these circumstances, and with this explanation, I shall be ready to render them, whenever it may suit you to require them."

⁂

38. JAMES MONROE TO JAMES MADISON MARCH 29, 1811

"DEAR SIR,—I have received your letter of the 26. instant. Its contents are very satisfactory to me. The just principles on which you have invited me into the department of State have removed every difficulty which had occurred to me to the measure, they afford also a strong ground for hope that the joint counsels & labours of those who are thus associated in the government will promote the best interests of our country. To succeed in that most desirable object my utmost exertions will be made. I add with pleasure that I shall carry into the government, a sincere desire to harmonize in the measures necessary to that end on the fair and liberal policies expressed in your letter."

⁂

39. JAMES MONROE TO THOMAS JEFFERSON APRIL 3, 1811

"DEAR SIR,—An unexpected change has taken place in my situation since I had last the pleasure to see you. An invitation from the President to enter into the department of state will take me to Washington. Having accepted the office, I set out tomorrow in the stage to commence its duties."

40. JAMES MONROE TO DR. CHARLES EVERETT APRIL 23, 1811

"I intimated to you from Richmond that the letter of invitation from the President into the office which I now hold was addressed on such fair & liberal principles, proposing a co-operation of our labours & efforts to promote the publick welfare by such means as our experience & judgments might suggest, as to remove all possible difficulty, in the view alluded to in yours, on my part."

41. JAMES MONROE TO DR. CHARLES EVERETT APRIL 23, 1811

"The conduct of the P[resident] since my arrival has corresponded with my previous anticipation; it is perfectly friendly, and corresponding with our antient relation, which I am happy to have restored. On publick affairs we confer without reserve, each party expressing his own sentiments, and viewing dispassionately the existing state, animated by a sincere desire to promote the public welfare. I have full confidence that this relation will be always preserved in the future."

42. LETTER FROM JAMES MONROE TO HENRY CLAY AUGUST 28, 1812

"I most sincerely wish that the President could dispose of me at this juncture, in the military line. If circumstances would permit, and it should be thought that I could render any service, I would, in a very few days, join our forces assembling beyond the Ohio, and endeavor to recover the ground which we have lost."

43. JAMES MONROE TO HENRY CLAY SEPTEMBER 17, 1812

"On the intelligence of the surrender of Detroit, the President expressed a desire to avail himself of my services in that quarter, and had partly decided so to do. He proposed that I should go in the character of a volunteer, with the rank of major general, to take command of the forces. I expressed my willingness to obey the summons, although it was sudden and unexpected, as indeed the event which suggested the idea was. On mature reflection, however, he concluded that it would not be proper for me to leave my present station at the present juncture. I had no opinion on the subject, but was prepared to act in any situation in which it might be thought I might be most useful."

44. JAMES MONROE TO JAMES MADISON DECEMBER 1813

"It is painful to me to make this communication to you nor should I do it if I did not most consciensiously believe that [John Armstrong] if continued in office will ruin not you and the administration only, but the whole republican party & cause. He has already gone far to do it and it is my opinion, if he is not promptly removed, he will soon accomplish it. Without repeating other objections to him & if the above facts are true none others need be urged, he wants a head fit for his station &, indolent except for improper purposes, he is incapable of that combination & activity which the times require. My advice to you therefore is to remove him at once."

45. JAMES MONROE TO THOMAS JEFFERSON JUNE 7, 1813

"When we were together last summer, we conferred on the then state of the departments of War & Navy, and agreed, that whatever might be the merit of the gentlemen in them, which was admitted in certain respects, a change in both was indispensable. I mentioned that I had intimated to the President, before we left Washington, my willingness to take the former, if he thought that the public interest would be advanced by it. It seemed to be your opinion that it would. On returning here, such was the pressure of public opinion, supported by all our friends in Congress, that a change in the department of war was soon decided on, & even solicited by Mr. Eustis himself. In conversation with the President I repeated what I had said before, and intimated that I would either take that department or a military station, as might be thought most adviseable. On the surrender of Hull, I had offered to proceed to the State of Ohio, and to take the command in that quarter, with a volunteer commission, to which he willingly assented. In consequence, I had, with his approbation, sent off the cannon &c. from this place, and made every other arrangement, for the prosecution of the campaign against Upper Canada, and was on the point of setting out when it was thought best to decline it. The President was particularly induced to adopt this latter counsel, by the appointment conferred on General Harrison, by the government of Kentuckey, and his apparent popularity in the western country. I do not recollect that I mentioned this to you before. To the offer which I now repeated the President replied, that he did not wish me to leave my present station, which tho' inactive at the time, might not long continue so, for an inferior one, to hold it while I remained in service."

46. JAMES MONROE TO THOMAS JEFFERSON JUNE 7, 1813

"The President was of the opinion that if I quitted my present station I ought to take command of the army. It being necessary to place some one immediately in the department of War, to supply the vacancy made by Mr. Eustis's retreat, the President requested me to take it *pro tempore,* leaving the ultimate decision on the other questions open to further consideration. I did so, and immediately set to work on the important duties of the office."

47. JAMES MONROE TO THOMAS JEFFERSON JUNE 28, 1813

"DEAR SIR,—From the date of my last letter to you the President has been ill of bilious fever; of that kind called the remittent. It has perhaps never left him, even for an hour, and occasionally simptoms have been unfavorable. This is I think the 15th. day. Elzey of this place, & Shoaff of Annapolis, with Dr. Tucker, attend him. They think he will recover. The first mentioned I have just seen, who reports that he had a good night, & is in a state to take the bark, which indeed he has done on his best day, for nearly a week. I shall see him before I seal this, & note any change, should there be any, from the above statement."

48. JAMES MONROE TO GENERAL HENRY DEARBORN JUNE 18, 1814

"You may recollect that you had been infirm, and had over estimated, no doubt, whether your health would permit you to retain the command of the troops. Of the President's constant friendship for you, and attention to every circumstance, interesting to your honor and feelings, I can speak with the utmost confidence, as I can, that this disposition towards you has undergone no change. I am satisfied that he had the highest confidence in your integrity, attachment to free government and ability to command, diminished only by the infirmity alluded to, which had more weight, considering the very active services imposed on you at your time of life. That confidence is unimpaired."

49. FROM JAMES MONROE TO THE CHAIRMAN OF MILITARY COMMITTEE OF THE SENATE FEBRUARY 1815

"In dividing the United States into military districts, and placing a General of the regular army in command in each, with such portions of the regular force, artillery and infantry, as could be spared from other service, it was the object of the President to afford the best protection to every part of the Union that circumstances would admit of, with the least burthen that might be possible to the people."

50. EXCERPT FROM JAMES MONROE'S FIRST INAUGURAL ADDRESS MARCH 4, 1817

"In the administrations of the illustrious men who have preceded me in this high station, with some of whom I have been connected by the closest ties from early life, examples are presented which will always be found highly instructive and useful to their successors. From these I shall endeavor to derive all the advantages which they may afford. Of my immediate predecessor, under whom so important a portion of this great and successful experiment has been made, I shall be pardoned for expressing my earnest wishes that he may long enjoy, in his retirement, the affections of a grateful country—the best reward of exalted talents and the most faithful and meritorious services."

51. JAMES MONROE TO JAMES MADISON OCTOBER 18, 1817

"DEAR SIR,—Our carriage arrived sooner; some days than we expected, in consequence of which and other considerations, connected with affairs at Washington (our horses also hired), I am forced to hurry on there. It was our intention to have been with you last night, but hearing that Mr. Bagot is with you we are under the necessity, on account of our equipment, our baggage being sent on, by Richmond, to decline calling. I think, also, it will be better to avoid a meeting at your house, with the British Minister. We beg you (Mrs. Monroe & Mrs. Hay) to present our respects to Mrs. Madison & to make our apology for not seeing her as we pass on."

52. JAMES MONROE TO JAMES MADISON OCTOBER 5, 1818

"DEAR SIR,—I had the pleasure to receive your letter of the 2nd. yesterday. We shall set out to-morrow & be with you the day after. I am much pushed by many important concerns to get to Washington as soon as possible, but will certainly remain a day with you."

53. JAMES MONROE TO JAMES MADISON MARCH 31, 1821

"DEAR SIR,—Since I have been in this office many newspapers have been sent to me, from every part of the Union, unsought, which having neither time nor curiosity to read, are in effect thrown away. I should have stopped the practice, but from the delicacy to the Editors, & expecting also that they would subject me to no charge. Lately I have been informed that the same practice took place in your time, & had been tolerated till you retired, when the Editors sent you bills for the amounts of the subscriptions to their papers, for eight years, making an enormous sum. Be so kind as to inform me whether this was the fact, as in case it was I may write to the Editors (a few excepted & very few) not to send them."

54. JAMES MONROE TO JAMES MADISON AUGUST 2, 1824

"Whether I shall be able to see you this summer is uncertain. I do not think that Mrs. Monroe could go with me, & doubt whether I can go without her. Her health is much impair'd by many causes, particularly by our long service, & the heavy burdens & cares to which she has been subjected, and to which the strength of her constitution has not been equal. If the retirement to the country, & change of air should relieve her, and other circumstances should permit, I will certainly see you as soon as I may be able."

55. JAMES MONROE TO JAMES MADISON OCTOBER 18, 1824

"I have long wished to visit Albemarle, & to pass some hours at least with you. I must be here the beginning of next month to prepare for the meeting of Congress. If I can go, I shall set out in a few days."

56. JAMES MONROE TO THOMAS JEFFERSON APRIL 9, 1826

"I did never ask, an indemnity for injuries done me, in the first mission, of you, or Mr. Madison, nor could I do it, with honor. To touch the subject after I came into the administration, was utterly impossible."

57. JAMES MONROE TO C. J. INGERSOLL NOVEMBER 25, 1827

"You judge correctly of my feelings and sentiments, in believing that every proof which is afforded, by my fellow citizens, of their approbation of the conduct of Mr. Madison in public office, & especially in his construction of the powers of the general government in regard to domestic manufactures, is very gratifying to me. The construction which he lately gave of those powers corresponds with his acts while in office, and is a confirmation of the opinion which he then entertained. In that construction I entirely concur."

58. JAMES MONROE TO COLONEL HUGH MERCER DECEMBER 10, 1827

"It comports, in my opinion, with the public interest that persons who have so long served their country in its highest offices, especially in the late one, as Mr. Madison and I have done, should take no part in contests of this kind."[88]

59. JAMES MONROE TO JAMES MADISON JANUARY 18, 1828

"DEAR SIR,—I presume you have heard that both of us are placed on the electoral ticket by the convention lately assembled at Richmond. I have received a letter from Col. Mercer apprizing me of it, and also a private letter from Judge Brooke, to the same effect. In complyance with your suggestion, I wrote, shortly after the receipt of your letter, to Col.

88 Monroe is referring to the presidential election of 1828.

Mercer, & intimated your desire not to be placed on the ticket, for reasons analogous to them, which I urged in my own case, & which I infer, from his last letter, that he had fully executed, by communication to the members of the committee of the convention, & to others. I have been much surprised, therefore, to find that we have been placed on the nomination. You will, I presume, have seen my reply to the committee of Aldie, who gave me an invitation to attend a dinner there, on the 8th., in favor of General Jackson, in which I state explicitly that I can take no position which may, by inference, arrange me on the side of either of the candidates against the other. I assign as the reason those which you gave to the Com: of your county last year, on a similar meeting. I shall be glad to know what course you intend to pursue. My intention is not to act, & the sooner this is made known, the better I think it will be, as to both of us, if such is likewise your decision, as it will be in regard to those affected by it. The position of neutrality being taken there is little cause for much deliberation on the subject. Delay, with a notification of that decision afterwards, may, by appearing to be the result of reflection, be considered as a proof, by partizans, that it was founded solely on insurmountable objections to Mr. Adams, & not on the professed desire of observing a neutrality between the candidates. I have written to Judge Brooke, & informed him, as I likewise have Col. Mercer, that I cannot act, & expressed a wish that official notice may be given me, without delay, that I may give a like answer to it, for the information of our fellow citizens. Should delay take place, it will merit consideration, as our answer is intended for the public, whether we should make the notice in the papers of the nomination, the ground of a letter to him, and cause it to be forthwith published in the *Intelligencer,* sending to the latter, or to the editors of some other paper, a copy of that to the Judge. I wish to hear from you as soon as convenient on the subject."

60. JAMES MONROE TO JAMES MADISON JANUARY 29, 1828

"DEAR SIR,—I have just received your of the 23d, and by the same mail a second from Judge Brooke, the purport of which I hasten to communicate to you. He is aware, as I infer, from the communications which were made to the members of the convention by Col. Mercer, & likewise, on your part, by Mr. Cabell, that we will not act, or remain on the ticket, and has assured me, in the letter just received, that, on obtaining an answer to one received from him some days past, if in the sense of that of which I advised you, he will immediately give us official notice of our nomination. In his first letter he requested me to communicate with you on the subject, and to take no decisive step until I heard from you. I shall intimate to him, in reply, by the next mail, which will be on Thursday, that I have done so, & that we act in accord in it. I presume that we shall obtain a regular notification, in the course of the next week, as he assures me that it shall not be delayed, after the receipt of the letter in reply to that of his, which I received to-day.

I am aware that a claim to exemption from the service, on account of the office which we lately held, or from considerations of private feeling, may not be considered by all as satisfactory. The claim, however, in both views, has weight, and I think that I shall avail myself of it. I contemplate, however, adding another motive, as a public one, alluded to in my letter to Col. Mercer, of which I sent you a copy, stating that instances might occur in which those who had had experience in public affairs, & by service in the late office, might render useful service to their country, provided they kept aloof from such elections & were held in estimation by the community; that if they became partizans, in elections to the chief office, they could have weight only with the party with which they arranged themselves; that they could have none with the other. I shall, of course state, that I hope no such event will ever occur, but that it is better that persons who have so long served should remain tranquil spectators of the mov'ment, than embark in it."

61. JAMES MONROE TO JAMES MADISON FEBRUARY 13, 1828

"From a view of the gazettes, I find that we stand in a very equivocal state before the nation, the presumption being, in many parts, that we wish to remain neutral, but are held in this state for a political purpose, by the committee, who are charged with availing themselves of our names, to favor their object. I think they act unwisely in delaying the notification, & that an injurious reaction is likely to follow the discloser of the fact that we will not serve. Several letters from friends at Washington complain of our silence. It remains for us to decide whether we will suffer ourselves to be held much longer in this state."

62. JAMES MONROE TO JAMES MADISON MARCH 28, 1828

"The incident with the Richmond convention has given us both much trouble. The difficulty we had to encounter was to answer calls from the other side which should declare our neutrality, and not compromit the nominators. I hope that we shall hear no more of it."

63. JAMES MONROE TO JAMES MADISON AUGUST 5, 1828

"DEAR SIR,—On my return home, which I did on the day contemplated when we parted, I had the satisfaction to find my daughter & Mr. Hay in good health, & to receive letters from Mr. Gouverneur, advising me that Mrs. Monroe's health had improved, & was improving. I hope that you & Mrs. Madison have been equally fortunate. I was so much overcome by the heat, & fatigue of the journey in consequence of it, that I have been incapable of any exertion since. I now send you the buckles which I promised, to repair the loss which you sustained in our interesting walk at Monticello."

64. JAMES MONROE TO JAMES MADISON MARCH 20, 1829

"I have heard of the attacks which have been made on you by Mr. Giles, but have not been able to read them. They will do you no injury. Our system is in operation on its principles, unaided, in the councils, by the props which supported it in the revolution, and by revolutionary characters since. A complete remedy to a political disease is seldom found until something like a crisis occurs, and this is promoted by the abuse of those who have rendered the most important services, and whose characters will bear the test of enquiry. I think the period not distant when a very different view will be taken of this, and many other subjects now in agitation."

65. JAMES MONROE TO JAMES MADISON JUNE 25, 1829

"DEAR SIR,—We heard with great regret of your serious indisposition, but were relieved from anxiety by a letter, sometime since, from Mr. R. Taliaferro, which assured us that you had nearly recovered to perfect health."

66. JAMES MONROE TO JAMES MADISON SEPTEMBER 10, 1829

"DEAR SIR,—I am anxious to know the state of your health, & whether it is such as will enable you to attend the convention. I most earnestly hope that you will be able to attend it, for, if I go, I shall be much gratified to meet you there, and, whether I do, or not, I am satisfied that your presence, altho' you may take no part in the discussion, would have a very useful effect."

67. JAMES MONROE TO JAMES MADISON JULY 2, 1830

"DEAR SIR,—Being very anxious to join, & proceed with you to the University, to perform our duties there, I have delayed answering your letter of May the 18, in hope that my health would be so far restored as to enable me to do it. In this I am disappointed. I am still too weak to sustain such an exertion. I am, and have been since my return, free from fever, and I take exercise on horseback in the morning, daily, and think that I gradually recover strength, but it is in a very limited degree. Through the heat of the day I am forced to repose on a bed, incapable of any effort, without exposing myself to injury. Under these circumstances it would be improper for me to make the attempt. Other obstacles present themselves; Mrs. Monroe could not accompany me; her weak state forbids it, and I could not leave her here alone."

68. JAMES MONROE TO JAMES MADISON APRIL 11, 1831

"It is very distressing to me to sell my property in Loudon, for, besides parting with all I have in the State, I indulged a hope, if I could retain it, that I might be able occasionally to visit it, and meet my friends, or many of them there. But ill health & advanced years prescribe a course which we must pursue. I deeply regret that there is no prospect of our ever meeting again, since so long have we been connected, and in the most friendly intercourse, in public & private life, that a final separation is among the most distressing incidents which could occur."

VI. JOHN QUINCY ADAMS ON JAMES MADISON

1. JOHN QUINCY ADAMS TO JOHN ADAMS APRIL 5, 1790

"I do not think indeed that the public opinion can always be collected from newspapers, but they are never silent upon unpopular topics of so great importance. Mr. Madison's reputation has suffered from his conduct in that affair; and Judge Dana is the only man I know whose character gives weight to his opinions, that has adopted those of Mr. Madison."

2. JOHN QUINCY ADAMS TO JOHN ADAMS MARCH 2, 1794

"DEAR SIR:

You will doubtless hear before this reaches you the event of a town meeting which was called here lately for the purpose of helping forward Mr. Madison's resolutions, and of intimidating our representatives who opposed them."[89]

3. JOHN QUINCY ADAMS TO JOSEPH PITCAIRN MAY 2, 1797

"Some of the French papers have announced *positively* the arrival of Mr. Madison at Paris as Envoy Extraordinary to settle the differences. I think it is impossible that this should be true, especially as I have this day a letter from my brother of the 26th which mentions nothing of it. I should like to know how and where the report originated. It has long been whispered about that such an appointment had been made. Perhaps it is spread abroad as a hint. Perhaps as a delusion, to keep up an expectation of accommodation, until it shall be too late to retreat, or to examine into the conduct of those who are driving into war. There appear to me to be many symptoms of such a policy. I think good advantage may be made of the disposition which it so manifestly dreads."

89 These resolutions dealt with punishing Great Britain with higher duties on imported manufactured goods. The resolutions were seen to be detrimental to the economy of the eastern states, particularly Massachusetts.

4. JOHN QUINCY ADAMS TO JOHN ADAMS MAY 11, 1797

"MY DEAR SIR:

I have before mentioned to you the accounts circulated, that Mr. Madison was appointed Envoy Extraordinary to France, and sent you the papers which announced his arrival at Paris. The present papers contradict that article, but repeat that he has been appointed. I suppose it is meant as a hint.

General Pinckney is still [at the Hague], and has done me the honor to communicate with me in the most unreserved and confidential manner upon the state of our affairs with France. He has also desired me to say to you, that it is his wish that no scruple whatever as it regards him may impede the appointment of Mr. Madison, or of any other person, who may be more like to succeed in arranging the differences with France."

5. AN EXCERPT FROM THE DIARY OF JOHN QUINCY ADAMS NOVEMBER 3, 1807

"Mr. Jefferson said that he had always been extremely fond of agriculture, and knew nothing about it, but the person who united with other sciences the greatest agricultural knowledge of any man he knew was Mr. Madison. He was the best farmer in the world."

6. AN EXCERPT FROM THE DIARY OF JOHN QUINCY ADAMS JANUARY 23, 1808

"On taking the ballots for the office of President, there were eighty-three votes for James Madison, three for James Monroe, and three for George Clinton. Before the ballot for Vice-President, Mr. Pope made a speech recommending unanimity for the choice of this office. The votes were seventy-nine for George Clinton, five for Henry Dearborn, three for John Langdon, and one for J. Q. Adams. The chairman then declared James Madison duly nominated, by a great majority of votes, as a candidate for the office of President, and George Clinton for that of Vice-President."

7. JOHN QUINCY ADAMS TO JOHN ADAMS JANUARY 27, 1808

"Notwithstanding the critical situation of the country the two Houses of Congress are acting very much at their leisure, and from their present proceedings one would imagine we were in a state of profound peace. The presidential election engrosses the principal attention of the members. About one-half the members of both houses here have declared in favor of Mr. Madison and to re-elect the Vice President.[90] In the legislature of Virginia, also, the friends of Mr. Madison have outnumbered those of Mr. Monroe nearly three to one."

8. JOHN QUINCY ADAMS TO GEORGE BOYD MAY 14, 1808

"I can see no impropriety in your intended application to Mr. Madison for the appointment as a messenger to bear dispatches to France, and I could indulge my feelings with no higher gratification than that of aiding your wishes by my recommendation. But my situation in relation to the Secretary of State, as well as to every other member of the administration, is such as to forbid me from even the most distant appearance of solicitation of any favor of any description whatsoever, for myself or for any of my relatives."

9. AN EXCERPT FROM THE DIARY OF JOHN QUINCY ADAMS MARCH 4, 1809

"I went to the Capitol, and witnessed the inauguration of Mr. Madison as President of the United States. The House was very much crowded, and its appearance very magnificent. He made a very short speech, in a tone of voice so low that he could not be heard, after which the official oath was administered to him by the Chief-Justice of the United States, the four other Judges of the Supreme Court being present and in their robes. After the ceremony was over I went to pay the visit of custom. The company was received at Mr. Madison's house; he not having yet removed to the President's house. Mr. Jefferson was among the visitors. The Court had adjourned until two o'clock. I therefore returned to them at that hour. Mr. Martin closed the argument in the cause of Fletcher and Peck; after which the Court adjourned. I came home to dinner, and in the evening went with the ladies to a ball at Long's, in honor of the new President. The crowd was excessive—the

90 George Clinton of New York

heat oppressive, and the entertainment bad. Mr. Jefferson was there. About midnight the ball broke up."

10. AN EXCERPT FROM THE DIARY OF JOHN QUINCY ADAMS MARCH 6, 1809

"This morning, while at breakfast, I received a not from Mr. Madison, the new President, requesting me, as I go up to the Capitol Hill, to call on him at his late residence, or at the President's house; which I accordingly did. He there informed me that he proposed to nominate me to the Senate as Minister Plenipotentiary to Russia. Mr. Jefferson had sent Mr. Short there last summer, but on his nominating him the Senate rejected the nomination. Mr. Madison said he had been informed the objection was not to the mission, but to the man; that the Emperor of Russia had so frequently and so strongly urged a wish for an interchange of Ministers with this country, that he, Mr. Madison, was very desirous of complying with that inclination; that the commercial relations between the two countries were important, and that in this desposition of the Emperor, perhaps some valuable advantages might be obtained. He apologized for not having given me earlier notice of this proposition, from the extraordinary pressure of business which the recent occurrences had thrown upon him; and observed that the nominations must be sent in within the course of half an hour. . .

I told him that, upon the little consideration I was able to give the subject upon this sudden notice, I could see no sufficient reason for refusing the nomination; though, from the circumstances, the confirmation by the Senate might be uncertain.

He again apologized for the shortness of the time, and said if, upon further consideration, I should perceive any insuperable obstacle to my acceptance, or the confirmation of the appointment, I might still reserve the right of finally declining.

On these grounds I consented that the nomination should be made. The report of the nomination was circulated within an hour of the time when I went into court."

11. JOHN QUINCY ADAMS TO LOUISA CATHERINE ADAMS MARCH 5, 1809

"The oath of office was yesterday administered to the new President in the chamber of the Representatives. He delivered a short speech, which you will without a doubt see in the newspapers before you can receive this letter. It is in very general terms, and was spoken in a tone of voice so low that scarcely any part of it was heard by three-fourths of the audience.

The body of the House was excessively crowded and the galleries were equally thronged, which gave it altogether a very magnificent appearance. The city was very much crowded with strangers, and I believe I may say without exaggeration that in the course of the day yesterday I saw more people than in the whole time I have ever been here.

Immediately after the ceremony was performed the President and his lady received company at their own house. I paid my visit with your mamma and Mr. and Mrs. Hellen. It was not at the President's house, which Mr. Jefferson has not yet left. He was with the company who visited his successor.

In the evening there was a ball at Long's on the Capitol Hill, the house which last winter was kept by Stelle. The crowd there was excessive; the rooms suffocating and the entertainment bad. Your sister Hellen literally took me with her, for I should not have gone but at special invitation that I would attend her. The President and his family were also there, and also Mr. Jefferson. I had some conversation with him in the course of the evening, in the course of which he asked me whether I continued as fond of POETRY as I was in my youth. I told him, yes; that I did not perceive I had lost any of my relish for good poetry, though my taste for the minor poets, and particular for *amatory verses*, was not so keen as it had been when I was young. He said he was still fond of reading Homer, but did not take much delight in Virgil."

12. JOHN QUINCY ADAMS TO LOUISA CATHERINE ADAMS MARCH 9, 1809

"On Monday morning Mr. Madison sent his nominations to the Senate. The heads of departments are as I wrote you they would be. He nominated me to go to Russia. But the Senate took no vote on his nomination. They pass'd a resolution that it was inexpedient or unnecessary in their opinion that a minister should be sent to Russia."

-ↈ-

13. JOHN QUINCY ADAMS TO LOUISA CATHERINE ADAMS MARCH 9, 1809

"I believe you will not be much disappointed at the failure of the proposition to go to Russia. In respect to ourselves and to our children it would have been attended with more trouble than advantage. I had as little desire as expectation of that or any other appointment; and although I feel myself obliged to the President for his nomination, I shall be better pleased to stay at home than I should have been to go to Russia."

-ↈ-

14. JOHN QUINCY ADAMS TO JAMES MADISON APRIL 30, 1809

"I cannot deny myself the pleasure which this opportunity affords me to offering you, sir, my congratulations upon the favorable change in the aspect of our public affairs, since your accession to the presidency, and of presenting you my most earnest hopes, that the just and honorable principles, which I have the most entire confidence will govern your administration, may be crowned with success beyond the expectation of our country's best friend, and equal to your own wishes."

-ↈ-

15. JOHN QUINCY ADAMS TO EZEKIEL BACON JUNE 15, 1809

"Mr. Randolph's speeches are very amusing, and very popular among the enemies of the administration. Among the federalists *with us*, however, there are great numbers who will finally support Mr. Madison, *provided he does not quarrel with England*, but on no other contingency."

-ↈ-

16. JOHN QUINCY ADAMS TO WILLIAM EUSTIS JUNE 22, 1809

"I rejoice that your conviction in the honesty of Mr. Madison has been confirmed by the opportunity you now have of ascertaining it conclusively. I have entertained that confidence in him at a time when, if I had lent an ear to prejudices, they would have led at least to suspicion; and although if the event had proved me mistaken in my confidence, I should not have renounced my theory of human nature, I should certainly have felt conscious that in the application of my principle I had committed an error of judgment. I hope you will not conclude from this reasoning that I mean to make Mr. Madison's honesty prove me a hero. I did not stake my life upon the issue."

17. JOHN QUINCY ADAMS TO WILLIAM EUSTIS JUNE 22, 1809

"I have no doubt that overtures of a very *conciliatory* nature have been made to Mr. Madison from the predominating party [in Boston], and I presume you know more of them than I can inform you. Perhaps you also know that among his and your friends, there is some uneasiness under the apprehension of a coalition from which, in respect to party views, they might be the sufferers. Of all this I have heard a little, but it being a subject in which I have no inclination to meddle, I have felt not much interest in the purposes of either side."

18. JOHN QUINCY ADAMS TO WILLIAM EUSTIS JUNE 22, 1809

"The readiness with which the propositions from England were received by Mr. Madison has given universal satisfaction in [Massachusetts], and rendered the commencement of his administration extremely popular. There is a wish, feebly intimated rather than directly asserted from a certain quarter, that measures hostile to France might be adopted. I observe the same thing in the congressional maneuvering at Washington, but I hope it will not be suffered to prevail. Senseless and cruel as the conduct of France towards this country has been, I still wish that a war with her may be avoided. As Great Britain is now upon her good behavior, I cherish a slight hope that Mr. Madison will yet signalize his administration by obtaining from her *justice* and our *rights*. At any rate that we shall escape a war with her, and yet surrender nothing essential. But no alliance with the British lion; no common cause against the Corsican!"

19. JOHN QUINCY ADAMS TO ROBERT SMITH JULY 5, 1809

"SIR:

I had the honor yesterday of receiving your letter of 29th ultimo, inclosing a commission as minister plenipotentiary to the Emperor of Russia. In requesting you, sir, to offer to the President my respectful acknowledgments for the expression of his wish that this appointment might be agreeable to me. . .".

-⊰⊱-

20. JOHN QUINCY ADAMS TO ROBERT SMITH JULY 5, 1809

"Considerations of a powerful nature, arising from my personal circumstances and those of my family, would at this time restrain me from leaving for so distant a region, and so incertain a period of absence, the land of my parents and of my children; and in consulting the operations of my own judgment, a doubt might perhaps remain, whether any service it may be in my power to render my country on this mission, can outweigh that which I must abandon in my present relations with society. Yet a firm conviction, that the first object of the President's administration is the welfare of the whole Union, and an ardent desire to contribute whatever aid I can give to a purpose which has all the wishes of my heart, reconcile me to the station where the regular authority of the country has deemed it best to place me, and induce my acceptance of the office."

-⊰⊱-

21. JOHN QUINCY ADAMS TO WILLIAM EUSTIS JULY 16, 1809

"I have determined to *go*. Inclining myself, to the belief, that home and private station was a position in which I could have served the country and aided Mr. Madison's administration, (which is the same thing) more usefully than upon this mission, I have yet acquiesced in the judgment of those to whom the Constitution has left it, and who have thought best to place me abroad. I could not be insensible to the spontaneous and unsolicited token of the President's confidence, manifested in the nomination at the commencement of his administration, nor was it consistent with my sense of my own duties, to meet that confidence with a temper of hesitation or of coolness in regard to the mode, or the place where, *he* conceived I might be useful to the cause. . .".

-⊰⊱-

22. JOHN QUINCY ADAMS TO JOSEPH HALL AUGUST 15 & 17, 1810

"As the leading federalists, some of whom at one time last summer professed a disposition to support Mr. Madison's administration, have so decidedly made their election to be in opposition to it, I cannot flatter myself with any prospect that their views of public affairs will soon, if ever, coincide with mine more than for the last three years."

23. JOHN QUINCY ADAMS TO SECRETARY OF STATE JAMES MONROE JUNE 2, 1811

"Deeply sensible of the honor done me by the President and Senate of the United States in the appointment to the bench of the Supreme Court, I lament, that circumstances beyond my control have prescribed to me the duty of declining it. As they are for the most part of a private nature I have taken the liberty to explain them in a letter to the President himself, herewith enclosed: and which I have to ask you the favor to deliver to him."

24. JOHN QUINCY ADAMS TO JAMES MADISON JUNE 3, 1811

"The new mark of confidence, which you have been pleased to show me in the nomination to an office so highly honorable, and so far as could relate to my own personal interest and concerns so acceptable, has made on my mind an impression which no time can obliterate, and which leaves me the more earnestly to regret my incapacity to meet it with a return, the most agreeable to you, by assuming and discharging its duties in a manner to justify that confidence, and do honor to your appointment."[91]

25. JOHN QUINCY ADAMS TO JAMES MADISON JUNE 3, 1811

"I cannot expect, nor however it might suit my convenience, can I permit myself to desire that you should keep an office of such importance vacant a full year longer to await my return, and this consideration is decisive to induce me to decline the appointment . . . .I must, therefore, intreat you, sir, to confer upon some other person the office as a judge of the Supreme Court,

91 President Madison nominated John Quincy Adams as an Associate Justice of the United States Supreme Court which the Senate approved on February 2, 1811.

to which you have had the goodness to appoint me. The impossibility of my return to the United States in due time to assume its duties must of itself forbid my acceptance of it. The other reasons which would in any case impel me to decline it I should have suppressed, but for the high sense of my personal obligation to you for the nomination, and the wish to be justified in your opinion for renouncing the post to which you have judged me suitably qualified."

26. JOHN QUINCY ADAMS TO JAMES MADISON JUNE 3, 1811

". . . I beg you to be assured that on my return to the United States, whenever you shall deem it proper, and I shall find it practicable, whether in public office of any kind or in retirement, the grateful sense of your kindness and the most fervent wishes for the prosperity of your public administration, and the promotion of your personal happiness, will be among the sentiments nearest to my heart."

27. JOHN QUINCY ADAMS TO ABIGAIL ADAMS MAY 28, 1812

"I have written to have the children sent to me, if they can be sent this year. I have also written to the President expressing my desire not to be left [in St. Petersburg, Russia] longer than another winter, which will accomplish the period of absence which he and myself had contemplated when he was pleased to make me the offer of this mission."

28. AN EXCERPT FROM THE DIARY OF JOHN QUINCY ADAMS AUGUST 6, 1812

"Mr. Proud dined with us, and brought with him the New York *Commercial Advertiser* of 22d June, containing the message of the President of the United States to Congress, communicating the sequel of the correspondence between Mr. Monroe and Mr. Foster, and recommending a declaration of war; the report of the Committee of Foreign Relations upon this message, also recommending an immediate appeal to arms; the act declaring war, approved 18th June; the proclamation of the President founded upon the act of Congress; and the yeas and nays in both Houses upon the act—seventy-nine to forty-nine in the House of Representatives, and nineteen to thirteen in the Senate; two Senators, Mr. Bradley and Mr. Whitesides, absent."

29. JOHN QUINCY ADAMS TO JOHN ADAMS FEBRUARY 15, 1813

"We are still ignorant of the issue of our presidential election, which the British ministry either believe or affect to believe to be the test of peace or war. It has even been asserted from publications in American gazettes to which I give not the least credit, that the candidate opposed against Mr. Madison was agreed upon by a coalition of very heterogeneous oppositions upon a special pledge that, if elected, he would within twenty-four hours after his installation suspend hostilities against Britain and commence a negotiation for peace.[92] The English gazettes have seized with avidity this absurd tale, and circulate it throughout Europe to propagate the opinion that the war is in America considered merely as Mr. Madison's war, and that if his antagonist should be elected, the new President would rush into the arms of England without asking a question of Congress, and take just such a peace as my Lord Castlereagh should be pleased to give him. That the chance of peace will depend upon the event of the American election the British ministry have explicitly avowed to be their expectation, and their ambassador [in St. Petersburg], Lord Cathcart, some months since intimated to me in conversation the same thing."

30. JOHN QUINCY ADAMS TO ABIGAIL ADAMS MARCH 25, 1813

"We have learnt through the only channel now open for news to reach us from America, that is, the English newspapers, that Mr. Madison has been re-elected and that Mr. Gerry is chosen Vice President.[93] It may give you a sample of the degree of ignorance in which we live of American affairs to be informed that we did not know until this account of the votes came who was the candidate for the Vice President to be run with Mr. Madison."

31. JOHN QUINCY ADAMS TO ABIGAIL ADAMS MARCH 25, 1813

"We have indeed had it repeated over to satiety here for the last twelve months, both from the English periodical journals and from private advices through federal sources, that the war was so extremely unpopular in the United States that it would occasion the loss of Mr. Madison's re-election. But now the tables are so completely turned that we hear it said Mr. Madison made the war for the sole purpose

92 DeWitt Clinton, New York

93 Madison received 128 Electoral Votes to DeWitt Clinton's 89.

of securing his election. Who shall decide when doctors disagree with themselves? The English journals tell us that in the debates of Congress Mr. Randolph and Mr. Quincy both charge this intention directly upon Mr. Madison. These are reproaches which for aught I know may gratify party feelings, but which appear neither very politic nor very liberal."

32. JOHN QUINCY ADAMS TO THOMAS BOYLSTON ADAMS APRIL 3, 1813

"Your remarks upon the issue of the presidential election have given me a fresh example of the identity in the process of our thoughts concerning the same event. I rejoice at Mr. Madison's reëlection and at Mr. Gerry's election, because it has proved the spirit of the nation to be still determined in support of their rights."

33. JOHN QUINCY ADAMS TO SECRETARY OF STATE JAMES MONROE JULY 14, 1813

"I must solicit the favor of you, sir, to make my warm and sincere acknowledgments acceptable to the President for the honor done me by this new appointment, to which I am the more sensible from the highly respectable and distinguished characters of the gentlemen with whom he was pleased to connect me in the mission.[94] I have only to add the most ardent wish that its result may prove satisfactory to him and propitious to our country."

34. JOHN QUINCY ADAMS TO JAMES MONROE AUGUST 9, 1813

"SIR:

In renewing my warmest acknowledgements for the approbation which the President has been pleased to express of my conduct in the mission to this country, and for the further tokens of his confidence which he has seen fit on this occasion to bestow, as well as for those which he had contemplated in the event of a successful termination to the present extraordinary mission, I can only add my earnest desire to deserve the continuance

94 President Madison appointed Adams as Chief Negotiator of a five man American delegation to mediate the Treaty of Ghent ending the War of 1812 with Great Britain.

of his good opinion, and my readiness to discharge to the best of my ability the duties of any station in which he may deem it expedient to require my coöperation in the public service."

35. JOHN QUINCY ADAMS TO WILLIAM PLUMER AUGUST 13, 1813

"I have seen it most eloquently demonstrated in the same papers, that eternal inextinguishable war with Britain is the master passion, the very Aaron's serpent of Mr. Madison's breast, and also that he is heartily tired and sick of the war, and ready to catch at any straw to get out of it."

36. JOHN QUINCY ADAMS TO ABIGAIL ADAMS MARCH 30, 1814

"Whatever may be the issue of the intended conferences at Gothenburg, I hope and believe they will not spin out beyond the bounds of the ensuing summer; and at all events I conclude it is not the President's intention that I should return to this place. If left to my own option I certainly shall not. After five winters passed at St. Petersburg, I have no wish to try in my own person, or to expose my family to the experience of this climate any longer."

37. JOHN QUINCY ADAMS TO LEVETT HARRIS JULY 9, 1814

"Queen Mab's thimble would have been a fire-bucket to extinguish the flames of Moscow, just as important as the place where we should meet the British commissioners was to the issue of the negotiation. But the President of the United States *felt,* and it was a feeling worthy of a Chief Magistrate of an independent and spirited people, that the metropolis of our enemy was not a suitable place to be substituted for the capital of a common friend and impartial mediator."

38. JOHN QUINCY ADAMS TO LOUISA CATHERINE ADAMS JULY 29, 1814

"Mr. Canning some time before in another debate had enjoined upon the ministry not to make peace without depriving America of her right to the fisheries; and one of the Lords of Admiralty is reported to have said in the same House of Commons, that the war with America would now be continued to accomplish the *deposition of Mr. Madison.* An article in the *Courier,* the ministerial paper, of the 22d, countenances the same idea. It states that the federalists in America are about taking a high tone; that they will address Congress for the removal of Mr. Madison, preparatory to his impeachment; on the ground that England will never make peace with him. . .".

39. JOHN QUINCY ADAMS TO LOUISA CATHERINE ADAMS AUGUST 5, 1814

"Mr. Beasley has sent us some of the latest American papers that have been received; they are to the 20th of June, and exhibit no indication of the intentions announced by the British gazettes on the part of the federalists to address Congress for the removal and impeachment of Mr. Madison. Quite the contrary. The New York election has given a great accession of strength to the government of the United States; and the Massachusetts governor and legislature are *retreating* and boast of their *forbearance.*"

40. JOHN QUINCY ADAMS TO LOUISA CATHERINE ADAMS OCTOBER 11, 1814

"A defence as despicable as the action it attempts to justify has been brought forward in one of the English newspapers; and its only artifice is to diminish the infamy by depreciating the importance of this vaunted exploit. They are compelled to urge how small and insignificant the distinction was which they could accomplish to ward off the shame of having destroyed everything in their power. The Capitol, they now say was only *an unfinished building*; the President's house was properly demolished because *the scoundrel* Madison lived in it, and to be sure they could not be blamed for having destroyed a navy yard. Let them lay this flattering unction to their soul. The ruins of the Capitol and other public buildings at Washington will remain monuments of British barbarism, beyond the reach of British destruction, when nothing of their oppressive power will be left but the memory of how much it was abused. . .".

41. JOHN QUINCY ADAMS TO LOUISA CATHERINE ADAMS NOVEMBER 11, 1814

"All the letters from England concur in stating that the popular sentiment from continuing the war is a perfect frenzy. The *Times* blubbers that all the laurels of Portugal, Spain, and France, have *withered* at Plattsburg, and threatens damnation to the ministry if they dare to make peace with Madison and his faction."

42. JOHN QUINCY ADAMS TO ABIGAIL ADAMS DECEMBER 24, 1814

"You know doubtless that heretofore the President intended in case of peace to send me to England. If the treaty should be ratified, I am uncertain whether he will still retain the same intention or not. I have requested to be recalled at all events from the mission to Russia. I shall proceed from this place in a few days to Paris, to be there in readiness to receive the President's orders, and I shall write immediately to my wife requesting her to come and join me there."

43. JOHN QUINCY ADAMS TO JAMES MONROE JUNE 23, 1815

"In delivering my credential letter to the Prince at the private audience previous to the levee, I had told him that I fulfilled the commands of my government in expressing the hope that it would be received as a token of the earnest desire of the President not only for the faithful and punctual observance of all our engagements contracted with Great Britain, but for the adoption of every other measure which might tend to consolidate the peace and friendship and to promote the harmony between the two nations."

44. JOHN QUINCY ADAMS TO JOHN ADAMS JANUARY 5, 1816

"We have, in the newspapers of last evening and this morning, the President's message at the opening of the session of Congress. It gives upon the whole a pleasing view of the state of our public affairs, but not quite so fair an aspect of the finances as were to be wished. Peace, however, will be the most healing of all medicines to them, and the complexion of the message is entirely pacific."

45. JOHN QUINCY ADAMS TO JOHN ADAMS JANUARY 3, 1817

"We have just received the President's message at the opening of the session of Congress. It has extorted a few sentences of unwilling and sulky approbation from the ministerial papers. Its contents are in a high degree gratifying to the friends of our country. Mr. Madison has the happiness of leaving the Union in a state of prosperity and of tranquility which did not accompany the retirement of either of his predecessors. For that very reason he leaves a more doubtful prospect to his successor. In the political as well as in the physical world the tempest must always alternate with fair weather. Hitherto, blessed be God, all our pilots have succeeded in weathering the storm. There are breakers ahead and all around us, however, and I hope your letter to the perpetual peace-mongers will give a lesson of useful instruction to our countrymen."

46. JOHN QUINCY ADAMS TO WILLIAM PLUMER JANUARY 17, 1817

"We have lately received what may be termed President Madison's valedictory message to Congress, and grateful indeed must it be to his feelings to compare the condition of the country at the close of his administration, with the turbulent and perilous state in which it was at the period of his first election. It will be the great duty of his successor, and of the Congress with which he is to cooperate, to use diligently the days of peace to prepare the nation for other trials which are probably not far distant, and which sooner or later cannot fail to arise."

47. JOHN QUINCY ADAMS TO JAMES MADISON DECEMBER 15, 1817

"I am happy to avail myself of this opportunity of expressing to you the high respect and veneration that I entertain for your character, and of renewing the personal acknowledgments which I feel to be due from me for the repeated instances of trust and confidence with which I was honored by you in the course of your public administration."

48. JOHN QUINCY ADAMS TO CHRISTOPHER HUGHES JUNE 22, 1818

"To the example which you allege of my predecessors, I have no other reply than 'non omnia possumus omnes.[95]' They must have had a greater degree of *facilite de*

95 "Not all of us are able to do all things."

travail than I have. It certainly was considered by Mr. Madison that the public duties of the Department of State were more than sufficient for one man, as you know one of the last acts of his administration was the proposal to take part of them off, by the establishment of a home department. Congress, however, thought otherwise."

49. AN EXCERPT FROM JOHN QUINCY ADAMS'S *PARTIES IN THE UNITED STATES* JANUARY 1824

"From the period of the peace with Great Britain in December 1814 the party conflict of Federalists and Republicans had ceased. All systematic opposition to the administration of Mr. Madison ceased at the same time. The Federalists retained their ascendency in Massachusetts in the state legislature until 1823, and the government of the state has been in constant harmony with that of the Union. At the expiration of the second term of Mr. Madison a division took place in the Republican Party upon the selection of his successor."

50. AN EXCERPT FROM JOHN QUINCY ADAMS'S *PARTIES IN THE UNITED STATES* JANUARY 1824

"Mr. Madison, perhaps without sharing the opinions in favor of constitutional limitation, indulged his own inclination in withdrawing from the public service at the close of his second term, and no attempt was made to urge his longer continuance in office. The public indifference indeed with which his retirement and that of Mr. Monroe were attended is among the remarkable characteristics of the time, and indicates an unusual calmness of the temperature of party spirit."

51. AN EXCERPT FROM JOHN QUINCY ADAMS'S *PARTIES IN THE UNITED STATES* JANUARY 1824

"The succession had from that time fallen upon the Secretary of State, the head of the most important of the executive departments. The transition of the administration from Mr. Jefferson to Mr. Madison had been thus effected almost without a struggle. It could scarcely be said that the administration had been changed. Had Mr. Jefferson been authorized by the Constitution of the law to appoint his successor he would have named Mr. Madison; and Mr. Madison would in like manner have conferred the office on Mr. Monroe. . .".

52. AN EXCERPT FROM THE DIARY OF JOHN QUINCY ADAMS MAY 18, 1825

"G. Sullivan came and took leave. Spoke of his visits to Mr. Jefferson and Mr. Madison, the latter of whom, he said, appeared cordially disposed to this Administration; Mr. Jefferson less so, and particularly with regard to Mr. Clay."

53. EXCERPT FROM JOHN QUINCY ADAMS'S *AN EULOGY ON THE LIFE AND CHARACTER OF JAMES MONROE, FIFTH PRESIDENT OF THE UNITED STATES* AUGUST 25, 1831

". . . I indulge the effusion of gratitude, and of public veneration, to share in your gladness, that he [Madison] yet lives—lives to impart to you, and to your children, the priceless jewel of his instruction: lives in the hour of darkness, and of danger, gathering over you, as if from the portals of eternity, to enlighten, and to guide."

54. AN EXCERPT FROM THE DIARY OF JOHN QUINCY ADAMS AUGUST 29, 1836

"Madison moderated some of his [Jefferson's] excesses, and refrained from following others. He was in truth a greater and a far more estimable man."

55. EXCERPT FROM JOHN QUINCY ADAMS'S *AN EULOGY ON THE LIFE AND CHARACTER OF JAMES MONROE, FIFTH PRESIDENT OF THE UNITED STATES* AUGUST 25, 1831

"Let us look *back* then for consolation from the thought of the shortness of human life, as urged upon us by the recent decease of James Madison, one of the pillars and ornaments of his country and of his age. His time on earth was short, yet he died full of years and of glory—less, far less than one hundred years have elapsed since the day of his birth—yet has he fulfilled, nobly fulfilled, his destinies as a man and a Christian. He has improved his own condition by improving that of his country and his kind."

56. EXCERPT FROM JOHN QUINCY ADAMS'S *AN EULOGY ON THE LIFE AND CHARACTER OF JAMES MONROE, FIFTH PRESIDENT OF THE UNITED STATES* AUGUST 25, 1831

"In the first and in the early part of the second stage of the revolution, the name of James Madison had not appeared. At the commencement of the contest he was but ten years of age. When the first blood was shed, here in the streets of Boston, he was a student in the process of his education at Princeton College, where the next year, 1771, he received the degree of bachelor of Arts. He was even then so highly distinguished by the power of application and the rapidity of his progress, that he performed all the exercised of the two senior Collegiate years in one—while at the same time his deportment was so exemplary, that Dr. Witherspoon, then at the head of that College, and afterwards himself one of the most eminent Patriots and Sages of our revolution, always delighted in bearing testimony to the excellency of his character at that early stage of his career; and said to Thomas Jefferson long afterwards, when they were all colleagues in the revolutionary Congress, that in the whole career of MR. MADISON at Princeton, he had never known him to say or do an indiscreet thing."

57. EXCERPT FROM JOHN QUINCY ADAMS'S *AN EULOGY ON THE LIFE AND CHARACTER OF JAMES MONROE, FIFTH PRESIDENT OF THE UNITED STATES* AUGUST 25, 1831

"On the 20th of March, 1780, he took his seat as a delegate in the Congress of the Confederation. It was then, in the midst of the revolution, and under the influence of its most trying scenes, that his political character was formed, and then it was that the virtue of discretion, the spirit of moderation, the conciliatory temper of compromise found room for exercise in its most comprehensive extent."

58. EXCERPT FROM JOHN QUINCY ADAMS'S *AN EULOGY ON THE LIFE AND CHARACTER OF JAMES MONROE, FIFTH PRESIDENT OF THE UNITED STATES* AUGUST 25, 1831

"Mr. Madison remained in Congress nearly four years from the 20th of March, 1780 till the first Monday in November, 1783. He was thus a member of that body during the last stages of the revolutionary war and for one year after the conclusion of the Peace. He had during that period, unceasing opportunities to observe the mortifying inefficiency of the merely federative principle upon which the Union of the States had been organized, and had taken an active part in all the remedial measures proposed by Congress for amending the Articles of Confederation."

59. EXCERPT FROM JOHN QUINCY ADAMS'S *AN EULOGY ON THE LIFE AND CHARACTER OF JAMES MONROE, FIFTH PRESIDENT OF THE UNITED STATES* AUGUST 25, 1831

"At the Session of 1785, a general revisal was made of the Statute Laws of Virginia, and the great burden of the task devolved upon Mr. Madison as chairman of the Judiciary Committee of the House. The general principle which pervaded this operation was the adaptation of the civil code of the Commonwealth, to its republican and unfettered independence as a Sovereign State, and he carried it through with that same spirit of liberty which had dictated the Act for the establishment of Religious Freedom. The untiring industry, the searching and penetrating application, the imperturbable patience, the moderation and gentleness of disposition, which smoothed his way over the ruggedest and most thorny paths of life, accompanied him through this transaction as through all the rest."

60. EXCERPT FROM JOHN QUINCY ADAMS'S *AN EULOGY ON THE LIFE AND CHARACTER OF JAMES MONROE, FIFTH PRESIDENT OF THE UNITED STATES* AUGUST 25, 1831

"The fourteenth number of the Federalist, the next in the series written by Mr. Madison, is an elaborate answer to an objection which had been urged against the Constitution, drawn from the extent of country, then comprised within the United States. From the deep anxiety pervading the whole of this paper, and a most eloquent and pathetic appeal to the spirit of union, with which it concludes, it is apparent that the objection itself was in the mind of the writer, of the most formidable and most plausible character. He encounters it with all the acuteness of his intellect and all the energy of his heart. His chief argument is a recurrence to his previous distinction between a Republic and a Democracy—and next to that by an accurate definition of the boundaries within which the United States were then compromised. The range between the 31st and 45th degree of North Latitude, the Atlantic and the Mississippi—he contends that *such* an extent of territory, with the great improvements which were to be expected in the facilities of communication between its remotest extremes, was *not* incompatible with the existence of a confederated republic—or at least that from the vital interest of the people of the Union, and of the Liberties of mankind in the success of the American Revolution, it was worthy of an experiment yet untried in the annals of the world."

61. AN EXCERPT FROM JOHN QUINCY ADAMS'S *AN EULOGY ON THE LIFE AND CHARACTER OF JAMES MADISON, FOURTH PRESIDENT OF THE UNITED STATES* SEPTEMBER 27, 1836

"The papers of the Federalist had a powerful, but limited influence upon the public mind. The Constitution was successively submitted to Conventions of the People, in each of the thirteen States, and in almost every one of them was debated against opposition of deep feeling, and strong party excitement. The authors of the Federalist were again called to buckle on their armour in defence of their plan. The Convention for the Commonwealth of Virginia, met in June, 1788, nine months after the Constitution had been promulgated. It had already been ratified by seven of the States, and New Hampshire, at an adjourned session of her Convention, adopted it while the Convention of Virginia were in session. The assent of that State was therefore to complete the number of nine, which the Constitution itself had provided should be sufficient for undertaking its execution between the ratifying States. A deeper interest was then involved in the decision of Virginia, than in any other member of the Confederacy, and in no State had the opposition to the plan been so deep, so extensive, so formidable as there. Two of her citizens, second only to Washington, by the weight of their characters, the splendor of their public services and the reputation of their genius and talents, Patrick Henry, the first herald of the Revolution in the South, as James Otis had been at the North, and Thomas Jefferson, the author of the Declaration of Independence, and the most intimate and confidential friend of Madison himself, disapproved the Constitution. Jefferson was indeed at that time absent from the State and the country, as the representative of the United States at the Court of France. His objections to the Constitution were less fervent and radical. Patrick Henry's opposition was to the whole plan, and to its fundamental principle the change from a confederation of Independent States, to a complicated government, party federal, and partly national. He was a member of the Virginia Convention; and there it was that Mr. Madison was destined to meet and encounter, and overcome the all but irresistible power of his eloquence, and the inexhaustible resources of his gigantic mind.

The debates in the Virginia Convention furnish an exposition of the principles of the Constitution, and a Commentary upon its provisions not inferior to the papers of the Federalist. Patrick Henry pursued his hostility to the system into all its details; objecting not only to the Preamble and the first Article, but to the Senate, to the President, to the Judicial Power, to the treaty making power, to the controul given to Congress over the militia, and especially to the omission of a Bill of Rights—seconded and sustained with great ability by George Mason, who had been a member of the Convention which formed the Constitution, by James Monroe and William Grayson, there was not a controvertible point, real or imaginary in the whole instrument which escaped their embittered opposition; while upon every point Mr. Madison was prepared to meet them, with cogent argument, with intense and anxious feeling, and with mild, conciliatory gentleness of temper, disarming the adversary by the very act of seeming to decline contention with him. Mr. Madison devoted himself particularly to the task of answering and replying to the objections of Patrick Henry, following him step by step, and meeting him at every turn. His principle co-adjutors were Governor Randolph, Edmund Pendleton, the President of the Convention, John Marshall, George Nicholas, and Henry Lee of Westmorland. Never was there assembled in Virginia a body of men, of more surpassing talent, of bolder energy, or of purer integrity than in that Convention. The volume of their debates should be the pocket and pillow companion of every youthful American aspiring to the honor of rendering important service to his country; and there as he reads and meditates, will he not fail to perceive the steady, unfaltering mind of James Madison, marching from victory to victory, over the dazzling but then beclouded genius and eloquence of Patrick Henry. "

62. AN EXCERPT FROM JOHN QUINCY ADAMS'S *AN EULOGY ON THE LIFE AND CHARACTER OF JAMES MADISON, FOURTH PRESIDENT OF THE UNITED STATES*

September 27, 1836

"Too happy should I be, if with a voice speaking from the last to the coming generation of my country, I could effectively urge them to seek in the temper and moderation of James Madison that healing balm which assuages the malignity of the deepest seated political disease, redeems to life the rational mind and restores to health the incorporated union of our country, even from the brain fever of party spirit."

63. AN EXCERPT FROM JOHN QUINCY ADAMS'S *AN EULOGY ON THE LIFE AND CHARACTER OF JAMES MADISON, FOURTH PRESIDENT OF THE UNITED STATES*

September 27, 1836

"Mr. Madison perhaps in some degree influenced by the opinions and feelings of his long cherished and venerated friend, Jefferson, was already harboring suspicions of a formal design on the part of Hamilton, and of the federal party generally to convert the government of the United States into a monarchy like that of Great Britain, and thought he perceived in these papers of Pacificus the assertion of a prerogative in the President of the United States to engage the nation in war. He therefore entered the list against Mr. Hamilton in the public journals and in five papers under the signature of Helvidius, scrutinized the doctrines of Pacificus with an acuteness of intellect never perhaps surpassed and with a severity scarcely congenial to his natural disposition and never on any other occasion indulged. Mr. Hamilton did not reply; nor in any of his papers did he notice the animadversions of Helvidius."

64. AN EXCERPT FROM JOHN QUINCY ADAMS'S *AN EULOGY ON THE LIFE AND CHARACTER OF JAMES MADISON, FOURTH PRESIDENT OF THE UNITED STATES*

September 27, 1836

"The papers of Pacificus and Helvidius are among the most ingenious and profound Commentaries on that most important part of the Constitution, the distribution of the Legislative and Executive powers incident to war, and when considered as supplementary to the joint labors of Hamilton and Madison in the Federalist, they possess a deep and monitory interest to the American philosophical Statesman. The Federalist exhibits the joint efforts of two powerful minds in promoting one great common object, the adoption of the Constitution of the United States. The papers of Pacificus and Helvidius present the same minds, in collision with each other, exerting all their energies in conflict, upon the construction of the same instrument which they had so arduously labored to establish; and it is remarkable that upon the points in the papers of Pacificus most keenly contested by his adversary, the most forcible of his arguments are pointed with quotations from the papers of the Federalist written by Mr. Hamilton.

But whether in conjunction with or in opposition to each other, the co-operation or the encounter of intellects thus exalted and refined, controled by that moderation and humanity, which have hitherto characterized the history of our Union, cannot but ultimately terminate in spreading light and promoting peace among men."

65. AN EXCERPT FROM JOHN QUINCY ADAMS'S *AN EULOGY ON THE LIFE AND CHARACTER OF JAMES MADISON, FOURTH PRESIDENT OF THE UNITED STATES*

September 27, 1836

"The influence of Mr. Jefferson over the mind of Mr. Madison, was composed of all that genius, talent, experience, splendid public services, exalted reputation, added to congenial tempers, undivided friendship and habitual sympathies of interest and of feeling could inspire. Among the numerous blessings which it was the rare good fortune of Mr. Jefferson's life to enjoy, was that of the uninterrupted, disinterested, and efficient friendship of Madison. But it was the friendship of a mind not inferior in capacity and tempered with a calmer sensibility and a cooler judgment than his own."

66. AN EXCERPT FROM JOHN QUINCY ADAMS'S *AN EULOGY ON THE LIFE AND CHARACTER OF JAMES MADISON, FOURTH PRESIDENT OF THE UNITED STATES*

September 27, 1836

"Upon the change of administration by the election of Mr. Jefferson as President of the United States in 1801, a new career was opened to the talents and wisdom of his friend, who thenceforth became his first assistant and his most confidential adviser in the administration of the Government."

67. AN EXCERPT FROM JOHN QUINCY ADAMS'S *AN EULOGY ON THE LIFE AND CHARACTER OF JAMES MADISON, FOURTH PRESIDENT OF THE UNITED STATES*

September 27, 1836

"Through this fiery ordeal the administration of Mr. Jefferson was to pass and the severest of its tests were to be applied to Mr. Madison.[96] His correspondence with the ministers of Great Britain, France, and Spain, and with the ministers of the United States to those nations during the remainder of Mr. Jefferson's administration constitute the most important and most valuable materials in its history. His examination of the British doctrines relating to neutral trade, will hereafter be considered a standard Treatise on the law of Nations; not inferior to the works of any writer upon those subjects since the days of Grotius and every way worthy of the author of Publius and of Helvidius. There is indeed in all the diplomatic papers of American Statesmen justly celebrated as they have been, nothing superior to this Dissertation, which was not strictly official. It was composed amidst the duties of the Department of State, never more arduous than at that time—in the summer of 1806. It was published inofficially and a copy of it was laid on the table of each member of Congress at the commencement of the session in December 1806.

68. AN EXCERPT FROM JOHN QUINCY ADAMS'S *AN EULOGY ON THE LIFE AND CHARACTER OF JAMES MADISON, FOURTH PRESIDENT OF THE UNITED STATES*

September 27, 1836

"The administration of Mr. Madison, was with regard to its most essential principles a continuation of that of Mr. Jefferson. He too was the friend of peace, and earnestly desirous of maintaining it. As a last resource for the preservation of it, an act of Congress prohibited all commercial intercourse with both [France and Great Britain], the prohibition to be withdrawn from either or both in the event of a repeal by either of the orders and decrees in violation of neutral rights. France ungraciously and equivocally withdrew her's. Britain refused, hesitated and at last conditionally withdrew her's when it was too late—after a

96 Adams is referring to the intense controversies surrounding the conflict of neutral and belligerent shipping rights between the United States and the enemies of Great Britain, namely France and Spain. The question of neutral shipping rights greatly strained the relationship between the United States and Great Britain.

formal declaration of war had been issued by Congress at the recommendation of President Madison himself."

69. AN EXCERPT FROM JOHN QUINCY ADAMS'S *AN EULOGY ON THE LIFE AND CHARACTER OF JAMES MADISON, FOURTH PRESIDENT OF THE UNITED STATES*

September 27, 1836

"For this state of unexampled prosperity a tribute of gratitude and applause is due to the administration of Madison, for the wise conciliatory policy upon which it was conducted from the close of the War [of 1812], until the end of his second Presidential term in March 1817, when he voluntarily retired from public life.

From that day, for a period advancing on upon its twentieth year, he lived in a happy retirement; in the bosom of a family and with a partner for life alike adapted to the repose and comfort of domestic privacy, as she had been to adorn and dignify the highest of public stations. Between the occupation of agriculture, the amusements of literature and the exercise of beneficence, the cultivation of the soil, of the mind and of the heart, the leisure of his latter days was divided."

70. AN EXCERPT FROM JOHN QUINCY ADAMS'S *AN EULOGY ON THE LIFE AND CHARACTER OF JAMES MADISON, FOURTH PRESIDENT OF THE UNITED STATES*

September 27, 1836

"In 1829 a Convention was held in Virginia for the revisal of the Constitution of the Commonwealth, in which transaction the people of the State again enjoyed the benefit of his long experience and his calm and conciliatory counsels. The unanimous sense of that body would have deferred to him the honor of presiding over their deliberations, but the infirmities of age had already so far encroached upon the vigor of his constitution, that he declined in the most delicate manner the nomination by proposing himself the election of his friend and successor to the Chief Magistracy of the Union, James Monroe."

71. AN EXCERPT FROM JOHN QUINCY ADAMS'S *AN EULOGY ON THE LIFE AND CHARACTER OF JAMES MADISON, FOURTH PRESIDENT OF THE UNITED STATES*

September 27, 1836

"Mr. Madison was associated with his friend Mr. Jefferson in the institution of the University of Virginia, and after his decease was placed at its head under the modest and unassuming title of Rector. He was also the President of an Agricultural Society in the county of his residence, and in that capacity delivered an address which the practical farmer and the classical scholar may read with equal profit and delight.

In the midst of these occupations and the declining days of the Philosopher, the Statesman and the Patriot were past, until the 28th day of June last, the anniversary of the day on which the ratification of the Convention of Virginia in 1788 had affixed the seal of James Madison as the father of the Constitution of the United States, when his earthly part sunk without a struggle into the grave, and a spirit bright as the seraphim that surrounded the throne of omnipotence, ascended to the bosom of God."

72. AN EXCERPT FROM JOHN QUINCY ADAMS'S *AN EULOGY ON THE LIFE AND CHARACTER OF JAMES MADISON, FOURTH PRESIDENT OF THE UNITED STATES*

September 27, 1836

"This Constitution, my countrymen, is the great result of the North American revolution. This is the giant stride in the improvement of the condition of the human race, consummated in a period of less than one hundred years. Of the signers of the address to George the Third in the Congress of 1774—of the signers of the Declaration of Independence in 1776—of the signers of the Articles of Confederation in 1781, and of the signers of the federal and national Constitution of Government under which we live, with enjoyments never before allotted to man, not one remains in the land of the living. The last survivor of them all was he to honor whose memory we are here assembled at once with mourning and with joy."

73. AN EXCERPT FROM JOHN QUINCY ADAMS'S *AN EULOGY ON THE LIFE AND CHARACTER OF JAMES MADISON, FOURTH PRESIDENT OF THE UNITED STATES*
September 27, 1836

"Not in the great and strong wind of a revolution, which rent the mountains and brake in pieces the rocks before the Lord—for the Lord is not in the wind—not in the earthquake of a revolutionary war, marching to the onset between the battle field and the scaffold—for the Lord is not in the earthquake—Not in the fire of civil dissension—In war between the members and the head—In nullification of the laws of the Union by the forcible resistance of one refractory State—for the Lord is not in the fire; and *that* fire was never kindled by your fathers! No! it is in the still small voice that succeeded the whirlwind, the earthquakes and the fire. The voice that stills the raging of the waves and the tumults of the people—that spoke the words of peace—of harmony—of union. And for that voice, may you and your children's children 'to the last syllable of recorded time,' fix your eyes upon the memory, and listen with your ears to the life of James Madison."

74. AN EXCERPT FROM THE DIARY OF JOHN QUINCY ADAMS SEPTEMBER 27, 1836

"Tuesday; Boston; eulogy on James Madison. . . Two hours and a half were occupied in the delivery, and yet I omitted much of the abridgment of my discourse in the copy made chiefly by my sons. The house was crowded to the utmost of its capacity. I had undertaken this task with a most painful anxiety and fear that I might be disabled from performing it altogether—an anxiety much sharpened by the illness which for the last three days had almost extinguished my voice. I did get through, but with extreme difficulty, with frequent imperfections of delivery, without being able to raise my voice to be heard throughout the house, and with entire conviction that I must never again engage to address such and auditory on a day fixed beforehand, or, indeed, upon any day, or any occasion. Forty-three years and more have passed away since I first spoke to a crowded audience in Boston. My voice is now gone; my eyes are in no better condition. The day was uncommonly darkened with clouds, and threatened rain the whole morning; there was a heavy shower while I was speaking, and, the house being lighted only by skylights from above, there were parts of the time when I found it impossible to read, and was obliged to pass over towards the end, or repeat from memory. The delivery was accordingly bad, and I was under much agitation, with the fear that I should be forced to break off in the midst of my address and declare my inability to proceed. There was, however, an uninterrupted and fixed attention of the auditory throughout the whole time, occasional slight cheerings of applause, and at the close a full and long-continued manifestation of satisfaction."

-ꕥ-

75. AN EXCERPT FROM THE DIARY OF JOHN QUINCY ADAMS SEPTEMBER 28, 1836

"I read the article from the *North American Review* upon nullification, sent to me by Mr. Edward Everett, and written by him in 1830. I read also the letters from Mr. Madison to him upon the subject, of the same date. I have undertaken to mark, in very explicit terms, the difference between the opinions, the purposes, and the conduct of Mr. Madison and Mr. Jefferson with reference to the Alien and Sedition Acts. They were remarkably different."

Chapter 5

JAMES MONROE

I. JAMES MONROE ON THE PRESIDENCY

1. AN EXCERPT FROM JAMES MONROE'S *SOME OBSERVATIONS OF THE CONSTITUTION, &C.* 1788

"I think I may venture to affirm that a confederacy formed of principalities would not last long, for the pride of princes would not brook those familiarities and insults which a free discussion of rights and interests, especially if they interfere, sometimes unavoidably occasions; and when an absolute prince takes offence he wields that state with him. But this is not the case with democracies, for although their chief magistrates may be offended, yet it is difficult for them to communicate at the same time, the same passions and dispositions to the whole community which they themselves possess."

2. AN EXCERPT FROM JAMES MONROE'S *OBSERVATIONS UPON THE PROPOSED PLAN OF FEDERAL GOVERNMENT. WITH AN ATTEMPT TO ANSWER SOME OF THE PRINCIPAL OBJECTIONS THAT HAVE BEEN MADE TO IT* 1788

"It has been urged by many, that the President should be continued in office, only a given number of years, and then be rendered ineligible.[97] To this it may be answered, were that to be the case, a good officer might be displaced, and a bad one succeed. Knowing that he could not be continued, he might be more attentive to enrich himself, should opportuni-

97 Monroe is here referring to Article II, Section 1 of the United States Constitution.

ties offer, than to the execution of his office. But as his continuance in office, will depend upon his discharging the duties of it with ability, and integrity, his eligibility will most probably be the best security for his conduct. The longer a man of abilities and virtue, fills an office, the better, and easier will the duties of it be discharged: The whole system of administration becomes well arranged; and every department in the government well filled. An election to this office once in every four years, is a sufficient curb upon the President. The Electors hold the reins. If he has misconducted himself, he will not be re-elected: if has governed with prudence, and ability, he ought to be continued. The Vice-President will probably be a candidate to succeed the President. The former will therefore be a perpetual centinel over the latter; will be a stimulus to keep him up to his duty, and afford an additional security for his upright conduct.

Notwithstanding these reasons, and the powerful checks opposed to the powers of the President, the enemies of the Constitution has sounded the alarm with great violence, upon the ground of his eligibility for life. Some tell us that it will be the means of his becoming the hereditary sovereign of the United States; whilst others hold up to our view the dangers of an elective monarchy.

It is pretty certain that the President can never become the sovereign of America, but with the voluntary consent of the people. He is re-elected by them; not by any body of men over whom he may have gained an undue influence. No citizen of America has a fortune sufficiently large, to enable him to raise and support a single regiment. The President's salary will be greatly inadequate either to the purpose of gaining adherents, or of supporting a military force: He will possess no princely revenues, and his personal influence will be confined to his native State. Besides, the Constitution has provided, that no person shall be eligible to this office, who is not thirty-five years old; and in the course of nature very few fathers leave a son who has arrived to that age. The powers of the President are not kingly, any more than the ensigns of his office. He has no guards, no regalia, none of those royal trappings which would set him apart from the rest of his fellow citizens. Suppose the first President should be continued for life: What expectations can any man in the Union have to succeed him, except such as are grounded upon the popularity of his character?

None of its citizens possess distinct principalities, from whence money may be drawn to purchase, or armies raised to intimidate the votes. Fortunately for America, she has no neighbouring Princess to interfere in her elections, or her councils: No Empress of Russia to place the Crown upon the head of her favorite Powniotosky.[98]

98 The King of Poland at the time of this entry was Stanislaus Leginski, Count Powniotowsky.

It has also been objected, that a Council of State ought to have been assigned the President. The want of it, is, in my apprehension, a perfection rather than a blemish. What purpose would such a Council answer, but that of diminishing, or annihilating the responsibility annexed to the character of the President. From the superiority of his talents, or the superior dignity of his place, he would probably acquire an undue influence over, and might induce a majority of them to advise measures injurious to the welfare of the States, at the same time that he would have the means of sheltering himself from impeachment, under that majority. I will here once for all observe, that descended as we are from the English, conversant as we are in the political history of that country, it is impossible not to derive both political opinions, and prejudices, from that source. The objectors probably considered, that as in the English government, the first Magistrate has a Council of State; there should be one also in the American. But they should at the same time have recollected, that the King of England is not personally responsible for his conduct; but that her Constitution looks up to his Ministers, that is, to his Council, to answer for the measures of the Sovereign. But in the American Constitution, the first Magistrate is the efficient Minister of the people, and as such, ought to be alone responsible for his conduct. Let him act pursuant to the dictates of his own judgment; let him advise with his friends; let him consult those of whom he has the highest opinion for wisdom, but let not his responsibility be diminished by giving him a Council."

3. AN EXCERPT FROM JAMES MONROE'S *OBSERVATIONS UPON THE PROPOSED PLAN OF FEDERAL GOVERNMENT. WITH AN ATTEMPT TO ANSWER SOME OF THE PRINCIPAL OBJECTIONS THAT HAVE BEEN MADE TO IT* 1788

"The powers vested in the President by this and the subsequent clause[99], belong, from the nature of them, to the Executive branch of government; and could be placed in no other hands with propriety.

So long as laws cannot provide for every case that may happen: So long as punishments shall continue disproportionate to crimes, the power of pardoning should somewhere exist. With whom could this power, so precious to humanity, be better entrusted, than with the President? An officer who, from his age and experience, will seldom be misled in the exercise of it; and who less liable to the influence of prejudice and passion than a popular assembly, will most probably be guided by discretion in the use of it."

99 Monroe is here referring to Article II, Section 2 of the United States Constitution.

4. AN EXCERPT FROM JAMES MONROE'S *OBSERVATIONS UPON THE PROPOSED PLAN OF FEDERAL GOVERNMENT. WITH AN ATTEMPT TO ANSWER SOME OF THE PRINCIPAL OBJECTIONS THAT HAVE BEEN MADE TO IT* 1788

"The Constitution has here lessened the authority of the President, by making the assent of two-thirds of the Senate necessary in the important cases of making treaties, in appointing Ambassadors, the Judges of the Supreme Court, and the great officers of the State.[100]

Writers upon the government have established it as a maxim, that the Executive and Legislative authority should be kept separate. But the position should be taken with considerable latitude. The Executive authority here given to a branch of the Legislature, is no novelty, in free governments. In England, the Executive, or Cabinet Council, is taken indifferently from either House of Parliament. In the States of New York and Jersey, the Senate not only act as an Executive Council, but also form a part of the Court of Appeals.

The following reasons suggest themselves in support of the propriety of vesting the President and Senate with the power of making treaties.

The President is the Representative of the Union: The Senate the Representatives of the respective States. The objects of treaties must always be either of great national import, or such as concern the States in their individual capacities; but never can concern the States in their individual capacities; but never can concern the individual members of the State. Secrecy and dispatch are necessary in making them: For without secrecy and dispatch, they are seldom made to purpose. Hence arises the impropriety of consulting either the Representatives of the people, or the different States. If the former were consulted, the interests of the small States might be sacrificed; if the latter, almost insurmountable obstacles would be thrown in the way of every negociation."

---

100 Monroe is referring to Article II, Section 2 of the United States Constitution.

5. AN EXCERPT FROM JAMES MONROE'S *OBSERVATIONS UPON THE PROPOSED PLAN OF FEDERAL GOVERNMENT. WITH AN ATTEMPT TO ANSWER SOME OF THE PRINCIPAL OBJECTIONS THAT HAVE BEEN MADE TO IT* 1788

"The powers given by this section are such as in all governments, have always been, and must necessarily be, vested in the first magistrate."[101]

6. AN EXCERPT FROM JAMES MONROE'S *OBSERVATIONS UPON THE PROPOSED PLAN OF FEDERAL GOVERNMENT. WITH AN ATTEMPT TO ANSWER SOME OF THE PRINCIPAL OBJECTIONS THAT HAVE BEEN MADE TO IT* 1788

"The persons subject to impeachment, are the President, Vice President, and all civil officers of the United States, and no others."

7. AN EXCERPT FROM JAMES MONROE'S *OBSERVATIONS UPON THE PROPOSED PLAN OF FEDERAL GOVERNMENT. WITH AN ATTEMPT TO ANSWER SOME OF THE PRINCIPAL OBJECTIONS THAT HAVE BEEN MADE TO IT* 1788

"All civilized societies have found it necessary to punish a variety of offences, with the loss of life. The life of man is a serious forfeiture: Our law has therefore humanely and justly said, that it shall not be affected, but by the unanimous opinion of twelve men. In political view, this mode of trial, in State prosecutions, is of still greater importance. The Chief Magistrate, or the Legislature itself, of a republic, is liable to personal prejudice, and to passion, as any King in Europe; and might prosecute a bold writer, or any other person, who had become obnoxious to their resentment, with as much violence and rigour. What so admirable a barrier to defend the innocent, and protect the weak from the attacks of power, as the interposition of a jury? In this respect, the trial by jury may well be called the palladium of liberty."

101 Monroe is referring to Article II, Section 3 of the United States Constitution.

8. EXCERPT FROM JAMES MONROE'S *SOME OBSERVATIONS ON THE CONSTITUTION, &C.* 1788

"It has been long established by the most celebrated writers, but particularly illustrated and explained by the President Montesquieu and Mr. Locke, that the division of the powers of a government over one state, or one people only, into three branches, the legislative, executive, and judiciary, is absolutely necessary for the preservation of liberty."

9. EXCERPT FROM JAMES MONROE'S *SOME OBSERVATIONS ON THE CONSTITUTION, &C.* 1788

"The ingenuity of man can devise no other, without an appeal to the people, which if possible should always be avoided, than that of giving the Executive, the other active branch an absolute negative on the laws; for otherwise its enterprises must be successful. Many restraints might be designated by the constitution, but without effect. And from this at the same time that it preserved the balance of the government, no injury could be sustained. Against the encroachments of the Executive the fears and apprehensions of the whole continent would be awake, with a watchful jealousy they would observe its movements."

10. EXCERPT FROM JAMES MONROE'S *SOME OBSERVATIONS ON THE CONSTITUTION, &C.* 1788

"The Executive is that upon which, in many respects, we should rest our hopes, for an equal, a fœderal, and a wise administration. Every possible effort should therefore be used to expel from the hearts of those who fill it, a preference of one part of the community to another."

11. EXCERPT FROM JAMES MONROE'S *SOME OBSERVATIONS ON THE CONSTITUTION, &C.* 1788

". . . I could likewise wish to see the citizen at the head of this department, capable of reelection at the expiration of his service which would be at the end of every three of four years, so long as he should merit the confidence of his country."

12. EXCERPT FROM JAMES MONROE'S *SOME OBSERVATIONS ON THE CONSTITUTION, &C.* 1788

"The mode of election should also be a fundamental in the organization of this branch. If the command of this office was placed within the reach of court influence, the most alarming consequences were to be apprehended from it. If the ultimate decision should happen at the metropolis, it is easy to be perceived what an opportunity this would present for venalty and corruption. It must be a great object particularly for either France or Britain to have the friend of their respective courts in this office, possessed of such extensive powers and which might dispense such important favors to them. The influence of the presiding magistrate himself, especially within the town in which he had for some time resided, and to whose citizens he had rendered many substantial services, and who of course would be averse to the introduction of a *novus homo* among them, would not be inconsiderable. In addition to which it is to be observed, that it forms a departure from a principle which should prevail through the whole, but particularly in the organization of this branch, a dependence of this officer, for every thing estimable among mankind, upon the people of America. By the people therefore should the appointment be made, not in person, but by the means of electors chosen for the purpose. To prevent the possibility of any interference, or byas on their free election, that of the electors by the people, should be on the same day in every state, and that of the President by the electors likewise on the same day and at some specific place in each, unless an invasion, or other extraordinary circumstance should prevent it; in which case perhaps the electors themselves, or the executive of the state might appoint some other. Whatever time might be employed in this mode of election is immaterial; it is of the first importance, and should never be dispensed with, that he be thus appointed."

13. EXCERPT FROM JAMES MONROE'S *SOME OBSERVATIONS ON THE CONSTITUTION, &C.* 1788

"But high powers in the Executive branch require in every respect, a direct and immediate responsibility; for although it should be so organized as that whilst to those who fill it, and act with propriety in the discharge of its functions, the door should be left open for a continuance of public favour, yet the sword of justice should be held constantly suspended over the heads of those, who shall be convicted of having barely sacrificed the interests, or made attempt upon the liberties of their country. There should be no constitutional restrain, no equivocation of office, to shield a traitor from the justice of an injured people. No circumstance to blunt or turn aside the keen edge of their resentment. With the charge should the powers of his office cease. He should stand alone unsupported, and unprotected except by the integrity of his heart and the rectitude of his conduct. For these reasons the executive power should be vested altogether in one person; unrestrained by a constitutional council, its operations will be more easy and regular, and its responsibility the greater and more immediate. And for these reasons if there is a constitutional council it must be from its nature the most improper tribunal, that can be formed or conceived, for the tryal of the offences of the principal, since they must be either partakers of the crime, or some way or other a party interested in it.

With an Executive organized on these principles, being independent of the legislature, and in a very responsible situation, I should be well content to entrust great powers, because I should calculate with tolerable certainty upon an honest and a wise execution of them. The constitution perhaps suggests those, with some exceptions that are proper; whether it would be safe to give it the absolute controul of the fleet and army at all time, in peace and war, the ordering them out, and laying them by, without consent of the legislature, or even knowledge, is at least doubtful. In Great Britain this power may be committed to the King with propriety; but he is the Lord of hereditary dominions, and transmits the inheritance in his line forever. By betraying his trust he might lose his crown, and perhaps gain nothing, even if he established despotism. But with the President who perhaps depends on a quadriennial election the case is different. It is certainly a formidable power to place in the hands of any one public servant. I would however in no event interpose the opinion of the legislature, so as to controul the movements of these forces, but merely to affix the condition, or emergency, upon which his absolute power over them should commence. As I would repose the whole trust of this department in one officer, so he alone should be responsible for all its transactions. He might associate whom he pleases, of the wise men of America in his councils, but they should be of his own association. An allowance might be made him, to compensate them for their services, for which he would be accountable."

14. EXCERPT FROM JAMES MONROE'S *SOME OBSERVATIONS ON THE CONSTITUTION, &C.* 1788

"The placing the executive power in the hands of one person, appears to be perfectly right. If this branch had been put into commission, the state spirit would have been communicated to it, and have tainted all its measures; in addition to this there would have been less responsibility. But the mode of election, does not in all respects appear, to merit such commendation."

15. JAMES MONROE TO JAMES MADISON APRIL 26, 1789

"We are happy to find that both branches of the legislature have formed a house; that the President & vice president are summon'd to fill the Executive department, and flatter ourselves that the government will immediately commence its operations."

16. JAMES MONROE TO THOMAS JEFFERSON JUNE 27, 1793

"I think the position incontrovertible that if he possesses the right to say we shall be neutral, he might say we shod. not be. The power in both instances must be in the same hands, for if the Executive could say we shod. be neutral, how could the legislature, that we shod. war. In truth a right to declare our neutrality, as a distinct authority, cannot exist, for that is only the natural state of things, when the positive power of declaring war is not exerted; and this belongs to the legislature only; any interference therefore with it, by the Executive, must be unconstitutional & improper."

17. JAMES MONROE TO FRANCE'S COMMITTEE OF PUBLIC SAFETY OCTOBER 18, 1794

"The Congress will commence its session in a few weeks, and it is the duty of the President to lay before that body, and at that time, the state of public affairs; comprising, as the most interesting particular, the conduct and disposition of other nations towards the United States."

18. JAMES MONROE TO JAMES MADISON JULY 5, 1796

"DEAR SIR,—Yesterday the Fourth of July was celebrated here [Paris] by the Americans. I intended to have done it, but having given them an entertainment last year they returned the compliment this. You will observe by the copy sent in, that [in the toast] to the American government the term 'executive' is used and not 'president.'"

19. JAMES MONROE TO THOMAS JEFFERSON JULY 6, 1797

"I request this statement as a matter of right and upon the principle that altho the Executive possesses the power to censure & remove a public minister, yet it is a power which ought to be exercised according to the rules of Justice: which only are too well defined, by the Principles of our government, to require illustration here."

20. JAMES MONROE TO THOMAS JEFFERSON JULY 19, 1797

"Do you suppose or contend that the power committed to the Executive by the Constitution, to remove and censure a public minister, or any other public servant, has authorized it so to do, without a sufficient cause? Or that the Executive is not accountable to the publick & the party injured for such an act, in like manner as it is accountable for any and every other act, it may perform by virtue of the Constitution? Upon what principle is a discrimination founded, which presumes restraints in certain cases, against the abuse of Executive power, and leaves that power without restraint in all other cases? And how do you designate, or where draw the line between these two species of power, so opposite in their nature & character? This doctrine is against the spirit of our Constitution which provides a remedy for every injury. It is against the spirit of elective government, which considers every public functionary as a public servant. It becomes the meridian of those countries only, where the monarch inherits the territory as his patrimony, and the people who inhabit it as his slaves.

That the right to censure and remove a public officer was delegated to the Executive with peculiar confidence, is a motive why it should be exercised with peculiar care; for the more confidential the trust which is committed to a public functionary, in a responsible station, the greater circumspection should he use in the discharge of it. It was not intended thereby to dispense with the principles of justice or the unalienable rights of freemen, in favor of Executive *pleasure.* On the contrary it was expected that that *pleasure* would be exercised with discretion, & that those principles & rights would be invariably observed. It is an incompetent recompense to a person who has been injured by the Executive, to be told that the Constitution permits the injury, if the power intrusted was hereby abused and the principles of the Constitution violated. And it is an unbecoming measure in the administration to defend by the argument of power, what it cannot justify at the tribunal of reason and justice."

21. JAMES MONROE TO THOMAS JEFFERSON JULY 31, 1797

"I forbear to discuss again the solidity of that principle which supposes every public officer of the United States (the judges excepted) a menial servant to the President: a principle which if established, banishes from the bosom of every such officer all regard for country; every noble and patriotic sentiment, and makes him dependant, not upon the integrity and propriety of his own conduct, but upon the personal favor of his superior. If such were the case what confidence could the people of America repose in any public functionary, since after he gets into office he sinks into a machine and ceases to be a watchful centinel over the public rights and interests. If such were the case the principles and practice of our free government are departed from, and the most slavish doctrines of the most slavish governments are introduced in their stead. And that such must be the case is obvious if the Executive can exercise the *discretion* you speak of, in the *pleasurable* manner you contend for, and without accounting for any of its acts, or the motives of them in any case to the party injured, the public, or any person whatever. This doctrine merits the attention of the people of America because it is a pernicious one. They have provided in the Constitution they have adopted, a suitable mode for the appointments of public officers, President and all liberally, and ought to be faithfully served. They have likewise provided for and wish a supervision of the superior over the inferior, but I trust it is their intention that the merits and character of the latter, should be estimated by the standards of his integrity and public services, and not by the whim, caprice or any less worthy motive of those above him."

22. JAMES MONROE TO THOMAS JEFFERSON MAY 4, 1801

"There is a subject to which I wish to engage yr. particular attention. Before I came into this office I was of opinion that the correspondence between the Executive of the Genl. Govt. and a State shod. be conducted as between parties that were mutually respectful but equally independent of each other. My idea appeared to me to be sound; indeed incontrovertible in principle, and it was matter of surprise how a contrary practice had been adopted...I consider the chief magistrate of the Union in reference to a like character in each State as first among equals, and admit the same priority in the legislative and judicial departments, and the departments under them, where the individual States have correspondent institutions. If this idea is just, it follows that the communication between the two govts. When carried on by the govr. Of a State, shod. be with the President of the U. States. To subject the State govrs. to the necessity of corresponding with the officers appointed by the President, seems to place them in the same grade, to deny the right of sovereignty in the individual States, and to consider them as subaltern inferior establishments, emanating from and dependent on the general government."

23. JAMES MONROE TO THOMAS JEFFERSON MAY 23, 1801

"If you differ with me in sentiment, and think the ch: magistrates of the States shod. correspond with the heads of Departments & not the President, it is very far from my wish that you shod. deviate from your opinion. Let it pass in silence."

24. JAMES MONROE TO JAMES MADISON SEPTEMBER 8, 1804

"I told him [Lord Harrowby] that business there [America] was conducted differently from what it was here [England]: that here the ministry in both houses proposed and carried publick measures: but that with us the members of the administration were excluded from the legislature: that the three branches were completely separate and distinct from each other: that altho' they were a check, each on the other, yet that neither was responsible for the acts of the other: that the passage of a bill by both houses, was no evidence of the sense of the Executive on the subject of it, till it had its sanction. . .".

25. JAMES MONROE TO THOMAS JEFFERSON FEBRUARY 27, 1808

"In regard to the approaching election I have been and shall continue to be an inactive Spectator of the movement. Should the nation be disposed to call any citizen to that station it would be his duty to accept it. On that ground I rest. I have done nothing to draw the attention of any one to me in reference to it, nor shall I in the future."

26. JAMES MONROE TO L. W. TAZEWELL OCTOBER 30, 1808

"With New York there is a good understanding. [Vice President George] Clinton has said to one of my friends that if I could be elected he would decline in my favor; he urged the propriety some months past to that friend of keeping me in the nomination here & elsewhere with a view to ascertain that point. My standing in the States Eastward of New York is said to be better than his. The reserve in pushing my pretentions heretofore, is I think in some measure imputable, to a feeling of delicacy for him. I am persuaded that he so considers it. The backwardness of the Eastern States to come forward against Mr. Madison, I mean of such as are so disposed, is believed by some who possess the means of information, to proceed from and indifference to the election of Clinton. My opinion decidedly is that he who stands the best prospect for success ought to be preferred. That arrangement can only be made after the Electors are chosen."

27. JAMES MONROE TO L. W. TAZEWELL OCTOBER 30 1808

"The result of this election will I presume be finally placed in the hands of the State of Massachusetts, perhaps [James Sullivan] the Governor of that State. The majority in both branches of the legislature is federal, & this majority in favor of the election of a federalist. But it is necessary to pass a law for the election of Electors, [Clinton] will never assent to one which opens the door to a federalist. To me he is personally well disposed, has full confidence in my principles &c.; his sons were known to me abroad, one, who was of the family of Mr. Bowdoin, in my confidence, and on a footing of friendship. From this latter a letter to me, was received, dated in June, while I was in Kentucky, on the subject of the election, and expressing the most favourable sentiments to me. It was lately only that I was enabled to answer, which I did with caution, but in terms correspondent with the relations subsisting between us. Mr. Bowdoin is personally friendly to me, as he certainly was to the object, not only unsolicited but discouraged by me, while abroad. He wrote to me on his return, and expressed his regret to hear, as he said, that my friends supported me for the secondary station only. I replied that they had nominated me for the primary one. I have not heard from him since. If the federalists cannot elect their own man, it is believed that they would prefer me to Mr. Madison, and there seems to me to be little prospect of their success in that respect. Those circumstances afford one of an arrangement between them in my favor. If Massachusetts supports me, the Eastern States generally will probably join her in it. The governor however is liable to be assailed in many ways and by many arguments. The support given me by the federalists will become a potent weapon in the hands of such men as [William Branch] Giles and [John] Nicholas to attack me with. It will be represented to him that by supporting me he will be throwing himself & the State into the hands of that party: that in case of my election the national government will assume a federal form & take a federal direction: that we shall sacrifice by it not only our personal fortunes but the cause. It will require much firmness in those who are profoundly & immovably attached to the cause, not in the way of correct information, and who have as yet kept in their minds the admn. & the cause together, to resist this kind of clamorous appeal."

28. JAMES MONROE TO L. W. TAZEWELL OCTOBER 30, 1808

"It is well known to our friends here that I have more than once pressed on them the consideration of the propriety of my withdrawal from the controversy not from any feeling of a personal nature, proceeding from the gloom of the prospect, at those periods, but from the relation which my support had to the publick interest & themselves. They resolved invariably & unanimously to continue the nomination, on the principle, that by so doing, be the success what it might, the cause of free government would be advanced not injured. Since the last decision on that point I have felt myself more at liberty to express my sentiments on the subject to them, as a member rather than a party that had a particular connection with it."

29. JAMES MONROE TO WILLIAM WIRT DECEMBER 20, 1808

"DEAR SIR,—Your letter of this day has equally surprised & hurt me, by intimating a suspicion that it was my desire and on acct. of the late Presidential contest to separate from such of my old friends as took part against me. I really thought that my conduct had in no instance given the slightest cause for such a suspicion. Let me ask has it done so in regard to you? Did I not consult you on some most important topicks, after I knew that you were not in my favor?"

30. JAMES MONROE TO COLONEL JOHN TAYLOR SEPTEMBER 10, 1810

"In the then pending election I never took any part. I knew that I should not be elected, and in all probability should have been withdrawn had it not been believed that such a step would be viewed in the light of a compromise, or concession, which would have been construed in some form or other unfavorable to my character, or to that of those who supported me."

31. JAMES MONROE TO COLONEL JOHN TAYLOR SEPTEMBER 10, 1810

"Every branch of government is elective. The President owes his appointment as much to the suffrage of his fellow-citizens as a representative in Congress, or a member of the State

Assembly. But the election of the Chief Magistrate is the more important act because it draws after it more important consequences. It is the great act which, in a peculiar manner, designates that the sovereignty is in the People. It is that act in the exercise of which the strongest appeal is made to them by the contending interests in society, and which produces the greatest, and most general, excitement. When it is performed everything seems to be done. The character of the administration, and the tone of public measures, are believed to be settled by it."

32. JAMES MONROE TO COLONEL JOHN TAYLOR SEPTEMBER 10, 1810

"After the hard rubs which I have received under two administrations, the last of which touched me most sensibly, believe me I have no hankering after public employment. My hankering is for peace, which is to be found in retirement only, which my circumstances imperiously require."

33. JAMES MONROE TO COLONEL JOHN TAYLOR NOVEMBER 19, 1810

"Happy indeed would it be if that state of things had arrived, for then would our government rest on its true principles;[102] then would the ch: Magistrate cease to be the head of a party, an event which, with you, I anxiously wish to see; then might all his acts be scrutinized and criticised without reference to an ulterior and greater cause."

34. JAMES MONROE TO THE HONORABLE ADAM SEYBERT JUNE 10, 1812

"I have always thought that every institution, of whatsoever nature it might be, ought to be comprised within some one of the departments of Government, the Chief of which only should be responsible to the Chief Executive Magistrate of the Nation. The establishment of inferior independent departments, the heads of which are not, and ought not to be members of the Administration, appears to me to be liable to many serious objections, which will doubtless occur to you. I will mention the following only. First, that the concerns of such inferior departments cannot be investigated and discussed with the same

102 Monroe is referring to the end of the Federalist Party.

advantage in the meetings and deliberations of the administration as they might be if the person charged with them was present. The second is, that to remedy this inconvenience the President would necessarily become the head of that department himself, and thus be drawn into much investigation in detail that would take his attention from more general and important concerns, to the prejudice of the public interest."

35. JAMES MONROE TO JAMES MADISON FEBRUARY 25, 1813

"The departments of the government being recognized by the Constitution have appropriate duties under it. As organs of the Executive will, they contain records of its transactions, and are, in that sense, checks on the Executive. If the Secretary at War leaves the seat of government, (the Chief Magistrate remaining there) and performs the duties of a General, the powers of a Chief Magistrate, of the Secretary at War, Lieutenant General, are all united in the latter. There ceases to be a check on the Executive power as to military operations; indeed the Executive power, as known to the Constitution, is destroyed. The whole is transferred from the Executive to the General at the head of the army. It is completely absorbed in hands where it is most dangerous. It may be said that the President is Commander in Chief; that the Secretary at War is his organ as to military operations, and that he may allow him to go to the army, as being well informed in military affairs, & act for himself. I am inclined to think that the President, unless he takes the command of the army in person, acts, in directing its movements, more as the Executive power than as Commander in Chief. What would become of the Secretary at War if the President took command of the army I do not know. I rather suppose, however, that, altho' some of his powers would be transferred to the military staff about the President, he would, nevertheless, retain his appropriate constitutional character in all other respects."

36. JAMES MONROE TO "THE CHAIRMAN OF MILITARY COMMITTEE OF SENATE" FEBRUARY 1815

". . . the Governors of Massachusetts, Connecticut & Rhode Island have objected to the requisitions made on the several States for parts of their respective quotas of militia on the following grounds: 1st., That the President has no right to make a requisition for any portion of the militia for either of the purposes specified by the Constitution unless the Executive of the State on whose militia such call is made admits that the case alleged exists, and approves the call. 2ndly. That when the militia of a State should be called into the service of the United States no officers of the regular army had a right to command them, or other person not an officer of the militia, except the President of the United States in person. These being the only difficulties which have arisen between the Executive of the United States and the Executive of any of the individual States relative to the command of the militia, known to the Department, are, it is presumed, those respecting which the Committee has asked information."

37. JAMES MONROE TO "THE CHAIRMAN OF MILITARY COMMITTEE OF SENATE" FEBRUARY 1815

"By the law of 1795 the President is authorized to call forth the militia, for the purposes mentioned in the Constitution, by a direct application to the militia officers, without any communication with, or reference to the Executives of the individual States, and penalties are prescribed for carrying the law into effect, should resort to them be necessary."

38. JAMES MONROE TO "THE CHAIRMAN OF MILITARY COMMITTEE OF SENATE" FEBRUARY 1815

"That the President alone has the right to command the militia in person, when called into the service of the United States, and that no officer of the regular army can take command in his absence, is a construction for which I can see nothing in the Constitution to afford the slightest pretext."

39. JAMES MONROE TO "THE CHAIRMAN OF MILITARY COMMITTEE OF SENATE" FEBRUARY 1815

"The President is in himself no bond of union in that respect. He holds his station as Commander in Chief of the land and naval forces, and of the militia, under a constitution which binds together as one people, for that, and many other important purposes. His absence would not dissolve the bond. It would not revive discordant, latent claims, or become a signal for disorganization."

40. JAMES MONROE TO GENERAL ANDREW JACKSON DECEMBER 14, 1816

"I agree with you decidedly in the principle that the Chief Magistrate of the Country ought not to be the head of a party, but of the nation itself."

41. JAMES MONROE TO JAMES MADISON NOVEMBER 24, 1817

"DEAR SIR,—I have been, since my return here, so incessantly engaged in the most interesting business, that I have not had a moment to say anything to you. I am now engaged in preparing the message to Congress, whose meeting is so near at hand, that I shall, I fear, be badly prepared. The question respecting canals & roads is full of difficulty, growing out of what has passed on it. After all the consideration I have given it, I am fixed in the opinion, that the right is not in Congress and that it would be improper in me, after your negative, to allow them to discuss the subject & bring a bill for me to sign, in the expectation that I would do it. I have therefore decided to communicate my opinion in the message & to recommend the procuring an amendment from the States, so as to vest the right in Congress in a manner to comprise in it a power also to institute seminaries of learning. The period is perhaps favorable to such a course."

42. AN EXCERPT FROM JAMES MONROE'S FIRST INAUGURAL ADDRESS MARCH 4, 1817

"I should be destitute of feeling, if I was not deeply affected by the strong proof which my fellow citizens have given me of their confidence, in calling me to the high office, whose functions I am about to assume. As the expression of their good opinion of my conduct in the public service, I derive from it a gratification, which those who are conscious of having done all that they could to merit it, can alone feel. My sensibility is increased by a just estimate of the importance of the trust and of the nature and extent of its duties; with the proper discharge of which, the highest interests of a great and free people are intimately connected. Conscious of my own deficiency, I cannot enter on these duties without great anxiety for the result. From a just responsibility I will never shrink; calculating with confidence that in my best efforts to promote the public welfare, my motives will always be duly appreciated and my conduct be viewed with that candour and indulgence which I have experienced in other stations."

43. AN EXCERPT FROM JAMES MONROE'S FIRST INAUGURAL ADDRESS MARCH 4, 1817

"Such, then, is the happy Government under which we live; a Government adequate to every purpose for which the social compact is formed; a Government elective in all its branches, under which every citizen may, by his merit, obtain the highest trust recognized by the Constitution."

44. AN EXCERPT FROM JAMES MONROE'S FIRST INAUGURAL ADDRESS MARCH 4, 1817

"The Executive is charged, officially, in the departments under it, with the disbursement of the public money and is responsible for the faithful application of it to the purposes for which it is raised. The Legislature is the watchful guardian over the Public purse. It is its duty to see that the disbursement has been honestly made. To meet the requisite responsibility, every facility should be afforded to the Executive to enable it to bring the public agents instructed with the public money strictly and promptly to account. Nothing should be presumed against them; but if, with the requisite facilities, the public money is suffered to lie long and uselessly in their hands, they will not be the only defaulters, nor will the demoralizing effect be confined to them. It will evince a relaxation and want of tone in the administration, which will be felt by the whole community."

45. AN EXCERPT TAKEN FROM JAMES MONROE'S SECOND INAUGURAL ADDRESS MARCH 5, 1821

"Fellow Citizens:

I shall not attempt to describe the grateful emotions which the new and very distinguished proof of the confidence of my fellow-citizen, evinced by my re-election to this high trust, has excited in my bosom. The approbation which it announces of my conduct in the preceding term affords me a consolation which I shall profoundly feel through life. The general accord with which it has been expressed adds to the great and never ceasing obligations which it imposes. To merit the continuance of this good opinion, and to carry it with me into my retirement as the solace of advancing years, will be the object of my most zealous and unceasing efforts."

46. AN EXCERPT TAKEN FROM JAMES MONROE'S SECOND INAUGURAL ADDRESS MARCH 5, 1821

"Having no pretensions to the high and commanding claims of my predecessors, whose names are so much more conspicuously identified with our Revolution, and who contributed so pre-eminently to promote its success, I consider myself rather as the instrument than the cause of the union which has prevailed in the late election. In surmounting, in favor of my humble pretensions, the difficulties which so often produced division in like occurrences, it is obvious that other powerful causes, indicating the great strength and stability of our Union, have essentially contributed to draw you together. That these powerful causes exist, and that they are permanent is my fixed opinion; that they may produce a like accord in all questions touching, however, remotely, the liberty, prosperity, and happiness of our country will always be the object of my most fervent prayers of the Supreme Author of All Good."

47. AN EXCERPT TAKEN FROM JAMES MONROE'S SECOND INAUGURAL ADDRESS MARCH 5, 1821

"In a government which is founded by the people, who possess exclusively the sovereignty, it seems proper that the person who may be placed by their suffrages in this high trust should declare on commencing its duties the principles on which he intends to conduct the administration. If the person thus elected has served the preceding term, an opportunity is afforded him to review its principal occurrences and to give such further explanation respecting them as in his judgment may be useful to his constituents. The events of one year have influenced on those of another, and, in like manner of a preceding on the succeeding administration. The movements of a great nation are connected in all their parts. If errors have been committed they ought to be corrected; if the policy is sound it ought to be supported. It is by a thorough knowledge of the whole subject that our fellow citizens are enabled to judge correctly of the past and to give a proper direction to the future."

48. AN EXCERPT FROM JAMES MONROE'S RESPONSE TO AN ADDRESS PRESENTED TO HIM BY THE MAYOR AND CITY COUNCIL OF BALTIMORE JUNE 2, 1817

"Experience has shown our dangers, and admonished us as to the means of averting them. Congress has appointed large sums of money for the fortifications of our coast and inland frontier, and for the establishment of naval dock yards, and building a navy. It is proper, that these works should be executed with judgment, fidelity, and economy; much depends, in the execution, on the executive, to whom extensive power is given as to the general arrangement, and to whom the superintendence exclusively belongs. You do me justice believing that it is to enable me to discharge these duties, with the best advantage to my country, that I have undertaken this tour."

49. AN EXCERPT FROM JAMES MONROE'S RESPONSE TO THE MEMBERS OF THE PENNSYLVANIA CINCINNATI OF PHILADELPHIA JUNE 6, 1817

"In attending to the military and naval defence of the United States, nothing can be more gratifying to me, than to meet the surviving members of my associates in arms, who distinguished themselves in our revolutionary contest. I can never forget the dangers of that great epoch, nor be indifferent to the merit of those who partook in them.

To promote tranquility at home, and respect abroad, by a firm and impartial administration, are among the highest objects of the chief magistrate of the United States. To acquit myself in the discharge of these duties, with advantage to my fellow citizens, will be the undeviating object of my zealous exertions. Their approbation will be the highest recompense which I can receive."

50. AN EXCERPT FROM JAMES MONROE'S RESPONSE TO THE COMMITTEE OF THE TOWN OF PROVIDENCE JUNE 30, 1817

"Living under a Constitution which secures equal, civil, religious and political rights to all, it is a great consolation in administering it, that the people have formed so just an estimate of its value, and from rational conviction and not from blind prejudices, are sincerely devoted to its preservation."

51. AN EXCERPT FROM JAMES MONROE'S RESPONSE TO A WELCOME ADDRESS PRESENTED TO HIM BY CHARLES BULFINCH ON BEHALF OF THE CITY OF BOSTON JULY 3, 1817

"I accepted the trust, to which I have been called by my fellow citizens, with diffidence, because, I well knew the frailty of human nature, and had often experienced my own deficiencies. I undertook this tour, with a view and in the hope of acquiring knowledge, which might enable me to discharge my various and important duties, with greater advantage to my country, to which my whole mind, and unwearied efforts shall always be directed. In pursuing objects so dear to us all, I rely with confidence on the firm and generous support of my fellow citizens, throughout our happy Union."

52. AN EXCERPT FROM JAMES MONROE'S REPLY TO AN ADDRESS PRESENTED TO HIM BY R. W. TREVEJI, CHAIRMAN OF THE COMMITTEE OF ARRANGEMENTS FOR LYNN, MASSACHUSETTS JULY 5, 1817

"The kind reception given me by the citizens of Lynn, has my hearty thanks.

It affords me pleasure that they so justly estimate the principles of our excellent constitution. It will be my faithful endeavor so to conduct my administration, as to realize their expectations; and the best reward of my exertions in the office lately conferred on me, will be the approbation of my fellow citizens."

53. AN EXCERPT FROM JAMES MONROE'S RESPONSE TO THE CITIZENS OF PORTSMOUTH, MAINE JULY 12, 1817

"This general movement of my fellow citizens, and the expression of their regard for the Chief Magistrate of the nation, is not directed to me personally. My humble services give me no such claim. I see in it the strongest evidence of their attachment to the free government under which we live, and of an enlightened and expanded patriotism from which the happiest effects may be anticipated."

54. AN EXCERPT FROM JAMES MONROE'S ADDRESS TO THE CITIZENS OF KENNEBUNK, MAINE JULY 15, 1817

"To behold a free, an enlightened, and a high minded people paying a spontaneous tribute of respect and affection to the man who is elevated to the Chief Magistracy of a nation, is in itself an imposing spectacle. To that individual, such a scene, you may well believe must possess a character of peculiar and appropriate interest. I have never before been so much affected. Such distinguished attentions, such unexpected effusions of regard, as I experience from my fellow citizens, do indeed sink into my heart. They make me feel, if possible, a deeper sense of my own obligations to devote all my faculties to their service."

55. JAMES MONROE TO THOMAS JEFFERSON SEPTEMBER 6, 1821

"DEAR SIR,—Your letter of the 13th. ulto. found me at the Shannondale Spring, to which I had taken my family, on account of the indisposition of Mrs. Monroe, & of our little grand child, the daughter of Mr. Gouverneur. The duties which I had to perform to my family in this distressing state, which terminated the day before yesterday in the death of the infant, superadded to those of the office I hold, prevented my giving an earlier answer to your letter."

56. JAMES MONROE TO JAMES MADISON MAY 10, 1822

"The approaching election, tho' distant, is a circumstance that excites greatest interest in both houses, and whose effect, already sensibly felt, is still much to be dreaded. There being three avowed candidates in the administration is a circumstance which increases the embarrassment.[103] The friends of each endeavour to annoy the others, as you have doubtless seen by the public prints. I many cases the attacks are personal, directed against the individual."

57. JAMES MONROE TO THOMAS JEFFERSON MARCH 22, 1824

"There have been several candidates, under me, in the administration, for the office which I hold, and such the activity & animosity of their respective advocates & friends, towards the rival candidates, that my situation has been peculiarly embarrassing."

58. AN EXCERPT FROM JAMES MONROE'S *EIGHT ANNUAL MESSAGE* DECEMBER 7, 1824

"I cannot conclude this communication, the last of the kind which I shall have to make, without recollecting with great responsibility and heartfelt gratitude the

103 Monroe is referring to Secretary of State John Quincy Adams, Secretary of the Treasury William H. Crawford, and Secretary of War John C. Calhoun.

many instances of the public confidence and the generous support which I have received from my fellow-citizens in the various trusts with which I have been honored. Having commenced my service in early youth, and continued it since with few and short intervals, I have witnessed the great difficulties to which our Union has been exposed, and admired the virtue and intelligence with which they have been surmounted. From the present prosperous and happy state I derive a gratification which I cannot express."

59. JAMES MONROE TO T. RINGGOLD MAY 8, 1826

"I declare most solemnly that I took no part in the [1816 presidential] election, being restrained from it both by principle & policy. To Mr. Adams & Mr. Crawford I gave proof of respect & confidence by bringing them into the administration. Neither of them gave me any aid in my own election, nor did I wish it. It is known to many, as it is to you, that I could hardly be considered a candidate, having authorized the two Senators from Pennsylvania, when I entered the Department of War in 1814, to announce to the Republican party that I thought they had better put me entirely out of view, for the reason that the country was in peril, that decisive measures alone could save it, that I should propose them, and that I should prose them, and that I knew that opposition would be made by some, not because they were wrong, but to defeat me in the other object should I be brought forward. These considerations did not operate when the peace took place, & in consequence my friends brought me forward, but still I took no part, but left the result entirely to the unbiased opinion of my fellow citizens."

60. JAMES MONROE TO JOHN C. CALHOUN DECEMBER 16, 1827

"As soon as my election to that high trust was announced to me, the manner in which the appointments to all the Departments should be distributed throughout the Union, and the persons who should be placed in them, received my immediate, and most deliberate attention. My object was to place a citizen from each of the greatest sections of the Union in one. The appointments which were immediately made of Mr. Adams from the East, of Mr. Crawford from the South, and of Mr. Shelby from the West, were exemplifications of my views in both instances, and the refusal of the latter to accept the Department of War, to which he was appointed, left me at liberty, on the principles on which I acted, to confer it on a citizen of any State, in either of the sections to which an appointment to one of the other Departments had not been made."

61. JAMES MONROE TO JUDGE FRANCIS T. BROOKE FEBRUARY 21, 1828

"After the long and laborious service in which I have been engaged, and in the most difficult conjunctions to which our country has been exposed, it is my earnest desire to cherish tranquility in my retirement. Important as this object is to me, I am satisfied, if I become a party to elections to the high office of Chief Magistrate of the U. States, that I cannot accomplish it. In the pending election I have motives of a personal nature, which would make it particularly painful to me to interfere. Having held, in the office from which I lately retired, a very friendly relation with both candidates, & given to each strong proofs of confidence & regard, it would be very repugnant to my feelings to take the part of either, against the other."

62. JAMES MONROE TO JUDGE FRANCIS T. BROOKE FEBRUARY 21, 1828

"As a permanent rule I was led to conclude, that it would be better for our country, and contribute more to the success of our excellent system of government, that those who have held the office of Chief Magistrate, should abstain, after their retirement, from becoming partisans in subsequent elections to that office."

63. JAMES MONROE TO JUDGE SAMUEL L. SOUTHARD FEBRUARY 8, 1831

"If the Chief Magistrate has any power of restraint while in office, it must cease after his retirement."

II. GEORGE WASHINGTON ON JAMES MONROE

1. LETTER FROM GEORGE WASHINGTON TO ARCHIBALD CARY MAY 30, 1779

"Dr. Sir: I very sincerely lament that the situation of our service will not permit us to do justice to the merits of Major Monroe, who will deliver you this, by placing him in the army upon some satisfactory footing. But as he is on the point of leaving us and expresses an intention of going to the South-ward where a new scene has opened, it is with pleasure I take occasion to express to you the high opinion I have of his worth. The zeal he discovered by entering the service at an early period, the character he supported in his regiment, and the manner in which he distinguished himself at Trenton, where he received a wound, induced me to appoint him to a captaincy in one of the additional regiments. This regiment failing from the difficulty of recruiting, he entered into Lord Sterlings family and has served two campaigns as a volunteer aid to his lordship. He has in every instance maintained the reputation of a brave active and sensible officer. As we cannot introduce him into the Continental line, it were to be wished the State follow the bent of his military inclination and render service to his country. If an event of this kind could take place it would give me particular pleasure, as the esteem I have for him, and a regard to merit conspire to make me earnestly wish to see him provided for in some handsome way."

2. GEORGE WASHINGTON TO JAMES MONROE FEBRUARY 23, 1789

"I received by the last Mail your letter dated the 15th of this month, accompanied with your printed observations on the new Constitution, and am much obliged by this token of your polite attention. However I may differ with you in sentiment on some of the points, which are advocated in your Treatise; I am pleased in discovering so much candour and liberality as seem to predominate in your Style and manner of investigation. That a Spirit of unanimity, accommodation and rectitude may prevail so extensively, as to facilitate the means for removing any well grounded apprehensions of the possible future ill consequences, which may result from the general government. . .".

3. GEORGE WASHINGTON TO JAMES MONROE APRIL 9, 1794

"Sir,

In reply to your letter of yesterday, I can assure you with the utmost truth, that I have no other object in nominating men to the offices than to fill them with such characters as, in my judgment, or (when they are unknown to me) from such information as I can obtain from others, are best qualified to answer the purposes of their appointment.

Having given you this assurance, I request, if you are possessed of any facts or information, which would disqualify Colo. Hamilton for the mission to which you refer, that you would be so obliging as to communicate then to me in writing. I pledge myself, they shall meet the most deliberate, impartial & candid consideration I am able to give them."

4. GEORGE WASHINGTON TO TIMOTHY PICKERING JULY 27, 1796

"Mr. Monroe in every letter he writes, relative to the discontents of the French government at the conduct of our own, always concludes without finishing his story; leaving great scope to the imagination to divine what the ulterior measures of it will be."

5. GEORGE WASHINGTON TO JAMES MONROE AUGUST 25, 1796

"Thus, Sir, you have the substance, candidly related, of a letter which you say, you have been told by a person 'who has read it, has produced an ill effect' when, in my opinion, the contrary (viewing it in the light of an unreserved and confidential communication) ought to have been produced. For I repeat it again, that unless my pacific disposition was displeasing, nothing else could have given umbrage by the most rigid construction of the letter; of that will shew in the remotest degree any disposition on my part to favor the British interests in their dispute with France."

6. GEORGE WASHINGTON'S REMARKS ON JAMES MONROE'S *VIEW OF THE CONDUCT OF THE EXECUTIVE OF THE UNITED STATES* MARCH 1798

"No one who will read the documents which he refers to, attentively can be at a loss for them; much less those who have the evidence the Executive[104] had that he was promoting the views of a party in his own Country that were obstructing every measure of the Administration, and by their attachment to France were hurrying it (if not with design, at least in its consequences) into a War with G[reat] Britain, in order to favour France."

7. GEORGE WASHINGTON'S REMARKS ON JAMES MONROE'S *VIEW OF THE CONDUCT OF THE EXECUTIVE OF THE UNITED STATES* MARCH 1798

"To state facts for the information of Congress, and not to write eulogiums on the French Nation, or conduct was the object of the then President.[105] If Mr. Monroe should ever fill the Chair of Government he may (and it is presumed he would be well enough disposed) let the French Minister frame his Speeches."

104 Washington is speaking of himself.

105 George Washington

III. JOHN ADAMS ON JAMES MONROE

1. JOHN ADAMS TO ABIGAIL ADAMS JANUARY 14, 1797

"Monroes House has been a School for Scandal against his Country, its Government and Governors."

2. JOHN ADAMS TO J. M. FORBES FEBRUARY 6, 1798

"I must avow that, upon the first publication of Mr. Monroe's work,[106] I was much hurt at that levity with which so many Americans, and among them some of respectable character, had taken an open part against the executive authority of their own government, especially when that authority was exercised by a character so universally respected as Washington. It looked as if Americans would be forever incapable of any kind of government."

3. JOHN ADAMS TO F. A. VANDERKEMP JULY 13, 1815

"'Monroe's Treaty!'[107] I care no more about it than about the mote that floats in the sunbeams before my eyes. The British minister [James Monroe] acted the part of a *horse-jockey.* He annexed a *rider* that annihilated the whole treaty."

4. JOHN ADAMS TO BENJAMIN WATERHOUSE JUNE 25, 1816

"I presume the *Parcae* have decreed that Monroe shall be P[resident]. Why should I grieve, when grieving I must bear: and take with Guilt what guiltless I might share? But I had rather have [Samuel] Dexter."[108]

5. JOHN ADAMS TO BENJAMIN WATERHOUSE JUNE 18, 1817

"Have you adjusted your Bib & Tucker to visit the President? There is no other theme of conversation at present. It is kind in him at this pressing time to give the Nation

106 *A View of the Conduct of the Executive in the Foreign Affairs of the United States*, 1797.

107 Commercial treaty negotiated and signed by Monroe and William Pinckney with Great Britain that was later rejected by President Thomas Jefferson as it failed to resolve the impressments issue with that nation.

108 Samuel Dexter, Secretary of War 1800-1801, Secretary of the Treasury January-May, 1801.

something to talk about. His plain manner will please in general. Tranquility & prosperity to his Administration. Amen."

-⁂-

6. JOHN ADAMS TO JAMES MONROE JUNE 23, 1817

"I congratulate you Sir on your election to the first office in the nation & on your visitation to the Eastern States, in which I hope you will find much satisfaction.
I hope also that you will do me the honour with the Gentlemen of your Suite, to dine with me in my Cottage in Quincy before you take leave of Massachusetts."

-⁂-

7. JOHN ADAMS TO JAMES MONROE JULY 1817

"In the good old English Language of your Virginian and my New England Ancestors, I am right glad to see you in the oldest Plantation, in Old Massachusetts, next to Salem, where you will be recd with more Splendor and I hope with equal cordiality."

-⁂-

8. VERBAL GREETING BY JOHN ADAMS TO NEWLY ELECTED PRESIDENT JAMES MONROE JULY 7, 1817

"Sir, I am happy to welcome you and your friends, and to acknowledge my high appreciation of the distinction which you propose to confer on my son as Secretary of State."

-⁂-

9. JOHN ADAMS TO RICHARD RUSH SEPTEMBER 15, 1817

"I could write you a Volume on the Visitation of the President to the Eastern States. The Result has been highly favourable to the Public Cause. Not an indiscretion has escaped from him. And his Patience and Activity have been such as I could never imitate and such as I could scarcely believe feasible."

-⁂-

10. JOHN ADAMS TO THOMAS JEFFERSON OCTOBER 18, 1817

"Mr. Monroe has got the un[i]versal Character among all our Common People of 'A very smart Man' And verily I am of the same Mind. I know of not another who could have executed so great a plan so cleverly.[109] I wish him the same happy Success through his whole Administration."

-⊰⊱-

11. JOHN ADAMS LETTER TO LOUISA CATHERINE ADAMS MAY 8, 1819

"I am Informed by your Son—my dear namesake—that you propose to be here by the first of July—I pray you to be sure that you arrive here before that day—bring your Husband with you. If the President can wander round the Universe and leave all the business of the Public to two or three of his ministers—I am sure your Husband can take upon himself to come to Quincy, and to Boston, for a couple of months—his business can be done by the Post Office better than the Presidents—What a Precedent is Monroe establishing for future Presidents? He will make the Office the most perfect Slavery that ever existed—The next president must go to Callifornia."

-⊰⊱-

12. JOHN ADAMS TO LOUISA CATHERINE ADAMS JUNE 11, 1819

"I rejoice to hear that the President intends to shorten his journey because I believe if he lengthens it, it will kill him—and I sincerely wish he may continue President another four years—after the expiration of this—and that your Husband will continue to be his Secretary—for a more happy combination is not to be expected."

-⊰⊱-

13. JOHN ADAMS TO THOMAS JEFFERSON NOVEMBER 23, 1819

"Congress are about to assemble and the Clouds look black and thick, Assembling from all points, threatening thunder and Lightning. The Spanish Treaty, the Missouri Slavery, the encouragement of Manufactures by protecting duties or absolute prohibitions, the project of a Bankrupt Act, the plague of Banks, perhaps even the Monument for Washington, and above all the bustle of Caucuses for the approaching Election for President and Vice President, will probably produce an effervescence, though there is no doubt that the present President and Vice President will be re-elected by great Majority's, as they ought to be, unless [Daniel D.] Tompkins should be chosen Governour of New York."

---

109 Capturing the Republican nomination over former Secretary of War William H. Crawford by a vote of 65-54.

IV. THOMAS JEFFERSON ON JAMES MONROE

1. THOMAS JEFFERSON TO BENJAMIN FRANKLIN OCTOBER 5, 1781

"The bearer hereof Colo. James Monroe who served some time as an officer in the American army and as such distinguished himself in the affair of Princetown as well as on other occasions, having resumed his studies, comes to Europe to complete them. Being a citizen of [Virginia], of abilities, merit and fortune, and my particular friend, I take the liberty of making him known to you, that should any circumstances render your patronage and protection as necessary as they would be always agreeable to him, you may be assured they are bestowed on one fully worthy of them.

He will be able to give you a particular detail of American affairs and especially of the prospect we have thro' the aid of our father of France, of making captives of Ld. Cornwallis and his army, of the recovery of Georgia and South Carolina, and the possibility that Charlestown itself will be opened to us."

2. THOMAS JEFFERSON TO W. T. FRANKLIN MAY 7, 1786

"You have formed a just opinion of Monroe. He is a man whose soul might be turned wrong side outwards, without discovering a blemish to the world."

3. THOMAS JEFFERSON TO JAMES MONROE MAY 10, 1786

"Information from other quarters gives me reason to suspect you have in negotiation a very important change in your situation.[110] You will carry into the execution all my wishes for your happiness. I hope it will not detach you from a settlement in your own country. I had even entertained hopes of your settling in my neighborhood: but these were determined by your desiring a plan of a house in Richmond. However reluctantly I relinquish this prospect, I shall not the less readily obey your commands by sending you a plan. Having been much engaged since my return from England in answering the letters & dispatching other business which had accumulated during my absence, & being still much

110 James Monroe married Elizabeth Kortright on February 16, 1786 in New York, New York.

engaged, perhaps I may not be able to send the plan by this conveyance. If I do not send it now, I will surely by the first conveyance after this."

-⁂-

4. THOMAS JEFFERSON TO JAMES MONROE AUGUST 11, 1786

"I look forward with anxiety to the approaching moment of your departure from Congress. Besides the interest of the Confederacy & of the State I have a personal interest in it. I know not to whom I may venture confidential communications after you are gone. [Richard Henry] *Lee I scarcely know.* [William] *Grayson is lazy.* [Edward] *Carrington is industrious but not always as discreet as well-meaning, yet* on the whole I believe *he would be the best* if you find him *disposed to the correspondence. Engage him* to *begin* it."

-⁂-

5. THOMAS JEFFERSON TO JAMES MONROE DECEMBER 18, 1786

"The revisal of the Congressional intelligence contained in your letters, makes me regret the loss of it on your departure. I feel, too, the want of a person there, to whose discretion I can trust confidential communications, and on whose friendship I can rely against the unjust designs of malevolence. I have no reason to suppose I have enemies in Congress; yet it is too possible to be without that fear."

-⁂-

6. THOMAS JEFFERSON TO JAMES MONROE DECEMBER 18, 1786

"On my return [from Paris], which will be early in the spring, I shall send you several livraisons of the Encyclopedie, and the plan of your house. I wish to heaven, you may continue in the disposition to fix it in Albemarle. [William] Short will establish himself there, and perhaps Madison may be tempted to do so. This will be society enough, and it will be the great sweetener of our lives. Without society, and a society to our taste, men are never contented. The one here supposed, we can regulate our minds, and we may extend our regulations to the sumptuary department, so as to set a good example to a country which needs it, and to preserve our own happiness clear of embarrassment."

-⁂-

7. THOMAS JEFFERSON TO JAMES MONROE DECEMBER 18, 1786

"You wish not to engage in the drudgery of the bar.[111] You have two asylums from that. Either to accept a seat in the Council, or in the judiciary department. The latter, however, would require a little previous drudgery at the bar, to qualify you to discharge your duty with satisfaction to yourself. Neither of these would be inconsistent with a continued residence in Albemarle. It is but twelve hours' drive in a sulky from Charlottesville to Richmond, keeping a fresh horse always at the half-way, which would be a small annual expense."

8. THOMAS JEFFERSON TO JAMES MONROE MAY 26, 1795

"Mr. Madison & myself examined your different situations for a house. We did not think it admitted any sort of question but that that on the east side of the road, in the wood, was the best. There is a valley not far from it to the southwest & on the western side of the road which would be a fine situation for an orchard. Mr. Jones having purchased in Loudon we shall hardly see him here, & indeed have hardly seen him. If I can get proper orders from him I will have the ground above mentioned planted in fruit."

9. THOMAS JEFFERSON TO WILLIAM BRANCH GILES DECEMBER 31, 1795

"I should not wonder if Monroe were to be recalled under the idea of his being of the partisans of France, whom the President considers as the partisans of *war & confusion* in his letter of July 31, and as disposed to excite them to hostile measures, or at least to unfriendly sentiments.[112] A most infatuated blindness to the true character of the sentiments entertained in favor of France."

10. THOMAS JEFFERSON TO JOHN FRANCIS MERCER SEPTEMBER 5, 1797

"We have now with us our friend Monroe. He is engaged in stating his conduct for the information of the public. As yet, however, he has done little, being too much occupied

111 In 1786 Monroe was admitted to the Virginia bar where he practiced law in Fredericksburg until 1790.

112 Monroe was serving as minister to France at the time and highly sympathetic to that nation and critical of the Jay Treaty leading to his recall by George Washington.

with re-arranging his household. His preliminary skirmish with the Secretary of state [Timothy Pickering] has, of course, bespoke a suspension of the public mind, till he can lay his statement before them."

11. THOMAS JEFFERSON TO JAMES MONROE DECEMBER 27, 1797

"Your book was later coming than was to have been wished: however it works irresistibly.[113] It would be very gratifying to you to hear the unqualified eulogies both on the matter & manner by all who are not hostile to it from principle. A pamphlet written by Fauchet (and now reprinting here) reinforced the views you have presented of the duplicity of the administration here. The Republican party in the H. of Representatives is stronger than its antagonistic party on all strong questions."

12. THOMAS JEFFERSON TO JAMES MADISON JANUARY 3, 1798

"Monroe's book is considered as masterly by all those who are not opposed in principle, and it is deemed unanswerable. An answer, however, is commenced in Fenno's paper yesterday, under the signature of Scipio. The real author not yet conjectured."

13. THOMAS JEFFERSON TO JAMES MONROE FEBRUARY 8, 1798

"It has been said here that C[harles] Lee was the author of Scipio, but I know of no authority for it. I had expected Hamilton would have taken the field, and that in that case you might have come forward yourself very shortly merely to strengthen and present in a compact view those points which you expected yourself they would lay hold of, particularly the disposition expressed to acquiesce under their spoiliatory decree. Scipio's attack is so weak as to make no impression. I understand that the opposite party admit that there is nothing in your conduct which can be blamed, except the divulging secrets: & this I think might be answered by a few sentences, discussing the question whether an Ambassador is the representative of his country or of the President."

113 Jefferson is referring to Monroe's, *A View of the Conduct of the Executive in the Foreign Affairs of the United States,* (1797) which was highly critical of the Washington Administration's foreign policy and as a defense of Monroe's actions in France.

14. THOMAS JEFFERSON TO JAMES MONROE FEBRUARY 8, 1798

"As to the question of your practicing law in Richmond, I have been too long out of the way in Virginia to give an opinion on it worth attention. I have understood the business is very profitable, much more so than in my time: and an opening of great importance must be made by the retirement of [John] Marshall & [Bushrod] Washington, which will be filled by somebody."

15. THOMAS JEFFERSON TO JAMES MONROE FEBRUARY 8, 1798

"I do expect that your farm will not sufficiently employ your time to shield you from ennui. Your mind is active, & would suffer if unemployed. Perhaps it's energies could not be more justifiably employed than for your own comfort. I should doubt very much however, whether you should combine with this the idea of living in Richmond, at least till you see farther before you. I have always seen that tho' a residence at the seat of government gave some advantages, yet it increased expenses also so seriously as to overbalance the advantages. I have always seen too that a good stand in the country intercepted more business than was shared by the residents of the city. Yours is a good stand. You need only to visit Staunton Cts. Some times to put yourself in the way of seeing clients."

16. THOMAS JEFFERSON TO JAMES MONROE MARCH 8, 1798

"How far it may be eligible for you to engage in the practice of the law I know not. On the question of your removal to Richmond, I may doubtless be under bias, when I suppose it's expediency questionable. The expense to be incurred in the first moments will certainly be great. Could it be only deferred for a while it would enable you to judge whether the prospect opened will be worth that dislocation of your affairs, or whether some other career may not open on you. Of these things nobody but yourself can judge. It is a question too for yourself whether a seat among the judges of the state would be an object for you. On all these points your friends can only offer motives for consideration: on which none but yourself can decide avec connoissance de cause. I really believe that some employment, more than your farms will furnish, will be necessary to your happiness. You are young, your mind active, and your health vigorous. The languor of ennui would, in such a condition of things, be intolerable."

17. THOMAS JEFFERSON TO JAMES MONROE APRIL 5, 1798

"Yesterday I had a consultation with mr. [John] Dawson on the matter respecting [Fulwar] Skipwith. We have neither of us the least hesitation, on a view of the ground, to pronounce against your coming forward in it at all. Your name would be the watchword of party at this moment, and the question would give opportunities of slander, personal hatred, and injustice, the effect of which on the justice of the case cannot be calculated. Let it therefore come forward in Skipwith's name without your appearing to even know of it. But is it not a cause which the auditor can decide? If it is, that tribunal must be first resorted to. I do not think Scipio worth your notice. He has not been noticed here but by those who were already determined. Your narrative and letters wherever they are read produce irresistable conviction, and cannot be attacked but by a contradiction of facts, on which they do not venture. Finding you unassailable in that quarter, I have reason to believe they are preparing a batch of small stuff, such as refusing to drink Genl. Washington's health, speaking ill of him, & the government, withdrawing civilities from those attached to him, countenancing Paine to which they add connivance at the equipment of privateers by Americans."

18. THOMAS JEFFERSON TO JAMES MONROE MAY 21, 1798

"You will have seen, among numerous addresses & answers, one from Lancaster [Pennsylvania], and it's answer. The latter traveling out of the topics of the address altogether, to mention you in a most injurious manner. Your feelings have no doubt been much irritated by it, as in truth it had all the characters necessary to produce irritation. What notice you should take of it is difficult to say. But there is one step in which two or three with whom I have spoken concur with me, feeble as the hand is from which this shaft is thrown, yet with a great mass of our citizens, strangers to the leading traits of the character from which it came, it will have considerable effect; & that in order to replace yourself on the high ground you are entitled to, it is absolutely necessary you should reappear on the public theatre, and take an independent stand, from which you can be seen & known to your fellow citizens. The H[ouse] of Repr[esentatives] appears the only place which can answer this end, as the proceedings of the other house are too obscure. [Samuel Jordan] Cabell has said he would give way to you, whenever you should chuse to come in, and I really think it would be expedient for yourself as well as the public, that you should not wait until another election, but come to the next session. No interval should be admitted between this last attack of enmity and your re-appearance with the approving voice of your constituents, & your taking a commanding attitude. I have not before been anxious for your return to public life, lest it should interfere with a proper pursuit of your private interests, but the next session will not at all interfere with your courts, because it must end Mar 4, and I verily believe the next election will give us such a majority in the He of R as to enable the republican party to shorten the alternate unlimited session, as it is evident that to shorten the sessions is to lessen the evils & burthens of the government on our country. The present session has already cost 200,000 D, besides the wounds it has inflicted on the prosperity of the Union. I have no doubt Cabell can be induced to retire immediately, & that a writ may be issued at once. The very idea of this will strike the public mind, & raise its confidence in you. If this be done, I should think it best you should take no notice at all of the answer to Lancaster. Because were you to shew a personal hostility against the answer, it would deaden the effect of everything you should say or do in your public place hereafter. All would be ascribed to an enmity of Mr. A[dams], and you know with what facility such insinuations enter the minds of men. I have not seen Dawson since this answer has appeared, & therefore have not yet learnt his sentiments on it."

19. THOMAS JEFFERSON TO JOHN TAYLOR JANUARY 24, 1799

"Mr. Tazewell died about noon this day after an illness of about 36. hours. On this event, so melancholy for his family and friends, the loss to the public of so faithful and able a servant no reflections can be adequate.

The object of this letter (and which I beseech you to mention as from me to no mortal) is the replacement of him *by the legislature.* Many points in Monro's character would render him the most valuable acquisition the republican interest in this legislature could make. There is no chance of bringing him into the other house as some had wished, because the present representative of his district will not retire."

20. THOMAS JEFFERSON TO JAMES MONROE JANUARY 10, 1803

"I have but a moment to inform you that the fever into which the western mind is thrown by the affair at N. Orleans stimulated by the mercantile, and generally the federal interest threatens to overbear our peace.[114] In this situation we are obliged to call on you for a temporary sacrifice of yourself, to prevent this greatest of evils in the present prosperous tide of our affairs. I shall to-morrow nominate you to the Senate for an extraordinary

114 France suspended the right of deposit for the United States at the Port of New Orleans; prompting Jefferson to say, "There is on the globe one single spot the possessor of which [France] is our natural and habitual enemy."

mission to France, and the circumstances are such as to render it impossible to decline; because the whole public hope will be rested on you. I wish you to be either in Richmond or Albermarle till you receive another letter from me, which will be written two days hence if the Senate decide immediately or later according to the time they will take to decide. In the meantime pray work night and day to arrange your affairs for a temporary absence; perhaps for a long one."

21. THOMAS JEFFERSON TO JAMES MONROE JANUARY 13, 1803

"DEAR SIR,—I dropped you a line on the 10th informing you of a nomination I had made of you to the Senate, and yesterday I enclosed you their approbation not then having time to write. The agitation of the public mind on occasion of the late suspension of our right of deposit at N. Orleans is extreme. In the western country it is natural and grounded on honest motives. In the seaports it proceeds from a desire for war which increases the mercantile lottery; in the federalists generally and especially those of Congress the object is to force us into war if possible, in order to derange our finances, or if this cannot be done, to attach the western country to them, as their best friends, and thus get again into power. Remonstrances memorials &c. are now circulating through the whole of the western country and signing by the body of the people. The measures we have been pursuing being invisible, do not satisfy their minds. Something sensible therefore was become necessary; and indeed our object of purchasing N. Orleans and the Floridas is a measure liable to assume so many shapes, that no instructions could be squared to fit them, it was essential then to send a minister extraordinary to be joined with the ordinary one,[115] with discretionary powers, first however well impressed with all our views and therefore qualified to meet and modify to these every form of proposition which could come from the other party. This could be done only in full and frequent oral communications. Having determined on this, there could not be two opinions among the republicans as to the person. You possess the unlimited confidence of the administration and of the western people; and generally of the republicans everywhere; and were you to refuse to go, no other man can be found who does this. The measure has already silenced the Feds. here. Congress will no longer be agitated by them: and the country will become calm as fast as the information extends over it. All eyes, all hopes, are now fixed on you; and were you to decline, the chagrin would be universal, and would shake under your feet the high ground on which you stand with the public. Indeed I know nothing which would produce such a shock, for on the event of this mission depends the future destines of this republic. If we cannot by a purchase of the country insure to ourselves a course of perpetual peace and friendship with all nations, then as war cannot be distant, it behooves

115 Robert Livingston

us immediately to be preparing for that course, without, however, hastening it, and it may be necessary (on your failure on the continent) to cross the channel.

We shall get entangled in European politics, and figuring more, be much less happy and prosperous. This can only be prevented by a successful issue to your present mission. I am sensible after the measures you have taken for getting into a different line of business, that it will be a great sacrifice on your part, and presents from the season and other circumstances serious difficulties. But some men are born for the public. Nature by fitting them for the service of the human race on a broad scale, has stamped with the evidences of her destination and their duty.

But I am particularly concerned that in the present case you have more than one sacrifice to make. To reform the prodigalities of our predecessors is understood to be peculiarly our duty, and to bring the government to a simple and economical course. They, in order to increase expenses, debt, taxation, and patronage tried always how much they could give. The outfit given to ministers resident to enable them to furnish their house, but given by no nation to a temporary minister, who is never expected to take a house or to entertain, but considered on a footing of a voyageur, they gave to their extraordinary missionaries by wholesale. In the beginning of our administration, among other articles of reformation in expense, it was determined not to give an outfit to missionaries extraordinary, and not to incur the expense with any minister of sending a frigate to carry him or bring him. The Boston happened to be going to the Mediterranean, and was permitted therefore to take up Mr. Livingstone and touch in a port of France. A frigate was denied to Charles Pinckney and has been refused to Mr. King for his return. Mr. Madison's friendship and mine to you being so well known, the public will have eagle eyes to watch if we grant you any indulgencies of the general rule; and on the other hand, the example set in your case will be more cogent on future ones, and produce greater approbation to our conduct. The allowance therefore will be in this and all similar cases, all the expenses of your journey and voiage, taking a ship's cabin to yourself, 9,000 D. a year from your leaving home till the proceedings of your mission are terminated, and then the quarter's salary for the expenses of the return as prescribed by law. As to the time of your going you cannot too much hasten it, as the moment in France is critical. St. Domingo delays [France's] taking possession of Louisiana, and they are in the last distress for money for current purposes. You should arrange your affairs for an absence of a year at least, perhaps for a long one. It will be necessary for you to stay here some days on your way to New York. You will receive here what advance you chuse. Accept assurances of my constant and affectionate attachment."

22. THOMAS JEFFERSON TO P. S. DUPONT DE NEMOURS FEBRUARY 1, 1803

"While we were preparing on this subject such modifications of the propositions of your letter of Oct 4, as we could assent to, an event happened which obliged us to adopt measures of urgency. The suspension of the right of deposit at New Orleans, ceded to us by our treaty with Spain, threw our whole country into such a ferment as imminently threatened its peace. This, however, was believed to be the act of the Intendant, unauthorized by his government. But it showed the necessity of making effectual arrangements to secure the peace of the two countries against the indiscreet acts of subordinate agents. The urgency of the case, as well as the public spirit, therefore induced us to make a more solemn appeal to the justice and judgment of our neighbors, by sending a minister extraordinary to impress them with the necessity of some arrangement. Mr. Monroe has been selected. His good dispositions cannot be doubted. Multiplied conversations with him, and views of the subject taken in all the shapes in which it can present itself, have possessed him with our estimates of everything relating to it, with a minuteness which no written communication to Mr. Livingston could ever have attained. These will prepare them to meet and decide on every form of proposition which can occur, without awaiting new instructions from hence, which might draw to an indefinite length a discussion where circumstances imperiously oblige us to a prompt decision. For the occlusion of the Mississippi is a state of things in which we cannot exist. He goes, therefore, joined with Chancellor Livingston, to aid in the issue of a crisis the most important the U S have ever met since their independence, and which is to decide their future character & career."

23. THOMAS JEFFERSON TO GENERAL HORATIO GATES JULY 11, 1803

"The territory acquired, as it includes all the waters of the Missouri & Mississippi, has more than doubled the area of the U.S. and the new part is not inferior to the old in soil, climate, productions & important communications. If our legislature dispose of it with the wisdom we have a right to expect, they may make it the means of tempting all our Indians on the East side of the Mississippi to remove to the West, and of condensing instead of scattering our population. I find our opposition is very willing to pluck feathers from Monroe, although not fond of sticking them into Livingston's coat. The truth is both have a just portion of merit and were it necessary or proper it could be shewn that each has rendered peculiar service, & of important value. These grumblers too are very uneasy lest the administration should share some little credit for the acquisition, the whole of which they ascribe to the accident of war."

24. THOMAS JEFFERSON TO JAMES MONROE JANUARY 8, 1804

"Congress is now engaged in a bill for the government of Louisiana. It is impossible to foresee in what shape it will come out. They talk of giving 5,000 D. to the Governor, but the bill also proposes to commence at the close of this session. I have in private conversations demonstrated to individuals that that is impossible; that the necessary officers cannot be mustered there under 6 months. If they give that time for it's commencement, it may admit our appointing you to that office, as I presume you could be in place with a term not much beyond that, & in the interval the Secretary of state would govern."

25. THOMAS JEFFERSON TO JAMES MONROE JANUARY 8, 1804

"You are not to calculate that 5,000 D. would place you by any means as much at your ease there as 9,000 D. where you are.[116] In that station you cannot avoid expensive hospitality. Where you are, altho' it is not pleasant to fall short in returning civilities, yet necessity has rendered this so familiar in Europe as not to lessen respect for the person whose circumstances do not permit a return of hospitalities. I see by your letters the pain which this situation gives you, and I can estimate its acuteness from the generosity of your nature. But, my dear friend, calculate with mathematical rigour the pain annexed to each branch of the dilemma & pursue that which brings the least. To give up entertainment, & to live with the most rigorous economy till you have cleared yourself of every demand is a pain for a definite time only: but to return here with accumulated encumbrances on you, will fill your life with torture. We wish to do everything for you which law & rule will permit. But more than this would injure you as much as us. Believing that the mission to Spain will enable you to suspend expense greatly in London, & to apply your salary during your absence to the clearing off your debt, you will be instructed to proceed there as soon as you shall have regulated certain points of neutral right for us with England, or as soon as you find nothing in that way can be done. This you should hurry as much as possible, that you may proceed to Spain, for settling with that court the boundaries of Louisiana."

116 Monroe was then serving as United States Minister to Great Britain and living in London; a position he held until 1807. Jefferson was referring to the $5,000 annual salary that the new position of Governor of Louisiana would earn.

26. THOMAS JEFFERSON TO JAMES MONROE JANUARY 8, 1804

"When mentioning your going to N. Orleans & that the salary there would not increase the ease of your situation, I meant to have added that the only considerations which might make it eligible to you were the facility of getting there the richest land in the world, the extraordinary profitableness of their culture, and that the removal of your slaves there might immediately put you under way. You alone however can weight these things for yourself, and after all, it may depend on the time the legislature may give for commencing the new government. But, let us hear from you as soon as you can determine, that we may not incur the blame of waiting for nothing."

27. THOMAS JEFFERSON TO JAMES MONROE MAY 4, 1806

"If you are here at any time before the fall, it will be in time for any object you may have, and by that time the public sentiment will be more decisively declared. I wish you were here at present, to take your choice of the two governments of Orleans & Louisiana, in either of which I could now place you; and I verily believe it would be to your advantage to be just that much withdrawn from the focus of the ensuing contest, until it's events should be known. The one has a salary of 5000 D., the other of 2000 D.; both with excellent hotels for the Governor. The latter at St. Louis, where there is good society, both French & American; a healthy climate, & the finest field in the U S for acquiring property. The former not unhealthy, if you begin a residence there in the month of November. The Mrs. Trists & their connections are established there. As I think you can within 4. months inform me what you say to this, I will keep things in their present state till the last day of August, for your answer."

28. THOMAS JEFFERSON TO JAMES MONROE OCTOBER 26, 1806

"To prevent that depression of spirits which experiences has taught me to expect on returning after a long absence from one's home, and that you may be prepared & fortified for a discouraging view, I will just observe that our neighborhood considers your manager Mr. Lewis as one of the honestest & best men in the world, but the poorest manager. They think he has not made your estate maintain itself, & that you will find it unprovided with present subsistence. Nobody has made this season half a year's provision of corn & your estate less than most others: & it is said there is no stock of any kind remaining on the farm for your immediate subsistence. To restock the farm with bread, requires a year, & with animals 2 or 3 years. A previous communication of these circumstances (if you have received them from no other) will enable you to come prepared to meet them."

-⁂-

29. THOMAS JEFFERSON TO JAMES MONROE MARCH 21, 1807

"The government of New Orleans is still without such a head as I wish. The salary of 5000 D. is too small; but I am assured the Orleans legislature would make it adequate, would you accept it. It is the 2d. office in the U S in importance, and I am still in hopes you will accept it. It is impossible to let you stay at home while the public has so much need of talents."

-⁂-

30. THOMAS JEFFERSON TO JAMES MONROE MAY 29, 1807

"I had intended to have written you to counteract the wicked efforts which federal papers are making to sow tares between you and me, as if I were lending a hand to measures unfriendly to any views which our country might entertain respecting you. But I have not done it, because I have before assured you that a sense of duty, as well as of delicacy, would prevent me from ever expressing a sentiment on the subject, and that I think you know me well enough to be assured I shall conscientiously observe the line of conduct I profess. I shall receive you on your return with warm affection I have ever entertained for you, and be gratified if I can in any way avail the public of your services."

-⁂-

31. THOMAS JEFFERSON TO JAMES MONROE FEBRUARY 18, 1808

"I see with infinite grief a contest arising between yourself and another,[117] who have been very dear to each other, and equally so to me. I sincerely pray that these dispositions may not be affected between you; with me I confidently trust they will not. For independently of the dictates of public duty, which prescribe neutrality to me, my sincere friendship for you both will ensure it's sacred observance. I suffer no one to converse with me on the subject. I already perceive my old friend [George] Clinton, estranging himself from me. No doubt lies are carried to him, as they will be to the other two candidates, under forms which however false, he can scarcely question. Yet I have been equally careful as to him also, never to say a word on this subject. The object of the contest is a fair & honorable one, equally open to you all; and I have no doubt the personal conduct of all will be so chaste, as to offer no ground of dissatisfaction with each other. But your friends will not be as delicate. I know too well from

117 James Madison

experience the progress of political controversy, and the exacerbation of spirit into which it degenerates, not to fear for the continuance of your mutual esteem. One piquing thing said draws on another, that a third, and always with increasing acrimony, until all restraint is thrown off, and it becomes difficult for yourselves to keep clear of the toils in which your friends will endeavor to interlace you, and to avoid the participation in their passions which they will endeavor to produce. A candid recollection of what you know of each other will be the true corrective. With respect to myself, I hope they will spare me. My longings for retirement are so strong, that I with difficulty encounter the daily drudgeries of my duty. But my wish for retirement itself is not stronger than that of carrying into it the affections of all my friends. I have ever viewed Mr. Madison and yourself as two principal pillars of my happiness. Were either to be withdrawn, I should consider it as among the greatest calamities which could assail my future piece of mind. I have great confidence that the candor & high understanding of both will guard me against this misfortune, the bare possibility of which has so far weighed on my mind, that I could not be easy without unburthening it."[118]

32. THOMAS JEFFERSON TO JAMES MONROE MARCH 10, 1808

"From your letter of the 27th ultimo, I perceive that painful impressions have been made on your mind during your late mission, of which I had never entertained a suspicion. I must, therefore, examine the grounds, because explanations between reasonable men can never but do good.

1. You consider the mission of Mr. Pinckney as an associate, to have been in some way injurious to you. Were I to take that measure on myself, I might say in its justification, that it has been the regular & habitual practice of the U S to do this, under every form in which their government has existed. I need not recapitulate the multiplied instances, because you will readily recollect them. I went as an adjunct to Dr. Franklin & Mr. Adams, yourself as an adjunct first to Mr. Livingston, and then to Mr. Pinckney, & I really believe there has scarcely been a great occasion which had not produced an extraordinary mission. Still, however, it is well known that I was strongly opposed to it in the case of which you complain. A committee of the Senate called on me with two resolutions of that body on the subject of impressment & spoliations by G. Britain, & requesting that I would demand satisfaction. After delivering the resolutions, the committee entered into free conversation, and observed, that although the Senate could not, in form, recommend any extraordinary mission, yet that as individuals, there was but one sentiment among

118 Jefferson would later openly favor James Madison for the presidency.

them on the measure, and they pressed it. I was so much averse to it, & gave them so hard an answer, that they felt it, and spoke of it. But it did not end here. The members of the other House took up the subject, and set upon me individually, and these the best friends to you, as well as myself, and represented the responsibility which a failure to obtain redress would throw on us both, pursuing a conduct in opposition to the opinion of nearly every member of the Legislature. I found it necessary, at length, to yield my own opinion to the general sense of the national council, and it really seemed to produce a jubilee among them; not from any want of confidence in you, but from a belief in the effect which an extraordinary mission would have on the British mind, by demonstrating the degree of importance which this country attached to the rights which we considered as infracted.

2. You complain of the manner in which the treaty was received. But what was the manner? I cannot suppose you to have given a moment's credit to the stuff which was crowded in all sorts of forms into the public papers, or to the thousand speeches they put into my mouth, not a word of which I had ever uttered. I was not insensible at the time of the views to mischief, with which these lies were fabricated. But my confidence was firm, that neither yourself nor the British government, equally outraged by them, would believe me capable of making the editors of newspapers the confidants of my speeches or opinions. The fact was this. The treaty was communicated to us by Mr. [David M.] Erskine on the day Congress was to rise. Two of the Senators inquired of me in the evening, whether it was my purpose to detain them on account of the treaty. My answer was, 'that it was not: that the treaty containing no provision against the impressment of our seamen, and being accompanied by a kind of protestation of the British ministers, which would leave that government free to consider it as a treaty or no treaty, according to their own convenience, I should not give them the trouble of deliberating on it.' This was substantially, & almost verbally, what I said whenever spoken to about it, and I never failed when the occasion would admit of it, to justify yourself and Mr. Pinckney, by expressing my conviction, that it was all that could be obtained from the British government; that you had told their commissioners that your government could not be pledged to ratify, because it was contrary to their instructions; of course, that it should be considered but as a project; and in this light I stated it publicly in my message to Congress on the opening of the session. Not a single article of the treaty was ever made known beyond the members of the administration, nor would an article of it be known at this day, but for it's publication in the newspapers, as communicated by somebody from beyond the water, as we have always understood. But as to myself, I can solemnly protest, as the most sacred of truths, that I never, one instant, lost sight of your reputation and favorable

standing with your country, & never omitted to justify your failure to attain our wish, as one which was probably unattainable. Reviewing therefore, this whole subject, I cannot doubt you will become sensible, that your impressions have been without just ground. I cannot, indeed, judge what falsehoods may have been written or told you; and that, under such forms as to command belief. But you will soon find, my dear Sir, that so inveterate is the rancor of party spirit among us, that nothing ought to be credited but what we hear with our own ears. If you are less on your guard than we are here, at this moment, the designs of the mischief-makers will not fail to be accomplished, and brethren & friends will be made strangers & enemies to each other, without ever having said or thought a thing amiss of each other. I presume that the most insidious falsehoods are daily carried to you, as they are brought to me, to engage us in the passions of our informers, and stated so positively & plausibly as to make even *doubt* a rudeness to the narrator; who, imposed on himself, has no other than the friendly view of putting us on our guard. My answer is, invariably, that my knoledge of your character is better testimony to me of a negative, than any affirmative which my informant did not hear *from yourself* with his own ears. In fact, when you shall have been a little longer among us you will find that little is to be believed which interests the prevailing passions, and happens beyond the limits of our own senses. Let us not then, my dear friend, embark our happiness and our affections on the ocean of slander, of falsehood & of malice, on which our credulous friends are floating. If you have been made to believe that I ever did, said, or thought a thing unfriendly to your fame & feelings, you do me injury as causeless as it is afflicting me. In the present contest in which you are concerned, I feel no passion, I take no part, I express no sentiment. Whichever of my friends is called to the supreme cares of the nation, I know that they will be wisely & faithfully administered, and as far as my individual conduct can influence, they shall be cordially supported. For myself I have nothing further to ask of the world, than to preserve in retirement so much of their esteem as I may have fairly earned, and to be permitted to pass in tranquility, in the bosom of my family & friends, the days which yet remain for me. Having reached the harbor myself, I shall view with anxiety (but certainly not with a wish to be in their place) those who are still buffeting the storm, uncertain of their fate. Your voyage has so far been favorable, & that it may continue with entire prosperity, is the sincere prayer of that friendship which I have ever borne you, and of which I now assure you, with the tender of my high respect & affectionate salutations."

33. THOMAS JEFFERSON TO JAMES MONROE APRIL 11, 1808

"Conscious that I never felt a sentiment towards you that was not affectionate it is a great relief to find that the doubts you have entertained on that subject are removed by an explanation of the circumstances which produced them."

34. THOMAS JEFFERSON TO JAMES MONROE APRIL 11, 1808

"Your letters from Madrid in 1804.5. expressed your anxious wish & intention to come home on your return to London. My extreme wish was that you should remain there, and I hoped by not being in a hurry to answer that manifestation of your desire, time might produce a change in your mind. But as soon as it was known (during the session of 1805.6) that yourself and Mr. Madison were both contemplated as candidates for the succession to the presidency, I became apprehensive that by declining longer to assent to your return, I might be suspected of a partial design to keep you out of the way. In fact it was openly said by some of those who were pressing your name and popularity into the service of their vindictive fashions. This produced the acquiescence in your desire to come home which then took place, and the commission to Mr. Pinckney to succeed you whenever you should determine to come. And these motives clearly show themselves in my letter of Mar. 16 which says 'I shall join Mr. Pinckney of Maryland as your associate for settling our differences with G. Britain. He will be authorized to take your place *whenever* you think yourself obliged to return. It is desirable for *your own*, as well as the *public* interest that you should join in the settlement of this business, and I am perfectly satisfied that if this can be done so as to be here *before the next meeting of Congress*, it will be greatly for your benefit. But I do not mean by this *to overrule your own determination* (i.e. either to stay or come home) which measures to be taken here will place in perfect freedom.' Here you will perceive how much I wished your aid in the joint commission, and that your longer continuance there could not but, in itself, be desirable, but that I did not ask it from an apprehension that your return before the next Congress might be important to your higher interests.

I consider it now as a great misfortune that my letter of Mar. 16 did not go on to you. I would, I trust, have corrected the inferences of a change in my affections towards you drawn from a combination of circumstances, which circumstances were produced from very different causes, and some of them from the strength of those very affections of which you thought that they noted a diminution, a desire to conform your movements, in point of time, to what I deemed your best interests. I have gone thus minutely into these details from as desire to eradicate from your mind every fiber of doubt as to my sentiments towards you; and I am persuaded they will satisfactorily solve every circumstance which might at any time have occasioned doubt. I have done it too the more cordially because I perceive from your letter that disposition to a correct view of the subject which I knew to be inherent in your mind. What I have hitherto said has been confined to my own part only of these transactions. Yet it would be a criminal suppression of truth were I not to add that in the whole course of them. Mr. Madison has appeared to be governed by the most cordial friendship for you, has manifested on every occasion the most attentive concern for whatever might befriend your fame or fortune, and been as much alive to whatever regarded you, as a brother could have been."

35. THOMAS JEFFERSON TO JAMES MADISON NOVEMBER 30, 1809

"I received last night yours of the 27th, and rode this morning to Col. Monroe's. I found him preparing to set out to-morrow morning for London, from whence he will not return till Christmas. I had an hour or two's frank conversation with him. The catastrophe of poor Lewis served to lead us to the point intended.[119] I reminded him that in the letter I wrote to him while in Europe, proposing the Government of Orleans, I also suggested that of Louisiana, if fears for health should be opposed to the other. I said something on the importance of the post, its advantages, &c.—expressed my regret at the curtain which seemed to be drawn between him and his best friends, and my wish to see his talents and integrity engaged in the service of his country again, and that his going into any post would be a signal of reconciliation, on which the body of republicans, who lamented his absence from the public service, would again rally to him. These are the general heads of what I said to him in the course of our conversation. The sum of his answers was, that to accept of that office was incompatible with the respect he owed himself; that he never would act in any office where he should be subordinated to any body but the President himself, or which did not place his responsibility with the President and the nation; that at your accession to the chair, he would have accepted a place in the cabinet, and would have exerted his endeavors most faithfully in support of your fame and measures; that he is not unready to serve the public and especially in the case of any difficult crisis in our affairs; that he is satisfied that such is the deadly hatred of both France and England, and such their self reproach and dread at the spectacle of such a government as ours, that they will spare nothing to destroy it; that nothing but a firm union among the whole body of republicans can save it, and therefore that no schism should be indulged on any ground; that in his present situation, he is sincere in his anxieties for the success of the administration, and in his support of it as far as the limited sphere of his action or influence extends; that his influence to this end had been used with those with whom

119 Jefferson is referring to Meriwether Lewis who committed suicide on October 11, 1809 in Tennessee.

the world had ascribed to him an interest he did not possess, until, whatever it was, it was lost, (he particularly named J. Randolph, who he said, had plans of his own, on which he took no advice;) and that he was now pursuing what he believed his properest occupation, devoting his whole time and faculties to the liberation of his pecuniary embarrassments, which, three years of close attention, he hoped, would effect. In order to know more exactly what were the kinds of employ he would accept, I adverted to the information of the papers, which came yesterday, that Gen. [Wade] Hampton was dead, but observed that the military life in our present state, offered nothing which could operate on the principle of patriotism; he said he would sooner be shot than take command under [General James] Wilkinson. In this sketch, I have given truly the substance of his ideas, but not always his own words. On the whole, I conclude he would accept a place in the cabinet, or a military command dependent on the Executive alone, and I rather suppose a diplomatic mission, because it would fall within the scope of his views, and not because he said so, for no allusion was made to anything of that kind in our conversation. Everything from his breathed the purest patriotism, involving, however, a close attention to his own honor and grade. He expressed himself with the utmost devotion to the interests of our own country, and I am satisfied he will pursue them with honor and zeal in any character in which he shall be willing to act.

I have thus gone far beyond the single view of your letter, that you may, under any circumstances, form a just estimate of what he would be disposed to do. God bless you, and carry you safely through all your difficulties."

36. THOMAS JEFFERSON TO JAMES MONROE MAY 5, 1811

"Your favor on your departure from Richmond, came to hand in due time. Although I may not have been among the first, I am certainly with the sincerest, who congratulate you on your entrance into the national councils. Your value there has never been unduly estimated by those whom personal feelings did not misguide. The late misunderstandings at Washington have been a subject of real concern to me. I know that the dissolutions of personal friendship are among the most painful occurrences in human life. I have sincere esteem for all who have been affected by them, having passed with them eight years of great harmony and affection. These incidents are rendered more distressing in our country than elsewhere, because our printers ravin on the agonies of their victims, as wolves do on the blood of the lamb."

37. THOMAS JEFFERSON TO WILLIAM DUANE OCTOBER 1, 1812

"I clearly think with you on the competence of Monroe to embrace great views of action. The decision of his character, his enterprise, firmness, industry, and unceasing vigilance, would, I believe, secure, as I am sure they would merit, the public confidence, and give us all the success which our means can accomplish."

38. THOMAS JEFFERSON TO JAMES MONROE JANUARY 1, 1815

"I much regretted your acceptance of the war department. Not that I know a person who I think would better conduct it. But, conduct it ever so wisely, it will be a sacrifice of yourself. Were an angel from Heaven to undertake that office, all our miscarriages would be ascribed to him. Raw troops, insubordinate militia, want of arms, want of money, want of provisions, all will be charged to want of management in you. I speak from experience, when I was Governor of Virginia. Without a regular in the State, and scarcely a musket to put into the hands of the militia, invaded by two armies, Arnold's from the sea-board and Cornwallis' from the southward, when we were driven from Richmond and Charlottesville, and every member of my council fled from their houses, it was not the total destitution of means, but the mismanagement of them, which, in the querulous voice of the public, caused all our misfortunes. It ended, indeed, in the capture of the whole hostile force, but not till means were brought us by General Washington's army, and the French fleet and army. And although the legislature, who were personally intimate with both the means and measures, acquitted me with justice and thanks, yet General Lee has put all those imputations among the romances of his historical novel, for the amusement of credulous and uninquisitive readers. Not that I have seen the least disposition to censure you. On the contrary, your conduct on the attack of Washington has met the praises of every one, and your plan for regulars and militia, their approbation. But no campaign is as yet opened. No generals have yet an interest in shifting their own incompetence on you, no army agents their rogueries. I sincerely pray you may never meet censure where you will deserve most praise, and that your own happiness and prosperity many be the result of your patriotic services."

39. THOMAS JEFFERSON TO THE MARQUIS DE LAFAYETTE MAY 14, 1817

"Nor is the election of Monroe an inefficient circumstance in our felicities. Four and twenty years, which he will accomplish, of administration in republican forms and principles, will so consecrate them in the eyes of the people as to secure them against the danger of change. The evanition of party dissensions has harmonized intercourse, and sweetened society beyond the imagination."

40. THOMAS JEFFERSON TO NATHANIAL MACON JANUARY 12, 1819

"I have had, and still have, such entire confidence in the late and present Presidents, that I willingly put both soul and body into their pockets. While such men as yourself and your worthy colleagues of the legislature, and such characters as compose the executive administration, are watching for us all, I slumber without fear, and review in my dreams the visions of antiquity."

41. THOMAS JEFFERSON TO JAMES MONROE JANUARY 18, 1819

"While on the subject of this correspondence, I will presume also to suggest to Mr. [John Quincy] Adams the question of whether he should not send back Onis's letters in which he has the impudence to qualify you by the term 'his Excellency'? An American gentleman in Europe can rank with the first nobility because we have no titles which stick him at any particular place in their line. So the President of the US. under that designation ranks with Emperors and kings, but add Mr. Onis's courtesy of 'his Excellency' and he is then on a level with Mr. Onis himself, with the Governors of provinces and even of every petty fort in Europe, or the colonies."

42. THOMAS JEFFERSON TO JAMES MONROE FEBRUARY 21, 1823

"I had had great hopes that while in your present office you would break up the degrading practice of considering the President's house as a general tavern and economise sffly to come out of it clear of difficulties. I learn the contrary with great regret. Your society during the little time I have left would have been the chief comfort of my life. Of the 3. portions into which you have laid off your lands here, I will not yet despair but that you may retain that on which your house stands. Perhaps you may be able to make an equivalent partial sale in Loudon before you can compleat one here...You have had some difficulties and contradiction to struggle with in the course of your admn but you will come out of them with honor and with the affections of your country. Mine to you have been & ever will be constant and warm."

43. THOMAS JEFFERSON TO JAMES MONROE FEBRUARY 22, 1826

"Your favor of the 13th was received yesterday. Your use of my letter with the alterns subsequently proposed, needs no apology. And it will be a gratifn to me if it can be of any service to you. I learn with sincere affection the difficulties with which you have still to struggle. Mine are considble, but the single permission given me by the legislature of such a mode of sale as ensures a fair value for what I must sell, will leave me still a competent provision. If sold under the hammer it must have been for whatever the bidder would gratuitously offer. For such a piece of property for example as my mills there could not have been two bona fide bidders in the state. A Virginia estate managed rigorously well yields a comfortable subsistence to it's owner living on it, but nothing more. But it runs him in debt annually if at a distance from him, if he is absent, if he is unskillful as I am, if short crops reduce him to deal on credit, and most assuredly if thunder struck from the hand of a friend as I was. Altho' all these causes conspired against me, and should have put me on my guard I had no suspicions until my grandson undertook the management of my estate and developed to me the state of my affairs, fortunately while yet retrievable in a comfortable degree. I hope they may prove to be so."

V. JAMES MADISON ON JAMES MONROE

1. JAMES MADISON TO JAMES MONROE NOVEMBER 1784

"DEAR SIR,—Your favor without date was brought by thursday's post. It inclosed a cypher, for which I thank you, and which I shall make use of as occasion may require, though, from the nature of our respective situations, its chief value will be derived from your use of it."

2. JAMES MADISON TO JAMES MONROE NOVEMBER 14, 1784

"DEAR SIR,—I had intended by this post to commence our correspondence with a narrative of what has been done and is proposed to be done at the present Session of the General Assembly, but, by your last letter to Mr. Jones, I find that it is very uncertain whether this will get to Trenton before you leave it for Virginia. I cannot, however, postpone my congratulations on your critical escape from the danger which lay in ambush for you, and your safe return to Trenton. My ramble extended neither into the dangers nor gratifications of yours. It was made extremely pleasing by sundry circumstances, but would have been more so, I assure you, Sir, if we had been contemporarys in the route we both passed."

3. JAMES MADISON TO JAMES MONROE MARCH 21, 1785

"You will not be disappointed at the barrenness which is hence to mark the correspondence on my part. In the recess of the Legislature, few occurrences happen which can be interesting, and in my retired situation, few even of these fall within my knowledge."

4. JAMES MADISON TO JAMES MONROE APRIL 12, 1785

"I wish much to throw our correspondence into a more regular course. I would write regularly every week if I had a regular conveyance to Fredericksburg. As it is I will write as often as I can find conveyances."

5. JAMES MADISON TO THOMAS JEFFERSON AUGUST 20, 1785
"I am invited by Col. Monroe to an option of rambles this fall, one of which is into the Eastern States. I wish much to accept so favorable an opportunity of executing the plan from which I was diverted last fall, but cannot decide with certainty whether it will be practicable or not."

6. JAMES MADISON TO THOMAS JEFFERSON OCTOBER 3, 1785
"Col. Monroe had left Philadelphia a few days before I reached it, on his way to a treaty to be held with the Indians about the end of this month on the Wabash. If a visit to the Eastern States had been his choice, short as the time would have proved, I should have made an effort to attend him. As it is, I must postpone that gratification, with a purpose, however, of embracing it on the first convenient opportunity."

7. JAMES MADISON TO JAMES MONROE AUGUST 17, 1786
"Your knowledge of all circumstances will make you a better judge of the solidity or fallacy of these reflections than I can be. I do not extend them because it would be superfluous, as well as because it might lead to details which could not prudently be committed to the mail without the guard of a cypher. Not forseeing that any confidential communication on *paper* would happen between us during my absence from Virginia, I did not bring mine with me."

8. JAMES MADISON TO JAMES MONROE MARCH 19, 1786
"A newspaper since the date of the latter has verified to me your inauguration into the mysteries of Wedlock, of which you dropped a previous hint in the former. You will accept my sincerest congratulations on this event, with every wish for the happiness it promises."

9. JAMES MADISON TO JAMES MONROE MARCH 19, 1786
"I join you cheerfully in the purchase from Taylor, as preferably to taking it wholly to myself. The only circumstance I regret is that the first payment will rest with you alone, if the conveyance should be accelerated. A few months will elapse inevitably before I shall be able to place on the spot my half of the sum but the day shall be shortened as much as possible. I accede also fully to your idea of extending the purchase in that

quarter. Perhaps we may be able to go beyond the thousand acres you have taken into view. But ought we not to explore the ground before we venture too far? Proximity of the situation is but presumptive evidence of the quality of soil. The value of land depends on a variety of little circumstances which can only be judged of from inspection, and a knowledge of which gives a seller an undue advantage over an uninformed buyer. Can we not about the last of May or June take a turn into that district, I am in a manner determined on it myself. It will separate you but for a moment from New York, and may give us lights of great consequence. I have a project in my head which if it hits your idea and can be effected may render such an excursion of decisive value to us I reserve it for oral communication."

10. JAMES MADISON TO THOMAS JEFFERSON MAY 12, 1786

"Monroe lost his election in King George by 6 votes."

11. JAMES MADISON TO JAMES MONROE MAY 13, 1786

"The encouragement you give me to expect your company has in a manner determined me to encounter a journey as soon as I can conveniently make preparation for it. I am the rather induced to do it as I shall be the more able by that means to accelerate a repayment of your kind advances, having some little resources in Philadelphia of which I must avail myself for that purpose. My next will probably tell you when I shall be able to set out."

12. JAMES MADISON TO JAMES MONROE MAY 13, 1786

"Great changes have taken place in the late elections. I regret much that we are not to have your aid. It will be greatly needed I am sure. Mercer it seems lost his election by the same number of votes as left you out."

13. JAMES MADISON TO JAMES MONROE JUNE 4, 1786

"DEAR SIR,—At the date of my last I expected I should by this time have been on the journey which promises the pleasure of taking you by the hand in New York. Several circumstances have produced a delay in my setting out which I did not calculate upon, and which are like to continue it for eight or ten days to come."

14. JAMES MADISON TO THOMAS JEFFERSON AUGUST 12, 1786

"My trip to N[ew] Y[ork] was occasioned chiefly by a plan concerted between Col. Monroe & myself for a purchase of land on the Mohawk. Both of us have visited that district and were equally charmed with it."

15. JAMES MADISON TO JAMES MONROE OCTOBER 5, 1786

"I fear I shall be obliged to accept of your very friendly procrastination of the repayment which ought long ago to have been made. The disappointments which have prevented it, contribute to my delay here at this time, and will together with a vicarious business which I have undertaken for a particular friend, probably spin it out a few days longer."

16. JAMES MADISON TO JAMES MONROE APRIL 19, 1787

"I hear with great pleasure that you are to aid the deliberations of the next Assembly, and with much concern that paper money will probably be among the bad measures which you will have to battle. Wishing you success in this and all your other labours for the public and for yourself. . .".

17. JAMES MADISON TO THOMAS JEFFERSON APRIL 22, 1788

"Monroe is considered by some as an enemy [of the Constitution]; but I believe him to be a friend though a cool one."

18. EXCERPT FROM JAMES MADISON'S *POWER TO LAY TAXES* JUNE 11, 1788

"My honorable friend, over the way [Mr. Monroe] yesterday, seemed to conceive, as an insuperable objection, that if land were made the particular object of taxation, it would be unjust, as it would exonerate the commercial part of the community—that if it were laid on trade, it would be unjust in discharging the landholders; and that any exclusive selection of it would be unequal and unfair."

---

19. JAMES MADISON TO GEORGE WASHINGTON JANUARY 14, 1789

"I fear, from the vague accounts which circulate, that the federal candidates are likely to stand in the way of one another. This is not the case however in my district. The field is left entirely to Monroe & myself. The event of our competition will probably depend on the part to be taken by two or three descriptions of people, whose decision is not known, if not yet to be ultimately formed."

---

20. JAMES MADISON TO THOMAS JEFFERSON MARCH 29, 1789

"It was my misfortune to be thrown into a contest with our friend, Col. Monroe. The occasion produced considerable efforts among our respective friends. Between ourselves, I have no reason to doubt that the distinction was duly kept in mind between political and personal views, and that it has saved our friendship from the smallest diminution. On one side I am sure it is the case."

---

21. JAMES MADISON TO EDMUND RANDOLPH JULY 15, 1789

"I am glad to find you concurring in the decision as to the power of removal. It seems to meet with general approbation North of Virginia, and there, too, as far as I yet learn. Mr. Pendleton is fully in opinion with you. So is Monroe, I am *told.*"

---

22. JAMES MADISON TO THOMAS JEFFERSON JUNE 12, 1792

"Monroe and his lady left us on Wednesday, on their way home. He is to meet the revisors at Richmond about the 15th. I understood Mrs. M. was to be added to the family at Monticello during his absence."

---

23. JAMES MADISON TO THOMAS JEFFERSON AUGUST 20, 1793

"I am just setting off to Monroe's, and hope to prevent the trouble of an express from Monticello with the letter referred to in it. I have already acquainted you with the immediate object of this visit. I have just received a line from him expressing a particular desire to communicate with me, and reminding me that he sets off the last of the month for the Courts, and of course will be occupied for some days before with preparations. This hurries me."

24. JAMES MADISON TO THOMAS JEFFERSON SEPTEMBER 2, 1793

"Monroe is particularly solicitous that you should take the view of your present position and opportunities above suggested. He sees so forcibly the difficulty of keeping the feelings of the people as to Genèt distinct from those due to his constituents, that he can hardly prevail on himself, absolutely and *openly*, to abandon him. I concur with him that it ought to be done no farther than is forced upon us; that general silence is better than open denunciation and crimination;"

25. JAMES MADISON TO JAMES MONROE OCTOBER 29, 1793

"I send the little balance of tea due Mrs. Monroe, which I intended, but failed, to procure before my late trip. As you are becoming a worshiper of Ceres, I add an ear of corn, which is forwarder, by three weeks, than the ordinary sort, and if given to your overseer, may supply a seasonable dish on your return next summer. Mr. Jefferson is so delighted with it, that he not only requested me to forward some to Mr. Randolph, but took an ear with him, to be brought back on his return, that there might be no possible disappointment. Should you have an opportunity, after you know the day of your setting out, be so good as to drop me a notice of it. My compliments to Mrs. Monroe."

26. JAMES MADISON TO THOMAS JEFFERSON JUNE 1, 1794

"Col. Monroe is busy in preparing for his embarkation. He is puzzled as to the mode of getting to France. He leans towards an American vessel, which is to sail for Baltimore for Amsterdam. A direct passage to France is scarcely to be had, and is incumbered with the risk of being captured and carried to England."

27. JAMES MADISON TO THOMAS JEFFERSON NOVEMBER 16, 1794

"Not a line, official or private, from Monroe. His enthusiastic reception you will have seen."

28. JAMES MADISON TO JAMES MONROE DECEMBER 4, 1794

"The account of your arrival [to France] and reception had some time ago found its way to us thro' the English Gazettes. The language of your address to the Convention was certainly very grating to the ears of many here; and would no doubt have employed the tongues and the pens too of some of them, if external as well as internal circumstances had not checked them; but more particularly, the appearance about the same time of the Presidents letter and those of the Secretary of State."

29. JAMES MADISON TO JAMES MONROE DECEMBER 4, 1794

"When in Albemarle last fall I visited your farm along with Mr. Jefferson, and viewed the sites out of which a choice is to be made for your house. The one preferred by us is that which we favored originally on the East side of the road, near the field not long since opened. All that could be suggested way of preparation was, that trees be planted promiscuously & pretty thickly in the field adjoining the wood. In general your farm appeared to be as well as was to be expected. Your upper farm I did not see, being limited in my stay in that quarter."

30. JAMES MADISON TO THOMAS JEFFERSON MARCH 23, 1795

"We have no private letters from Monroe. His last public ones were no later than November. They contained a history of the Jacobin clubs, in the form of an apology for the Convention. Extracts on that subject were immediately put into the newspapers, and are applied to party purposes generally, particularly in New York, where the election of Governor is on the anvil."

31. JAMES MADISON TO JAMES MONROE MARCH 26, 1795

"From as near a view as I have yet been able to take of your letter to Mr. R[andolph], I see no reason why I should hesitate to deliver it. I cannot forbear believing that the Report of stipulations, offensive and defensive, is quite without foundation; but your view of things, on the contrary supposition, involves a variety of interesting ideas; and your communications and reflections in general with regard to the Treaty, as proceeding from one in your position and of your sentiments, merit too much attention in the Executive Department to be withheld altogether from it."

32. JAMES MADISON TO THOMAS JEFFERSON JANUARY 10, 1796

"I have letters from Col. Monroe of the 23 and 24 of October. His picture of the affairs of France, particularly of the prospect exhibited in the approaching establishment of the Constitution, is very favorable. This, as far as we know, has had an easy birth, and wears a promising countenance. He had not learnt with certainty the ratification of the Treaty by the President, but wrote under the belief of it. His regrets, and his apprehensions, were as strong as might be expected."

33. JAMES MADISON TO JAMES MONROE FEBRUARY 26, 1796

"It has been whispered that you are to be recalled, and Bingham to replace you. I entirely disbelieve it; but the whisper marks the wishes of those who propagate it."

34. JAMES MADISON TO JAMES MONROE APRIL 7, 1796

"Some of your enemies here have been base enough to throw into circulation insinuations that you have launched into all the depths of speculation. It has even been propagated that you and [Fulwar] Skipwith, or perhaps you, through Skipwith, had purchased Chantilly, the magnificent estate of the late Prince of Condé. I was joined by others of your friends in the roundest contradictions of such malicious reports, and in explaining the incredibility and palpable falsehood of them. Having heard nothing latterly on the subject, I concluded that the antidote has effectually destroyed the poison. I understand, however, that the circumstance of the money of which you were robbed, and which is said ought to have gone long before to Amsterdam, where the public faith was violated by the delay, is a topic of unfavorable conversation within the Treasury Department and in unfriendly circles. If you ever wrote any thing to me on the subject, it has totally miscarried. The first account I had of it was very lately, from Mr. Swan, who threw the whole blame on Skipwith, who was charged with the operation of remitting the money to Holland. I am not apprehensive that any impressions can be entertained, even among your enemies in the Cabinet, of anything more than incaution on your part; I am sure that nothing beyond that can be impressed on others. In the mean time, it is right you should know every handle that can be taken against you. It continues to be the suspicion of some that the Cabinet meditates your recall, and, of course, that they may possible lay hold of the slightest pretext. I retain my opinion that such a step will never be hazarded on a slight pretext, and, consequently, that it will never be hazarded at all."

35. JAMES MADISON TO THOMAS JEFFERSON JANUARY 8, 1797

"Not a word from Monroe, or any other quarter, relating to his recall, or enabling us to judge on the question whether Pinckney will be received. We wait with anxiety for the light that will probably be thrown on the first point by the expected communication."

36. JAMES MADISON TO THOMAS JEFFERSON DECEMBER 25, 1797

"The attack on Monroe's publication evidently issues from, or is aided by, an official source, and is a proof that the latter bites.[120] I have not yet seen a copy of it, and was astonished to learn in Richmond, where I passed a day, that a single copy only had reached that place, which, from the length of it, not more than two or three persons had read. By them it was said, that if this did not open the eyes of the people, their blindness must be incurable. If a sufficient number of copies do not arrive there before the adjournment of the Assembly, the only opportunity of circulating the information in this State will be lost for a year, that it, till the subject has lost its flavor. The enormous price, also, was complained of, as a probable obstacle to an extensive circulation."

37. JAMES MADISON TO JAMES MONROE FEBRUARY 5, 1798

"DEAR SIR,—The calls of my carpenters, and the fineness of the weather, have induced me to hurry my wagon up for the nails. It will receive the few articles which you have been so good as to offer from the superfluities of your stock, and which circumstances will permit me now to lay in; to wit, Two table cloths for a dining-room of about 18 feet; two, or three, or four, as may be convenient, for a more limited scale; four dozen napkins; and two

120 Madison is referring to Monroe's book, *A View of the Conduct of the Executive in the Foreign Affairs of the United States* (1797).

mattresses. We are so little acquainted with the culinary utensils in detail, that it is difficult to refer to such by name or description as would be within our wants. We conclude it best, therefore, not to interfere with any opportunity you may have of gratifying your other friends, and to reserve our demands on your kindness till we can have the pleasure of seeing you, as well as have it in our power to compare the undisposed-of remains with our probable wants."

38. JAMES MADISON TO JAMES MONROE FEBRUARY 5, 1798

"Calling to mind the difficulty you may experience from the general failure of the potato crop last year, I beg you to accept by the bearer a couple of bushels, which may furnish the seed for your garden, if nothing more. Mrs. Madison insists on adding for Mrs. Monroe a few pickles and preserves, with half a dozen bottles of gooseberries and a bag of dried cherries, which will not be wanted by us till another season will afford a supply, and which the time of your return home must have deprived her of, as the fruit of the last season. We both wish we could substitute something more worthy of acceptance."

39. JAMES MADISON TO THOMAS JEFFERSON FEBRUARY 12, 1798

"I was astonished to find that even Monroe himself had not yet seen a printed copy of his publication. In the mean time, Scipio's misrepresentations and sophistries are filling the public mind with all the poison which [Timpthy] P[ickering]'s malice can distil into it. Where the book is not seen first, and an antidote does not quickly follow from the same centre which gives circulation to the poison, innocence and truth cannot have fair play."

40. JAMES MADISON TO JAMES MONROE JUNE 9, 1798

"The sortie of Mr. [John] Adams presents, as you observe, more difficult questions. On one hand, silence may beget misconstructions from opposite quarters. On the other, it is not easy to find an objectionable, and at the same time adequate mode of repelling the aggression. A *repetition* of your demand for the reasons of your recall does not appear eligible after what has passed on that subject, though it must be owned the ground taken by Pickering is materially changed by the language of Mr. Adams. Any summons of a personal nature on Mr. Adams is, I think, forbidden by the considerations you have glanced at. Nor is it, perhaps, unworthy of consideration, that in the present composition and spirit of the two Houses anything like an occasion may be seized for wreaking party revenge through the forms of the Constitution. It is even possible that the fury of the moment may have suggested the unwarrantable attack as a snare that might answer the purpose. Whatever difficulties might obstruct such a proceeding, they would probably be got over by the same spirit which is overleaping so many others.

If the case admits of any formal interposition on your part, it would seem to be in the way of a temperate and dignified animadversion, published with your name on it. In such a publication there would be room for such ideas relative to yourself as justice to yourself might render eligible, and also for such relative to Mr. Adams as prudence would permit. This is an idea, however, that has perhaps rather grown out of the difficulties of the case than is recommended by its own merit. You will be able to decide on it with more deliberation than I have bestowed on it."

41. JAMES MADISON TO THOMAS JEFFERSON JUNE 10, 1798

"Monroe is much at a loss what course to take in consequence of the wicked assault on him by Mr. A., and I am as much so as to the advice that ought to be given him. It deserves consideration, perhaps, that if the least occasion be furnished for reviving Governmental attention to him, the spirit of party revenge may be wreaked thro' the forms of the Constitution. A majority in the H. of R. and 2/3 of the Senate seem to be ripe for everything. A temperate and dignified animadversion on the proceeding, published with his name, as an appeal to the candor and justice of his fellow-citizens against the wanton and unmanly treatment, might, perhaps, be of use. But it would be difficult to execute it in a manner to do justice to himself, and inflict it on his adversary, without clashing with the temper of the moment."

42. JAMES MADISON TO CHARLES PINCKNEY JANUARY 18, 1803

"In these debates, as well as in indications from the press, you will perceive, as you would readily suppose, that the Cession of Louisiana to France has been associated as a ground of much solicitude, with the affair at New Orleans. Such indeed has been the impulse given to the public mind by these events, that every branch of the Government has felt the obligation of taking the measures most likely, not only to re-establish our present rights, but to promote arrangements by which they may be enlarge and more effectually secured. In deliberating on this subject, it has appeared to the President, that the importance of the crisis, called for the experiment of and Extraordinary Mission, carrying with it the weight attached to such a measure, as well as the advantage of a more thorough knowledge of the views of the Government and the sensibility of the public, than could be otherwise conveyed. He has accordingly selected for this service, with the approbation of the Senate Mr. Monroe formerly our Minister Plenipotentiary at Paris, and lastly Governor of the State of Virginia, who will be joined with Mr. Livingston in a Commission extraordinary to treat with the French Republic, and with yourself in a like Commission, to treat, if necessary with the Spanish Government."

43. JAMES MADISON TO JAMES MONROE MARCH 10, 1806

"I fear you will have considered me as a delinquent in my correspondence, but it is an appearance I could not possible avoid. For the last year, especially the last 5 or 6 months, the weight of business has almost broke me down, and robbed me of every leisure for writing to my friends, even where public considerations, as well as private inclination, recommended it. I beg you to be assured that the privation could in no case be more sincerely regretted than it has been in yours; that I feel myself much indebted for the numerous private communications I have received from you; and that, with the united regards of Mrs. M. and myself for you and Mrs. Monroe, I remain, dear sir."

44. JAMES MADISON TO JAMES MONROE MARCH 20, 1807

"The President and all of us are fully impressed with the difficulties which your negociation had to contend with, as well as with the faithfulness and ability with which it was supported, and are as ready to suppose, in as far as there may be variance in our respective view of things, that in your position we should have had yours, as that, in our position, you would have ours. What may be the effect of further efforts in another form, or on other grounds, if these can be devised, remains to be seen. The President has, doubtless, given you to understand as well the choice left you as to a participation in these efforts, as the satisfaction which will be felt in case your arrangements admit your stay for the purpose. If he has been silent, it is because he assures himself that his sentiments cannot be misconstrued by you. The uncertainty whether you may not have carried into effect the purpose intimated in your private letter by Mr. P., before this reaches London, concurs with the urgency of the opportunity in rendering it shorter than it would be otherwise."

45. JAMES MADISON TO THOMAS JEFFERSON DECEMBER 11, 1809

"The state of Col. Monroe's mind is very nearly what I had supposed. His willingness to have taken a seat in the Cabinet is what I had not supposed."

46. JAMES MADISON TO THOMAS JEFFERSON APRIL 1, 1811

"You will have inferred the change which is taking place in the Department of State. Col. Monroe agrees to succeed Mr. Smith, who declines however the mission to Russia, at first not unfavorably looked at. I was willing, notwithstanding many trying circumstances, to have smoothed the transaction as much as possible, but it will be pretty sure to end in secret hostility, if not open warfare. On account of my great esteem & regard for common friends such a result is truly painful to me. For the rest, I feel myself on firm ground, as well in the public opinion as in my own consciousness."

47. JAMES MADISON TO JAMES MONROE MARCH 31, 1811

"I am particularly glad to find that you will be able to set out at so early a day for Washington. To the advantage of preventing an inconvenient chasm in the public business, will be added the opportunity of a provident attention to the accommodations required by your establishment here. The House occupied by Mr. Smith is the best in the place, and I believe is not yet out of reach. He means also to dispose of certain portions of his furniture which might suit your purpose. These considerations taken together recommend strongly that you should not wait for the receipt of your commission, but consider what has passed between us, as sufficient ground for a communication to the council. The actual receipt of the commission cannot be a necessary preliminary. As well as I recollect I did not receive mine, as Secretary of State till it was handed to me on the spot, by Mr. Jefferson. In case of appointments at a great distance, it might be extremely inconvenient for any other course to be observed. It is the more desirable that you should not wait for your commission, as I find that it will be tuesday morning before its date will be consistent with the understanding & arrangement here, & that your arrival would of consequence be thrown forward till the beginning of the next week. I might indeed, as the law authorizes, provide an interim Functionary, for the current business requiring his signature, & not admitting delay; but there are objections to this resort where it can be avoided. I hope therefore you will find no difficulty in the mode of anticipation recommended; the more especially as your communication to the council may be delayed till tuesday morning the time proposed for your setting out, and at which time your commission will have been formally consummated, & ready to be delivered."

-⁂-

48. JAMES MADISON TO JOHN GRAHAM AUGUST 28, 1813

"I am very sorry to hear of the indisposition of Col. Monroe. I hope it will be found to justify the term *slight* which you apply to it."

-⁂-

49. EXCERPT FROM A MEMORANDUM WRITTEN BY PRESIDENT JAMES MADISON AUGUST 29, 1814

". . . I had within a few hours received a message from the commanding General of the Militia informing me that every officer would tear off his epauletts if General [John] Armstrong was to have anything to do with them; that before his arrival there was less difficulty, as Mr. Monroe who was very acceptable to them, had, as on preceding occasions of his absence, though very reluctantly on this, been the medium for the functions of Secretary of War, but that since his return and presence the expedient could not be continued, and the question was, what was best to be done."

-⁂-

50. JAMES MADISON TO MR. DALLAS SEPTEMBER 27, 1816

"Mr. Clay declines the War Department. The task now to be fulfilled is not without its delicacies, as you know. I shall avail myself of a conversation with Mr. Monroe, which his journey back to Washington will afford me in a day or two. I could wish for a similar opportunity with others, whose sentiments would be valuable on the occasion."

-⁂-

51. JAMES MADISON TO JAMES MONROE AUGUST 22, 1817

"DEAR SIR,—Your favor of July 27, from Pittsburg, was duly received, and I am very glad to learn from it that the fatiguing scenes through which you have passed had not prevented some improvement in your health. The sequel of your journey will have been still more friendly to it, as affording a larger proportion of the salutary part of your exercise. I hope you will find an ample reward for all the inconveniences to which you have been subjected in the public benefit resulting from your tour. The harmony of sentiment so extensively manifested will give strength to the Administration at home, and command abroad additional respect for our Country and its institutions. The little vagaries which have excited criticism, whether proceeding from the fervor of patriotism or from selfish views, are light in the scale against the consideration that an opportunity has been given and seized for a return to the national family of the prodigal part which had been seduced from it, and for such a commitment of the seducers themselves, that they cannot resume their opposition to the Government without a public demonstration that their conversion was inspired by the mere hope of sharing in the loaves and fishes."

52. JAMES MADISON TO JOHN GRAHAM 1817

"The friendship which has long subsisted between the President of the United States [Monroe] and myself gave me reason to expect, on my retirement from office, that I might often receive applications to interpose with him on behalf of persons desiring appointments. Such an abuse of his dispositions towards me would necessarily lead to the loss of them, and to the transforming me from the character of a friend to that of an unreasonable and troublesome solicitant. It therefore became necessary for me to lay down as a law for my future conduct never to interpose in any case, either with him of the Heads of Departments (from whom it must go to him) in any case whatever for office."

53. JAMES MADISON TO JAMES MONROE NOVEMBER 29, 1817

"Your favor of the 24th. has just been received. I am fully aware of the load of business on your hands preparatory to the meeting of Congress. The course you mean to take in relation to Roads & Canals, appears to be best adapted to the posture in which you find the case."

54. JAMES MADISON TO JAMES MONROE DECEMBER 9, 1817

"DEAR SIR,—The mail of Saturday brought me the Copy of your message. It is a fine landscape of your situation; and cannot fail to give pleasure at home, and command respect abroad."

55. JAMES MADISON TO JAMES MONROE DECEMBER 27, 1817

"DEAR SIR,—Your favor of the 22d has been duly received. I am so much aware that you have not a moment to spare from your public duties, that I insist on your never answering my letters out of mere civility. This rule I hope will be applied to the present as well as future letters."

56. JAMES MADISON TO RICHARD RUSH MAY 10, 1817

"The P[resident] is executing the Southern half of his projected tour, and is every where greeted with Public testimonies of affection & confidence. Whatever may be the motives of some who join in the acclamations the unanimity, will have the good effect of strengthening the administration at home and inspiring respect abroad."

57. JAMES MADISON TO JAMES MONROE MAY 21, 1818

"I hope you will dispose of yourself during the summer in the manner most friendly to your health. As nature does less for us, we should take more care of ourselves. We shall count, of course, on the pleasure of seeing you all in your transits between Washington and Albemarle, if the latter, as we presume will be the case, should be the scene of your relaxations."

58. JAMES MADISON TO JAMES MONROE NOVEMBER 19, 1820

"The view you have taken of our public affairs cannot but be well received at home, and increase our importance abroad. The state of our finances is the more gratifying, as it so far exceeds the public hopes."

59. JAMES MADISON TO JAMES MONROE MAY 6, 1822

"DEAR SIR,--This will probably arrive at the moment for congratulating you on the close of the scene in which your labours are blended with those of Congress. When will your recess from those which succeed commence, and when and how much of it will be passed in Albemarle? We hope for the pleasure of halts with us, and that Mrs. M. and others of your family will be with us."

60. JAMES MADISON TO JAMES MONROE AUGUST 5, 1824

"We had looked for the greater pleasure of giving a welcome about this time to you and Mrs. Monroe, being informed from Albemarle that you were to be there in a few days. We are very sorry for the uncertainty you intimate, but still hope that Mrs. Monroe's health will not only permit you to make the journey, but her to join you in it. It could not fail to be beneficial to both; and you owe it to yourself as well as to your friends to take some repose with them after the vexations which have beset you. Come, I pray you, and be not in your usual hurry."

61. JAMES MADISON TO JAMES MONROE DECEMBER 16, 1824

"The effect of the delay in your receiving your outfit, in occasioning the sale of your land near Charlottesville, is a subject of peculiar regret. It is difficult to estimate the sacrifice when the price obtained is compared with the value given to the property by the subsequent establishment of the University at the spot."

62. JAMES MADISON TO JAMES MONROE JANUARY 23, 1828

"You were not more surprised than I had a right to be at seeing our names on the electoral ticket. After my letter to you, which you made known to Col. Mercer, I wrote to Mr. Cabell in the most *decided* terms; and he informs me he made the proper use of it. I have a letter from Col. Mercer also, corresponding, doubtless, with his to you. The awkwardness thrown upon us is much increased by the delay in giving regular notice. To anticipate it might mark an unsuitable feeling of one sort, as well as censure on the delay. To be silent too long leaves room for inferences of another sort, also to be avoided. The latter effect will, however, be corrected by our answers, which seem to be sufficiently foretold, whilst there would be no opportunity of doing away with the former."

63. JAMES MADISON TO GENERAL LA FAYETTE FEBRUARY 20, 1828

"In the zeal of party, a large and highly respectable meeting at Richmond, in recommending Presidential electors, were led by a misjudging policy to put on their tickets the names of Mr. Monroe and myself, not only without our sanction, but on sufficient presumptions that they would be withdrawn. In my answer to that effect, I have ventured to throw in a dehortation from the violent manner in which the contest is carried on. How it may be relished by the parties I know not."

-⁂-

64. JAMES MADISON TO JAMES MONROE FEBRUARY 26, 1828

"The course pursued has been misjudged, and will probably receive adversary comments proving it to be so. To us it has been particularly unpleasant from the awkward position into which it threw us before the public, and from the task, delicate as troublesome, of answering friendly letters addressed to us on the occasion. It may happen, too, that our public answers are not to escape newspaper remarks, for which neither of us has any appetite."

-⁂-

65. JAMES MADISON TO JAMES MONROE MAY 18, 1830

"We had been led to hope that your health was better re-established than you represent it. As it is progressive, and your constitution, though, like mine, the worse for wear, has remains of good stamina, I will not despair of the pleasure of seeing you in July, and of making our visit together to the University. Should prudence forbid such a journey, I think you ought not to resign the trust. It is probable there will be a quorum without you, and I would prefer the risk of failure to a loss of your name and your future aid. I should myself resign, but for considerations belonging to you as well as myself. I do not think your weakness, unless positively disabling you for the journey, should deter you from it. The moderate exercise in a carriage and a change of air, with a cheerful meeting with your friends, may stimulate your convalescence. You have heretofore found the experiment beneficial."

-⁂-

66. JAMES MADISON TO JAMES MONROE APRIL 21, 1831

"I considered the advertisement of your estate in Loudon as an omen that your friends in Virginia were to lose you. It is impossible to gainsay the motives to which you yielded in making N. York your residence, though I fear you will find its climate unsuited to your period of life and the state of your health. I just observe, and with much pleasure, that the sum voted by Congress, however short of just calculations, escapes the loppings to which it was exposed from the accounting process at Washington, and that you are so far relieved from the vexations involved in it. The result will, I hope, spare you at least the sacrifice of an untimely sale of your valuable property; and I would fain flatter myself, that with an encouraging improvement of your health, you might be brought to reconsider the arrangement which fixes you elsewhere. The effect of this, in closing the prospect of our ever meeting again, afflicts me deeply; certainly not less so than it can you. The pain I feel at the idea, associated as it is with a recollection of the long, close, and uninterrupted friendship which united us, amounts to a pang which I cannot well express, and which makes me seek for an alleviation in the possibility that you may be brought back to us in the wonted degree of intercourse. This is a happiness my feelings covet, notwithstanding the short period I could expect to enjoy it; being now, though in comfortable health, a decade beyond the canonical three-score-and-ten, an epoch which you have by just passed. As you propose to make a visit to Loudon previous to the notified sale, if the state of your health permits, why not, with the like permission, extend the trip to this quarter? The journey, at a rate of your own choice, might co-operate in the re-establishment of your health, whilst it would be a peculiar gratification to your friends, and, perhaps, enable you to join your colleagues at the University once more at least. It is much to be desired that you should continue, as long as possible, a member of the Board, and I hope you will not send in your resignation in case you find your cough and weakness giving way to the influence of the season and the innate strength of your constitution. I will not despair of your being able to keep up your connexion with Virginia by retaining Oak Hill and making it not less than an occasional residence. Whatever may be the turn of things, be assured of the unchangeable interest felt by Mrs. M, as well as myself, in your welfare, and in that of all who are dearest to you."

67. JAMES MADISON TO JOHN W. FRANCIS JULY 9, 1831

"DEAR SIR,—Your favor of the 4th, communicating the death of Mr. Monroe, was duly received. I had been prepared for the event, by information of its certain approach. The time of it was so far happy, as it added another to the coincidences before so remarkable and so memorable. You have justly ranked him with the heroes and patriots who have deserved best of their country. No one knew him better than I did, or had a sincerer affection for him, or condoles mire deeply with those to whom he was most dear."

68. JAMES MADISON TO ALEXANDER HAMILTON, JR. JULY 9, 1831

"DEAR SIR,—Your letter of June 30 was duly received, and the death of Mr. Monroe, which it anticipated, became, I learn, a sad reality on the 4th instant, its date associating it with the coincidences before so remarkable and so memorable.

The feelings with which the event was received by me may be inferred from the long and uninterrupted friendship which united us, and the intimate knowledge I had of his great public merits, and his endearing private virtues. I condole in his loss most deeply with those to whom he was most dear. We may cherish the consolation, nevertheless, that his memory, like that of the other heroic worthies of the Revolution gone before him, will be embalmed in the grateful affections of a posterity enjoying the blessings which he contributed to procure for it."

69. JAMES MADISON TO TENCH RINGGOLD JULY 12, 1831

"DEAR SIR,—I received in the due times your two favors of July 7 and 8, the first giving the earliest, the last the fullest account that reached me of the death of our excellent friend; and I cannot acknowledge these communications without adding the thanks which I owe, in common with those to whom he was most dear, for the devoted kindness on your part during the lingering illness which he could not survive.

I need not say to you, who so well know, how highly I rated the comprehensiveness and character of his mind; the purity and nobleness of his principles; the importance of his patriotic services; and the many private virtues of which his whole life was a model; nor how deeply, therefore, I must sympathize, on his loss, with those who feel it most. A close friendship, continued through so long a period and such diversified scenes, had grown into an affection very imperfectly expressed by that term; and I value accordingly the manifestation in his last hours that the reciprocity never abated."

70. JAMES MADISON TO JOHN QUINCY ADAMS SEPTEMBER 23, 1831

"J. M., with his best respects to Mr. Adams, thanks him for the copy of his eulogy on the life and character of James Monroe.

Not only must the friends of Mr. Monroe be gratified by the just and happy tribute paid to him memory; the historian, also, will be a debtor for the interesting materials and the eloquent samples of the use to be made of them which will be found in its pages."

VI. JOHN QUINCY ADAMS ON JAMES MONROE

1. JOHN QUINCY ADAMS TO JAMES MONROE NOVEMBER 22, 1794

"I am well assured, Sir, that your zeal for the interests of the United States in general, and for the security and efficacy of their rights to all your fellow citizens individually, is too ardent and active to be susceptible of any accession from my solicitations. It would therefore be unnecessary, though I hope it will not be improper for me to add, that in the particular instance upon which I now address you me feelings of private friendship coincide with my concern for the public welfare. That the gentlemen to whom the property was addressed and belonged are all personally known to me. That Mr. Gill is Lieutenant Governor of Massachusetts, and Messrs. Head and Amory are among the most respectable citizens in Boston, and that in recommending the case to your attention I follow the impulse of my inclination no less than the dictate of my duty.

I am happy, Sir, that this opportunity is given me to return you my best acknowledgments for you kind offer of a good understanding and correspondence between us, of which my father informed me at the time when I had the honor of being appointed to my present station. I should have notified you of my arrival here before this but for the interruption of the communication between France and this country, consequent upon the present state of affairs. When the regular intercourse shall again be restored I shall feel myself honored by a correspondence as frequent and considerable as my consist with propriety and the public service."

2. AN EXCERPT FROM THE DIARY OF JOHN QUINCY ADAMS JANUARY 22, 1795

"They spoke of Mr. Monroe's reception by the National Convention. 'Parbleu,' said one, 'it was a scène attendrissante.' It was '*une des plus fameuses séances*' of the Convention. There were more than ten thousand persons present. 'He shed tears, he was so much affected. I saw him cry.' 'Ah!' said another, 'ç'était aussi bien de quoi faire pleurer.'[121] Then they said one of the flags had been sent to America. In short, the national character appeared in nothing more conspicuous than in the manner in which they spoke of this occurrence."

121 Translation: "It was a touching scene. It was one of the most famous parts of the Convention." "It was so good it could make you cry."

3. JOHN QUINCY ADAMS TO JOHN ADAMS FEBRUARY 12, 1795

"The apartments of the Princess of Orange are occupied by the Commissaries of the National Convention, who are styled the Representatives of the French people. They received the visit from the Minister of the United States at Amsterdam, where he happened to be at the time of their arrival. They assure him that they considered it altogether as a fraternal visit, and expressed themselves in terms of the utmost civility towards the United States, their President and Vice President. They appear to be well pleased with Mr. Monroe, but as to his predecessor, they spoke of [Gouverneur Morris] too, more than once."

4. JOHN QUINCY ADAMS TO JOHN ADAMS AUGUST 13, 1796

"They tell me of the *rage* of the French government at our treaty with Britain, of their *inflexible* determination to resent it by *some determined act*, of their *raising their tone* as they advance in victory, of the dreadful consequences to be apprehended from their resentments, and which nothing under Heaven can avert, unless it be peradventure the extreme prudence of Mr. Monroe in whom they have *very great confidence*."

5. JOHN QUINCY ADAMS TO TIMOTHY PICKERING NOVEMBER 16, 1796

"I understand that Mr. Monroe has received his recall. General Pinckney has not yet arrived."

6. JOHN QUINCY ADAMS TO RUFUS KING NOVEMBER 26, 1796

"Mr. Monroe, I have been informed, is very much incensed at his recall. I presume you have had occasion to observe the menacing tone which is attributed by some to the intentions of the French government. I hope and persuade myself that General Pinckney will be as far from encouraging or provoking any such disposition as his predecessor has been. I have been often assured, that Mr. Monroe enjoyed very highly the confidence of the Directory; that he had great personal influence with them, and was exceedingly beloved."

7. JOHN QUINCY ADAMS TO JOSEPH PITCAIRN DECEMBER 2, 1796

"I am glad to hear that Mr. Pinckney has arrived at Bordeaux and am anxious to hear what his reception will be at Paris. I had heard before receiving your letter that Mr. Monroe was highly incensed at his recall, and that the reception of his successor was to be questioned. Mr. Monroe's conduct in refusing to receive an address, dictated not by regard for him but by hostility to the government, is altogether honorable to him. I most cordially hope that he has recognized the character and views of those who have advised him with sentiments so deeply hostile to the American government."

8. JOHN QUINCY ADAMS TO DAVID HUMPHREYS DECEMBER 10, 1796

"Some of the Americans at Paris drew up and signed an address to Mr. Monroe, expressive of their thanks for his services and regret at his recall; others refused to sign it, and Mr. Monroe himself, aware of the real design which was proposed by this address, refused to receive it. He is, however, as I have heard, very much offended at his recall."

9. JOHN QUINCY ADAMS TO JOSEPH PITCAIRN DECEMBER 22, 1796

"With regard to Mr. Monroe, it is my wish and hope, that he too will not chose to place his dependence upon a state of separation and opposition to the government which he has represented; that he has always been the Minister of United America, and not the minister of particular interests and opinions. The present circumstances make it impossible not to consider this as a question, which is only to be decided by his future conduct."

10. JOHN QUINCY ADAMS TO JOSEPH PITCAIRN JANUARY 13, 1797

"What Mr. Monroe's opinion may be of personal compliments to him, coupled with scorn and indignity to his country and the Government which employed him, is not my business to inquire. I have hoped he would remember above all that he was an American, and as he boasts his military services against one nation, his hatred of which I believe nobody doubts, that he would not contribute to the servility of his own country towards another nation, however ardent his own attachment to its interests, or his inclination to gratify its will might be. It is very evident that the French government will do for him all that it can. I presume he is prepared to return the same for them. The Frenchmen who, as you observe, think he ought to have mentioned Mr. Pinckney's mission, do not perhaps reflect that it might have displeased the Directory. The reason is indeed not sufficient, but it might in that instance be effectual."

11. JOHN QUINCY ADAMS TO JOHN ADAMS JANUARY 14, 1797

"I have already written you an account of the refusal of the French Directory to receive Mr. Pinckney, and the apparent alliance between then and the internal enemies of the American government. But since my last letter Mr. Monroe has delivered his letters of recall, and upon that occasion made a speech which was answered by the President of the Directory, Barras. Mr. Monroe's address indicates what his language and conduct will be upon his return. The same unqualified devotion to the French will, which made him so confidential with Fauchet upon the parties within the United States before he set out upon his mission, has influenced him in this last transaction; and at the moment when a national indignity, outrageous as it was unprovoked, was offered to his country, he still condescends to flatter them, by an eulogy upon the *generous services*, which they themselves have long since publicly and officially declared to have been *merely the fruit of a vile speculation;* by a declaration as false as it is dishonorable to America, that the principles of their Revolution and of ours were the same; and by an ostentatious avowal of his partiality for the present cause of France, and all this without even hinting the mission of Mr. Pinckney, whose personal and patriotic merits are surely not inferior to his own."

12. JOHN QUINCY ADAMS TO JOHN ADAMS JANUARY 14, 1797

"During several months, if the concurring reports of many different persons may be believed, Mr. Monroe made no scruple or hesitation to say in public and mixed companies, that he had not the smallest doubt but Mr. Jay was bribed to sign the treaty, and to one person he added that *to his certain knowledge,* when Mr. Jay was employed to negotiate for our navigation of the Mississippi, he did in fact negotiate against it."

13. JOHN QUINCY ADAMS TO JOHN ADAMS FEBRUARY 7, 1797

"I saw Mr. Monroe almost every day while he was [at the Hague]. He conversed with me but little upon public affairs, and with great reserve particularly concerning our situation with France. His deportment evidently discovered an exasperated and strongly agitated mind, though his conversation was in every particular extremely guarded. He went from this place to Amsterdam, where he stayed only a few days, and from whence he very suddenly set out for Utrecht on his return to Paris, on the same day when news arrived here of the order to depart given to Mr. Pinckney."

14. JOHN QUINCY ADAMS TO JOHN ADAMS FEBRUARY 23, 1797

"DEAR SIR:

General Pinckney and his family have arrived at Amsterdam, but as I have not seen him I presume he did not pass through [the Hague]. On the other hand Mr. Monroe has arrived in Paris, upon his return from his tour through this country. What was the cause of Mr. Pinckney's being ordered to leave France is yet unknown. But the conduct of the French government and its dependents at the same time towards Mr. Monroe, and his conduct towards them, give me serious uneasiness. The views and designs which these circumstances seem to indicate are of a nature so important to the Constitution and even to the union of our country, that I cannot but feel anxious to discover how far they really extend, and cannot but observe with concern the apparent concert of an internal American party with the present government of France to overthrow that of the United States."

15. JOHN QUINCY ADAMS TO JOHN ADAMS MARCH 4, 1797

"The most unaccountable circumstance to me, in the present state of affairs, is the refusal to receive Mr. Pinckney, and the order given him to leave France, if as they pretend they do not mean an absolute rupture. The only manner in which I can explain it is by the supposition that they are trying to force the American government upon a reappointment of Mr. Monroe."

16. JOHN QUINCY ADAMS TO JOHN ADAMS MARCH 30, 1797

"It is said Mr. Monroe is upon the point of his departure to return home, and I understand that he has frequent interviews with the French Minister of Foreign Affairs. The report adds that he will charge himself with the terms which the Directory think proper to prescribe to the American government, and that among other proposals will be that of a loan by the United States to pay the debts of France to American citizens. I saw in a Philadelphia paper some time ago a piece of evidently Gallic composition and saying that there was nothing but water and milk in the veins of Americans! The Directory seem to entertain the same opinion."

17. JOHN QUINCY ADAMS TO JOHN ADAMS APRIL 3, 1797

"You will find in the newspapers which I send at this time, that Thomas Paine has left Paris, and is going to America. Another of the French papers says that he is going with Mr. Monroe 'to repair the mischief done by the administration of Washington.'"

18. JOHN QUINCY ADAMS TO JOHN ADAMS APRIL 3, 1797

"Paine indeed is pursuing his vocation. He has no country; no affections that constitute the pillars of patriotism. But going with Mr. Monroe—where can the imagination stop in reflecting upon these things? Can Monroe? Can — I have done. I remember the late President's advice not to admit hastily suspicions against the designs of citizens in distant parts of the Union, and I will yet hope that a formal purpose to sever the Union into two parts, by the help of a French war against the whole, is at least not extensively intended or known; and that it will never meet with encouragement or support from men, who *ought* to consider the Union as the principle paramount to all others in the policy of every American."

19. JOHN QUINCY ADAMS TO JOHN ADAMS APRIL 30, 1797

"Mr. Monroe has indeed enjoyed the favor of the French government constantly and to a very high degree. I have indeed been a little surprised to hear as coming from himself since his recall, that he had been treated for a long time with extraordinary coolness by them. This account is so different from all the unanimous accounts of the last summer, stating how highly he possessed their confidence; so different from all that I have constantly heard and seen, from the very direct evidence that has been displayed to me of their benevolence towards him and patronage of him, that I could not help supposing the coolness about which we are now told, to be represented as strongly as the reality could warrant. The Director Barras has indeed in a very formal manner declared their sense of Mr. Monroe's merits, and very explicitly shown what care had been taken by him to convince them how much he disapproved the measures and general policy of the government which he represented."

20. JOHN QUINCY ADAMS TO WILLIAM VANS MURRAY OCTOBER 26, 1797

"Mr. Monroe has called upon the Secretary of State for the reasons of his recall; he seems to think that the tenure of the President's pleasure, expressed in his commission meant the pleasure of Mr. Monroe. He is trying to make a noise, and add one more puff to the bellows of faction, but his breath happens to be weak. He talks about liberty, and enlightened principles, and despotism, and coalition, as much as Molière's Tartuffe talks of piety, devotion, the love of God and sin. Mr. Pickering has answered him by plainly referring to the constitutional principles, which made an assignment of the reasons demanded improper; but at the same time gives him to understand what the reasons were, and offers in his individual character to tell him the reasons why *he* advised to it. This however, Mr. Monroe, chooses to decline, and the offer appears to have vexed him. He is going to publish a pamphlet; for you know with us everything ends in a pamphlet, as in France all ends in a song."

21. JOHN QUINCY ADAMS TO WILLIAM VANS MURRAY JANUARY 27, 1798

"Monroe especially has shown himself at this time, what he was when he set Tom Paine to howl at his benefactor Washington, silencing him in word, while he instigated him in deed. There is no distinction of weapons in the modern philosophy; poison is just as freely used as the sword."

22. JOHN QUINCY ADAMS TO ABIGAIL ADAMS FEBRUARY 22, 1798

"The solicitude to escape from a charge of speculation has compelled a reluctant disclosure of a different sort of error. It might be unnecessary. But we must remark the extreme industry with which Monroe labored to foster and preserve a malversation which at the same time he dared not avow. His correspondence upon this subject amounts to this. 'I do not believe you guilty, but I wish the world to think you so; I cannot accuse you, but I will not disculpate you.' He used his benefactor the late President, no better. For he fed and boarded Tom Paine to abuse him in the most false and scurrilous manner, and made Tom at the same time certify that he had checked his malicious effusions. Monroe justly says that speculation in our funds would have been criminal in a Secretary of the Treasury, but he does not tell us what he thinks of an American Minister in France speculating in assignats and confiscated property. Of the policy or morality of this he could not properly decide. No man is a judge in his own cause."

23. JOHN QUINCY ADAMS TO WILLIAM VANS MURRAY DECEMBER 8, 1798

"Monroe's greatest enemy is himself, and his own book.[122] The most malignant foe could not pronounce so complete a sentence of damnation both upon his head and heart as that work. It is so unanswerably bad that you see even faction is ashamed of it. . .".

24. AN EXCERPT FROM THE DIARY OF JOHN QUINCY ADAMS JANUARY 17, 1806

"The message from the President was accompanied by very voluminous documents on the subject of our differences with Great Britain; and particularly a letter from Mr. Monroe, our Minister at London, to the Secretary of State, full of bitterness against England, and urging strong and decisive measures."

25. AN EXCERPT FROM THE DIARY OF JOHN QUINCY ADAMS MARCH 6, 1806

"It is said there is now very warm electioneering in the party for the next presidential election, and that Mr. Randolph's object in his present denunciation is to prevent Mr. Jefferson from consenting to serve again, and Mr. Madison from being his successor. Mr. Randolph's man is said to be Mr. Monroe. Sed quære de hoc."

122 *A View of the Conduct of the Executive in the Foreign Affairs of the United States*, (1797).

26. JOHN QUINCY ADAMS TO JOHN ADAMS DECEMBER 27, 1807

"Mr. Monroe is [in Washington, D. C.] and has been received with great demonstrations of respect and affection by his own state. There is said to be some electioneering on foot, of which he is one of the objects. Electioneering, indeed, is reported to be very active, but I know nothing of its course of proceedings."[123]

-❧-

27. JOHN QUINCY ADAMS TO JOHN ADAMS JANUARY 27, 1808

"The presidential election engrosses the principal attention of the members. About one-half the members of both houses here have declared in favor of Mr. Madison and to re-elect the Vice President. In the legislature of Virginia, also, the friends of Mr. Madison have outnumbered those of Mr. Monroe nearly three to one. I understand that by way of making a temporary provision for Mr. Monroe he is to be chosen Governor of Virginia."

-❧-

28. AN EXCERPT FROM THE DIARY OF JOHN QUINCY ADAMS FEBRUARY 13, 1808

"There were at the Capitol several members of both Houses, and Mr. [William Branch] Giles appeared much exasperated at a threat which has appeared from Mr. Monroe, of publishing another book—an electioneering book, to defeat Madison's election and promote his own."

-❧-

29. JOHN QUINCY ADAMS TO THOMAS BOYLSTON ADAMS JANUARY 24, 1812

"I join very cordially in the wish of Mr. Monroe that *all* the difference between us and England could be accommodated in like manner. But I fear that day is yet remote."

-❧-

123 Upon his return from Great Britain in December 1807, Monroe put himself forward as a candidate for the Democratic-Republican presidential nomination challenging Secretary of State James Madison.

30. JOHN QUINCY ADAMS TO LOUISA CATHERINE ADAMS DECEMBER 2, 1814

"Mr. Monroe has been appointed Secretary of War. The Department of State is not yet filled."[124]

⁂

31. JOHN QUINCY ADAMS TO JOHN ADAMS JANUARY 3, 1817

"About the middle of November last Mr. George Boyd arrived here, and among the rumors of news circulating at Washington at the time of his departure, told me it was said by some that the State Department would be offered to me by the next President.[125] Since then numerous suggestions to the same effect have reached me, and the report has finally been distributed throughout this country by the paragraphs of newspapers, extracted from those of the United States. Although these circumstances have been sufficient to induce me very seriously to deliberate in my own mind upon the determination which it may be proper for me to come to, if the proposal should really be made, yet nothing has yet occurred which would justify me in taking any step on the presumption that it will. No direct communication, either from the present President, or from his expected successor, has made it necessary or proper for me to inform either of them what my decision would be upon it, and I think it due both to them and to myself to reserve my answer and my resolution upon the offer, until it is made."

⁂

32. JOHN QUINCY ADAMS TO PRESIDENT JAMES MONROE APRIL 17, 1817

"SIR:

I had the honor of receiving yesterday the quadruplicate of your favor of 6 March, informing me that you have been pleased with the concurrence of the Senate to commit to me the Department of State. For this distinguished mark of your confidence, and for the obliging terms in which you have the goodness to communicate it, I pray you to be assured of the grateful sense which I entertain. I accept it with no other hesitation than that with

124 Monroe served in this position from 1814-1815 while retaining his duties as the Secretary of State.

125 Democratic-Republican James Monroe defeated Federalist Rufus King 183 to 34 in the Electoral College.

which I cannot but be affected in contemplating the arduous duties assigned to me by this appointment, and the consciousness of needing your indulgence and that of our country in the endeavor faithfully to discharge them."

33. JOHN QUINCY ADAMS TO ABIGAIL ADAMS APRIL 23, 1817

"MY DEAR MOTHER:

Your kind letters of 12 and 17 March, the latter enclosing one (copy) from Mr. H. G. Otis to my father, reached me on the day with a letter from the new President of the United States, informing me that with the concurrence of the Senate he had appointed me to the office just vacated by himself. I had never received from him any previous intimation that it was his intention to make this nomination, although from various sources, and among others the public newspapers, suggestions had found their way to me that it would probably be made. I am duly sensible of this mark of his confidence, and devoutly wish that he may never have occasion to regret that it was misplaced. The only hesitation that I could feel with regard to my duty on the occasion arose from a very serious doubt of my competency for the place. You will give me credit when I assure you that this doubt has weighed more heavily upon my mind than it ever did upon the occasion of any former appointment with which I have been honored."

34. JOHN QUINCY ADAMS TO ABIGAIL ADAMS MAY 16, 1817

"The manner in which the President has thought proper to nominate me was certainly honorable to himself, as it was without any intimation from me, or, as far as I know, from any of my friends, which could operate as an inducement to him. His motives were altogether of a public nature, and I trust I shall be duly sensible of the personal, as well as of the political duties which this unsolicited and spontaneous confidence imposes upon me."

35. JOHN QUINCY ADAMS TO ABIGAIL ADAMS MAY 16, 1817

"You observe that among the various public speculations there have been some expressing apprehensions that my public opinions and feelings would not harmonize with those of the President. It is certain that our sentiments upon subjects of great public interest have at particular periods of our public life been much at a variance. That they may be so again is as certainly not impossible. If I had any present reason for expecting it, I should deem it my duty to decline the office which he has tendered to me; but I have none. Ever since his appointment to the Department of State has brought me into official relations with him, I have known few of his opinions with which I did not cordially concur, and where there might be shades of difference, have had ample reasons to be satisfied with the consideration which he has given to the candid expressions of mine. I am aware, however, how much more delicate and difficult a task it will be to conciliate the duties of self-respect and the spirit of personal independence, with the deference of personal obligation and the fidelity of official subordination, under the new station assigned to me than it has hitherto been in those which I have held."

36. JOHN QUINCY ADAMS TO ABIGAIL ADAMS MAY 16, 1817

"For myself I shall enter upon the functions of my office with a deep sense of the necessity of union with my colleagues, and with a suitable impression that my place is *subordinate.* That my duty will be to *support,* and not to counteract or oppose, the President's administration, and that if from any cause I should find my efforts to that end ineffectual, it will be my duty seasonably to withdraw from the public service, and to leave to more competent persons the performance of the duties to which I should find myself inadequate. The President, I am sure, will neither require nor expect from me any sacrifice of principles inconsistent with my own sense of right, and I hope I shall never be unmindful of the respect for his character, the deference to his sentiments, and the attachment to his person, due from me to him, not only by the relative situation which he has placed me to himself, but by the gratitude with which his kindness ought to be required."

37. AN EXCERPT FROM THE DIARY OF JOHN QUINCY ADAMS SEPTEMBER 20, 1817

"The President, James Monroe, returned last Wednesday from a tour of nearly four months to the eastern and western parts of the United States. He is in the President's House, which is so far restored from the effects of the British visit in 1814 that it is now for the first time again habitable. But he is apprehensive of the effects of the fresh painting and plastering, and very desirous of visiting his family at his seat in Virginia. He is therefore going again to leave the city in two or three days, but said his absence would only be for a short time."

38. JOHN QUINCY ADAMS TO ABIGAIL ADAMS SEPTEMBER 21, 1817

"The President had arrived [at Washington, D. C.] on Wednesday and occupies the official mansion, where I had an interview with him last evening. But the walls are fresh plastered, and the wainscoting is new painted, and they render it so insalubrious for present residence, that the President proposes immediately to leave it again and to pass some time at his estate in Virginia."

39. AN EXCERPT FROM THE DIARY OF JOHN QUINCY ADAMS OCTOBER 3, 1817

"I had visits this morning from Mr. Levett Harris, Mr. Nourse, the Registrar of the Treasury, and Mr. Correa de Serra, the Portuguese Minister. Harris had just returned from visits to Mr. Jefferson, Mr. Madison, and President Monroe, and Correa was going to pay them. Correa says he calls them the Presidential Trinity, and that last year he called them the past, the present, and the future."

40. JOHN QUINCY ADAMS TO JOHN ADAMS SMITH OCTOBER 8, 1817

"From the latter end of May until the middle of September the President was absent from this place on a tour through the eastern and part of the western states. He was everywhere received with the strongest demonstrations of respect, and met with the most assiduous attentions from that part of the country which has been conspicuous for the violence of its opposition to the administration of his immediate predecessor. Party spirit has indeed subsided throughout the union to a degree that I should have thought scarcely possible."

41. AN EXCERPT FROM THE DIARY OF JOHN QUINCY ADAMS OCTOBER 24, 1817

"It was past three before I could call at the President's, and I was with him upwards of an hour. I asked him at what time it would best suit his convenience that I should call upon him daily. He said he had given a general order to receive me at all times, but in a few days he would fix upon some regular hour to see me, as it would be necessary for him to take some part of the day for exercise."

42. JOHN QUINCY ADAMS TO WILLIAM PLUMER OCTOBER 27, 1817

"The President has but within these few days [on the 20th] returned from Virginia; and the cabinet, as it is sometimes called, is not yet fully constituted. That in the views which the President may take of measures to promote the public interest there may be cordial and harmonious coöperation among those whom he has called and may call to the executive departments is my earnest desire, and as far as can depend upon me, my intention—co-incidence of opinion even between four or five persons upon all great political questions is not to be expected. I hope there is no danger that differences of opinion will lead to dissensions detrimental to the public interest."

43. AN EXCERPT FROM THE DIARY OF JOHN QUINCY ADAMS MARCH 28, 1818

"At the President's this morning I had the voluminous dispatches from G. W. Erving, at Madrid, and from Worthington and Halsey, at Buenos Ayres, to read. But the President, though convalescent, is yet so weak that he declined hearing them wholly read, and asked me to state the substance of them to him. When I told him that Worthington, one of the informal agents sent to South America to collect information, had been concluding a treaty there, he said, with quick and irritated tone, 'Dismiss him instantly. Recall him! Dismiss him! Now, to think what recommendations that man had! Dismiss him at once, and send him the notice of his demission by every possible channel."

44. JOHN QUINCY ADAMS TO RICHARD RUSH MAY 29, 1818

"The President's health during the last winter has been infirm, and he had one severe attack of illness which confined him three weeks to his chamber. He has however entirely recovered, and yesterday left the city with the Secretaries of War and the Navy upon a tour down the Chesapeake to Norfolk, upon which he expects to be absent about three weeks. He will not extend his journey further south this winter."

45. EXCERPT FROM THE DIARY OF JOHN QUINCY ADAMS JUNE 26, 1818

"At the President's. He had concluded to go from the city this evening to his farm, in Loudoun County, Virginia, thirty-three miles distant from hence; and, though the moment is very critical, and a storm is rapidly thickening, he has not read many of the papers that I left with him, and he puts off everything for a future time."

46. EXCERPT FROM THE DIARY OF JOHN QUINCY ADAMS JULY 28, 1818

"There is in the country a great mass of desire to be in opposition to the Administration. It is a sort of instinctive impression that Mr. Monroe's Administration will terminate by bringing in an *adverse* party to it. This of itself engages all the newspapers not employed by public patronage, but desiring it, and many of those possessing it, against the Administration. This propensity to blame is still increased by an affection of showing their independence, and escaping the charge of subserviency to the Executive. All the restless and uneasy spirits naturally fall into the ranks of opposition, and Clay, who has seen all this, has, from the time of Mr. Monroe's election, squared his conduct accordingly. He has been constantly looking out for positions upon which to erect his batteries against the Administration."

47. AN EXCERPT FROM THE DIARY OF JOHN QUINCY ADAMS JULY 28, 1818

"The truth is, that there is in this, and perhaps must be in every Administration in this country, a perpetual tendency to fall, as well as leaders of opposition always on the watch to trip them up or pull them down. Whatever their management may be, nothing but success can keep them up. Success is undoubtedly the effect partly of judicious management and partly of good fortune."

48. AN EXCERPT FROM THE DIARY OF JOHN QUINCY ADAMS DECEMBER 8, 1818

"There is what in vulgar language is called an undertow always working upon and about the President—what used in England to be called a back-stairs influence—of which he never says anything to me, and which I discover only by its effects."

49. AN EXCERPT TAKEN FROM THE DIARY OF JOHN QUINCY ADAMS DECEMBER 11, 1818

"At the President's, where I met Mr. Crawford and Mr. Calhoun. The President found, upon enquiry of Major Jackson, that President Washington never had been at the house of any foreign Minister; nor had any other President. He determined, therefore, not to break through the established usage."

50. AN EXCERPT TAKEN FROM THE DIARY OF JOHN QUINCY ADAMS FEBRUARY 26, 1819

"Some of the men of the highest standing and greatest abilities in Virginia are personal rivals and adversaries of Mr. Monroe. His popularity, however, throughout the State, supported by the weight and influence of Mr. Jefferson and Mr. Madison, is so great that they do not venture to assail him directly and in front. They are therefore constantly on the watch for any occasion upon which they can attack his Administration;"

51. AN EXCERPT TAKEN FROM THE DIARY OF JOHN QUINCY ADAMS AUGUST 8, 1819

"After dinner Mr. Calhoun called upon me, and rode with me to the President's house. We found him returned from his journey, with his companions, Mr. Gouverneur and Lieutenant Monroe. He is in good health, though much exhausted by a journey of five thousand miles, all south of this latitude and almost all in the summer."

52. AN EXCERPT TAKEN FROM THE DIARY OF JOHN QUINCY ADAMS NOVEMBER 26, 1819

"This I readily admitted, but observed it was one of those cases in which no course which the Administration could steer would be free from censure. If the President recommended delay, he would be charged with weakness and pusillanimity. If he proposed immediate action, he would be accused of rashness and violence."

53. AN EXCERPT TAKEN FROM THE DIARY OF JOHN QUINCY ADAMS NOVEMBER 26, 1819

"Lately, and particularly yesterday, I saw that my advice had become irksome to the President—that he was verging to a suspicion that I was spurring him to rash and violent measures. I fell, therefore, entirely into his own views of the subject, and Crawford, having discovered this, immediately took the ground I had abandoned, and is for at once assuming the offensive with Spain. The enemies of Mr. Monroe's Administration, and my enemies, have been continually laboring with the industry and venom of spiders to excite in his mind a jealousy of me. They have so far succeeded that whatever I earnestly recommend, he distrusts."

54. AN EXCERPT TAKEN FROM THE DIARY OF JOHN QUINCY ADAMS JANUARY 8, 1820

"In short, as the first Presidential term of Mr. Monroe's Administration has hitherto been the period of the greatest national tranquility enjoyed by this nation at any portion of its history, so it appears to me scarcely avoidable that the second term will be among the most stormy and violent. I told him this day that I thought the difficulties before him were thickening and becoming hourly more and more formidable."

55. AN EXCERPT TAKEN FROM THE DIARY OF JOHN QUINCY ADAMS JANUARY 10, 1820

"The time may, and I think will, come when it will be my duty equally clear to give my opinion, and it is even now proper for me to begin the preparation of myself for that emergency. The President thinks this question will be winked away by compromise.[126] But so do not I. Much am I mistaken if it is not destined to survive his political and individual life and mine."

56. AN EXCERPT TAKEN FROM THE DIARY OF JOHN QUINCY ADAMS MARCH 3, 1820

"When I came this day to my office, I found there a note requesting me to call at one o'clock at the President's house. It was then one, and I immediately went over. He expected that the two bills, for the admission of Maine, and to enable Missouri to make a Constitution, would have been brought to him for his signature, and he had summoned all the members of the Administration to ask their opinions in writing, to be deposited in the Department of State, upon two questions: 1, Whether Congress had a Constitutional right to prohibit slavery in a Territory: and 2, Whether the eight section of the Missouri bill (which interdicts slavery *forever* in the Territory north of thirty-six and a half latitude) was applicable only to the Territorial State, or could extend to it after it should become a state."

57. AN EXCERPT TAKEN FROM THE DIARY OF JOHN QUINCY ADAMS APRIL 6, 1820

"There is at present no ostensible intention to oppose the re-election of Mr. Monroe as President in any part of the Union. Every attempt to form a new fixed opposition party has hitherto failed."

58. AN EXCERPT TAKEN FROM THE DIARY OF JOHN QUINCY ADAMS MAY 15, 1820

"There is at the new Capitol a chamber assigned for the President of the United States and the President of the Senate. There I found the President, and there he remained till the session closed. He signed thirty-four Acts, which passed in the course of the day. All the members of the Administration occasionally attended, and, as usual, read the Acts, to see that they were correctly enrolled before he signed them. The President had been a few minutes into the House, but did not remain long. Nothing in the Constitution precludes

126 Adams is referring to the Missouri Compromise question.

the personal appearance of the President of the United States in either House while they are sitting, though it has very seldom, if ever, happened."

59. AN EXCERPT TAKEN FROM THE DIARY OF JOHN QUINCY ADAMS JUNE 23, 1820

"The censorial power of the President of the United States over the moral and official conduct of the officers appointed and subject to removal by him, is one of those the exercise of which is of the most extreme delicacy. There are cases when it is proper to mark disapprobation without expressing it; others in which it must be unequivocally expressed, and among them such as require different degrees of severity; others, finally, which demand the permission to resign, or, last of all, peremptory removal. In the discharge of this most painful and ungracious duty the President seems to me more governed by momentary feelings, and less by steady, and inflexible principle, than I think he ought. But his failing leans to virtue's side. He is universally indulgent, and scrupulously regardful of individual feelings. He is perhaps too reluctant to exercise this power at all. He rather turns his eyes from misconduct, and betrays a sensation of pain when it is presented directly to him. Whether this weakness, as it appears to me to be, is not better than its proximate energy, is perhaps doubtful. In the theory of a President's duties, with almost as much indulgence, and the same tenderness for the feelings of individuals, I should look for a little more vigilance to observe, and a little more rigor to control, the faults of Executive officers. One of the consequences of this tendency to censorial laxity is the necessity under which I have often found myself, of presenting to the President cases requiring censure, and, after having presented them, of bringing them again and again before him, until something is done; for whatever he consents to do, unless it is to be executed immediately, he never thinks of it afterwards; and in the way of censure or punishment, if an order that he gives should not be executed, I doubt whether he would ever notice it, unless by having it again called to his attention."

60. AN EXCERPT TAKEN FROM THE DIARY OF JOHN QUINCY ADAMS JANUARY 1, 1821

". . . At the drawing-room at the President's. It was more thronged with the company than I ever saw it on any similar occasion. 'Donec eris felix, multos numerabis amicos.'[127]

127 "When you are successful, everyone wants to be your friend."

Mr. Monroe, by a vote, with a single exception unanimous, of all the electoral colleges of this Union, has just been re-elected President of the United States for a second term of four years. No such state of things as the present has existed since the establishment of the present Constitution; for although the second election of Washington, like the first, was unanimous, yet the opposition to his Administration was more organized and more violent than it now is to that of Mr. Monroe."

61. AN EXCERPT TAKEN FROM THE DIARY OF JOHN QUINCY ADAMS FEBRUARY 23, 1821

"The President read to me some detached paragraphs of the address he proposes to deliver at his second inauguration. Some question has been suggested to the President whether he should deliver on that occasion *any* address; some of his Virginian friends having taken a fancy that it is anti-republican and not authorized by the Constitution. I entertained no such opinion, but told him that if he concluded to omit the address, notice of his intention should be given in the newspapers, as there would be a great concourse of people to witness his taking the oath, and they would be much disappointed if there should be nothing but that naked ceremony. He will refer the question to a Cabinet consultation."

62. AN EXCERPT TAKEN FROM THE DIARY OF JOHN QUINCY ADAMS FEBRUARY 26, 1821

"A joint committee of both Houses of Congress waited this day upon the President and informed him of his re-election. The President told them that he proposed to take the oath of office next Monday. The 4th of March, the day upon which the Presidential term of four years commences, happens this year to fall on Sunday, for the first time since the establishment of the present Constitution, and the question occurred whether the President should take the official oath on that day or postpone it to the next. He wrote to the Chief Justice of the Supreme Court requesting their opinion upon it, and they advised postponing the ceremony till Monday. The question yet remains undetermined whether any inaugural address is to be delivered or not."

63. AN EXCERPT TAKEN FROM THE DIARY OF JOHN QUINCY ADAMS MARCH 5, 1821

"Second inauguration of James Monroe as President of the United States. The arrangements were made at the hall of the House of Representatives, by the Marshal of the District, in concert with the Clerk, and by consent of the late Speaker of the House. There were seats reserved for the ladies of the heads of Departments, and others for the members of the Diplomatic Corps and members of Congress. The President had requested the heads of Departments to assemble at his house and accompany him to the Capitol. The Marshal had recommended that the ladies should go early, to secure their admission into the hall and their seats. Mrs. Adams went first to the Capitol, and sent back the carriage for me. Madame De Neuville went in company with her. A quarter before twelve I went to the President's house, and the other members of the Administration immediately afterwards came there. The Marshal and one of his deputies was there, but no assemblage of people. The President, attired in a full suit of black broadcloth of somewhat antiquated fashion, with shoe- and knee-buckles, rode in a plain carriage with four horses and a single colored footman. The Secretaries of State, the Treasury, War, and the Navy followed, each in a carriage-and-pair. There was no escort, nor any concourse of people on the way. But on alighting at the Capitol a great crowd of people were assembled, and the avenues to the hall of the House were so choked up with persons pressing for admittance that it was the utmost difficulty that the President made his way through them into the House. Mr. [George] Canning and Mr. [G. Crawford] Antrobus, in full Court-dress uniforms, were in the midst of this crowd, unable to obtain admission. We got in at last, after several minutes of severe pressure. There was not a soldier present, nor a constable distinguishable by any badge of office. The President took a seat on a platform just before the Speaker's chair. The Chief Justice was seated at his right hand, the other Judges of the Supreme Court in chairs fronting him; the President of the Senate and late Speaker of the House at his left hand; the heads of Department sidelong at the right; and the foreign Ministers in the seats of the members at the left. The House and galleries were as thronged as possible. There was much disorder of loud talking and agitation in the gallery, not altogether ceasing even while the President was reading his address, which he did immediately after taking the oath. At this ceremony the Chief Justice merely held the book, the President repeating the oath in the words prescribed by the Constitution. The address was delivered in a suitably grave and rather low tone of voice. After it was finished, several persons came up to the President and shook hands with him by way of congratulation. At his departure from the House there was a cheering shout from the people in the galleries, and the music of the Marine Band played both at his entrance and departure. I returned home with my family, and immediately afterwards went to the President's house, where there was a numerous circle for congratulation. I then passed a couple of hours at my office, and in the evening attended a ball at Brown's Hotel. The President and his family were there, but retired before supper. We came home immediately after, and finished a fatiguing and bustling day about midnight."

64. AN EXCERPT TAKEN FROM THE DIARY OF JOHN QUINCY ADAMS MARCH 9, 1821

"Mr. Monroe had just been re-elected with apparent unanimity, but he had not the slightest influence in Congress. His career was considered as closed. There was nothing further to be expected by him or from him. Looking at Congress, they were a collection of *materials*, and how much good and how much evil might be done with them, accordingly as they should be well or ill directed. But henceforth there was and would not be a man in the United States possessing less *personal* influence over them than the President."

65. EXCERPT FROM JOHN QUINCY ADAMS'S *PARTIES IN THE UNITED STATES* JANUARY 1822

"The succession of Presidents from Virginia terminated with the administration of Mr. Monroe. The collisions of opinion upon the principles of government had lost all their asperity and much of their ardor, the results of the French Revolution had disappointed the enthusiast of democracy, and the Republican administration had adopted and practiced upon most of the principles which they had strenuously contested while the government was in Federal hands.

The example of Presidents Washington, Jefferson, and Madison had accustomed the people to the voluntary retirement of the Presidents after a service of two successive terms. It was taken for granted that this example would be followed by Mr. Monroe, and although it is probable his inclination would have been to retire, there can be little doubt that had it been otherwise he would not have been gratified with a second re-election."

66. AN EXCERPT TAKEN FROM THE DIARY OF JOHN QUINCY ADAMS APRIL 30, 1822

"'*Your* report!' said the President, in a tone of sharp anger. '*Tis* my report. It is no report at all until I have accepted it.' My feelings were wound up to a pitch at which it was with extreme difficulty that I preserved the control of my temper and the command of my expressions. I did so, however, and said, 'Sir, it is *your* report, to do what you please with it, when received; but so far as I understand the Constitution of this country it is my report to make, and I am the responsible person in making it.'

He said that he had always, when Secretary of State, considered the reports he had made to Mr. Madison as subject entirely to the control of the President, and had always felt himself bound to make any alteration in a report required by him.

I replied that I had invariably observed the same rule with him. I had never in a single instance written a public paper to be submitted to him without making every alteration in it suggested by him and insisted on. I was now willing to make any alteration that he would desire in this report, and had told him so when I presented the report to him. But the report when made I considered as mine."

67. AN EXCERPT TAKEN FROM THE DIARY OF JOHN QUINCY ADAMS JUNE 2, 1822

"The President had little personal influence in Congress. He was now no longer the centre of hopes and expectations. He was independent of all, and had no lures for retainers or baits for ambition to hold out."

68. AN EXCERPT TAKEN FROM THE DIARY OF JOHN QUINCY ADAMS SEPTEMBER 11, 1822

"It has also an article in reply to a very foolish one of the National Advocate, which denied the existence of any opposition to Mr. Monroe's Administration, declared that he had faithfully and zealously discharged his duties as President of the United States, but that he had a private account to settle with the Democratic party, which must now go on by the election of a suitable President for his successor. The shamelessness with which this principle is advanced, that the President, by faithfully performing his duty as Chief Magistrate of the nation, had violated his allegiance to the party which brought him into power, and that therefore a successor to him must be chosen who will violate his duty to the whole nation by exclusively favoring his own party, is characteristic of the electioneering in favor of Mr. Crawford."

69. JOHN QUINCY ADAMS TO LOUISA CATHERINE ADAMS OCTOBER 7, 1822

"Of the public history of Mr. Monroe's administration, all that will be worth telling to posterity hitherto has been transacted through the Department of State. The treaties with Great Britain, with Spain, with France, and with Russia, and the whole course of policy with regard to South America, have been all under the immediate management of that Department. They are all events affecting not only the present interests, but the future condition of this people. The acquisition of Florida and the extension of the territories of the Union to the Pacific Ocean have been accomplished through that Department, and the formal admission of our right to border upon the South Sea, both by Spain and Great Britain, has been first obtained, I might confidentialy say by me. That it has been obtained through the Department of State in Mr. Monroe's administration, is beyond the reach of contradiction or of events."

70. AN EXCERPT TAKEN FROM THE DIARY OF JOHN QUINCY ADAMS AUGUST 2, 1823

"The President was suddenly seized this morning with cramps or convulsions, of such extreme violence that he was at one time believed to be dying, and he lay upwards of two hours in a state of insensibility. I did not hear of it till the fit was over. I called at his house, and saw there Dr. Washington and Mr. Hay. The Doctor said the President was disposed to sleep, and it would be best that no person should see him. Mr. Hay said Dr. Sim had pronounced the danger to be past, and did not apprehend a renewal of the attack. But, Hay added, he thought it would be some time before it would be prudent to lay before him business of any kind. Before returning home to dinner, I sent to enquire how he was, and the answer to the messenger was, 'much better.'"

71. AN EXCERPT TAKEN FROM THE DIARY OF JOHN QUINCY ADAMS AUGUST 9, 1823

"The President is often afraid of the skittishness of mere popular prejudices, and I am always disposed to brave them. I have much more confidence in the calm and deliberate judgment of the people than he has."

72. AN EXCERPT TAKEN FROM THE DIARY OF JOHN QUINCY ADAMS NOVEMBER 18, 1823

"The President appears yet to be in an extraordinary degree of dejection. There must be something that affects him besides the European news."

73. AN EXCERPT TAKEN FROM THE DIARY OF JOHN QUINCY ADAMS APRIL 11, 1824

"I read this day the President's memoir upon the transactions relating to the appropriations for furnishing the President's house. It enters into details of a very humiliating character, and which ought never to have been, or to be, required of him. The principal difficulty appears to have sprung from his having used his own furniture until that provided for by the appropriations could be procured, and having received for it six thousand dollars, to be repaid upon the redelivery of his furniture to him. This produced an intermingling of Lane's public and private accounts with him, which, by Lane's sickness and death, remained unsettled at his decease. There arises from all this an exposure of domestic and household concerns almost as incongruous to the station of the President of the United States as it would be to a blooming virgin to exhibit herself naked before a multitude. The malignity of political opposition has no feeling of delicacy. There appears to be nothing really censurable in all these transactions, but Lane was an unfortunate selection of an agent, and his final insolvency has produced all these awkward consequences."

74. AN EXCERPT TAKEN FROM THE DIARY OF JOHN QUINCY ADAMS AUGUST 31, 1824

"The President again said that the object of his Administration had been to draw the parties of this country together and unite them all as one people; but that to effect this it was essential that he should proceed cautiously, and avoiding to shock the prejudices of his own party."

-⁂-

75. AN EXCERPT TAKEN FROM THE DIARY OF JOHN QUINCY ADAMS NOVEMBER 30, 1824

"As the *last* session message that the President is to deliver, it contains more matter of a general character than any of the preceding, and a summary review of the policy of the Administration throughout its career. There was no discussion upon any of the *topics* introduced into the message, and no diversity of opinion with regard to any of the recommendations in it. There never has been a period of more tranquility at home and abroad since our existence as a nation than that which now prevails."

-⁂-

76. AN EXCERPT TAKEN FROM THE DIARY OF JOHN QUINCY ADAMS FEBRUARY 2, 1825

"The nominations belonged properly to his Administration, and my wish was that it should be really his Administration to the last moment of its existence. If the election should fall upon me, I should therefore entreat him, as a favor, that he would make the nominations as his own, and as he would have made then at any other period of his Administration."

-⁂-

77. AN EXCERPT TAKEN FROM THE DIARY OF JOHN QUINCY ADAMS FEBRUARY 25, 1825

"At the President's. I read to him my intended address, excepting the part relating to his Administration. He said he had done the same with Mr. Madison. He also said he had drawn up a paper concerning parties, the views of which exactly corresponded with those of my address."

-⁂-

78. AN EXCERPT TAKEN FROM THE DIARY OF JOHN QUINCY ADAMS MARCH 3, 1825

"This day closed the second session of the Eighteenth Congress, and the Administration of James Monroe as President of the United States. I had passed a sleepless night, occasioned by the unceasing excitement of many past days;"

79. EXCERPT FROM JOHN QUINCY ADAMS'S INAUGURAL ADDRESS MARCH 4, 1825

"Passing from this general review of the purposes and injunctions of the Federal Constitution and their results as indicating the first traces of the path of duty in the discharge of my public trust, I turn to the Administration of my immediate predecessor as the second. It has passed away in a period of profound peace, how much to the satisfaction of our country and to the honor of our country's name is known to you all. The great features of its policy, in general concurrence with the will of the Legislature, have been to cherish peace while preparing for defensive war; to yield exact justice to other nations and maintain the rights of our own; to cherish the principles of freedom and of equal rights wherever they were proclaimed; to discharge with all possible promptitude the national debt; to reduce within the narrowest limits of efficiency the military force; to improve the organization and discipline of the Army; to provide and sustain a school of military science; to extend equal protection to all the great interests of the nation; to promote the civilization of the Indian tribes, and to proceed in the great system of internal improvements within the limits of the constitutional power of the Union. Under the pledge of these promises made by that eminent citizen at the same time of his first induction to this office, in his career of eight years the internal taxes have been repealed; sixty millions of the public debt have been discharged; provision has been made for the comfort and relief of the aged and indigent among the surviving warriors of the Revolution; the regular armed force has been reduced and its constitution revised and perfected; the accountability for the expenditure of public moneys has been made more effective; the Floridas have been peaceably acquired, and our boundary has been extended to the Pacific Ocean; the independence of the southern nations of this hemisphere has been recognized, and recommended by example and by counsel to the potentates of Europe; progress has been made in the defense of the country y fortifications and the increase of the Navy, toward the effectual suppression of the African traffic in slaves, in alluring the aboriginal hunters of our land to the cultivation of the soil and of the mind, in exploring the interior regions of the Union, and in preparing by scientific researches and surveys for the further application of our national resources to the internal improvement of our country.

In this brief outline of the promise and performance of my immediate predecessor the line of duty for his successor is clearly delineated. To pursue to their consummation those purposes of improvement in our common condition instituted or recommended by him will embrace the whole sphere of my obligations. To the topic of internal improvement, emphatically urged by him at his inauguration, I recur with peculiar satisfaction."

80. AN EXCERPT TAKEN FROM THE DIARY OF JOHN QUINCY ADAMS APRIL 9, 1825

"In the evening I visited Mr. Monroe, at the President's house. He is making preparations for his departure, with his family, but is somewhat delayed by the illness of Mrs. Monroe."

81. AN EXCERPT TAKEN FROM THE DIARY OF JOHN QUINCY ADAMS DECEMBER 14, 1825

"He [Asbury Dickins] then enlarged upon the services he had rendered, especially during the last two years, in the Treasury—intimating that he had really performed all the duties of the Secretary; and he added he supposed I knew that he had been the medium of communication between the Treasury Department and the President after all personal communications between Mr. Monroe and Mr. Crawford had ceased.

His fact had not been before known to me, and I told Dickins so.

He said that a few weeks before the close of the Administration, some words used by Mr. Monroe to Mr. Crawford had induced the latter to abstain thenceforward from coming to this house, or ever seeing Mr. Monroe again.

When Mr. Southard came in, I asked him if this fact had been known to him. He said, yes; that one day last winter, on coming here on business, he found Mr. Monroe walking to and fro across the room in great agitation; that he told him Crawford had just left him; he had come to him concerning the nomination of certain officers of the Customs in the Northern ports; that Crawford recommended the nomination of several persons, against whom Mr. Monroe expressed several objections; that Mr. Crawford at last rose in much irritation, gathered the papers together, and said, petulantly, 'Well, if you will not appoint the persons well qualified for the places, tell me whom you will appoint, that I may get rid of their importunities.' Mr. Monroe replied with great warmth, saying that he considered Crawford's language as extremely improper and unsuitable to the relations between them; when Crawford, turning to him, raised his cane, as in the attitude to strike, and said, 'You damned infernal old scoundrel!' Mr. Monroe seized the tongs at the fireplace for self-defence, applied a retaliatory epithet to Crawford, and told him he would immediately ring for servants himself and turn him out of the house; upon which Crawford, beginning to recover himself, said he did not intend, and had not intended, to insult him, and left the house. They never met afterwards."

82. AN EXCERPT TAKEN FROM THE DIARY OF JOHN QUINCY ADAMS MARCH 5, 1828

"Mr. Rush was here with sundry papers from the Treasury Department. . . He spoke also of the letters from Messrs. Madison and Monroe declining to stand as candidates to serve as Electors of President and Vice President at the next election. He thought the letter of Mr. Monroe would be liable to be criticised."

83. AN EXCERPT TAKEN FROM THE DIARY OF JOHN QUINCY ADAMS MAY 12, 1828

"I told him [James Barbour] it was my belief that the debt hanging so heavily upon the old age of Mr. Monroe was chiefly contracted by the expensive establishment of his household in London after his return from Spain in 1805."

84. AN EXCERPT TAKEN FROM THE DIARY OF JOHN QUINCY ADAMS JUNE 30, 1828

"I received shortly before dinner a note from Marshal Ringgold, with a letter from J. S. Skinner, the Postmaster at Baltimore, informing him that Mr. Monroe had spent the day, yesterday, with Mr. Charles Carroll of Carrollton, and would be here this afternoon.

He came and spent an hour with me in the evening, and promised to dine with me to-morrow. He has left Mrs. Monroe with her daughter, Mrs. Gouverneur, near New York, where she is to pass the summer. We conversed together upon indifferent topics, and upon European politics, without touching upon the present state of our own affairs or the convulsive agitation of the public mind at the approach of the Presidential election. He is going to attend a meeting of the Visitors of the University of Virginia."

85. AN EXCERPT TAKEN FROM THE DIARY OF JOHN QUINCY ADAMS JANUARY 17, 1830

"I received a note from Mr. Ringgold, written last evening, informing me that Mr. Monroe was at his house, and I immediately went to see him. General Mason and General Jessup were there, and Mr. White, a member of the House of Representatives from Louisiana, came in. Mr. Monroe had been dangerously ill, and, although convalescent, is much emaciated."

86. AN EXCERPT TAKEN FROM THE DIARY OF JOHN QUINCY ADAMS DECEMBER 12, 1830

"After dinner, I visited Mr. Monroe at his son-in-law's, Samuel L. Gouverneur's. Mrs. Hay was also there. Gouverneur is going to-morrow for Washington. Mr. Monroe's health is infirm, and his appearance feeble and emaciated."

87. AN EXCERPT TAKEN FROM THE DIARY OF JOHN QUINCY ADAMS APRIL 27, 1831

"I paid a visit to the ex-President, Monroe, at the house of his son-in-law, Samuel L. Gouverneur. He was confined to his chamber, and extremely feeble and emaciated. Congress passed at their last session an Act making a further allowance to him, for his claims, of thirty thousand dollars, which have been paid him. He has advertised for sale his estate in Loudoun County, Virginia, and proposes to go there in a few weeks; but it is doubtful whether he will ever be able to leave his chamber. Mr. Monroe is a very remarkable instance of a man whose life has been a continued series of the most extraordinary good fortune, who has never met with any known disaster, has gone through a splendid career of public service, has received more pecuniary reward from the public than any other man since the existence of the nation, and is now dying, at the age of seventy-two, in wretchedness and beggary. I sat with him perhaps half an hour. He spoke of the commotions now disturbing Europe, and of the recent quasi revolution at Washington; but his voice was so feeble that he seemed exhausted by the exertion of speaking. I did not protract my visit and took leave of him, in all probability for the last time."

88. AN EXCERPT TAKEN FROM THE DIARY OF JOHN QUINCY ADAMS JULY 7, 1831

"Received this morning a letter from Samuel L. Gouverneur of the 4th, and one from George Sullivan of the 5th, at New York, announcing the decease, at three o'clock in the afternoon of the 4th, of the ex-President of the United States, James Monroe, a man whose life has been marked with vicissitudes as great as have befallen any citizen of the United States since the beginning of our national existence. An officer of the Revolutionary army, wounded at Princeton in December, 1776; a member of the Confederation Congress; then of the Senate of the United States; Minister to France under Washington's Administration; next Governor of Virginia; then Minister to France, Great Britain, and Spain; Governor of Virginia again; Secretary of State, Secretary of War, and eight years President of the United States—elected for the second term by a vote of the Electors unanimous save one. His life for the last six years has been one of abject penury and distress, and they have brought him to a premature grave, though in the seventy-third year of his age. His Administration, happening precisely at the moment of the breaking up of old party divisions, was the period of the greatest tranquility which has ever been enjoyed by this country; it was a time of great prosperity, and his personal popularity was unrivalled. Yet no one regretted the termination of his Administration, and less of popular veneration followed him into retirement than had accompanied all his predecessors. His last days have been much afflicted, contrasting deeply with the triumphal procession which he made through the Union in the years 1817 and 1819."

89. AN EXCERPT TAKEN FROM THE DIARY OF JOHN QUINCY ADAMS JULY 15, 1831

"Mr. Harrison, Alderman, and Mr. Wetmore, a member of the Common Council of Boston, came out as a sub-committee of the committee of arrangements appointed by the city government to take order for the delivery of an eulogy of the late ex-President Monroe. These gentlemen informed me that it had been determined to invite me to undertake the task.

I told them that the relation in which I had stood to Mr. Monroe, and the respect that I entertained for his character, would forbid me to decline the invitation, and that the high gratification I should derive from contributing any assistance I could give to an object in which the city government of Boston took an interest would induce me to undertake the service with pleasure. I then asked them at what time they proposed that the eulogy should be pronounced.

They said they were instructed to enquire what time would best suit my convenience.

I said that in a performance of that nature a number of biographical notices would be expected—for the facts concerning which I should be under the necessity of resorting to Mr. Monroe's family. I should immediately write to his son-in-law, Samuel L. Gouverneur, at New York, and could not anticipate with certainty the time when I might receive his answer—probably in a week or ten days—after which I should want about a fortnight to prepare. I supposed it might be about a month before I should be prepared.

They said it had been supposed about three weeks would be a suitable interval, but that the city government would readily fix the time which would be convenient to me.

I said I would make it as early as possible, and give them notice as soon as I should be ready."

90. AN EXCERPT TAKEN FROM THE DIARY OF JOHN QUINCY ADAMS JULY 18, 1831

"I was occupied from breakfast to dinner-time almost entirely in refreshing my memory upon the important military events of our Revolutionary War. Mr. Monroe's career of public life began with it. From 1776 to 1779 he was in General Washington's army, and was present at the most important events in it through the series of those years. He was also occasionally engaged in other military service till the close of the war. He was wounded by a ball through the shoulder at the battle of Princeton. It will be indispensable to notice this part of his life in delivering his eulogy. I must, therefore, renew my familiarity with the history of the war, for which purpose I read many pages of Pitkin's and Belsham's Histories, of Stedman's History of the War, of the Remembrancer, and of Washington's Letters to Congress. These gave me distinct recollections of the campaign of 1776, and of the affair at Princeton, in January, 1777. Going back to those times seems almost like a resurrection from the dead; but while reading so much I could write but little, and made scarcely any progress with my eulogy, and otherwise fell in arrear of my ordinary tasks."

91. AN EXCERPT TAKEN FROM THE DIARY OF JOHN QUINCY ADAMS AUGUST 6, 1831

"I am still toiling upon the eulogy on Mr. Monroe, my plan of which forms itself as I proceed. It has assumed the shape of a memoir upon his life. It was long, eventful, and connected with the principal events of our history, from the Declaration of Independence, for a full half-century."

92. AN EXCERPT TAKEN FROM THE DIARY OF JOHN QUINCY ADAMS AUGUST 18, 1831

"Finished the eulogy upon James Monroe. I have been obliged to abridge this, and have omitted much of what I wished to say. It is now so long that more than half of it must be suppressed at the delivery; and yet I shall be much perplexed to select the part to be spoken. A much more serious inconvenience is that I have not time to write it over a second time, and it will be a performance much more crude than the Fourth of July oration."

93. EXCERPT FROM JOHN QUINCY ADAMS'S *AN EULOGY ON THE LIFE AND CHARACTER OF JAMES MONROE, FIFTH PRESIDENT OF THE UNITED STATES* AUGUST 1831

"Had he [Monroe] been born ten years before, it can scarcely be doubted that he would have been one of the members of the first Congress, and that his name would have gone down to posterity among those of the signers of the Declaration of Independence."

---

94. EXCERPT FROM JOHN QUINCY ADAMS'S *AN EULOGY ON THE LIFE AND CHARACTER OF JAMES MONROE, FIFTH PRESIDENT OF THE UNITED STATES* AUGUST 1831

"Of this race of men, James Monroe was one—not of those who did, or could take a part in the preliminary controversy, or in the Declaration of Independence. He may be said almost to have been born with the question, for at the date of the Stamp-Act, he was in the fifth year of his age; but he was bred in the school of the prophets, and nurtured in the detestation of tyranny. His patriotism outstripped the lingering march of time, and at the dawn of manhood, he joined the standard of his country. It was at the very period of the Declaration of Independence, issued as you know at the hour of severest trial to our country; when every aspect of her cause was unpropitious and gloomy. Mr. Monroe commenced his military career, as his country did that of her Independence, with adversity. He joined her standard when others were deserting it. He repaired to the head quarters of Washington at New York, precisely at the time when Britain was pouring her thousands of native and foreign mercenaries, upon our shores; when in proportion as the battalions of invading armies thickened and multiplied, those of the heroic chieftain of our defence were dwindling to the verge of dissolution."

---

95. EXCERPT FROM JOHN QUINCY ADAMS'S *AN EULOGY ON THE LIFE AND CHARACTER OF JAMES MONROE, FIFTH PRESIDENT OF THE UNITED STATES* AUGUST 1831

"And in this career both of adverse and of prosperous fortune, James Monroe was one of that little Spartan band, scarcely more numerous, though in the event more prosperous, than they who fell at Thermopylœ. At the Heights of Haerlem, at the White Plains, at Trenton he was present, and in leading the vanguard at Trenton, received a ball, which sealed his patriotic devotion to his country's freedom with his blood.—The superintending Providence which had decreed that on that, and a swiftly succeeding day, Mercer, and Haselet, and Porter, and Neal, and Fleming, and Shippen, should join the roll of warlike dead, martyrs to the cause of liberty, reserved Monroe for higher services, and for a long and illustrious career, in war and in peace."

96. EXCERPT FROM JOHN QUINCY ADAMS'S *AN EULOGY ON THE LIFE AND CHARACTER OF JAMES MONROE, FIFTH PRESIDENT OF THE UNITED STATES* AUGUST 1831

"The first fruits of his youth had been given to her defence in war: the rigour and maturity of his manhood was now to be devoted to her welfare in council."

97. EXCERPT FROM JOHN QUINCY ADAMS'S *AN EULOGY ON THE LIFE AND CHARACTER OF JAMES MONROE, FIFTH PRESIDENT OF THE UNITED STATES* AUGUST 1831

"In all the proceedings, relating to the navigation of the Mississippi, from the reception of Mr. Gardoqui, till the acquisition of Louisiana and its annexation to the United States, the agency of Mr. Monroe was conspicuous above all others. He took the lead in the opposition to the recommendation of Mr. Jay. He signed, in conjunction, with another eminent citizen of the State of New-York, Robert R. Livingston, the Treaty which gave us Louisiana: and, during his administration, as President of the United States, the cession of the Floridas was consummated. His system of policy, relating to this great interest, was ultimately crowned with complete success. That which he opposed, might have severed or dismembered the Union."

98. EXCERPT FROM JOHN QUINCY ADAMS'S *AN EULOGY ON THE LIFE AND CHARACTER OF JAMES MONROE, FIFTH PRESIDENT OF THE UNITED STATES* AUGUST 1831

"Mr. Monroe was deeply penetrated with the conviction that a great and radical change, in the Articles of Confederation, was indispensible, even for the preservation of the Union. But, in common with Patrick Henry, George Mason, and many other patriarchs of the Revolution, his mind was not altogether prepared for that which was, in truth, a revolution, far greater than the severance of the United American Colonies from Great Britain: a revolution accomplishing that which the Declaration of Independence had only conceived and proclaimed: substituting a Constitution of Government for a people, instead of a mere Confederation of States."

-⁂-

99. EXCERPT FROM JOHN QUINCY ADAMS'S *AN EULOGY ON THE LIFE AND CHARACTER OF JAMES MONROE, FIFTH PRESIDENT OF THE UNITED STATES* AUGUST 1831

"That Mr. Monroe, then, was one of those enlightened, faithful, and virtuous patriots, who opposed the adoption of the Constitution, can no more detract from the eminence of his talents, or the soundness of his principles, than the project for the temporary abandonment of the right to navigate the Mississippi, can impair those of the eminent citizens of New-York and Massachusetts, by whom that measure was proposed. During a Statesman's life, an estimate of his motives will necessarily mingle itself with every judgment upon his conduct, and that judgment will often be swayed more by the concurring or adverse passions of the observer, than by reason, or even by the merits of the cause. Candour, in the estimate of motives, is rarely the virtue of an adversary; but it is an indispensable duty before the definitive tribunal of posthumous renown."

-⁂-

100. EXCERPT FROM JOHN QUINCY ADAMS'S *AN EULOGY ON THE LIFE AND CHARACTER OF JAMES MONROE, FIFTH PRESIDENT OF THE UNITED STATES* AUGUST 1831

"The contemporaneous missions of Mr. Jay to Great Britain, and of Mr. Monroe to France, are among the most memorable events in the history of this Union. There are in the annals of all nations occasions, when wisdom and patriotism, and the brightest candour and the profoundest sagacity, are alike unavailing for success. There are sometimes elements of discord, in the social relations of men, which no human virtue or skill can reconcile. Mr. Jay and Mr. Monroe, each within his own sphere of action, executed with equal faithfulness, perhaps with equal ability, the trust committed to him, in the spirit of his appointment and of his instructions."

-⁂-

101. EXCERPT FROM JOHN QUINCY ADAMS'S *AN EULOGY ON THE LIFE AND CHARACTER OF JAMES MONROE, FIFTH PRESIDENT OF THE UNITED STATES* AUGUST 1831

"Arriving in France, at the precise moment when the excesses of the revolutionary parties were on the turning spring tide of their highest flood, Mr. Monroe was received, with splendid formality, in the bosom of the National Convention, when not another civilized nation upon the earth, had a recognized representative in France. He there declared, in perfect consistency with his instructions, the fraternal friendship of his country and her government, for the French people, and their devoted attachment to her cause, as the cause of Freedom."

102. EXCERPT FROM JOHN QUINCY ADAMS'S *AN EULOGY ON THE LIFE AND CHARACTER OF JAMES MONROE, FIFTH PRESIDENT OF THE UNITED STATES* AUGUST 1831

"It was, perhaps, rather the misfortune of all, than the fault of any one, that the views of Mr. Monroe, with regard to the policy of the American Administration, did not accord with those of President Washington. He thought that France had just cause of complaint; and, called to the painful and invidious task of defending and justifying that which he personally disapproved, although he never, for a moment, forgot the duties of his station, it was, perhaps, not possible that he should perform them entirely to the satisfaction of his Government. He was recalled, towards the close of Washington's administration, and Charles Cotesworth Pinckney was appointed in his place."

103. EXCERPT FROM JOHN QUINCY ADAMS'S *AN EULOGY ON THE LIFE AND CHARACTER OF JAMES MONROE, FIFTH PRESIDENT OF THE UNITED STATES* AUGUST 1831

"Thus it was, that the congenial mind of James Monroe, at the zenith of his public honours, and in the retirement of his latest days, cast off, like the suppuration of a wound, all the feeling of unkindness, and all the severities of judgment, which might have intruded upon his better nature, in the ardour of civil dissension. In veneration for the character of Washington, he harmonized with the now unanimous voice of his country; and he has left recorded, with his own hand, a warm and unqualified testimonial to the pure patriotism, the pre-eminent ability and the spotless integrity of John Jay."

104. EXCERPT FROM JOHN QUINCY ADAMS'S *AN EULOGY ON THE LIFE AND CHARACTER OF JAMES MONROE, FIFTH PRESIDENT OF THE UNITED STATES* AUGUST 1831

"Soon after these deep and trying afflictions, he removed his residence to the city of New-York; where, surrounded by filial solicitude and tenderness, the flickering lamp of life held its lingering flame, as if to await the day of the nation's birth and glory; when the soldier of the Revolution, the statesman of the Confederacy, the chosen chieftain of the constituted nation, sank into the arms of slumber to awaken no more upon earth, and yielded his pure and gallant spirit to receive the sentence of his Maker."

105. EXCERPT FROM JOHN QUINCY ADAMS'S *AN EULOGY ON THE LIFE AND CHARACTER OF JAMES MONROE, FIFTH PRESIDENT OF THE UNITED STATES* AUGUST 1831

"It may suffice to say that, until the war [of 1812] broke out, and during its continuance, the duties of the offices held by Mr. Monroe, at the head of, successively, of the Departments of State and War, were performed with untiring assiduity, with universally acknowledged ability, and, with zeal of patriotism, which counted health, fortune, and life itself, for nothing, in the ardour of self-devotion to the cause of his country."

106. EXCERPT FROM JOHN QUINCY ADAMS'S *AN EULOGY ON THE LIFE AND CHARACTER OF JAMES MONROE, FIFTH PRESIDENT OF THE UNITED STATES* AUGUST 1831

"A combined system of efficient fortification arming the shores and encircling the soil of the republic, and the gradual establishment of a powerful navy, were from the restoration of the peace unto his latest hour, among the paramount and favorite principles in the political system of Mr. Monroe for the government of the Union. In these objects, he had the good fortune to be supported as well by the opinions of his immediate predecessor, as by the predominant sentiments of the people."

107. EXCERPT FROM JOHN QUINCY ADAMS'S *AN EULOGY ON THE LIFE AND CHARACTER OF JAMES MONROE, FIFTH PRESIDENT OF THE UNITED STATES* AUGUST 1831

"On the retirement of Mr. Madison from the office of chief magistrate in 1817, Mr. Monroe was elected by a considerable majority of the suffrages in the electoral colleges as his successor. This election took place at a period of tranquillity in the public mind, of which there had been no previous example since the second election of Washington. To this tranquillity, many concurring causes, such as are never likely to meet again, contributed, and among them, of no inferior order was the existing state of the foreign, and especially the European world. It continued through the four years of his first Presidential term, at the close of which he was re-elected without a show of opposition, and by the voice little less than unanimous of the whole people."

108. EXCERPT FROM JOHN QUINCY ADAMS'S *AN EULOGY ON THE LIFE AND CHARACTER OF JAMES MONROE, FIFTH PRESIDENT OF THE UNITED STATES* AUGUST 1831

"Viewed as a whole, throughout its extent, can there be a doubt in considering it as the most magnificent supplement to our national Independence presented by our history, and will there arise an historian of the Republican empire, who shall fail to perceive or hesitate to acknowledge, that throughout the long series of these transactions, which more than doubled the territories of the North-American Confederation, the leading mind of that great movement in the annals of the world, and thus far in the march of human improvement upon the earth, was the mind of James Monroe?"

109. EXCERPT FROM JOHN QUINCY ADAMS'S *AN EULOGY ON THE LIFE AND CHARACTER OF JAMES MONROE, FIFTH PRESIDENT OF THE UNITED STATES* AUGUST 1831

"In his Inaugural Address, delivered according to a prevailing usage, upon his induction to office, he took a general view of the existing condition and general interests of the nation, and marked out for himself a path of policy, which he faithfully pursued. The first of the objects to which he declared that his purposes would be directed, was the preparation of the country for future defensive war. Fortification of the coast and inland frontiers—peace establishments of the army and navy, with an improved system of regulation and discipline for the militia, were the means by which this was to be effected, and to which his indefatigable labours were devoted. The internal improvements of the country, by roads and canals; the protection and encouragement of domestic manufactures; the cultivation of peace and friendship with the Indian tribes—tendering to them, always, the hand of cordiality, and alluring them by good faith, kindness, and beneficent instruction, to share and to covet the blessings of civilization; a prudent, judicious, and economical, administration of the Treasury; with the profitable, and, at the same time liberal, management of the public lands, then first beginning to disclose their active and appreciating value, as national property: all these were announced as the interests of the great community, which he surveyed as committed to his charge, and to the faithful custody and advancement of which, his unremitted exertions should be directed: and never was pledge with more entire self-devotion redeemed."

110. EXCERPT FROM JOHN QUINCY ADAMS'S *AN EULOGY ON THE LIFE AND CHARACTER OF JAMES MONROE, FIFTH PRESIDENT OF THE UNITED STATES* AUGUST 1831

"The opinions of James Monroe upon doubtful or controverted points of Constitutional Law, can never cease to be deserving of profound respect. They were never lightly entertained. They were always deliberate, always disinterested, always sincere."

111. EXCERPT FROM JOHN QUINCY ADAMS'S *AN EULOGY ON THE LIFE AND CHARACTER OF JAMES MONROE, FIFTH PRESIDENT OF THE UNITED STATES* AUGUST 1831

"And, in his last annual Message to Congress, on the seventh of December, 1824, announcing his retirement from public life, after the close of that session of the Legislature, he reviewed the whole course of his administration, comparing it with the pledges which he had given at its commencement, and at its middle term, appealing to the judgment and consciousness of those whom he addressed, for its unity of principle a one consistent whole, not exempt indeed, from the errors and infirmities incident to all human action, but characteristic of purposes always honest and sincere, of intentions always pure, of labours outlasting the daily circuit of the sun, and outwatching the vigils of the night—and what *he* said not, but a faithful witness is bound to record; of a mind anxious and unwearied in the pursuit of truth and right; patient of inquiry; patient of contradiction; courteous, even in the collision of sentiment; sound in its ultimate judgments; and firm in its final conclusions."

112. EXCERPT FROM JOHN QUINCY ADAMS'S *AN EULOGY ON THE LIFE AND CHARACTER OF JAMES MONROE, FIFTH PRESIDENT OF THE UNITED STATES* AUGUST 1831

"Such my fellow citizens was James Monroe. Such was the man, who presents the only example of one whose public life, commenced with the War of Independence, and is identified with all the important events of your history from that day forth for a full half century. And now, what is the purpose for which we have here assembled to do honour to his memory? Is it to scatter perishable flowers upon the yet unsodded grave of a public benefactor? Is it to mingle tears of sympathy and of consolation, with those of mourning and bereaved children? Is it to do honour to ourselves, by manifesting a becoming sensibility, at the departure of one, who by a long career of honour and of usefulness has been to us all as a friend and brother? Or is it not rather to mark the memorable incidents of a life signalized by all the properties which embody the precepts of virtue and the principles of wisdom? Is it not to pause for a moment from the passions of our own bosoms, and the agitations of our own interests, to survey in its whole extent the long and little-beaten path of the great and the good: to fix with intense inspection our own vision, and to point the ardent but unsettled gaze of our children upon that resplendent row of cresset lamps, fed with the purest vital air, which illuminate the path of the hero, the statesman and the sage. Have you a son of ardent feelings and ingenuous mind, docile to instruction, and panting for honorable distinction? point him to the pallid cheek and agonizing form of James Monroe, at the opening blossom of life, weltering in his blood on the field of Trenton, for the cause of his country. Then turn his eye to the same form, seven years later, in health and vigour, still in the bloom of youth, but seated among the Conscript Fathers of the land to receive entwined with all its laurels the sheathed and triumphant sword of Washington. Guide his eye along to the same object, investigating by the midnight lamp, the laws of nature and nations, and unfolding them, at once with all the convictions of reason and all the persuasions of eloquence to demonstrate the rights of his countrymen to the contested Navigation of the Mississippi, in the Hall of Congress. Follow him with this trace in his hand, through a long series of years, by laborious travels and intricate Negotiations, at Imperial Courts, and in the Palaces of Kings, winding his way amidst the ferocious and party coloured Revolutions of France, and the life-guard favourites and Camarillas of Spain. Then look at the Map of United North America, as it was at the definitive peace of 1783. Compare it with the map of that same Empire as it is now; limited by the Sabine and the Pacific Ocean, and say, the change, more than of any other man, living or dead, was the work of James Monroe. See him pass successively from the Hall of the Confederation Congress to the Legislative Assembly of his native commonwealth; to their Convention which ratified the Constitution of the North American people; to the Senate of the Union; to the Chair of Diplomatic Intercourse with ultra Revolutionary France; back to the Executive honours of his native state; again to the embassies of transcendant magnitude, to France, to Spain, to Britain; restored once more to retirement and his country; elevated again to the highest trust of his State; transferred successively to the two preeminent Departments of Peace and War, in the National Government; and at the most momentous crisis burthened with the duties of both—and finally raised, first by the suffrages of a majority, and at last by the unanimous call of his countrymen to the Chief Magistracy of the Union. There behold him for a term of eight years, strengthening his country for a defence by a system of combined fortifications, military and naval, sustaining her rights, her dignity and honour abroad; soothing her dissensions, and conciliating her acerbities at home; controuling by a firm though peaceful policy the hostile spirit of European Alliance against Republican Southern America; extorting by the mild compulsion of reason, the shores of the Pacific from the stipulated acknowledgment of Spain; and leading back the imperial autocrat of the North, to his lawful boundaries, from his hastily asserted dominion over the Southern Ocean. Thus strengthening and consolidating the federative edifice of his country's Union, till he was entitled to say like Augustus Cœsar of his imperial city, that he had found her built of brick and left her constructed of marble."

Chapter 6

JOHN QUINCY ADAMS

I. JOHN QUINCY ADAMS ON THE PRESIDENCY

1. AN EXCERPT FROM JOHN QUINCY ADAMS'S *LETTERS OF PUBLICOLA* JULY 20, 1791

"By the Constitution of the United States, it is true, the right of declaring war is vested in the Congress, that is, in the legislative power. But it is in the point of form that it agrees with the Constitution of France; it has wisely placed the management of all negotiations and treaties, and the appointment of all agents and ministers in the executive department; and it has so thoroughly adopted in this instance the *principles* of the English Constitution, that although it has given the Congress the right of declaring war, which is merely a difference of form, it has vested in the President, with advice of the Senate as his executive council, the right of making peace, which is implied in that of forming treaties."

2. AN EXCERPT FROM JOHN QUINCY ADAMS'S *COLUMBUS* DECEMBER 4, 1793

"They had delegated to the President, the power of negotiating with the ministers of foreign power, and with the concurrence of the Senate, to make treaties with them. They had specially directed their President in the Constitution, which defined his authority and prescribed his duties, to 'take care, that the laws be faithfully executed;' and, if, in the course of his administration, a difference of opinion upon the meaning of a national compact should arise between him and the agent of a foreign power, they had not reserved to themselves the right of judging between them. Nor did they imagine, that they had thereby imparted to their Chief Magistrate, a power in the smallest degree arbitrary. For if the construction, upon which his measures were grounded, should be erroneous, they had provided a judiciary power, competent to correct his mistakes. If he proceeded upon a wilful and treacherous misinterpretation, they had secured the means of removing him from his office by impeachment; but in either case, they had retained no appellate jurisdiction to themselves."

3. AN EXCERPT FROM JOHN QUINCY ADAMS'S *COLUMBUS* DECEMBER 7, 11, & 14, 1793

"The Constitution of the United States says that *the executive power* shall be vested in the President. That he shall receive Ambassadors and other public Ministers, and that he shall *take care that the laws be faithfully executed.* In committing this trust, the people of the United States, undoubtedly gave to the office which they invested with this authority, all the powers which are essential to its fulfillment; to suppose otherwise would be absurd in the extreme. The idea of expressly commanding a man to do a particular act, and at the same instant of prohibiting all the means, without the use of which that act becomes impossible, is too ridiculous to require a refutation. When therefore the constitution of the United States commands the President of the Union to take care that the laws be faithfully executed, this prescription is of itself a warrant, authorizing him to do any act consistent with the laws of the land, which may be necessary to answer that valuable purpose."

4. AN EXCERPT FROM JOHN QUINCY ADAMS'S *COLUMBUS* DECEMBER 7, 11, & 14, 1793

"The Constitution of the United States has made the *Declaration of War a Legislative Act*, and thereby has expressly vested the right of making it in the Congress, to whom it has entrusted the *Legislative Power.* This principle was, no doubt, adopted upon the mature deliberation, and upon the conclusion drawn by the framers of the Constitution, and by the people of America, that this declaration properly belongs to the Legislative Department of Government. But the Constitution has not said, that the President shall perform no function which in its consequence might be productive of a war. Such a provision would have been tantamount to a declaration that the President should have no powers at all."

⁂

5. JOHN QUINCY ADAMS TO JOHN ADAMS APRIL 12, 1794

"My business I can hope will increase.[128] But as it is I have no disposition to complain. It gives me bread and I find myself so well satisfied with that, that my greatest apprehension is of growing indolent and listless. It is hardly possible to obtain a conquest over the ambitious principle without subduing in some measure that of an honorable activity. You recommend to me to attend the town meetings and make speeches; to meet with caucuses and join political clubs. But I am afraid of all these things. They might make me a better politician, and give me an earlier chance of appearing as a public man; but that would throw me completely in the power of the people, and all my future life would be a life of dependence. I had rather continue some time longer in obscurity, and make some provision for fortune, before I sally out in quest of fame or public honors. . .".

⁂

6. JOHN QUINCY ADAMS TO CHARLES ADAMS SEPTEMBER 15, 1795

"You observe that there are many people who wish to raise a jealousy between Mr. Jay and another public character nearly connected with us.[129] It appears to me very probable that such attempts will be made, and I hope with you that they will prove abortive; but if I have one wish in my heart more forcible than any other, it is that the occasion for which you suppose the plan is laid may never happen. Whoever may be the successor of the present first magistrate will hold a situation so uncomfortable and so dangerous, that there is nothing in its possession to make it desirable. I am so far from looking on that place as an object worthy of ambition, that if my unequivocal wishes could decide the point on the supposition of the contingency, which we all deprecate, the election would be declined in the most decisive and explicit manner."

⁂

128 In 1790 John Quincy Adams had opened a law office in Boston; however, he experienced difficulty attracting clients.

129 John Adams

7. JOHN QUINCY ADAMS TO JOHN ADAMS APRIL 4, 1796

"The removal of the President, however effected in the tactics of the combined French and party powers, is to be followed by a plan for introducing into the American Constitution a Directory instead of a President, and for taking from the supreme Executive the command of the armed force. This hopeful project has been intimated to you in a former letter. How far it has been shaped and organized I know not; whether the course of events will prevent its advancement as a practical measure I shall not pretend to say; but of the design to bring it forward at the first favorable moment I have not the shadow of a doubt."

8. JOHN QUINCY ADAMS TO SYLVANUS BOURNE DECEMBER 22, 1796

"You dread the influence of frothy newspaper declamations, and of party spirit and heats encouraged by this example of foreign interference. I see their activity and their malignancy no less clearly than yourself, but not with quite so much apprehension. Suppose its effects should be to turn the election? This is probably one of its principal objects, but should it succeed, what then? Is the devil to be raised, or are we to be set all by the ears for having a Virginian instead of New England man for President? One honest and able man instead of another? Indeed these ideas may pass among Europeans, but they are not worthy of an American."

9. JOHN QUINCY ADAMS TO SYLVANUS BOURNE DECEMBER 22, 1796

"You have now as you requested the state of my hopes and fears on this business. I fear (or rather I do not fear, I *know*) that faction in America will make of its French patronage the most that it possibly can. I hope (or rather I have no doubt), but that the justice, the virtue, and the spirit of the American people and government will prove triumphant over the patronage, as well as over the spirit of faction; and as to the decision upon the presidential election, I am not alarmed about it at all, but have the most unequivocal confidence, that in either of the probable alternatives, the chief magistracy of the Union will be administered with wisdom and integrity, with moderation and spirit, equal to every exigency to which it may be exposed. . .".

10. JOHN QUINCY ADAMS TO W. & J. WILLINK AND N. & J. VAN STAPHORST & HUBBARD DECEMBER 22, 1796

"The real intelligence from America of a later date countenances no such expectations of a dissolution of the American union, and I trust, gentlemen, that the course of events will soon show, that the American people can elect a President without involving themselves either in a civil or foreign war."

11. JOHN QUINCY ADAMS TO JOHN ADAMS MAY 20, 1797

"If I could without ridiculous presumption venture a word of advice to a President of the United States, it would be to fasten an eternal seal upon his lips, and burn his pen of private correspondence with regard to public affairs."

12. JOHN QUINCY ADAMS TO WILLIAM VANS MURRAY JANUARY 25, 1800

"There is no more comparison between the powers of a President of the United States and a premier consul, than between the character of Washington and Buonaparte."

13. JOHN QUINCY ADAMS TO ABIGAIL ADAMS MARCH 10, 1801

"To be relieved from the labors and responsibility of such a station as that of an American President, is a great consolation for all the pain of being removed from it, and will I hope have its full weight as such."

14. JOHN QUINCY ADAMS TO ABIGAIL ADAMS MAY 16, 1817

"I know something of the difficulty of moving smoothly along with associates, equal in trust, justly confident of their abilities, disdainful of influence, yet eager to exercise it, impatient of control, and of opposing real, stubborn resistance to surmises and phantoms of encroachment, and I see that in the nature of the thing an American President's Cabinet must be composed of such materials."

15. AN EXCERPT FROM THE DIARY OF JOHN QUINCY ADAMS MARCH 18, 1818

"When Everett was here, he asked me if it would not be advisable to expose Clay's conduct and motives in the newspapers, to which I answered very explicitly in the negative. He also asked me if I was determined to do nothing with a view to promote my future election to the Presidency as the successor of Mr. Monroe. I told him I should do absolutely nothing. He said that as others would not be so scrupulous, I should not stand upon equal footing with them. I told him that was not my fault—my business was to serve the public to the best of my abilities in the station assigned to me, and not to intrigue for further advancement. I never, by the most distant hint to any one, expressed a wish for any public office, and I should not now begin to ask of that which of all others ought to be most freely and spontaneously bestowed."

16. JOHN QUINCY ADAMS TO WILLIAM PLUMER JULY 6, 1818

"Many of the members of the former Congress had shown dissatisfaction at this course, and had urged that it would be fairer and save the time of Congress and the nation if the chief magistrate should explicitly make know his opinion beforehand, so as to spare the majority of the legislature the necessity of coming in direct collision with his negative. These reasons certainly have their weight, but in fact the exercise of actual control by the President over the opinions and wishes of a majority of the legislature will never be very palatable in what form soever it may be administered."

17. AN EXCERPT FROM THE DIARY OF JOHN QUINCY ADAMS JANUARY 25, 1819

"Caballing with members of Congress for future contingency has become so interwoven with the practical course of our Government, and so inevitably flows from the practice of caucussing by the members to fix on candidates for President and Vice-President, that to decline it is to pass upon myself a sentence of total exclusion. Be it so! Whatever talents I possess, that of intrigue is not among them. And instead of toiling for a future election, as Pope recommends, my only wisdom is to prepare myself for voluntary or for unwilling retirement."

18. AN EXCERPT FROM THE DIARY OF JOHN QUINCY ADAMS MARCH 13, 1819

"At the legislative caucus preliminary to the last election, Crawford was the candidate, and came near to be the successful candidate, against Mr. Monroe. As the candidate of a very powerful minority, then, he stands naturally the most prominent candidate after the close of Mr. Monroe's Presidential career. He is a native Virginian, and has all the sympathies of Southern interests and Southern feelings in his favor. On the ordinary impulses to human opinions and conduct, Mr. Monroe must ultimately favor Crawford's pursuits, and this occurrence, trivial as it is, furnishes one among many proofs that such will be the fact. I can see nothing in it of which I have any right to complain. It proves that the relative position of Mr. Monroe, of Crawford, and of myself towards each other is a very bad one; that mine, in particular, is peculiarly bad, and probably to be remedied in no other manner than by my withdrawing from it—an event for which I have only to wish that my mind may be duly prepared."

19. AN EXCERPT FROM THE DIARY OF JOHN QUINCY ADAMS MAY 29, 1819

"We had an evening tea-party and dancing of cotillions at our house; about sixty persons came, and as many more were prevented from coming by the weather. Poletica asked me this evening what style of address he should use in writing official notes or letters. I told him without giving any titles of honor to the President or the Secretary of State. He said he had always been aware that the title of 'His Excellency' was not suitable to the President, but he had observed it was given here to the Governors of the States, and it was everywhere given in Europe to the officers corresponding to our heads of Departments. I told him the Governors of the States were 'Excellencies' by the State Constitutions, but that the Constitution of the United States recognized no titles of honor in the officers appointed under it, and that our point of honor consisted in the exclusion of all such titles. 'Præfulgebant Cassius atque Brutus, eo ipso, quod effigies eorum non visebantur.'"[130]

130 "Cassius and Brutus outshone them, by that very fact, their likenesses were not to be seen."

20. AN EXCERPT FROM THE DIARY OF JOHN QUINCY ADAMS NOVEMBER 26, 1819

"The President said it was an exceedingly difficult question, and he would think profoundly upon it before coming to his final determination. I told him that I had the more freely given him all my present impressions from a consideration that it was by our Constitution the President himself who was responsible for all the great national measures recommended by him. The heads of Departments are responsible only as his subalterns."

21. AN EXCERPT FROM THE DIARY OF JOHN QUINCY ADAMS NOVEMBER 27, 1819

". . .but the seeds of this discord are sown in the practice which the Virginia Presidents have taken so much pains to engraft upon the Constitution of the Union, making it a principle that no President can be more than twice elected, and that whoever is not thrown out after one term of service must decline being a candidate after the second. This is not a principle of the Constitution, and I am satisfied that it ought not to be. Its inevitable consequence is to make every Administration a scene of continual and furious electioneering for the succession to the Presidency."

22. AN EXCERPT FROM THE DIARY OF JOHN QUINCY ADAMS NOVEMBER 27, 1819

"[William] Crawford was made a candidate against Monroe, and in the legislative caucus very nearly outvoted him. He therefore considers himself as the natural successor, and has made all his arrangements accordingly. During the first year of the Administration, seeing that I had no personal friends, or at least no political partisans, and numerous inveterate opponents in Congress, he probably took it for granted that I should in no event be an obstacle in his way. Within the last eighteen months he has begun to fear that I might, and although he sees that I have gained nothing of electioneering force in Congress, but that, on the contrary, strong new electioneering force will be brought to bear against me, he has seen some indications of popular sentiment in my favor in quarters where he did not expect them, and feels a necessity of working against my influence with the President and with the public."

23. AN EXCERPT FROM THE DIARY OF JOHN QUINCY ADAMS MAY 2, 1820

"Fuller said it was apparent that preparations were making for a violent canvass for the Presidential election of 1824. I said there had been scarcely anything but such canvassing since 1816. He said he hoped I did not intend to withhold myself from the contest. I told him the principle of my life had been never to ask the suffrage of my country, and never to shrink from its call. If life, health, and private circumstances admitting of it, and a belief of competency to the station, not inferior to others who may be competitors for it, should be mine after the vicissitudes of the next four years, I shall adhere to the principle upon which I have always acted. Whether any portion of the country will think of calling for my services will certainly depend upon the series of future events. I know the disadvantages on which I now stand, and am conscious of my inability to make interest by caballing, bargaining, place-giving, or tampering with members of Congress."

24. AN EXCERPT FROM THE DIARY OF JOHN QUINCY ADAMS MAY 2, 1820

"In the course of three sessions I have formed slight personal acquaintances with most of the members [of the House of Representatives], but have had neither time nor opportunity to become intimate with any of them. My means of acquiring personal adherents, therefore, are nothing. Upon the foundation of public service alone must I stand; and when the nation shall be called to judge of that, by the result, whatever it may be, I must abide. Were it in my power, I would sink in oblivion the very idea of a Presidential election in 1824; but, forget it as I might, it would be ever present to the minds of my adversaries."

25. AN EXCERPT FROM THE DIARY OF JOHN QUINCY ADAMS MAY 2, 1820

"The three sessions of Congress have been three wresting-matches to bring me down by the ruins of Mr. Monroe's Administration. The first and second attempts failed. That of the present session has been favored by circumstances."

26. AN EXCERPT FROM THE DIARY OF JOHN QUINCY ADAMS JUNE 14, 1820

"It is, in theory, one of the duties of a President of the United States to superintend in some degree the moral character of the public officers who hold their places at his pleasure. But the difficulty of carrying it into practice is great, and the number of instances in which I see corruption of the deepest dye, without being able to punish or even to displace it, is among the most painful appendages to my situation."

27. AN EXCERPT FROM THE DIARY OF JOHN QUINCY ADAMS NOVEMBER 24, 1820

"[William] Plumer spoke to me on two subjects. One, the appointment of a District Attorney in New Hampshire, upon which he expressed a wish for the reappointment of Mr. Humphreys. The other related to the approaching election of President and Vice-President of the United States. His father is chosen one of the electors for the State of New Hampshire, and has intimated to him that there and in Massachusetts there are persons unwilling to vote for the re-election of D. D. Tompkins as Vice-President, and disposed to vote for me; not with an expectation or intention of success, but with a prospective view of holding up my name to view at a future period; and has enquired whether it was with my approbation. I answered, Certainly not; that my wish was that both Mr. Monroe as President and Mr. Tompkins as Vice-President should be re-elected unanimously; but, however that might be, that there should not be a single vote given for me, and I requested him to write so immediately. As to Massachusetts, I told him it would be peculiarly disagreeable to me that any such votes should be given, because my own father had been chosen one of the electors."

28. AN EXCERPT FROM THE DIARY OF JOHN QUINCY ADAMS NOVEMBER 24, 1820

"Literature has been the charm of my life, and, could I have carved out my own fortunes, to literature would my whole life have been devoted. I have been a lawyer for bread, and a statesman at the call of my country."

29. AN EXCERPT FROM THE DIARY OF JOHN QUINCY ADAMS JANUARY 22, 1821

". . .that as the second election of Mr. Monroe as President of the United States was now completed, it was natural to look forward to the next Presidential term and enquire who would be the fittest person for his successor; that he had reflected much upon this subject, and had come to the conclusion that I was the most suitable person, and that he should be disposed to exercise his influence in my favor.[131]

I tendered him my thanks for his good opinion, and told him I could make him no better return for it than to give him a candid and explicit statement of my principles. I did not know that it was Mr. Monroe's intention to retire from public life at the expiration of his second Presidential term. If he should not decline a third election, I should not consent, were it even in my power, to have my name held up as a candidate to oppose him. If he should decline, and my life and health after four years remain as at present, I shall with others be before the nation to be disposed of as they may think proper. If others should be disposed to hold me up as a candidate for the suffrages of my country, I shall not, as at present advised, withhold my name; but I shall neither solicit the nomination nor take any part whatever in procuring or supporting it."

30. AN EXCERPT FROM THE DIARY OF JOHN QUINCY ADAMS FEBRUARY 25, 1821

"[Joseph] Hopkinson dined with us, and, according to his engagement, came and sat with me an hour before dinner. The object of his seeking this conversation with me was the next Presidential election. He gave me to understand that he was disposed to consider me as a candidate for that occasion; that others were of similar disposition, but that it was necessary there should be a concert and understanding between them, as there already was, and long had been, between the partisans of Mr. Crawford. He said that the extent and activity of their intrigues was incredible, and unless systematically counteracted would infallibly be successful.

I told Mr. Hopkinson that I was perfectly aware of the exertions making by Mr. Crawford himself and his friends to secure the Presidency at the next election. There were others making exertions not less ardent and persevering for Mr. Clinton, of

131 Adams is referring to a Dr. Allison. Adams writes, "He is an old Baptist clergyman, who was a chaplain in our army during the Revolutionary War."

New York. There was a third party, less apparent now, and the struggle of which was eventual, to depend upon the conflict now raging in that State between Clinton and Tompkins. The State was now about equally divided, and, as there is no marked difference of principle to contend for, they are squabbling for men. If either party should obtain over the other such an ascendency as would carry a large majority of the State, its leader would be the candidate of New York for the Presidency. The only question between them will be which shall be the man. New York, at any rate, will have a candidate of her own, and if both these rivals should be out of the way she would sooner take up Mr. King than resort to any other State. The politics of Pennsylvania will be greatly influenced by those of New York. She too is a divided State; but the scuffle for her Governor is between men neither of whom has any prospects in the General Government. She will probably be an accessory to New York. Whether any party, or any one individual, would support or propose me as a candidate, I could not tell; but even in my own native State of Massachusetts the predominating party, the federalists, had a grudge against me, which they would not lose the opportunity of indulging. To one thing, however, I had made up my mind: I would take no one step to advance or promote pretensions to the Presidency. If that office was to be the prize of cabal and intrigue, of purchasing newspapers, bribing by appointments, or bargaining for foreign missions, I had no ticket in that lottery. Whether I had the qualifications necessary for a President of the United States was, to say the least, very doubtful to myself. But that I had no talent for obtaining the office by such means was perfectly clear. I had neither talent nor inclination for intrigue. I can do nothing either to canvass for myself or to counteract the canvassing of others. I will have no stipendiary editor of newspapers to extol my talents and services and to criticise or calumniate my rivals. I will devote none of my time to devising laws to increase my own patronage and multiply canvassers in my favor. My time is now not sufficient to discharge the duties of my office; any part of it which I should spend in efforts to make partisans or to pull down competitors would be an abandonment of public for personal aims. For this, if I had the talent, I have not the will; and if I had the will, I have not the talent."

31. JOHN QUINCY ADAMS TO LOUISA CATHERINE ADAMS AUGUST 11, 1821

". . . I well know that I never was and never shall be what is commonly termed a popular man, being as little qualified by nature, education, or habit for the arts of a courtier as I am desirous of being courted by others. Such as I am I envy not the reputation of any other man in the Union. There is not another man in the Union, excepting the Presidents past and present, who receives or continues to receive from the people of this country indications of esteem and confidence more distinguished and flattering than I have. With the exception of one single mark of dissatisfaction from the legislature of my native state thirteen years since, my life has been one continual succession for more than five and twenty years of high, of honorable and important trusts, and of literary and scientific distinctions—all conferred without any of those blandishments by which some others acquire esteem or favors. If ever a man had reason to be grateful for the portion of public consideration which has been shown him, it is I, and I trust I am grateful for it. I am certainly not intentionally repulsive in my manners and deportment, and in my public station I never made myself inaccessible to any human being. But I have no powers of fascination; none of the honey which the profligate proverb says is the true fly-catcher; and be assured, my dear friend, it would not be good policy for me to affect it. The attempt would make me ridiculous because it would be out of nature. . .".

32. EXCERPT FROM JOHN QUINCY ADAMS'S *PARTIES IN THE UNITED STATES* JANUARY 1822

"In all governments of which the chief magistrate is elective, the organizations, the character and the movements of parties will depend in great degree upon the anticipation to the succession. Among the citizens most distinguished for their talents and services, it is to be expected there will always be several ambitious of attaining the summit of honor and power, around whom others of considerable influence will rally, and whose conflicting pretensions will be supported by partisans more or less numerous and pressed forward for the popular suffrages with degrees of zeal and address not always proportioned to their merit. The prospect of succession to the presidency must in the ordinary course of events be confined to the vice-president, the heads of the executive departments, and a very small number of citizens of great eminence in the several states of the Union. The election of the second and third Presidents of the United States had fallen upon incumbents of the vice-presidency; but those persons, even when elected to the vice-presidency, had been voted for as candidates for the presidency. An amendment to the Constitution then prescribed that the office should be voted for distinctly, and since that time the Vice-President's office had been an insuperable barrier to that of President."

33. AN EXCERPT FROM THE DIARY OF JOHN QUINCY ADAMS JANUARY 2, 1822

"The next day, in a Gazette of this city, a piece of three columns of the vilest and foulest slander upon me is published, and from that day no conclave of cardinals was ever more belabored with caballing than Congress have been to make partisans for the new candidate. All this was a natural consequence of the position in which the members of the Administration were placed towards one another by Mr. Jefferson's principle of limiting the Presidential service to eight years. I could solemnly declare that all my views hitherto had been exclusively confined to the support of his Administration. It was with that view alone that I had proposed to accept the proffer of Mr. Taylor. It was very unfortunate for the Administration that this offer had not been accepted. I should continue to act on the same principles as long as it would be possible; but, in the way things were now working, I knew not how long this might be.

The President said he was fully aware that such always had been my conduct; that he had been perfectly satisfied with my service, and hoped I should continue it during the remainder of his Administration; that from the interest always taken by the members of Congress in the Presidential election, it was natural that the prominent members of an Administration should, by their respective friends, be considered as competitors for the succession to the Presidency, and there was no question but that the diverse views of different members of Congress with reference to the succession would affect very materially their conduct in relation to depending measures. He believed that any movement by members of Congress now would be premature, and of little effect upon the ultimate result. He had been during a certain period of Mr. Madison's Administration in a predicament not unlike that of the present time. With regard to the management of the war, General Armstrong being at the head of that Department, he (Mr. Monroe) had from various circumstances entertained the opinion that Mr. Madison did not give due weight to his own opinions of military measures to be adopted. The succession then, too, mingled itself with everything in Congress, and at a most critical period of the war. In order to take away from those who were thus disposed the motive for such caballing, he had requested some of his particular friends, among whom Mr. Hugh Nelson was one, to say that he desired his name might be discarded as a candidate for the succession to the Presidency; and if the war had continued, an arrangement to that effect was actually made, and the name of another person was to have been brought forward. After the close of the war, however, no great interest of the country being at stake, it was not thought necessary further to pursue that plan. With regard to the person who might be chosen as his successor, from the relations between the several members of the Administration and himself, he felt it his duty to take no part in favor of or against any one.

I said this was what I should have expected, and was in my own opinion the only proper course to be pursued by him; and I added that if in the progress of his Administration any similar crisis to that of which he had spoken should arise, wherein the withdrawal of my name from all consideration as a candidate would subserve any purpose useful to the country, I should very cheerfully imitate his example.

He said he could see no possible occasion for that, and there might be occasions on which a vindication of my character from obloquy in the public prints would be proper."

34. AN EXCERPT FROM THE DIARY OF JOHN QUINCY ADAMS JANUARY 3, 1822

W[illiam] Plumer, of New Hampshire, was at the office, and told me he had this morning seen and conversed with Mr. Calhoun, who had assured him that his assent to stand as a candidate at the next election for the Presidency was qualified—a candidate against any Southern man. His own opinion had invariably been in favor of a Northern man for the next President, and personally for me. But the intimation given to him had been that I should have no support from the North; and in that case he had been willing to stand against any Southern man, and particularly against Mr. Crawford, whose principles and character he could not approve."

35. JOHN QUINCY ADAMS TO JOHN D. HEATH JANUARY 7, 1822

"By the practical operation of our government, and the experience of the two most recent successive Presidential elections, it was probable that if the duties of the Department should be performed to the satisfaction of the country, the person holding [the office of Secretary of State] would be one of those towards whom the public attention would be turned as a suitable candidate to succeed the President upon his retirement from office. This was an incident arising from my position as much unsought by me as the position itself. I had indulged the hope that the agitations which must be expected to attend the canvassing for a successor to the President would have been postponed at least until the last year preceding the election, and until Mr. Monroe should have signified his own intention to retire. I regret exceedingly that a different course should have been pursued, and that both in the state legislature and in the Congress of 1821 great and systematic exertions should have been concerted to forestall the public opinion of the country for the Presidential election of 1825. It could not be observed that *all* these exertions hitherto have been directed to the positive purpose of excluding me from the field of competition, when its proper time shall arrive. That in connection with them many of the public presses throughout the Union should have teemed with slander, false and foul, upon my character was of course to be expected, and has been and continues to be realized. So far have I been from contributing to this premature fermentation by any act on my part, that it is but very recently indeed that I have had more than the general reason resulting from my position to believe that the people of any portion of the Union would probably look to me as a candidate for the succession to the Executive chair. That such a disposition may, since what has happened, be manifested at no distant day is now probable. It will proceed from the Republicans of my native section of the Union, but to what extent, and with what degree of unanimity I am not informed. I have hitherto discouraged and, as far as I have been able, restrained the exhibition of any such movement, and shall now barely leave it to take its course. The time of election is yet so far distant, and the events which must finally decide it are so contingent, that it may be for time only to disclose who shall be the real candidate of that day. From facts within my knowledge I incline to the belief that the legislative caucus in South Carolina was a *feint*, marking other purposes than those of advancing Mr. [William] Lowndes, although one of them was undoubtedly that which you mention, of setting aside any purpose of which the danger might be apprehended that my name might be hereafter held up for the favorable consideration of the citizens of South Carolina. Efforts of the same kind, though connected with other names, have been and are making probably in every state in the Union, certainly in my own native state and its immediate vicinity. With the rule which I have adopted as the first principle of my relations with public concerns, that these efforts should succeed is to be foreseen as highly probable, and if your kind opinion in my favor were less pure, disinterested and patriotic than it is, I should advice you to devote your talents and your friendly offices to some candidate more able and willing to toil for the advancement of his own pretensions than I am or can be. For if the old prudential maxim that God helps those who help themselves is morally applicable to the pursuit of public honors and trust, I shall certainly be the most helpless candidate that ever was presented to the view of the American people. Whatever the event may prove, it will not be without precious consolation to me while testimonials like those contained in your letter shall be left me. While citizens of distinguished merit and respectable standing, viewing public men and their conduct only through the pure atmosphere of public spirit, personally strangers to me, and guided by public motives alone, shall estimate my services to the country by honesty of intention and faithfulness of diligence, the suffrage of five such men, unbiased as it must and ineffective as it may be, will be dearer to me than that of a whole Sodom of political chapmen, who would barter a Presidency for a department or an embassy, or stoop to spread the table of greatness for the promise of the crumbs which may fall from it."

36. AN EXCERPT FROM THE DIARY OF JOHN QUINCY ADAMS MAY 9, 1822

"Were it consistent with my principles to work for my own advancement any otherwise than by public service, it is now too late for me to commence bidding for the Presidency. Neither have I any faculty at driving such bargains. I told Cook that I thought it impossible the present Executive Administration should hold together through another session of Congress. It is now nothing but a system of mining and countermining between Crawford and Calhoun to blow up each other, and a continual underhanded working of both, jointly, against me, which has been the more effective because I have neither creature nor champion in either House of Congress. At this game Crawford is a much superior artist to Calhoun, whose hurried ambition will probably ruin himself and secure the triumph of Crawford. Such is the present situation."

37. AN EXCERPT FROM THE DIARY OF JOHN QUINCY ADAMS JUNE 2, 1822

". . . I doubted whether the Cabinet, as it is called, of Mr. Monroe would continue entire through the next session of Congress. Mr. [William] Crawford or Mr. [John C.] Calhoun, and most probably the latter, would be compelled to resign. Very probably the case might be my own. For the attacks upon me at the late session of Congress had been from masked batteries, but they had been of the most deadly character, and, as they imputed to me as a crime that which I believed to be the greatest service I had rendered my country, I could not possibly foresee what the next charge against me would be. All I knew was, that it became me to be prepared for my political decease at a moment's warning."

38. JOHN QUINCY ADAMS TO JOHN D. HEATH JUNE 21, 1822

"The *Richmond Enquirer* does not approve of me for next President of the United States. This declaration is fair and candid, nor have I a word to say in objection to it; but when in setting forth my sins it charges me with a proposal to let the British into the heart of our country, it is neither fair, nor candid, nor true. And as it considered me *hors de combat* for the Presidency even before the last kick which is to prove my *coup de grâce*, to join in the slander upon me was as needless as it was ungenerous. If the editors of the *Richmond Enquirer* and of a dozen other newspapers in the United States would sincerely and honestly consider me as *hors de combat*, they would save themselves much of the labor they are yet to undergo in flirting from their scavenger carts mud in my face to finish me.

Situated as I am I well know how hopeless a task it would be to attempt the refutation of the falsehoods which are constantly circulating against me in the newspapers. For every amputated head of the hydra there will always be two new ones to shoot up. Slander is the first and most efficacious of electioneering engines among us, but newspaper slander is not that which had operated or will operate most unfavorably to me. An undercurrent of calumny has been flowing and will continue to flow in every direction throughout the Union, nothing of which appears in the newspapers, but it goes in whispers and in private correspondence. It is a branch of the caucusing system, and it adapts its movements to the feelings and prejudices of the different sections of the country. It has a story for Pittsburg and a story for Portland, a misrepresentation for Milledgeville and a lie for Lexington. I have noticed of all this undermining from every quarter of the Union, and in several instances from persons total strangers to me, in others by anonymous letters. I have no countermining at work to blast the reputation of others and seldom attempt even to defend my own. I make no *bargains*. I listen to no overtures for *coalition*. I give no money. I push for no appointments of canvassing partisans to office. This utter inability to support my own cause passes among the caucus mongers for simplicity approaching to idiotism. I know it has been an avowed motive to some and a successful argument to others for resorting to other standards, and during the late session of Congress there was so animated a recruiting service and so general an enlistment, that Duane and Ritchie had good reason for concluding that I, who had neither Captain Plume nor Sergeant Kite to recruit for me, was *hors de combat*."

39. JOHN QUINCY ADAMS TO PETER PAUL FRANCIS DEGRAND JULY 5, 1822

"They who want a President with a cool head must vote for one. And so must they who want a President with an honest heart. If they can hit upon a man uniting both, so much the better for them."

40. AN EXCERPT FROM THE DIARY OF JOHN QUINCY ADAMS JULY 8, 1822

"In the evening Mr. [John C.] Calhoun was here, and afterwards General [Winfield] Scott, with Mr. Dick, the District Judge of the United States in Louisiana. They came while Mr. Calhoun was with me, and interrupted our conversation. The relations in which I now stand with Calhoun are delicate and difficult. At the last session of Congress he suffered a few member of Congress, with an Irishman named Rogers, editor of a newspaper at Easton, Pennsylvania, at their head, to set him up as a candidate for the succession to the Presidency. From that moment the caballing in Congress, in the State Legislatures, in the newspapers, and among the people, against me, has been multiplied tenfold. The Franklin Gazette, of Philadelphia, under the direction of R. Bache, G. M. Dallas, T. Sergeant, and Ingham, in concert with Rogers, opened immediately upon me, and has kept up ever since an insidious fire against me. Calhoun's partisans have countenanced it, and have been as busy as those of Mr. Crawford in their efforts to degrade me in the public opinion. Meanwhile, Calhoun has always professed to be a friend and admirer of mine, and to persons whom he knows to be my friends has said that he did not mean to be a candidate against a Northern man, and that he himself was decidedly for a Northern President."

41. AN EXCERPT FROM THE DIARY OF JOHN QUINCY ADAMS AUGUST 19, 1822

"Answered General Dearborn's letter, and received one from my wife, chiefly upon an attack against me in one of the Philadelphia newspapers on account of the negligence of my dress. It says that I wear neither waistcoat nor cravat, and sometimes go to church barefoot. My wife is much concerned at this, and several of my friends at Philadelphia have spoken to her of it as a serious affair. In the Washington *City Gazette*, some person unknown to me has taken the cudgels in my behalf, and answered the accusation gravely as if the charge were true. It is true only as regards the cravat, instead of which, in the extremity of the summer heat, I wear round my neck a black silk riband. But even in the falsehoods of this charge, what I may profitably remember is the perpetual and malignant watchfulness with which I am observed in my open day and secret night, with the deliberate purpose of exposing me to public obloquy or public ridicule. There is nothing so deep and nothing so shallow which political enmity will not turn to account. Let it be a warning to me to take heed to my ways."

42. JOHN QUINCY ADAMS TO LOUISA CATHERINE ADAMS OCTOBER 7, 1822

"Your letter and journal to the 3rd have come to hand. If I should give you the reasons why I cannot go and spend a week at Philadelphia, to show my friends there how much I long to be President, you would think them very ridiculous, and me not less so for detailing them. My friends at Philadelphia are not the only ones who send me kind messages to inform me that unless I mend my manners, I shall never be President. Well, and what then? There will be candidates enough for the Presidency without me, and if my delicacy is not suited to the times, there are candidates enough who have no such delicacy. It suits my temper to be thus delicate. Do they call it aristocratic hauteur and learned arrogance? Why, so be it, my worthy friends and approve good masters. It is not then cringing servility, nor insatiate importunity.

If my friends will neither say nor write to me a single word about the Presidency, from this time forward until the election is over, I believe it would be better for me and perhaps for them. The event will neither depend upon them nor upon me. They and you think I am panting to be President, when I am much more inclined to envy Castlereagh the relief he has found from a situation too much like mine, though I implore the mercy of God that I may be never so deserted of him as to seek relief in the same manner. I have reliance upon God, and therefore while possessed of my reason, I shall never cut the thread of my own life. I have reliance upon my country, and therefore will never flinch from the duties or the dangers of any situation to which she will call me. I have reliance upon *myself* (with God's blessing), and hope I have resources to bear the neglect or the rejection of my services by my country. If I should tell you that I dread infinitely more than I wish to be President, you would not believe me. But suppose it for a moment to be true. How could you advise me to act? Will you say it is very easy? Decline publicly to be a candidate? No. That would be political suicide. It would be to distrust myself and my country. It is my situation that makes me a candidate, and you at least know that my present situation was neither of my own seeking, nor of my choice."

43. JOHN QUINCY ADAMS TO LOUISA CATHERINE ADAMS OCTOBER 7, 1822

"So much for the *public* history of Mr. Monroe's administration. Now for its secret history. This has been one continued series of intrigues, from the Amelia Island expedition, to the senatorial *etiquette* and the Seminole war debates, down to Jackson's quarrel in Florida, and Jonathan Russell's duplicate, to bar my access to the next Presidency. All the leading members of both houses of Congress, all the editors of accredited printing presses throughout the Union, and all the caucussing managers of the state legislatures, have been engaged, each with his own views, and as retainers to their respective *patrons,* in crying me down and disgracing me in the estimation of the people. Meanwhile I have not a single active partisan in Congress; not a single printing press in pay or in promise; not one member of any one state legislature disposed to caucus for me, or connected with my interest by any stimulant expectation of his own. Do my friends in Philadelphia suppose me so totally blind to what is passing around me, as not to see what my situation is, or not to foresee what its result must be? Do they suppose that, while I see *all* the avenues to the temple preoccupied one by one, and a crowd rushing to the gate, already stifling one another, I expect to obtain admission by standing still? Or do they think me besotted enough to believe that I could, if I would, turn the current of public opinion in my favor by a week's visit to Philadelphia? Tell them that I am going by another road and to another temple. That if they must have a President to whom they dare speak, and if they dare not speak to me, they must vote for another man. That I am *not* bound to be President of the United States, but that I *am* bound to perform the duties of Secretary of State as long as I hold that office, and that Washington and not Philadelphia is the place where those duties must be performed."

44. A PORTION OF AN OPEN LETTER APPEARING IN THE *RICHMOND ENQUIRER* WRITTEN BY JOHN QUINCY ADAMS TO THE FREEHOLDERS OF WASHINGTON, WYTHE, GRAYSON, RUSSELL, TAZEWELL, LEE AND SCOTT COUNTIES, VIRGINIA JANUARY 4, 1823

"I believe that the constitution of the United States had not authorized the Congress to invest the President with all the absolute powers of a Spanish monarch over a Spanish colony; to annex the people of that colony to our federal union, and to give them without naturalization, and to thrust upon them without their consent, all the rights, privileges and immunities, duties and burdens of the constituent members of the confederation."

45. AN EXCERPT FROM JOHN QUINCY ADAMS'S *THE MACBETH POLICY* JANUARY 1823

"The law of friendship is a reciprocation of good offices. He who asks or accepts the offer of friendly service contracts the obligation of meeting it with a suitable return. He who asks or accepts the offer of aid to promote his own views necessarily binds himself to promote the views of him from whom he receives it. Whatever may be the wishes of an individual, nothing but the unbiassed voice of many others can make him even a candidate for the chief magistracy. If he asks or accepts the aid of one, he must ask or accept the aid of multitudes. Between the principle, of which much has been said in the newspapers, that *a President of the United States must remember those* to whom he owes his elevation, and the principle of accepting no aid on the score of friendship or personal kindness to him, there is no alternative. The former, as it has been announced and urged, I deem to essentially and vitally corrupt. The latter is the only principle to which no exception can be taken."

46. AN EXCERPT FROM THE DIARY OF JOHN QUINCY ADAMS NOVEMBER 28, 1823

"It was possible, perhaps not improbable, that there should be three candidates for the Presidency, to be chosen by the House of Representatives, and no majority be found practicable for either of them—in which case the Executive Government must be administered by the Vice-President; though [John W. Taylor] knew not whether for a whole Presidential term or only until a new election for President could be held.

I told him I had seen a paragraph in the Richmond Enquirer stating that there was a plan to that effect on foot, and that the Vice-President thus to be chosen had been named to them. This was all that I knew of the matter. But there would be so great inconvenience in devolving upon the Vice-President the Executive power, from mere inability to choose a President, that if the case should occur of three candidates, as he had supposed, and no majority could be formed for either, I should expect one of them would ultimately withdraw.

He said neither of them could withdraw, as he could not prevent those who adhered to him from voting for him.

I said if the case was supposable that I should be one of them, and should have of the three smallest number of electoral votes, I should not only think it my duty to withdraw, but to declare that if elected I would not accept—rather than that the election should fail."

47. AN EXCERPT FROM THE DIARY OF JOHN QUINCY ADAMS JANUARY 23, 1824

"Mr. [Benjamin] Crowninshield told me that William King, at my house last Tuesday evening, warmly urged to him that my friends ought to go into caucus with those of Mr. Crawford to vote for him as President and me as Vice-President, upon the principle that it is impossible I should be elected as President, and that, the first place being unattainable, it will be the part of wisdom to secure the second. Crowninshield said he gave King no encouragement to expect the acquiescence of my friends in this arrangement, and he agreed with me that it ought not be accepted."

48. AN EXCERPT FROM THE DIARY OF JOHN QUINCY ADAMS JANUARY 25, 1824

"I told Taylor that my mind was made up. I was satisfied there was at this time a majority of the whole people of the United States, and a majority of the States, utterly averse to a nomination by Congressional caucus, thinking it adverse to the spirit of the Constitution, and tending to corruption. I thought it so myself; and therefore would not now accept a Congressional caucus nomination, even for the Presidency. And of course a nomination for the Vice-Presidency, in cooperation with one for Mr. Crawford as President, could have no charms for me. Not that I despised the Vice-Presidency, or wished peevishly to reject the second place because I could not obtain the first; but because the people disapproved of this mode of nomination, and I disapproved of it myself. I added that in opposition to such nomination I wished my friends to take any measures in concert with others opposed to it as might be proper. In effecting this concert, I wished them to dispose of me as they should think best for the public service. I was entirely prepared to consider the election by the people of another person to the Presidency as an indication of their will that I should retire to private life.

Taylor said he thought my determination perfectly correct as to the Vice-Presidency; but that I should reconsider that of retiring to private life; that the mere failure of an election to the Presidency could not be considered as indicative of the will of the people that I should retire from the place that I now hold. A multitude of causes and of motives contributed to the issue of a Presidential election—sectional feelings, party prejudices, political management, and many others. I might still without dishonor retain my place under another Administration."

49. AN EXCERPT FROM THE DIARY OF JOHN QUINCY ADAMS JANUARY 30, 1824

"Colonel R. M. Johnson, Mr. R. King, and Mr. Fuller had long conversations with me concerning the movements of the parties here for the Presidential succession. Johnson says that Calhoun proposed to him an arrangement by which I should be supported as President, General Jackson as Vice-President, Clay as Secretary of State, and he himself Secretary of the Treasury; not as a bargain or coalition, but by the common understanding of our mutual friends."

50. AN EXCERPT FROM THE DIARY OF JOHN QUINCY ADAMS FEBRUARY 4, 1824

"There was in the genius of our institutions a graduated subordination among the persons by whom the Government was administered. Reputation was the basis of our elections, and the emblem of its organization was a pyramid, at the point of which was the chief, under whom men of high consideration, though not equal to his, naturally found their places. Among the sources of this consideration, age and experience had their share, and, unless superseded by very transcendent merit, a decisive share. This had never yet been otherwise under our present Constitution. Not a single instance had occurred of a person older than the President of the United States accepting office as a head of Department under him. This was not the result of any written law, but it arose from the natural operation of our system. What effect of such a departure from it as the election of Mr. Calhoun might be, I could not undertake to say. But this I would say, and had said to those of my friends who had spoken to me on the subject: that if the harmony of the country could be promoted by setting me altogether aside, I would cheerfully acquiesce in that disposition, and never would be the occasion or the supporter of factious opposition to any Administration whatsoever."

51. AN EXCERPT FROM THE DIARY OF JOHN QUINCY ADAMS FEBRUARY 4, 1824

"I attended in the evening the drawing-room at the President's. On returning home, I found J. W. Taylor at my house, and had a long conversation with him. He told me that Jesse B. Thomas, a Senator from Illinois, had strongly urged upon him the expediency of my acquiescing in the nomination as Vice-President, with

Mr. Crawford for the Presidency. He said that Mr. Crawford would certainly be elected, and he spoke of certain members of Congress as ultimately to vote for him who appear to be far otherwise disposed at this time; that it was, however, very desirable that he should carry with him the strength which he would derive from the co-operation of my friends; that from the state of Mr. Crawford's health it was highly probable the duties of the Presidency would devolve upon the Vice-President, which had made it necessary to select with peculiar anxiety a person qualified for the contingency which was to be anticipated; that a compliance with the views of Mr. Crawford's friends on this occasion would be rendering them a service which would recommend me to their future favor, and would doubtless secure my election hereafter to the Presidency. Taylor said he had answered that admitting even the certainty that Mr. Crawford should be elected, that was not sufficient reason for the acquiescence of my friends in the proposed arrangement. If the election should be carried against them, they will at least have followed their own sense of what was right and fit."

52. AN EXCERPT FROM THE DIARY OF JOHN QUINCY ADAMS MARCH 19, 1824

"[Richard Mentor] Johnson says Mr. Crawford's friends, particularly Governor [James] Barbour, are very sanguine of his election, and entirely sure of the vote of New York. They consider all prospect of my being supported as having vanished, and that all New England will abandon me and vote for Crawford. I believe Mr. Crawford's prospects and mine equally unpromising. Intrigue against the voice of the people will probably give him New York. Virginia, Georgia, North Carolina, and Delaware will also probably be for him; but not others; and if New York fails him he will decline and withdraw. Whether all New England will support me is yet problematical, and the rest is yet more uncertain. The issue must be where it ought to be, and my duty is cheerful acquiescence in the event."

53. AN EXCERPT FROM THE DIARY OF JOHN QUINCY ADAMS MARCH 23, 1824

"The mining and countermining upon this Presidential election is an admirable study of human nature. The mist into which Calhoun's bubble broke settles upon Jackson, who is now taking the fragments of Clinton's party. Those of Clay will also fall chiefly to him and his sect, and Crawford's are now working for mine. They both consider my prospects as desperate, and are scrambling for my spoils. I can do no more than satisfy them that I have no purchasable interest. My friends will go over to whomsoever they may prefer—some to one and some to another."

54. AN EXCERPT FROM THE DIARY OF JOHN QUINCY ADAMS MARCH 25, 1824

"Wyer was here, and told me Colonel Taylor of Caroline, the Senator from Virginia, had mentioned to him that there was a rumor circulated in that State that my father had made his will, bequeathing his estate to a public institution, or to his native town, and that from this is was inferred that I was laboring under his displeasure, and it was producing unfavorable political impressions concerning my personal character. He said Colonel Taylor had thoughts of writing to my father about it. I told Wyer that I should be glad if Colonel Taylor would write; that my father's conduct to me had been that of a most affectionate father; and that he had not left it to the disposal of a will to bestow upon me my portion of his estate. He had conveyed it to me by deed, irrevocable by himself. I stated to him the various dispositions advantageous to me already made by my father, and his undeviating kindness to me. This utterly groundless rumor is a new ingredient in the electioneering cauldron. What next?"

55. AN EXCERPT FROM THE DIARY OF JOHN QUINCY ADAMS MARCH 27, 1824

"[Horatio] Seymour appeared anxious to ascertain for whom it would be best to vote as Vice-President. I said I believe the popular feeling in New England had already received such an impulse that it was no longer controllable, nor did I think it worth while to attempt the control of it. I was convinced it would give no dissatisfaction to General Jackson, or his friends, that he should be voted for as Vice-President by those who should support me for the Presidency, and if others should carry him to the Presidency itself, we must, as in every other event of the same election, acquiesce in the voice of the nation, as delivered through its constitutional organs. I told them I was very sure I had nothing to expect, and was not willing to have anything to ask, in the way of support to me from any other candidate or his friends. I desired to stand only upon my own ground, and would not crave assistance from any other quarter. I wished my friends to vote for Jackson as Vice-President, because I thought the place suited to him and him suited to the place. The thing was fitting in itself, and perfectly well suited to the usual geographical distribution of the two offices. On public principles it was unexceptionable, and I would not look further for determining motives."

56. AN EXCERPT FROM THE DIARY OF JOHN QUINCY ADAMS APRIL 22, 1824

"Mr. Moore came at seven o'clock this evening, according to his appointment. He announced himself as the most intimate friend but one to Mr. De Witt Clinton that he had in the world. He wished that my friends and Mr. Clinton's friends should harmonize; for the Clintonians would certainly turn the scale in New York; Mr. Clinton was against Mr. Crawford for President, and wished for an honest man in that office; that Mr. Clinton's friends, until very lately, had thought they could bring him forward with prospects of success, but they had now given it up as hopeless; that I was very strong in New York, and the attempt to set up General Jackson would only terminate in giving the vote to Crawford. His wish was that I should be chosen President, and General Jackson Vice-President. But he wished to know what were my sentiments with regard to Mr. Clinton.

I told him that whether the people of New York would vote for me or not I should leave entirely to themselves; that my feelings towards Mr. Clinton were altogether friendly."

57. AN EXCERPT FROM THE DIARY OF JOHN QUINCY ADAMS MAY 1, 1824

"I asked [John Reed, Jr.] if he thought there was a doubt of my election by a large majority of the electoral votes but for an opposition from the Republican party on the very ground of my being suspected of too much federalism. He said there were not. I told him I had originally been a federalist, just such as President Washington had been. But of the course that had been pursued by the federalists during and preceding the late war my opinion was well known, and had been fully manifested by my conduct. Personally, the federalists had done me wrong, and I expected no favor from them. But during the whole of the present Administration it had been at least as much supported by the federalists as by the Republicans. If it should be the pleasure of the people of the United States that I should serve them as their President, I should be the President not of a section, nor of a faction, but of the whole Union."

58. AN EXCERPT FROM THE DIARY OF JOHN QUINCY ADAMS MAY 8, 1824

"To suffer without feeling is not in human nature; and when I consider that to me alone, of all the candidates before the nation, failure of success would be equivalent to a vote of censure by the nation upon my past service, I cannot dissemble to myself that I have more at stake upon the result than any other individual in the Union. Yet a man qualified for the elective Chief Magistracy of ten millions of people should be a man proof alike to prosperous and to adverse fortune. If I am able to bear success, I must be tempered to endure defeat. He who is equal to the task of serving a nation as her chief ruler must possess resources of a power to serve her even against her own will. This is the principle that I would impress indelibly upon my own mind, and for the practical realization of which in its proper result I look to wisdom and strength from above."

59. AN EXCERPT FROM THE DIARY OF JOHN QUINCY ADAMS MAY 24, 1824

"David Trimble, member of the House of Kentucky, came and took leave. He spoke of his earnestness in support of the election of Mr. Clay to the Presidency, and said he hoped there was less of personal animosity between him and me than there had been heretofore. I told him there never had been on my part any animosity other than that which Mr. Clay had chosen to raise. Trimble said he did not wish to enter upon this subject, and, after some other remarks, said all he could tell me was, that of the candidates before the public for the Presidency, Mr. Clay would be his first choice, but I should not be his last. He meant I should take this as a proof of his friendly disposition to me."

60. AN EXCERPT FROM THE DIARY OF JOHN QUINCY ADAMS JUNE 10, 1824

"Could the President sign an Act, Congress not being in session? Wirt thought he could. So did I. The article of the Constitution concerning the signature of the President to Acts of Congress was read and analyzed. Nothing in it requiring that the President should sign while Congress are in session.

Calhoun said that uniform practice had established a practical construction of the Constitution.

I observed that the practice had merely grown out of the precedents in the British Parliament. But the principles were different. The King was a constituent part of Parliament, and no Act of Parliament could be valid without the King's approbation. But the President is not a constituent part of Congress, and an Act of Congress may be valid as law without his signature or assent."

61. AN EXCERPT FROM THE DIARY OF JOHN QUINCY ADAMS JULY 29, 1824

"*Day.* I rise between five and six, and, when the tide serves, swim between one and two hours in the Potomac. Breakfast about nine, then write or meditate or receive visitors till one or two. Attend at my office till six, then home to dine. Take an evening walk of half an hour, and from ten to eleven retire to bed. There are eight or ten newspapers of extensive circulation published in various parts of the Union acting in close concert with each other and pouring forth continual streams of slander upon my character and reputation, public and private. No falsehood is too broad, and no insinuation too base, for them, and a great portion of their calumnies are of a nature that no person could show or even assert their falsehood but myself. As the Presidential election approaches, numerous correspondents from every quarter write me letters professing good will, or enquiring of my opinions, from men most of them entirely unknown to me. I answer very few, and perhaps ought to answer none of them. Particular friends write to me by way of consultation and of anxiety; and they can seldom be answered with entire freedom. The result is a great waste of time and of mental occupation upon subjects personal to myself, to the necessary neglect of public business and detriment to the public service. I have no reason to hope to be released from this state of trial for many months to come. To pass through it with a pure heart and a firm spirit is my duty and my prayer."

62. AN EXCERPT FROM THE DIARY OF JOHN QUINCY ADAMS AUGUST 27, 1824

"About fifteen newspapers in various parts of the United States, several of them daily papers, others printed twice or three times a week, are, and for the ensuing four or five months at least will be, filled column upon column with everything that truth, misrepresentation, or falsehood can supply to defame and disgrace me. In passing through this ordeal, may the Spirit which has hitherto sustained me still by my staff and guide."

63. AN EXCERPT FROM THE DIARY OF JOHN QUINCY ADAMS AUGUST 31, 1824

"*Day.* The distribution of my time differs not from that of the last month. The bitterness and violence of Presidential electioneering increase as the time advances. The uncertainty of the event continues as great as ever. It seems as if every liar and calumniator in the country was at work day and night to destroy my character. It does not surprise me, because I have seen the same species of ribaldry year after year heaped upon my father, and for a long time upon Washington. But it is impossible to be wholly insensible to this process while it is in operation. It distracts my attention from public business, and consumes precious time. I have finally concluded to take a month of holiday, to visit my father and dismiss care."

64. AN EXCERPT FROM THE DIARY OF JOHN QUINCY ADAMS JANUARY 25, 1825

"There is at this moment a very high state of excitement in the House, Mr. Clay and the majority of the Ohio and Kentucky delegations having yesterday unequivocally avowed their determination to vote for me. This immediately produced an approximation of the Calhoun, Crawford, and Jackson partisans, and will effectually knit the coalition of the South with Pennsylvania."

65. AN EXCERPT FROM THE DIARY OF JOHN QUINCY ADAMS JANUARY 25, 1825

"The impression almost universal, made yesterday, was that the election was settled in my favor; but the result of the counter-movement will be the real crisis, and I have little doubt that will be decisive the other way. My situation will be difficult and trying beyond my powers of expression. May but my strength be proportioned to my trial."

66. AN EXCERPT FROM THE DIARY OF JOHN QUINCY ADAMS FEBRUARY 5, 1825

". . . that if I should be elected, it would only be by Clay's corrupt coalition with me, and that the people would be so disgusted with this that there would be a systematic and determined opposition from the beginning, so that the Administration could not get along. It would be overthrown, and he would be involved in its ruin."

67. AN EXCERPT FROM THE DIARY OF JOHN QUINCY ADAMS FEBRUARY 9, 1825

"May the blessing of God rest upon the event of this day!—the second Wednesday in February, when the election of a President of the United States for the term of four years, from the 4th of March next, was consummated. Of the votes in the electoral colleges, there were ninety-nine for Andrew Jackson, of Tennessee; eighty-four for John Quincy Adams, of Massachusetts; forty-one for William Harris Crawford, of Georgia; and thirty-seven for Henry Clay, of Kentucky: in all, two hundred and sixty-one. This result having been announced, on opening and counting the votes in joint meeting of the two Houses, the House of Representatives immediately proceeded to the vote by ballot from the three highest candidates, when John Quincy Adams received the votes of thirteen, Andrew Jackson of seven, and William H. Crawford of four States. The election was thus completed, very unexpectedly, by a single ballot. Alexander H. Everett gave me the first notice, both of the issue of the votes of the electoral colleges as announced in the joint meeting, and of the final vote as declared. Wyer followed him a few minutes afterwards. Mr. Bolton and Mr. Thomas, the Naval Architect, succeeded; and B. W. Crowninshield, calling, on his return from the House to his lodgings, at my house, confirmed the report. Congratulations from several of the officers of the Department of State ensued—from D. Brent, G. Ironside, W. Slade, and Josias W. King. Those of my wife, children, and family were cordial and affecting, and I received an affectionate note from Mr. Rufus King, of New York, written in the Senate-chamber after the event."

68. AN EXCERPT FROM THE DIARY OF JOHN QUINCY ADAMS FEBRUARY 9, 1825

"After dinner, the Russian Minister, Baron Tuyl, called to congratulate me upon the issue of the election. I attended, with Mrs. Adams, the drawing-room at the President's. It was crowded to overflowing. General Jackson was there, and we shook hands. He was altogether placid and courteous. I received numerous friendly salutations. D. Webster asked me when I could receive the committee of the House to announce to me my election. I appointed to-morrow noon, at my own house."

69. AN EXCERPT FROM THE DIARY OF JOHN QUINCY ADAMS FEBRUARY 9, 1825

"I enclosed Mr. R[ufus] King's note, with a letter of three lines, to my father, asking for his blessing and prayers on the event of this day, the most important day of my life, and which I would close as it began, with supplications to the Father of mercies that its consequences may redound to His glory and to the welfare of my country. After I returned from the drawing-room, a band of musicians came and serenaded me at my house. It was past midnight when I retired."

70. JOHN QUINCY ADAMS TO JOHN ADAMS FEBRUARY 9, 1825

"MY DEAR AND HONORED FATHER:—

The enclosed note from Mr. King will inform you of the event of this day, upon which I can only offer you my congratulations and ask your blessings and prayers.

Your affectionate and dutiful son,

JOHN QUINCY ADAMS"

71. AN EXCERPT FROM THE DIARY OF JOHN QUINCY ADAMS FEBRUARY 10, 1825

"At noon, Daniel Webster, of Massachusetts, Joseph Vance, of Ohio, and William S. Archer, of Virginia, came as a committee of the House of Representatives and announced to me that in the recent election of a President of the United States, no person having received a majority of all the votes of the elector's appointed, and the choice having consequently devolved upon the House of Representatives, that House, proceeding in the manner prescribed in the Constitution, did yesterday choose me to be President of the United States for four years, commencing on the 4th day of March next.

I observed to the committee that the only preceding occasion since the establishment of the Constitution of the United States upon which a similar notification had been made from the House of Representatives was at the election of Mr. Jefferson, who had returned to the committee a written answer. I had thought it would be proper to follow this example, and I read, and delivered to Mr. Webster, the answer that I had prepared.

The committee informed me that they had already notified the President of the election."

72. AN EXCERPT FROM THE DIARY OF JOHN QUINCY ADAMS FEBRUARY 11, 1825

"I was at the President's, and again repeated the request that he would make the nominations which had been postponed till after the election. He said he would take it into consideration. I told the President I had invited Mr. Crawford to remain at the head of the Treasury Department, and showed him the letter I had received from him this morning, in very friendly terms declining the offer. I then said that I should offer the Department of State to Mr. Clay, considering it due to his talents and services, to the Western section of the Union, whence he comes, and to the confidence in me manifested by their delegations; that for the Treasury and War Departments I should be glad to take his advice, and to consult him with reference to other objects of public interest, if it would be agreeable to him."

73. AN EXCERPT FROM THE DIARY OF JOHN QUINCY ADAMS MARCH 4, 1825

"After two successive sleepless nights, I entered upon this day with a supplication to Heaven, first, for my country; secondly, for myself and for those connected with my good name and fortunes, that the last results of its events may be auspicious and blessed. About half-past eleven o'clock I left my house with an escort of several companies of militia and a cavalcade of citizens, accompanied in my carriage by Samuel L. Southard, Secretary of the Navy, and William Wirt, Attorney-General, and followed by James Monroe, late President of the United States, in his own carriage. We proceeded to the Capitol, and to the Senate-chamber. The Senate were in session, and John C. Calhoun presiding in the chair, having been previously sworn into office as Vice-President of the United States and President of the Senate. The Senate adjourned, and from the Senate-chamber, accompanied by the members of that body and by the Judges of the Supreme Court, I repaired to the hall of the House of Representatives, and, after delivering from the Speaker's chair my inaugural address to a crowded auditory, I pronounced from a volume of the laws held up to me by John Marshall, Chief Justice of the United States, the oath faithfully to execute the office of President of the United States, and, to the best of my ability, to preserve, protect, and defend the Constitution of the United States. After exchanging salutations with the late President, and many other persons present, I retired from the hall, passed in review the military companies drawn up in front of the Capitol, and returned to my house with the same procession which accompanied me from it. I found at my house a crowd of visitors, which continued about two hours, and received their felicitations. Before the throng had subsided, I went myself to the President's house, and joined with the multitude of visitors to Mr. Monroe there. I then returned home to dine, and in the evening attended the ball, which was also crowded, at Carusi's Hall. Immediately after supper I withdrew, and came home. I closed the day as it had begun, with thanksgiving to God for all His mercies and favors past, and with prayers for the continuance of them to my country, and to myself and mine."

74. AN EXCERPT FROM THE DIARY OF JOHN QUINCY ADAMS MARCH 8, 1825

"The usual appropriation of fourteen thousand dollars for refurnishing the President's house was made by an Act of Congress at the close of the session. Mr. Crawford being desirous to dispose of his plate, and as there was no probability that he could dispose of it here, I agreed to take it for the public service and pay for it from this appropriation. There were during Mr. Monroe's Administration fifty thousand dollars appropriated for furnishing the house. He had placed the fund under the management of Colonel Lane, who, two or three years since, died insolvent, with twenty thousand dollars of public moneys unaccounted for, which has given rise to much obloquy upon Mr. Monroe. I have determined, therefore, to charge myself with the amount of the new appropriation, and to be myself accountable to the Treasury for its expenditure."

75. AN EXCERPT FROM THE DIARY OF JOHN QUINCY ADAMS NOVEMBER 7, 1830

"Spent the evening in writing and reflecting upon this new incident, which has drifted me back again amidst the breakers of the political ocean. It is also a novelty in the history of the country, and as a precedent may have no unimportant bearing upon future events. By the Constitution of the United States, the President is re-eligible as long as he lives. Washington, Jefferson, and Madison voluntarily retired after one re-election, and Jefferson no doubt intended to make the example a practical exposition of constitutional principle. It was followed by Mr. Monroe, perhaps with not much cordiality, and will be continued as long as a Presidential term of eight years shall wear out the popularity of the person holding the office. One of the consequences of this has been and will be that ex-Presidents will survive for many years the termination of their offices; that as individuals they will take a part in public affairs, and that they will sometimes solicit, and sometimes be elected to, subordinate offices. All the preceding Presidents have held offices of a public nature after the expiration of their Presidential service; none, however, as a member of either House of Congress; and there are many who think it now a derogatory descent. This is a mere prejudice; and had I alleged my former station as a reason for rejecting the suffrages of the people assigning me a seat in the House of Representatives, I should not merely have been chargeable with arrogance, but should have exposed myself to ridicule. So far as concerns myself, I consider this new call to the public service as a misfortune, inasmuch as it takes from me the last hope of an old age of quiet and leisure. I am still to be buffeted with political rancor and personal malignity, with more than equal chances of losing the favor even of those who now think they honor themselves by their suffrages more than me. My return to public life in a subordinate station is disagreeable to my family, and disapproved by some of my friends; though no one of them has expressed that disapprobation to me. For the discharge of the duties of this particular station I never was eminently qualified, possessing no talent for extemporaneous public speaking, and at this time being in the decline of my faculties, both of mind and body. This event, therefore, gives me deep concern and anxious forebodings. Yet can I not withhold my grateful acknowledgement to the Disposer of human events, and to the people of my native region, for this unexpected testimonial of their continued confidence after all the combinations of personal rivals and political competitors to shake it. 'The hearth knoweth its own bitterness, and a stranger intermeddleth not with its joys.' No one knows, and few conceive, the agony of mind that I have suffered from the time that I was made by circumstances, and not by my volition, a candidate for the Presidency till I was dismissed from that station by my failure of my re-election. They were feelings to be suppressed; and they were suppressed. No human being has ever heard me complain. Domestic calamity, far heavier than any political disappointment or disaster can possibly be, overtook me immediately after my fall from power, and the moment of my distress was seized by an old antagonist to indulge a hatred overflowing with the concentrated rancor of forty years, and who could not resist the pleasure of giving me what he thought the finishing blow at the moment when he saw me down. It seemed as if I was deserted by all mankind; and precisely at that time the American Academy of Arts and Sciences, a literary and scientific institution of my native State, which for a series of years during my prosperity had annually elected me their President when it was impossible for me to attend their meetings, thought proper to substitute another President in my place. In the French opera of Richard Cœur-de-Lion, the minstrel, Blondel, sings under the walls of his prison a song, beginning:

'O, Richard! O, mon Roi!
L'univers t'abandonne.'

When I first heard this song, forty-five years ago, at one of the first representations of that delightful play, it made and indelible impression upon my memory, without imagining that I should ever feel its force so much closer to home. In the year 1829 scarce a day passed that did not bring it to my thoughts. In the course of last winter a vacancy occurred in the Board of Overseers of Harvard University. Absent, I was very unexpectedly elected to fill that vacancy. I attributed this to the personal friendship and influence of President Quincy. But this call upon me by the people of the district in which I reside, to represent them in Congress, has been spontaneous, and, although counteracted by a double opposition, federalists and Jacksonite, I have received nearly three votes in four throughout the district. My election as President of the United States was not half so gratifying to my inmost soul. No election or appointment conferred upon me ever gave me so much pleasure. I say this to record my sentiments; but no stranger intermeddleth with my joys, and the dearest of my friends have no sympathy with my sensations."

76. AN EXCERPT FROM JOHN QUINCY ADAMS'S *AN EULOGY ON THE LIFE AND CHARACTER OF JAMES MADISON, FOURTH PRESIDENT OF THE UNITED STATES* SEPTEMBER 27, 1836

"If there be a duty, binding in chains more adamantine than all the rest the conscience of a Chief Magistrate of this Union, it is that of preserving peace with all mankind—peace with the other nations of the earth—peace among the several States of this Union—peace in the hearts and temper of our own people. Yet must a President of the United

States never cease to feel that his charge is to maintain the rights, the interests and the honor no less that the peace of his country—nor will he be permitted to forget that peace must be the offspring of two concurring wills. That to seek peace is not always to ensue it."

II. GEORGE WASHINGTON ON JOHN QUINCY ADAMS

1. GEORGE WASHINGTON COMMISSIONING JOHN QUINCY ADAMS AS UNITED STATES MINISTER TO THE NETHERLANDS MAY 30, 1794

"GEORGE WASHINGTON,
President of the United States of America

To John Quincy Adams.—Greeting.

Reposing especial trust and confidence in your integrity, prudence and ability, I have nominated, and by and with the advice and consent of the Senate, do appoint you the said JOHN QUINCY ADAMS Minister Resident for the United States of America with their High Mightiness the States General of the United Netherlands, authorizing you hereby to do and perform all such matters and things as to the said place or office doth appertain, or as may be duly given you in charge hereafter, and the said office to hold and exercise during the pleasure of the President of the United States for the time being. IN TESTIMONY whereof I have caused the seal of the United States to be hereunto affixed. Given under my hand at the City of Philadelphia the thirtieth day of May, in the year of our Lord, one thousand seven hundred and ninety four, and of the Independence of the United States of America the eighteenth.

GEO. WASHINGTON.

By the President of the United States of America,
(SEAL) EDMOND RANDOLPH, *Secretary of State*"

2. GEORGE WASHINGTON TO ALEXANDER HAMILTON JUNE 7, 1794

"I presume that the power, which you design for Mr. Adams, will be of the same kind with that formerly given to his predecessor Mr. Short. I wish you to have the two powers prepared in conformity with this letter."

3. GEORGE WASHINGTON TO EDMUND RANDOLPH JUNE 19, 1794

"At five o'clock this afternoon I reached this place, and shall proceed on in the morning.

Mr. Adams' Commission, as Minister Resident to the United Netherlands, was signed, if I recollect rightly, before I left Philadelphia. If his letters of Credence are forwarded to me by the Post, they also shall be signed & returned to you; to supersede the necessity of his waiting for them in case every thing else should be in readiness, before I return.

As his duties at the Hague, will be few, & simple; chiefly of a pecuniary sort; there will be no necessity for detaining him to obtain my approbation of his instructions but I would have the Secretary of the Treasury consulted thereon."

4. GEORGE WASHINGTON TO JOHN ADAMS AUGUST 20, 1795

"Mr. John Adams, your son, must not think of retiring from the walk he is now in: his prospects if he pursues it are fair: and I shall be much mistaken, if in as short a time as can well be expected, he is not found at the head of the Diplomatic Corps, let the government be administered by whomever the people may choose."

5. MESSAGE FROM PRESIDENT WASHINGTON TO THE UNITED STATES SENATE INFORMING THEM OF HIS NOMINATION OF JOHN QUINCY ADAMS AS AMERICAN AMBASSADOR TO SPAIN MAY 28, 1796

"GENTLEMEN OF THE SENATE:—

I nominate John Quincy Adams, at present Minister Resident of the United States at the Hague, to be their Minister Plenipotentiary at Lisbon.

G°˙ Washington"

6. OFFICIAL LETTER BY GEORGE WASHINGTON, COMMISSIONING JOHN QUINCY ADAMS AS UNITED STATES MINISTER TO PORTUGAL MAY 30, 1796

"GEORGE WASHINGTON, President of the United States of America

To John Quincy Adams—Greeting

Reposing especial Trust and Confidence in your Integrity, Prudence and Ability, I have nominated and by and with the advice and consent of the Senate, do appoint you the said John Quincy Adams, Minister Plenipotentiary for the United States of America at the court of her most Faithful Majesty, authorizing you hereby to do and perform all such matters and Things as to the said Place of Office doth appertain, or as may be duly given you in charge hereafter, and the said office to hold and exercise during the pleasure of the President of the United States for the time being. IN TESTIMONY whereof I have caused the seal of the United States to be hereunto affixed. Given under my hand at the City of Philadelphia, the Thirtieth day of May, in the year of our Lord one thousand seven hundred and ninety-six, and of the Independence of the United States of America the twentieth.

GEO. WASHINGTON.

By the President of the United States of America,
(SEAL) TIMOTHY PICKERING, *Secretary of State,*

7. GEORGE WASHINGTON TO THE BATAVIAN REPUBLIC NATIONAL ASSEMBLY FEBRUARY 17, 1797

"Deeming it expedient that John Quincy Adams, Minister Resident from the United States of America to the Batavian Republic, should enter on another mission, he is instructed to take leave of you; and in doing it to express to you the continuance of our friendship and our sincere desire to render perpetual that harmony and good understanding which has ever subsisted between the two Republics. We are persuaded that he will do this in a manner corresponding with these sentiments and to the respect we bear you. And we pray God to have you, Great and good Friends, in his holy keeping. Written at the City of Philadelphia, the 17th day of February 1797."

8. GEORGE WASHINGTON TO MARIA I OF PORTUGAL FEBRUARY 17, 1797

"Desirous of continuing a friendly and useful intercourse between the subjects of your Majesty and the Citizens of these States, and the proofs or our good will and considerations towards your Majesty, I have named John Quincy Adams, one of our distinguished Citizens, Minister Plenipotentiary for the United States of America near your Majesty. He knows the interests we take, and shall ever take, in your prosperity and happiness; and I beseech your Majesty to give entire Credence to whatever he shall deliver on our part, and most of all when he shall assure you of the sincerity of our friendship."

9. GEORGE WASHINGTON TO JOHN ADAMS FEBRUARY 20, 1797

"Dear Sir: I thank you for giving me the perusal of the enclosed, The sentiments do honor to the head and heart of the writer, and if my wishes would be of any avail they should go to you in a *strong hope* that you will not withhold merited promotion for Mr. John Adams because he is your Son. For without intending to compliment the father or the mother, or to censure any others, I give it as my decided opinion that Mr. Adams is the most valuable public character we have abroad, and that he will prove himself to be the ablest of all our Diplomatic Corp.

If he was now to be brought into *that* line, or into any other public walk, I could not, upon the principle which has regulated my own conduct, disapprove the caution which is hinted at in the letter. But he is already entered; the public more and more, as he is known, are appreciating his talents and worth; and his country would sustain a loss if these are checked by over delicacy on your part."

10. GEORGE WASHINGTON TO JOHN QUINCY ADAMS JUNE 25, 1797

"I am now, as you supposed the case would be when you then wrote, seated under my Vine and Fig-tree; where, I am permitted to enjoy the shade of it, my vows will be continually offered for the welfare and prosperity of our country; and for the support, ease and honor of the Gentleman to whom the Administration of its concerns are entrusted. I have expressed to him my sentiments, and wishes, that you may be induced to continue in the Diplomatic line; and these sentiments and wishes, are the result of the surest conviction of its utility, as it relates to the public interest.

For the kind expressions you have extended to me, and the approbation of those sentiments, I took the liberty of submitting to my countrymen, in my late Valedictory, I have a grateful sense; and thank you for communicating them, and the approbation of good and Virtuous Men, is the most pleasing reward my mind is susceptible of, for any Service it has been in my power to render my Country."

III. JOHN ADAMS ON JOHN QUINCY ADAMS

1. JOHN ADAMS TO ABIGAIL ADAMS JUNE 29, 1777

"Tell Mr. John, that I am under no Apprehensions about his Proficiency in Learning. With his Capacity, and Opportunities, he can not fail to acquire Knowledge. But let him know, that the moral Sentiments of his Heart, are more important than the Furniture of his Head. Let him be sure that he possesses the great Virtues of Temperance, Justice, Magnanimity, Honour and Generosity, and with these added to his Parts he cannot fail to become a wise and great Man."

2. JOHN ADAMS TO JOHN QUINCY ADAMS JULY 27, 1777

"If it should be the Design of Providence that you should live to grow up, you will naturally feel a Curiosity to learn the History of the Causes which have produced the late Revolution of our Government. No Study in which you can engage will be more worthy of you.

It will become you to make yourself Master of all the considerable Characters, which have figured upon the Stage of civil, political of military Life. This you ought to do with the Utmost Candour, Benevolence and Impartiality, and if you should now and then meet with an Incident, which shall throw some Light upon your Fathers Character, I charge you to consider it with an Attention only to Truth."

3. JOHN ADAMS TO JOHN QUINCY ADAMS AUGUST 11, 1777

"As the War in which your country is engaged will probably hereafter attract your Attention, more than it does at this Time, and as the future Circumstances and Negotiations, similar to those which are now in Agitation, I wish to turn your Thoughts early to such Studies, as will afford you the most solid Instruction and Improvement for the Part which may be allotted you to act on the Stage of Life.

There is no History, perhaps, better adapted to this useful Purpose than that of Thucidides, an Author, of whom I hope you will make yourself perfect Master, in original Language, which is Greek, the most perfect of all human languages. In order to understand him fully in his own Tongue, you must however take Advantage, of every Help you can procure and particularly of Translations of him into your Mother Tongue."

-⁂-

4. JOHN ADAMS TO JOHN QUINCY ADAMS DECEMBER 28, 1780

"The Ice is so universal now that I suppose you spend some Time in Skaiting every day. It is a fine Exercise for young Persons, and therefore I am willing to indulge you in it, provided you confine yourself to proper Hours, and to strict Moderation. Skaiting is a fine Art. It is not Simple Velocity or Agility that constitutes the Perfection of it but Grace. There is an Elegance of Motion, which is charming to the sight, and is useful to acquire, because it obliges you to restrain that impetuous Ardour and violent Activity, into which the Agitation of Spirits occasioned by this Exercise is apt to hurry you, and which is inconsistent both with your Health and Pleasure."

-⁂-

5. JOHN ADAMS TO JOHN QUINCY ADAMS APRIL 28, 1782

"I am well pleased with your learning German for many Reasons, and principally because I am told that Science and Literature flourish more at present in Germany than any where. A Variety of Languages will do no harm unless you should get an habit of attending more to Words than Things.

But, my dear boy, above all Things, preserve your Innocence, and a pure Conscience. Your morals are more importance, both to yourself and the World than all Languages and all Sciences. The least Stain upon your Character will do more harm to your Happiness than all Accomplishments will do it good."

-⁂-

6. JOHN ADAMS TO JOHN QUINCY ADAMS AUGUST 18, 1782

"It is with Pleasure that I enclose this amiable Letter from your Sister, which breaths a very commendable affection for You and solicitude for your Welfare. There is nothing more tender than these Correspondences between Families, as there is nothing more sacred than the relations of a Brother and a sister, except that of Parent and Child. It is your duty to answer her.

I say again, it is a moral and religious duty to cultivate these amiable Connections by constant Correspondence, when We cannot by Conversation. But I need not recur to any Thing so austere as the Idea of Duty. The Pleasure of corresponding with a sister so worthy of you ought to be Motive sufficient. Subjects can never be wanting. Descriptions of Cities, Churches, Palaces, Paintings, Spectacles, all the Objects around you, even the manners and Dress of the People will furnish ample materials."

7. JOHN ADAMS TO HIS DAUGHTER ABIGAIL ("NABBY") ADAMS AUGUST 13, 1783

". . . I have had of the society of your brother, whom I brought with me from the Hague. He is grown to be a man, and the world says they should take him for my younger brother, if they did not know him to be my son. I have great satisfaction in his behaviour, as well as in the improvements he has made in his travels, and the reputation he has left behind him wherever he has been. He is very studious and delights in nothing but books, which alarms me for his health; because, like me, he is naturally inclined to be fat. His knowledge and his judgment are so far beyond his years, as to be admired by all who have conversed with him."

8. JOHN ADAMS TO ABIGAIL ADAMS JULY 26, 1784

". . . I Send you a son who is the greatest Traveller, of his Age, and without Partiality, I think as promising and manly a youth as is in the World."

9. JOHN ADAMS TO BENJAMIN WATERHOUSE APRIL 23, 1785

"Dear Sir,—This Letter will be delivered you, by your old Acquaintance, John Quincy Adams, whom I beg leave to recommend to your attention and favor. He is anxious to study sometime, at [Harvard] before he begins the Study of the Law which appears at present to be the Profession of his Choice.

He must undergo an Examination, in which I suspect he will not appear exactly what he is; in Truth there are few who take their Degrees at College, who have so much Knowledge; but his Studies having been pursued by himself, on his travels without any steady Tutor, he will be found awkward in speaking Latin, in Prosody, in Parsing, and even, perhaps, in that accuracy of Pronunciation in reading orations or Poems in that Language, which is often chiefly attended to in such Examinations.

It seems to be necessary therefore that I make this Apology for him to you, and request you to communicate it in confidence to the Gentlemen who are to examine him, and such others as you think prudent. If you were to examine him in English and French Poetry, I know not where you would find any body his Superior. in Roman and English History few Persons of his Age;[132] it is rare to find a youth possessed of so much knowledge."

-⊰⊱-

10. JOHN ADAMS TO JOHN QUINCY ADAMS MARCH 19, 1786

"This Letter, I presume, will find you at the University, where I hope you will pass your time both pleasantly and profitably. Let Us know how you find Things, and take care of your health. You have in your Travels had so much Exercise, that it is not Safe to discontinue it, and indulge your self too much in a Sedentary Life. Never fail to walk an hour or two every day."

-⊰⊱-

11. JOHN ADAMS TO JOHN QUINCY ADAMS MAY 26, 1786

"Give me leave to congratulate you on your Admission into the Seat of the Muses, our dear Alma Mater, where I hope you will find a Pleasure and Improvements equal to your Expectations. You are now among Magistrates and Ministers, Legislators and Heroes, Ambassadors and Generals, I mean among Persons who will live to Act in all these Characters. If you pursue your Studies and preserve your Health you will have as good a Chance as most of them, and I hope you will take Care to do nothing now which you will in any future Period have reason to recollect with shame or Pain."

-⊰⊱-

12. JOHN ADAMS TO JOHN QUINCY ADAMS JANUARY 10, 1787

". . . You must all attend to your health. All depends upon that. I found it difficult to persuade you, while in Europe, to take your fresh Air, and active Exercise regularly.

---

132 At the time this letter was written John Quincy Adams was 18 years of age.

When you come into a Lawyers office, you will find it more necessary Still. At present, Attendance on Prayers, Recitations and public Exhibitions, and the Amusements of Conversation with your fellow Students, are instead of Exercise. But when you come to pore alone over Law, which is not very entertaining, you will find a difference.

But at all times and in all Places, above all Things, preserve the Sentiments and the delicate sensibilities of youth, throughout your whole Life. Honour and Integrity, Humanity and Modesty are natural to Man. Let not the Commerce of the World, ever wear them out or blunt the Edge of your sensibility of them."

13. JOHN ADAMS TO ABIGAIL ADAMS JANUARY 21, 1794

"John may pursue his Studies and Practice with confidence as well as Patience.

His Talents, his Virtues his studies and his Writings are not unknown, nor will they go without their Recompence, if Trouble is a Recompence for Trouble, If the People neglect him the Government will not: of the Government neglect him the People will not, as least very long."

14. JOHN ADAMS TO ABIGAIL ADAMS MAY 19, 1794

"Mr. John I hear rises in his Reputation at the Bar as well as in the Esteem of his fellow Citizens. His Writings have given him a greater Consideration in [Philadelphia] than he is aware of. I am Sometimes told that I ought to be proud of him; and truly I dont want to be told this. He will be made a Politician too soon. But he is a Man of great Experience, and I hope sound Philosophy. He was a greater statesman at Eighteen, than Some Senators I have known at fifty. But he must learn Silence and Reserve, Prudence, Caution – above all to curb his Vanity and collect himself, faculties or Virtues that his Father has often much wanted. I have often thought he has more Prudence at 27, than his Father at 58."

15. JOHN ADAMS TO JOHN QUINCY ADAMS MAY 26, 1794

"The Secretary of State called upon me this morning to inform me by the order of the President, that it was determined to nominate you to go to Holland as Resident

Minister. The President desired to know if I thought you would accept. I answered that I had no authority from you, but it was my opinion that you would accept, and that it would be my advice that you should. . . Your knowledge of Dutch and French, your education in that country, your acquaintance with my old friends there, will give you advantages beyond many others. It will require all your prudence and all your other virtues as well as all your talents. . . Be secret. Don't open your mouth to any human being on the subject except your mother. Go and see with how little wisdom this world is governed."

16. JOHN ADAMS TO JOHN QUINCY ADAMS MAY 29, 1794

"The nomination, which is the result of the President's own observations and reflections, is as politic, as it is unexpected. It will be a proof that sound principles in morals and government are cherished by the executive of the United States, and that study, science and literature are recommendations which will not be overlooked. It will, or at least it ought to have in England and Holland more effect than any thing that has been done, except perhaps the appointment of Mr. [John] Jay. It is a pledge given by the American cabinet, that they are not enemies to a rational form of government, and that they are not hurried away by a wild enthusiasm for every unmeaning cry of Liberty, Republicanism and Equality."

17. JOHN ADAMS TO JOHN QUINCY ADAMS APRIL 26, 1795

"I have no language to express to you the pleasure I have received from the satisfaction you have given to the President and Secretary of State, as well as from the clear, comprehensive and mastery accounts in your letters to me of the public affairs of nations in Europe, whose situation and politics it most concerns us to know. Go on, my dear son, and by a diligent exertion of your genius and abilities, continue to deserve well of you father, but especially your country. The more faithfully you have discharged and fulfilled your duty to me, the more anxious I have been lest I may not have fulfilled mine to you with so much punctuality."

18. AN EXCERPT FROM A MESSAGE FROM PRESIDENT JOHN ADAMS TO THE UNITED STATES SENATE MAY 20, 1797

"GENTLEMEN OF THE SENATE:—

I nominate John Quincy Adams, of Massachusetts, to be Minister Plenipotentiary from the United States to the King of Prussia."

JOHN ADAMS"

19. PRESIDENT JOHN ADAMS'S OFFICIAL APPOINTMENT OF JOHN QUINCY ADAMS AS AMERICAN AMBASSADOR TO PRUSSIA JUNE 1, 1797

"JOHN ADAMS, President of the United States of America

To John Quincy Adams — Greeting

Reposing especial Trust and Confidence in your Integrity Prudence and Ability, I have nominated and by and with the Advice and Consent of the Senate, do appoint you the said John Quincy Adams Minister Plenipotentiary for the United States of America at the Court of His Majesty the King of Prussia, authorizing you hereby to do and perform all such Matters and things as to the said Place of Office doth appertain, or as may be duly given you in charge hereafter, and the said office to hold and exercise during the pleasure of the President of the United States for the time being. IN TESTIMONY whereof I have caused the seal of the United States to be hereunto affixed. Given under my hand at the City of Philadelphia, the first day of June, in the year of our Lord one thousand seven hundred and ninety-seven, and of the Independence of the United States of America the Twenty-first.

JOHN ADAMS"

20. JOHN ADAMS TO JOHN QUINCY ADAMS NOVEMBER 3, 1797

"Your reasons will not bear examination. Your own disqualifications, if they had existed, would have been the same at Lisbon as at Berlin. The superior title of many other American citizens, if that had existed, would have been the same in Portugal as in Prussia. But if there is any authority in the opinion of Washington and all his ministers, with which mine concurs, and it is supported by the opinions of all men I know or hear of, and by the general sense of America, your qualifications and title to the mission either to Portugal or Prussia, are equal to those of any one of your fellow citizens, be he who he may. Your disapprobation of a nomination by the President of his own son, is founded on a principle which will not bear the test. It is a false principle. It is an unjust principle. The sons of Presidents have the same claim to liberty, equality, and the benefit of the laws with all other citizens. It is downright injustice to them to prescribe a law of proscription against them. The law considers it as one of the severest punishments to declare a man incapable of serving in any office under the government. Shall an infamous disqualification to serve their country, the punishment of the highest crimes, be arbitrarily inflicted on the sons of a President, merely because they are his sons? Why has not the Constitution, or the Legislature, made such a law of exclusion? Upon my honor, if such a law had existed, I would not have accepted the office at my time of life, at least that is my present feeling and judgment.

It gives no color of reason to those who represent you (if any such there are, which I do not believe, because it is well understood that Mr. Washington appointed you not only without my solicitation, but without my desire) as the creature of favor: because you stand exactly as you did, and there is no favor in it."

21. JOHN ADAMS TO JOHN MARSHALL JANUARY 31, 1801

"I request you would cause to be prepared letters for me to sign, to the King of Prussia, recalling Mr. John Quincy Adams, as minister plenipotentiary from his court. You may express the thanks of the President to his Majesty for the obliging reception and kind treatment this minister has met with at his court, and may throw the letter into the form of leave to return to the United States. . . It is my opinion this minister ought to be recalled from Prussia. Justice would require that he should be sent to France or England, if he should be continued in Europe. The mission to St. James is perfectly well filled by Mr. King; that to France is no doubt destined for some other character. Besides, it is my opinion that it is my duty to call him home."

22. JOHN ADAMS TO JOHN QUINCY ADAMS JANUARY 8, 1808

"Your situation you think critical, I think it is clear, plain and obvious. You are supported by no party. You have too honest a heart, too independent a mind and too brilliant talents, to be sincerely and confidentially trusted by any man who is under the dominion of party maxims or party feelings, and where is there another man who is not you? You may depend upon it then that you fate is decided. You will be countenanced neither by France, Spain or England. You will be supported neither by Federalists nor Republicans. In the next Congress, Dr. Eustis will be chosen Senator, and your will be numbered among the dead like Jay, Elsworth, King, Ames, Dexter and an hundred others of the brightest geniuses of this country. You ought to know and expect this, and by no means regret it.—Return to your professorship but above all to your office as a lawyer devote yourself to your profession and the education of your children."

23. JOHN ADAMS TO WILLIAM CUNNINGHAM SEPTEMBER 27, 1808

"As you have mentioned my son, I shall only take the liberty to say that his conduct as far as I know it, has been able, upright, candid, impartial & Independent. His letter to Mr. Otis I applaud and admire. His resignation I approve. He would have been more politic if he had declined his invitation to the caucus, though the question was only between Mr. Madison and Mr. Monroe, and, knowing both, I should certainly as he did prefer the former to the latter."

24. JOHN ADAMS TO WILLIAM CUNNINGHAM, JR. OCTOBER 13, 1808

"Washington was indeed under obligations to [John Quincy], for turning the tide of sentiment against Genet, and he was sensible of it and grateful for it. The enthusiasm for Genet and France and the French Revolution was, at this time, almost universal throughout the United States, but in Pennsylvania, and especially in Philadelphia, the rage was irresistible. . . J. Q. Adams' writings first turned this tide; and the yellow fever completed the salvation of Washington. . . . Not all Washington's ministers, Hamilton and Pickering included, could have written those papers, which were so fatal to Genet.[133] Washington saw

133 John Adams is referring to the *Publicola* essays May-July 1791, authored by John Quincy Adams in defense of President Washington's policy of neutrality.

it, and felt his obligations. He took great pains to find out their author. The first notice I had of his design to appoint my son to a mission abroad, was from his Secretary of State Randolph, who told me he had been ordered to enquire of the members of Congress, and others, concerning the life and character of J. Q. Adams, and, he was, that day to report in favor of his appointment."

25. JOHN ADAMS TO WILLIAM CUNNINGHAM DECEMBER 13, 1808

"Your designation of Mr. J. Q. A. to the office Mr. Madison now holds, will be as erroneous as the other to that of Vice President.- Mr. Giles, Mr. Monroe, Mr. Pope, Mr. Mitchell, Mr. Twenty others, will be more likely. No! Mr. Adams must be left where he is.- He is now at his ease, is happy and useful: more useful perhaps than he could be in any public station, in these times of anarchy, violence and fury. No! The old Whigs and their posterity must all go in to obscurity, and all the public offices must be monopolized by the blood of the old refugees."

26. JOHN ADAMS TO WILLIAM CUNNINGHAM DECEMBER 13, 1808

"I may mention to you, in confidence, that considerable pains have been taken to persuade your friend J. Q. A. to consent to be run by the Republicans. But he is utterly adverse to it: and so am I: for many reasons among which are 1. The office, tho a precious Stone, is but a carbuncle, shining in the dark. 2. It is a state of perfect slavery: the drudgery of it is extremely oppressive. 3. The compensation is not a living for a common Gentleman. 4. He must resign his professorship. 5 He must renounce his practice at the Bar. 6. He must stand in competition with Mr. Lincoln, which would divide the Republican interest and certainly prevent the election of either. 7 It would produce an eternal separation between him and the federalists, at least that part of them, who now constitute the absolute oligarchy. This I own however, I should not much regret, for this nation has more to fear from them than any other source. 8. Finally and above all there is as little prospect of doing any good, as acquiring any honor or receiving any comfort. For these reasons I am decidedly against the project, and so is he. Private station in my opinion has no equal for him."

27. JOHN ADAMS TO JOHN QUINCY ADAMS FEBRUARY 11, 1811

"In absolute private life, scorning all intrigue, but employing your studies for the solid interest of mankind and your country, you may do more real good in my opinion than in any public station."

28. JOHN ADAMS TO THOMAS JEFFERSON FEBRUARY 3, 1812

"The Material of the Samples of American Manufacture which I sent you was not Wool or Cotton, nor Silk nor Flax nor Hemp nor Iron nor Wood. They were spun from the Brain of John Quincy Adams and consist in two Volumes of his lectures on rhetorick and oratory, delivered when he was Professor of that Science in our University of Cambridge.[134] A relation of mine, a first cousin of my ever honoured, beloved and revered mother, Nicholas Boylston, a rich merchant of Boston, bequeathed by his will a donation for establishing a professorship, and John Quincy Adams, having in his veins so much of the blood of the founder, was most earnestly solicited to become the first professor. The volumes I sent you are the fruit of his labour during the short time he held that office. But it ought to be remembered that he attended his duty as a Senator of the United States during the same Period. It is with some anxiety submitted to your judgment."

29. JOHN ADAMS LETTER TO BENJAMIN WATERHOUSE MARCH 31, 1813

"Talk not to me of my Son for Governor or any Thing else. He is gone, as his Father did before him on a Romantic Expedition to Muscovy to his own Ruin and the Ruin of his Children. I pray God he [*torn*] return this Summer, whatever may become of M[*torn*] but Gull Traps."

30. JOHN ADAMS TO JOHN QUINCY ADAMS MAY 1 & 14, 1815

"My son! No man except your father was ever placed in a more delicate or dangerous situation than you are... What shall I say to you, my son? Shall I recommend

134 John Quincy Adams wrote the two volume *Lectures on Rhetoric and Oratory* while serving as Boylston Professor of Rhetoric and Oratory at Harvard University from 1805-1809. The elder Adams sent copies to Jefferson who included the books in his personal library.

to you the eternal taciturnity of Franklin, and Washington? I believe your nature is as incapable of it, as mine. Yet, without it you will be exposed to innumerable dangers... Your providence I know is greater than mine ever was, and hitherto has been *a toute epreuve*, but still I hope these anxious hints will not be thought impertinent."

31. JOHN ADAMS TO THOMAS JEFFERSON OCTOBER 10, 1817

"I thank you for your kind congratulations on the return of my little family from Europe. To receive them all in fine health and good Spirits, after so long an absence, was a greater Blessing, than at my time of Life when they went away I had any right to hope or reason to expect. If the Secretary of State can give Satisfaction to his fellow Citizens in his new Office it will be a Source of consolation to me while I live: though it is not probable that I shall long be a Witness of his good Success or ill Success. I shall be obliged to say to him and to your and to your Country and mine, God bless you all! Fare Ye Well. Indeed I need not wait a moment. I can say all that now with as good a Will and as clear a conscience as at any time past or future."

32. JOHN ADAMS TO THOMAS JEFFERSON JANUARY 22, 1825

"The presidential election has given me less anxiety than I, myself could have imagined. The next administration will be a troublesome one to whomsoever it falls. And our John has been too much worn to contend much longer with conflicting factions. I call him our John, because when you was at Cul de sac at Paris, he appeared to me to be almost as much your boy as mine. I have often speculated upon the consequences that would have ensued from my taking your advice, to send him to William and Mary College in Virginia for an Education."

33. JOHN ADAMS TO JOHN QUINCY ADAMS FEBRUARY 18, 1825

"My dear Son;—I have received your letter of the 9th. Never did I feel so much solemnity as upon this occasion. The multitude of my thoughts and the intensity of my feelings are too much for a mind like mine, in its ninetieth year. May the blessing of God Almighty continue to protect you to the end of your life, as it has heretofore protected you in so remarkable a manner from your cradle! I offer the same prayer for your lady and your family, and am your affectionate father."

IV. THOMAS JEFFERSON ON JOHN QUINCY ADAMS

1. THOMAS JEFFERSON TO ABIGAIL ADAMS AUGUST 9, 1786

"This proposition about the exchange of a son for my daughter puzzles me. I should be very glad to have your son, but I cannot part with my daughter. Thus you see I have such a habit of gaining in trade with you that I always expect it."

2. THOMAS JEFFERSON TO JAMES MADISON JUNE 28, 1791

"Nobody doubts here who is the author of *Publicola*, any more than of *Davila*. He is very indecently attacked in Brown's & Bache's papers."

3. THOMAS JEFFERSON TO JAMES MONROE JULY 10, 1791

"A writer under the name of Publicola, in attacking all Paine's principles, is very desirous of involving me in the same censure with the author. I certainly merit the same, for I profess the same principles; but it is equally certain I never meant to have entered as a volunteer into the cause. My occupations do not permit it."

4. THOMAS JEFFERSON TO JOHN ADAMS JULY 17, 1791

". . . I found on my return from a journey of a month that a writer came forward under the signature of Publicola, attacking not only the author & principles of the pamphlet, but myself as it's sponsor, by name. Soon after came hosts of other writers defending the pamphlet & attacking you by name as the writer of Publicola. Thus were our names thrown on the public stage as public antagonists."

5. THOMAS JEFFERSON TO THOMAS PAINE JULY 29, 1791

"Indeed I am glad you did not come away till you had written your 'Rights of man." That has been much read here, with avidity and pleasure. A writer under the signature Publicola has attacked it. A host of champions entered the arena immediately in your defence.

The discussion excited the public attention, recalled it to the 'Defense of the American constitutions' and the 'Discourses on Davila,' which it had kindly passed over without censure in the moment, and very general expressions of their sense have been now drawn forth; & I thank God that they appear firm in their republicanism, notwithstanding the contrary hopes & assertions of a sect here, high in names, but small in numbers. These had flattered themselves that the silence of the people under the 'Defence' and 'Davila' was a symptom of their conversion to the doctrine of kings, lords, & commons. They are checked at least by your pamphlet, & the people confirmed in their good old faith."

6. THOMAS JEFFERSON TO JAMES MADISON JUNE 1, 1797

"Yesterday they put up the nomination of John Quincy Adams to Berlin, which had been objected to as extending our diplomatic establishment. It was approved 18 to 14."

7. THOMAS JEFFERSON TO JAMES MADISON MARCH 15, 1798

"The President has nominated John Quincy Adams Commissioner Plenipotentiary to renew the treaty with Sweden. Tazewell made a great stand against it, on the general ground that we should let our treaties drop, & remain without any. He could only get 8. votes against 20. A trial will be made to-day in another form, which he thinks will give 10. or 11. against 16. or 17. declaring the renewal inexpedient. In this case, notwithstanding the nomination has been confirmed, it is supposed the President would perhaps not act under it, on the probability that more than a third would be against the ratification. I believe, however, that he would act, and that a third could not be got to oppose the ratification."

8. THOMAS JEFFERSON TO JOHN QUINCY ADAMS DECEMBER 6, 1805

"Thomas Jefferson requests the favour of Mr. Adams to dine with him on Monday the 9th. instant—Dinner will be on the table precisely at sunset.

The favour of an Answer is asked."

9. THOMAS JEFFERSON TO WILLIAM SHORT MARCH 8, 1809

"DEAR SIR,—It is with much concern I inform you that the Senate has negatived your appointment. We thought it best to keep back the nomination to the close of the session, that the mission might remain secret as long as possible, which you know was our purpose from the beginning. It was then sent in with an explanation of its object and motives. We took for granted, if any hesitation should arise, that the Senate would take time, and that our friends in that body would make inquiries of us, and give us the opportunity of explaining and removing objections. But to our great surprise, and with an unexampled precipitancy, they rejected it at once. This reception of the last of my official communications to them, could not be unfelt, nor were the causes of it spoken out by them. Under this uncertainty, Mr. Madison, on his entering into office, proposed another person, (John Q. Adams.) He was also negatived, and they adjourned *sine die.*"

10. THOMAS JEFFERSON TO JOHN ADAMS SEPTEMBER 8, 1817

"I congratulate Mrs. Adams and yourself on the return of your excellent and distinguished son, and our country still more on such a minister of their foreign affairs; and I renew to both the assurance of my high and friendly respect and esteem."

11. THOMAS JEFFERSON TO JOHN QUINCY ADAMS NOVEMBER 1, 1817

"I have barely left myself room to express my satisfaction at your call to the important office you hold, and to tender you the assurance of my great esteem and respect."[135]

12. THOMAS JEFFERSON TO JAMES MONROE JANUARY 18, 1819

"On the subject of these communications, I will venture a suggestion which, should it have occurred to yourself or to Mr. Adams as is probable, will only be a little labor lost. I propose then that you select Mr. Adams's 4. principal letters on the Spanish subject, to wit, that which establishes our right to the Rio-bravo which was laid before the Congress of 1817 .18. His letters to Onis of July 23. & Nov. 30. and to Erving of Nov. 28 perhaps also that of Dec. 2. Have them well translated into French, and send English & French

135 John Quincy Adams had recently been appointed Secretary of State under President James Monroe. Adams served in this position from 1817-1825.

copies to all our ministers at foreign courts, and to our consuls. The paper on our right to the Rio-bravo, and the letter to Erving of Nov. 28. are the most important and are among the ablest compositions I have ever seen, both as to logic and style. A selection of these few in pamphlet form will be read by every body; but, by nobody, if buried among Onis's long-winded and tergiversating diatribes, and all the documents; the volume of which alone will deter an European reader from ever opening it. Indeed it would be worth while to have the two most important of these published in the Leyden gazette, from which it would go into the other leading gazettes of Europe. It is of great consequence to us, & merits every possible endeavor, to maintain in Europe a correct opinion of our political morality. These papers will place the event with the world in the important cases of our Western boundary, of our military entrance into Florida, & of the execution of Arbuthnot and Ambrister. On the two first subjects it is very natural for an European to go wrong, and to give into the charge of ambition, which the English papers (read every where) endeavor to fix on us. If the European mind is once set right on these points, they will go with us in all the subsequent proceedings, without further enquiry.

While on the subject of this correspondence, I will presume also to suggest to Mr. Adams the question whether he should not send back Onis's letters in which he has the impudence to qualify you by the term 'his Excellency'? An American gentleman in Europe can rank with the first nobility because we have no titles which stick him at any particular place in their line. So the President of the US. under that designation ranks with Emperors and kings, but add Mr. Onis's courtesy of 'his Excellency' and he is then on a level with Mr. Onis himself, with the Governors of provinces and even of every petty fort in Europe, or the colonies."

13. THOMAS JEFFERSON TO JOHN QUINCY ADAMS OCTOBER 23, 1822

"Thomas Jefferson returns his thanks to Mr. Adams for the copy of the Ghent Documents which he has been so kind as to send him. So far as concerns Mr. Adams personally, the respect and esteem of the public for him was too firmly and justly fixed, to need this appeal to them but the volume is a valuable gift to his fellow citizens generally, and especially to the future historians whom it will enable to give correct ideas of the views of that treaty and to do justice to the abilities with which it was negociated. He begs leave to salute Mr. Adams with assurances of his highest esteem and respect."

14. THOMAS JEFFERSON TO THE MARQUIS DE LA FAYETTE OCTOBER 28, 1822

"You will have seen how prematurely they have begun to agitate us with the next presidential election. Many candidates are named: but they will be reduced to two, Adams & Crawford. Party principles, as heretofore will have their weight, but the papers tell you there are no parties now, republicans and federalists forsooth are all amalgamated. This, my friend, is not so. The same parties exist now which existed before. But the name of Federalist was extinguished in the battle of New Orleans; and those who wore it now call themselves republicans. Like the fox pursued by the dogs, they take shelter in the midst of the sheep. They see that monarchism is a hopeless wish in this country, and are rallying anew to the next best point a consolidated government. They are therefore endeavoring to break down the barriers of the state rights, provided by the constitution against consolidation. Hence you will see in the debates of Congress these new republicans maintaining the most ultra doctrines of the old federalists. This new metamorphosis is the only clue which will enable you to understand these strange appearances. They will become more prominent in the ensuing discussions. One candidate is supposed to be a consolidationist, the other a republican of the old school, a friend to the constitutional organization of the government, and believing that the strength of the members can alone give real strength to the body. And this is the sentiment of the nation, and will probably prevail if the principle of the Missouri question should not mingle itself with those of the election. Should it do so, all will be uncertain. This uncertainty however gives me no uneasiness. Both are able men, both honest men, and whatever be the bias, the good sense of our people will direct the boat ultimately to it's proper point."

15. THOMAS JEFFERSON TO HENRY DEARBORN OCTOBER 31, 1822

"Take into account also that you will escape the two years agitation just commencing with us. Even before you had left us our newspapers had already begun to excite the question of the next president. They are advancing fast into it. Many candidates are named, but they will settle down, as is believed, to Adams and Crawford. If the Missouri principle should mingle itself with the party divisions the results will be very doubtful. For altho' it is pretended there are no longer any parties among us, that all are amalgamated, yet the fact is that the same parties exist now that ever existed, not indeed under the old names of Republicans and Federalists. The Hartford Convention and battle of New Orleans extinguished the latter name. All now call themselves republicans, as the fox when pursued by dogs takes shelter in the midst of the sheep.

Finding monarchy desperate here, they rally to their next hope, a consolidated government, and altho' they do not avow it (as they never did monarchism) yet it is manifestly their next object.

Hence you see so many of these new republicans maintaining in Congress the rankest doctrines of the old federalists. The judges aid in their old way as sappers and miners. One of the candidates is supposed to be a Consolidationist, the other for maintaining the banner of state rights as provided by the constitution against the fear of Consolidation."

16. THOMAS JEFFERSON TO JUDGE WILLIAM JOHNSON MARCH 4, 1823

"We have been too careless of our future reputation, while our tories will omit nothing to place us in the wrong. Besides the five-volumed libel which represents us as struggling for office, and not at all to prevent our government from being administered into a monarchy, the life of Hamilton is in the hands of a man who, to the bitterness of the priest, adds the rancor of the fiercest federalism. Mr. Adams's papers, too, and his biography, will descend of course to his son, whose pen, you know, is pointed, and his prejudices not in our favor. And doubtless other things are in preparation, unknown to us. On our part we are depending on truth to make itself known, while history is taking a contrary set which may become too inveterate for correction."

17. THOMAS JEFFERSON TO RICHARD RUSH JUNE 5, 1824

"The question will ultimately be, as I suggested in a former letter to you, between Crawford and Adams, with this in favor of Crawford that altho' many states have a different 1st favorite, he is the second with nearly all, and that if it goes into the legislature he will surely be elected."

18. THOMAS JEFFERSON TO JOHN QUINCY ADAMS JULY 18, 1824

"I have safely received the two copies of the facsimile of the Declaration of Independence which you have been so kind as to send me under a resolution of Congress. With a due sense of respect for this mark of attention to myself I contemplate with pleasure the evidence afforded of reverence for that instrument, and view in it a pledge of adhesion to it's principles, and of a sacred determination to maintain and perpetuate them. As toward this holy purpose no one has it more in their powers to contribute with effect, than yourself so I am equally happy in the confidence that none will do it with more zeal and fidelity, and I pray you to accept the assurance of my great esteem and respectful consideration."

19. THOMAS JEFFERSON TO RICHARD RUSH OCTOBER 13, 1824

"The éclat of this visit has almost merged the Presidential question, on which nothing scarcely is said in our papers.[136] That question will lie ultimately between Crawford and Adams; but, at the same time, the vote of the people will be so distracted by subordinate candidates, that possibly they may make no election, and let it go to the House of Representatives. There, it is thought, Crawford's chance is best."

20. THOMAS JEFFERSON TO WILLIAM SHORT JANUARY 8, 1825

"Can any one read Mr. Adams' defence of the American constitutions without seeing that he was a monarchist? And J. Q. Adams, the son, was more explicit than the father, in his answer to Paine's rights of man. So much for leaders. Their followers were divided. Some went the same lengths, others, and I believe the greater part, only wished a stronger executive."

21. THOMAS JEFFERSON TO JOHN ADAMS JANUARY 8, 1825

"This Presidential election has given me few anxieties. With you this must have been impossible. . .".

22. THOMAS JEFFERSON TO WILLIAM B. GILES DECEMBER 25, 1825

"My memory is indeed become almost a blank, of which no better proof can probably be given you than by my solemn protestation, that I have not the least recollection of your intervention between Mr. John Q. Adams and myself, in what passed on the subject of

136 Jefferson is referring to the Marquis de La Fayette's visit to the United States. In the same letter Jefferson writes to Rush, "You will have seen by our papers the delirium into which our citizens are thrown by a visit from General La Fayette. He is making a triumphant progress through the States, from town to town, with acclamations of welcome, such as no crowned head ever received." Jefferson to Rush, October 13, 1824.

the embargo. Not the slightest trace of it remains in my mind. Yet I have no doubt of the exactitude of the statement in your letter. And the less, as I recollect the interview with Mr. Adams, to which the previous communications which had passed between him and yourself were probably and naturally the preliminary. That interview I remember well; not indeed in the very words which passed between us, but in their substance, which was of a character too awful, too deeply engraved in my mind, and influencing too materially the course I had to pursue, ever to be forgotten. Mr. Adams called on me pending the embargo, and while endeavors were making to obtain its repeal. He made some apologies for the call, on the ground of our not being then in the habit of confidential communications, but that that which he had then to make, involved too seriously the interest of our country not to overrule all other considerations with him, and make it his duty to reveal it to myself particularly. I assured him there was no occasion for any apology for his visit; that, on the contrary, his communications would be thankfully received, and would add a confirmation the more to my entire confidence in the rectitude and patriotism of his conduct and principles. He spoke then of the dissatisfaction of the eastern portion of our confederacy with the restraints of the embargo then existing, and their restlessness under it. That there was nothing which might not be attempted, to rid themselves of it. That he had information of the most unquestionable certainty, that certain citizens of the eastern States (I think he named Massachusetts particularly) were in negotiation with agents of the British government, the object of which was an agreement that the New England States should take no further part in the war then going on; that, without formally declaring their separation from the Union of the States, they should withdraw from all aid and obedience to them; that their navigation and commerce should be free from restraint and interruption by the British; that they should be considered and treated by them as neutrals, and as such might conduct themselves towards both parties; and, at the close of the war, be at liberty to rejoin the confederacy. He assured me that there was eminent danger that the convention would take place; that the temptations were such as might debauch many from their fidelity to the Union; and that, to enable its friends to make head against it, the repeal of the embargo was absolutely necessary. I expressed a just sense of the merit of this information, and of the importance of the disclosure to the safety and even the salvation of our country; and however reluctant I was to abandon the measure, (a measure which persevered in a little longer, we had subsequent and satisfactory assurance would have effected its object completely,) from that moment, and influenced by that information, I saw the necessity of abandoning it, and instead of effecting our purpose by this peaceful weapon, we must fight it out, or break the Union. I then recommended to yield to the necessity of a repeal of the embargo, and to endeavor to supply its place by the best substitute, in which they could procure a general concurrence.

I cannot too often repeat, that this statement is not pretended to be in the very words which passed; that it only gives faithfully the impression remaining on my mind. The very words of a conversation are too transient and fugitive to be so long retained in remembrance. But the substance was too important to be forgotten, not only from the revolution of measures it obliged me to adopt, but also from the renewals of it in my memory on the frequent occasions I have had of doing justice to Mr. Adams, by repeating this proof of his fidelity to his country, and of his superiority over all ordinary considerations when the safety of that was brought into question."

23. THOMAS JEFFERSON TO WILLIAM B. GILES DECEMBER 26, 1825

"You asked my opinion of the propriety of giving publicity to what is stated in your letter, as having passed between Mr. John Q. Adams and yourself. Of this no one can judge but yourself. It is one of those questions which belong to the forum of feeling. This alone can decide on the degree of confidence implied in the disclosure; whether under no circumstances it was to be communicated to others? It does not seem to be of that character, or at all to wear that aspect. They are historical facts which belong to the present, as well as future times. I doubt whether a single fact, known to the world, will carry as clear conviction to it, of the correctness of our knowledge of the treasonable views of the federal party of that day, as that disclosed by this, the most nefarious and daring attempt to dissever the Union, of which the Hartford convention was a subsequent chapter; and both of these having failed, consolidation becomes the fourth chapter of the next book of their history. But this opens with a vast accession of strength from their younger recruits, who, having nothing in them of the feelings or principles of '76, now look to a single and splendid government of an aristocracy, founded on banking institutions, and moneyed incorporations under the guise and cloak of their favored branches of manufactures, commerce and navigation, riding and ruling over the plundered ploughman and beggared yeomanry. This will be to them a next best blessing to the monarchy of their first aim, and perhaps the surest stepping stone to it."

V. JAMES MADISON ON JOHN QUINCY ADAMS

1. JAMES MADISON TO THOMAS JEFFERSON JUNE 23, 1791

"Mr. King tells me an attack on Payne has appeared in a Boston paper under the name of Publicola, and has an affinity in the stile as well as sentiments to the discourses on Davila."[137]

2. JAMES MADISON TO THOMAS JEFFERSON JULY 13, 1791

"Beckley has just got back from his eastern trip. He says that the partizans of Mr. Adams's heresies in that quarter are perfectly insignificant in point of number; that particularly in Boston he is become distinguished for his unpopularity; that Publicola is probably the manufacture of his son, out of materials furnished by himself, and that the publication is generally as obnoxious in New England as it appears to be in Pennsylvania. If young Adams be capable of giving the dress in which Publicola presents himself, it is very probable he may have been made the Editor of his father's doctrines.

I hardly think the printer would so directly disavow the fact if Mr. Adams was himself the writer. There is more of method, also, in the arguments, and much less of clumsiness and heaviness in the style, than characterize his writings."

3. JAMES MADISON TO JOHN QUINCY ADAMS MARCH 6, 1809

"J. Madison presents his compts. To Mr. Adams & asks the favor of a call on him at his house this morning for a few minutes, as he may be passing to the Capitol Hill. As J. M. may happen at the moment to be at the President's House, it may perhaps be as well for Mr. Adams to take that in his way."

137 *Discourses on Davila* (1790) were written by John Adams; however, *Publicola* was penned by John Quincy Adams.

4. AN EXCERPT FROM A MESSAGE BY JAMES MADISON TO THE UNITED STATES SENATE JUNE 26, 1809

"To the Senate of the United States.

The considerations which led to the nomination of a Minister Plenipotentiary to Russia, being strengthened by evidence of the earnest desire of the Emperor to establish a diplomatic intercourse between the two Countries, and of a disposition in his Councils favorable to the extension of a commerce mutually advantageous; as will be seen by the extracts from letters from General Armstrong and Consul Harris, herewith *confidentially* communicated;

I nominate John Quincy Adams, of Massachusetts, to be Minister Plenipotentiary of the United States to the Court of St. Petersburg."

5. JAMES MADISON TO THOMAS JEFFERSON JULY 4, 1809

"You will have seen that a renomination of J. Q. Adams for Russia has succeeded with the Senate."

6. JAMES MADISON TO ABIGAIL ADAMS AUGUST 15, 1810

"MADAM

I have received your letter of the 1st. instant. Altho' I have not learned that Mr. Adams has yet signified to the Department of State his wish to return from the Mission to St. Petersburg, it is sufficiently ascertained by your communication, as well as satisfactorily explained by the considerations suggested. I have accordingly desired the Secretary of State to let him understand that as it was not the purpose of the Executive to subject him to the personal sacrifices which he finds unavoidable, he will not, in retiring from them, impair the sentiments which led to his appointment."

7. JAMES MADISON TO JOHN QUINCY ADAMS OCTOBER 16, 1810

"DEAR SIR,— Previous to my return to this City, I received a letter from Mrs. Adams, your highly respectable mother, communicating your anxiety to leave a situation rendered insupportable by the ruinous expenses found to be inseparable from it, and taking it for granted that you had written or would write to the Secretary of State to the same effect. The answer to her was, that as it was not the intention of the Executive to expose you to unreasonable sacrifices, it could not withhold a permission to retire from them, and that you would be so informed from the Department of State. You will accordingly receive a letter of leave, and a blank commission, providing for the care of your affairs till a successor may be appointed. As no communication of your wishes, however, has yet been received from yourself, I cannot but hope that the peculiar urgency manifested in the letter of Mrs. Adams was rather hers than yours, or that you have found the means of reconciling yourself to a continuance in your station. Beside that confidence in the value of your services which led to the call upon them, there are considerations, which you will readily appreciate, bearing against a sudden return from a short mission, the occasion for which has been made the subject of so much lubrication."

8. JAMES MADISON TO THOMAS JEFFERSON DECEMBER 7, 1810

"They wish for J. Q. Adams as honest, able, independent, & untainted with such objections."[138]

9. JAMES MADISON TO TZAR ALEXANDER I OF RUSSIA FEBRUARY 25, 1811

"John Quincy Adams who has for sometime resided near your Majesty in quality of Minister Plenipotentiary of the United States, having been selected to fill a distinguished and important office at Home, we have desired him to take leave of your Majesty, and to embrace that occasion to assure you of our continued friendship and sincere desire to preserve and strengthen the harmony and good understanding so happily subsisting between the two nations, and which will be further manifested by his Successor."[139]

138 In this letter Madison is expressing to Jefferson a desire to appoint John Quincy Adams to the United States Supreme Court.

139 On February 22, 1810 John Quincy Adams was appointed by President Madison to fill a vacancy on the United States Supreme Court as an Associate Justice. Adams declined the appointment and remained in Russia.

10. JAMES MADISON TO JOHN QUINCY ADAMS NOVEMBER 15, 1811

"I need not say how agreeable it would have been to me, and I am persuaded satisfactory to the public, if your inclination & circumstances had favored the new allotment of your services. Being ignorant of the obstacle arising from the particular state of your family, and inferring from considerations known to you, that such an exchange might not be unwelcome, I had proceeded so far in anticipating a decision different from that which took place in your mind, as to hold out the station at St. Petersburg to another. It has happened that no disappointment of any sort ensued to your contemplated successor. But I ought not to omit, that I did not so far lose sight of the possibility that you might be induced to decline the new appointment, as not to have meditated a provision for that event which would have probably deprived of its embarrassments. In the present state of things, I have only to wish that your diplomatic situation many continue to be less incommodious than it was at first found; and that opportunities of rendering it useful to your Country may equal her confidence in the fidelity and ability which you will apply to them."

11. JAMES MADISON TO JOHN QUINCY ADAMS DECEMBER 23, 1817

"I cannot be insensible to the terms in which you refer to the official relations which have subsisted between us, but must disclaim the obligations which you consider as lying on your side. The results of what took place on mine prove that I only avoided the demerit of a different course. Be pleased Sir to accept assurances of my continued esteem and of my friendly respects."

12. JAMES MADISON TO JAMES MONROE FEBRUARY 13, 1819

"It would be a happiness, also, if the subject, as it relates to General Jackson, could have an issue satisfactory to his feelings, and to the scruples of his friends and admirers. Mr. Adams has given all its luster to the proof that the conduct of the General is invulnerable to complaints from abroad; and the question between him and his country ought to be judged under the persuasion that if he has erred, it was in the zeal of his patriotism, and under a recollection of the great services he has rendered."

13. JAMES MADISON TO JOHN QUINCY ADAMS JULY 16, 1821

"J. Madison presents his respects to Mr. Adams with many thanks for his 'Address' on the 4th. of July, which is not less rich in excellent thoughts, than eloquent in the enunciation of them."

14. JAMES MADISON TO JOHN QUINCY ADAMS OCTOBER 24, 1822

"The Treaty of Ghent forms a prominent epoch in our National History; and will be a lasting monument of the Ability and patriotism with which it was negotiated. Incidents elucidating the transaction, cannot therefore but be interesting, and they are made the more so by the eloquent strain in which they are presented. Accept my thanks Sir for the little volume containing them, with assurances of my continued esteem and cordial respects."

15. JAMES MADISON TO JOHN QUINCY ADAMS MARCH 27, 1826

"J. Madison has received, under the President's name, a copy of the Message and documents transmitted to the House of Representatives, relating to the proposed Congress at Panama; and he ought not to make his acknowledgments for the politeness to which he is indebted, without expressing, at the same time, his sense of the ability and eloquence, as well as of the intrinsic interest by which the communication is characterized."

16. JAMES MADISON TO JOHN QUINCY ADAMS DECEMBER 20, 1826

"The copy of your Message to Congress transmitted under your Cover, having arrived during an absence at our University from which I am but just returned, a regretted delay has taken place in acknowledging the favor. I now offer my thanks for it, with an expression of the due sense I have of the increased interest given to the topics embraced in the Communication, by the eloquent and impressive form in which they are presented."

17. JAMES MADISON TO JOSEPH C. CABELL MARCH 22, 1827

"Every President, from General George Washington to Mr. J. Q. Adams, inclusive, has recognised the power of a tariff in favor of manufacturers, without indicating a doubt, or that a doubt existed anywhere."

18. JAMES MADISON TO JOHN QUINCY ADAMS DECEMBER 9, 1827

"DEAR SIR,—I return my thanks for the copy of your Message to Congress on the 3d instant, politely forwarded under your cover. Its very able view of blessings which distinguish our favored country is very gratifying; and the feelings inspired by our condition find an expanded scope in the meliorations infused into that of all other people, by a progress of reason and truth, in the merit of which we may justly claim a share."

19. JAMES MADISON TO GENERAL LA FAYETTE FEBRUARY 20, 1828

"You sympathize too much with a country that continues its affection for you without abatement, not to be anxious to know the probable result, as well as the present state of the ardent contest.[140] I can only say that the party for General Jackson are quite confident, and that for Mr. Adams apparently with but faint hopes. Whether any change, for which there is time, will take place in the prospect, cannot be foreseen. A good deal will depend on the vote of New York, and I see by the newspapers that the sudden death of Mr. Clinton is producing in both parties rival appeals, through obituary eulogies, to the portion of the people particularly attached to him."

20. JAMES MADISON TO JOHN QUINCY ADAMS DECEMBER 8, 1828

"J. Madison with his respectful compliments to the President of the U. States, returns many thanks for the copy of his Message to Congress, politely forwarded by him. It could not be read without a lively sense of the interesting features it presents of the National prosperity; nor without recognizing the ability & eloquence of which previous occasions had furnished like examples."

---

140 Madison is referring to the 1828 presidential election.

21. JAMES MADISON TO JOHN QUINCY ADAMS FEBRUARY 24, 1829

"DEAR SIR,—I have received, in your kind letter of the 21st instant, the little pamphlet containing the correspondence between yourself and 'several citizens of Massachusetts,' with 'certain additional papers.'

The subjects presented to view by the pamphlet will, doubtless, not be overlooked in the history of our country. The documents not previously published are of a very interesting cast."

22. JAMES MADISON TO JOHN QUINCY ADAMS AUGUST 2, 1831

"J. Madison presents his best respects to Mr. Adams, and thanks him for the Copy of his Oration on the 4th. of July. It is recommended to the public attention; not only by the characteristic ability & eloquence of the author; but by some of the views taken of its topics, which render it particularly interesting."

23. JAMES MADISON TO JOHN QUINCY ADAMS SEPTEMBER 23, 1831

"J. Madison, with his best respects to Mr. Adams, thanks him for the copy of his 'Eulogy on the Life & Character of James Monroe.'

Not only must the friends of Mr. Monroe be gratified by the just & happy tribute paid to his memory: The Historian also will be a debtor for the interesting materials and the eloquent samples of the use to be made of them, which will be found in its pages."

24. JAMES MADISON TO DR. BENJAMIN WATERHOUSE MARCH 1, 1834

"I have not yet seen the 'History of the Hartford Convention;' and such are the arrears in the reading I have assigned to myself, that I am not sure, if I possessed the book, that I should ever be able, with my waning strength and fading vision, to examine a work filling so many pages. It will be fortunate for the historical truth, and for individual as well as political justice, if a chastising notice of its spurious contents should fall within the scope of the masterly pen you refer to."[141]

25. JAMES MADISON TO JOHN QUINCY ADAMS JULY 30, 1834

"DEAR SIR,—The copy of your intended speech on the 'Removal of the Deposits' was received in the due time; but such was and has since been the deterioration of my health, that I could not give it a proper perusal. Being at present somewhat relieved from the supervening malady under which I have been more particularly suffering, I avail myself of this circumstance to thank you for your polite attention. I have found in the pamphlet, as was anticipated, the very able and impressive views which have always distinguished your investigations of important subjects."

26. JAMES MADISON TO JOHN QUINCY ADAMS JULY 30, 1834

"On the supposition that you are on a visit to Quincy, I address my letter accordingly. Wherever it may find you, it will faithfully express the high esteem and cordial regard, with the best wishes for a prolonged and happy life."

27. JAMES MADISON TO JOHN QUINCY ADAMS FEBRUARY 4, 1835

"J. Madison with his best respects to Mr. Adams returns him many thanks for his 'Oration on the Life & Character of De Lafayette.' J. M. has read it with a deep impression of the abounding merits which render it worthy of the source from which it comes, and of the object & the occasion which inspired it."

28. JAMES MADISON TO MARTIN VAN BUREN FEBRUARY 18, 1835

"J. Madison, with his respectful compliments to Mr. Van Buren, returns his thanks for the copy of Mr. Adams's Oration on the 'Life and character of La Fayette.' It is s single illustration of the powers and resources of the Orator, and will deservedly aid in making known a character which will be the more admired the more its known."

141 Madison is referring to John Quincy Adams.

VI. JAMES MONROE ON JOHN QUINCY ADAMS

1. JAMES MONROE TO JOHN QUINCY ADAMS APRIL 2, 1795

"In removing the embarrassment to which our Commission was subjected, it became indispensably necessary that application should be made to the competent authority, and to which your powers were certainly competent, whether French or Dutch; for unless that government was totally & permanently absorbed in this, it followed that you were the party thro' all the intermediate modifications, to whom it belonged to take cognizance of the affairs, and redress the grievances, if any there be, of our countrymen there.[142] It gives me pleasure to hear that you have experienced no difficulty upon this head, because thereby the interest of the United States will be greatly promoted: I take it for granted you will experience the like facility in the future but if the contrary should be the case and any arrangement on the part of this government here appears to you necessary, to facilitate your operations & you will be pleased to communicate the same to me & point out the line in which I may be serviceable, be assured that I shall be happy to cooperate with you in obtaining it."

2. JAMES MONROE TO JOHN QUINCY ADAMS APRIL 2, 1795

"I beg of you, to command me in all cases wherein I can be serviceable."

3. JAMES MONROE TO THOMAS JEFFERSON FEBRUARY 25, 1798

"I think the discussion on the foreign intercourse bill will produce a good effect. The principle taken by the republicans is sound. If we had had no ministers abroad thro' this war, I am sure we should have had no dispute with France. And Mr. Adams's appointment of his son to the mission, was a most reprehensible act.[143] If you had appointed (being in his place) a near relation to such an office, the noise which the royalists would have made, would never have ceased. The inattention which the enemies of such a mission, enemies from principle too, have previously shewn to the measure is a proof of their extreme supineness, in cases where they ought to be active, & might be active with effect."

142 John Quincy Adams served as Minister to the Netherlands from 1794-1797.

143 On June 1, 1797 President John Adams appointed his son, John Quincy, as minister plenipotentiary to Prussia.

4. JAMES MONROE TO JAMES MADISON   FEBRUARY 2, 1806

"DEAR SIR, — It is said that a letter is just received in town from Philadelphia of the last of December which state that Mr. Adams of the Senate is or will be appointed Envoy Extraordinary to [Great Britain] to adjust the commercial differences between it and the United States. The gentleman who gave me the information declined mentioning the name either of the author of the letter or receiver, tho' the fact might be relied on. On my part I can form no opinion respecting the report, having received no letter from you since my return to England to authorize one of any kind."

5. JAMES MONROE TO JOHN ADAMS   FEBRUARY 15, 1813

"From your son we have received no letters of a late date. The Baltic being frozen up, & the communication by land cut off by the war between France and Russia, have prevented it. His view of the present state of affairs between those powers, and in the north generally, will be very interesting, & is looked for with anxiety by the President."

6. JAMES MONROE TO ABIGAIL ADAMS   APRIL 10, 1813

"It is impossible for me to state the precise time when your son will return to the United States. He is associated in the negotiation with Great Britain to be commenced in St. Petersburgh under the mediation of the Emperor of Russia. His service in that negotiation is deemed of high importance to his country. Whenever he resolves to return home, every facility in the power of the government will be rendered to him."

7. JAMES MONROE TO JOHN ADAMS   APRIL 10, 1813

"Dear Sir

Since writing the letter—enclosed, to Mrs. Adams, I have conferred with the President on the subject of your son's return, and am authorised to state to you, that in case of peace with Great Britain, the mission to London will be offered to him. The conduct of your son, it gives me pleasure to state, has obtained the [entire] approbation of the President.—It is hoped that it will suit his convenience to take part in the negotiation for peace, should Great Britain accept the mediation of Russia as is presumed, and in forming a commercial treaty with both those powers, as is contemplated. His knowledge of the subject in relation to both, makes it of great importance that his country should have the advantage of his services, in those important transactions. In regard to his personal views, and to those of Mrs. Adams & yourself, respecting his making a visit home, whenever-desired, the utmost facility will be given in the powers of the government."

8. JAMES MONROE TO JOHN ADAMS APRIL 19, 1813

"DEAR SIR, — The arrangement being completed relative to the negotiations to be conducted at St. Petersburg, I have the pleasure to apprise you of it, as that there will still be time to enable you to write to your son, by the vessel which takes his colleagues there. The occasion was thought to be of that high importance to require according to the usage of our country, a special mission of three. Mr. Gallatin & Mr. Bayard are the two others. There will be two commissions for treating with Great Britain; One, for peace, including a definition of neutral rights, under the mediation of Russia; a second to form a treaty of commerce. In these the order will be, Mr. Gallatin, your Son & Mr. Bayard. There will also be a Commission to form a commercial treaty. In this the order will be, your Son, Mr. Gallatin & Mr. Bayard. The first two commissions contemplating negotiations which might be carried on at any other place, being with another power and Mr. G being a member of the administration, it was thought correct to give him the priority. The other contemplating a treaty with Russia with whom your son is accredited, that circumstance seemed to justify the propriety of giving the priority to him. They are all Envoys Extraordinary & Ministers Plenipotentiary. They are also allowed an outfit upon the principle that they must be presented in a distinguished manner to the Court & be drawn much into Society of the first rank & greatest expence. In truth, if we allowed our Ministers abroad all that the law permits, in every case we shall hardly be able to put them at their ease there, & shall certainly never recompense them for their services & sufferings. Presuming that it would be satisfactory to you to have these details I have taken an interest in communicating them. You will have sufficient time to write by these gentlemen after receiving this letter provided you forward to them without delay your dispatches to Philadelphia."

9. JAMES MONROE TO THOMAS JEFFERSON JUNE 7, 1813

"The mediation of Russia offers some prospects of accommodation with Great Britain, but no certainty of it. It is not known that she has accepted the overture. The Russian minister was informed that the President accepted it because he wished peace on honorable conditions, and was willing to avail himself of every fair opportunity to promote it: that he did not ask whether Great Britain had accepted the mediation, because it was sufficient that the Emperor had offered it; and that the President sought by the manner of accepting it to evince his high respect for the character of the Emperor. It became a question whether authority should be given Mr. Adams alone to manage the negotiation, or éclat be attached to the Mission, by adding two Envoys to it, to be sent from this country. The latter course was preferred, and Mr. Gallatin being desirous, of acting in it, he was employed."

10. JAMES MONROE TO JOHN ADAMS JULY 15, 1813

"From your son no late letters have been received. The Baltic being frozen up, & the communication by land interrupted, by the war, between France & Russia, have prevented it. His view of the present state of affairs, between those powers, & in the north generally, will be very interesting & is looked for with anxiety by the President."

11. JAMES MONROE TO JOHN QUINCY ADAMS MARCH 13, 1815

"SIR, —The restoration of peace having afforded an opportunity to renew the friendly intercourse with Great Britain, the President availed himself of it without delay by the appointment of a Minister Plenipotentiary to the British Government. Your long and meritorious services induced him, with the advice and consent of the Senate, to confer that appointment on you, for which I have the honor to transmit to you a commission and letter of credence. Of this intention you were sometime since advised.

On entering on the duties of this trust your attention will naturally be drawn to the means of preserving the peace which has been so happily restored by a termination, so far as it may be practicable, of all causes of future variance. These will form the subject of a more full communication hereafter. I shall confine this letter to some objects incident to the new state of things which will probably come into discussion in your first interviews."

12. JAMES MONROE TO THOMAS JEFFERSON FEBRUARY 23, 1817

"To your friendship, & good wishes in my favor, I have always had the greatest sensibility, and shall continue to have. The time is approaching, when I shall commence the duties of the trust suggested in your last, the difficulties of which have been felt, in a certain degree, even in the present stage; particularly in the formation of the administration with which I am to act. On full consideration of all circumstances, I have thought that it would produce a bad effect, to place any one from this quarter of the Union, in the dept. of State, or from the south or west. You know how much has been said to impress a belief, on the country, north & east of this, that the citizens from Virginia, holding the Presidency, have made appointments to that dept., to secure the succession, from it, to the Presidency, of the person who happens to be from that State. My opinion is, that those of that State, who have been elected to the Presidency, would have obtained that proof of the public confidence had they not previously filled the dept. of State, except myself, & that my service in any other dept., contributed more to overcome prejudices against my election than that in the dept. of State. It is, however, not sufficient that this allegation is unfounded. Much effect has been produced by it, so much, indeed, that I am inclined to believe, that if I nominated any one from this quarter (including the south and west, which in relation to such a nomination at this time, would be viewed in the same light) I should embody against the approaching administration, principally, to defeat, the suspected arrangement for the succession, the whole of the country, north of the Delaware, immediately, and that the rest of the Potomac would likely to follow it. My wish is to prevent such a combination, the ill effect of which would be so sensibly felt, on so many important public interests, among which, the just claims, according to the relative merit of the party of persons, in this quarter, ought not to be disregarded. With this view, I have thought it advisable to select a person for the dept. of State, from the Eastern States, in consequence of which my attention has been turned to Mr. Adams, who by his age, long experience in our foreign affairs, and adoption into the republican party, seems to have superior pretentions to any there."

13. JAMES MONROE TO JOHN QUINCY ADAMS MARCH 6, 1817

"DEAR SIR,—Respect for your talents and patriotic services has induced me to commit to your care, with the sanction of the Senate, the Department of State. I have done this in confidence that it will be agreeable to you to accept it, which I can assure you will be very gratifying to me. I shall communicate your appointment by several conveyances to multiply the chances of your obtaining early knowledge of it, that, in case you accept it, you may be enabled to return to the United States, and enter on the duties of the office, with the least delay possible."[144]

-⁂-

14. JAMES MONROE TO COLONEL BARBOUR OCTOBER 20, 1826

"Of Mr. Adams's friendship I never entertained a doubt, nor do I of the Administration generally. No difficulty therefore arises from that source."

-⁂-

15. JAMES MONROE TO JUDGE JOHN MCLEAN OCTOBER 1827

"It has been my object since I left office, as it was before, to take no part in the election between the competitors, & in which I have been guided equally by feeling & principle.[145] I had given to each, while in office, strong proofs of confidence & regard, which I have wished to preserve. To be made a partizan of either against the other, in the pending contest, would be very distressing to me. I had rather submit to some transitory injury, for such it could only be, than be placed in that state, at this time, even in vindication of my character, if to be avoided on just principles."

-⁂-

16. JAMES MONROE TO JUDGE JOHN MCLEAN DECEMBER 5, 1827

"By the faithful & useful discharge of your public duties, you have given the best support which could be rendered to the administration of Mr. Adams, & of which he must be sensible. No person at the head of the government has, in my opinion, any claim to the active, partizan exertions of those in office under him. Justice to his public acts, friendly feelings, and a candid & honorable deportment towards him, without forgetting what is due to others, are all he has a right to expect, and in these, I am satisfied, you have never failed."

-⁂-

17. JAMES MONROE TO JAMES MADISON DECEMBER 10, 1827

"Presuming it may be useful to you to see what has passed between Col. Mercer & me, respecting the measure, contemplated by some persons, to place us on the ticket of one of

144 John Quincy Adams, then serving as United States Minister to Great Britain, accepted President Monroe's offer and on September 22, 1817 was sworn in as the eighth Secretary of State.

145 Monroe is referring to the presidential election of 1828 between political rivals John Quincy Adams and Andrew Jackson.

the candidates in the approaching election, I send you his two letters to me, and a copy of my answer to the last, of this date, which I have authorized him, in a separate one, to shew, if necessary, in profound confidence, to the committee of the convention. In the latter I have stated that I did not know how you would act, should you be nominated, but that I concluded from what passes between us when we were last together, that it was likewise your wish to preserve a state of perfect neutrality between the candidates. I observed to him that it would be improper that it should be known that such application had been made to me, & declined, lest improper inferences might be drawn from it, to the prejudice of Mr. Adams, & forming a departure, in a degree, from that state of neutrality."

18. JAMES MONROE TO WILLIAM WIRT OCTOBER 24, 1828

In Mr. Gouverneur's appointment I take great interest, but I well know that you, and several other friends, will do all in your power to promote it. I am now satisfied, also, that the President entertains a very friendly feeling for me, and will with pleasure confer it on him, should it comport with his views of propriety and policy."

19. JAMES MONROE TO WILLIAM WIRT OCTOBER 24, 1828

"On all subjects, public and private, I should be happy to have an opportunity of communicating with you, as we have always done, with the most intimate confidence in each other. Whether the present Administration ought to withdraw, in the event that Mr. Adams should not be reelected, is a question of great delicacy, as to the numbers, & of interest, by way of example, as to principle. They hold their offices, as others do, as servants of the public, not his. Their appointments do not cease with his. They are responsible, each, for the faithful performance of their duties. He likewise is responsible for them. In this respect there is a difference between our government and that of Great Britain; in the latter the Minister alone is responsible. The office of the Chief being hereditary, he is beyond the reach of impeachment. With us, both may be impeached, the Chief and Minister. They are also his counsellors. In some views, therefore, they may be considered as holding an independent ground, that is, as depending on their good conduct in office, and not on the change of the incumbent. In others, the opposite argument appears to have force. Where a difference of principle is involved, it would seem as if a change would be necessary; but where such difference does not exist the danger is, by connecting the members with the fortune of the incumbent, of making them the mere appendages & creatures of the individual, which may have, in certain views, in the progress of affairs, an unfavorable effect on our system. Whenever things get to that state, that manners are approved, or disapproved, by parties contending for power, to promote the success of their favorite, principle is lost sight of, and the people cease to be the sovereign, or rather to exercise the sovereign power in a manner to preserve it. They become instruments, whereby the basis of the system will be shaken. Still as the heads of the Dept. are her Counsellors, and wield important branches of the Government, I do not see how they can remain in office without her sanction, or wait after his election till apprised of his decision by himself. This view is much less applicable, in every instance and circumstance, to your case than to theirs. Your duties are different. He has less connection with, and less responsibility for the performance of them. Your standing is likewise such, nothing unfriendly having occurred between you, that I should think he would wish to retain you."

20. JAMES MONROE TO JOHN QUINCY ADAMS DECEMBER 17, 1828

"DEAR SIR,—I have received the copy of your late message to Congress, which you were so kind as to send me, & have perused it with great attention & interest. I consider it a candid & able exposition of our affairs, foreign & domestic, & have no doubt that it will be so considered by the nation. It was very gratifying to me to see you enter so fully into the subjects, on which you were called on to act during your Administration, from a belief that the illustration which you have given, in each instance, will be useful to our country, & leave an impression of your conduct, in those affairs, very favorable to yourself. The calm & deliberate manner in which you have given this illustration, without making any allusion to yourself, will likewise have a good effect. In your friendship I have the most perfect confidence, having seen in your conduct, while I was in the Administration, and since my retirement, the most uniform & satisfactory proofs of it. My indisposition, proceeding from the accidents with which you are acquainted, has ceased. I am still weak, but daily recover my strength. I shall always be happy to see you here, & wherever we may chance to meet, as I shall, thro' life, take a sincere & great interest in your welfare and happiness."

NOTES

Chapter I
George Washington
I. George Washington on the Presidency

1. Thomas J. Fleming, ed., *Affectionately Yours, George Washington: A Self-Portrait in Letters of Friendship,* New York: W. W. Norton & Company, Inc., 1967, p. 192-193.
2. W. B. Allen, ed., *George Washington: A Collection,* Indianapolis: Liberty Classics, 1988, pp. 392-393.
3. Dorothy Twohig, ed., *The Papers of George Washington: Presidential Series, September 1788—March 1789,* Charlottesville: University Press of Virginia, 1987, vol. 1, pp. 32-33.
4. Ibid, pp. 71-73.
5. Ibid, p. 136.
6. Ibid, p. 159.
7. Ibid, pp. 198-199.
8. Ibid, p. 200.
9. Ibid, pp. 263-264.
10. Ibid, p. 376.
11. John C. Fitzpatrick ed., *The Writings of George Washington from the Original Manuscript Sources, 1745-1799,* Washington: United States Government Printing Office, 1939, vol. 30, pp. 255-256.
12. Allen, p. 436.
13. Dorothy Twohig ed., *The Papers of George Washington: Presidential Series, April 1789—June 1789,* Charlottesville: University of Virginia Press, 1987, vol. 2, pp. 245-247.
14. Fitzpatrick, 30: pp. 322-323.
15. Twohig, 2: pp. 390-391.
16. Fitzpatrick, 30: pp. 360-362.
17. Allen, p. 537.
18. Ibid.
19. Ibid, p. 538.
20. Ibid, pp. 537-538.
21. "From George Washington to the Virginia Legislature, 27 April 1790," Founders Online, National Archives (http://founders.archives.gov/documents/Washington/05-05-02-0228 [last update: 2015-09-29]).

22. John C. Fitzpatrick ed., *The Writings of George Washington from the Original Manuscript Sources, 1745-1799,* Washington: United States Press, 1939, vol. 31, pp. 53-55.
23. Dorothy Twohig ed., *The Papers of George Washington: Presidential Series, January 1790-June 1790,* Charlottesville: University of Virginia Press, 1996, vol. 5, p. 526.
24. "From George Washington to Tobias Lear, 5 September 1790," Founders Online, National Archives (http://founders.archives.gov/documetns/Washington/05-06-02-0190 [last update: 2015-09-29]).
25. John C. Fitzpatrick, ed., *The Writings of George Washington from the Original Manuscript Sources, 1745-1799,* Washington: United States Government Printing Office, 1939, vol. 32, pp. 46-49.
26. "Second Inaugural Address, 4 March 1793," Founders Online, National Archives (http://founders.archives.gov/documents/Washington/05-12-02-0200 [last update: 2015-09-29]).
27. Allen, p. 655.
28. "From George Washington to John Sinclair, 6 March 1797," Founders Online, National Archives (http://founders.archives.gov/documents/Washington/06-01-02-0010 [last update: 2015-09-29]).
29. "From George Washington to John Quincy Adams, 20 January 1799," Founders Online, National Archives (http://founders.archives.gov/documents/Washington/06-03-02-0227 [last update: 2015-09-29]).
30. Allen, p. 666.

II. John Adams on George Washington

1. Letter from John Adams to Abigail Adams, 29 May 1775 [electronic edition]. *Adams Family Papers: An Electronic Archive.* The Massachusetts Historical Society. *Available at* http://www.masshist.org/digitaladams/
2. L. H. Butterfield, ed., *Diary and Autobiography of John Adams,* Cambridge: The Belknap Press of Harvard University Press, 1962, vol. 3, pp. 322-323.
3. Frank Shuffelton, ed., *The Letters of John and Abigail Adams,* New York: Penguin Books, 2004, p. 63.
4. Charles Francis Adams, ed., *The Works of John Adams, Second President of the United States,* Boston: Little, Brown and Company, 1854, vol. IX, pp. 358-359.

5. L. H. Butterfield, ed., *Diary and Autobiography of John Adams,* Cambridge: The Belknap Press of Harvard University Press, 1961, vol. 4, p. 5.
6. Shuffelton, p. 259.
7. Ibid, p. 306.
8. Ibid, pp. 306-307.
9. Charles Francis Adams, ed., *The Works of John Adams, Second President of the United States,* Boston: Little, Brown and Company, 1852, vol. VII, p. 282.
10. Richard Alan Ryerson, ed., *Adams Family Correspondence,* Cambridge: The Belknap Press of Harvard University, 1993, vol. 5, pp. 315-316.
11. Adams, 9: pp. 540-541.
12. Lester J. Cappon, ed., *The Adams-Jefferson Letters: The Complete Correspondence Between Thomas Jefferson and Abigail and John Adams,* Chapel Hill: The University of North Carolina Press, 1959, vol. I, p. 202.
13. Cappon, 1: p. 236.
14. Richard Rosenfeld, *American Aurora, A Democratic-Republican Returns: The Suppressed History of Our Nation's Beginnings and the Heroic Newspaper that Tried to Report It,* New York: St. Martin's Press, 1997, p. 485.
15. Charles Francis Adams, ed., *The Works of John Adams, Second President of the United States,* Boston: Little, Brown and Company, 1853, vol. VIII, pp. 486-487.
16. Adams, 9: p. 569.
17. Letter from John Adams to Abigail Adams, 25 March 1796 [electronic edition]. *Adams Family Papers: An Electronic Archive.* The Massachusetts Historical Society. *Available at* http://www.masshist.org/digitaladams/
18. Letter from John Adams to Abigail Adams, 16 December 1796 [electronic edition]. *Adams Family Papers: An Electronic Archive.* The Massachusetts Historical Society. *Available at* http://www.masshist.org/digitaladams/
19. Letter from John Adams to Abigail Adams, 3 March 1797 [electronic edition]. *Adams Family Papers: An Electronic Archive.* The Massachusetts Historical Society. *Available at* http://www.masshist.org/digitaladams/
20. Adrienne Koch and William Peden, eds., *The Selected Writings of John and John Quincy Adams,* New York: Alfred A. Knopf, 1946, p. 141-142.
21. Letter from John Adams to Abigail Adams, 5 March 1797 [electronic edition]. *Adams Family Papers: An Electronic Archive.* The Massachusetts Historical Society. *Available at* http://www.masshist.org/digitaladams/
22. Letter from John Adams to Abigail Adams, 14 April 1797 [electronic edition]. *Adams Family Papers: An Electronic Archive.* The Massachusetts Historical Society. *Available at* http://www.masshist.org/digitaladams/

23. Adams, 9: pp. 142-143.
24. "From John Adams to John Trumbull, 18 November 1805," Founders Online, National Archives (http://founders.archives.gov/documents/Adams/99-02-02-5108 [last update: 2015-09-29]).
25. Charles Francis Adams, ed., *The Works of John Adams, Second President of the United States,* Boston: Charles C. Little and James Brown, 1851, vol. VI, p. 546.
26. "From John Adams to Benjamin Rush, 20 June 1808," Founders Online, National Archives (http://founders.archives.gov/documents/Adams/99-02-02-5242 [last update: 2015-09-29]).
27. "From John Adams to Benjamin Rush, 10 October 1808," Founders Online, National Archives (http://founders.archives.gov/documents/Adams/99-02-02-5263 [last update: 2015-09-29]).
28. "From John Adams to Boston Patriot, 8 June 1809," Founders Online, National Archives (http://founders.archives.gov/documents/Adams/99-02-02-5375 [last update: 2015-09-29]).
29. "From John Adams to Boston Patriot, 27 June 1811," Founders Online, National Archives (http://founders.archives.gov/documents/Adams/99-02-02-5651 [last update: 2015-09-29]).
30. "From John Adams to John Holmes, 10 August 1815," Founders Online, National Archives (http://founders.archives.gov/documents/Adams/99-02-02-6501 [last update: 2015-09-29]).
31. "From John Adams to John Randolph, Jr., 1816," Founders Online, National Archives (http://founders.archives.gov/documents/Adams/99-02-02-6683 [last update: 2015-09-29]).
32. Rosenfeld, p. 476.

III. Thomas Jefferson on George Washington

1. Sarah N. Randolph, ed., *The Domestic Life of Thomas Jefferson,* New York: F. Unger Publishing Company, 1958, p. 358.
2. Paul Leicester Ford, ed., *The Writings of Thomas Jefferson, 1781-1784*, New York: G. P. Putnam's Sons, 1894, vol. III, p. 168.
3. Paul Leicester Ford, ed., *The Writings of Thomas Jefferson, 1784-1787,* New York: G. P. Putnam's Sons, 1894, vol. IV, p. 26.

4. H. A. Washington, ed., *The Writings of Thomas Jefferson: Being His Autobiography, Correspondence, Reports, Messages, Addresses, and Other Writings, Official and Private*, Washington, D.C.: Taylor & Maury, 1853, vol. II, p. 465.
5. Paul Leicester Ford, ed., *The Writings of Thomas Jefferson, 1788-1792*, New York: G. P. Putnam's Sons, 1894, vol. V, p. 70.
6. Ibid, pp. 94-95.
7. Ibid, p. 282.
8. Ibid, pp. 300-301.
9. Paul Leicester Ford, ed., *The Writings of Thomas Jefferson, 1792-1794*, New York: G. P. Putnam's Sons, 1895, vol. I, p. 1.
10. Ibid.
11. Paul Leicester Ford, ed., *The Writings of Thomas Jefferson, 1760-1775*, New York: G. P. Putnam's Sons, 1892, vol. I, p. 198.
12. Ibid, p. 202.
13. Ford, 6: pp. 292-293.
14. Ibid, 1: p. 254.
15. Paul Leicester Ford, ed., *The Writings of Thomas Jefferson, 1795-1801*, New York: G. P. Putnam's Sons, 1896, vol. VII, p. 41.
16. Ibid, pp. 101-102.
17. Ibid, p. 104.
18. Ibid, 1: p. 284.
19. Paul Leicester Ford, ed., *The Writings of Thomas Jefferson, 1801-1806*, New York: G. P. Putnam's Sons, 1897, vol. VIII, p. 5.
20. Mary A. Hackett, J.C.A. Stagg, Jeanne Kerr Cross, and Susan Holbrook Perdue, eds., *The Papers of James Madison: Secretary of State Series, 1 August 1801 to 28 February 1802*, Charlottesville: University of Virginia Press, 1993, vol. 2, p. 228.
21. H. A. Washington, ed., *The Writings of Thomas Jefferson: Being His Autobiography, Correspondence, Reports, Messages, Addresses, and Other Writings, Official and Private*, Washington, D.C.: Taylor & Maury, 1854, vol. IV, p. 494.
22. H. A. Washington, ed., *The Writings of Thomas Jefferson: Being His Autobiography, Correspondence, Reports, Messages, Addresses, and Other Writings, Official and Private*, Washington, D. C.: Taylor & Maury, 1853, vol. V, pp. 213-214.
23. Paul Leicester Ford, ed., *The Writings of Thomas Jefferson, 1807-1815*, New York: G. P. Putnam's Sons, 1898, vol. IX, pp. 449-450.
24. Ibid, pp. 448-449.
25. Ibid, p. 450.

26. Ibid, pp. 450-451.
27. Ibid, 1: p. 155.
28. Ibid.
29. Ibid, p. 165.
30. Ibid, p. 168.
31. Paul Leicester Ford, ed., *The Writings of Thomas Jefferson, 1816-1826*, New York: G. P. Putnam's Sons, 1899, vol. X, p. 228.
32. Ibid.
33. Ibid, pp. 310-311.
34. Ibid, p. 314.
35. Ibid, pp. 314-315.
36. Ibid, pp. 313-314.

IV. James Madison on George Washington

1. Gaillard Hunt, ed., *The Writings of James Madison, 1769-1783*, New York: G. P. Putnam's Sons, 1900, vol. I, p. 65.
2. James Madison, *Letters and Other Writings of James Madison: Fourth President of the United States.* vol. I, 1769-1793, Philadelphia: J.B. Lippincott and Company, 1865, vol. I, p. 56.
3. Ibid, p. 107.
4. Ibid, p. 127.
5. Ibid, p. 140.
6. Ibid, p. 148.
7. Ibid, p. 198.
8. Ibid, p. 214.
9. Ibid, p. 263.
10. Ibid, p. 267.
11. Ibid, p. 284.
12. Ibid, p. 328.
13. Gaillard Hunt, *The Writings of James Madison, 1787*, New York: G. P. Putnam's Sons, 1902, vol. III, p. 3.
14. Ibid, pp. 3-4.
15. James Madison, *Letters and Other Writings of James Madison: Fourth President of the United States, 1769-1793*, Philadelphia: J. B. Lippincott & Company, 1865, vol. I, p. 329.
16. Ibid, p. 332.

17. Ibid, pp. 330-331
18. Ibid, p. 421.
19. Ibid, p. 422.
20. Ibid, p. 441.
21. Ibid, p. 457.
22. Ibid, pp. 461-462.
23. Ibid, p. 468.
24. Ibid, pp. 470-471.
25. Charles F. Hobson, et al., eds., *The Papers of James Madison, 2 March 1789-20 January 1790*, Charlottesville: University Press of Virginia, 1979, vol. 12, p. 249.
26. Madison, 1: p. 479.
27. Ibid, p. 519.
28. Ibid, pp. 554-558.
29. Ibid, pp. 559-560.
30. Ibid, pp. 563-568.
31. Gaillard Hunt, *The Writings of James Madison*, New York: G.P. Putnam's Sons, 1906, vol. VI, p. 127.
32. Madison, 1: pp. 581-582.
33. Ibid, p. 66.
34. Ibid, p. 600.
35. James Madison, *Letters and Other Writings of James Madison: Fourth President of the United States, 1794-1815*, Philadelphia: J. B. Lippincott and Company, 1865, vol. II, pp. 3-4.
36. Ibid, p. 17.
37. Ibid, p. 18.
38. Ibid, pp. 24-25.
39. James Madison, *Letters and Other Writings of James Madison: Fourth President of the United States, 1829-1836*, Philadelphia: J. B. Lippincott and Company, 1865, vol. IV, p. 495.
40. Madison, 2: p. 83.
41. Ibid, p. 85.
42. Ibid, pp. 96-97.
43. Ibid, p. 103.
44. Ibid.
45. Ibid, p. 109.
46. Ibid, pp. 114-115.
47. Ibid, p. 127.
48. Ibid, p. 130.
49. Ibid, p. 463.
50. James Madison, *Letters and Other Writings of James Madison: Fourth President of the United States, 1816-1828*, Philadelphia: J.B. Lippincott and Company, 1865, vol. III, pp. 323-324.

51. Ibid, pp. 482-483.
52. Ibid, p. 495.
53. Ibid, p. 573.
54. Ibid, pp. 582-583
55. Ibid, p. 584.
56. Madison, 4: p. 68.
57. Ibid, p. 174.
58. Ibid, p. 297.
59. Ibid, pp. 376-377.

V. James Monroe on George Washington

1. Stanislaus Murray Hamilton, ed., *The Writings of James Monroe, 1778-1794*, New York: G.P. Putnam's Sons, 1898, vol. I, p. 2.
2. Ibid, pp. 19-22.
3. Daniel Preston and Marlena C. DeLong, eds., *The Papers of James Monroe: Selected Correspondence and Papers, 1776-1794,* Westport: Greenwood Press, 2006, vol. 2, p. 238.
4. Hamilton, 1: pp. 173-174.
5. Ibid, p. 186.
6. Preston, 2: p. 497.
7. Ibid, p. 543.
8. Ibid, pp. 626-627.
9. Ibid, p. 637.
10. Ibid, p. 641.
11. Ibid, p. 665.
12. Hamilton, 1: p. 298.
13. Stanislaus Murray Hamilton, ed., *The Writings of James Monroe, 1794-1796*, New York: G. P. Putnam's Sons, 1899, vol. II, p. 403.
14. Stanislaus Murray Hamilton, ed., *The Writings of James Monroe, 1794-1796*, New York: G. P. Putnam's Sons, 1899, vol. III, pp. 19-20.
15. Ibid, pp. 20-21.
16. Ibid, p. 24.
17. Ibid, pp. 53-54.
18. Ibid, p. 161.
19. Ibid, pp. 165-166.

20. Stanislaus Murray Hamilton, ed., *The Writings of James Monroe, 1803-1806*, New York: G. P. Putnam's Sons, 19oo, vol. IV, p. 238.
21. Daniel Preston and Marlena C. DeLong, eds., *The Papers of James Monroe: A Documentary History of the Presidential Tours of James Monroe, 1817, 1818, 1819,* vol. 1, Westport: Greenwood Press, 2003, vol. 1, p. 52.
22. Ibid, p. 196.
23. Ibid, p. 526.
24. Ibid, p. 587.
25. Stanislaus Murray Hamilton, ed., *The Writings of James Monroe, 1817-1823*, New York: G.P. Putnam's Sons, 1902, vol. VI, p. 150.
26. Ibid, p. 192
27. Stanislaus Murray Hamilton, ed., *The Writings of James Monroe, 1824-1831*, New York: G.P. Putnam's Sons, 1903, vol. VII, p. 244.
28. Ibid, pp. 129-130.
29. Brown, Stuart Gerry Brown, ed., *The Autobiography of James Monroe,* Syracuse: Syracuse University Press, 1959, p. 24.
30. Ibid.
31. Ibid, pp. 24-25.
32. Ibid, pp. 28-29.
33. Ibid, p. 34.
34. Ibid, p. 50.
35. Ibid, p. 51.
36. Ibid, p. 52.
37. Ibid, p. 53.
38. Ibid, p. 146.
39. Ibid, pp. 146-147.
40. Ibid, p. 150.

VI. John Quincy Adams on George Washington

1. Worthington Chauncey Ford, ed., *Writings of John Quincy Adams, 1779-1796*, New York: The Macmillan Company, 1913, vol. I, pp. 43-44.
2. Ibid, p. 43.
3. Ibid, p. 120.
4. Ibid, pp. 150-151.
5. Ibid, p. 152.

6. Allan Nevins, ed., *The Diary of John Quincy Adams, 1794-1845, American Political, Social and Intellectual Life from Washington to Polk*, New York: Longmans, Green and Company, 1928, p. 1.
7. Charles Francis Adams, ed., *Memoirs of John Quincy Adams, Comprising Portions of His Diary From 1795 to 1848*, Philadelphia: J. B. Lippincott & Company, 1874, vol. I, pp. 34-35.
8. Ibid, p. 61.
9. Ibid, pp. 96-97.
10. Ibid, pp. 110-111.
11. Ford, 1: p. 360.
12. Ibid, p. 408.
13. Ibid, p. 428.
14. Adams, 1: pp. 141-142.
15. Ford, 1: pp. 453-454.
16. Ibid, p. 466.
17. Ibid, pp. 467-468.
18. Ibid, p. 475.
19. Ibid, pp. 476-477.
20. Ibid, p. 477.
21. Ibid, p. 484.
22. Ibid, pp. 485-486.
23. Worthington Chauncey Ford, ed., *Writings of John Quincy Adams, 1796-1801*, New York: The Macmillan Company, 1913, vol. II, p. 13.
24. Ibid, pp. 21-22.
25. Ibid, p. 42.
26. Ibid, p. 46.
27. Ibid, pp. 49-51.
28. Ibid, pp. 64-65.
29. Ibid, pp. 109-110.
30. Ibid, pp. 119-120.
31. Ibid, pp. 133-134.
32. Ibid, p. 359.
33. Ibid, p. 378.
34. Ibid, p. 449.
35. Ibid, p. 451.
36. Ibid, p. 451.
37. Ibid, p. 453.
38. Ibid, pp. 454-455.

39. Ibid, p. 460.
40. Adrienne Koch and William Peden, eds., *The Selected Writings of John and John Quincy Adams*, New York: Alfred A. Knopf, 1946, p. 263.
41. Ibid, pp. 263-264.
42. Worthington Chauncey Ford, ed., *Writings of John Quincy Adams, 1801-1810*, New York: The Macmillan Company, 1913, vol. III, p. 342.
43. Charles Francis Adams, ed., *Memoirs of John Quincy Adams, Comprising Portions of His Diary From 1795 to 1848*, Philadelphia: J. B. Lippincott & Company, 1875, vol. V, p. 401.
44. Koch, p. 335.
45. Charles Francis Adams, ed., *Memoirs of John Quincy Adams, Comprising Portions of His Diary From 1795 to 1848*, Philadelphia: J. B. Lippincott & Company, 1875, vol. VI, p. 427.
46. Walter LaFeber, ed., *John Quincy Adams and American Continental Empire, Letters, Papers and Speeches*, Chicago: Quadrangle Books, 1965, pp. 135-137.
47. Charles Francis Adams, ed., *Memoirs of John Quincy Adams, Comprising Portions of His Diary From 1795 to 1848*, Philadelphia: J. B. Lippincott & Company, 1875, vol. VII, p. 218.
48. Adams, Charles Francis Adams, ed., *Memoirs of John Quincy Adams, Comprising Portions of His Diary From 1795 to 1848*, Philadelphia: J. B. Lippincott & Company, 1876, vol. III, pp. 187, 219.
49. John Quincy Adams, *An Eulogy on the Life and Character of James Monroe, Fifth President of the United States,* Boston: J. H. Eastburn, City Printer, 1831, p. 20.
50. Ibid, pp. 20-21.
51. Adams, 8: pp. 468-479.
52. Charles Francis Adams, ed., *Memoirs of John Quincy Adams, Comprising Portions of His Diary From 1795 to 1848*, Philadelphia: J. B. Lippincott & Company, 1876, vol. IX, p. 344.
53. Nevins, p. 497.
54. Charles Francis Adams, ed., *Memoirs of John Quincy Adams, Comprising Portions of His Diary From 1795 to 1848*, Philadelphia: J. B. Lippincott & Company, 1876, vol. X, p. 117.
55. Nevins, p. 498.
56. Charles Francis Adams, ed., *Memoirs of John Quincy Adams, Comprising Portions of His Diary From 1795 to 1848*, Philadelphia: J. B. Lippincott & Company, 1877, vol. XII, pp. 11-12.

Chapter II
John Adams
I. John Adams on the Presidency

1. Charles Francis Adams, ed., *The Works of John Adams, Second President of the United States,* Boston: Little, Brown and Company, 1853, vol. VIII, pp. 464-465.
2. Ibid, pp. 492-493.
3. Charles Francis Adams, ed., *The Works of John Adams, Second President of the United States,* Boston: Little, Brown and Company, 1851, vol. VI, p. 430.
4. Ibid, pp. 430-431.
5. Adams, 8: p. 494.
6. Ibid, pp. 512-513.
7. Letter from John Adams to Abigail Adams, 2 February 1796 [electronic edition]. *Adams Family Papers: An Electronic Archive.* The Massachusetts Historical Society. *Available at* http://www.masshist.org/digitaladams/
8. Letter from John Adams to Abigail Adams, 15 February 1796 [electronic edition]. *Adams Family Papers: An Electronic Archive.* The Massachusetts Historical Society. *Available at* http://www.masshist.org/digitaladams/
9. Letter from John Adams to Abigail Adams, 13 March 1796 [electronic edition]. *Adams Family Papers: An Electronic Archive.* The Massachusetts Historical Society. *Available at* http://www.masshist.org/digitaladams/
10. Letter from John Adams to Abigail Adams, 9 April 1796 [electronic edition]. *Adams Family Papers: An Electronic Archive.* The Massachusetts Historical Society. *Available at* http://www.masshist.org/digitaladams/
11. Letter from John Adams to Abigail Adams, 7 December 1796 [electronic edition]. *Adams Family Papers: An Electronic Archive.* The Massachusetts Historical Society. *Available at* http://www.masshist.org/digitaladams/
12. Letter from John Adams to Abigail Adams, 1 January 1797 [electronic edition]. *Adams Family Papers: An Electronic Archive.* The Massachusetts Historical Society. *Available at* http://www.masshist.org/digitaladams/
13. Letter from John Adams to Abigail Adams, 31 January 1797 [electronic edition]. *Adams Family Papers: An Electronic Archive.* The Massachusetts Historical Society. *Available at* http://www.masshist.org/digitaladams/
14. Letter from John Adams to Abigail Adams, 5 March 1797 [electronic edition]. *Adams Family Papers: An Electronic Archive.* The Massachusetts Historical Society. *Available at* http://www.masshist.org/digitaladams/

15. Letter from John Adams to Abigail Adams, 9 March 1797 [electronic edition]. *Adams Family Papers: An Electronic Archive.* The Massachusetts Historical Society. *Available at* http://www.masshist.org/digitaladams/
16. Adrienne Koch and William Peden, eds., *The Selected Writings of John and John Quincy Adams,* New York: Alfred A. Knopf, 1946, p. 144.
17. Charles Francis Adams, ed., *The Works of John Adams, Second President of the United States*, Boston: Little, Brown and Company, 1854, vol. IX, p. 181.
18. "From John Adams to Mercy Otis Warren, 8 August 1807," Founders Online, National Archives (http://founders.archives.gov/documents/Adams/99-02-02-5203 [last update: 2015-09-29]).
19. "From John Adams to Benjamin Rush, 25 July 1808," Founders Online, National Archives (http://founders.archives.gov/documents/Adams/99-02-02-5245 [last update: 2015-09-29]).
20. Adams, 6: pp. 539-540.
21. Adams, 9: p. 281.
22. "From John Adams to John Adams Smith, 22 December 1811," Founders Online, National Archives (http://founders.archives.gov/documents/Adams/99-03-02-2076 [last update: 2015-09-29]).
23. "From John Adams to Benjamin Rush, 24 June 1812," Founders Online, National Archives (http://founders.archives.gov/documents/Adams/99-02-02-5814 [last update: 2015-09-29]).
24. Charles Francis Adams, ed., *The Works of John Adams, Second President of the United States*, Boston: Little, Brown and Company, 1854, vol. X, pp. 153-154.
25. David B. Mattern, J.C.A. Stagg, Mary Parke Johnson, and Anne Mandeville Colony, eds., *The Papers of James Madison: Retirement Series, 4 March 1817 to 31 January 1820,* Charlottesville: University of Virginia Press, vol. 1, p. 60.

II. George Washington on John Adams

1. "To John Adams from George Washington, 15 January 1776," Founders Online, National Archives (http://founders.archives.gov.documents/Adams/06-03-02-0206 [last update: 2015-09-29]).
2. "From George Washington to Major General Philip Schuyler, 18 January 1776," Founders Online, National Archives (http://founders.archives.gov/documents/Washington/03-03-02-0096 [last update: 2015-09-29]).

3. "From George Washington to Benjamin Lincoln, 14 November 1788," Founders Online, National Archives (http://founders.archives.gov/documents/Washington/05-01-02-0084 [last update: 2015-09-29]).
4. W. B. Allen, ed., *George Washington: A Collection,* Indianapolis: Liberty Classics, 1988, p. 430.
5. John C. Fitzpatrick, ed., *The Writings of George Washington from the Original Manuscript Sources, 1745-1799*, Washington: United States Government Printing Office, 1939, vol. 30, p. 219.
6. Ibid, p. 174.
7. "[Diary entry: 6 April 1790]," Founders Online, National Archives (http://founders.archives.gov/documents/Washington/01-06-02-0001-0004-0006 [last update: 2015-09-29]).
8. "From George Washington to John Adams, 14 June 1790," Founders Online, National Archives (http://founders.archives.gov/documents/Washington/05-05-02-0327 [last update: 2015-09-29]).
9. Letter from John Adams to Abigail Adams, 7 December 1796 [electronic edition]. *Adams Family Papers: An Electronic Archive.* Massachusetts Historical Society. *Available at* http://www.masshist.org/digitaladams/
10. John C. Fitzpatrick, ed., *The Writings of George Washington from the Original Manuscript Sources, 1745-1799*, Washington: Government Printing Office, 1940, vol. 35, p. 410.
11. Ibid, p. 428.
12. "From George Washington to Oliver Wolcott, Jr., 29 May 1797," Founders Online, National Archives (http://founders.archives.gov/documents/Washington/06-01-02-0129 [last update: 2015-09-29]).
13. John C. Fitzpatrick, ed., *The Writings of George Washington from the Original Manuscript Sources, 1745-1799,* Washington: Government Printing Office, 1941, vol. 36, pp. 291-292.
14. W. W. Abbot, ed., *The Papers of George Washington, Retirement Series, January 1798—September 1798,* Charlottesville: University of Virginia Press, 1998, vol. 2, p. 334.
15. "To John Adams from George Washington, 4 July 1798," Founders Online, National Archives (http://founders.archives.gov/documents/Adams/99-02-02-2696 [last update: 2015-09-29]).
16. John Rhodehamel, ed., *George Washington: Writings,* New York: Literary Classics of the United States, 1997, p. 1005.
17. Abbot, 2: p. 403.
18. Ibid.

19. "To John Adams from George Washington, 25 September 1798," Founders Online, National Archives (http://founders.archives.gov/documents/Adams/99-02-02-3028 [last update: 2015-09-29]).
20. Rhodehamel, p. 1014.
21. W. W. Abbot and Edward G. Lengel, eds., *The Papers of George Washington Retirement Series, September 1798—April 1799,* Charlottesville: University of Virginia Press, 1999, vol. 3, p. 404.
22. W. W. Abbot, ed., *The Papers of George Washington. Retirement Series, vol. 4, April 1799—December 1799,* Charlottesville: University of Virginia Press, 1999, vol. 4, p. 203.
23. Ibid, p. 239.
24. Ibid, pp. 238-239.

III. Thomas Jefferson on John Adams

1. Paul Leicester Ford, ed., *The Writings of Thomas Jefferson, 1781-1784*, New York: G. P. Putnam's Sons, 1894, vol. III, pp. 309-310.
2. Paul Leicester Ford, ed., *The Writings of Thomas Jefferson, 1784-1787,* New York: G. P. Putnam's Sons, 1894, vol. IV, pp. 325-326.
3. Lester J. Cappon, ed., *The Adams-Jefferson Letters: The Complete Correspondence Between Thomas Jefferson and Abigail and John Adams,* Chapel Hill: The University of North Carolina Press, 1959, vol. I, p. 172.
4. John P. Foley, ed., *The Jeffersonian Cyclopedia,* New York: Russell & Russell, 1967, vol. I, p. 7.
5. Paul Leicester Ford, ed., *The Writings of Thomas Jefferson, 1788-1792*, New York: G. P. Putnam's Sons, 1895, vol. V, p. 104.
6. Ibid, p. 329.
7. Julian P. Boyd, ed., *The Papers of Thomas Jefferson*, Princeton: Princeton University Press, 1982, vol. 20, p. 293.
8. Worthington Chauncey Ford, ed., *Writings of John Quincy Adams, 1779-1796*, New York: The MacMillan Company, 1913, vol. I, p. 65.
9. Cappon, 1: p. 246.
10. Boyd, 20: pp. 310-311.
11. Paul Leicester Ford, ed., *The Writings of Thomas Jefferson, 1792-1794*, New York: G. P. Putnam's Sons, 1895, vol. VI, p. 144.
12. Paul Leicester, ed., *The Writings of Thomas Jefferson, 1795-1801*, New York: G. P. Putnam's Sons, 1896, vol. VII, pp. 91-92.

13. Ibid, pp. 95-97.
14. Worthington Chauncey Ford, 1: pp. 107-108.
15. Ibid, p. 115.
16. Paul Leicester Ford, ed., *The Writings of Thomas Jefferson, 1760-1775*, New York: G. P. Putnam's Sons, 1892, vol. I, p. 273.
17. Ibid, p. 274.
18. Paul Leicester Ford, 7: p. 338.
19. Paul Leicester Ford, ed., *The Writings of Thomas Jefferson, 1801-1806*, New York: G. P. Putnam's Sons, 1897, vol. VIII, p. 265.
20. Ibid, pp. 306-307.
21. Ibid, p. 307.
22. Ibid, p. 309.
23. Paul Leicester Ford, ed., *The Writings of Thomas Jefferson, 1807-1815*, New York: G. P. Putnam's Sons, 1898, vol. IX, p. 295.
24. Ibid, pp. 296-297.
25. Ibid, p. 298.
26. Ibid, pp. 298-299.
27. Ibid, pp. 297-29.
28. Ibid, pp. 300-301.
29. Lester J. Cappon, ed., *The Adams-Jefferson Letters: The Complete Correspondence Between Thomas Jefferson and Abigail and John Adams,* Chapel Hill: The University of North Carolina Press, 1959, vol. II, p. 291.
30. Ibid, p. 292.
31. Paul Leicester Ford, vol. IX: pp. 377-378.
32. Ibid, p. 387.
33. H. A. Washington, ed., *The Writings of Thomas Jefferson: Being His Autobiography, Correspondence, Reports, Messages, Addresses, and Other Writings, Official and Private,* Washington, D.C.: Taylor & Maury, 1854, vol. VII, p. 62.
34. Paul Leicester Ford, 1: p. 166.
35. Ibid, p. 167.
36. Paul Leicester Ford, ed., *The Writings of Thomas Jefferson, 1816-1826*, New York: G. P. Putnam's Sons, 1899, vol. X, p. 268.
37. Ibid.
38. Ibid, p. 298.
39. Ibid, p. 331.
40. Washington, 7: p. 431.

IV. James Madison on John Adams

1. James Madison, *Letters and Other Writings of James Madison, Fourth President of the United* States, *1769-1793*, Philadelphia: J. B. Lippincott & Co., 1865, vol. I, p. 63.
2. Gaillard Hunt, ed., *The Writings of James Madison, 1783-1787*, New York: G. P. Putnam's Sons, 1901, vol. 2, pp. 129-130.
3. Ibid, p. 211.
4. Merrill D. Peterson, ed., *James Madison: A Biography in His Own Words*, New York: Harper & Row Publishers, 1974, p. 132.
5. Gaillard Hunt, ed., *The Writings of James Madison, 1787-1790*, New York: G. P. Putnam's Sons, 1904, vol. V, p. 37.
6. Ibid, p. 99.
7. Ibid, pp. 270-271.
8. Ibid, pp. 302-303.
9. Peterson, p. 166.
10. Hunt, 5: p. 335.
11. Charles F. Hobson, et al., eds., *The Papers of James Madison, 2 March 1789-20 January 1790,* Charlottesville: University Press of Virginia, 1979, vol. 12, pp. 182-183.
12. Gaillard Hunt, ed., *The Writings of James Madison, 1790-1802*, New York: G. P. Putnam's Sons, 1906, vol. VI, pp. 50-51.
13. Ibid, p. 53.
14. Madison, 1: p. 539.
15. Hunt, 6: p. 109.
16. Ibid, p. 121.
17. James Madison, *Letters and Other Writings of James Madison, Fourth President of the United States, 1829-1836*, Philadelphia: J. B. Lippincott & Co., 1865, vol. IV, pp. 498-499.
18. Madison, 1: p. 63.
19. James Madison, *Letters and Other Writings of James Madison, Fourth President of the United States, 1794-1815*, Philadelphia: J. B. Lippincott & Co., 1865, vol. II, p. 106.
20. Peterson, p. 209.
21. Hunt, 6: pp. 300-302.
22. Madison, 2: 109.
23. Ibid, p. 110.

24. Hunt, 6: pp. 302-304.
25. Madison, 2: pp. 114-115.
26. Ibid, pp. 114-116.
27. Ibid, pp. 116-117.
28. Peterson, p. 218.
29. Hunt, 6: pp. 309-310.
30. Ibid, pp. 310-311.
31. Madison, 2: p. 130.
32. Hunt, 6: pp. 312-314.
33. Ibid, pp. 315-316.
34. Ibid, p. 318.
35. Peterson, pp. 220-221.
36. Hunt, 6: pp. 320-321.
37. Ibid, p. 323.
38. Ibid, pp. 324-325.
39. Madison, 2: p. 149.
40. Hunt, 6: p. 330.
41. Peterson, pp. 232-233.
42. Madison, 2: pp. 166-167.
43. Hunt, 6: p. 417.
44. Gaillard Hunt, ed., *The Writings of James Madison, 1808-1819*, New York: G. P. Putnam's Sons, 1908, vol. VIII, p. 375.
45. David B. Mattern, J. C. A. Stagg, Mary Parke Johnson, and Anne Mandeville Colony, eds., *The Papers of James Madison: Retirement Series, 4 March 1817 to 31 January 1820*, Charlottesville: University of Virginia Press, 2009, vol. 1, p. 13.
46. James Madison, *Letters and Other Writings of James Madison: Fourth President of the United States, 1816-1828*, Philadelphia: J. B. Lippincott and Company, 1865, vol. III, p. 41.
47. Hunt, 8: p. 392.
48. Madison, 3: p. 105.
49. Ibid, p. 336.
50. Ibid, p. 527.
51. Madison, 4: pp. 175-176.

V. James Monroe on John Adams

1. Daniel Preston, ed., *The Papers of James Monroe: Selected Correspondence and Papers, 1776-1794,* Westport: Greenwood Press, 2006, vol. 2, p. 78.
2. Ibid, p. 97.
3. Stanislaus Murray Hamilton, ed., *The Writings of James Monroe, 1778-1794*, New York: G. P. Putnam's Sons, 1898, vol. I, p. 99.
4. Ibid, p. 189.
5. Ibid, pp. 225-226.
6. Ibid, p. 226.
7. Daniel Preston, ed., *The Papers of James Monroe: A Documentary History of the Presidential Tours of James Monroe, 1817, 1818, 1819,* Westport: Greenwood Press, 2003, vol. 1, p. 559.
8. Hamilton, 1: p. 245.
9. Preston, 2: p. 572.
10. Hamilton, 1: p. 442.
11. Ibid, p. 443.
12. Ibid, p. 444.
13. Stanislaus Murray Hamilton, ed., *The Writings of James Monroe, 1796-1802,* New York: G. P. Putnam's Sons, 1900, vol. III, p. 67.
14. Ibid, pp. 70-72.
15. Ibid, p. 72.
16. Ibid, p. 73.
17. Ibid, p. 77.
18. Ibid, p. 83.
19. Ibid.
20. Ibid, p. 90.
21. Ibid, pp. 102-103.
22. Ibid, p. 106.
23. Ibid, pp. 115-118.
24. Ibid, p. 120.
25. Ibid, p. 122.
26. Ibid, pp. 125-126.
27. Ibid, p. 126.
28. Ibid, pp. 127-128.
29. Ibid, pp. 131-132.

30. Ibid, p. 132.
31. Ibid, p. 138.
32. Ibid, pp. 136-137.
33. Ibid, p. 139.
34. Ibid, p. 149.
35. Ibid, pp. 151-152.
36. Ibid, p. 161.
37. Ibid, p. 168.
38. Ibid.
39. Ibid, p. 178.
40. "To James Madison from James Monroe, 4 June 1800," *Founders Online*, National Archives, last modified July 12, 2016, http://founders.archives.gov/documents/Madison/02-08-02-0577.
41. Hamilton, 3: pp. 219-220.
42. Ibid, pp. 249-250.
43. Ibid, p. 250.
44. Ibid.
45. Ibid.
46. Ibid, p. 251.
47. Ibid.
48. Ibid, p. 252.
49. Ibid, p. 264.
50. Ibid, p. 265.
51. Ibid, pp. 284-285.
52. Stanislaus Murray Hamilton, ed., *The Writings of James Monroe, 1807-1816*, New York: G. P. Putnam's Sons, 1902, vol. V, p. 132.
53. Ibid, pp. 134-135.
54. Ibid, p. 189.
55. Ibid, pp. 243-244.
56. Ibid, p. 250.
57. Stanislaus Murray Hamilton, ed., *The Writings of James Monroe, 1817-1823*, New York: G. P. Putnam's Sons, 1902, vol. VI, p. 68.
58. "To John Adams from James Monroe, 4 July 1817," *Founders Online*, National Archives, last modified July 12, 2016, http://founders.archives.gov/documents/Adams/99-02-02-6786.
59. Hamilton, 7: pp. 116-117.

VI. John Quincy Adams on John Adams

1. Worthington Chauncey Ford, ed., *Writings of John Quincy Adams, 1779-1796*, New York: The MacMillan Company, 1913, vol. I, p. 27.
2. Ibid, p. 30.
3. Ibid, p. 44.
4. Ibid, p. 54.
5. Ibid, pp. 57-58.
6. Ibid, p. 107.
7. Ibid, p. 112.
8. Ibid, p. 120.
9. Ibid, pp. 125-126.
10. Ibid, pp. 130-131.
11. Alan Nevins, ed., *The Diary of John Quincy Adams, 1794-1845,* New York: Charles Scribner's Sons, 1951, pp. 1-2.
12. Worthington Chauncey Ford, 1: pp. 197-198.
13. Ibid, p. 371.
14. Ibid.
15. Ibid, p. 417.
16. Ibid, p. 424.
17. Worthington Chauncey Ford, ed., *Writings of John Quincy Adams, 1796-1801*, New York: The MacMillan Company, 1913, vol. II, p. 13.
18. Ibid, pp. 17-18.
19. Ibid, p. 46.
20. Ibid, p. 82.
21. Ibid, pp. 102-103.
22. Ibid, p. 108.
23. Nevins, p. 15.
24. Worthington Chauncey Ford, 2: p. 142.
25. Ibid.
26. Ibid, p. 167.
27. Ibid, pp. 179-180.
28. Ibid, p. 181.
29. Ibid, pp. 253-254.
30. Ibid, p. 302.
31. Ibid, p. 473.

32. Ibid, pp. 480-481.
33. Ibid, pp. 482-484.
34. Ibid, p. 484.
35. Ibid, p. 487.
36. Ibid, pp. 488-489.
37. Ibid, pp. 489-490.
38. Ibid, pp. 490-491.
39. Worthington Chauncey Ford, 2: p. 491.
40. Ibid, p. 496.
41. Ibid, p. 510.
42. Ibid, pp. 511-512.
43. Ibid, p. 527.
44. Ibid.
45. Worthington Chauncey Ford, ed., *Writings of John Quincy Adams, 1801-1810,* New York: The MacMillan Company, 1914, vol. III, p. 6.
46. Ibid, p. 82.
47. Ibid, pp. 84-85.
48. Ibid, pp. 105-106.
49. Ibid, p. 122.
50. Ibid, p. 295.
51. Ibid, p. 296.
52. Ibid, p. 297.
53. Ibid, p. 301.
54. Ibid, p. 319.
55. Ibid, p. 427.
56. Worthington Chauncey Ford, ed., *Writings of John Quincy Adams, 1811-1813*, New York: The MacMillan Company, 1914, vol. IV, p. 71.
57. Ibid, p. 101.
58. Ibid.
59. Ibid, pp. 120-121.
60. Ibid, p. 122.
61. Ibid, pp. 196-197.
62. Ibid, p. 452.
63. Ibid, p. 512.
64. Worthington Chauncey Ford, ed., *Writings of John Quincy Adams, 1814-1816*, New York: The MacMillan Company, 1915, vol. V, p. 23.
65. Ibid, p. 166.

66. Worthington Chauncey Ford, ed., *Writings of John Quincy Adams, 1816-1819*, New York: The MacMillan Company, 1916, vol. VI, p. 2.
67. Nevins, p. 172.
68. Worthington Chauncey Ford, 6: p. 109.
69. Ibid, p. 112.
70. Ibid, pp. 462-463.
71. Nevins, p. 233.
72. Adrienne Koch and William Peden, ed., *The Selected Writings of John and John Quincy Adams,* New York: Alfred A. Knopf, 1946, pp. 326-327.
73. Nevins, pp. 300-301.
74. Charles Francis Adams, ed., *Memoirs of John Quincy Adams, Comprising Portions of His Diary from 1795 to 1848,* Philadelphia: J. B. Lippincott & Co., 1875, vol. VI, pp. 415-416.
75. Ibid, p. 416.
76. Ibid, p. 417.
77. Ibid, p. 418.
78. Ibid, p. 358-363.
79. Ibid, p. 471.
80. Charles Francis Adams, ed., *Memoirs of John Quincy Adams, Comprising Portions of His Diary from 1795 to 1848*, Philadelphia: J. B. Lippincott & Co., 1876, vol. XI, p. 263.

Chapter III
Thomas Jefferson
I. Thomas Jefferson on the Presidency

1. H. A. Washington, ed., *The Writings of Thomas Jefferson: Being His Autobiography, Correspondence, Reports, Messages, Addresses, and Other Writings, Official and Private,* Washington, D. C.: Taylor & Maury, 1853, vol. II, pp. 355-356.
2. Ibid, p. 375.
3. Paul Leicester Ford, ed., *The Writings of Thomas Jefferson, 1788-1792,* New York: G. P. Putnam's Sons, 1895, vol. V, pp. 20-21.
4. Paul Leicester Ford, ed., *The Writings of Thomas Jefferson, 1795-1801,* New York: G. P. Putnam's Sons, 1896, vol. VII, pp. 9-10.
5. H. A. Washington, ed., *The Writings of Thomas Jefferson: Being His Autobiography, Correspondence, Reports, Messages, Addresses, and Other Writings, Official and Private,* Washington, D. C.: Taylor & Maury, 1854, vol. IV, pp. 151-152.
6. Ford, 7: p. 91.
7. Ibid, pp. 116-117.
8. Ibid, pp. 119-120.
9. Paul Leicester Ford, ed., *The Writings of Thomas Jefferson, 1801-1806,* New York: G. P. Putnam's Sons, 1897, vol. VIII, p. 5.
10. Ibid, p. 12.
11. Washington, 4: p. 380.
12. Ibid, pp. 536-537.
13. Paul Leicester Ford, ed., *The Writings of Thomas Jefferson, 1807-1815,* New York: G. P. Putnam's Sons, 1898, vol. IX, pp. 9-10.
14. H. A. Washington, ed., *The Writings of Thomas Jefferson: Being His Autobiography, Correspondence, Reports, Messages, Addresses, and Other Writings, Official and Private,* Washington, D. C.: Taylor & Maury, 1853, vol. V, pp. 432-433.
15. Washington, H. A., ed., *The Writings of Thomas Jefferson: Being His Autobiography, Correspondence, Reports, Messages, Addresses, and Other Writings, Official and Private,* vol. VIII, Washington, D. C.: Taylor & Maury, 1854, p. 158.
16. Washington, 5: p. 472.
17. Ibid, pp. 532-533.
18. Paul Leicester Ford, ed., *The Writings of Thomas Jefferson, 1816-1826,* New York: G. P. Putnam's Sons, 1899, vol. X, p. 263.

II. George Washington on Thomas Jefferson

1. John Rhodehamel, ed., *George Washington: Writings,* New York: Literary Classics of the United States, 1997, p. 485.
2. Ibid, p. 597.
3. Ibid, p. 687.
4. Ibid, pp. 754-755.
5. John C. Fitzpatrick, ed., *The Writings of George Washington from the Original Manuscript Sources, 1745-1799,* Washington: United States Government Printing Office, 1931, vol. 31, p. 12.
6. Rhodehamel, p. 826.
7. Ibid, p. 825.
8. John C. Fitzpatrick, ed., *The Writings of George Washington from the Original Manuscript Sources, 1745-1799,* Washington: United States Government Printing Office, 1940, vol. 33, p. 216.
9. Rhodehamel, p. 864.
10. Ibid, p. 878.
11. Ibid, pp. 951-952.

III. John Adams on Thomas Jefferson

1. John Adams autobiography, part 1, "John Adams," through 1776, sheet 41 of 53 [electronic edition]. *Adams Family Papers: An Electronic Archive.* Massachusetts Historical Society. *Available at* http://www.masshist.org/digitaladams/
2. L. H. Butterfield, ed., *The Adams Papers: Series I, Diaries, Diary and Autobiography of John Adams,* Cambridge: The Belknap Press of Harvard University Press, 1961, vol. 3, pp. 336-337.
3. Ibid, pp. 335-336.
4. Julian P. Boyd, ed., *The Papers of Thomas Jefferson,* Princeton: Princeton University Press, 1953, vol. 7, p. 382.
5. Ibid.
6. Richard Alan Ryerson, ed., *Adams Family Correspondence,* Cambridge: The Belknap Press of Harvard University Press, 1993, vol. 6, p. 111.

7. Boyd, 7: p. 383.
8. Charles Francis Adams, ed., *The Works of John Adams, Second President of the United States,* Boston: Little, Brown and Company, 1853, vol. VIII, pp. 508-509.
9. Ibid, p. 508.
10. Letter from John Adams to Abigail Adams, 28 December 1792 [electronic edition]. *Adams Family Papers: An Electronic Archive.* The Massachusetts Historical Society. *Available at* http://www.masshist.org/digitaladams/
11. "John Adams to John Quincy Adams, 3 January 1793," *Founders Online*, National Archives, last modified July 12, 2016, http://founders.archives.gov/documents/Adams/04-10-02-0003.
12. Letter from John Adams to Abigail Adams, 3 February 1793 [electronic edition]. *Adams Family Papers: An Electronic Archive.* The Massachusetts Historical Society. *Available at* http://www.masshist.org/digitaladams/
13. Letter from John Adams to Abigail Adams, 26 December 1793 [electronic edition]. *Adams Family Papers: An Electronic Archive.* The Massachusetts Historical Society. *Available at* http://www.masshist.org/digitaladams/
14. Letter from John Adams to Abigail Adams, 6 January 1794 [electronic edition]. *Adams Family Papers: An Electronic Archive.* The Massachusetts Historical Society. *Available at* http://www.masshist.org/digitaladams/
15. Lester J. Cappon, ed., *The Adams-Jefferson Letters: The Complete Correspondence Between Thomas Jefferson and Abigail and John Adams*, Chapel Hill: The University of North Carolina Press, 1959, vol. I, p. 255.
16. Letter from John Adams to Abigail Adams, 20 December 1796 [electronic edition]. *Adams Family Papers: An Electronic Archive.* The Massachusetts Historical Society. *Available at* http://www.masshist.org/digitaladams/
17. Letter from John Adams to Abigail Adams, 27 December 1796 [electronic edition]. *Adams Family Papers: An Electronic Archive.* The Massachusetts Historical Society. *Available at* http://www.masshist.org/digitaladams/
18. Letter from John Adams to Abigail Adams, 1 January 1797 [electronic edition]. *Adams Family Papers: An Electronic Archive.* The Massachusetts Historical Society. *Available at* http://www.masshist.org/digitaladams/
19. Letter from John Adams to Abigail Adams, 3 January 1797 [electronic edition]. *Adams Family Papers: An Electronic Archive.* The Massachusetts Historical Society. *Available at* http://www.masshist.org/digitaladams/
20. Letter from John Adams to Abigail Adams, 5 January 1797 [electronic edition]. *Adams Family Papers: An Electronic Archive.* The Massachusetts Historical Society. *Available at* http://www.masshist.org/digitaladams/
21. Charles Francis Adams, 8: p. 535.

22. Harold C. Syrett, ed., *The Papers of Alexander Hamilton,* New York: Columbia University Press, 1976, vol. XXIV, p. 557.
23. Charles Francis Adams, ed., *The Works of John Adams, Second President of the United States,* Boston: Little, Brown and Company, 1854, vol. IX, pp. 577-578.
24. "From John Adams to Boston Patriot, 8 June 1809," Founders Online, National Archives (http://founders.archives.gov/documents/Adams/99-02-02-5375 [last update: 2015-09-29]).
25. Charles Francis Adams, 9: p. 285.
26. "From John Adams to Joseph Ward, 8 January 1810," Founders Online, National Archives (http://founders.archives.gov/documents/Adams/99-02-02-5495 [last update: 2015-09-29]).
27. Charles Francis Adams, ed., *The Works of John Adams, Second President of the United States,* Boston: Little, Brown and Company, 1856, vol. X, p. 10.
28. Ibid.
29. Ibid, p. 11.
30. Lester J. Cappon, ed., *The Adams-Jefferson Letters: The Complete Correspondence Between Thomas Jefferson and Abigail and John Adams, 1812-1826*, Chapel Hill: The University of North Carolina Press, 1959, vol. II, pp. 293-294.
31. "From John Adams to Thomas Jefferson, 1 May 1812," Founders Online, National Archives (http://founders.archives.gov/documents/Adams/99-02-02-5781 [last update: 2015-09-29]).
32. "From John Adams to Benjamin Rush, 27 December 1812," Founders Online, National Archives (http://founders.archives.gov/documents/Adams/99-02-02-5916 [last update: 2015-09-29]).
33. "From John Adams to Richard Rush, 24 November 1814," Founders Online, National Archives (http://founders.archives.gov/documents/Adams/99-02-02-6353 [last update: 2015-09-29]).
34. Charles Francis Adams, 10: p. 155.
35. Cappon, 2: p. 507.
36. "From John Adams to Thomas Jefferson, 26 May 1817," Founders Online, National Archives (http://founders.archives.gov/documents/Adams/99-02-02-6762 [last update: 2015-09-29]).
37. Cappon, 2: p. 601.

IV. James Madison on Thomas Jefferson

1. Gaillard Hunt ed., *The Writings of James Madison, 1769-1783*, New York: G. P. Putnam's Sons, 1900, vol. I, pp. 132-133.
2. Ibid, pp. 142-143.
3. Ibid, p. 167.
4. Ibid, p. 170.
5. Ibid, p. 195.
6. Ibid, pp. 207-208.
7. Ibid, p. 225.
8. Ibid, pp. 259-260.
9. Hunt, Gaillard ed., *The Writings of James Madison*, 1783-1787, New York: G. P. Putnam's Sons, 1901, vol. II, p. 5.
10. Ibid, p. 50.
11. Ibid, p. 51.
12. Gaillard Hunt, ed., *The Writings of James Madison, 1787-1790*, New York: G. P. Putnam's Sons, 1904, vol. V, pp. 175-176.
13. Ibid, p. 235.
14. Ibid, pp. 435-436.
15. Gaillard Hunt, ed., *The Writings of James Madison, 1790-1802*, New York: G. P. Putnam's Sons, 1906, vol. VI, p. 9.
16. Ibid, p. 15.
17. Ibid, p. 109.
18. Ibid.
19. Ibid, pp. 129-130.
20. Ibid, pp. 177-178.
21. Ibid, pp. 296-302.
22. Ibid, pp. 307-308.
23. James Madison, *Letters and Other Writings of James Madison: Fourth President of the United States, 1794-1815*, Philadelphia: J.B. Lippincott and Company, 1865, vol. II, p. 163.
24. Ibid.
25. Mary A. Hackett, J.C.A. Stagg, Ellen J. Barber, Anne Mandeville Colony, and Angela Kreider, eds., *The Papers of James Madison: Secretary of State Series, 1 November 1803 to 31 March 1804*, Charlottesville: University of Virginia Press, 2002, vol. 6, p. 362.

26. Gaillard Hunt, ed., *The Writings of James Madison, 1803-1807*, New York: G. P. Putnam's Sons, 1908, vol. VII, pp. 120-121.
27. Madison, 2: p. 209.
28. Ibid, p. 221.
29. Hunt, Gaillard Hunt ed., *The Writings of James Madison, 1808-1819*, New York: G. P. Putnam's Sons, 1908, vol. VIII, pp. 49-50.
30. James Madison, *Letters and Other Writings of James Madison: Fourth President of the United States, 1816-1828,* Philadelphia: J.B. Lippincott and Company, 1865, vol. III, pp. 115-116.
31. Hunt, 8: p. 421.
32. Madison, 3: p. 265.
33. Ibid, p. 282.
34. Ibid, p. 301.
35. Ibid, pp. 304-305.
36. Ibid, p. 342.
37. Ibid.
38. Ibid, p. 476.
39. Ibid, p. 492.
40. Ibid, p. 517.
41. Ibid.
42. Ibid, p. 518.
43. Ibid, p. 525.
44. Ibid, p. 526.
45. Ibid, pp. 531-535.
46. Ibid, pp. 538-540.
47. Ibid, p. 549.
48. Ibid, p. 570.
49. Ibid, pp. 573-574.
50. Ibid, pp. 579-580.
51. Ibid, p. 593.
52. Ibid, p. 594.
53. Ibid, pp. 617-619.
54. Ibid, p. 629.
55. Ibid, pp. 629-630.
56. Ibid, pp. 659-660.
57. James Madison, *Letters and Other Writings of James Madison: Fourth President of the United States, 1829-1836,* Philadelphia: J. B. Lippincott and Company, 1865, vol. IV, p. 18.

58. Ibid, pp. 70-71.
59. Ibid, pp. 85-86.
60. Ibid, pp. 109-110.
61. Ibid, pp. 111-112.
62. Ibid, pp. 157-158.
63. Ibid, p. 175.
64. Ibid, pp. 199-200.
65. Ibid, pp. 206-207.
66. Ibid, p. 218.
67. Ibid, p. 229.
68. Ibid, p. 279.
69. Ibid, p. 303.
70. Ibid, p. 314.
71. Ibid, p. 341.
72. Ibid, p. 410.
73. Ibid.
74. Ibid, p. 435.

V. James Monroe on Thomas Jefferson

1. Stanislaus Murray Hamilton, ed., *The Writings of James Monroe, 1778-1794*, New York: G. P. Putnam's Sons, 1898, vol. I, pp. 8-11.
2. Ibid, pp. 11-12.
3. Ibid, p. 12.
4. Ibid, pp. 13-14.
5. Ibid, p. 15.
6. Ibid, p. 16.
7. Ibid, p. 24.
8. Ibid, pp. 54-55.
9. Ibid, p. 64.
10. Ibid, p. 106.
11. Ibid, p. 119.
12. Ibid, p. 128.
13. Ibid, p. 173.
14. Ibid, p. 175.
15. Ibid, p. 181.

16. Ibid, p. 195.
17. Ibid, pp. 199-200.
18. Ibid, p. 207.
19. Ibid, p. 223.
20. Ibid.
21. Ibid, pp. 275-276.
22. Ibid, pp. 225-226.
23. Ibid, p. 281.
24. Stanislaus Murray Hamilton, ed., *The Writings of James Monroe, 1794-1796*, New York: G. P. Putnam's Sons, 1899, vol. II, p. 9.
25. Ibid, p. 54.
26. Ibid, pp. 269-270.
27. Ibid, p. 312.
28. Ibid, pp. 410-412.
29. Ibid, p. 413.
30. Ibid, p. 444.
31. Stanislaus Murray Hamilton, ed., *The Writings of James Monroe, 1796-1802*, New York: G. P. Putnam's Sons, 1900, vol. III, p. 25.
32. Ibid, p. 47.
33. Ibid, pp. 69-70.
34. Ibid, pp. 86-87.
35. Ibid, p. 102.
36. Ibid, p. 103.
37. Ibid, pp. 118-119.
38. Ibid, p. 125.
39. Ibid, pp. 244-245.
40. Ibid, pp. 256-257.
41. Ibid, pp. 262-263.
42. Ibid, p. 264.
43. Ibid, pp. 268-269.
44. Ibid, pp. 269-270.
45. Ibid, p. 273.
46. Ibid, p. 287.
47. Ibid, p. 295.
48. Ibid, pp. 298-299.
49. Ibid, pp. 316-317.
50. Ibid, pp. 343-344.
51. Ibid, p. 351.

52. Stanislaus Murray Hamilton, ed., *The Writings of James Monroe, 1803-1806*, New York: G. P. Putnam's Sons, 1900, vol. IV, p. 5.
53. Ibid, pp. 15-16.
54. Ibid, pp. 26-27.
55. Ibid, p. 28.
56. Ibid, pp. 48-49.
57. Ibid, p. 57.
58. Ibid, p. 59.
59. Ibid, p. 62.
60. Ibid, p. 76.
61. Ibid, p. 78.
62. Ibid, pp. 110-111.
63. Ibid, p. 116.
64. Ibid, pp. 122-123.
65. Ibid, p. 128.
66. Ibid, p. 141.
67. Ibid, p. 238.
68. Ibid, p. 239.
69. Ibid, pp. 266-267.
70. Ibid, p. 349.
71. Ibid, p. 392.
72. Ibid, pp. 441-442.
73. Ibid, pp. 450-451.
74. Ibid, p. 477.
75. Ibid, pp. 489-490.
76. Stanislaus Murray Hamilton, ed., *The Writings of James Monroe, 1807-1816*, New York: G. P. Putnam's Sons, 1901, vol. V, pp. 24-25.
77. Ibid, p. 26.
78. Ibid, p. 28.
79. Ibid, pp. 32-33.
80. Ibid, p. 51.
81. Ibid, pp. 61-62.
82. Ibid, p. 71.
83. Ibid, pp. 73-74.
84. Ibid, p. 100.
85. Ibid, p. 101.
86. Ibid, p. 122.
87. Ibid, p. 123.

88. Ibid, p. 131.
89. Ibid, p. 136.
90. Ibid, pp. 152-153.
91. Ibid, pp. 184-185.
92. Ibid, pp. 200-201.
93. Ibid, pp. 268-269.
94. Ibid, pp. 298-299.
95. Ibid, p. 299.
96. Stanislaus Murray Hamilton, ed., *The Writings of James Monroe, 1817-1823*, New York: G. P. Putnam's Sons, 1902, vol. VI, p. 23.
97. Ibid, p. 103.
98. Ibid, p. 115.
99. Ibid, p. 298.
100. Ibid, p. 399.
101. Ibid.
102. Stanislaus Murray Hamilton, ed., *The Writings of James Monroe, 1824-1831*, New York: G. P. Putnam's Sons, 1903, vol. VII, p. 11.
103. Ibid, p. 12.
104. Ibid, pp. 28-29.
105. Ibid, p. 42.
106. Ibid, p. 69.
107. Ibid, pp. 69-70.
108. Ibid, p. 246.
109. Stuart Gerry Brown, ed., *The Autobiography of James Monroe,* Syracuse: Syracuse University Press, 1959, p. 31.
110. Ibid, p. 33.
111. Ibid, p. 35.
112. Ibid, p. 38.
113. Ibid, pp. 149-150.
114. Ibid, p. 153.
115. Ibid, p. 154.

VI. John Quincy Adams on Thomas Jefferson

1. Worthington Chauncey Ford, ed., *Writings of John Quincy Adams, 1779-1796*, New York: The MacMillan Company, 1913, vol. I, p. 69.

2. Worthington Chauncey Ford, ed., *Writings of John Quincy Adams, 1796-1801,* New York: The MacMillan Company, 1913, vol. II, p. 42.
3. Ibid, pp. 53-54.
4. Ibid.
5. Ibid, p. 96.
6. Ibid, pp. 507-508.
7. Worthington Chauncey Ford, ed., *Writings of John Quincy Adams, 1801-1810,* New York: The MacMillan Company, 1914, vol. III, p. 4.
8. Ibid, p. 7.
9. Ibid, p. 57.
10. Ibid, p. 59.
11. Ibid, p. 67.
12. Ibid, p. 71.
13. Ibid, pp. 75-76.
14. Ibid, p. 78.
15. Ibid, p. 79.
16. Ibid, p. 81.
17. Allan Nevins, ed. *The Diary of John Quincy Adams, 1794-1845,* New York: Charles Scribner's Sons, 1951, pp. 24-26.
18. Ford, 3: p. 86.
19. Nevins, pp. 28-29.
20. Ibid, p. 31.
21. Ford, 3: p. 117.
22. Nevins, p. 37.
23. Ibid, pp. 37-38.
24. Ibid, p. 40.
25. Ibid, pp. 44-45.
26. Nevins, p. 47.
27. Ford, 3: p. 164.
28. Adrienne Koch and William Peden, ed., *The Selected Writings of John and John Quincy Adams,* New York: Alfred A. Knopf, 1946, p. 261.
29. Ford, 3: p. 200.
30. Nevins, p. 55.
31. Ford, 3: p. 236.
32. Ibid, p. 236.
33. Ibid, p. 289.
34. Ibid, pp. 315-316.
35. Worthington Chauncey Ford, ed., *Writings of John Quincy Adams,* 1811-1813, New York: The MacMillan Company, 1914, vol. IV, pp. 315-316.

36. Ibid, p. 342.
37. Ibid, p. 457.
38. Ibid, p. 181.
39. Ibid.
40. Charles Francis Adams, ed., *Memoirs of John Quincy Adams, Comprising Portions of His Diary from 1795 to 1848,* Philadelphia: J. B. Lippincott & Co., 1875, vol. V, pp. 317-324.
41. Worthington Chauncey Ford, ed., *Writings of John Quincy Adams. 1820-1823*, New York: The MacMillan Company, 1917, vol. VII, pp. 270-271.
42. Ibid, p. 299.
43. Nevins, p. 289.
44. Ford, 7: p. 338.
45. Koch, p. 327.
46. Ibid, pp. 330-331.
47. Ibid, pp. 332-333.
48. Ford, 7: pp. 352-353.
49. Koch, p. 335.
50. Nevins, p. 324.
51. Ibid, p. 346.
52. Ibid, pp. 356-357.
53. Ibid, p. 357.
54. Ibid, p. 358.
55. Ibid.
56. Koch, p. 369.
57. Ibid, p. 371.
58. Nevins, p. 408.
59. Ibid, p. 409.
60. Ibid, pp. 410-412.
61. Ibid, p. 412.
62. Ibid, pp. 416-417.
63. Ibid, p. 453.
64. Koch, p. 384.
65. Ibid, pp. 385-387.
66. Nevins, p. 468.
67. Charles Francis Adams, ed., *Memoirs of John Quincy Adams, Comprising Portions of His Diary from 1795 to 1848,* Philadelphia: J. B. Lippincott & Co., 1876, vol. IX, pp. 306-307.
68. Koch, p. 393.
69. Ibid, p. 394.

Chapter IV
James Madison
I. James Madison on the Presidency

1. Robert A. Rutland, et al., eds., *The Papers of James Madison, 27 May 1787-3 March 1788,* Chicago: University of Chicago Press, 1977, vol. 10, p. 16.
2. Ibid, p. 22.
3. Ibid, pp. 22-23.
4. Ibid.
5. Ibid, p. 25.
6. Ibid, pp. 107-108.
7. Ibid, p. 108.
8. Ibid, p. 110.
9. Ibid, pp. 115-117.
10. Ibid, p. 166.
11. Saul K. Padover, *The Complete Madison: His Basic Writings,* New York: Harper and Brothers Publishers, 1953, pp. 199-200.
12. Ibid, p. 99.
13. Robert A. Rutland, et al., eds., *The Papers of James Madison, 7 March 1788-1 March 1789,* Charlottesville: University Press of Virginia, 1977, vol. II, pp. 154-155.
14. James Madison, *Letters and Other Writings of James Madison: Fourth President of the United States, 1769-1793,* Philadelphia: J. B. Lippincott and Company, 1865, vol. I, p. 422.
15. Ibid, p. 467.
16. Padover, pp. 201-202.
17. Charles F. Hobson, et al., eds., *The Papers of James Madison, 2 March 1789-20 January 1790,* Charlottesville: University Press of Virginia, 1979, vol. 12, pp. 173-174.
18. Madison, 1: p. 471.
19. Padover, p. 200.
20. Hobson, 12: pp. 225-227.
21. Ibid, pp. 233-239.
22. Charles F. Hobson, et al., eds., *The Papers of James Madison, 20 January 1790-31 March 1791,* Charlottesville: University Press of Virginia, 1981, vol. 13, p. 319.
23. Galliard Hunt, *The Writings of James Madison, 1790-1802,* New York: G. P. Putnam's Sons, 1906, vol. VI, p. 15.
24. Madison, 1: p. 549.

25. Thomas A. Mason, et al., eds., *The Papers of James Madison, March 1793-20 April 1795*, Charlottesville: University Press of Virginia, 1985, vol. 15, pp. 66-73.
26. Ibid, pp. 81-82.
27. Ibid, pp. 83-84.
28. Ibid, pp. 108-110.
29. Ibid, p. 521.
30. James Madison, *Letters and Other Writings of James Madison: Fourth President of the United States, 1794-1815,* Philadelphia: J. B. Lippincott and Company, 1865, vol. II, pp. 131-132.
31. Padover, p. 321.
32. Madison, 2: p. 157.
33. Galliard Hunt, ed., *The Writings of James Madison, 1808-1819*, New York: G. P. Putnam's Sons, 1908, vol. VIII, p. 47.
34. Ibid, p. 48.
35. Ibid, pp. 235-236.
36. Padover, pp. 183-184.
37. James Madison, *Letters and Other Writings of James Madison, Fourth President of the United States, 1816-1828*, Philadelphia: J. B. Lippincott and Company, 1865, vol. III, p. 417.
38. Ibid, pp. 282-283
39. Madison, 2: pp. 332-336.
40. Madison, 3: pp. 360-361.
41. Ibid, pp. 599-600.
42. James Madison, *Letters and Other Writings of James Madison, Fourth President of the United States, 1829-1836*, Philadelphia: J. B. Lippincott and Company, 1865, vol. IV, pp. 66-67.
43. Ibid, pp. 77-79.
44. Ibid, pp. 299-300.

II. George Washington on James Madison

1. John C. Fitzpatrick, ed., *The Writings of George Washington from the Original Manuscript Sources, 1745-1799,* Washington: United States Government Printing Office, 1939, vol. 29, pp. 188-189.
2. Ibid, p. 286.
3. Ibid, pp. 188-189.

4. John C. Fitzpatrick, ed., *The Writings of George Washington from the Original Manuscript Sources, 1745-1799,* Washington: United States Government Printing Office, 1939, vol. 30, p. 96.
5. Ibid, p. 415.

III. John Adams on James Madison

1. Letter from John Adams to Abigail Adams, 28 April 1796 [electronic edition]. *Adams Family Papers: An Electronic Archive.* The Massachusetts Historical Society. *Available at* http://www.masshist.org/digitaladams/
2. "John Adams to Abigail Adams, 14 January 1797," Founders Online, National Archives (http://founders.archives.gov/documents/Adams/04-11-02-0257 [last update: 2015-09-29]).
3. Charles Francis Adams, ed., *The Works of John Adams, Second President of the United States,* Boston: Little, Brown and Company, 1854, vol. IX, p. 286.
4. Ibid.
5. "From John Adams to John Trumbull, 27 July 1805," Founders Online, National Archives (http://founders.archives.gov/documents/Adams/99-02-02-5089 [last update: 2015-09-29]).
6. "From John Adams to John Trumbull, 18 November 1805," Founders Online, National Archives (http://founders.archives.gov/documents/Adams/99-02-02-5108 [last update: 2015-09-29]).
7. "From John Adams to Benjamin Rush, 26 March 1806," Founders Online, National Archives (http://founders.archives.gov/documents/Adams/99-02-02-5129 [last update: 2015-09-29]).
8. "From John Adams to Mercy Otis Warren, 26 March 1806," Founders Online, National Archives (http://founders.archives.gov/documents/Adams/99-02-02-5203 [last update: 2015-09-29]).
9. "From John Adams to John Quincy Adams, 8 January 1808," Founders Online, National Archives (http://founders.archives.gov/documents/Adams/99-03-02-1629 [last update: 2015-09-29]).
10. "From John Adams to John Quincy Adams, 19 February 1808," Founders Online, National Archives (http://founders.archives.go/documents/Adams/99-03-02-1644 [last update: 2015-09-29]).

11. "From John Adams to Benjamin Rush, 20 June 1808," Founders Online, National Archives (http://founders.archives.gov/documents/Adams/99-02-02-5242 [last update: 2015-09-29]).
12. "From John Adams to Benjamin Rush, 10 October 1808," Founders Online, National Archives (http://founders.archives.gov/documents/Adams/99-02-02-5263 [last update: 2015-09-29]).
13. "From John Adams to John Quincy Adams, 23 December 1808," Founders Online, National Archives (http://founders.archives.gov/documents/Adams/99-03-02-1696 [last update: 2015-09-29]).
14. Letter from John Adams to Benjamin Rush, 4 March 1809 [electronic edition]. *Available at* http://www.digitalhistory.uh.edu/documents/documents_p2.cfm?doc=366
15. "From John Adams to François Adriaan Van der Kemp, 4 April 1811," Founders Online, National Archives (http://founders.archives.gov/documents/Adams/99-02-02-5625 [last update: 2015-09-29]).
16. Worthington Chauncey Ford, *Statesman and Friend: Correspondence of John Adams with Benjamin Waterhouse, 1784-1822,* Boston: Little, Brown, and Company, 1927, p. 77.
17. Letter from John Adams to Benjamin Rush, 14 May 1812 [electronic edition]. Department of History, University of Wisconsin-Madison, Center for the Study of the American Constitution. *Available at* https://history.wisc.edu/csac/founders/madison/
18. Lester J. Cappon, ed., *The Adams-Jefferson Letters: The Complete Correspondence Between Thomas Jefferson and Abigail and John Adams,* Chapel Hill: The University of North Carolina Press, 1959, vol. II, p. 304.
19. "From John Adams to Benjamin Rush, 3 July 1812," Founders Online, National Archives (http://founders.archives.gov/documents/Adams/99-02-02-5819 [last update: 2015-09-29]).
20. "From John Adams to Benjamin Rush, 10 July 1812," Founders Online, National Archives (http://founders.archives.gov/documents/Adams/99-02-02-5824 [last update: 2015-09-29]).
21. "From John Adams to William Stephens Smith, 15 October 1812," Founders Online, National Archives (http://founders.archives.gov/documents/Adams/99-03-02-2202 [last update: 2015-09-29]).
22. J. C. A. Stagg, ed., *The Papers of James Madison, Presidential Series,* Charlottesville: University of Virginia Press, 2004, vol. 5, pp. 455-456.
23. Charles Francis Adams, ed., *The Works of John Adams, Second President of the United States,* Boston: Little, Brown, and Company, 1856), vol. X., p. 23.

24. "From John Adams to John Quincy Adams, 30 November 1812," Founders Online, National Archives (http://founders.archives.gov/documents/Adams/99-03-02-2210 [last update: 2015-09-29]).
25. Stagg, 5: pp. 642-643.
26. "From John Adams to James Madison, 14 May 1813," Founders Online, National Archives (http://founders.archives.gov/documents/Adams/99-02-02-6030 [last update: 2015-09-29]).
27. "From John Adams to Richard Rush, 15 July 1813," Founders Online, National Archives (http://founders.archives.gov/documents/Adams/99-02-02-6104 [last update: 2015-09-29]).
28. "From John Adams to Richard Rush, 6 September 1813," Founders Online, National Archives (http://founders.archives.gov/documents/Adams/99-02-02-6145 [last update: 2015-09-29]).
29. Adams, 10: p. 73.
30. "From John Adams to Richard Rush, 8 October 1813," Founders Online, National Archives (http://founders.archives.gov/documents/Adams/99-02-02-6176 [last update: 2015-09-29]).
31. "From John Adams to Thomas McKean, 30 October 1814," Founders Online, National Archives (http://founders.archives.gov/documents/Adams/99-02-02-6347 [last update: 2015-09-29]).
32. Adams, 10: p. 109
33. Adams, 10: p. 113.
34. "From John Adams to John Taylor, 5 March 1815," Founders Online, National Archives (http://founders.archives.gov/documents/Adams/99-02-02-6425 [last update: 2015-09-29]).
35. "From John Adams to Thomas McKean, 6 July 1815," Founders Online, National Archives (http://founders.archives.gov/documents/Adams/99-02-02-6489 [last update: 2015-09-29]).
36. Cappon, 2: p. 455.
37. Adams, 10: p. 181.
38. "From John Adams to Jedidiah Morse, 5 December 1815," Founders Online, National Archives (http://founders.archives.gov/documents/Adams/99-02-02-6550 [last update: 2015-09-29]).
39. "From John Adams to John Quincy Adams, 19 December 1815," Founders Online, National Archives (http://founders.archives.gov/documents/Adams/99-03-02-3008 [last update: 2015-09-29]).
40. Cappon, 2: pp. 507-508.
41. Adams, 10: p. 258.

42. Ibid, p. 267.
43. Ibid, p. 268.
44. "From John Adams to John Quincy Adams, 13 January 1818," Founders Online, National Archives (http://founders.archives.gov/documents/Adams/99-03-02-3433 [last update: 2015-09-29]).
45. Adams, 10: p. 378.

IV. Thomas Jefferson on James Madison

1. Paul Leicester Ford, ed., *The Writings of Thomas Jefferson, 1784-1787*, New York: G. P. Putnam's Sons, 1894, vol. IV, pp. 17-19.
2. Paul Leicester Ford, ed., *The Writings of Thomas Jefferson, 1788-1792*, New York: G. P. Putnam's Sons, 1894, vol. V, pp. 70-71.
3. Paul Leicester Ford, ed., *The Writings of Thomas Jefferson, 1792-1794*, New York: G. P. Putnam's Sons, 1894, vol. VI, p. 519.
4. Paul Leicester Ford, ed., *The Writings of Thomas Jefferson, 1795-1801*, New York: G. P. Putnam's Sons, 1896, vol. VII, pp. 8-9.
5. Ibid, pp. 32-33.
6. Ibid, p. 91.
7. H. A. Washington, ed., *The Writings of Thomas Jefferson: Being His Autobiography, Correspondence, Reports, Messages, Addresses, and Other Writings, Official and Private*, Washington, D. C.: Taylor & Maury, 1854, vol. IV, pp. 169-170.
8. Ford, 7: p. 132.
9. Ibid, p. 231.
10. Ibid, p. 318.
11. Ibid, p. 344.
12. H. A. Washington, ed., *The Writings of Thomas Jefferson: Being His Autobiography, Correspondence, Reports, Messages, Addresses, and Other Writings, Official and Private*, Washington, D. C.: Taylor & Maury, 1853, vol. V, p. 433.
13. Ibid, p. 435.
14. Ibid, p. 437.
15. Paul Leicester Ford, ed., *The Writings of Thomas Jefferson, 1807-1815*, New York: G. P. Putnam's Sons, 1898, vol. IX, p. 252.
16. Washington, 5: pp. 450-451.
17. Ibid, p. 451.
18. Ibid, p. 473.

19. John P. Foley, ed., *The Jeffersonian Cyclopedia,* New York: Russell and Russell, 1967, vol. II, p. 524.
20. Washington, 5: p. 533.
21. Ibid, p. 555.
22. Ford, 9: p. 321.
23. H. A. Washington, ed., *The Writings of Thomas Jefferson: Being His Autobiography, Correspondence, Reports, Messages, Addresses, and Other Writings, Official and Private,* Washington, D. C.: Taylor & Maury, 1854, vol. VI, pp. 82-83.
24. Paul Leicester Ford, ed., *The Writings of Thomas Jefferson, 1807-1815*, New York: G. P. Putnam's Sons, 1898, vol. IX, p. 369.
25. Ibid, p. 384.
26. H. A. Washington, ed., *The Writings of Thomas Jefferson: Being His Autobiography, Correspondence, Reports, Messages, Addresses, and Other Writings, Official and Private,* Washington, D. C.: Taylor & Maury, 1854, vol. VI, p. 123.
27. Ford, 9: pp. 483-484.
28. Ibid, p. 512.
29. Ibid, p. 521.
30. Lester J. Cappon, ed., *The Adams-Jefferson Letters: The Complete Correspondence Between Thomas Jefferson and Abigail and John Adams, 1812-1826,* Chapel Hill: The University of North Carolina Press, 1959, vol. II, p. 453.
31. H. A. Washington, ed., *The Writings of Thomas Jefferson: Being His Autobiography, Correspondence, Reports, Messages, Addresses, and Other Writings, Official and Private,* Washington, D. C.: Taylor & Maury, 1854, vol. VII, pp. 62-63.
32. Paul Leicester Ford, ed., *The Writings of Thomas Jefferson, 1816-1826*, New York: G. P. Putnam's Sons, 1899, vol. X, p. 170.
33. Paul Leicester Ford, ed., *The Writings of Thomas Jefferson, 1760-1775*, New York: G. P. Putnam's Sons, 1892, vol. I, pp. 56-57.
34. Ford, 10: pp. 377-378.
35. Ibid, p. 395.

V. James Monroe on James Madison

1. Stanislaus Murray Hamilton, ed., *The Writings of James Monroe, 1778-1794,* New York: G. P. Putnam's Sons, 1898, vol. I, pp. 59-60.
2. Ibid, pp. 94-95.
3. Ibid, p. 139.

4. Ibid, p. 165.
5. Ibid, p. 169.
6. Ibid, p. 171.
7. Ibid, p. 172.
8. Ibid, p. 174.
9. Ibid, p. 199.
10. Ibid, pp. 206-207.
11. Ibid, p. 246.
12. Ibid, p. 278.
13. Stanislaus Murray Hamilton, ed., *The Writings of James Monroe, 1794-1796*, New York: G. P. Putnam's Sons, 1899, vol. II, p. 11.
14. Ibid, p. 37.
15. Ibid, p. 216.
16. Ibid, p. 444.
17. Stanislaus Murray Hamilton, ed., *The Writings of James Monroe, 1796-1802*, New York: G. P. Putnam's Sons, 1900, vol. III, p. 48.
18. Ibid, p. 70.
19. Ibid, p. 86.
20. Ibid, p. 156.
21. Ibid, p. 158.
22. Ibid, pp. p. 159-160.
23. Ibid, p. 200.
24. Ibid, p. 201.
25. Stanislaus Murray Hamilton, ed., *The Writings of James Monroe, 1803-1806*, New York: G. P. Putnam's Sons, 1900, vol. IV, p. 77.
26. Ibid, p. 217.
27. Stanislaus Murray Hamilton, ed., *The Writings of James Monroe, 1807-1816*, New York: G. P. Putnam's Sons, 1901, vol. V, p. 20.
28. Ibid, p. 26.
29. Ibid, pp. 26-27.
30. Ibid, p. 27.
31. Ibid, p. 80.
32. Ibid.
33. Ibid, pp. 135-136.
34. Ibid, p. 138.
35. Ibid, pp. 148-149.
36. Ibid, pp. 181-182.
37. Ibid, pp. 182-183.

38. Ibid, pp. 183-184.
39. Ibid, p. 184.
40. Ibid, p. 185.
41. Ibid, p. 186.
42. Ibid, p. 218.
43. Ibid, p. 222.
44. Ibid, pp. 276-277.
45. Ibid, pp. 260-261.
46. Ibid, p. 263.
47. Ibid, p. 271.
48. Ibid, p. 283.
49. Ibid, p. 318.
50. Ibid, p. 14.
51. Stanislaus Murray Hamilton, ed., *The Writings of James Monroe, 1817-1823*, New York: G. P. Putnam's Sons, 1902, vol. VI, pp. 29-30.
52. Ibid, pp. 73-74.
53. Ibid, pp. 174-175.
54. Stanislaus Murray Hamilton, ed., *The Writings of James Monroe, 1824-1831*, New York: G. P. Putnam's Sons, 1903, vol. VII, p. 31.
55. Ibid, pp. 40-41.
56. Ibid, p. 79.
57. Ibid, p. 126.
58. Ibid, p. 135.
59. Ibid, pp. 144-146.
60. Ibid, pp. 149-150.
61. Ibid, pp. 150-151.
62. Ibid, p. 164.
63. Ibid, p. 177.
64. Ibid, p. 193.
65. Ibid, p. 205.
66. Ibid, pp. 205-206.
67. Ibid, pp. 213-214.
68. Ibid, pp. 233-234.

VI. John Quincy Adams on James Madison

1. Worthington Chauncey Ford, ed., *Writings of John Quincy Adams. vol. I, 1779-1796*, New York: The MacMillan Company, 1913, vol. I, pp. 53-54.
2. Ibid, pp. 179-180.
3. Worthington Chauncey Ford, ed., *Writings of John Quincy Adams, 1796-1801*, New York: The MacMillan Company, 1913, vol. II, p. 164.
4. Ibid, pp. 165-166.
5. Allan Nevins, ed., *The Diary of John Quincy Adams, 1794-1845,* New York: Charles Scribner's Sons, 1951, p. 47.
6. Ibid, p. 52.
7. Worthington Chauncey Ford, ed., *Writings of John Quincy Adams, 1801-1810*, New York: The MacMillan Company, 1914, vol. III, p. 189.
8. Ibid, p. 235.
9. Nevins, p. 58.
10. Ibid, pp. 58-59.
11. Ford, 3: pp. 288-289.
12. Ibid, p. 291.
13. Ibid.
14. Ibid, p. 312.
15. Ibid, p. 314.
16. Ibid, p. 319.
17. Ibid, pp. 319-320.
18. Ibid, p. 320.
19. Ibid, pp. 328-329.
20. Ibid, p. 329.
21. Ibid, p. 332.
22. Ibid, p. 474.
23. Worthington Chauncey Ford, ed., *Writings of John Quincy Adams, 1811-18*13, New York: The MacMillan Company, 1914, vol. IV, p. 90.
24. Ibid, pp. 93-94.
25. Ibid, pp. 94-97.
26. Ibid, pp. 97-98.
27. Ibid, p. 340.
28. Nevins, p. 96.
29. Ford, 4: p. 438.

30. Ibid, p. 456.
31. Ibid, p. 457.
32. Ibid, p. 462.
33. Ibid, pp. 493-494.
34. Ibid, p. 498.
35. Ibid, pp. 504-505.
36. Worthington Chauncey Ford, ed., *Writings of John Quincy Adams, 1814-1816*, New York: The MacMillan Company, 1915, vol. V, pp. 23-24.
37. Ibid, p. 58.
38. Ibid, p. 68.
39. Ibid, p. 72.
40. Ibid, pp. 157-158.
41. Ibid, p. 182.
42. Ibid, p. 247.
43. Ibid, pp. 323-324.
44. Ibid, p. 461.
45. Worthington Chauncey Ford, ed., *Writings of John Quincy Adams, 1816-1819*, New York: The MacMillan Company, 1916, vol. VI, p. 136.
46. Ibid, p. 140.
47. Ibid, p. 273.
48. Ibid, p. 354.
49. Adrienne Koch and William Peden, ed., *The Selected Writings of John and John Quincy Adams,* New York: Alfred A. Knopf, 1946, p. 334.
50. Ibid, pp. 335-336.
51. Ibid, p. 336.
52. Nevins, p. 346.
53. John Quincy Adams, *An Eulogy on the Life and Character of James Monroe, Fifth President of the United States,* Boston: J. H. Eastburn, City Printer, 1831, p. 73.
54. Ibid, 468.
55. John Quincy Adams, *An Eulogy on the Life and Character of James Madison, Fourth President of the United States,* Boston: American Stationers' Company, 1936, pp. 4-5.
56. Ibid, p. 10.
57. Ibid, p. 11.
58. Ibid, p. 12.
59. Ibid, pp. 19-20.
60. Ibid, pp. 32-33.
61. Ibid, pp. 35-37.
62. Ibid, p. 41.

63. Ibid, pp. 46-47.
64. Ibid, pp. 47-48.
65. Ibid, p. 54.
66. Ibid, pp. 61-62.
67. Ibid, pp. 71-72.
68. Ibid, pp. 74-75.
69. Ibid, pp. 81-82.
70. Ibid, p. 82.
71. Ibid, p. 84.
72. Ibid, pp. 84-85.
73. Ibid, p. 87.
74. Nevins, p. 470.
75. Ibid, pp. 470-471.

Chapter V
James Monroe
I. James Monroe on the Presidency

1. Stanislaus Murray Hamilton, ed., *The Writings of James Monroe, 1778-1794*, New York: G. P. Putnam's Sons, 1898, vol. I, p. 312.
2. Ibid, pp. 378-380.
3. Ibid, p. 381.
4. Ibid, pp. 382-383.
5. Ibid, p. 383.
6. Ibid.
7. Ibid, p. 388.
8. Ibid, p. 325.
9. Ibid, p. 327.
10. Ibid, p. 328.
11. Ibid, p. 329.
12. Ibid, pp. 329-330.
13. Ibid, pp. 330-331.
14. Ibid, p. 336.
15. Ibid, p. 201.
16. Ibid, p. 262.
17. Stanislaus Murray Hamilton, ed., *The Writings of James Monroe, 1794-1796*, New York: G. P. Putnam's Sons, 1899, vol. II, p. 262.
18. Stanislaus Murray Hamilton, ed., *The Writings of James Monroe, 1796-1802*, New York: G. P. Putnam's Sons, 1900, vol. III, p. 19.
19. Ibid, p. 67.
20. Ibid, pp. 71-72.
21. Ibid, pp. 77-78.
22. Ibid, pp. 282-284.
23. Ibid, p. 287.
24. Stanislaus Murray Hamilton, ed., *The Writings of James Monroe, 1803-1806*, New York: G. P. Putnam's Sons, 1900, vol. IV, p. 242.
25. Stanislaus Murray Hamilton, ed., *The Writings of James Monroe, 1807-1816*, New York: G. P. Putnam's Sons, 1901, vol. V, p. 26.
26. Ibid, p. 74.
27. Ibid, pp. 74-79.

28. Ibid, pp. 80-81.
29. Ibid, p. 84.
30. Ibid, p. 136.
31. Ibid, p. 144.
32. Ibid.
33. Ibid, pp. 156-157.
34. Ibid, p. 203.
35. Ibid, pp. 245-246.
36. Ibid, pp. 308-309.
37. Ibid, pp. 312-313.
38. Ibid, p. 315.
39. Ibid, p. 317.
40. Ibid, p. 342.
41. Stanislaus Murray Hamilton, ed., *The Writings of James Monroe, 1817-1823*, New York: G. P. Putnam's Sons, 1902, vol. VI, pp. 32-33.
42. Ibid, p. 6.
43. Ibid, p. 8.
44. Ibid, pp. 12-13.
45. Ibid, p. 163.
46. Ibid.
47. Ibid, pp. 163-164.
48. Richard Radcliffe, ed., *The President's Tour: A Collection of Addresses Made to James Munroe, Esq. President of the United States, On His Tour Through the Northern and Middle States. A. D. 1817, Accompanied with Answers from the President,* New Ipswich: Salmon Wilder, 1822, p. 17.
49. Ibid, p. 19.
50. Ibid, p. 21.
51. Ibid, p. 29.
52. Ibid, p. 41.
53. Ibid, p. 60.
54. Ibid, p. 51.
55. Hamilton, 6: pp. 191-192.
56. Ibid, p. 286.
57. Stanislaus Murray Hamilton, ed., *The Writings of James Monroe, 1824-1831*, New York: G. P. Putnam's Sons, 1903, vol. VII, p. 11.
58. Ibid, pp. 49-50.
59. Ibid, p. 81.
60. Ibid, p. 136.

61. Ibid, pp. 153-154.
62. Ibid, p. 154.
63. Ibid, p. 220.

II. George Washington on James Monroe

1. John C. Fitzpatrick, ed., *The Writings of George Washington from the Original Manuscript Sources, 1745-1799,* Washington: United States Government Printing Office, 1936, vol. 15, pp. 198-199.
2. "From George Washington to James Monroe, 23 February 1789," *Founders Online,* National Archives, last modified July 12, 2016, http://founders.archives.gov/documents/Washington/05-01-02-0249
3. "From George Washington to James Monroe, 9 April 1794," *Founders Online,* National Archives, last modified July 12, 2016, http://founders.archives.gov/documents/Washington/05-15-02-0434
4. John C. Fitzpatrick, ed., *The Writings of George Washington from the Original Manuscript Sources, 1745-1799,* Washington: United States Government Printing Office, 1940, vol. 35, p. 156.
5. "From George Washington to James Monroe, 25 August 1796," *Founders Online,* National Archives, last modified July 12, 2016, http://founders.archives.gov/documents/Washington/99-01-02-00883
6. John C. Fitzpatrick, ed., *The Writings of George Washington from the Original Manuscript Sources, 1745-1799,* Washington: United States Government Printing Office, 1941, vol. 36, p. 215.
7. Ibid.

III. John Adams on James Monroe

1. Letter from John Adams to Abigail Adams, 14 January 1797 [electronic edition]. *Adams Family Papers: An Electronic Archive.* The Massachusetts Historical Society. *Available at* http://www.masshist.org/digitaladams/
2. Charles Francis Adams, ed., *The Works of John Adams, Second President of the United States,* Boston: Little, Brown and Company, 1853, vol. VIII, p. 565.
3. Charles Francis Adams, ed., *The Works of John Adams, Second President of the United States,* Boston: Little, Brown and Company, 1856, vol. V, p. 170.

4. Worthington Chauncey Ford, ed., *Statesman and Friend: Correspondence of John Adams with Benjamin Waterhouse, 1784-1822,* Boston: Little, Brown, and Company, 1927, p. 122.
5. Daniel Preston, ed., *The Papers of James Monroe: A Documentary History of the Presidential Tours of James Monroe, 1817, 1818, 1819,* Westport: Greenwood Press, 2003, vol. 1, p. 101.
6. Ibid, p. 162.
7. Ibid, p. 198.
8. Ibid, p. 226.
9. Ibid.
10. Lester J. Cappon, ed., *The Adams-Jefferson Letters: The Complete Correspondence Between Thomas Jefferson and Abigail and John Adams,* Chapel Hill: The University of North Carolina Press, 1959, vol. II, p. 522.
11. Preston, 1: p. 756.
12. Ibid, p. 762.
13. Cappon, 2: p. 548.

IV. Thomas Jefferson on James Monroe

1. Lester J. Cappon, ed., *The Adams-Jefferson Letters: The Complete Correspondence Between Thomas Jefferson and Abigail and John Adams, 1812-1826*, Chapel Hill: The University of North Carolina Press, 1959, vol. II, pp. 11.
2. H. A. Washington, ed., *The Writings of Thomas Jefferson: Being His Autobiography, Correspondence, Reports, Messages, Addresses, and Other Writings, Official and Private,* Washington, D. C.: Taylor & Maury, 1853, vol. I, p. 555.
3. Paul Leicester Ford, ed., *The Writings of Thomas Jefferson, 1784-1787,* New York: G. P. Putnam's Sons, 1899, vol. IV, p. 395.
4. Ibid, p. 265.
5. H. A. Washington, ed., *The Writings of Thomas Jefferson: Being His Autobiography, Correspondence, Reports, Messages, Addresses, and Other Writings, Official and Private,* Washington, D. C.: Taylor & Maury, 1853, vol. II, p. 70.
6. Ibid, p. 71.
7. Ibid.
8. Paul Leicester Ford, ed., *The Writings of Thomas Jefferson, 1795-1801,* New York: G. P. Putnam's Sons, 1896, vol. VII, p. 17.
9. Ibid, p. 44.
10. Ibid, p. 171.

11. Ibid, p. 183.
12. Ibid, p. 190.
13. Ibid, pp. 197-198.
14. Ibid, p. 198.
15. Ibid.
16. Ibid, p. 216.
17. Ibid, p. 232.
18. Ibid, pp. 257-260.
19. Ibid, pp. 322-323.
20. Paul Leicester Ford, ed., *The Writings of Thomas Jefferson, 1801-1806*, New York: G. P. Putnam's Sons, 1897, vol. VIII, p. 188.
21. Ibid, pp. 190-192.
22. Ibid, pp. 204-205.
23. Ibid, pp. 249-250.
24. Ibid, p. 288.
25. Ibid, p. 288.
26. Ibid, p. 290.
27. Ibid, pp. 448-449.
28. Ibid, p. 478.
29. Paul Leicester Ford, ed., *The Writings of Thomas Jefferson, 1807-1815*, New York: G. P. Putnam's Sons, 1898, vol. IX, p. 37.
30. H. A. Washington, ed., *The Writings of Thomas Jefferson: Being His Autobiography, Correspondence, Reports, Messages, Addresses, and Other Writings, Official and Private,* Washington, D.C.: Taylor & Maury, 1853, vol. V, pp. 82-83.
31. Ford, 9: pp. 177-178.
32. Ibid, pp. 178-181.
33. Ibid, p. 181.
34. Ibid, p. 184.
35. Ibid, pp. 265-267.
36. Ibid, pp. 323-324.
37. Ibid, pp. 368-369.
38. Ibid, pp. 498-499.
39. Paul Leicester Ford, ed., *The Writings of Thomas Jefferson, 1816-1826*, New York: G. P. Putnam's Sons, 1898, vol. X, p. 84.
40. Ibid, pp. 120-121.
41. Ibid, p. 123.
42. Ibid, p. 246.
43. Ibid, p. 379.

V. James Madison on James Monroe

1. James Madison, *Letters and Other Writings of James Madison: Fourth President of the United States,* 1769-1793, Philadelphia: J. B. Lippincott and Company, 1865, vol. I, p. 107.
2. Ibid, p. 108.
3. Galliard Hunt, ed., *The Writings of James Madison, 1783-1787,* New York: G. P. Putnam's Sons, 1901, vol. II, p. 128.
4. Ibid, p. 132.
5. Ibid, p. 165.
6. Madison, 1: p. 195.
7. Ibid, p. 249.
8. Hunt, 2: pp. 231-232.
9. Ibid, pp. 232-233.
10. Ibid.
11. Ibid, p. 242.
12. Ibid, p. 243.
13. Ibid, p. 244.
14. Ibid, p. 265.
15. Ibid, p. 274.
16. Ibid, p. 353.
17. Galliard Hunt, ed., *The Writings of James Madison, 1787-1790,* New York: G. P. Putnam's Sons, 1904, vol. V, p. 121.
18. Ibid, pp. 156-157.
19. Ibid, p. 319.
20. Madison, 1: p. 458.
21. Ibid, p. 488.
22. Ibid, p. 562.
23. Ibid, p. 593.
24. Ibid, p. 598.
25. Ibid, p. 606.
26. James Madison, *Letters and Other Writings of James Madison, Fourth President of the United States, 1794-1815,* Philadelphia: J. B. Lippincott & Company, 1865, vol. II, p. 18.
27. Ibid, p. 20.

28. Galliard Hunt ed., *The Writings of James Madison, 1790-1802,* New York: G. P. Putnam's Sons, 1906, vol. VI, p. 219.
29. Ibid, p. 226.
30. Madison, 2: p. 39.
31. Ibid, p. 41.
32. Ibid, p. 72.
33. Ibid, p. 84.
34. Ibid, p. 92.
35. Ibid, p. 111.
36. Ibid, pp. 121-122.
37. Ibid, p. 123.
38. Ibid, p. 124.
39. Ibid, p. 126.
40. Ibid, pp. 146-147.
41. Ibid, pp. 148-149.
42. Gaillard Hunt, ed., *The Writings of James Madison, 1803-1807,* New York: G. P. Putnam's Sons, 1908, vol. VII, p. 3.
43. Madison, 2: p. 221.
44. Ibid, p. 404.
45. Ibid, p. 460.
46. Galliard Hunt ed., *The Writings of James Madison, 1808-1819,* New York: G. P. Putnam's Sons, 1908, vol. VIII, p. 136.
47. Ibid, pp. 136-137.
48. Ibid, p. 261.
49. Ibid, p. 301.
50. James Madison, *Letters and Other Writings of James Madison, Fourth President of the United States, 1816-1828,* Philadelphia: J. B. Lippincott & Company, 1867, vol. III, p. 23.
51. Ibid, pp. 46-47.
52. Hunt, 8: p. 389.
53. Ibid, p. 397.
54. Ibid, p. 399.
55. Ibid, pp. 403-404.
56. Ibid, p. 435.
57. Madison, 3: p. 98.
58. Ibid, p. 186.
59. Ibid, p. 267.
60. Ibid, p. 446.

61. Ibid, p. 474.
62. Ibid, pp. 613-613.
63. Ibid, p. 620.
64. Ibid, p. 624.
65. James Madison, *Letters and Other Writings of James Madison, Fourth President of the United States, 1816-1828,* Philadelphia: J. B. Lippincott & Company, 1865, vol. IV, p. 82.
66. Ibid, pp. 178-179.
67. Ibid, p. 188.
68. Ibid, pp. 188-189.
69. Ibid, p. 189.
70. Ibid, p. 196.

VI. John Quincy Adams on James Monroe

1. Worthington Chauncey Ford, ed., *Writings of John Quincy Adams, 1779-1796,* New York: The MacMillan Company, 1913, vol. I, pp. 236-237.
2. Charles Francis Adams, ed., *Memoirs of John Quincy Adams, Comprising Portions of His Diary from 1795 to 1848,* Philadelphia: J. B. Lippincott & Co., 1874, vol. I, p. 62.
3. Ford, 1: pp. 283-284.
4. Worthington Chauncey Ford, ed., *Writings of John Quincy Adams, 1796-1801,* New York: The MacMillan Company, 1913, vol. II, p. 22.
5. Ibid, p. 43.
6. Ibid, p. 51.
7. Ibid, pp. 54-55.
8. Ibid, p. 55.
9. Ibid, p. 62.
10. Ibid, pp. 74-75.
11. Ibid, pp. 79-80.
12. Ibid, p. 85.
13. Ibid, pp. 107-108.
14. Ibid, pp. 126-127.
15. Ibid, p. 136.
16. Ibid, p. 151.
17. Ibid, p. 156.
18. Ibid, p. 157.

19. Ibid, p. 161.
20. Ibid, pp. 217-218.
21. Ibid, pp. 245-246.
22. Ibid, pp. 262-263.
23. Ibid, pp. 379-380.
24. Adams, 1: p. 386.
25. Ibid, p. 418.
26. Worthington Chauncey Ford, ed., *Writings of John Quincy Adams, 1801-1810,* New York: The MacMillan Company, 1914, vol., III, pp. 172-173.
27. Ibid, p. 189.
28. Adams, 1: p. 514.
29. Worthington Chauncey Ford, ed., *Writings of John Quincy Adams, 1811-1813*, New York: The MacMillan Company, 1914, vol. IV, p. 291.
30. Worthington Chauncey Ford, ed., *Writings of John Quincy Adams, 1814-1816*, New York: The MacMillan Company, 1915, vol. V, p. 221.
31. Worthington Chauncey Ford, ed., *Writings of John Quincy Adams, 1816-1819,* New York: The MacMillan Company, 1916, vol. VI, pp. 132-133.
32. Ibid, p. 177.
33. Ibid, pp. 178-179.
34. Ibid, p. 180.
35. Ibid, p. 181.
36. Ibid, p. 182.
37. Charles Francis Adams, ed., *Memoirs of John Quincy Adams, Comprising Portions of His Diary from 1795 to 1848,* Philadelphia: J. B. Lippincott & Co., 1875, vol. IV, p. 7.
38. Ford, 6: p. 188.
39. Adams, 4: p. 12.
40. Ford, 6: p. 211.
41. Adams, 4: p. 13.
42. Ford, 6: pp. 225-226.
43. Adams, 4: p. 70.
44. Ford, 6: p. 342.
45. Adams, 4: pp. 103-104.
46. Ibid, p. 119.
47. Ibid, p. 120.
48. Ibid, p. 187.
49. Ibid, p. 188.
50. Ibid, p. 279.
51. Ibid, p. 405.

52. Ibid, p. 449.
53. Ibid, p. 450.
54. Ibid, p. 497.
55. Adrienne Koch and William Peden, ed., *The Selected Writings of John and John Quincy Adams,* New York: Alfred A. Knopf, 1946, p. 302.
56. Ibid, p. 304.
57. Charles Francis Adams, ed., *Memoirs of John Quincy Adams, Comprising Portions of His Diary from 1795 to 1848,* Philadelphia: J. B. Lippincott & Co., 1875, vol. V, p. 58.
58. Ibid, pp. 118-119.
59. Ibid, p. 158.
60. Ibid, pp. 224-225.
61. Ibid, p. 292.
62. Ibid, p. 302
63. Ibid, pp. 317-318.
64. Ibid, p. 324.
65. Koch, p. 335.
66. Adams, 5: pp. 508-509.
67. Charles Francis Adams, ed., *Memoirs of John Quincy Adams, Comprising Portions of His Diary from 1795 to 1848,* Philadelphia: J. B. Lippincott & Co., 1875, vol. VI, p. 8.
68. Ibid, pp. 62-63.
69. Worthington Chauncey Ford, ed., *Writings of John Quincy Adams, 1820-1823*, New York: The MacMillan Company, 1917, vol. VII, pp. 316-317.
70. Adams, 6: p. 168.
71. Ibid, p. 170.
72. Ibid, p. 190.
73. Ibid, p. 289.
74. Ibid, p. 415.
75. Ibid, p. 432.
76. Ibid, p. 491.
77. Ibid, p. 512
78. Ibid, p. 516.
79. Koch, pp. 358-359.
80. Koch, p. 528.
81. Charles Francis Adams, ed., *Memoirs of John Quincy Adams, Comprising Portions of His Diary from 1795 to 1848,* Philadelphia: J. B. Lippincott & Co., 1875, vol. VII, pp. 80-81.
82. Ibid, p. 463.
83. Ibid, p. 539.

84. Charles Francis Adams, ed., *Memoirs of John Quincy Adams, Comprising Portions of His Diary from 1795 to 1848,* Philadelphia: J. B. Lippincott & Co., 1876, vol. VIII, p. 46.
85. Ibid, p. 173.
86. Ibid, p. 249.
87. Ibid, p. 360.
88. Ibid, pp. 377-378.
89. Ibid, pp. 380-381.
90. Ibid, pp. 381-382.
91. Ibid, pp. 389.
92. Ibid, pp. 399.
93. John Quincy Adams, *An Eulogy on the Life and Character of James Monroe, Fifth President of the United States,* Boston: J. H. Eastburn, City Printer, 1831, p. 8-9.
94. Ibid, pp. 16-17.
95. Ibid, p. 18.
96. Ibid, p. 19.
97. Ibid, pp. 38-39.
98. Ibid, pp. 40-41.
99. Ibid, p. 44.
100. Ibid, p. 52.
101. Ibid, p. 53.
102. Ibid, p. 55.
103. Ibid, p. 57.
104. Ibid, pp. 71-72.
105. Ibid, p. 72.
106. Ibid, pp. 81-82.
107. Ibid, p. 85.
108. Ibid, pp. 85-86.
109. Ibid, pp. 86-87.
110. Ibid, p. 88.
111. Ibid, pp. 91-92.
112. Ibid, pp. 92-94.

Chapter VI
John Quincy Adams
I. John Quincy Adams on the Presidency

1. Worthington Chauncey Ford, ed., *Writings of John Quincy Adams, 1779-1796*, New York: The MacMillan Company, 1913, vol. I, p. 106.
2. Ibid, pp. 151-152.
3. Ibid, p. 169.
4. Ibid, p. 175.
5. Ibid, pp. 185-186.
6. Ibid, p. 417.
7. Ibid, p. 486.
8. Worthington Chauncey Ford, ed., *Writings of John Quincy Adams, 1796-1801*, New York: The MacMillan Company, 1913, vol. II, p. 60.
9. Ibid.
10. Ibid, p. 63.
11. Ibid, p. 170.
12. Ibid, p. 449.
13. Ibid, p. 511.
14. Worthington Chauncey Ford, ed., *Writings of John Quincy Adams, 1816-1819*, New York: The MacMillan Company, 1916, vol. VI, pp. 181-182.
15. Charles Francis Adams, ed., *Memoirs of John Quincy Adams, Comprising Portions of His Diary from 1795 to 1848,* Philadelphia: J. B. Lippincott & Co., 1875, vol. IV, p. 64.
16. Ford, 6: p. 381.
17. Adams, 4: pp. 230-231.
18. Ibid, pp. 297-298.
19. Ibid, pp. 381-382.
20. Ibid, pp. 449-450.
21. Ibid, pp. 451-452.
22. Ibid, p. 452.
23. Charles Francis Adams, ed., *Memoirs of John Quincy Adams, Comprising Portions of His Diary from 1795 to 1848,* Philadelphia: J. B. Lippincott & Co., 1875, vol. V, pp. 89-90.
24. Ibid, p. 90.
25. Ibid, pp. 90-91.
26. Ibid, p. 151.
27. Ibid, pp. 205-206.

28. Ibid, pp. 219-220.
29. Ibid, p. 242.
30. Ibid, pp. 297-299.
31. Adrienne Koch and William Peden, ed., *The Selected Writings of John and John Quincy Adams,* New York: Alfred A. Knopf, 1946, p. 320.
32. Ibid, p. 336.
33. Adams, 5: pp. 475-476.
34. Ibid, pp. 477-478.
35. Worthington Chauncey Ford, ed., *Writings of John Quincy Adams, 1820-1823*, New York: The MacMillan Company, 1917, vol. VII, pp. 193-195.
36. Adams, 5: p. 525.
37. Charles Francis Adams, ed., *Memoirs of John Quincy Adams, Comprising Portions of His Diary from 1795 to 1848,* Philadelphia: J. B. Lippincott & Co., 1875, vol. VI, pp. 7-8.
38. Ford, 7: pp. 271-272.
39. Ibid, p. 281.
40. Adams, 6: pp. 42-43.
41. Ibid, p. 54-55.
42. Ford, 7: pp. 315-316.
43. Ibid, pp. 317-318.
44. Ibid, p. 346.
45. Ibid, pp. 357-358.
46. Adams, 6: p. 217.
47. Ibid, p. 235.
48. Ibid, pp. 237-238.
49. Ibid, pp. 241-242.
50. Ibid, p. 246.
51. Ibid, pp. 246-247.
52. Ibid, p. 261.
53. Ibid, p. 265.
54. Ibid, pp. 266-267.
55. Ibid, p. 269.
56. Ibid, p. 302.
57. Ibid, pp. 312-313.
58. Ibid, pp. 323-324.
59. Ibid, p. 355.
60. Ibid, pp. 379-380.
61. Ibid, pp. 403-404.
62. Ibid, pp. 412-413.
63. Ibid, p. 415.

64. Ibid, p. 478.
65. Ibid, pp. 478-479.
66. Ibid, p. 496.
67. Ibid, pp. 501-502.
68. Ibid, p. 502.
69. Ibid, p. 503.
70. Ibid, p. 505.
71. Ibid.
72. Ibid, p. 508.
73. Ibid, pp. 518-519.
74. Ibid, pp. 526-527.
75. Charles Francis Adams, ed., *Memoirs of John Quincy Adams, Comprising Portions of His Diary from 1795 to 1848,* Philadelphia: J. B. Lippincott & Co., 1876, vol. VIII, pp. 245-247.
76. John Quincy Adams, *An Eulogy on the Life and Character of James Madison, Fourth President of the United States,* Boston: American Stationers' Company, 1936, pp. 72-73.

II. George Washington on John Quincy Adams

1. Worthington Chauncey Ford, ed., *Writings of John Quincy Adams, 1779-1796,* New York: The Macmillan Company, 1913, vol. I, pp. 191-192.
2. "From George Washington to Alexander Hamilton, 7 June 1794," Founders Online, National Archives (http://founders.archives.gov/documents/Washington/05-16-02-0162 [last update: 2015-09-29]).
3. "From George Washington to Edmund Randolph, 19 June 1794," Founders Online, National Archives (http://founders.archives.gov/documents/Washington/05-16-02-0198 [last update: 2015-09-29]).
4. John C. Fitzpatrick, ed., *The Writings of George Washington from the Original Manuscript Sources, 1745-1799,* Washington: United States Government Printing Office, 1940, vol. 34, p. 279.
5. Charles Francis Adams, ed., *Memoirs of John Quincy Adams, His Diary From 1795 to 1848*, Philadelphia: J. B. Lippincott and Company, 1874, vol. I, p. 195.
6. Worthington Chauncey Ford, ed., *Writings of John Quincy Adams, 1779-1796*, New York: The Macmillan Company, 1913, vol. I, p. 488.

7. "From George Washington to Batavian Republic National Assembly, 17 February 1797," Founders Online, National Archives (http://founders.archives.gov/documents/Washington/99-01-02-00303 [last update: 2015-09-29]).
8. "From George Washington to Maria I, 17 February 1797," Founders Online, National Archives (http://founders.archives.gov/documents/Washington/99-01-0c2-00306 [last update: 2015-09-29]).
9. John C. Fitzpatrick, ed., *The Writings of George Washington from the Original Manuscript Sources, 1745-1799,* Washington: United States Government Printing Office, 1940, vol. 35, p. 394.
10. Ibid, p. 476.

III. John Adams on John Quincy Adams

1. L. H. Butterfield, ed., *Adams Family Correspondence, June 1776-March 1778,* Cambridge: The Belknap Press of Harvard University Press, 1963, vol. 2, p. 271.
2. Ibid, pp. 289-290.
3. Ibid, pp. 307-308.
4. L. H. Butterfield, ed., *Adams Family Correspondence, October 1780-September 1782,* Cambridge: The Belknap Press of Harvard University Press, 1973, vol. 4, pp. 55-56.
5. Ibid, p. 317.
6. Ibid, pp. 366-367.
7. Richard Alan Ryerson, ed., *Adams Family Correspondence, October 1782-November 1784*, Cambridge: The Belknap Press of Harvard University Press, 1993, vol. 5, p. 223.
8. Ibid, p. 399.
9. Worthington Chauncey Ford, ed., *Statesman and Friend: Correspondence of John Adams with Benjamin Waterhouse, 1784-1822,* Boston: Little, Brown, and Company, 1927, pp. 5-6.
10. Margaret A. Hogan, C. James Taylor, Celeste Walker, Anne Decker Cecere, Gregg L. Lint, Hobson Woodward, and Mary T. Claffey, eds., *Adams Family Correspondence, January 1786-February 1787*, Cambridge: The Belknap Press of Harvard University Press, 2005, vol. 7, p. 96.
11. Ibid, p. 205.
12. Ibid, p. 429.

13. Letter from John Adams to Abigail Adams, 21 January 1794 [electronic edition]. *Adams Family Papers: An Electronic Archive.* The Massachusetts Historical Society. *Available at* http://www.masshist.org/digitaladams/
14. Letter from John Adams to Abigail Adams, 9 May 1794 [electronic edition]. *Adams Family Papers: An Electronic Archive.* The Massachusetts Historical Society. *Available at* http://www.masshist.org/digitaladams/
15. Worthington Chauncey Ford, ed., *Writings of John Quincy Adams, 1779-1796*, New York: The Macmillan Company, 1913, vol. I, p. 190.
16. Ibid.
17. Ibid, p. 408.
18. Charles Francis Adams, ed., *Memoirs of John Quincy Adams, His Diary From 1795 to 1848*, Philadelphia: J. B. Lippincott and Company, 1874, vol. I, p. 195.
19. Worthington Chauncey Ford, ed., *Writings of John Quincy Adams, 1796-1801,* New York: The MacMillan Company, 1913, vol. II, p. 173.
20. Ibid, p. 174.
21. Ibid, p. 498.
22. "From John Adams to John Quincy Adams, 8 January 1808," Founders Online, National Archives (http://founders.archives.gov/documents/Adams/99-03-02-1629 [last update: 2015-09-29]).
23. "From John Adams to William Cunningham, 27 September 1808," Founders Online, National Archives (http://founders.archives.gov/documents/Adams/99-02-02-5259 [last update: 2015-0929]).
24. Ford, 1: p. 148.
25. "From John Adams to William Cunningham 13 December 1808," Founders Online, National Archives (http://founders.archives.gov/documents/Adams/99-02-02-5275 [last update: 2015-09-29]).
26. "From John Adams to William Cunningham 13 December 1808," Founders Online, National Archives (http://founders.archives.gov/documents/Adams/99-02-02-5275 [last update: 2015-09-29]).
27. Worthington Chauncey Ford, ed., *Writings of John Quincy Adams, 1811-1813*, New York: The MacMillan Company, 1914, vol. IV, p. 98.
28. Lester J. Cappon, ed., *The Adams-Jefferson Letters: The Complete Correspondence Between Thomas Jefferson and Abigail and John Adams,* Chapel Hill: The University of North Carolina Press, 1959, vol. II, p. 294.
29. Ford, *Statesman and Friend*, p. 97.
30. Samuel Flagg Bemis, *John Quincy Adams and the Foundations of American Foreign Policy*, New York: Alfred A. Knopf, Inc., 1949, p. 224.

31. Lester J. Cappon, ed., *The Adams-Jefferson Letters: The Complete Correspondence Between Thomas Jefferson and Abigail and John Adams*, Chapel Hill: The University of North Carolina Press, 1959, vol. II, p. 521.
32. Ibid, pp. 606-607.
33. Adrienne Koch and William Peden, *The Selected Writings of John and John Quincy Adams*, New York: Alfred A. Knopf, 1946, p. 218.

IV. Thomas Jefferson on John Quincy Adams

1. Paul Leicester Ford, ed., *The Writings of Thomas Jefferson, 1784-1787*, New York: G. P. Putnam's Sons, 1894, vol. IV, p. 261.
2. Paul Leicester Ford, ed., *The Writings of Thomas Jefferson, 1788-1792*, New York: G. P. Putnam's Sons, 1895, vol. V, pp. 346-347.
3. Ibid, p. 351.
4. Ibid, pp. 354-355.
5. Ibid, p. 366.
6. Paul Leicester Ford, ed., *The Writings of Thomas Jefferson, 1795-1801*, New York: G. P. Putnam's Sons, 1896, vol. VII, p. 132.
7. Ibid, p. 218.
8. "From Thomas Jefferson to John Quincy Adams, 6 December 1805," Founders Online, National Archives (http://founders.archives.gov/documents/Jefferson/99-01-02-27708 [last update: 2015-12-30]).
9. Paul Leicester Ford, ed., *The Writings of Thomas Jefferson*, 1807-1815, New York: G. P. Putnam's Sons, 1898, vol. IX, p. 218.
10. H. A. Washington, ed., *The Writings of Thomas Jefferson: Being His Autobiography, Correspondence, Reports, Messages, Addresses, and Other Writings, Official and Private*, Washington, D. C.: Taylor & Maury, 1859, vol. VII, p. 83.
11. Ibid, p. 90.
12. Paul Leicester Ford, ed., *The Writings of Thomas Jefferson*, 1816-1826, New York: G. P. Putnam's Sons, 1899, vol. X, pp. 122-123.
13. "From Thomas Jefferson to John Quincy Adams, 23 October 1822," Founders Online, National Archives (http://founders.archives.gov/documents/Jefferson/98-01-02-3108 [last update: 2015-12-30]).
14. Ford, 10: pp. 233-234.
15. Ibid, p. 237.
16. Ibid p. 247.
17. Ibid, p. 305.

18. "From Thomas Jefferson to John Quincy Adams, 18 July 1824," Founders Online, National Archives (http://founders.archives.gov/documents/Jefferson/98-01-02-4413 [last update: 2015-12-30]).
19. Ford, 10: p. 322.
20. Ibid.
21. Washington, 7: p. 387.
22. Ibid, pp. 424-426.
23. Ford, 10: pp. 356-357.

V. James Madison on John Quincy Adams

1. Gaillard Hunt, ed., *The Writings of James Madison, 1790-1802*, New York: G. P. Putnam's Sons, 1906, vol. VI, p. 52.
2. James Madison, *Letters and Other Writings of James Madison, Fourth President of the United States, 1769-1793*, Philadelphia: J. B. Lippincott & Co., 1865, vol. I, p. 539.
3. "From James Madison to John Quincy Adams, 6 March 1809," *Founders Online*, National Archives, modified June 29, 2016, http://founders.archives.gov/documents/Madison/03-01-02-0022.
4. "From James Madison to the Senate, 26 June 1809," *Founders Online*, National Archives, last modified June 29, 2016, http://founders.archives.gov/documents/Madison/03-01-02-0287.
5. James Madison, *Letters and Other Writings of James Madison, Fourth President of the United States, 1794-1815,* Philadelphia: J. B. Lippincott & Co., 1865, vol. II, p. 445.
6. "From James Madison to Abigail Adams, 15 August 1809," *Founders Online*, National Archives, (http://founders.archives.gov/documents/Madison/03-02-02-0597 [last update: 2016-03-28]).
7. Madison, 2: p. 483.
8. Galliard Hunt, ed., *The Writings of James Madison, 1808-1819*, New York: G. P. Putnam's Sons, 1908, vol. VIII, p. 111.
9. "From James Madison to Alexander I, 25 February 1811 (Abstract)," *Founders Online*, National Archives, last modified June 29, 2016, http://founders.archives.gov/documents/Madison/03-03-02-0242.
10. Hunt, 8: pp. 165-166.
11. Ibid, p. 402.
12. James Madison, *Letters and Other Writings of James Madison, Fourth President of the United States, 1816-1828,* Philadelphia: J. B. Lippincott & Co., 1865, vol. III, p. 117.

13. "From James Madison to John Quincy Adams, 16 July 1821," *Founders Online*, National Archives, last modified June 29, 2016, http://founders.archives.gov/documents/Madison/04-02-02-0302.
14. Madison, 3: p. 288.
15. "From James Madison to John Quincy Adams, 27 March 1826," *Founders Online*, National Archives, last modified June 29, 2016, http://founders.archives.gov/documents/Madison/99-02-02-0640.
16. "From James Madison to John Quincy Adams, 20 December 1826," *Founders Online*, National Archives, last modified June 29, 2016, http://founders.archives.gov/documents/Madison/99-02-02-0841.
17. Madison, 3: p. 573.
18. Ibid, p. 602.
19. Ibid, p. 620.
20. "From James Madison to John Quincy Adams, 8 December 1828," *Founders Online*, National Archives, last modified June 29, 2016, http://founders.archives.gov/documents/Madison/99-02-02-1625.
21. James Madison, *Letters and Other Writings of James Madison, Fourth President of the United States, 1829-1836,* (Philadelphia: J. B. Lippincott & Co., 1865), vol. IV, p. 31.
22. "From James Madison to John Quincy Adams, 2 August 1831," *Founders Online*, National Archives, last modified June 29, 2016, http://founders.archives.gov/documents/Madison/99-02-02-2415.
23. "From James Madison to John Quincy Adams, 23 September 1831," *Founders Online*, National Archives, last modified June 29, 2016, http://founders.archives.gov/documents/Madison/99-02-02-2437.
24. Madison, 4: p. 340.
25. Ibid, p. 345.
26. Ibid, p. 346.
27. "From James Madison to John Quincy Adams, 4 February 1835," *Founders Online*, National Archives, last modified June 29, 2016, http://founders.archives.gov/documents/Madison/99-02-02-3088.
28. Madison, 4: p. 376.

VI. James Monroe on John Quincy Adams

1. Stanislaus Murray Hamilton, ed., *The Writings of James Monroe, 1794-1796*, New York: G. P. Putnam's Sons, 1899, vol. II, p. 237.
2. Ibid, p. 238.
3. Stanislaus Murray Hamilton, ed., *The Writings of James Monroe, 1796-1802*, New York: G. P. Putnam's Sons, 1900, vol. III, p. 106.
4. Stanislaus Murray Hamilton, ed., *The Writings of James Monroe, 1803-1806*, New York: G. P. Putnam's Sons, 1901, vol. IV, p. 398.
5. Stanislaus Murray Hamilton, ed., *The Writings of James Monroe, 1807-1816*, New York: G. P. Putnam's Sons, 1901, vol. V, p. 244.
6. Ibid, p. 250.
7. "To John Adams from James Monroe, 10 April 1813," *Founders Online*, National Archives, last modified July 12, 2016, http://founders.archives.gov/documents/Adams/99-02-02-5995.
8. Hamilton, 5: pp. 251-252.
9. Ibid, p. 267.
10. "To John Adams from James Monroe, 15 July 1815," *Founders Online*, National Archives, last modified July 12, 2016, http://founders.archives.gov/documents/Adams/99-02-02-6106.
11. Hamilton, 5: p. 375.
12. Stanislaus Murray Hamilton, ed., *The Writings of James Monroe, 1817-1823*, New York: G. P. Putnam's Sons, 1902, vol. VI, pp. 2-4.
13. Ibid.
14. Stanislaus Murray Hamilton, ed., *The Writings of James Monroe, 1824-1831*, New York: G. P. Putnam's Sons, 1903, vol. VII, p. 87.
15. Ibid, pp. 122-123.
16. Ibid, pp. 128-129.
17. Ibid, pp. 133-134.
18. Ibid, p. 180.
19. Ibid, pp. 181-182.
20. Ibid, pp. 186-187.

ABOUT THE AUTHOR

David Anthony Clark was born and raised in Reno, Nevada and graduated summa cum laude from the University of San Francisco with a Bachelor of Arts degree in American history. He also holds a Master of Arts degree in American history from Villanova University. Clark is also a graduate of the USAF's Squadron Officer School, Air Command and Staff College, and Air War College.

Clark resides in Reno, Nevada with his two daughters where he teaches American history and serves as a colonel in the Nevada Air National Guard. He has served in the United States military for 26 years and has completed over a dozen deployments overseas including three tours of duty to Iraq in support of Operation Iraqi Freedom. He has served as the Commander of the 152nd Maintenance Group and Vice Commander of the 152nd Airlift Wing. He currently serves as the Nevada Air National Guard's Director of Strategic Plans and Programs.

INDEX

CPSIA information can be obtained
at www.ICGtesting.com
Printed in the USA
LVHW062315200321
682006LV00032B/452

9 781981 55020